*Number Ten: The Centennial Series of
the Association of Former Students,
Texas A&M University*

TEXAS' LAST FRONTIER

Texas' Last Frontier

Fort Stockton and the Trans-Pecos,

1861–1895

By

CLAYTON W. WILLIAMS

Edited by

ERNEST WALLACE

TEXAS A&M UNIVERSITY PRESS

College Station

Library of Congress Cataloging in Publication Data

Williams, Clayton.
   Texas' last frontier.

   (The Centennial series of the Association of Former Stu-
dents, Texas A&M University; no. 10)
   Bibliography: p.
   Includes index.
   1. Pecos County (Tex.)—History.   I. Wallace, Ernest.
II. Title.   III. Title: Fort Stockton and the Trans-Pecos,
1861–1895.   IV. Series.
F392.P28W54   976.4′92305   81-48379
ISBN 0-89096-126-3   AACR2

Manufactured in the United States of America
FIRST EDITION

My family is the greatest thing in my life. My wife, Chicora (Chic) Graham Williams, is and has always been my best publicity agent.

So I dedicate this book to my wife, to my fine son, Clayton Williams, Jr., to my dear daughter, Janet Pollard, and to their families.

Contents

I. Soldiers and Forts

II. Indians and Settlers

III. Law, Outlaws, and Feuds

IV. Tragedy and Success

List of Illustrations

H. Koehler General Merchandise Store

Friedlander building and Heid saloon, Fort Stockton

Fort Stockton scene, 1899

F. W. Young store, Fort Stockton

Grey Mule Saloon, Fort Stockton

Orient Saloon, Pecos

Group of Fort Stockton citizens, ca. 1893

Group of Pecos citizens, ca. 1883

Early Fort Stockton settlers

Edward Armon Sieker, Jr.

Company D, Texas Rangers, 1894

Judge O. W. Williams, ca. 1940

Preface

On the arid plateau plain on a direct line from the town of McCamey about forty-five miles northeast to Fort Davis in the rugged Davis Mountains, thence about sixty-five miles to the southwest is Comanche Springs, one of the largest springs in Texas. Until recently it provided a permanent source of water that flowed thirty-seven miles northeast to join the Pecos River near Horsehead Crossing, the most noted of the Pecos River crossings. Before the arrival of the Anglo-Americans, the springs were a popular camping site for Indians, particularly the Comanches and Kiowas, who traveled the Great Comanche Trail when raiding for horses and captives in Mexico. Before the outbreak of the Civil War, Comanche Springs had become a well-known rest station on several routes of commerce and travel—the San Antonio–Chihuahua Trail, the Lower San Antonio–San Diego Mail Route, the Upper San Antonio–San Diego Mail Route (the branch from Horsehead Crossing by way of Fort Davis to El Paso), and the Butterfield Overland Mail Route. As a protection for the mail service, travelers, and freighters, the army in 1859 established Fort Stockton at the springs. The garrison was abandoned in 1861 but reestablished in 1866 and for most of the next two decades served as the command post for the lower Pecos and Davis Mountain area.

Some enterprising San Antonio businessmen, seeing the possibility of agriculture by use of the water from Comanche Springs and the potential revenue to be derived by providing supplies to the garrison, which was almost four hundred miles from the San Antonio supply depot, and to the weary freighters and travelers, opened a store adjacent to the fort. Other settlers, many of whom were German, Irish, or Mexican, soon followed, and by 1877, 8,000 acres were in cultivation. The little town adjacent to the fort, originally named Saint Gall, became Fort Stockton, the county seat of Pecos County, and the pivotal point on the crossroads of Texas' last frontier. After the subjugation of the Apaches in the early 1880s, the area was victimized for a time by a dangerous criminal element. Simultaneously, cattlemen and sheepmen began moving large herds of their stock into the region. In the 1890s Fort Stockton and the surrounding area typified the lawless character of the American frontier. Some of the most respectable citizens became involved in deadly feuds.

Regarding the feuds, always a highly volatile subject, I feel obligated as a historian to give a rather full account. Many facts are not known and probably will never be known, but enough time has passed since those tragic events occurred, I believe, that no living person will suffer injury by the narration.

My friends and family ask why I am so dedicated to writing this book. Fort Stockton and the surrounding area, I believe, epitomize the American frontier, and local people, still noticeably characterized by their frontier heritage, long to have that heritage recorded for their posterity. It would be a rare person indeed who could examine the historical markers in and around Fort Stockton, the old guardhouse, the renovated officers' quarters, the ruins of the cavalry barns, the men's barracks, the Oldest House in Town, and the irrigation ditches without being overwhelmed with a feeling of admiration for the stamina and optimism of the pioneers they commemorate. In some respects, this volume is a continuation of my three-volume historical background of Fort Stockton and western Texas.

For an accurate and detailed account of the history of this pioneer town and surrounding area, I have for many years searched the state and national archives, military and county records, newspaper files, and the writings, both published and unpublished, of many of the pioneers. The diary and voluminous writings of my father, Judge O. W. Williams, who was one of the Fort Stockton pioneers, provided the major source and incentive for this work. As a result of my long personal acquaintance, I have been able to obtain a great amount of invaluable information from many of the pioneers, their children, and their grandchildren.

In the preparation of this volume, I am indebted to my good friend Dr. Ernest Wallace, Horn Professor of History, Emeritus, at Texas Tech University, for streamlining and editing my unduly lengthy manuscript. Also, I wish to give special acknowledgment to my friend and assistant, Gaines Kincaid, who searched the archives in Washington, D.C., Austin, Texas, and several county courthouses in western Texas and interviewed numerous persons in his search for information that had not been recorded or that needed verification.

Clayton Williams

I.
Soldiers and Forts

CHAPTER 1

The Civil War to August, 1861

SLAVERY was only one of the issues that culminated in secession and the bloody Civil War. More fundamental was the issue of state sovereignty. In the early 1830s the doctrine of nullification (the right of a state to ignore a federal law it considered abhorrent) was propounded in response to tariff legislation and was related only indirectly to slavery. Still a part of Mexico at the time, Texas had no role in that "prelude to civil war."[1]

The institution of slavery, nevertheless, was a major part of the states' rights issue—and Texas was a slave region. Although Mexican laws at times had attempted to prohibit slavery, by 1836 the slave population of Texas was estimated at 5,000. The constitution of the Republic of Texas guaranteed the institution, and the number of slaves thereafter increased rapidly. Between 1850 and 1860, the slave population increased by 213.8 percent, while the free population increased by only 179.73 percent. In 1860, there were 21,878 slaveholders in Texas—5.7 percent of the total for the entire United States. Thus, it was obvious which side the majority of Texans would choose in 1861.[2]

Not all Texans, however, favored secession. As early as 1848, Senator Sam Houston had indicated his feelings by voting for the creation of the Oregon Territory without slavery, contrary to the contention of some of his most influential constituents that neither Congress nor a territorial government had the power to abolish the institution.[3] As governor, Houston continued to oppose secession.

Following the election of Abraham Lincoln as president in 1860,

[1]William W. Freehling, *Prelude to Civil War: The Nullification Controversy,* preface.
[2]Rupert Norval Richardson, *Texas: The Lone Star State,* pp. 88–90, 219–220.
[3]Ibid., p. 241.

secessionists petitioned Houston to call the legislature into session to resolve the matter, but he refused. In late December, South Carolina seceded, and she was soon followed by Mississippi, Florida, Alabama, Georgia, and Louisiana. Finally, after a group of Texas secessionists on December 8, 1860, issued a call for an election for delegates to a state convention to decide the issue, the governor, hoping to circumvent secession, called for a special session of the legislature to convene on January 21, 1861, seven days before the convention was to begin.

The special session of the legislature was tumultuous. The governor pleaded for "the proud structure of government, built by our fathers," but the legislature approved the convention. The convention met as scheduled and on February 2 by a vote of 166 to 8 repealed the ordinance by which Texas had joined the United States. Apart from the issues of states' rights and slavery, the convention gave as a reason that the United States had failed to protect Texas against Indians and Mexican bandits and had refused to reimburse the state for expenditures made in her own defense.

In the statewide election that followed, the Texans voted 46,129 for to 14,697 against secession. Of the then 154 counties, 122 reported the election returns, and of these only 19 voted against secession. Bexar County's vote was 827 for and 709 against. El Paso County cast 871 votes for and only 2 against. Presidio County, which then included the present Pecos County, did not report.

On March 4, 1861, the secession convention recommended and declared Texas a "separate sovereign state" as of March 2. A Lone Star flag, presented to the convention by a group of Texas women, was planted on the dome of the capitol and saluted with a discharge of artillery. Almost immediately, the convention directed its delegates to apply for admission to the newly established Confederate States government at Montgomery, Alabama. This was unnecessary, for the Confederate Congress had already passed an act to admit Texas.

The convention set twelve o'clock noon, March 16, as the deadline for all public officers to declare allegiance to the new government. Governor Houston refused, whereupon Lieutenant Governor Edward Clark, who was then called upon to take the oath, answered in the affirmative and was declared governor.[4]

[4] Marquis James, *The Raven: A Biography of Sam Houston*, pp. 404–408, 411–412; Richardson, *Texas*, pp. 246–249; Ernest Wallace, *Texas in Turmoil, 1849–1875*, pp.

Meanwhile, the Confederacy had been organized. Jefferson Davis, of Mississippi, and other Southerners resigned from the United States Senate on January 21, 1861. Delegates from the seceded states, in convention in Montgomery, organized a new government and inaugurated Davis as provisional president of the Confederacy on February 18, just two weeks before Lincoln's inauguration in Washington. On March 6 the new government called for 100,000 volunteers; on March 11 a permanent constitution was adopted; and on April 12 Confederate troops opened fire on Fort Sumter. The war had begun. On April 18 Robert E. Lee declined an offer to command the United States Army, and two days later he resigned his commission. On May 16, the Confederate Congress authorized the recruiting of 400,000 men, and five days later that body voted to move the capital to Richmond, Virginia.[5]

Meanwhile, in Texas, the Secession Convention had acted to neutralize the 2,700 Union soldiers in the state. Georgia-born Confederate sympathizer Major General D. E. Twiggs was in command of the Union soldiers in Texas, with his headquarters and a small detachment of troops in San Antonio. In February, 1861, Colonel Ben McCulloch, acting under the authority of the Secession Convention's Committee of Public Safety, with a greatly superior force of volunteers marched into San Antonio and coerced Twiggs into surrendering that post along with his supplies and artillery, excepting only the soldiers' sidearms and camp and garrison equipment. On February 18 Twiggs agreed to similar terms for the capitulation and evacuation of all other government military posts in Texas. Shortly thereafter, he resigned his commission and joined the Confederate Army.

Henry McCulloch, Ben's brother, was commissioned by the Committee of Public Safety to bring about the capitulation of the posts in the northern portion of the state. He encountered no difficulty. During the evacuation of the Eighth U.S. Infantry from the West Texas posts, the committee placed Henry in charge of that operation and simultaneously put him in command of the frontier from Fort Chadbourne to the Red River. In the southern part of the state, Colonel John S. (Rip) Ford and his hastily recruited volunteers took control.

60–64, 70–73; Ernest W. Winkler, ed., *Journal of the Secession Convention of Texas, 1861*, pp. 10, 15–66, 70–80, 88–90, 183–184.

[5] *American Heritage Civil War Chronology.*

After the first shots of the war were fired at Fort Sumter, the evacuation terms were considered to be no longer in effect.[6]

The company of William (Bill) C. Adams was among the first organized as state militia or minutemen to take over the posts from the Federals. Adams played a major role in this capacity. His orders from Colonel Ben McCulloch, on February 21, stated: "It will be your duty to have your Command ready to accompany the persons appointed by the commissioners to receive the Federal Property at Camp Wood and Fort Inge." Adams received the order at Uvalde a few days later, and during the next month or so he organized a company of mounted volunteers.

The recruiting was probably not easy, because a large majority of the citizens of Uvalde County opposed secession. (In the referendum earlier, the county's vote had been seventy-six against secession and only sixteen in favor.[7]) There were very few slaveowners in the area, as this part of Texas was not suitable for a plantation system, and many citizens of Uvalde County were Germans who opposed slavery and disunion. Adams, however, completed the enrollments and presumably fulfilled his assignment.

For some reason, nearly half of Lieutenant Adams' company withdrew from service within a week or two. Perhaps some simply did not have their hearts in the Southern cause, but more likely the Federal troops were cooperative and there was no need for them. Apparently, members of Adams' company were not obligated to serve out their three-month enlistment.[8]

When the Second Regiment, Texas Mounted Rifles, came into existence at Fort Brown on March 19, 1861, Colonel John S. Ford, its commanding officer, was given jurisdiction over the entire Rio Grande

[6]Richardson, *Texas*, pp. 249–250; Walter P. Webb and H. Bailey Carroll, eds., *The Handbook of Texas*, 2:812; J. Evetts Haley, *Fort Concho and the Texas Frontier*, pp. 100, 101; W. C. Holden, "Frontier Defense in Texas during the Civil War," *West Texas Historical Association Year Book* 4 (1928): 16–18; Martin Hardwick Hall, "The Formation of Sibley's Brigade and the March to New Mexico," *Southwestern Historical Quarterly* 61 (January, 1958): 383; Winkler, *Secession Convention of Texas*, pp. 20, 22, 264, 266, 375–383.

[7]Winkler, *Secession Convention of Texas*, p. 90.

[8]Texas, Militia, Muster Rolls, Lieutenant William C. Adams' Company, Archives, Texas State Library (TSL), Austin; Ike Moore, arranger, *The Life and Diary of Reading W. Black: A History of Early Uvalde*, p. 27.

frontier. Lieutenant Colonel John R. Baylor then was assigned the duty of getting all of the Union soldiers out of the extreme portion of West Texas.[9] Commissioners Samuel Maverick, Thomas J. Devine, and P. N. Luckett repeatedly urged in their communications to John C. Robertson, chairman of the Committee of Public Safety, that none of the Federal units be permitted to evacuate in any direction except by way of the Texas coast. The commissioners greatly feared that, if any of the Federals went to New Mexico, Arizona, or Kansas, they might set up "a free State to injure and annoy us in the not very remote future."[10]

The accounts of the Confederate occupation of West Texas and its abandonment by the Eighth United States Infantry vary considerably, but on paper, at least, everything appeared fairly well organized. Colonel C. A. Waite, Twiggs's successor, in February issued orders for twenty-six wagons and teams to be sent to aid in the evacuation of Forts Bliss, Quitman, Davis, Stockton, and Camp Hudson, and that: "The most remote garrison will move first, & the garrison of each succeeding post 2 days after the passage of the command which precedes it. They will direct their march upon Indianola [on the Texas coast], where transports will be in readiness for their embarkation. The troops will march with their arms & ammunition, the necessary clothing & camp equipage, and, as the means of transportation are limited, no extra baggage will be allowed."[11] Agents acting on behalf of the state were to accompany the train to receive the public property. Apparently doubtful that the evacuation would go as planned, Waite added that, should agents for the state fail to appear or anyone refuse to give the proper receipts, the commanding officer was to have inventories made of the property to be abandoned.

Baylor's advance detachment gave the Federal troops the choice of changing their allegiance or leaving. At most posts, which were distantly separated and indefensible in enemy territory, the Union sol-

[9] George Wythe Baylor, *John Robert Baylor, Confederate Governor of Arizona*, p. 4; Hall, "Formation of Sibley's Brigade," p. 4.

[10] Winkler, *Secession Convention of Texas*, pp. 270, 272–273, 275, 404.

[11] C. A. Waite, San Antonio, Texas, Special Orders No. 32, February 24, 1861, in United States, *War of the Rebellion: Official Records of the Union and Confederate Armies* (hereafter cited as *Official Rebellion Records*), Series I, 1:594.

diers had left before the Texas troops arrived.[12] By mid-April all the posts in West Texas had been evacuated.

In far western Texas, the center of evacuation was Fort Davis. According to Lieutenant Z. R. Bliss, who was there, a Captain Parker, in command of the Baylor detachment, and Captain Edward D. Black met at Fort Davis and negotiated the evacuation terms. Bliss later wrote that James Magoffin of El Paso, who had been appointed by the Committee of Public Safety to receive the property "at [Fort] Quitman from me, did not come in person, but sent his son, Samuel, who receipted to me for all the property, and with his team helped move our supplies to San Antonio. He and his brother-in-law, Gabriel Valdez, went with us."[13]

After a march of 140 miles to Fort Davis, the Fort Quitman evacuees met a company of Baylor's Confederates and there transferred to it all its government property. Within a few days, the six companies of the Eighth Infantry, with Captain I. V. D. Reeve in command, commenced the eastward journey. Among the company commanders were Lieutenants James J. Van Horn, Henry M. Lazelle, Frank Beck, W. G. Jones, and assistant surgeon DeWitt C. Peters. The group also included Major James V. Bomford, First Lieutenant Zenas R. Bliss, six second lieutenants, one woman, and about 250 enlisted men, who departed Fort Davis eastward to "they knew not where." The Fort Davis sutler, Alexander Young, also went along, with about $40,000 to $50,000 worth of goods for which there were no purchasers. Most of the officers mentioned by Bliss returned to the Union army, but a few joined the Confederates. Some of the Union soldiers may have crossed into Mexico, gone down the Rio Grande to the Gulf, and shipped out to the United States.[14]

Because hostility already existed between the Confederate States and the United States, the Confederate authorities did not comply with their agreement with Twiggs. On April 11, Confederate Colonel Earl Van Dorn, who had been appointed in March to command the

---

[12] Waite, Special Orders No. 36, February 27, 1861, in ibid., 1:596; Carlysle Graham Raht, *The Romance of Davis Mountains and Big Bend Country*, p. 145.

[13] Mrs. O. L. Shipman, *Taming the Big Bend*, pp. 33–34, quoting Zenas R. Bliss, "Reminiscences," Eugene C. Barker Texas History Center, Austin.

[14] Ibid. For information regarding army officers, see Francis B. Heitman, *Historical Register and Dictionary of the United States Army, 1789–1903*, 1:204, 223, 225, 229, 435, 583, 620, 786, 822, 982.

Confederate troops in Texas, was instructed "to intercept and prevent the movement of the United States troops from the State of Texas." Reportedly, 815 Union soldiers were captured, some of whom accepted parole under protest; others refused parole and were kept in prison. The captured men had the option of joining the Confederate military or of taking an oath not to fight with the North under penalty of death if captured.[15] On April 25, seven companies under Major C. C. Sibley, of the Third Infantry, surrendered to Van Dorn after trying unsuccessfully to reach the transports in Matagorda Bay. These men were paroled as prisoners of war. Some units of the Eighth Infantry were captured near San Antonio and paroled, but others were imprisoned.[16]

During the latter part of January and all of February, 1861, Fort Stockton was garrisoned by Company C, Eighth Infantry. Its officers were the artistic Captain Arthur T. Lee and Second Lieutenant Edwin W. H. Reed. The rolls for Company C contained thirty-nine enlisted men available for duty and eight on detached service. Sixty-five men had been transferred out in January, and Company H of the First Infantry had been moved on January 3 to Camp Cooper. Colonel Waite's orders were received at Stockton early in March. On January 29 Captain Lee, having received a leave of absence, left ahead of his company. He was captured in San Antonio but was released by special orders dated April 22, and his parole was signed the following day on promise that he would not do army duty against the Confederacy. With that parole he returned through the Confederate States to his home and afterward rejoined the Union army.

Stockton's post returns for March were not received in San Antonio until April 25, indicating that they were either sent by mail or were brought in with the captured Eighth Infantry units. At any rate, Fort Stockton, like other West Texas posts, had been evacuated by mid-April.[17]

Because they were no longer safe, many civilian Unionists also left

[15] Thomas Yoseloff, *Battles and Leaders of the Civil War*, p. 39.

[16] Ibid.; Barry Scobee, *Old Fort Davis*, p. 46; Dudley G. Wooten, ed., *A Comprehensive History of Texas, 1685–1897*, 2:521–522.

[17] U.S. Department of War, Post Returns, Fort Stockton, Texas, for January, February, and March, 1861, Records of the Adjutant General's Office (AGO), Record Group (RG) 94, National Archives (NA), Washington, D.C.; W. Stephen Thomas, *Fort Davis and the Texas Frontier: Paintings by Captain Arthur T. Lee, Eighth U.S. Infantry*, p. 9, 29–30. Lee built Fort Croghan in the fall of 1849.

Texas. Some found their way out via the coast; some fled to Mexico; others made their way to California. One of the most dangerous areas for Union sympathizers was Franklin (El Paso), where, it will be re- called, only 2 of the 873 votes had been against secession. Living there at the time were the three Mills brothers: Anson, who in 1859 made the first land survey in the future Pecos County (a part of which falls inside the present city of Fort Stockton), William Wallace, and Emmett —all staunch Unionists from Indiana. Each chose a different method of leaving.

Anson Mills had been admitted to the Military Academy in 1855 but was there only about a year and a half and did not again become involved with the military until a couple of months after his dramatic flight from El Paso. In his memoirs, published nearly sixty years later, Anson Mills described his hasty departure: "We left in the coach on the 9th of March, 1861. I was one of eight passengers. Some were going to Richmond and some to Washington, but we agreed, as this was ex- pected to be the last coach to go through, to stand by each other and declare we were all going on business."[18]

The Butterfield Overland route went by way of Fort Chadbourne, north of present San Angelo, but, by the time the stage from El Paso reached there, Colonel H. E. McCulloch had secured the evacuation of the Federal troops. Mills continued:

> We met part of this force near Fort Chadbourne, and we were all excite- ment to know what they would do, as it was rumored they would seize the mail company horses for cavalry. Marching in columns of two, they separated, one column to the right and the other to the left side of the stagecoach.
>
> We told the driver to drive fast and to say he was carrying United States mail. The soldiers laughed at this, and four of them taking hold of the right- hand wheels and four of the left, the driver could not, with the greatest whip- ping, induce the horses to proceed. They laughed again, and called out: "Is Horace Greeley aboard?"

Greeley, taking his own famous advice, had gone west—temporarily. This staunch proponent of abolition had been lecturing in California and had announced that he intended to return east on the Butterfield route. Fortunately for Anson Mills and his companions, McCulloch's men were familiar with Greeley's picture, and after the passengers

---

[18] Heitman, *Historical Register*, 1:713; Anson Mills, *My Story*, p. 62.

were examined the stage was allowed to proceed. Two months later, Anson Mills became a first lieutenant in the United States Army.[19]

Shortly after Baylor's command arrived in Franklin, Emmett Mills and six other young men attempted to go to California. At Cook's Spring, near Deming, New Mexico, the seven youths, all well armed, were attacked by Mangas Coloradas and his Apaches. After quickly reaching the top of a small hill and constructing a stone breastwork, they held out for two days. A few days later, Alejandro Daguerre (or Deguerre or Dagare) found their bodies and a penciled note, dated July 23, 1861, which said the fight had lasted two days, many Indians had been killed, and five of their group were dead or seriously injured. When Colonel Baylor learned of this, he sent George M. Frazer with fifteen men to examine and report on the incident. The bodies, two or three of which had been scalped, were buried at the scene. When the Indians later sold the captured arms in Mexico, they reported that Cochise had joined in the fight and that forty warriors had been slain.[20]

A large number of people living in eastern Texas headed for California. Many of these, according to Noah Smithwick, the veteran of the Battle of Concepción and other engagements, had voted for secession but did not choose to take part in the fighting. Smithwick, who was among one group, left an account of his preparations for the trip:

> As the son of a revolutionary soldier, I could not raise my hand against the Union he had fought to establish. I had fought to make Texas a member of the Union, and I would not turn around and fight to undo my work. . . . When the ordinance of secession passed, I immediately set about getting away. I sold my farm for $2,000. The mill for which I had been offered $12,000 I could not cash at any price. I was, however, bent on fleeing from the wrath to come, so I turned the property over to my nephew, John Hubbard, who, though also a Unionist, decided to stay and face the consequences; a decision that cost him his life. I didn't get a dollar for the mill, but took promissory notes, secured by mortgages, for $4,000. A fine young negro man that had a few months before the election been assessed at $1,500, I sold to Governor Houston for $800, and everything else in proportion.

Smithwick and a number of his friends, in prairie schooners pulled

[19] Heitman, *Historical Register*, 1:713; Mills, *My Story*, p. 62. Anson Mills later became a captain and received several brevets for meritorious conduct in battles.

[20] *El Paso Herald*, March 17, 1923; *Texas, A Guide to the Lone Star State*, p. 249; Oscar Waldo (O. W.) Williams, "An Old Timer's Reminiscences of Grant County [N. Mex.]," *West Texas Historical Association Year Book* 16 (1940): 139; W. W. Mills, *Forty Years at El Paso, 1858–1898*, pp. 53, 195.

by long-horned Texas steers, started on April 14, 1861. At Fort Chadbourne Smithwick noted the absence of the American flag and the
presence of a few Texas Rangers. Farther on, the travelers viewed dismantled and deserted stage stations. Near the crossing of the Concho
on the Butterfield route they were joined by a Dr. Ferguson and a
large train of emigrants from Dallas. Upon trudging west across the dry
stretch from the Concho to the Pecos at Horsehead Crossing, they
found that the ferry had been destroyed and the river was flush; consequently, they raised their wagon beds by placing blocks under them in
order to keep the goods dry while crossing at a lower ford.

At Fort Stockton, likely in early June, Smithwick reported the
post was occupied by a company of state troops (apparently an advance
detachment of Baylor's command). Here, he wrote, the stage route
from San Antonio to El Paso connected with the Overland route. The
post's adobe buildings with dirt floors were beginning to deteriorate.
The roofs had heavy supporting timbers, and the heavy doors and
doorframes were being torn out and used for firewood by the emigrants. Two families and several single men joined the Smithwick
wagon train between Fort Stockton and Fort Davis. Fort Davis was also
occupied by a small group of Texans. Since James Walker's company
had not yet reached there, the Texans must have been a part of Baylor's
advance detachment.

After passing El Muerto Springs and Van Horn's Well and arriving
on the Rio Grande, the Smithwick party found Fort Quitman occupied
by four men who were awaiting Baylor's arrival. Here, the travelers
were joined by a large wagon train of emigrants from McKinney, Texas.
In El Paso, Smithwick got an explanation for the one-sided vote in
favor of secession in a country so sparsely settled. "'Oh, that was a light
vote,' the man I asked replied. 'We could have polled twice that number if the river hadn't taken a rise.'"[21]

The large Smithwick train continued through Tucson and Fort
Yuma in Arizona, reaching the latter place in mid-August, and finally
arrived at its destination, Tulare County, California. Several other emigrant trains were only a short distance ahead of Lieutenant Colonel
Baylor, who was en route to Fort Bliss.[22]

[21] Noah Smithwick, *The Evolution of a State: Or, Recollections of Old Texas Days*,
p. 343.
[22] Ibid., pp. 331–351.

WING OF WEST TEXAS & SOUTHEASTERN
NEW MEXICO TERRITORY   1861—1865
CIVIL WAR

NEW MEXICO TERRITORY

TEXAS

MILES
0 20 40 60 80 100

RIO GRANDE RIVER

FT. UNION
LAS VEGAS
SANTA FE
BATTLE OF GLORIETA

ALBUQUERQUE
PERALTA

FT. SUMNER

SOCORRO
BATTLE OF VAL VERDE
FT. CRAIG

PECOS RIVER

FT. STANTON

DOÑA ANA
LAS CRUCES
MESILLA
FT. FILLMORE

CAMP COOPER
BRAZOS RIVER
FT. PHANTOM HILL

TRAIL

EMIGRANTS
BIG SPRING
RED FORK
FT. CHADBOURNE

FRONTERA
FT. BLISS
FRANKLIN
ISLETA
PASO DEL
NORTE
SOCORRO
SAN ELI ZARIO

CAMP COLORADO
COLORADO

SAN SABA
FT. McKAVETT   FT. MASON
COLORADO

FT. QUITMAN
VAN HORN'S WELL
FT. STOCKTON
PECOS
SPRING
FT. LANCASTER
FT. MARTIN SCOTT

RIO GRANDE

FT. DAVIS
BURGESS
SPRING
FT. HUDSON
CAMP WOOD
CAMP VERDE

MEXICO

FT. LEATON
PERSIMMON GAP
ROSILLA MTS.
COROZONES PKS.
FT. CLARK
UVALDE
SAN ANTONIO
CASTROVILLE

RIVER

PRESIDIO
DEL NORTE
CHISOS MTS

FT. INOE

RIO FRIO RIVER

FT. DUNCAN

NUECES RIVER

Although small detachments of Baylor's force were left at the posts in West Texas, mainly Fort Davis, the posts were not fully occupied by the Texans until midsummer, and during the remainder of the year they were garrisoned in a random manner. Detachments of Baylor's companies moved back and forth from place to place primarily because considerable time elapsed before Van Dorn's messages, transmitted through Ford on the lower Rio Grande, reached him.

Meanwhile, the Confederates were attempting to consolidate their occupation of West Texas. General Order No. Eight informed Ford that one company of his mounted rifles was to go to Fort McIntosh, one to Fort Clark, and one to Fort Inge. Fort Davis, Fort Lancaster, Camp Cooper, and Fort McIntosh were to be occupied by one company of cavalry each and Fort Clark by two. Fort Inge was also to have a battalion of light artillery. But Van Dorn, by then a brigadier general, convinced that there were more posts between the coast and Fort Bliss (El Paso) than necessary, had Fort Quitman abandoned in favor of a strong garrison at Fort Bliss. About the same time, the Texas units were transferred to the army of the Confederacy.[23]

The first Confederate troops to occupy any Texas Trans-Pecos posts, excluding Baylor's advance guard, were the companies of the Second Cavalry of Captains James Walker at Fort Davis and Charles L. Pyron at Fort Stockton. Both units had taken part in the surrender of the six companies of the Eighth Infantry under I. V. D. Reeve, near San Antonio, on May 9. Pyron arrived at Fort Stockton in the latter part of June. In an affidavit made on April 13, 1863, John D. Holliday, a freighter who had acquired ownership of Camp Stockton in 1859, stated that Pyron's troops "took possession of the premises known as Fort Stockton, on or about the 26th day of June, A.D. 1861, and occupied the same until on or about the 1st of July, 1862."[24] Pyron's company was mustered into service in April, 1861, and was transferred to the Confederacy on May 23. At the time, Captain Pyron was forty-two; his first lieutenant, William Glenn Jett, was forty; and Second Lieutenant

---

[23] Earl Van Dorn, San Antonio, Texas, May 27, 1861, General Order No. 8 of May 24, in United States, *Official Rebellion Records*, Series I, 1:574–575, 577–578.

[24] Roscoe P. Conkling and Margaret B. Conkling, *The Butterfield Overland Mail, 1857–1869*, 2:1; Clayton Williams, *Never Again*, 3:212; Pecos County, Texas, Deed Records, 18:339, 341.

David M. Poor was twenty-two. Thomas Reeves, twenty-seven, was added as another second lieutenant after the unit was transferred to the Confederate States.

Born in Alabama in 1819, Charles L. Pyron came to Texas in 1848, where he became a cattle raiser. During much of the time that his company occupied Fort Stockton, Pyron with a part of his company was elsewhere, leaving Lieutenant Jett in command at Stockton. Jett, who was born in White County, Tennessee, on April 5, 1821, had come to Gonzales, Texas, when he was about nineteen. Subsequently, he had served as a lieutenant in Captain John Conner's company of Texas Rangers and had continued in that capacity when the company was mustered into the service of the United States at the outbreak of the war with Mexico.[25]

Captain James Walker, age forty-eight, organized his company in Lavaca County in April, 1861. His first lieutenant was Daniel D. Lattimer, twenty-five, and his second lieutenant was Ruben E. Mays, twenty-six, whose tragic death in the Mays Massacre will be described later. James Walker, born in London about 1812, migrated with his parents to Ohio when he was about three. In 1828 he was admitted to the United States Military Academy but after three years left West Point to become a doctor. He studied medicine in Ohio, Kentucky, and Philadelphia and began his practice in Hinds County, Mississippi. In 1854, Walker and his family moved to Texas to be near some of Mrs. Walker's relatives. Walker's three years at West Point obviously influenced his being chosen to command a company of Texas Mounted Rifles. Like Pyron, Captain Walker with a part of his company joined the Confederate invasion of New Mexico.[26]

When Pyron and Walker left for New Mexico, Captain William C. Adams, as previously mentioned, was given command of Forts Lancaster, Stockton, and Davis. Adams' company had been organized in February for the purpose of receiving Federal property at Camp Wood and

[25] Texas, Militia, Muster Rolls, Captain Charles L. Pyron's companies; *New Encyclopedia of Texas*, p. 1906; *Dallas Herald*, September 4, 1869; Eldon Stephen Branda, ed., *The Handbook of Texas: A Supplement*, 3:763; "Memoirs of Mrs. Ruth Clarinda Joff," *Frontier Times* 12, no. 3 (December, 1934): 99–104; A. J. Sowell, *Early Settlers and Indian Fighters of Southwest Texas*, 2:353, 376.

[26] Texas, Militia, Muster Rolls, Captain James Walker's Company; *New Encyclope-*

Fort Inge. Forty-two men, including the officers, were mustered in during March and April. Within a few short weeks, the company had completed its duties and was virtually disbanded. On June 8, the same day its disbandment became official, it was reorganized as Company C of Ford's Second Regiment of Texas Mounted Rifles, with Adams as its captain. Although most of the men were mustered in at Fort Inge on that date, others joined along its march into western Texas. For the most part, it was a very young group; only three or four were over forty, and several who signed as being eighteen were actually younger. Adams was thirty-seven, First Lieutenant John C. Ellis was thirty, and Second Lieutenant Emory Gibbons was twenty-eight.[27]

Between the departure of the Union soldiers and the arrival of Baylor at Fort Bliss, many El Pasoans (Franklinites, for at the time only the Mexican side of the river was called El Paso) carried arms and kept on the alert, for Fort Fillmore, only a few miles away, was still occupied by the Federals. Some Federal officers, including Captain H. H. Sibley, in New Mexico, however, favored the Confederacy. Originally from Louisiana and an 1838 graduate of the Military Academy, Sibley had served in Florida during the Seminole War and had been breveted a major during the United States–Mexican War. In May, 1850, while stationed forty miles from Austin, Sibley was informed that Wildcat and his Seminoles were headed his way. When Sibley contacted Wildcat, his band numbered 600 warriors and their families. Wildcat declared that he and his people had been mistreated by the United States, that they were on their way to Mexico, and that, unless provided food, they would fight. Wisely, Sibley furnished the Indians with twenty beeves and fifteen pounds of bread, and the band went peacefully on its way. Later, Sibley took part in two Utah expeditions to quell the Mormon disturbances, and in 1860 he was sent to New Mexico to engage in a campaign against the Navajo Indians.

On May 13, 1861, Sibley was promoted to the rank of major, but on

---

dia of Texas, p. 2146; biographical sketch of James Walker, supplied by Mr. and Mrs. John W. Walker, Midland, Texas.

[27] Texas, Militia, Muster Rolls, William C. Adams' Company; list of men in Company C over 35 and under 18, signed by William C. Adams, Fort Davis, Texas, June, 1862, William C. Adams Papers, in possession of Mrs. Brawley Adams, Balmorhea, Texas.

that same day he resigned to join the Confederate Army. A few days later, he was at Simeon Hart's mill, near El Paso (Franklin), waiting for transportation eastward, and on June 12 he wrote his former commander, Colonel William W. Loring, also a Confederate sympathizer, that "we are at last under the glorious banner of the Confederate States of America." The Federals, he continued, had evacuated Bliss, leaving behind much valuable public property; however, since Baylor and his troops were not expected for at least a couple of weeks, there was danger that Federal soldiers would attempt to retrieve the material. To prevent this, Sibley suggested that Loring delay resigning his commission until Baylor reached Bliss. Loring, however, had resigned on the same date as Sibley, but apparently his resignation had not yet been accepted. In the same letter, Sibley bemoaned his own "sickly sentimentality," which had overruled his desire to bring with him his entire company, as he felt that the best of the soldiers in New Mexico were pro-Southern. A short time later, Sibley departed on the eastbound stage. In early July he was in Richmond, Virginia, where he obtained a commission as a brigadier general in the Confederate Army and an authorization to raise a brigade of volunteer troops to drive the Federals from New Mexico.[28]

Eleven days after Sibley wrote to Loring, Unionist W. W. Mills in a letter to Judge John S. Watts described the situation at Mesilla, New Mexico, as anti-Unionist. A Confederate flag was flying from the house in which he wrote, and the country "is now as much in the possession of the enemy as Charleston is." All but two officers at Fort Fillmore were avowedly pro-Southern and were only holding on to their commissions "to embarrass our Government, and at the proper time to turn over everything to the South, after the manner of General Twiggs." The *Mesilla Times*, Mills continued, was "bitterly disunion, and threatens with death any one who refuses to acknowledge this usurpation. There is, however, a latent Union sentiment here, especially among

[28] *El Paso Herald*, March 17, 1923; Hall, "Formation of Sibley's Brigade," pp. 384–385; Edward R. S. Canby to Major I. Lynde, Santa Fe, June 30, 1861, in United States, *Official Rebellion Records*, Series I, 4:57; Williams, *Never Again*, 3:54–55; William Banta and J. W. Caldwell, *Twenty-seven Years on the Texas Frontier*, pp. 54–56. General Henry Hopkins Sibley was the grandson of Dr. John Sibley, who served as the United States Indian agent on the Louisiana-Texas border during the first decade of 1800, according to Dr. D. J. Sibley, Austin, Texas, grandnephew of H. H. Sibley.

the Mexicans, but they are effectually overawed." Mills also informed Judge Watts that about three hundred Texas troops were expected to reach Fort Bliss around July 7, 1861. Shortly thereafter, W. W. Mills experienced serious trouble with the Confederates, likely as a result of the letter quoted.[29]

In June, 1861, John R. Baylor started westward on the stage. One or more of his advance detachments had preceded him, including, it appears, the troops that Noah Smithwick had seen at Forts Stockton and Davis. Perhaps Pyron was at Stockton and Walker at Davis by the time Baylor arrived; it is even possible that these two companies traveled westward with Baylor's stage. At any rate, by midsummer Stockton and Lancaster were occupied by Pyron's Company B, and Davis was occupied by Walker's Company D. Fort Davis was left in the command of Lieutenants William P. White and Ruben E. Mays, for Walker and most of his men either accompanied Baylor to Fort Bliss or joined him there a short time later. Baylor, with his brother George as his adjutant, lost little time before marching into New Mexico.[30]

Baylor bypassed Fort Fillmore and set up his headquarters in the town of Mesilla on July 23. Fort Fillmore, almost in sight of Mesilla, was indefensible for various reasons, not the least being that the nearest water supply was a mile and a half away. Consequently, Major Isaac Lynde, its commander, had been authorized to abandon the place when the troops withdrawing from Arizona had joined him. With Baylor's arrival in the area, further delay became infeasible, but, fortunately, the Arizona units were alerted and by changing their route reached Fort Craig, halfway between Fort Fillmore and Albuquerque.

Before evacuating Fillmore, Major Lynde elected to test the

[29] W. W. Mills, La Mesilla, N. Mex., to John S. Watts, June 23, 1861, in United States, *Official Rebellion Records*, Series I, 4:56.

[30] Baylor, *John Robert Baylor*, p. 30; Raht, *Romance of Davis Mountains*, p. 147; *El Paso Herald*, March 17, 1923. In July, 1861, Lieutenant Donald C. Stith, United States Fifth Infantry, while officially in Chihuahua to recover a stolen Federal train and other materials, reportedly was captured by a "Lt. Adams," incorrectly identified as Confederate Captain W. C. Adams, who at the time was with his company east of the Pecos (E. R. S. Canby, Santa Fe, to the governor of Chihuahua, June 23, 1861, and D. C. Stith, Fort Bliss, to A. L. Anderson, July 20, 1861, both in United States, *Official Rebellion Records*, Series I, 4:43, 59–60; Heitman, *Historical Register*, 1:163, 926; D. C. Stith [for H. E. McCulloch], San Antonio, to commanding officer at Fort Davis, September 9, 1861, Adams Papers).

strength of Baylor's outfit. About 4:30 P.M. on July 25, with some 380 men and a battery of howitzers, he advanced toward Mesilla. Two miles south of Mesilla, he sent forward Lieutenant E. J. Brooks, the post adjutant, under a flag of truce to demand the "unconditional and immediate surrender of the town and the Texas forces."[31] According to Baylor, the Texans numbered fewer than 200, although it was rumored that they had been reinforced by local enlistments. Brooks was told that if Lynde wanted the town he would have to take it. Thus began the conquest of the New Mexico Territory.[32]

After the engagement that followed, in which both sides suffered a few casualties, Major Lynde on July 27 evacuated Fort Fillmore and marched northeastward. Because of insufficient water at San Augustín Springs, where he had expected to find an adequate supply, his men and horses suffered terribly from thirst along the march. Baylor's pursuing troops captured many Federals even before they reached San Augustín Springs. By taking a shortcut, the Texans suffered somewhat less than the Federals. According to Baylor, "The road for five miles was lined with fainting, famished [Federal] soldiers who threw down their arms as we passed and begged for water." After a brief attempt to resist capture and without consulting this staff, Lynde sent for Baylor and surrendered. Baylor continued his march to Fort Stanton, but prior to his arrival the Federals had set fire to the buildings and abandoned the post. Captain Walker's Company D, however, succeeded in recovering a portion of the post's stolen property.

By August 1, Baylor was back in Mesilla. There he issued a proclamation, "To the People of the Territory of Arizona," which, among other things, designated Mesilla as the seat of the new government. On the following day, Governor Baylor appointed as marshal George M. Frazer, who later was to have a prominent role in the history of Pecos County.[33] Although Mesilla was the seat of government, Baylor spent much of his time at Fort Bliss. While he was there, W. W. Mills

[31] Heitman, *Historical Register*, 1:249.

[32] Raymond McCoy, "Victory at Fort Fillmore," *New Mexico Magazine*, August, 1961, pp. 20–23, 35; J. R. Baylor, Doña Ana, N. Mex., to T. A. Washington, September 21, 1861, in United States, *Official Rebellion Records*, Series I, 4:17–20.

[33] John R. Baylor, Proclamation and appointments, and John R. Baylor, Fort Bliss, Texas, to Earl Van Dorn, August 14, 1861, both in United States, *Official Rebellion Records*, Series I, 4:20–21, 22–23.

was captured in El Paso del Norte, Mexico, and taken to Fort Bliss, but eventually he was released. Mills then recrossed the river and from there went to join the Union Army at Fort Craig.[34]

[34] *El Paso Herald*, March 17, 1923; E. R. S. Canby, Fort Craig, N. Mex., to Adjutant General, February 22, 1862, and B. S. Roberts, Fort Craig, N. Mex., to W. J. St. Nicodemus, February 23, 1862, both in United States, *Official Rebellion Records*, Series I, 9:487; W. W. Mills, in United States, *Official Rebellion Records*, Series I, 13:50, 103, 107; Heitman, *Historical Register*, 1:713; Webb and Carroll, *Handbook of Texas*, 2:201.

CHAPTER 2

War Preparations to August, 1861

CAPTAIN William C. Adams and his Company C of the Second Regiment of Texas Mounted Rifles did not reach the Pecos country until the last week in July, 1861. Organization and supplies were likely a problem contributing to the delay.[1] As previously noted, Adams' original company had been disbanded early in June but immediately reorganized as a company in Ford's regiment. Between June 8 and June 18, sixty-two men were enlisted, and two men sent from Fort Clark were mustered into the unit on June 25. The company had orders to march westward by the Lower San Antonio–El Paso Road. This route went through Fort Clark and San Felipe (Del Rio), then to and up the Devils River to Fort Hudson and Beaver Lake, and west to Howard's Well, Fort Lancaster, the Pecos River, Escondido (Tunas) Springs, Fort Stockton, Fort Davis, Van Horn's Well, and San Elizario.[2] At Fort Clark on July 1, Captain H. A. Hamner, Company H, transferred First Sergeant William H. A. Mattison, age twenty-two, and Second Sergeant John M. Elkins, age twenty-one, both from Weatherford, to Adams' company, which by that time had moved farther west.[3] At least two of these men had been with Baylor two years earlier, when he had formed a company of citizens and attempted to chase the reservation Indians out of Texas. Hamner had been captain of that company, and Elkins (and possibly Mattison) had served on the campaign.[4]

---

[1] The information in this chapter is largely from the post returns and muster rolls (Texas, Militia) of the Adams, Walker, and Pyron companies, Archives, Texas State Library, Austin, and the William C. Adams Papers, in possession of Mr. Brawley Adams, Balmorhea, Texas.

[2] Clayton Williams, *Never Again*, 3:156.

[3] Ibid., p. 180; Barry Scobee, *Fort Davis, Texas, 1853–1960*, p. 23.

[4] John M. Elkins, *Indian Fighting on the Texas Frontier*, pp. 15ff.

Between June 30 and July 17, fourteen men and boys were added to Adams' company at a place called Pedro Pinto, possibly a grazing camp or stage station on Piedra Pinta Creek (presently called Pinto Creek) about halfway between Fort Clark and present Del Rio. Except for Samuel Miller, age thirty-eight, all these were under twenty-eight; four claimed to be eighteen, but one, at least, was lying. Charles Montague, Jr., claimed that he was older because he was told he would be discharged if the War Department found out that he was only sixteen. Buglers Alonza G. Russell and Leonadas Fleming were each sixteen years old at the time of their enlistment.[5] Leonadas' father, Monroe Fleming, thirty-five, joined the Adams company on the same day that Leonadas did.[6]

At the time of his enlistment in Company C, Charles Montague, Jr., had a horse named Crockett, horse equipment valued at eighty dollars, and arms (a Sharp's rifle and a six-shooter) worth sixty-five dollars, altogether more than many of the officers could claim.[7] The teenage buglers were not so well equipped. Fleming had a rifle, but Russell had no arms at all. Thomas J. Johnson and six other youngsters who signed up at Pedro Pinto together had only one rifle and one six-shooter.

Adams and his company of eighty volunteers arrived at Fort Lancaster on July 28, about the same time Colonel Baylor was receiving the surrender of Major Isaac Lynde at San Augustín Springs in New Mexico. There Adams found First Lieutenant William G. Jett with a detachment of Pyron's company, which had been sent back from Fort Stockton to guard the public property. Also there he received orders from Colonel Baylor, dated July 12, to march immediately for Fort Bliss, leaving at Lancaster only twenty men under a second lieutenant. By then, however, it was too late for Company C to join Baylor on his campaign in New Mexico. Furthermore, the men were too weary to continue without rest, and besides the company supply train, under thirty-six-year-old Lieutenant John M. Ingram and an escort of thirteen

[5] List of men in Company C over 35 and under 18, signed by William C. Adams, Fort Davis, Texas, June 3, 1862, Adams Papers.

[6] In a letter dated April 3, 1967, to Clayton Williams, Mrs. Paul Coffer, Lovington, N. Mex., stated that Monroe Fleming, her grandfather, died at Fort Stockton during its occupation by the Confederates.

[7] J. Marvin Hunter, *Pioneer History of Bandera County*, pp. 124–125; Scobee, *Fort Davis, Texas*, p. 43; *New Encyclopedia of Texas*, p. 1378.

soldiers, had not yet arrived. Two weeks later Adams did start for Fort Bliss, but he got only as far as Van Horn's Well, where he received new orders from Baylor, directing him to return to his post.[8] Ingram, who had enlisted at Fort Inge on June 8, had been elected a second lieutenant when the company was transferred to the Confederate Army at Fort Clark on June 25.

On July 29, Adams took command at Fort Lancaster, allowing Lieutenant Jett to return to Fort Stockton. Three days later, August West, age nineteen, was mustered into Company C at Lancaster. His equipment included a horse valued at fifty dollars. During the first two weeks at Lancaster, the men under Adams did little except guard duty and occasional escort for a wagon train to Fort Stockton. Elsewhere, during the spring of 1861, thirty Comanches besieged the Butterfield mail station on Grape Creek, sixteen miles west of Fort Chadbourne and captured all of the station's horses and mules. Soon afterward, the Butterfield route was abandoned, and all its employees departed except those at Grape Creek. The same Comanches returned and besieged and set fire to the station. The inmates, Joel Pennington, his wife, his brother-in-law Charles Cox, and Elija Helms, came out shooting. During their escape, Helms and Cox managed to put the Indians on the defensive, but Pennington was badly injured on the face by a shotgun blast and was brought to Fort Chadbourne for medical attention. Several days later, the brothers of Mrs. John Elkins, Jesse and Dudley Johnson, twenty-two and eighteen, respectively, were attacked by Indians a short distance from Fort Chadbourne. The young men mounted their horses and fled to the safety of the post, with the attackers in close pursuit.[9]

As a result of the troop reduction, Indian attacks in Southwest

[8] John R. Baylor, Fort Bliss, Texas, to William C. Adams, July 12, 1861, Adams Papers. The name of Van Horn has appeared in various forms on old maps and in old accounts and records: Van Horn Wells, Van Horn's Well(s), Van Horne Wells, etc. The *Handbook of Texas* states that the wells and the modern city of Van Horn were named for James Judson Van Horn (Walter P. Webb and H. Bailey Carroll, eds. *The Handbook of Texas*, 2:831). As mentioned previously, J. J. Van Horn was one of the U. S. Army officers who evacuated the West Texas posts in 1861. The late Barry Scobee found this to be illogical, since the wells had been named (with or without the final *e* on Van Horn) years before J. J. Van Horn was commissioned and sent to West Texas. Scobee concluded that the name came from Major Jefferson Van Horne, who began his military service in West Texas in 1849 (*Fort Davis, Texas*, p. 25).

[9] Elkins, *Indian Fighting*, pp. 85–87.

Texas became more frequent. During July, the Apaches under Chief
Nicolas, near Fort Davis, pretended to be friendly and received rations
from the post.[10] And here begins a story relating to the "massacre" of
Lieutenant Ruben Mays and his men, the incident with the most contradictory accounts of all those that happened in West Texas during the
Civil War. While Adams was at Fort Lancaster and Captain James
Walker was with Baylor in New Mexico, Fort Davis and a part of
Walker's Company D were under the command of Lieutenants William P. White and Ruben E. Mays. White, age twenty-nine, originally
enrolled in the commissary unit but later became a second lieutenant
when his company was transferred to the Confederate Army. While
commanding at Fort Davis, White had a good lesson in Indian diplo-
macy. Chief Nicolas, who was drawing free rations at Fort Davis, requested Lieutenant White's permission to visit Colonel Baylor to make
a more lasting peace or, perhaps, a better deal. White approved, and a
James McCarty and Nicolas proceeded toward Fort Bliss on the stage.
John M. Elkins wrote that when the stage was only a mile from the
post Nicolas "snatched the stage driver's pistol and conductor's gun,
then jumped off the stage into the darkness."[11]

Elkins was confused as to where and when Nicolas left the stage,
unless he meant on the return trip. In his official report of the incident,
John R. Baylor stated that, because he could not stop at Fort Davis to
negotiate with the formidable Apache Indians, he had the head chief
brought to Fort Bliss by stage and there made with him a treaty. "I
loaded him with presents and sent him back by stage. . . . But he left
the stage after stealing two pistols, and a few nights afterward" his
band, after stealing all the horses possible and killing a number of cattle, left the Fort Davis area.[12]

Another version, slightly different, was told by Frank Fritter,

[10] Ibid., p. 37.

[11] The main sources used in this account of the Mays Massacre are: Elkins, *Indian
Fighting*, pp. 37–40 (quote from p. 37); John M. Elkins, *Life on the Texas Frontier*, pp.
25–27; E. E. Townsend, "Deed of a Frontier Hero," *Frontier Times* 5, no. 9 (June,
1928): 368; E. E. Townsend, "The Mays Massacre," West Texas Historical and Scientific
Society Publications *Bulletin* 48, no. 5 (1933): 29–43; *San Antonio Daily Express*, February 14, 1904 (article by John Buchanan reprinted from the Hallettsville, Texas, *Herald*);
Carlysle Graham Raht, *The Romance of Davis Mountains and Big Bend Country*, pp.
145–147; Scobee, *Fort Davis, Texas*, pp. 44–46, 205; Barry Scobee, *Old Fort Davis*, pp.
47–48.

[12] John R. Baylor to J. B. Magruder, December 29, 1862, in United States, *War of*

stage driver and a scout for the Confederates, whose source of information was a Mexican guide, the only survivor of a punitive expedition sent against Nicolas' thieving band. James Magoffin of El Paso and three Confederate commissioners, he related, had hired Chief Espejo and war captains Nicolas and Antonio as scouts. After drawing their blankets and supplies, they had "deserted and made this raid on the beef herd of the post [Fort Davis]."[13]

To punish the offenders, Lieutenant White on August 5 sent Lieutenant Ruben Mays with fourteen men in pursuit of the guilty Indians.[14] In addition to Mays and a Mexican guide named Juan Fernandez, the detachment included John Deprose, Joseph Lambert, and John Woodland.[15] According to the 1860 census, Deprose was a Canadian working as a teamster for James Urguhart, a Scottish stockraiser. Lambert, a clerk born in Ohio, and Woodland, a trader born in England, were both working for B. G. DeWitt, a sutler for the army before the Federal troops evacuated West Texas in 1861. Ten days later, on August 15, Juan, the guide, arrived at Fort Davis with a tale of tragedy. Mays's detachment, he said, had engaged a large force of Apaches on August 11, and he was the only survivor.[16]

Soon thereafter, Lieutenant White dispatched Lieutenant William Jett with eighteen men to rescue the survivors, if any, to ascertain the details of what had happened, and to bury the dead, if any were

---

the Rebellion: *Official Records of the Union and Confederate Armies* (hereafter cited as *Official Rebellion Records*), Series I, 9:916.

[13] Townsend, "Mays Massacre," p. 34.

[14] Letter from William P. White, Fort Davis, to Dr. W. E. East, Hallettsville, Texas, August 24, 1861, in Archives, University of Texas, Austin.

[15] "Sketches of Early Times in Western Texas," *State Gazette* (Austin), June 12, 1852; John Henry Brown, "The Great Indian Raid of 1840," *Dallas Herald*, August 15, 1874; Olive Todd Walker, "Major Whitfield Chalk, Hero of the Republic of Texas," *Southwestern Historical Quarterly* 60 (January, 1957): 360. The men of the detachment, like nearly all those in Walker's company, were from Lavaca County. According to the muster rolls and census reports, the soldiers were: Ruben E. Mays, 26; Thomas E. Carroll, 25; John C. Brown, 20, a bugler; Samuel R. Desper, 19; Frederick Perkins, 24; Samuel Shelby, 20; and John S. Walker, 20; the civilians were: John Turner, post guide at Fort Davis; John Deprose, 19; R. H. Spence; Jack or John Woodland, 34; Joseph Lambert (variously spelled Lampert and Lamport), 22; and Juan Fernandez, a guide.

[16] U.S. Department of the Interior, Bureau of the Census, "Eighth Census of the United States, 1860. Population. Texas," Bexar County and Lavaca County; Elkins, *Indian Fighting*, pp. 37–40; Elkins, *Life on the Texas Frontier*, pp. 25–27; Baylor to Magruder, December 29, 1862, in United States, *Official Rebellion Records*, Series I, 9:916.

found. In his report on the affair to General Earl Van Dorn on August 25, Colonel Baylor, at Fort Bliss, stated that the rescue party consisted of eight soldiers, three Anglo civilians, an unnamed Frenchman, six Mexicans, including the guide—a total of nineteen, counting Lieutenant Jett.[17] One of the soldiers was Joel Pontoon, about nineteen, whose father, also named Joel and a native of Maine, had migrated to DeWitt's colony, where he became well-known for being a good farmer and medical doctor and for calling the frontiersmen to arms when they defeated the Indians at Plum Creek in 1840 after their great raid on Linnville.[18] John M. Elkins was the only member of the rescue party to publish a detailed account of the Mays incident—and that after he was a very old man.[19]

According to Elkins, the Mays detachment probably had gone down Musquiz Canyon, southeast of Fort Davis, and from there headed in the direction of Cathedral Peak. From there, about a month later, the rescue party, consisting of Lieutenant Jett and "fifty men" (Elkins either exaggerated considerably or else had a very poor memory) from Forts Stockton, Davis, and Lancaster, led by Juan, followed the trail southeast through Persimmon Gap. James Dawson, who was also with the rescue party, told his son Jack that he thought the battle took place near Tornillo Creek at a site later called Grapevine Spring. The evidence indicates otherwise. The Mexican guide stated that the massacred party had followed a trail easterly for several days until signs indicated the proximity of the Indians. Then, while cautiously passing through a valley between two high mountains, it had encamped behind a large rock on a steep ascent of one of the mountains. The rescue party, Elkins continued, then made its way to the site of the encampment. According to Elkins, the rock (about twenty-five feet long by four feet high) appeared to provide a good defensive position.

At midnight on August 10, while camped at this site, Mays and his troops were awakened by some of the Indians' horses, which were grazing nearby. Mays ordered his men to herd those horses slowly and

[17] John R. Baylor, Fort Bliss, Texas, to Earl Van Dorn, August 25, 1861 (two letters), in United States, *Official Rebellion Records*, Series I, 4:24–26.

[18] U.S. Department of Interior, "Eighth Census, 1860," Lavaca County; "Sketches of Early Times," *State Gazette*, June 12, 1852; Brown, "The Great Indian Raid of 1840"; Olive Todd Walker, "Major Whitfield Chalk," p. 360.

[19] Elkins, *Indian Fighting*, pp. 25–27.

silently forward until they located the Indian encampment about three miles distant. (Lieutenant White in a letter to Dr. W. E. East of Hallettsville, Texas, stated that Mays "captured 100 head of horses without a fight.") Before sunrise on August 11, Mays and his troops attacked an encampment of Mescalero Apaches, but they were soon in full retreat before a very superior force (about 80 or 100, Lieutenant White stated in the aforementioned letter). In the confusion, according to Elkins, who obtained the information from Juan, Mays passed the order for a helter-skelter run for the camp at the large rock. Some made it, and there Mays, whose arm was broken, handed his rifle to the Mexican guide and with the other arm and hand continued to use his pistol. The guide, realizing that the survivors had been trapped, thereupon climbed quickly up the mountain behind the rock, passed through a gap, and made his way on foot in four days to Fort Davis.[20]

The rescue party, Elkins wrote, found at the rock encampment signs of a bloody battle and much shooting, including dead horses and some underclothes that had been torn, apparently for dressing wounds. Elkins apparently was not a close observer or else he either neglected or forgot to mention other signs of the battle, for Lieutenant White in his letter of August 24 to Dr. East stated that Jett's party had also found at the site hats, boots, parts of pants and coats of most of the missing men, and the body of John Deprose. In 1927, Jack Dawson stated that he had been told by his father, James Dawson, who was with the rescue party, that "the bodies [of the Mays party] were found and buried on the flat," a statement that appears somewhat questionable, since neither Elkins nor White mentioned such. Although not mentioned by Elkins, Dawson related and John Buchanan published accounts that credited Juan with a story that one of the men had an opportunity to escape but elected instead to die fighting with his comrades. Thomas Carroll (Carl or Carlton, as Jack Dawson remembered the name) and Juan were in the rear out of danger. Carroll called on Juan to go with him to the aid of their companions, but the guide said they would all be killed and refused. According to Dawson, Carroll "with a six-shooter in each hand, . . . rode into that swarm of murdering Apaches."[21] In

[20] White to East, August 24, 1861; Elkins, *Indian Fighting*, pp. 38–39; Baylor to Van Dorn, August 25, 1861 (two letters), in United States, *Official Rebellion Records*, Series I, 4:24–26.

[21] Townsend, "Mays Massacre," pp. 29–42.

the other version, the major facts are essentially the same, except Carroll (called Riley) and the guide were already out of the canyon, the
guide expressed his belief that all the others were dead by then, and
"Riley" said, "Well, I am going back to see if I can help them."[22]

After finishing the inspection of the battle site, Lieutenant Jett
and his men followed the trail of the Indians to the Rio Grande, where
it crossed into Mexico. They then returned to Fort Stockton, except
seven, including Elkins, who went to Fort Davis.

As previously related, on the night of August 13, 1861, a week after
Mays departed Fort Davis, Captain Bill Adams was "6 miles above Van
Horns Wells," more than halfway from Stockton to Bliss with a majority of his company. Upon his arrival at Fort Lancaster on July 28, he
had found waiting for him orders to march immediately to Bliss with 80
percent of his Company C, but at 10:00 P.M. on August 13 he received
new orders from Baylor, issued the previous day, to garrison half his
company at Lancaster and the other half at Stockton. In a P.S., Baylor
added that "Lt. Jutt [sic] will command at Ft. Stockton," and Adams
was to relieve the detachment of Captain Pyron's company at Fort
Hudson (at least the word appears to be Hudson) on the Devils River
and order it to join its company at Fort Bliss or Fort Stockton.[23] Perhaps, when ordering Company C to return to Lancaster and Stockton,
Baylor felt that the Indian menace in the lower Pecos country created
a more urgent need for troops than his plans for the conquest of New
Mexico.

[22] O. L. Shipman, *Taming the Big Bend*, pp. 35–36.
[23] John R. Baylor to Adams, August 12, 1861, Adams Papers.

CHAPTER 3

The Confederate Takeover, August, 1861, until March 29, 1862

FOR a time after the Mays Massacre, the only troops in the lower Pecos region were a few of Charles L. Pyron's men, under Lieutenant William G. Jett, a small detachment of James Walker's company, and William C. Adams' full company.[1]

As previously mentioned, on the night of August 13, 1861, while camped near Van Horn's Well, Adams received orders from Lieutenant Colonel John R. Baylor to place half of his company at Lancaster and half at Stockton. Fearing an attack by Union forces, Baylor on August 18 reversed his orders and instructed Adams to leave twenty men under a lieutenant at Lancaster and with the remainder to proceed as quickly as possible to Fort Bliss.[2] Because the nearest post office was at Fort Stockton, seventy-five or eighty miles distant,[3] Adams did not receive the first orders until August 25. By then, Baylor, having been informed of the Mays incident and realizing that Fort Davis needed additional soldiers, had dispatched orders to Adams to occupy Fort Davis with his entire company, except for a small guard at Fort Lancaster.

---

[1] Much information in this chapter is from the William C. Adams Papers, in possession of Mrs. Brawley Adams, Balmorhea, Texas. These papers contain muster rolls, post returns, correspondence, and other documents, many of which are also in the Archives, Texas State Library, Austin. The Adams muster rolls and post returns (which are not cited individually in this chapter) show the location of detachments, what men from other units were "casually" at the post (that is, passing through or laying over because of sickness), who had been killed or arrested, and what orders had been received. The United States, *War of the Rebellion: Official Records of the Union and Confederate Armies* (hereafter cited as *Official Rebellion Records*), Series I, vols. 9, 15, and 16, pt. 2, and Series II, vol. 2, also have been used extensively.

[2] John R. Baylor, Fort Bliss, to William C. Adams, August 18, 1861, Adams Papers.

[3] Adams, Fort Lancaster, to postmaster general, August 31, 1861, Adams Papers.

Meanwhile, Adams had left a detachment under First Lieutenant John C. Ellis at Lancaster, and, when Baylor's orders of the twenty-fifth arrived, he was with most of his company at Pecos Spring on the Pecos River, not far from the present site of Sheffield.[4] While at Pecos Spring, he received notice stating that Dr. Edwin Downs had been assigned to Lancaster, as an assistant surgeon, to relieve a Dr. Johnson. This arrangement united a father and son, for Downs's eighteen-year-old son, also named Edwin, was a member of the Company C detachment stationed at Lancaster.[5] Another surgeon or assistant surgeon was still needed, and Claudius Edward Richard King, later considered dean of San Antonio physicians, was subsequently assigned to Adams' company.[6]

Arriving at Fort Davis on September 7, Adams found that the post was garrisoned by only sixteen of Walker's men: Second Lieutenant William P. White, Sergeant J. B. Hawkins, and fourteen privates. The eight soldiers sent out to find Mays were members of this detachment. At the end of September, Adams' Company C was split into four parts. Captain Adams and about thirty-five of his men and a small detachment of Company D under Lieutenant White were at Fort Davis. A detachment under Lieutenant Ellis and Lieutenant William G. Jett with his small group from Pyron's company were at Stockton. Lieutenant Ingram supposedly had another detachment at Fort Bliss, but his supply officer, Adams complained, had failed to keep him informed.[7]

Adams received conflicting orders from Colonel H. E. McCulloch, in San Antonio, almost as frequently as he did from Baylor. Most were written by McCulloch's assistant adjutant general, Captain Donald C. Stith, who had been captured in Chihuahua by Baylor's men during the previous July while he was a lieutenant in the Union Army, had been paroled, and had promptly switched allegiance. On September 27 Adams received from McCulloch an order to proceed with his company to Fort Bliss as soon as Captain S. J. Richardson's command of W. P. Lane's Rangers arrived.[8] But this change never occurred. Rich-

[4] Baylor to Adams, August 25, 1861, Adams Papers.

[5] J. Marvin Hunter, *100 Years in Bandera*, pp. 16, 59.

[6] H. E. McCulloch, San Antonio, to Commanding Officer at Fort Davis, September 16, 1861, Adams Papers; *New Encyclopedia of Texas*, p. 1556.

[7] Adams, Fort Davis, to Baylor, November 5, 1861, Adams Papers.

[8] H. E. McCulloch, San Antonio, to Commanding Officer at Fort Davis, September 9, 1861, Adams Papers.

ardson disliked the idea of moving to far West Texas, and, according to one of his men, managed to get the order countermanded.[9]

Baylor, fearing that the Union forces in New Mexico might force the Texans to retreat, made plans in mid-October to get supplies and to withdraw to Fort Davis if necessary.[10] In the process, he dispatched a number of orders, many of which he countermanded before they could be carried out. He directed Adams to send the surplus (then later, all) ammunition at Fort Stockton to Doña Ana, New Mexico, and to send some of Adams' and Lieutenant White's men to Eagle Springs, about twenty miles from Van Horn's Well. The latter order did not arrive at Fort Davis until twenty-six days after it was written, and there is no evidence that the thoroughly confused Adams complied. Some of the orders issued in October, however, were eventually carried out. A detachment of Captain Richardson's Company F moved to Lancaster in November, Lieutenant Jett and his detachment from Company B joined their commander, Captain Pyron, in New Mexico, and a detachment of Adams' company moved to Fort Stockton.[11]

Because of wretched health, Richardson and the remainder of his company did not arrive at Lancaster until December. W. W. Heartsill, the diarist who was with the captain, found Lancaster to be "a beautiful place . . . on Live Oak Creek, half mile above it's [*sic*] junction with the Pecos River." The best part of the new post, he said, was the food, for his comrades who had arrived earlier had been "trafficking with a Mexican train; and have Cornbread, El Passo Onions and Dried Apples; besides have a new Mexican cook, the other-one refused to leave Fort Clark." There was not much to do at Lancaster except play "Town-Ball" and to trap or shoot "Kiotas" (coyotes), hundreds of which came around the soldiers' quarters at night. Unfortunately, Heartsill noted, "the big yellow Dog from the Stage stand" got caught in one of the "Kiota" traps and "soon bid farewell to earthly cares." John Duke was "a 'dead shot' at a Kiota in the dark, every night he gets one to three. If Kiota skins were valuable, John would soon rival the Hudson Bay Company." Heartsill discovered that West Texas weather was extremely erratic. On Christmas Day, 1861, it was so hot that he was "bothered to

[9]W. W. Heartsill, *Fourteen Hundred and 91 Days in the Confederate Army*, pp. 42–43.

[10]Capt. James Walker, Fort Bliss, to Adams, October 26, 1861, Adams Papers.

[11]H. E. McCulloch, San Antonio, to Adams, October 7, 1861, Adams Papers. During the Sibley Expedition, Jett served with Pryon in a number of engagements.

bind a shard [erect a shade] to escape from an oppresively warm Sun." On the following day, his Company F suffered through a norther that brought sleet.[12]

Early in October, Captain Adams went to Lancaster for six recruits, leaving Lieutenant Emory Gibbons in command at Fort Davis. During his absence, Gibbons took a small detachment of Company C to kidnap and arrest a prominent person on the south side of the Rio Grande. He received a directive from Colonel Baylor at Doña Ana, dated October 3, that read: "I am informed that there is a man at Presidio del Norte by the name of [A. F.] Wulff who is a spy. I want him *enticed* over on this side of the river and taken prisoner and sent to these headquarters in irons" (emphasis in original). According to Adams, Gibbons, on receiving this order, asked R. C. Daly, a clerk at Pat Murphy's store, to read it—aloud.[13] The action raises some question since the lieutenant could read, and Wulff was the partner of Pat Murphy, the sutler at Fort Davis.

The twenty-eight-year-old Lieutenant Emory Gibbons, a native of Arkansas and more recently a farmer in Uvalde County, Texas,[14] with a detachment of nine men left Fort Davis on October 12 to carry out the orders. Evidently, the small detachment took the eighty-eight-mile trail to Fort Leaton, located on the Texas side of the river, three miles below Presidio del Norte (present Ojinaga). Fort Leaton's occupants, who traded with the Indians for stolen horses and property, were not popular with the inhabitants of Presidio del Norte.[15]

Evidently, after some investigation at Fort Leaton and in the small Mexican village of Presidio, five members of the detachment, accompanied by Joseph Leaton (son of the deceased Ben Leaton), attended a dance in Presidio on the night of the fourteenth. Soon after the dance, the four men went to the residence of A. F. Wulff and took him captive when he answered a knock on the door. No sooner had Wulff been "yanked out by his head of hair" than he let out a yell for help. Al-

[12] Heartsill, *In the Confederate Army*, pp. 45–49.

[13] Adams, Fort Davis, to McCulloch, October 21, 1861, and Baylor, Doña Ana, N. Mex., to Adams, October 3, 1861, both in United States, *Official Rebellion Records*, Series II, 2:1526–1527; Adams to Baylor, October 21, 1861, Adams Papers.

[14] U.S. Department of the Interior, Bureau of the Census, "Eighth Census of the United States, 1860. Population. Texas," Uvalde County.

[15] Zenas R. Bliss, "Reminiscences," 1:261–263, in Eugene C. Barker Texas History Center, University of Texas, Austin.

though he was silenced by the threat of death, his wife and brother-in-law took up the cry. Presumably Wulff had been warned from Fort Davis and was prepared. Within a few minutes, a large number of shots were exchanged between Gibbons' men and the Mexicans. Troopers Thomas B. Wren, thirty, and John B. Boles, twenty-six, and one Mexican were killed. Not long afterward, Joseph Leaton was seen crossing to the Texas side of the river.

Meanwhile, Adams had returned to Fort Davis, and on the night of the ill-fated venture in Presidio del Norte, unaware of the state of affairs there, he sent First Sergeant Thomas L. Wilson with five soldiers to the Rio Grande to recall Lieutenant Gibbons' detachment. After he learned the details, he reported that the mission had failed because Wulff had been apprised of the plan.[16]

There was strong competition for army trade at frontier posts, particularly at Davis. Pat Murphy, the storekeeper there, and his partner, A. F. Wulff, had contracts with the Confederates, but the firm of Moke and Brother had a more legitimate claim to the sutlership. On September 17, 1861, John James, at San Antonio, wrote to Captain Adams, saying: "Mr. Moke who I understand is the sutler of Fort Davis, and [I] being the owner of it [Fort Davis], have rented it to our Government, reserving the sutlers store, having the privilege to rent it to the person who may be selected as sutler at $20 per month should he desire to occupy it at that price. Mr. Moke has agreed to pay the rent. And as you are the commanding officer, you will please put the sutler in possession."[17]

Apparently Wulff, a Union sympathizer, intended to keep Murphy from getting any Confederate business. After the Presidio affair, Colonel Baylor informed Adams that he was not to issue any voucher to Murphy and Wulff, or to either of them, until further orders.[18] About four months later, Adams was instructed to remove Murphy and put Moke and Brother in possession of the sutlership. In a strong letter to

[16] Adams, Fort Davis, to McCulloch, March 6, 1862, Adams Papers; Emory Gibbons to Benigno Contreras, October 16, 1861, Contreras to Gibbons, October 16, 1861, A. F. Wulff to Adams, October 16, 1861, and Wulff to Pat Murphy, November [October] 16, 1861, all in United States, *Official Rebellion Records*, Series II, 2:1527–1530.

[17] John James, San Antonio, to William C. Adams, September 17, 1861, Adams Papers.

[18] Baylor, La Mesilla, N. Mex., to Commanding Officer at Fort Davis, November 23, 1861, Adams Papers.

Colonel H. E. McCulloch in March, 1862, Adams denied that he had ever disobeyed orders regarding the sutlership and asserted that he had long before bestowed upon Moke and Brother the coveted business, as per instructions issued during the previous December.[19]

Meanwhile, Sergeant Wilson returned to Fort Davis with the Gibbons party on October 18, and Adams immediately placed Gibbons under arrest. Adams sent a report on the Gibbons affair and related documents to Colonel McCulloch, but he was unable to give full details because no one at Fort Davis could read the communications in Spanish from Presidio.[20] Gibbons, however, was "in arrest" only a short time. There appears to have been no court-martial, and soon he was again in command of the Company C detachment at Fort Stockton.

Since only an advance party of Richardson's Company F of Lane's Rangers had arrived at Lancaster by late November, 1861, Company C was still scattered. Captain Adams was at Davis, Gibbons was at Stockton, Ellis was at Lancaster, and Ingram was with Baylor in New Mexico or at Fort Bliss. Private Mattison, who had earlier transferred from Hamner's company, and John Elkins were on detached service with Ingram, but Mattison spent most of his time in sick bay at Fort Bliss. John W. Chitwood, another private, had never made it west; for an unreported reason he had been in confinement at Fort Clark since July 20.

There was not much for the soldiers to do. Occasionally there was escort duty for the mails or for an occasional drove of cattle. With most of the far West Texas posts occupied by at least a detachment, Indians usually stayed clear, but on the night of December 27, 1861, Apaches slipped into Pat Murphy's corral at Fort Davis and drove off a number of cattle. A punitive force of thirty-three men was sent in pursuit, and on the second day afterward Murphy wrote his friend, John Spencer, at Presidio that he thought the group was "hot on the trail, and I hope will be successful."[21] Apparently it was not.

Early in 1862, Captain Adams went to San Antonio, leaving Lieutenant Ellis in command at Davis. Although the reason is not clear, Adams may have had to answer charges regarding the sutler affair at

[19]Adams, Fort Davis, to McCulloch, March 6, 1862, Adams Papers.

[20]Adams, Fort Davis, to McCulloch, October 21, 1861, in United States, *Official Rebellion Records*, Series II, 2:1526–1527.

[21]Carlysle Graham Raht, *The Romance of Davis Mountains and Big Bend Country*, pp. 145–146.

Fort Davis. By then, Ingram and his detachment had returned from New Mexico and were assigned to Lancaster to relieve Richardson's Company F, whose enlistment period was about to expire. By April, 1862, the change at Lancaster had been completed. Heartsill's diary, relating to affairs at the post, is relatively dull. It has notations about an occasional norther, the stage from "Santa Fee," the smallpox at Fort Davis, and the burning of Pecos Station by the Indians, but no mention of the tragic deaths of two of Adams' men during his absence.[22] In April, twenty-one-year-old Private John W. O'Bryant, a native of Arkansas who had joined the company at Pedro Pinto, was shot to death in an affray at Fort Stockton,[23] and at Fort Davis on May 4 George T. Haynie, the eighteen-year-old bugler, a native of Kentucky, shot himself to death.[24]

By midsummer, Adams' company had returned to his command, but its days in West Texas were numbered. In New Mexico Baylor and H. H. Sibley had been unsuccessful, and a general evacuation was imminent. The last West Texas muster roll made out by Adams was on July 15, 1862, at Fort Lancaster, an indication that Company C was already on its way home. In June, when the one-year enlistments expired, Adams was ordered to designate which of his eighty-three men were over thirty-five or under eighteen at the time they were mustered into service. Then some of the youngsters who had lied about their ages when they had enlisted, including Charles Montague, Leonadas Fleming, and Alonza G. Russell, claimed that they had been sixteen (or younger) at the time.[25] Later Judge Joe Montague, Charles' son, wrote about his father's service at Fort Davis:

During the time my father remained at Fort Davis it is recorded that he was the only Confederate to kill an Indian. He and a Scotch seagoing man who had not left with the Federals were sent out with the horse herd. The sailor was no cowboy. As soon as the herd was conveniently out of sight of the post the sailor dismounted and walked. My father saw six Indians appearing over a ridge.

[22] Heartsill, *In the Confederate Army*, pp. 50–55.

[23] Return of Soldiers in Co. C, 2nd Regt., Texas Mounted Rifles, who have died since the 15th of October, 1861, signed by 1st Lt. Ellis, Fort Davis, May 1, 1862, Adams Papers.

[24] Return of Soldiers in Co. C, 2nd Regt., Texas Mounted Rifles, who have died since the 4th of April, 1862, signed by Lt. Ellis, Fort Davis, June 3, 1862, Adams Papers.

[25] Various documents, dated June and July, 1862, pertaining to discharges of Co. C troops over 35 and under 18, Adams Papers.

They were mounted bareback and without bridles. One rode a roan horse. He cut in after the man on foot, and also cut out some of the Confederate saddle animals. My father tried to head the Indian off. He saw that he could not succeed if the Indian stayed alive. So he hauled out his cap-and-ball pistol and began to shoot. The redman was effectively stopped, according to the account of the affair, and the grounded sailor and horses saved.[26]

Most of Adams' men reenlisted in other units, and Company C, Second Regiment, Texas Mounted Rifles, ceased to exist. During its assignment at Stockton, Lancaster, and Davis, the men had done everything that was required. Despite boredom and deprivations, there was apparently very little dissension among the troops, and there were no desertions. Five men lost their lives: Wren and Bowles were killed in Presidio by Mexicans; O'Bryant died in an affray at Stockton; Haynie shot himself at Davis; and Christopher C. Rine, a twenty-one-year-old Pedro Pinto boy, died of an undisclosed cause.

Meanwhile, the campaigns in New Mexico had greatly affected the West Texas posts. As previously stated, Major H. H. Sibley resigned his commission in the army in New Mexico and went to Richmond to seek a commission in the Confederate Army. Sibley informed Jefferson Davis of conditions in New Mexico and submitted a plan of campaign. The president approved, appointed Sibley a brigadier general, and ordered him to organize, "in the speediest manner possible," two full regiments of cavalry and one battery of howitzers, and "such other forces as he deemed necessary."[27]

Later Sibley was authorized to enlist more troops for his brigade. Getting the authorization and getting the troops, however, were two different things. Brigadier General Sibley set up his headquarters in San Antonio in mid-August, 1861, confident that he would soon have all the men, supplies, and arms needed and that he would be in New Mexico by September. His dream was soon shattered. Recruiting went wrong from the start. Many companies called up by Governor Edward Clark to join Sibley had been disbanded or too reduced in numbers to meet the requirements; a few units were not aware that they could join

[26] Barry Scobee, *Fort Davis, Texas, 1583–1960*, p. 43; Gertrude Harris, *A Tale of Men Who Knew No Fear*, p. 26.

[27] Martin Hardwick Hall, "The Formation of Sibley's Brigade and the March to New Mexico," in *Southwestern Historical Quarterly* 61 (1958):386.

without being called; and still others were being drained off to the eastern theaters.

To further complicate preparations, Texas military officers, expecting to be attacked on the coast, were reluctant to dispense with their war materiel. When General Van Dorn was transferred from Texas, Colonel H. E. McCulloch and his ordnance officer went to Galveston to confer with the new departmental commander, General P. O. Hébert, and, consequently, for several weeks Sibley had no responsible officer through whom he could obtain the needed ordnance supplies. As a result, he overstepped his authority by ordering subordinates to issue the materiel. He also sought to purchase firearms and have lances manufactured, but, as his disbursing officers were penniless, he had to rely on the credit of the Confederate government.

By some miracle, Sibley's Brigade finally came into existence, with three regiments of Texas Cavalry, the Fourth, Fifth, and Seventh, commanded respectively by Colonels James Reily, Tom Green, and William Steele. As each new company was added, it was subjected to a rigid period of training. Most of the men were under age twenty-five. The Fourth and Fifth regiments each had a battery of mountain howitzers, but for the most part the men in all the companies were poorly armed. "Few armies," wrote one of its historians, "probably have ever had a more motley collection of weapons." There were squirrel guns, bear guns, minié muskets, shotguns, navy revolvers, and common rifles. But what the men lacked in arms they made up for in exuberance and in eagerness to face the enemy.[28]

In late October, the first units of the army began the 700-mile march to Fort Bliss. Because of the scarcity of water and grass along parts of the route, it would have been impossible for the three regiments to travel as one unit. In fact, not even an entire regiment could march as a unit. Reily's Fourth left on October 26; Green's Fifth got under way on November 2; and Steele's regiment broke camp on November 20. Sibley, traveling in a coach, departed San Antonio on November 18. By December 15, all companies had started, except one that remained behind to escort Captain W. H. Harrison, the brigade paymaster. They all followed the San Antonio–El Paso route, by way

[28] Ibid., p. 393.

of Forts Clark, Hudson, Lancaster, Stockton, Davis, and Quitman. The detachments reunited on the Rio Grande, near old Fort Quitman, on Christmas night and after a week continued to Fort Bliss.

For most of the men, it was a wretched trip, and many did not make it to Fort Bliss. Because of illness, especially measles, a number of the soldiers were left at Fort Clark and perhaps at a few other posts along the way. Captain Adams reported that several of the enlisted men had been left at Fort Davis, either because of their own sickness or to attend sick comrades.

At Fort Bliss the situation was even worse. Dreaded smallpox had broken out among Baylor's men, and by the middle of January, 1862, there were over a hundred cases and six deaths. In addition, as a result of the cold weather and inadequate clothing, many of the troops took pneumonia.

Other troubles plagued Sibley's men along the route. Often there was not enough food. Horses got scours from drinking bad water. Colonel Green's slave stole his horse and disappeared into Mexico. A private who had struck a captain was court-martialed and sentenced to be "chained hard and fast" to a baggage wagon for a month. At San Felipe Springs, near Fort Clark, three soldiers were court-martialed for sleeping on sentry duty and condemned to close confinement on bread and water for ten days, but these sentences were later remitted. Major S. A. Lockridge, Fifth Regiment, while camped on a creek in present Val Verde County, lost all his beef cattle and work steers.[29]

At the time Sibley passed through Fort Lancaster, the post was garrisoned by a detachment of Captain Richardson's Company F. Although he did not arrive until later, Heartsill, the diarist with Richardson's company, made note of Sibley's brief stopover. On November 28 the Company F detachment was ordered to "appear in Uniform and mounted, with their Arms, at 7 o'clk A.M. for the purpose of escorting Gen'l Sibley and paying necessary honors." The ceremony was conducted with "great gusto, especially when Gen'l Sibley took charge of the Company to see how well they were drilled; Serg't Harwell was on the right, marching by two's; the command was given by the Gen'l,

---

[29] Lockridge, whose real name was William Kissane, had left Cincinnati five or six years earlier after being implicated in the burning of a steamer. He was with William Walker, the American filibuster, in the ill-fated attempt to invade Nicaragua in the 1850s.

'file left,' which was of course unheard, and on they went at a brisk trot, ascended the Mountain, and as they disappeared the General turned around muttering 'gone to h——l.' In the evening the Company returned, and found that the General had gone on his way rejoicing to New Mexico."[30]

By mid-December, Sibley had arrived at Fort Bliss and assumed command of the "Army of New Mexico," which included, in addition to those he had recruited, all the soldiers of Baylor's command. Within another two or three weeks, all the brigade, except the men left behind because of sickness, were united at Bliss, and Sibley began his campaign to chase the Federals out of New Mexico (which until February, 1863, included Arizona). After that, if his dreams materialized, he would establish Confederate posts at the head of the Gulf of Lower California and unite with the Mormons in Utah.

In mid-January, 1862, Sibley started up the Rio Grande. He occupied Doña Ana, near Las Cruces, and Fort Thorn, northwest of present Hatch, and established hospitals at both places. The men lacked proper clothing and blankets. "The ranks were becoming daily thinned," wrote Sibley, "by those two terrible scourges to an army," smallpox and pneumonia. Baylor's forces had about exhausted what little food existed in southern New Mexico, the quartermaster had no money for purchases of that available, and the plan to supply the troops with captured Federal goods did not materialize. Furthermore, Sibley, by his own later admission, was unfit for command because of ill health and, though he did not admit it, because of his addiction to John Barleycorn.

After a desperate battle at Val Verde, near Fort Craig, the Texans occupied Socorro, Albuquerque, and Santa Fe with little trouble. There remained to the northeast of Santa Fe, however, Fort Union and Las Vegas, where the retreating government was located. The Confederates, of course, must occupy those places.

In Glorietta Pass, about midway between Santa Fe and Fort Union, Sibley's command unexpectedly met head-on a large Federal force marching westward from Fort Union, and a fierce battle ensued. The Confederates were on the verge of victory, but during the engage-

[30] Heartsill, *In the Confederate Army*, p. 49.

ment, the Unionists discovered sixty to eighty Confederate supply wagons to the rear in the corrals at Johnson's Ranch. These and a six-pound field piece were captured. For the Texans the loss of the supply train was a disaster, for it deprived them of their already short supply of ammunition, forage, and provisions.[31] The only alternatives were surrender or retreat. Naturally, they chose to retreat.

[31] Theophilus Noel, *Autobiography and Reminsicences*, p. 23.

CHAPTER 4

From Glorietta to the War's End

AFTER their dead at Glorietta were buried, the Union commanders were anxious to follow up their victory. Colonel E. R. S. Canby, U.S. military commander of the Department of New Mexico, who had been isolated at Fort Craig, about halfway between El Paso and Albuquerque, ordered a contingent of the Union force to retreat to Fort Union, but his attempt at remote control caused utter confusion. Then deciding to catch Sibley before he could recover, he left the sick and wounded and ten companies at Fort Craig, with Christopher (Kit) Carson in command, and on April 1, 1862, with the remainder of his troops headed north. Before mid-April, his force had a minor engagement with some Confederates at Albuquerque and then proceeded northward and joined the advance units from Fort Union.[1]

Two days before, the retreating Confederates had reached Santa Fe, where they obtained food. Soon afterward, Sibley received word from Albuquerque that without reinforcements that place could not be held. "In our straightened [sic] circumstances," Sibley later wrote, "the question now arose in my mind whether to evacuate the country or take the desperate chance of fighting the enemy in his stronghold." With the Unionists advancing on him from two directions, he headed south. The retreat turned into panic. "The retreat of the Army of New Mexico, as we were called," wrote Theo Noel, "from Santa Fe down the Rio Grande to Socorro was like that of the skedaddling of a crowd of urchins who had been caught in a melon patch."[2]

---

[1]In this chapter extensive use has been made of Martin Hardwick Hall, "The Formation of Sibley's Brigade and the March to New Mexico," *Southwestern Historical Quarterly* 61 (January, 1958):383–405; and United States, *War of the Rebellion: Official Records of the Union and Confederate Armies* (hereafter cited as *Official Rebellion Records*), Series I, vols. 9, 15.

[2]H. H. Sibley to S. Cooper, May 4, 1862, in United States, *Official Rebellion Rec-*

All along the way, the fleeing Texans destroyed or abandoned equipment that impeded their progress. In many cases, the units disintegrated into small parties without any authority or discipline. Noel wrote that "we walked and staggered along like the reeling, hungry, thirsty wretches that we were, with no head, nobody to direct or command, with the bloodthirsty Dog Canyon Apache Indians following in our wake and scalping the poor unfortunate boys whose blistered feet and enfeebled frame made it impossible for them to march farther. . . . No army or body of men on the American continent ever suffered as did the men on this retreat."[3] Hospitals were set up but quickly evacuated; there was no time to attend to or carry along the sick and wounded. Some who died along the road were left unburied.

Even so, Sibley planned to capture the bypassed Fort Craig, but the plan was abandoned when Colonel Tom Green, due to the high waters, was unable to cross to the east side of the Rio Grande. It was then decided to continue the retreat on the west side of the river through the awesome mountains, a route almost impossible to traverse. By May, Sibley and a large part of his command were at Fort Bliss. The rear guard, under Colonel William Steele, and two or three hundred Confederates were in the Mesilla–Doña Ana area.

The Confederate commanders in San Antonio and Richmond still felt that with assistance Sibley would be able to hold his position. For that purpose, General P. O. Hébert, commander of the Department of Texas, ordered two regiments to be sent west. President Jefferson Davis expressed optimism that the two regiments would save Sibley, and General Robert E. Lee praised Hébert for having ordered the assistance and felt that the governor of Texas should send Sibley everything that could be spared. But none of this assistance ever materialized, and Sibley's situation daily grew more desperate. On May 27, Sibley wrote to General Hamilton P. Bee, commander of the Western District of Texas, that "the army is absolutely subsisting on poor meat and bread, with a limited supply. . . . Our ammunition may be said to be exhausted. For heavy guns we have perhaps 100 rounds. Clothing completely exhausted, with no means of renewing the supply."[4]

---

ords, Series I, 9:510 (in this letter Sibley gave an account of his New Mexico campaign, pp. 505–512); Theophilus Noel, *Autobiography and Reminiscences*, p. 63.

[3] Noel, *Reminiscences*, pp. 63–64.

[4] Sibley, Fort Bliss, Texas, to Gen. H. P. Bee, May 27, 1862, in United States, *Offi-*

New Mexico, he continued, was "not worth a quarter of the blood and treasure expended in its conquest," for the "indispensable element, food, cannot be relied on." It was unfortunate indeed that he had not agreed with the opinion a year and a half earlier of John C. Robertson, chairman of the Texas Committee of Public Safety, who had stated that if the Union Army decided to concentrate in New Mexico and Arizona Texans could not prevent it. "It is a matter of importance," Robertson had added, "to know how they could subsist in those territories."[5] It was for this reason that, until he had verification, General Canby doubted that troops from California were coming to his aid.

The Californians, nevertheless, were on their way. By April they had reached Fort Yuma and soon thereafter occupied Tucson, a Confederate post, without firing a shot.[6] When the retreating Southerners brought this news eastward, the Confederate Army of New Mexico—what was left of it—started for San Antonio. The rear guard under Steele at Mesilla was in a critical position. The retreating Confederates had already stripped the area of many of its meager supplies, and the local citizens refused to sell them any they had left, thereby forcing them to impress what they could. This caused, of course, ill feeling on both sides, and the troops became so disgusted and so impatient to return to Texas that at times they were near rebellion against their own leaders. They knew that if the Californians cut their retreat route they would be entrapped and forced to surrender. Thus, Steele had to withdraw to El Paso as soon as Sibley could evacuate Fort Bliss. On June 17 Sibley started his weary troops for San Antonio in small parties of fifteen to twenty men, and on July 8 Steele began withdrawing his "almost naked" rear guard from Mesilla to Fort Bliss, leaving behind the dream of a Confederate empire to the Pacific. There, while waiting for the main command to keep sufficient distance ahead, he traded across the river for food and money in preparation for the long and hazardous march across the barren West Texas desert to San Antonio. George M.

---

cial Rebellion Records, Series I, 9:714. One authority concluded that Sibley's failure in New Mexico was mainly due to logistical inadequacy and alcohol (Jerry Don Thompson, "Henry Hopkins Sibley: Military Inventor on the Texas Frontier," paper presented at a meeting of West Texas Historical Association, Abilene, Texas, April 7, 1973).

[5] Sibley to Bee, in United States, *Official Rebellion Records*, Series I, 9:714; Jno. C. Robinson, Austin, Tex., Feby 12, 1861, to [Texas] Commissioners, in *Journal of the Secession Convention of Texas, 1861*, ed. Ernest W. Winkler, p. 273.

[6] Sidney R. De Long, *The History of Arizona*, p. 19.

Frazer and other soldiers, according to Frazer's grandson, Ernest Riggs, gathered sufficient teams, food, and other necessities for the arduous retreat.

When James H. Carleton and his California Column arrived (having started from Tucson on August 16), it found, Carleton reported, that the retreating Texans had carried off, disposed of, or destroyed all equipment and supplies along their route, except in Mesilla and Franklin. Some public property that had originally belonged to the United States government had been traded across the river for breadstuff and specie. Over $800 in specie had been left with Dr. Southworth, the Confederate surgeon who had remained behind with twenty-six disabled men in the hospital, and a larger amount had been left in credit with parties in Mexico. Carleton managed to recover from rooms adjoining the customhouse in El Paso, Mexico, twelve wagonloads of hospital supplies and quartermaster property that, in all probability, were public property Steele had traded to Mexicans. Carleton also learned of some Confederate deserters on both sides of the river.

Theo Noel, a member of the retreating army, related a tale of horrible suffering. The soldiers, he wrote, had thrown away their guns, except their six-shooters. "There were six or eight horses and a wagon with four mules to the first party of six hundred men. . . ." After a long and weary march of nearly one hundred miles to Fort Quitman, the troops ascended Eagle Canyon twenty miles to the ruins of the old overland stage station. Eagle Springs, where there was a well forty feet deep, sixty feet in diameter, and with circling steps carved in its wall, were fed by a subterranean stream that flowed through a cavernous rock. The well had been filled with sheep, put there, Noel believed, by Indians hired by Canby, but what Indians and where the sheep came from were mysteries.

Already thirsty and with no water kegs, the weary soldiers continued their march for another twenty-two miles to Van Horn's Well, very similar to that at Eagle Springs, only to find it also filled with sheep. From here, Noel continued, "it was thirty-six miles to the Dead Man's Water Holes, making a distance of eighty-five miles that we had to tramp afoot over this desert road under a hot burning sun facing *sirocco* winds which blew from the southwest over the parched plains with heat that, once felt, can never be forgotten." The suffering, famishing, perishing men, strung out for twenty miles on the desert road, were reeling as though mad or drunk. Many died of measles, smallpox, mumps, or lack of food or water. The first to reach the water, about midnight, passed the word back. By daylight supposedly all had reached the water hole, but there was no roll call or any official check. Noel continued with his dramatic description:

As each famishing individual quenched his thirst he would go back and lie down across the road, the only place to lie, for it was all cactus, cat-claw and sage brush on each side. . . . At sunrise I started to the rear, where the wagon had been left and the mules turned loose. In the wagon there was a pick, a spade, and a shovel, and the corpse of a young friend who had perished on the road, which I had lifted into the wagon without aid.

I could have killed every man with that pickax as they lay there, so sound asleep were they. And a more ghastly sight I never beheld than those men lying on their backs, the sun shining in their faces. For forty-eight hours we had had nothing to eat. We had walked eighty-five miles without a drop of water. We had had no salt in anything we had eaten for nearly twenty days. Men whose ordinary weight was one hundred and eighty-five pounds weighed less than one hundred and fifteen.

At Fort Davis the troops with whom Noel marched found wood with which to build fires to bake unbolted flour that they kneaded into a dough, which was then wound around iron ramrods and held over the fire. After resting that day and night, this group again headed eastward.[7] Because of the hardships, one of the retreating parties buried two cannons somewhere west of Fort Davis, and apparently they have never been recovered. Supposedly the soldiers also buried many other articles they no longer had the strength to transport.[8]

A few days after his arrival at Bliss, Carleton and part of his cavalry started for Fort Quitman. He hoped to capture fifty or sixty wounded, sick, and disabled men Steele reportedly had left at Fort Davis. From Fort Quitman on the morning of August 23 he sent Cap-

[7]Noel, *Reminiscences*, pp. 64–66. Noel's group had left Fort Bliss in June or July rather than April as Noel stated. Otherwise, Captain Adams' Company C still would have had more food than unbolted flour. As previously stated, Adams' company did not move to Fort Lancaster until July.

[8]Barry Scobee, *Fort Davis, Texas, 1583–1960*, pp. 48–49, 51; A. M. Whetstone, son of Confederate soldier Thomas E. Whetstone, oral statement, to Clayton Williams, ca. 1940.

tain Edmond D. Shirland with a detachment to Fort Davis. (Apparently, Carleton immediately returned to Fort Bliss.) Shirland found the first two watering holes in about the condition Noel had described: Eagle Springs were "filled with rubbish and carrion," and Van Horn's Well was "entirely filled up." The men were able to clean out the Eagle Springs well enough to get water for both horses and soldiers but not the well at Van Horn.

Consequently, Shirland sent all but twenty of his men and some "picked horses" back to Eagle Springs to wait there and to clean the water hole thoroughly. Farther on, Shirland, like the Confederates before him, found ample water at Dead Man's Hole (El Muerto) and at Barrel Springs, less than twenty miles from Fort Davis. From this point, Shirland sent a corporal, a private, and a Mexican guide to reconnoiter Fort Davis. When the trio reported the next day that the post was unoccupied, Shirland went there and found it, indeed, entirely deserted. In one of the buildings of the Overland Mail Company he found lying on the floor a dead man, who had been shot through the body with a bullet and had an arrow wound on the head and one on the arm. He concluded that the room had been used as a hospital and that the victim, too ill to travel, had been killed by Indians. Shirland had the body buried.

In his report, dated September 2, 1862, Shirland gave a lengthy description of the buildings at Fort Davis, a number of which had been partially destroyed or damaged, especially the doors, windows, and roofs. The destruction was done both by retreating Confederates, who needed firewood, and by Indians, who apparently thought that the post had been completely deserted. Actually, a small group of refugees were hiding on a roof at the time the Indians were tearing up the place. According to Shirland, some materials had been hauled off; others had been burned. A wagon was loaded with lumber. Other property included some iron in the quartermaster's storehouse, some one hundred horseshoes, two old citizen-wagons, several wagon and cart wheels, some empty barrels, several chains, and many hospital bedsteads, all broken or in dilapidated condition.

Shirland also stated that he heard that a Confederate officer had sold the fort to a party in Del Norte, Mexico. Some Confederate officer at Fort Davis may have sold supplies, but it is extremely doubtful that anyone sold the post, for it belonged to John James of San Antonio, who had leased the site to the Confederates during the war and to the United States both before and after the war.[9]

If any Confederate officer did make such a deal, the victimized "buyer" might have been Edward Hall or someone Hall represented. Hall, it was reported in 1862, was a desperado who supposedly robbed Fort Davis of much public property and sold it in Chihuahua under the guise of an agent of the Confederate government, legally empowered to dispose of property taken from Fort Davis. Furthermore, when the Confederates evacuated the post, Diedrick Dutchover was assigned the job of looking after it and the equipment and supplies that were left behind. Dutchover was one of those on the roof while the Apaches were ransacking the buildings.

The dead man Shirland had buried at Fort Davis was probably on the roof with Dutchover (whose name had evolved from Anton Diedrick to Diedrick "Dutch All Over" and finally to Diedrick Dutchover), who had been with the mail service for years. Dutchover operated a small ranch five miles down Limpia Canyon from Fort Davis, had taken no part in either the struggle between the North and the South or in any of the fights against the Indians, who considered him to be harmless. Shortly after the Confederate troops left, Chief Nicolas appeared, with an estimated 250 Apache warriors. Seeing that Nicolas was in an ugly mood, the whites took refuge on the top of a building.

The refugees were Dutchover, a Mexican woman with two children, and four Americans, one of whom was quite ill. They managed to carry with them a sack of flour and two barrels of water. Fortunately, on the roof were some old wagon-wheel spokes, which provided a fire for cooking. Precaution was used to avoid betraying their position, but the Indians were actually too busy pillaging to discover the refugees. For two days and nights, the whites remained on the housetop. By then, the Indians had left the post and scattered over the countryside in search of stray cattle left by the troops. During the third night, under cover of darkness, Dutchover and his party, other than the sick man, struck out for Presidio, ninety-two miles away, and four days later, in

---

[9] Scobee, *Fort Davis, Texas*, pp. 20–21; United States, *Official Rebellion Records*, Series I, 9:577–579.

an exhausted and starving condition, they staggered into Presidio.[10]
When the stage arrived at Fort Davis the day after the departure of the
escapees, the driver found a man dead but not scalped, an indication
that, contrary to Shirland's surmise, the Indians likewise had found
him dead.[11] If it was the same corpse that Shirland later found, then
the stagecoach crew perhaps feared to tarry in that Indian-infested
area long enough to bury it.

After flying the Union flag over Fort Davis for a full day, Shirland
and his men returned to Dead Man's Hole, watered their animals, and
made a dry camp on the prairie. There, on the following day, they
were attacked by a superior force of Mescaleros. After a running battle,
four of the Indians were dead and about twenty wounded; Shirland had
two men wounded, one slightly and one painfully, and one horse
wounded. At Eagle Springs, the captain found sufficient water, but the
men he had sent there had not been able to get enough water for their
needs and had gone. On the next day, the two parties reunited on the
Rio Grande and then returned to Fort Bliss.

In September, Canby and his regulars were transferred to another
theater, and Carleton was placed in command of the Department of
New Mexico. Before departing for Santa Fe, Carleton paroled the
twenty-six men in the hospital at Franklin, furnished them with provisions and transportation, and ordered a party of soldiers under Lieutenant French (presumably Captain H. French, who later killed the
Confederate spy Henry Skillman) to escort them partway across West
Texas. Then, while en route to Santa Fe, he met another group of
ninety-three paroled Confederates, most, if not all, from the hospitals
at Santa Fe, Socorro, and Albuquerque, in the charge of a Confederate
surgeon named Covey. Displeased that he had received no word that
the men were being paroled and had been given arms for protection
against hostile Indians without any provision for returning the weapons, Carleton sent instructions to Lieutenant French to escort the pa-
rolees from Franklin to some point in West Texas relatively free from
attack and there take possession of the arms.

Meanwhile, General Hébert had ordered the abandonment of all
forts west of Fort Clark. By the time he issued the order, the abandon-

[10]Carlysle Graham Raht, *The Romance of Davis Mountains and Big Bend Country*, pp. 129–130, 149–150.
[11]Barry Scobee, *Old Fort Davis*, pp. 49–50.

ment had already taken place, and never again did the Confederates attempt to secure a foothold between Fort Clark and Fort Bliss. Likewise, the Federals made no attempt to garrison any post east of Bliss. Occasionally, however, both Federal and Texas units scouted Davis, Stockton, Quitman, and Lancaster. Once, in late 1862, upon the receipt of "circumstantial rumors that 6,000 Confederates [were] about to make another demonstration against this territory" and that Henry Skillman was planning to launch an attack on Franklin and Fort Bliss, Carleton sent troops to Horsehead Crossing on the Pecos River "to watch the enemy." Skillman, however, did nothing more than throw a scare into the Federals and the citizens of Franklin.[12]

When Texas militia ventured into West Texas, in most cases their object was to ascertain whether Federals were there. R. H. Williams, a member of a state outfit, recalled in his memoirs that his commanding officer believed "a yarn that two companies of Federal troops from California were coming down on Fort Lancaster . . . , and even now must have taken it." So off "to Fort Lancaster we went, a week's march there and back, only to find the whole story was a hoax." Not long afterward, the same officer "was greatly minded to march off to Fort Lancaster again, to attack another imaginary force of 'Feds' said to be in that neighborhood. This time, however, we managed to dissuade him from such a wild-goose chase, and got him to set about our legitimate business of Indian-hunting." On still another occasion, while looking for Indian camps near Fort Lancaster, Williams was sent to reconnoiter the fort, and the rest of the command soon followed. "Of course," said Williams, "I found no sign of the enemy, nor indeed of any other living creature; and as to the fort itself, the Indians had burned everything about it that was consumable, leaving nothing but the walls standing, bare and gaunt." (Much of the damage probably had been done by deserters and emigrants who needed firewood.)

In April, 1864, however, one rumor proved true, except that the enemy consisted of deserters, freebooters, and perhaps emigrants bound for California. "Three or four hundred Californians," Williams wrote, "established themselves at Fort Lancaster . . . , where they were assuming a threatening attitude, and attracting to themselves

[12]James H. Carleton, Santa Fe, to Captain Joseph Updegraff, December 8, 1862, Letters Sent, Records of the United States Army Commands, Record Group 98, National Archives, Washington, D.C.; Thompson, "Henry Hopkins Sibley."

many deserters from our service." Williams' outfit found Lancaster deserted, but the "Californians," who were located some distance beyond the fort, were attacked and routed. The Texans had four men killed and ten wounded. According to Williams' unreliable account, the Californians lost thirty-five killed, twenty wounded, and 250 horses captured. The survivors crossed the river into Mexico, where "we heard afterwards, they met with a hot reception from the ranchers and the people of the settlements they had plundered so that many were killed, the rest scattered to the four winds of heaven." In the aftermath, Williams wrote:

> We feasted royally on the ample provisions left behind by the enemy, and then, after a brief rest, having burned the tents and what plunder we couldn't carry away, set off for Fort Clark, with the wounded borne on improvised litters. . . . There . . . four of our own poor fellows died of their wounds, but the rest being soon fit to travel, we borrowed four ambulances and brought them back with us to our camp. . . . The captured horses and other plunder were sent into San Antonio, and sold for the benefit of the command in general.[13]

After the posts were abandoned in 1862, very few encounters with Indians in the Trans-Pecos region were recorded. The Apaches controlled the area, while the Comanches concentrated on a war against the United States in western Kansas, eastern Colorado, and eastern New Mexico and only occasionally raided the Texas frontier and into Mexico. During the raids into Mexico, the Comanches sometimes encountered the Apaches in the Trans-Pecos country. The two tribes had been fierce enemies since time immemorial. In one engagement, it seems, Comanche Chief Bajo el Sol defeated the Apaches at their ranchería on Toyah Creek, but in another in the same area he was killed. The brother of Bajo el Sol then took the band northward to the vicinity of the Canadian River, the region occupied by the northern bands of Comanches.[14]

During the Civil War, very few stockmen even considered the possibility of acquiring grazing lands in West Texas. But Richard Franklin Tankersley was foolhardy enough to do so. Tankersley, born in Mississippi in 1829, had moved to Texas in 1853 and had resided for a time

[13] R. H. Williams, *With the Border Ruffians, Memories of the Far West, 1852–1868*, pp. 325, 343, 347–348, 363–372.
[14] S. D. Myres, *Pioneer Surveyor—Frontier Lawyer: The Personal Narrative of O. W. Williams, 1877–1902*, pp. 270, 277–281, 289, 291, 296, 299.

in Round Rock and later in Cherokee and Brown counties. In 1863–1864 he and his family moved, in ox-drawn wagons, from Brown County to the South Concho, trailing seven hundred head of longhorn cattle.

After he selected the location for his ranch quarters, his family slept in the wagons and cooked over open fires until log cabins could be built. The cowboys looked after the stock closely until the herds became adjusted to the new country. Brownwood, about one hundred miles to the east, was his nearest source for supplies. Thus, the Tankersley family existed as much as possible off the land. It took ten longhorn cows to supply the ranch with milk, as each cow gave only about one pint a day. Bread and meat, supplemented by fruits, honey, and pecans, were the principal foods. Coffee, when available at all, was purchased green, parched in big pans, and then ground at the ranch kitchen. Ropes, bridles, except for the bits, and all saddle riggings were made from rawhide. The best ropes and girths, according to Tankersley's granddaughter, Fay Mason, were made from hair from the "mops" of buffalo.[15]

The final major encounter during the Civil War between whites and Indians in Southwest Texas took place near the Tankersley ranch. It was a tragic fiasco. In 1862 a group of Kickapoo Indians from Kansas and Oklahoma, discontented with the policies of the United States, migrated to Mexico. In December, while camped on the Little Concho, near present San Angelo, it was attacked by a mounted Confederate patrol. After shooting sixteen Texans out of their saddles, the Kickapoos hurried southward into Mexico, where they received a grant of land in return for a pledge to defend the country against Comanche and Kiowa raiders.

Favorably impressed with the treatment accorded their kinsmen, another group of Kickapoos started for Mexico in the fall of 1864. On New Year's Day, 1865, it camped on Dove Creek, eight miles east of present Mertzon and a few miles south of present San Angelo, and reported in a friendly mood to the Tankersley ranch on Dove Creek. Both the rancher and the Indians had horses missing, and the Kickapoos rounded up the missing animals and returned to their camp. A scouting party of Texas militia under Captain N. W. Gillentine unfortunately had crossed the trail of the Mexico-bound Kickapoos. Gillen-

[15] Fay Tankersley Mason, Colorado Springs, Colo., to Clayton Williams, April 14, 1965.

tine immediately reported his discovery. Captain S. S. Totten with a
Texas militia force rushed westward and joined Confederate Captain
Henry Fossett from Fort Chadbourne, giving a combined force of
about 360 men. Led by Gillentine's scouts, the Texans attacked the
Kickapoo camp on the morning of January 8. One detachment quickly
killed four or five Indians who were guarding the remuda. One participant later stated that an Indian bearing a white flag and accompanied
by two younger Indians approached and in good English asked for the
commander. He explained that the Kickapoos had killed no white people and had not stolen or destroyed any property; they had taken advantage of a permit to leave the reservation and were on their way to
Mexico to keep out of a war that did not concern them. Before Captain
Fossett could reply, the account continued, a buck private named Bed-
ford said, "Captain, you are not taking any prisoners, are you?" and
without waiting for an answer "ups his musket and shoots the Indian
through the chest." By this time the militia had opened fire on the
Kickapoo camp.[16]

The Kickapoos, more in numbers and better armed than the
Texans, occupied an excellent defensive position. After a half-hour of
close fighting, the Texans ran in panic for their horses. When they
reached safety, they counted twenty-six dead and sixty others critically
wounded. During a dreary snowstorm, the Texans began their retreat,
carrying on several travois, each between two horses, the severely
wounded and dead and pausing only at John Chisum's ranch on the
Colorado, where their names can still be seen on a ledger they signed
while there. The Kickapoos likewise decamped that night in the bitter
snowstorm and hastened to Mexico. From their new location in Mexico, they sought revenge on the Texans for this disgraceful attack.[17]

Before the outbreak of war, Texans had begun to drive some cattle
to California. After the Sibley disaster, these drives, of course, ceased,
and until after the war very few crossed West Texas. One that did belonged to W. A. Peril of Harper, Texas, and it was driven to Mexico.

---

[16] *Standard Times* (San Angelo), November 30, 1930, and January 10, 1965.

[17] Ibid.; J. Marvin Hunter, "The Battle of Dove Creek," *West Texas Historical Association Year Book* 10 (1934):74–84; *Houston Telegraph*, March 14, 1865; various documents, written in January and February, 1865, regarding the Dove Creek affair, in Texas
Adjutant General's Papers, Record Group 401, Archives, Texas State Library, Austin.

Peril went by way of Fort McKavett, the Concho River, Horsehead Crossing, Fort Stockton, and Presidio.[18] The little traffic that did cross in the latter part of the war was made largely by Confederate deserters and others who wanted to get out of the state before the inevitable defeat of the South. The deserters, according to W. C. Holden, during the winter of 1864–1865 flocked to the frontier in ever-increasing numbers. From both Confederate and state organizations, they came individually and, sometimes, in groups. "An examination of the muster rolls at the time of surrender shows that from one-fourth to one-half of the active force of the state companies were listed 'deserters'."[19]

One of the deserters, John Taylor, of Comanche, Texas, recorded in his diary that, upon learning in February, 1864, that an emigrant train was gathering on the Concho to start to California, he hurried to buy a wagon and team to join them. This was not easy, for he had to keep his plans secret and

go clear to Williamson County, 100 miles, for a wagon and team, there being none for sale any nearer than that. I traded off some of [my] cattle, the balance (about 30 head) I left together with my place consisting of 160 acres of land, improvement, etc. Several head of hogs; one share in school house in Comanche. . . .

I set out on the 15th of April, with a well-written transfer from Major [George B.] Erath to Concho County, there to report to a Captain of Militia in ten days.

There was but few that knew my intentions, it being reported that I was going to Concho to attend to a stock of cattle belonging to one W. W. Chandler living on Pecan Bays [Pecan Bayou, near present Brownwood].

I traveled on the 15th only five miles to the Widow Liggin[']s, where her son Giles Liggin joined me for the purpose of traveling with me as far as the Concho, where he had a brother, both deserters. . . .

On the 17th we traveled about 15 miles to Pecan Bays. Mr. Chandler visited our camp tonight and expressed himself uneasy for fear that the military authorities should deal harshly with him for helping me off, but I told him that when they found out I was gone to express himself surprised, that I had disappointed him. . . .

The emigrants that started on May 11 consisted of three separate trains traveling together. Taylor joined John Ward from "Vernon, Texas" (perhaps Mt. Vernon, since Vernon had not been founded), whose

[18] J. Marvin Hunter, ed., *The Trail Drivers of Texas*, pp. 411–412.

[19] W. C. Holden, "Frontier Defense in Texas during the Civil War," *West Texas Historical Association Year Book* 4 (1928):30.

train consisted of five families. One train, led by a man named Ball, consisted of ten wagons, ten families, and several young men, and a train from San Saba had six wagons, four families, and a few young men. On May 27, the wagons reached Antelope Spring, and at Fort Stockton on the following day Taylor wrote: "Here is good water and grass. We lay over 4 days; rained all the time. This post was destroyed, I suppose by General Sibley on his return; it is a beautiful place. Here there was a company of 40 or more deserters [who] overtook us, making their way into Mexico, some for El Paso with the intention of making their way into Missouri."

After many hardships with Indians and Mexicans along the way, the train finally reached California in October of 1864.[20] Almost exactly a year after deserter Taylor was at Fort Stockton, General E. Kirby Smith surrendered the Confederate Trans-Mississippi Department,[21] and a short time later Southwest Texas entered a new era of soldiers and settlers, who contested the Apaches for its possession.

[20] *Standard Times* (San Angelo), January 25, 1970.
[21] Holden, "Frontier Defense," p. 30.

II.
Indians and Settlers

CHAPTER 5

April, 1865, to April, 1867

$\mathbf{A}$LTHOUGH most traffic across West Texas during the Civil War consisted of military outfits, deserters, emigrants, and Indian raiders, occasionally a strongly guarded wagon carrying freight traversed the hazardous route between San Antonio and El Paso. The *San Antonio Ledger* of April 21, 1865, mentioned two recent arrivals but failed to explain what method of travel they had used. One of those, William Wilson, reported that El Paso was in "sad condition," that business was dull, and that money was scarce. The other arrival, Major W. B. Gillock, reported that a Mexican train loaded with salt had been attacked near Fort Quitman, and the entire party of thirteen men had been killed, the wagons burned, and the oxen captured.[1]

In all probability, the two travelers had used one of the two routes, both hazardous, that had been established between San Antonio and Franklin (El Paso) in 1849. The northern route was by way of Fredericksburg, the San Saba, the Middle Concho, Castle Gap, and Horsehead Crossing on the Pecos. From there, the road divided: one branch wound south to join the southern route at Fort Stockton; the other went up one side or the other of the Pecos almost to the mouth of Delaware Creek, followed the Delaware to near its head, skirted the south end of the Guadalupe Mountains, and passed by Hueco Tanks before ending at El Paso. The southern route went by Fort Clark, struck the Devils River not far from present Del Rio, worked its way up the Devils and across to Fort Lancaster and the Pecos, went up the Pecos some distance before crossing to Tunas (Escondido) Springs, and then went through Forts Stockton, Davis, and Quitman. After the war, these forts were gradually reoccupied by the United States Army for the same reasons as originally: to protect travelers; to provide guards for the

[1] *Southern Intelligencer* (Austin), April 26, 1865 (quoting from *San Antonio Ledger*, April 21, 1865).

mails, stages, and commercial trains; to encourage settlement; to chastise marauding Indians; and to prevent raids into Mexico by Indians
from the United States.

A month after Lee's surrender, about 300 Federal troops, most of
them blacks, were sent from Brazos Santiago port up the Rio Grande
to take possession of Brownsville. A Confederate force under Colonel
John S. (Rip) Ford, however, on May 13 at Palmito Ranch, near Brownsville, completely routed the Federals and sent them running back to
Brazos Island in the last battle of the war. The Confederates had only 3
men captured and 5 wounded; the Federals had about 30 killed and
wounded and 113 taken prisoner. From the prisoners Ford's men first
learned that the war had ended.[2] Four days later, General Philip
Henry Sheridan was placed in command of the Military Division of the
Southwest, and on June 19 General Gordon Granger arrived at Galveston with 1,800 troops and on the same day issued a proclamation
that "all slaves are free."[3] Shortly, Companies G and H, 125th Negro
Infantry, were dispatched to Fort Bliss and, more or less, were also to
occupy the neighboring towns of Ysleta, San Elizario, and Franklin.
The posts in the 400-mile stretch between Bliss and the nearest settlements to the east remained unoccupied.

The War Department deemed it more expedient to concentrate
its troops along the lower Rio Grande to prevent a possible invasion by
the French-installed emperor of Mexico, Archduke Maximilian, with
the aid of the self-exiled Confederates or the possible retreat of the op-
posing Mexican army under Benito Juárez into the United States.
Ringgold Barracks, not far from present McAllen, and Fort McIntosh,
at Laredo, were reoccupied in June and October, 1865, respectively,
and to support them construction was started on a railroad from Brazos
Santiago up the Rio Grande.[4] Maximilian, the brother of Austrian Emperor Francis Joseph I, became the supreme (but shaky) monarch of
Mexico through the auspices of Emperor Napoleon III of France. He

    [2] Walter P. Webb and H. Bailey Carroll, eds., *The Handbook of Texas*, 2:327.
    [3] Ibid., 1:934; 2:602.
    [4] U.S. Congress, House, "Distribution of troops in the department of Missouri on
the 31st of December, 1866," *Message of the President of the United States. Report of the
Secretary of War*, November [?], 1867, 40 Cong., 2 sess., 1868, House Exec. Doc. No. 1,
part 1, p. 43; U.S. Congress, House, "Railroads constructed by the railroad department,"
Message of the President of the United States. Report of the Secretary of War, November
14, 1866, 39 Cong., 2 sess., 1867, House Exec. Doc. No. 1, p. 167.

and his consort, Carlotta, arrived in Mexico during the summer of 1864. Since the French government had been sympathetic toward the South, General Joseph O. Shelby's Confederates, at the end of the Civil War, offered their services to Maximilian. The United States, however, demanded that the French withdraw from Mexico and to back up its demand sent an estimated 50,000 troops to Texas, with the majority concentrated along the lower Rio Grande. In April, 1866, Napoleon ordered the withdrawal of his troops to begin in November, and by March 12, 1867, all the French military had departed except the emperor and some of his retinue. Maximilian, left without military support, was captured and executed, and in December Benito Juárez was again elected president.[5]

Meanwhile, according to several legends, "Maximilian's millions" and Carlotta's valuables, or both, had been secretly transported into West Texas. Like most, the legends are vague, contradictory, and confusing. Whether the transportation was arranged by Maximilian, by Carlotta, or by others is not clear. The late Dan Bihl, of Fort Stockton, said that his father, who lived near Presidio del Norte during the Civil War and drove a stage from Fort Davis to Eagle Springs after the war, claimed that a caravan carrying a part of Carlotta's fortune across West Texas was wiped out by desperadoes or by Indians at Horsehead Crossing on the Pecos River.

The late O. W. Williams of Fort Stockton obtained another version of the story from Truman H. Conner, chief justice of the Court of Civil Appeals, at Fort Worth. According to Conner, a party of seven outlaws, evidently having decided that California or some place on the way would be more healthy, met on the west side of the Pecos River an old Mexican, who with his family and followers and their wagons was on his way from Chihuahua to San Antonio. Hired by the Mexican as a guard until he reached the safety of the settlements, the outlaws concluded that the wagon in the rear contained gold, silver, or other valuables and after crossing to the east side of the Pecos River killed all the Mexican entourage and took its cargo. The site was near a small spring. Surprised by the large amount of wealth they had taken and afraid of being caught with it, the villains buried the plunder. The next morning, Indians killed five of the seven. The two survivors succeeded in

[5] "A Reference History of the World," *Webster's New International Dictionary of the English Language* (1924 ed.), pp. 100, 127.

getting to San Antonio, where shortly afterward one died. The other was unable to secure the aid necessary to recover the treasure and eventually died in an asylum in Oklahoma. On his deathbed, Conner's story continued, he gave to an attendant who had been kind to him a statement of the circumstances of the robbery and an itinerary to the location of the hidden loot. The friend repeated the story to his friend Judge Conner, but the two were unable to find at Castle Gap adequate evidence to validate the story.[6]

The late Bill Cope of Fort Stockton obtained from his older brother Tom another version of the story. Tom, who came to Fort Stockton about 1890, only twenty-five years after the treasure was supposedly buried nearby, heard the story from William Forest Black, who claimed to have been the half-blood son of a member of the outlaw gang that perpetrated the massacre. While fleeing from the possibility of prosecution, the outlaws met a train of about seventeen Mexican men, women, and children, riding in several covered wagons and followed by a small oxcart carrying two barrels, and were employed by the Mexicans to escort them through the dangerous Comanche country. Along the way, the villains concluded that the barrels contained gold and silver coins, and after crossing the Pecos, possibly near Castle Gap, they attacked the Mexicans. In the fierce battle that followed, everyone was killed except two of the outlaws, an adult and a sixteen-year-old lad.

Afterward, the man burned the wagons and rearranged the scene to make it appear that Indians had caused the carnage. When the boy, who was keeping a lookout from atop a small, two-story, rock building, sighted dust caused, he believed, by approaching persons, the man hurriedly buried most of the gold and silver coins, deserted the wounded lad, and fled eastward with as much loot as he could easily carry. Although the account does not indicate what happened to the boy, Cope's story was given considerable credence by residents of the area. The outlaw who fled, after encountering Rangers and promising to leave Texas, lived out his life in Oklahoma and never had an opportunity to return for the loot. Supposedly, when on his deathbed, he related the incident and described the location.

[6] O. W. Williams, undated manuscript containing an account given to Williams by Judge Conner, Fort Worth, in possession of Clayton Williams, Fort Stockton, Texas. Truman H. Conner also served as a district judge and as president of Polytechnic College in Fort Worth (See *Fort Worth Record*, July 24, 1904).

Over a century later, people with metal detectors still search and dig in the vicinity of Castle Gap. Recently, lawyers for the kinsmen of George Shepherd, thought to have been a member of Quantrill's raiders and later of the outlaw gang that took the treasure, were inquiring about land that Shepherd had reportedly purchased in Ward, Crockett, or Pecos County.[7]

The stories of Maximilian's buried millions perhaps are nothing more than tall tales, but the accounts of Indian depredations in the Trans-Pecos country were not fictitious. The wagon train of N. Webb and Company left El Paso on February 1, 1866, bound for San Antonio. Near Eagle Springs it encountered a small party of Indians herding a few cattle and horses. In the fight that followed, the whites captured all of the Indians' stock, but the Indians, reenforced, harassed the caravan until nightfall and then bombarded the camp with heavy gunfire and attempted unsuccessfully to stampede all its stock. One Indian may have been wounded, but none of the Webb men was injured. The Webb party reported that Forts Quitman, Davis, Stockton, and Lancaster were in a state of desolation.[8]

About a month later, John and James Edgar, veterans of the Mexican and Civil wars and brothers-in-law of George M. Frazer, were in charge of two loaded freight trains on their way from San Antonio to El Paso. The trains, each with twenty wagons and 200 mules, were several days apart when John's train reached Wild Rose Pass in Limpia Canyon near Fort Davis. There it was attacked by Apaches led by Espejo. Noting that the train was well prepared for the attack, Espejo asked for a peace parley. When Edgar refused, the Indians withdrew. Fearing an ambush farther up the canyon, Edgar turned his wagons and headed back toward Fort Stockton. En route he met his brother's courier, who related that on April 26, between the Pecos River and Escondido, James's train had encountered a fierce storm that turned into sleet and snow. William Edgar, who obviously was with his brother James and who in 1902 published his account of the trip, wrote that after crossing the Pecos "we were overtaken by a frightful storm which

[7]John C. Gage, Kansas City, Mo., to Clayton Williams, February 26, 1964; Webb and Carroll, *Handbook of Texas*, 2:423. The San Antonio *Herald*, October 12 and October 21, and November 6, 1866, carried articles about coins discovered some four hundred miles west of San Antonio.

[8]San Antonio *Herald*, March 5, 1866.

held us three days in camp without wood, and killed one hundred and five mules." (The site later became known as Edgar's Boneyard.) James managed to get a part of his train into the ruins of Fort Stockton, where John joined him. There the two trains combined and eventually succeeded in reaching El Paso with about half of their original cargo.[9]

William devoted most of his account to the experiences of the return train to Limpia Canyon. On its return to San Antonio, the train (or that part of it William was with) consisted of twenty-eight male employees and the families of two of its teamsters, two women and two children, most of whom were Mexican. The train lay over a day at the abandoned Fort Davis to await the arrival of corn that William had ordered from Presidio. On the morning of June 1, the wagons traveled ten miles into the canyon for a noonday camp. That afternoon Edgar, his cook, and a man named Forbes rode forward into Wild Rose Pass in search of a place to camp for the night. Here they were attacked by Indians, and simultaneously sixty or seventy Lipans and Mescaleros opened fire upon the wagons. Before getting back to the train, William killed, he wrote, a number of Indians. "On arriving at the train, my men . . . seemed to look upon me as a superhuman." On the second day some Navajos from Bosque Redondo joined the siege. After several days, a parley ensued, and the Indians stated that they were starving and that they would depart if given some corn. Edgar agreed, but to avoid being entrapped he allowed only twenty Indians at a time to approach his wagons. After receiving the corn, Chief Gordo rather reluctantly withdrew.[10]

Although it was some time after the Civil War ended before Federal troops provided protection to the mail coaches that ran across West Texas, some drivers in the meantime made the run unmolested by Indians. When the stage lines resumed business across West Texas, the managers, to attract customers, assured the public that travel over

[9]There are a number of discrepancies in the various accounts of this episode. Some sources give William in place of John.

[10]Mrs. O. L. Shipman, *Taming the Big Bend*, pp. 37–38, 201–202; Carlysle Graham Raht, *The Romance of Davis Mountains and Big Bend Country*, pp. 153–154, 237; L. F. Durrell, grandson of George M. Frazer, San Antonio, to Clayton Williams, February 26 and April 30, 1967; Barry Scobee, *Old Fort Davis*, pp. 64–65; Barry Scobee, *Fort Davis, Texas, 1583–1960*, pp. 52–53; William M. Edgar, "One Wagon-train Boss of Texas, An Adveture with Indians on the Frontier," *Outing* 39, no. 4 (January, 1902):381–383.

the routes between San Antonio and El Paso would be safe. One such message that appeared in the San Antonio *Herald* on May 4, 1866, was typical: "U.S. mail stage line from San Antonio to El Paso—leaves both places on Mondays at 5 o'clock, A.M. An escort sufficient to prevent attacks will run with the coaches. Offices, at Menger's Hotel, San Antonio, and the house of Messrs. Louthan & Know, El Paso."

The first official stagecoach to carry the mail from San Antonio through far West Texas after the Civil War reached El Paso on May 6, 1866. It also carried James Wiley Magoffin, age about sixty-seven, a long-time merchant and trader who had settled in present El Paso after the Mexican War. Magoffin had been a staunch supporter of the Confederacy, and he, like Simeon Hart, had contributed greatly to the early success of Baylor and Sibley in their campaigns in New Mexico. Magoffin carried a proclamation signed by the Texas Reconstruction governor, A. J. Hamilton, authorizing him to organize El Paso County. Captain David Hammett Brotherton, an 1854 graduate of the Military Academy who had been breveted a major for his gallant and meritorious service in the Battle of Val Verde, then in command at Fort Bliss, refused to recognize Magoffin's authority, however, claiming that he had already appointed officers to organize the county. Thus, in West Texas military rule took precedence over civil authority.[11]

Apparently the stage that carried Magoffin was accompanied by a party of forty soldiers under Captain Theodore Alexander Wilson and Sam R. Miller, a civilian guard. Both men had been with Sibley, and Wilson was an experienced Indian fighter. The party saw Indian signs but no Indians until it reached Escondido, east of abandoned Fort Stockton. Here the men were besieged for forty-eight hours by some 350 Apache Indians. Occasionally the warriors circled within range of the stage guards' rifles, but each time a volley from the Texans forced them to retreat. Chief Espejo then resorted to his ruse of proposing a treaty. Captain Wilson, however, refused, and the Apaches finally withdrew.[12]

[11] Webb and Carroll, *Handbook of Texas*, 2:130; Francis B. Heitman, *Historical Register and Dictionary of the United States Army*, 1:250; J. Morgan Broaddus, *The Legal Heritage of El Paso*, pp. 85–88; San Antonio *Herald*, June 17, 1866.

[12] Raht, *Romance of Davis Mountains*, pp. 155–156; Scobee, *Fort Davis, Texas*, p. 53; Shipman, *Taming the Big Bend*, pp. 38–39.

Early in July, 1866, the eastbound stage, carrying a small guard and a few passengers, was attacked by about 125 Apaches at Varela Spring. One person, a man by the name of Davis, was killed. That evening, in the darkness, the besieged stole away and walked by way of Leon Springs to Fort Stockton, a distance of about forty miles.

When William Smith, the driver of the next westbound stage, arrived at Fort Stockton, he found six poor, hungry, barefooted, and almost naked souls, two of whom were wounded, in the old, deserted sutler store of J. D. Holliday. The only food the survivors had had for the last two days had been about a quart of corn found scattered over the earthen floor and boiled in an empty oyster can. Picking up the wretched group, Smith cautiously continued without incident to El Paso.[13]

The sutler store of J. D. Holliday, which in 1981 can still be seen, is the only remains of the first military post established at Fort Stockton. Now marked with a medallion that declares it to be the Oldest House in Fort Stockton, it was built by Company H, First Infantry, in 1859. The original Camp Stockton was almost destroyed by Indians and travelers who made fires with the thatch roofs and the frames of doors and windows. The land on which the original post was established was owned by Holliday, who operated the post office and served as post sutler, that is, provisioner for the troops. In 1862, G. H. Giddings bought from Holliday the land and, in addition, his holdings at Comanche Springs and a 160-acre tract in El Paso (now Pecos) County, all for a total of $3,475.75.[14]

George H. Giddings, a native of Pennsylvania, came to Texas in 1846. For years he was involved with the mail service between San Antonio, Texas, and San Diego, California. In 1861, President Lincoln sent him to Austin to try to prevent Texas' secession. He arrived too late, and, anyway, he probably did not have his heart in the task. He soon joined the Confederate Army and served as an officer in John S. Ford's regiment at the Battle of Palmito Ranch.[15]

About the time of the Varela incident, another stage party was attacked by a large band of Indians a short distance east of old Fort Lan-

---

[13] San Antonio *Herald*, July 20 and July 22, 1866.

[14] Clayton Williams, *Never Again*, 3:200–202, 224; Pecos County, Texas, Deed Records, 18:339, 341.

[15] Webb and Carroll, *Handbook of Texas*, 1:687.

caster. The road circled down Live Oak Creek along a slow grade to reach Lancaster. A steep, narrow route, barely wide enough for one wagon, went more directly down the escarpment to the ruins of the old fort. To escape, the driver took that dangerous route with his team on a dead run, risking the possibility of overturning and careening off bluffs 75 to 100 feet high rather than face torture and certain death at the hands of the Indians. This dangerous drive may have been the incident described many years later by Mrs. Josephine Couch of Ozona, Texas. Near the ruins of Fort Lancaster she once encountered an old man paying his last respects at the grave of his wife, who, he stated, had been in a vehicle that had dashed down Lancaster Hill to escape an Indian attack and soon afterward had died.[16]

Among the Confederate veterans that year to use commercially the dangerous San Antonio–El Paso road was Charles L. Pyron, who during the war had served with Baylor and Sibley. Pyron with a six-man party, after three weeks en route, arrived in San Antonio with his wagon train on August 24, 1866, and reported that four troops of blacks had replaced the California Volunteers at Fort Bliss. Pyron had followed the Upper Road by way of the Guadalupe Mountains and Horsehead Crossing. In the Pecos River region, he had met a herd of 10,000 cattle being driven to New Mexico, one of the first drives, if not the very first, over the route that soon became known as the Goodnight-Loving Trail.[17]

Since Confederate money was worthless, Texans were looking for negotiable paper or United States money. During the war, the unattended range cattle in Texas had greatly multiplied. Because steaks in the eastern market were selling for thirty cents a pound and Texas range steers could be bought for five to ten dollars each, numerous cattle drives were made from Texas to New Mexico, Kansas, and other states. The government began purchasing beef for the Indian reservation at Bosque Redondo, where 7,000 Apaches and Navajos created a ready market, and for other reservations in New Mexico and Arizona. It was this ready market that brought about the establishment, in 1866, of the Goodnight-Loving Trail, which became one of the most widely

---

[16]Zenas R. Bliss, "Reminscences," 2:24–25, in Eugene C. Barker Texas History Center, University of Texas, Austin; Josephine Couch, "At the Ruins of Old Fort Lancaster," *Pioneer Magazine of Texas* 4 (November, 1923):20.

[17]San Antonio *Herald*, August 28, 1866.

used cattle routes in the Southwest. It was named for cattlemen Charles Goodnight and Oliver Loving.

Charles Goodnight, born in Illinois in 1836, came to Texas ten years later with his mother and stepfather. In 1857, young Goodnight moved to Palo Pinto County and became a Ranger and Indian scout, and during the Civil War he served in a similar capacity with a Texas frontier regiment. Soon after the war, Goodnight entered the cattle business with Oliver Loving, a native of Kentucky who had come to Texas in 1845, when he was about thirty-three years old. In 1855, Loving moved his herds to Palo Pinto County, and during the next few years he made a number of drives to the north, at one time taking his cattle all the way to Chicago. During the Civil War, he furnished beef for the Confederacy.

In September, 1865, Goodnight collected a herd to drive to New Mexico, but before he could start the Indians stole most of it. The next spring he and Loving joined their respective herds and on June 6 started southwest along the Southern Overland (Butterfield) Mail Route for New Mexico by way of abandoned Forts Phantom Hill and Chadbourne, up the Middle Concho, along the waterless sixty-odd-mile ruts made by the Overland Mail stages through Castle Gap to the Pecos River at Horsehead Crossing, and then up the Pecos River to the Indian reservation of Fort Sumner. Although they were not the first to use the Pecos route, this drive in 1866 marked the opening of the Goodnight-Loving Trail. Goodnight and Loving drove their surplus cattle on northward into Colorado over a route later followed by an untold number of herds of Texas cattle.[18]

Goodnight and Loving became associated with John Chisum, a famous cattleman on the Pecos (not to be confused with the famous Jesse Chisholm, who in 1867 blazed a trail from the Red River to Abilene, Kansas). John Simpson Chisum, born in Tennessee in 1824, came to Texas in 1837. In the mid-1850s, he entered the cattle business with S. K. Fowler, of New York; their outfit, headquartered in Denton County, became one of the biggest in the state prior to the Civil War. During the war, Chisum, like Oliver Loving, became a beef contractor for the Confederate Army. In 1862, he located a new ranch in Concho County, near the Colorado River. At the close of the war, he dissolved

[18] Webb and Carroll, *Handbook of Texas*, 1:709, and 2:87.

his partnership with Fowler, sold his Denton County land, and moved his herds to the new location. By placing his profits into livestock, he avoided getting stuck with a lot of useless Confederate money.

For his cattle brand, Chisum used a "rail," a streak from shoulder to thigh, making any alteration rather evident. He marked his stock with the "jingle-bob," a slit in the ears so deep that they dangled limply. For this Chisum was often referred to as "Jinglebob John."

Soon after Goodnight and Loving returned from their first delivery of cattle to Fort Sumner, Chisum became associated with them in the cattle business. Thereafter, for several years, Jinglebob steers moved from Concho County to New Mexico, driven either by Goodnight and Loving hands or by Chisum's men. During the late 1860s, two of these herds were lost to Indians.[19]

According to a cowboy with Oliver Loving's herds, while the drovers were returning from a drive to New Mexico, a pack mule broke away in the darkness and scattered its load of provisions, including $6,000 in gold. "The gold was saved though all the provisions were lost and we had no way to get them replaced. We traveled nearly 100 miles without a bite to eat. At the Pecos River we ran across a man who divided a meager stock of food with us."[20]

Ornery pack mules were not the only causes of loss along the Goodnight-Loving Trail. Thirst, alkali water, and Indian raiders each took a heavy toll of cattle. Stockmen lost numerous cattle when the thirsty animals drank the alkali water of China Ponds, fifteen miles east of Castle Gap.[21] The Indians, however, exacted the heaviest losses. On one of his stagedriver trips from El Paso to San Antonio, J. D. Holliday on September 1, 1866, spotted in the vicinity of Escondido (Tunas) Springs a party of fifty-four Indians with a large drove of cattle. Some of these Indians attempted, without success, to ambush the stage while it was crossing the mesa north of the springs.[22]

Finally, pressured by petitions and letters, General P. H. Sheridan on October 8, 1866, wired Governor Throckmorton that additional troops had been ordered to the state "and that as much protection as we possibly can give to the frontier, will be cheerfully given and

[19] Ibid., 1:341–343; J. Marvin Hunter, ed., *The Trail Drivers of Texas*, p. 951.
[20] Otho Anne Hanscom, ed., *Parade of the Pioneers*, p. 236.
[21] Henry N. Strong, *My Frontier Days and Indian Fights on the Plains of Texas*, p. 41.
[22] San Antonio *Herald*, September 19, 1866.

that by early spring the frontier posts will be established." Fort Clark
was reoccupied by Company C, Fourth Cavalry, on December 12.[23]

In 1866 Messrs. Sawyer, Risher, and Hall acquired control of the
Overland Mail route between San Antonio and El Paso and put J. D.
Holliday in charge of operating the route. Before the end of November, Holliday was preparing the 150 miles of road to Piedra Pinta, by
way of stations at Castroville, D'Hanis, Rio Frio, Turkey Creek, and
Elm Creek, for the establishment of a regular weekly stage service. In
time, the company planned to build a station at Fort Stockton. By the
end of November, it was apparent that the stage companies would be
receiving the needed military protection, for Fort Mason had already
been garrisoned and others soon would be. Members of the mule train
of F. R. Diffenderffer and Company, which arrived in San Antonio
from El Paso on December 4 with $3,500 in specie, some gold dust,
and five tons of onions, brought word that the mail contractors were
busy repairing stations and putting livestock at each end and that very
soon they would begin weekly schedules.[24]

A number of farsighted Texans were risking capital on promotional
projects in Trans-Pecos Texas. Some were planning an irrigation ditch
along the Rio Grande across the desert from the New Mexico border to
Fort Quitman. Giddings got a contract for the construction of a double
row of "telegraph" from New Orleans to San Francisco. By early 1867,
however, none of the big promotions had made anyone rich, but the
cattle industry was improving and business was doing well in the area
around Presidio del Norte and Fort Leaton. Milton Faver, who had a
large, open-range cattle domain 150 miles southeast of El Paso, had
nearly always prospered. Not far distant, John B. Davis had established a ranch on the free rangeland in the mountains. Mose Kelly,
who established a customhouse on the Rio Grande in the home of John
Spencer, also operated a general merchandise store across the river in
Mexico.[25]

During the early part of 1867, the Texas frontier was plagued by
incessant Indian raiders. People were killed or captured all along the
frontier from the Red River to the Rio Grande, and the line of settle-

[23] Ibid., October 16, 1866; Webb and Carroll, *Handbook of Texas*, 1:622.
[24] San Antonio *Herald*, October 9, November 27 and 30, and December 4, 1866.
[25] Ibid., December 6 and 2, 1866; Raht, *Romance of Davis Mountains*, p. 162.

ments retreated eastward by more than a county.[26] The Pecos River country did not escape. Captain John A. Wilcox, Company C, Fourth Cavalry, while camped near Live Oak Creek and the abandoned Fort Lancaster, picked up a fresh trail that appeared to have been made by about 200 Indians and followed it for four days to the hills west of the Pecos. Upon overtaking the Indians on March 12, he engaged them in a running fight that lasted for four hours and about fifteen miles. Wilcox reported that he had four men missing in action, five wounded, and a guide killed and that forty Indians had been killed and a number wounded.[27]

[26] "Report of Major General W. S. Hancock," in U.S. Congress, House, *Message of the President of the United States. Report of the Secretry of War*, November 20, 1868, 40 Cong., 3 sess., 1869, House Exec. Doc. No. 1, p. 204; Joseph Carroll McConnell, *The West Texas Frontier*, 2:183–211.

[27] *Galveston Daily News*, March 29, 1867 (quoting from the *San Antonio Ledger*, n.d.); Heitman, *Historical Register*, 1:1034 and 2:427; Raht, *Romance of Davis Mountains*, p. 198; Shipman, *Taming the Big Bend*, p. 198; *Austin Republican*, April 13 and 20, 1867; *Dallas Herald*, April 13, 1867.

CHAPTER 6

January to September, 1867

SOME adventurers who risked their lives in the Trans-Pecos Indian country in 1867 were more interested in finding rich ore than in getting across the region or in locating "Maximilian's millions." The best known of this group was Jacob Snively. Snively, who spent much of his life searching for the pot at the end of the rainbow, was in Texas at least as early as April, 1835. Thereafter, he served in the Texas Army and held a number of prominent offices during the days of the Republic. Best remembered for the Snively Expedition in 1843, an unsuccessful attempt to capture a rich Mexican caravan en route from Missouri to Santa Fe, he was an expert surveyor and civil engineer. After the gold discovery in California, he became incurably smitten with gold fever and spent the next couple of decades seeking a fortune in California, Arizona, and Texas.[1]

Having heard rumors of a rich gold mine in the region of old Fort Quitman, Snively in January, 1867, set out for that area with more than a dozen men, including ex-Confederate Colonel William Cornelius Dalrymple, Moses Carson (brother of Kit), and possibly David Snively, Jacob's twin brother, and about thirty horses and mules. In February, somewhere between the head of the Middle Concho River and Horsehead Crossing of the Pecos, the party was attacked by a band of an estimated 60 to 200 Kickapoos or Kiowas and Comanches. The Indians, well armed with six-shooters, rifles, lances, and bows and arrows, engaged the prospectors in a running battle for a few hundred yards. After the prospectors took refuge in a gully, the Indians stampeded and captured all their pack animals and killed or captured all of the saddle animals. After the Indians withdrew, the prospectors started on foot for Frank Tankersley's ranch on Dove Creek. En route, they were rescued

---

[1]Walter P. Webb and H. Bailey Carroll, eds., *The Handbook of Texas*, 2:631.

by Rich Coffey, a rancher at the junction of the Concho and Colorado rivers, and his party, who were headed for the salt lake in present Crane County.[2]

Shortly after the Snively incident, on Live Oak Creek near Fort Lancaster, Indians, probably Kickapoos, variously estimated from 40 to 200, attacked the mail stage and on the following morning captured it and the mules. According to a Mexican who escaped during the siege, the warriors were armed with "the best quality of rifles." The leaders, the Mexican claimed, spoke excellent colloquial English that "savors very much of hellish whites," and they exhibited skill in harnessing the mules and handling "the 'ribbons' in the most graceful jockey style."[3]

Nearby, the W. B. Knox mule train of sixteen wagons, loaded with machinery for a large cotton factory in the State of Chihuahua, had a similar experience. Leaving San Antonio on March 17, the train was joined a short time later by George M. Frazer, who took charge of the caravan. At midnight on April 8, it was attacked by either Lipans or Mescaleros, or both, at Pecos Spring, near the Pecos River. The Indians drove off about 175 mules but, except for 3 that were killed in the exchange of gunfire, all were recaptured.[4]

Not long afterward, Jacob Snively and Dalrymple organized another expedition to search for minerals in the Trans-Pecos country. They designated Georgetown as the rendezvous site, where all those who wanted to go along were to report in the early part of May, "duly equipped in a manner to protect themselves from any attacks that may be made by savages."[5] While a part of the group was waiting for the others on the Concho River, Ben F. Gooch and his cowboys passed by, trailing about 500 cattle to New Mexico and accompanied by a man and his wife headed for Fort Sumner. The Gooch outfit was attacked at the head draws of the Middle Concho by a large party of unidentified Indians, and several white men were killed. After considerable hardship, Gooch, two other men, and the woman wandered back to the Concho.

[2] Ibid., 1:462, and 2:631; Steven Wilson, "Indians and Treasure Don't Mix," *Frontier Times* 48, no. 1 (January, 1974):8–13, 40–41; *Dallas Herald*, March 16, 1867; Joseph Carroll McConnell, *The West Texas Frontier*, 2:184–185.

[3] San Antonio *Herald*, February 24, 1867; *Dallas Herald*, March 16, 1867 (quoting the *San Antonio Express*).

[4] San Antonio *Herald*, March 20, 1867.

[5] Ibid., April 24, 1867.

The other cowboys managed to hold most of the herd until they were rejoined by Gooch and his party. Gooch then proceeded to Horsehead Crossing, where he was besieged by Indians for three days before Dalrymple and his prospectors galloped up. Meanwhile, the Indians had captured the herd, which they later took into New Mexico.

While on this trip, the Snively-Dalrymple party also saved another group that was driving a herd of cattle across the area. J. D. Hoy brought his wife and daughters from their home near Camp Saba in McCulloch County, because he thought they would be safer on the trip with twelve or thirteen cowboys than alone at home. The party had successfully pushed the herd across the seventy-mile dry stretch from the headwaters of the Middle Concho to the Pecos. Soon afterward, the wagon with the women arrived. While they were preparing dinner, Indians attempted to steal the remuda. Hoping to avert an attack on his family, Hoy released some of the horses to the Indians. The women were then hurriedly placed in the wagon and instructed to drive into a gully. As Mrs. Hoy rapidly loaded guns, the Indians took turns riding in close and shooting at them. One Indian was shot off his horse but was retrieved by his comrades. Several cowboys were wounded. Mrs. Hoy received a flesh wound in the hip, and a Mexican cowboy drowned while trying to escape by swimming across the Pecos.

After getting away with the cattle, the Indians quit the siege. Hoy and his cowboys then gathered the remaining horses and moved the women to the old Butterfield Stage house, a short distance above Horsehead Crossing. Although the route had been abandoned, the walls of the building were still intact. One morning a few days later, the Indians again unsuccessfully attempted to lure the weary defenders into ambush. The siege continued until the prospectors arrived. Informed that his other wagons and supplies had been ransacked and burned, Hoy was not surprised, for the chief had been seen sporting strips of a dress that belonged to one of the girls. Some of the cowboys had had enough of Indians and left for the Texas settlements. Although in a destitute condition, the Hoys continued toward New Mexico but sent a cowboy ahead to obtain food. Meanwhile, the main party lived on the meat of their oxen.[6]

[6] McConnell, *West Texas Frontier*, 2:185–186; Claim No. 2626 (J. D. Hoy), Indian Depredation Case Records, Records of U.S. Court of Claims, Record Group 123, National Archives, Washington, D.C.; John Beasley, McCulloch, Texas, to General D. R.

Unfortunately, members of the Hoy party did not know that food was within thirty-five miles of them at the abandoned site of Fort Stockton. There, William Russell had set up his stand and was advertising that "persons traveling from San Antonio to El Paso can be supplied with corn, flour, and beans at Comanche or Fort Stockton."[7]

Russell, no doubt, kept his wagons with their cargoes of corn, flour, and beans in a protected position behind the adobe walls of the fort's ruins. The teams, horses, and stagecoach animals were under the constant vigilance of one or two attendants along Comanche Creek as they grazed on the salt grass or cattails that abounded in the marshes. At night the animals were driven to the protective walls of the stagecoach pens and guarded by sentinels.

Perhaps because the men rarely received anything to eat other than beans, a disgruntled stage attendant at the Fort Stockton site had previously nicknamed the place "Beans Station." But the name did not last. Presumably, the diet improved after Russell set up his stand.[8]

The hazardous conditions in the vicinity of the Pecos were described by E. C. Powell, who arrived in San Antonio from Fort Stockton in early April. The route for 300 miles, Powell reported, was very dangerous. In traveling from Fort Stockton to Fort Hudson, his train "was constantly trailed and watched by the red savage. . . . Captain Wilcox, commanding at Fort Clark, was about to depart on an expedition against the Lipans, now in strong numbers in a village on the Pecos River, about ninety miles from the Fort."[9]

In late April, 1867, a mail party was attacked by Indians near Horseshoe Bend of the Pecos, some twelve or fifteen miles above the present town of Iraan. The well-armed Indians held the occupants of the stage and a squad of soldiers under siege from early afternoon until midnight. J. D. Holliday and a Dr. Burgess were credited with having shot one of the Indians.[10]

Gurley, July 10, 1867, Papers of Governor James Webb Throckmorton, Archives, Texas State Library (TSL), Austin; James E. Rauk, San Antonio, to E. M. Pease, August 17, 1867, Papers of Governor Elisha Marshall Pease, Archives, TSL; Katie Longfield, "Pioneer Woman Tells of a Perilous Trip," *Frontier Times* 14, no. 2 (November, 1936):56–57; *Austin Republican*, July 20, 1867.

[7] San Antonio *Herald*, April 21, 1867.
[8] Ibid., May 12, 1867.
[9] Ibid., April 17, 1867.
[10] Ibid., May 5, 1867.

All the members of at least three wagon trains also survived fierce Indian attacks that spring and summer while crossing the Trans-Pecos country. John Crandel Baker, the father of the late J. T. Baker of Fort Stockton, and several others, eager to trade their pecans, bacon, and lard for negotiable cash, started from Austin to El Paso with several wagons. After crossing the Pecos River they spotted in tall grass an Indian squaw, who jumped up and ran. Almost immediately the wagon train was surrounded by Indians, who stayed at a safe distance but kept up the siege for about twenty-four hours before leaving. Although no one was killed, so many horses were killed or disabled that the train could not proceed until some replacements were obtained.[11]

On another occasion, when John Burgess, with forty well-armed wagons loaded with grain, camped at Burgess Spring (Charco de Alsate or Kokernot Spring) at present Alpine, he was surrounded by Chief Leon and his warriors. Seeing that the train was corralled and the whites were prepared to fight, the Apaches sent for reinforcements and settled down to wait. During the night, Burgess padded the hooves of his fine racehorse to deaden their noise and sent a rider into the darkness to seek relief. The messenger outran his Indian pursuers, but he rode his horse to death and had to walk the last fifteen of the ninety-five miles to Presidio. On the second morning, the Apaches abandoned the siege when they saw a cloud of dust that was being made by a column of Mexican cavalry commanded by Captain Francisco Arzate from Presidio.[12]

As a result of a later encounter between John Burgess and the Apaches, Chief Alsate and some of his warriors were jailed and tried for a murder that was never committed. Burgess, John Davis, and William Brooks combined their freight outfits at Presidio del Norte to deliver corn and grain to the soldiers at Fort Stockton. A week or ten days thereafter, Mrs. Burgess saw at Presidio an Indian wearing her husband's coat and sent for the alcalde. As a result, Alsate and some of his warriors were thrown into the hoosegow and charged with murder. At the trial Mrs. Davis identified the coat as belonging to her husband, and nobody believed Alsate's explanation. Alsate claimed that he and Chief Leon with a large party of Apaches had attacked the train near

[11] Mrs. J. T. Baker, oral statement, to Clayton Williams, 1959.
[12] Mrs. O. L. Shipman, *Taming the Big Bend*, pp. 71–72; Carlysle Graham Raht, *The Romance of Davis Mountains and Big Bend Country*, pp. 164–165.

Burgess Spring, but the defenders had been able to circle their wagons into a defensive position with all the stock within. Finding a victory would be costly, Alsate and Leon agreed to a conference with the wagon masters. But when the negotiators met, Burgess and Davis drew their concealed weapons and demanded that the chiefs order their warriors to leave. This, Alsate said, was pure trickery, but Burgess had paid for it by giving him the overcoat. He felt that the trade was not so bad. Fortunately, before the trial ended John Burgess arrived—to the relief of his wife, and, no doubt, of Chief Alsate, and verified that he had indeed given the overcoat to the chief. The Indians were then released.[13]

After unloading their wagons at Stockton, the Burgess party had proceeded to the salt lakes in present Crane County, loaded their wagons with salt and then headed for Presidio. Incidentally, Chief Alsate was named for Lieutenant Francisco Arzate of the Mexican Army, whose company had been stationed at Presidio and whose uncle, Manuel Músquiz, previously had owned a ranch between Fort Davis and the Charco de Alsate.[14]

Even before the reestablishment of the military posts, the cattle frontier by the spring of 1867 had spread westward into Indian country, and the cattlemen were driving many thousands of beeves on the hoof northward to the railroads in Missouri and Kansas for the northeastern market. The Indian reservations and army posts of eastern New Mexico and the rangeland of New Mexico and Colorado also provided an affluent market for those who successfully made the hazardous drive. The trails to this market converged at Horsehead Crossing and from there went up the Pecos River.

By 1867 trail driving had become big business but hard work and extremely hazardous. The cowboys' wages were from fifteen to twenty-five dollars per month. Their chuck wagon provided them with coffee, beans, potatoes, salt pork, bread, and, for dessert, some "lick" (molasses). Each cowboy furnished his own saddle, blanket, bridle, quirt, spurs, rope, tying string, bedroll, slicker, and clothing.

Usually supplied with a string of seven horses previously "topped-off" by a broncobuster, each cowboy had the responsibility of training

---

[13] Raht, *Romance of Davis Mountains*, pp. 167–169.

[14] Ibid., pp. 167–170; Joe Cordero, Fort Stockton, grandson of Francisco Arzate, oral statement, to Clayton Williams.

his mounts. During a drive, horses were driven during the day by the wrangler and at night carefully watched by one or two wranglers and hobbled with a soft rope or rawhide. A horse was hobbled by tying together its two front feet, so that it could jump—but not walk—its front feet forward and walk its hind feet. As an alternative, it could be sidelined by tying the two feet on the same side. The horses were trained to remain in an improvised pen, made by tying ropes to trees, shrubs, wagons, or other available objects. When untrained horses were placed in such an enclosure, cowboys stood ready to lasso the front feet and yank them out from under any horse that tried to jump from the enclosure, generally causing the horse to fall hard on its head. After a time or two of this treatment, a horse made no further attempt to escape. The practice, known as forefoot'n (forefooting), required special skill and, although common then, is today an almost-forgotten art.

The chuck wagon, a sort of carryall with a big wooden box in the rear, held tin dishes, coffee pots, Dutch ovens, tin knives, forks, spoons, lard, salt, pepper, salt pork, baking soda, baking powder, flour, and most other items necessary for cooking. Barrels of water for cooking and drinking and pots and pans that could not be stored within the wagon or chuck box were strapped on the sides of the wagon. When empty, the barrels could be used to float the wagon across streams.

Extra supplies, such as beans and flour, the bedrolls, and other cowboy rigging were carried within the wagon. The door of the chuck box let down to form a table upon which the cook prepared meals and later set the plates and utensils at meal times. The cook, and an occasional helper, prepared the meals and drove the wagon. The cook was the absolute boss in his area and assessed penalties against those who broke the rules of the camp.

Before sunup, the cowboys had rolled up and put away their beds, helped themselves to coffee and breakfast, and caught their horses, which had been corralled by the wrangler. Once mounted, they relieved the last shift of the night watch, who in turn ate breakfast, saddled new mounts, and joined the others in pushing the herd. On each side of the herd and toward the front, two pointers guided and controlled the pace of the cattle and prevented stray cattle from wandering into the herd. Other men on the sides kept the herd under control and prevented stray cattle from joining the drive, and cowboys at the rear urged forward the stragglers. At noon, the men ate in relays since the cattle must be kept from scattering. At night, the herd was bedded down, and the crew divided into three shifts. Those on night watch usually circled around and around the herd until relieved or until the drive was resumed.

Stampedes, started by thunder, lightning, or other sudden noises or movements, were frequent. In the dark, with thousands of frightened animals charging madly behind the leaders, the cowboys dashed to the front of the stampede and attempted to turn the head of the herd back into the rear, thereby forcing the cattle to mill. During these wild and hazardous night rides, the men were in danger of being trampled or even being killed. The late E. L. Brown of Fort Stockton recalled a stampede that was caused by a tired horse. When the weary animal shook himself and snorted loudly, the startled steers were up and off. Another instance occurred when James H. Cook was on night watch. One placid old cow insisted on bedding down one very dark night a short distance from the herd. Cook drew closer to the animal each time he circled the herd. Eventually, Cook touched her neck with his foot. The startled cow jumped to her feet, snorted, and plunged toward the herd—rather, the spot where the herd had been, for before she could reach her bovine companions there was a roar and the earth trembled as thousands of cattle thundered across the plains.[15]

Stampedes also were caused occasionally by Indians who raced in among a herd of horses or longhorns, shouting, shooting, and thrashing buffalo hides on the end of a short lariat. Once the herd stampeded, the Indians were able to steal many of the animals.

Day and night the cowboy was exposed to the elements—Indians, stampedes, and other hazards. Two ballads repeated here tell of these tragedies. The first is "Little Joe, the Wrangler," one of the many collected by John and Allen Lomax:

> He said if we would give him work, he'd do the best he could.
> Though he didn't know straight up about a cow;
> So the boss he cut out a mount and kindly put him on,
> For he sorta liked this little kid somehow;
>
> Learned him to wrangle horses and to try to know them all,
> And get them in at daylight if he could;
> To follow the chuck-wagon and always hitch the team,
> And to help the Cocinero rustle wood.

[15] James H. Cook, *Fifty Years on the Old Frontier*, pp. 36–37.

We had driven to the Pecos, the weather being fine;
We camped on the south side in a bend;
When a norther commenced blowin', we had doubled up our guard,
For it taken all of us to hold them in.

Little Joe, the wrangler, was called out with the rest;
Though the kid had scarcely reached the herd,
When the cattle they stampeded, like a hailstorm long they fled,
Then we were all a-ridin' for the lead.

Midst the streaks of lightnin' a horse we could see in the lead,
'Twas Little Joe, the wrangler in the lead;
He was riding Old Blue Rocket with a slicker o'er his head,
A tryin' to check the cattle in their speed.

At last we got them milling and kinda quieted down,
And the extra guard back to the wagon went;
But there was one a'missin' and we knew it at a glance,
'Twas our little Texas stray, poor wrangling Joe.

The next morning just at daybreak, we found where Rocket fell,
Down in a washout twenty feet below;
And beneath the horse, mashed to pulp, his spur had rung the knell,
Was our little Texas stray, poor Wrangling Joe.[16]

The other, "The Dying Cowboy," is the last plea of a lonely
cowboy:

> Oh, bury me not on the lone prairie,
> These words came low and mournfully
> From the pallid lips of a youth who lay
> On his dying bed at the close of day.
>
> Oh, bury me not on the lone prairie
> Where the wild coyotes will howl o'er me,
> In a narrow grave just six by three,
> Oh, bury me not on the lone prairie.
>
> Oh, we buried him there on the lone prairie
> Where the wild rose blooms and the wind blows free;
> Oh, his pale young face nevermore to see—
> For we buried him there on the lone prairie.[17]

At the beginning of the drive, one steer usually took and kept the
lead. One of the cowboys led the way until the lead steer got in the

---

[16] John A. Lomax, *Cowboy Songs and Other Frontier Ballads*, pp. 167–169.
[17] Ibid., pp. 3–6.

habit of following a horseman. Once well-trained, the lead steer usually would follow the rider across a stream, and, as a result, the herd would follow. Otherwise, the herd had to be "choused" across.

In June, 1867, Oliver Loving, Charles Goodnight, and W. J. Wilson combined their herds to trail to New Mexico. They had just gotten underway when they were attacked at night by Indians near abandoned Camp Cooper on the Clear Fork of the Brazos. One man was wounded in the head by an arrow, and Goodnight escaped injury only because the buffalo robe in which he was sleeping deflected an arrow.

Slowly, the sixteen cowboys trailed the herd past the ruins of Phantom Hill, Buffalo Gap, Fort Chadbourne, and up the Middle Concho, where the cattle got their fill of water and grass before beginning the seventy-mile trek to Horsehead Crossing. China Ponds, on the route, was often dry, and Grierson Spring had not yet been discovered. Although there was rain nearly every day as far as the Pecos, it was not enough to provide water for the cattle. For three days and nights the cowmen drove without sleep, losing 300 cattle from dehydration. At the Pecos, the remaining cattle went crazy with thirst, stampeded, and plunged into the river, or were pushed in by those behind, and swam and wallowed around. Taking advantage of this confusion, a group of Indians drove off most of the surviving herd. After hunting for three days, the drovers still had about 300 head of cattle missing. During the search Wilson with six men returned eastward along the outbound trail more than twenty-five miles to a fresh trail that led to an Indian camp. Seeing that he was greatly outnumbered by the Indians, Wilson turned back and arrived at his party's camp on the Pecos River the next day.

The trail herd, now reduced to about 350 head, was then trailed up the Pecos River almost to the New Mexico line, where Loving and Wilson set out at a faster pace to reach Fort Sumner before the beef contracts were let in July. On the first day, the pair reached Blue River (also called Black River). Eighteen miles farther they sighted an estimated six hundred Indians and took cover in a cave in the bank of the Pecos. Each man had two six-shooters, Wilson had a six-shooting rifle, and Loving had a Henry rifle that was capable of firing sixteen or eighteen shots. Faced with such firepower, the Indians were held at bay until late in the evening and then called in Spanish for a powwow. Loving and Wilson agreed, but as Loving stepped out from his hiding place the Indians shot him in the side and another shot broke his arm at the wrist. The besieged pair held off the Indians until after midnight. Then Loving instructed Wilson to slip out for help and, if Loving died, to tell his family where and how and to inform Goodnight that he would not be captured alive, but if the Indians quit the siege he would wait for the herd two miles down the river.

Under cover of darkness, Wilson made his escape. During the next few days, the Indians used every effort to reach Loving. They cut tunnels through the dirt to within a few feet of where the wounded man lay, but they did not dare show their heads. They threw almost a cartload of boulders, obtained from the nearby bluffs, over the riverbank but with no more effect than to annoy the suffering Loving.

Since the Indians had taken the horses, Wilson had to go on foot. He was found by Goodnight's men after he had wandered around in a bewildered, half-starved condition for three or four days. Goodnight at once took six or seven men and started to Loving's relief. He rode all night through a violent rainstorm and until the middle of the next afternoon, but he found no trace of Loving. Goodnight wrongly concluded that his friend had been killed or had taken his own life rather than allowing himself to be captured. Rather, Loving had remained optimistic. With remarkable nerve and determination and his deadly fire, he stood the Indians off until the siege was abandoned. He then made his way some miles up the river to where the trail crossed it, thinking that would be a likely place to encounter assistance. Hungry and weak, he hid in the only clump of bushes in that vicinity and tried to obtain food by shooting birds, but his ammunition had become water-soaked. He then lay on the bank a few feet above the river, tied a cloth around a stick, and dipped it into the water to quench his thirst. Having gone without food for five days, he attempted to make a fire in order to burn his leather gloves to a crisp so that he might eat them— but in vain. On the third day that he lay there, by then helpless and delirious, three Mexicans and a German boy arrived at the crossing en route from New Mexico to Texas. The boy, while gathering sticks for a fire, discovered Loving. The wounded man, thinking he was again being attacked by Indians, tried but was unable to shoot. Loving was cautiously given food and water, and, when able to travel, he gave the Mexicans $250 to take him to Fort Sumner.

Within seventy-five miles of their destination, Loving met an old friend, who rushed to Fort Sumner and returned with an ambulance and doctors. Loving was treated and carried to the fort, but gangrene developed, and the amputation of an arm failed to save the life of one of the great cattle trail blazers.[18]

Meanwhile, the army was slowly moving to provide protection to the Texas frontier and the travelers along the Butterfield Overland Mail and the two San Antonio–El Paso roads. For a time, however, the army sent to the posts officers with raw recruits entirely unfamiliar with the country and furthermore did insufficient planning. As an example, in July, 1867, it established a "permanent" post at Buffalo Springs in present Clay County in North Texas, but because the area lacked water and timber the site was abandoned a few months later. The army reoccupied Forts Chadbourne and Belknap in May, 1867, but abandoned Belknap in September and founded Fort Griffin. Fort Hudson, on the lower Pecos, was occupied that year but abandoned in April, 1868.[19] No garrison was located anywhere near Horsehead Crossing, where cattlemen were having, and for years continued to have, trouble with Indians.

Preparatory to restoring forts on the southern San Antonio–El Paso route, the Quartermaster's Department at San Antonio solicited sealed bids in May, 1867, for transportation of military supplies for a year, beginning July 1, from San Antonio to Forts Inge, Clark, Stockton, Davis, and Bliss, "and all military posts or camps as are or may be established on the western and northwestern frontiers of Texas, south of latitude 32 north."[20] Then, in June, troops began arriving at the posts in the Pecos and Trans-Pecos region, an area swarming with hostile Indians. The Valdez brothers' wagon train from El Paso, comprising twenty-two wagons, arrived in San Antonio on June 13 after thirty

---

[18] J. Marvin Hunter, ed., *The Trail Drivers of Texas*, pp. 908–913; McConnell, *West Texas Frontier*, 2:194–198; J. Evetts Haley, *Charles Goodnight: Cowman and Plainsman*, pp. 162–184; L. S. Kinder, "A Chapter in the Life of Col. Chas. Goodnight," undated, typescript, sent by Judge Kinder, Plainview, Texas, to Judge O. W. Williams, now in possession of Clayton Williams.

[19] Allen W. Hoffman, "Findings along a Segment of the California Trail of 1849," *West Texas Historical Association Year Book* 33 (1957):113; Webb and Carroll, *Handbook of Texas*, 1:620, 622, 626–627.

[20] San Antonio *Herald*, May 21, 1867.

days on the road. Its members had seen on the Pecos the site of a recently abandoned Indian camp that appeared to have been occupied by about 1,500 Comanches. Farther east, the Valdez party saw westbound black troops of the Ninth Cavalry at the abandoned Fort Hudson and at Fort Clark.[21]

Apparently, some or all of the troops seen by the Valdez brothers were headed for posts beyond the Pecos. On June 29, 1867, Lieutenant Colonel Wesley Merritt arrived at the ruins of Fort Davis, where the town by that name is now located, 466 miles from San Antonio and in the Davis Mountains. Merritt brought with him the newly organized Negro Companies C, F, H, and I, Ninth Cavalry, and Companies B and E, Forty-first Infantry. The troops soon commenced the work of building barracks adjacent to the ruins of the old fort, near a spring of excellent water in Limpia Canyon.[22]

In September, sawmills began operating on the creek there. Pine logs were procured from Limpia Canyon, a distance of twenty-five miles. Simultaneously, carpenters and masons arrived from San Antonio. Quarries of red sandstone were within half a mile of the post, and limestone was available at a distance of about twenty-five miles, at a site where a kiln was built and lime was burned. By December 31, quarters for the commanding officer, except for the shingling of the roof, and the stonework for a captain's quarters had been completed. Foundation rock for the officers' quarters had been quarried; the mills had sawed 2,500 logs, which had been hauled from the pineries; and more than 422 bushels of lime had been burned. The civilian force during the time varied from 124 to 168 persons.[23]

Meanwhile, General Edward Hatch on July 21 had reoccupied Fort Stockton and made it the headquarters for the Ninth Cavalry. Hatch had with him Companies A, B, E, and K of the newly enlisted blacks from the vicinity of New Orleans. With the exception of the post trader's building, the pre-war, one-company fort was in ruins. The post, located at Comanche Springs on the route from San Antonio to El Paso and astride the great Comanche War Trail, was 70 miles northeast

[21] Ibid., June 13, 1867.

[22] Barry Scobee, *Fort Davis, Texas, 1583–1960*, p. 54.

[23] U.S. Congress, House, "Report of the Quartermaster General," *Message of the President of the United States. Report of the Secretary of War*, November 20, 1868, 40 Cong., 3 sess., 1869, House Exec. Doc. No. 1, pp. 865–866.

of Fort Davis and 260 miles west of Fort Clark, on Las Moras Creek in Kinney County. The clear, hard waters of Comanche Creek gushed from a number of springs, at one time the third largest source in Texas. A salt grass flat, varying from one hundred to several hundred yards, bordered the stream on its east side. A small undulating rise of about fifteen feet edged the stream's western bank.

The temporary quartermaster's tent and camp bakery were situated at the ruins of the old post at the present site of the Catholic church, county jail, courthouse, and old school. The new fort was constructed one-half mile to the north, on the west side of the creek, on what is now known as the Old Fort Addition to the city of Fort Stockton.

General Hatch had Mexicans, instead of enlisted men, employed to make the adobes for the fort's walls and had the storehouses and shops covered with dirt roofs to prevent fire. The 119 civilians employed by the government on September 30, 1867, included a superintendent, 2 engineers, 2 sawyers, 57 masons, 43 carpenters, 1 wheelwright, 2 blacksmiths, 6 quarrymen, 1 lime burner, and 4 cooks. With the exception of a stone guardhouse, the buildings for the four companies of cavalry were designed to have stone foundations and adobe walls. Although one-half of the mechanics, who arrived in November, were discharged because of indolence and drunkenness, by December 31, 1867, four stables, 33 ⅓ feet by 250 feet, had been completed, except for roofs, doors, and stalls; stone foundations for two company quarters had been laid and were ready for joists; 656 perch of stone had been quarried and laid in foundations, and 200 other perch were ready for use; and 450 bushels of lime had been burned.

Although an early plan specified that a rock quarry was available three miles to the west, the quarry actually used was on the south end and on top of Five Mile Mesa. At the base of the mesa and on the east side, a small spring flowed during rainy seasons. Thirty-six mule teams and wagons and one twelve-ox team and truck were provided to haul the stone and other materials. On top of the mesa, a ledge of rock could be worked easily. Evidence abounds that the mesa was worked for its rock. A road from the top of the south end of the mesa, usable until a few years ago, ran northwest toward the post. The limekiln, between the guardhouse and the creek, was covered up after the city's Spring Drive and First Street were constructed.

Patrols and other detached service got underway almost immediately after the post was reoccupied. A detachment of Company K established a courier line to Fort Clark, the nearest post office to the east, by way of the abandoned Fort Lancaster. During late July and early August, Captain George Gamble, a lieutenant, and thirty-six men scouted in the region of the Pecos River and Horsehead Crossing, and in September Gamble's detachment moved up the Pecos as far as the Guadalupe Mountains, while Lieutenant Fred Smith's detachment searched among the piñons for suitable timber.

In August a steam sawmill arrived for use in sawing timber. Since the closest suitable timber was in the mountains some forty miles away, it was soon sent to Fort Davis, where there was timber nearby. Apparently, the mill, while in Fort Stockton, was located where present Mill Street intersects the creek. Mesquite roots, obtained from a distance of twenty-eight miles, were used for fuel. Stock could graze on the salt grass flats adjoining the post during the growing season. Following a killing frost, other kinds of grass had to be cut and hauled from a distance of fifteen miles. Carpenters waited idly for the arrival of lumber, which was freighted from Uvalde, over three hundred miles to the east.

In all, the government spent $465,000 for construction work on Forts Richardson, Griffin, Chadbourne, Concho, Stockton, and Davis. Of that amount, $81,978.26 was spent on Fort Stockton on the construction of buildings on land the government had neither bought nor leased. Since a large portion of the supplies and building materials had to be hauled to Stockton from San Antonio, a distance of 391.8 miles, progress was understandably slow.

The fort, constructed more as quarters for cavalry than for defense, consisted of officers' quarters, barracks, stables, guardhouse, and quartermaster buildings bordering the perimeter of a rectangular parade ground, about 1,000 by 450 feet. The quartermaster building was at the north end; the guardhouse and ammunition storage building were at the south end. Seven officers' quarters bordered the west side, and adjoining each of these on the west was a tall adobe wall enclosing servants' quarters, fodder and grain rooms, horse stalls, a yard, and a privy. The wall protected both the officers' quarters and the parade ground. The only exit from the yard of each officer's house was a gate that opened onto the parade ground.

Four barracks bordered the parade ground on the east side, and behind the barracks were four long horse barns, extending lengthwise east and west. The blacksmith shop was located between the barns and the creek. Had the Indians realized how vulnerable to attack the horse barns were, the horses there surely would have been stolen a number of times.[24]

[24] Ibid., pp. 710–711, 766–767, 864–870; U.S. Department of War, Post Returns, Fort Stockton, 1867 and 1868, Records of the Adjutant General's Office (AGO), Record Group (RG) 94, National Archives (NA), Washington, D.C.; Edward Hatch, Fort Stockton, Texas, to Charles E. Morse, February 20, 1868, U.S. Department of War, Records of United States Army Commands, RG 98, NA, Washington, D.C.; personal observations of the ruins of the forts.

CHAPTER 7

June, 1867, to September, 1868

MANY herds of cattle were driven through the Pecos country in 1867. John C. Cureton moved several thousand steers from Coleman County by way of Horsehead Crossing and the military stage route to El Paso and thence into New Mexico, but the majority of herds were driven up the Pecos River. In anticipation of the cattlemen's trade, Dick Reed late in 1867 established Seven Rivers Trading Post between the sites of present Carlsbad and Artesia, New Mexico, where seven streams entered the west side of the Pecos River.[1]

Because the Indians were stealing cattle and killing travelers between the Concho River and Horsehead Crossing, Lieutenant Peter Martin Boehm and a company of cavalry in June, 1867, set up Camp Charlotte on the headwaters of the Middle Concho. While scouting to Horsehead Crossing and Salt Lake on the eighteenth and nineteenth, Boehm saw plenty of Indian signs but no Indians. Returning to Camp Charlotte on the twenty-fourth, he sent a sergeant and twenty men to escort a herd of cattle to Horsehead Crossing. This was the first military protection provided drovers over this stretch of the old Butterfield Trail. On the eighth of July, Boehm was relieved by Brevet Major M. J. Kelly, with Company G, Fourth Cavalry.[2]

In late July, Captain George Gamble with forty men found signs of a large Indian party on the old Comanche War Trail some seventeen miles north of Fort Stockton. The trail led to Horsehead Crossing, where the troops arrived on July 29 in time to prevent two large herds of cattle being driven to Fort Sumner from being raided by Indians,

---

[1]John A. Richard, "Ere the Coming of the Cattlemen," *Frontier Times* 6, no. 5 (February, 1929):193; Doris Gregory, "Seven Rivers," *New Mexico Magazine*, May, 1961, p. 25.

[2]J. Evetts Haley, *Fort Concho and the Texas Frontier*, p. 124; Francis B. Heitman, *Historical Register and Dictionary of the United States Army*, 1:590.

who remained for some time in the vicinity of the cattle.[3] On August 22, Indians attacked a paymaster and a small escort about forty miles from Fort Chadbourne, killing two privates, and on September 10 a scouting party of Company K, Fourth Cavalry, from Fort Inge, attacked a small Indian party, capturing forty-six horses, one mule, eight saddles, and one Mexican boy.[4]

As a result of the Indian problems in the area, Captain George Huntt, in early November, 1867, established a location for Camp Hatch (later to become Fort Concho) at the junction of the North and Middle Concho rivers. Afterward, the place was occupied by Captain James Callahan with a detachment of Company H, Fourth Cavalry. Nearby, Bart DeWitt established a trading post, known first as Over-the-River then as Santa Angela, which eventually became the present city of San Angelo.[5]

Fort Hudson was occupied in November and December by Companies D and G, Ninth Cavalry. Company D was temporarily stationed at the head of Devils River, twenty-eight miles west of the fort, for the purpose of digging water wells at Johnson's Run and deepening the one known as Howard's Well.[6]

The presence of troops, however, did not prevent Indian attacks. Fort Davis had hardly been reoccupied when the Indians struck. Mexicans employed by Sam Miller were herding 150 work oxen and 165 head of cattle near the fort when Apaches stampeded the stock and killed the herders. A detachment from the post, guided by Miller, followed the trail down Limpia Canyon, out past Gomez Peak, then north toward the Guadalupe Mountains, but the search was futile.[7]

Mail coaches were easy prey for the Indians. On September 30, 1867, Ben Ficklin took over the government contract to carry the mail some 650 miles from San Antonio to El Paso del Norte.[8] Considering

[3] U.S. Department of War, Post Returns, Fort Stockton, July, 1867, Records of the Adjutant General's Office (AGO), Record Group (RG) 94, National Archives (NA), Washington, D.C.; Edward Hatch, Fort Stockton, to the Assistant Adjutant General (AAG), August 5, 1867, Records of the United States Army Commands, RG 98, NA.

[4] U.S. Department of War, Post Returns, Fort Chadbourne, August, 1867, and Fort Inge, September, 1867.

[5] Haley, *Fort Concho*, pp. 128–132.

[6] U.S. Dpartment of War, Post Returns, Fort Hudson, November and December, 1867.

[7] Barry Scobee, *Old Fort Davis*, pp. 65–66.

[8] J. Evetts Haley, "Ben Ficklin, Pioneer Mail Man," *Shamrock*, Spring, 1959, p. 11.

it safer from Indian attack, he had the stage follow the Upper San Antonio–El Paso Road to Horsehead Crossing and from there the Lower
Road to Fort Stockton. The new route, nevertheless, traversed a frontier frequently raided by Comanches and Kiowas.

Travel and military-post mail, however, continued on the Lower
Road, but at a great price. On October 1 two black troopers of the
Ninth Cavalry, while escorting the military mail between Fort Clark
and Fort Stockton, were killed near Howard's Well, and the driver and
passengers were severely wounded. In the frantic efforts to escape the
Indians, the mail was dropped four miles from Howard's Well.[9]

In late October, Indians ambushed the stage en route from Camp
Hudson to Fort Stockton, killing its escorts, Corporal Wright and Private Jones. A few weeks afterward, over one hundred Apaches attacked the eastbound stage and gave up the chase only when, in sight
of Eagle Springs, they encountered Captain Henry Carroll's Company
F, Ninth Cavalry regiment. Again, on December 13, the stage, with
an escort of a corporal and six men, was attacked by about a hundred
Indians at Eagle Springs. It got through, but one man was killed and
four horses were wounded.[10]

About half the Comanches and some Kiowas did not sign the
Medicine Lodge Treaty in 1867, and some who did refused to comply
with its terms. When the supplies promised by the government failed
to arrive that winter on schedule, many Indians who had signed the
treaty left the reservation in disgust to gather loot on the Texas frontier
and in northern Mexico.[11] The lower Pecos country lay along the route
to Mexico.

By November 29, 1867, the army had scattered its limited forces
over a large portion of the vast state of Texas. For the most part, the
cavalry was on the frontier, and the infantry in the cities. Two companies of the 125th Infantry were at El Paso. The Fourth Cavalry had
two companies and its headquarters at Camp Verde, five at Fort Chadbourne, and one each at Forts Clark, Mason, Inge, and Jefferson. The

[9] U.S. Department of War, Post Surgeon's Report, Fort Stockton, October, 1867,
AGO, RG 94, NA; M. L. Crimmins, "Fort Lancaster, Crockett County, Texas," *Frontier
Times* 10, no. 5 (February, 1933):198.

[10] William H. Leckie, *The Buffalo Soldiers*, pp. 84–85; U.S. Department of War,
Post Surgeon's Report, Fort Stockton, December, 1867.

[11] Rupert Norval Richardson, *The Comanche Barrier to South Plains Settlement*,
pp. 313–314.

Ninth Cavalry, with its temporary headquarters at Fort Stockton, had four companies at that post, three at Fort Davis, one at Fort Hudson, and two at Brownsville. The Ninth also had detachments at Horsehead Crossing, Lancaster, and Quitman. During the last three months of 1867, patrols from these outfits scouted over 1,220 miles along the Pecos, Concho, Devils, Colorado, and Nueces rivers and through the counties of Shackelford, Stephens, Palo Pinto, Montague, and Clay, but only one of the scouting parties engaged any raiders in the lower Pecos area, at which time three braves and one squaw were killed and nineteen horses and one mule were captured. Five men returning from New Mexico after delivering a herd of cattle were killed by Indians at the head of the Concho and buried by Fort Concho soldiers on December 21.[12]

On December 26, Captain William Thompson Frohock, Lieutenant Fred W. Smith, and Company K, Ninth Cavalry, from Fort Stockton, while camped in the ruins of Fort Lancaster, were attacked by a large party of Kickapoos, Lipans, and renegades. One party of the Indians roped and dragged off the troopers' three horse wranglers and drove off the remuda, while another party charged the soldiers within the ruins of the old post. Two attempts were made to take the troopers' positions, and, reportedly, two brave women with the defenders helped distribute ammunition during the heat of the three-hour attack. The troops lost three men, thirty-one horses, and six mules. The Indians' loss was estimated at twenty dead and a large number wounded.[13]

The mail coach from Fort Hudson, carrying the driver, W. Hobkins, passengers Cesario Torres and Ed Gallagher, and five black troopers of the Ninth Cavalry, arrived at the scene a few hours after the siege was lifted. The occupants had seen numerous horse tracks across the road some twelve miles east of Howard's Well and again about one mile before they reached Lancaster Hill. Among the trophies taken by the soldiers at the scene of the Fort Lancaster fight

---

[12] "Report of Brevet Major General J. J. Reynolds Commanding Fifth Military District," in U.S. Congress, House, *Message of the President of the United States. Report of the Secretary of War*, November 20, 1868, 40 Cong., 3 sess., 1869, House Exec. Doc. No. 1, pp. 706–707, 711–712; Haley, *Fort Concho*, p. 155.

[13] U.S. Department of War, Post Returns, Fort Stockton, 1867; Leckie, *Buffalo Soldiers*, p. 85.

were bows and arrows, a Remington six-shooter, a new infantry coat, and a magnificent headdress ornamented with thirty silver plates. After laying over for a night, the mail party started early on the twenty-eighth for Fort Stockton. Within a mile of the Pecos, Hobkins saw an Indian and, fearing an ambush, returned to Lancaster. On the following day, a few Mexicans with carts, arriving at Lancaster, reported that unshod horses recently had crossed the Pecos.[14]

Shortly afterward and 200 miles farther west, all wagon trains on the western side of Eagle Springs were besieged by Indians until a detachment arrived from Fort Davis.[15] To provide the segment of the route from Fort Davis to El Paso additional protection, Fort Quitman was reoccupied by Captain Carroll with one company of Ninth Cavalry on January 1, 1868. Carroll found that much of the fort had been dismantled for firewood and that all that remained were the adobe walls and a few roofs. The company made repairs, hospital patients were placed in tents, and medical supplies were obtained from New Orleans every six months. Dairy products, eggs, chickens, vegetables, and fruit were hauled some 50 to 75 miles from the Mexican town of San Ignacio Guadalupe or from San Elizario. At the point of purchase, milk cost $0.05 cents per gallon; butter, about $1.00 per pound; eggs, $0.50 per dozen; chickens, $1.00 per pair; and vegetables and fruits, including cabbage, onions, turnips, and oranges, from $0.08 to $0.12 per pound.[16] But one company at Quitman was inadequate, and, after inspecting the region around Eagle Springs, General Hatch recommended that more troops be sent to that place. He suggested the following garrisons: one company at Barilla (Varela) Spring, two companies at Fort Davis, one company at El Muerto, forty miles west of Fort Davis, one company at Eagle Springs, a detachment at Van Horn's Well, and two companies at Quitman.[17]

During January and February of 1868, the Texas frontier caught hell. Raids were made from Montague and Cooke counties on the

[14] *San Antonio Express*, January 9, 1868; San Antonio *Herald*, January 8, 1868.

[15] Edward Hatch, Fort Stockton, to AAG, January 3, 1868, Army Commands, RG 98, NA; U.S. Department of War, Post Returns, Fort Stockton, January, 1868.

[16] Acting Assistant Surgeon J. J. Culver, "Report, Fort Quitman, Texas," 1868–1869, in U.S. Department of War, Surgeon General, *A Report on Barracks and Hospitals with Descriptions of Military Posts*, Circular No. 4, December 5, 1870.

[17] U.S. Department of War, Post Surgeon's Report, Fort Stockton, January and February, 1868.

north southward through Wise, Jack, Denton, Bosque, Comanche, and Kendall counties to the Rio Grande. The army was not yet very effective on the frontier. During January and March, 1868, seventeen cavalry patrols covered thousands of miles, but only two encountered Indians.[18] Nevertheless, beginning on March 1, 1868, triweekly mail service between San Antonio and El Paso was started through Fredericksburg, Mason, Fort Stockton, Fort Davis, and Fort Quitman. Another triweekly stage line under the same management connected San Antonio and Eagle Pass by way of Castroville, D'Hanis, Fort Inge, and Fort Clark. Apparently, the service was a success from the start. By April the San Antonio *Herald* was praising the line and its manager, Ben Ficklin, who had earlier been invovled in the Overland Pony Express between Kansas and California, for the comfort, the speed, and, especially, the safety it provided. The road was protected by one infantry and one cavalry company and a picket station at Fort Mason; four companies of cavalry and two of infantry at Fort McKavett; four companies of cavalry and two of infantry at Fort Concho; one company of cavalry at Camp Charlotte on the head of the Concho; a picket station at Wild China Ponds (more often called China Ponds); one company of infantry at Horsehead Crossing; one company of cavalry at Pecos Station (at or near Horseshoe Bend and "S" Crossing on the Pecos); four companies of cavalry and two of infantry at Fort Stockton; a picket at Varela Spring; three companies of cavalry and two of infantry at Fort Davis; a picket station at Barrel Springs; a picket station of one cavalry company at Van Horn's Well; a picket station of one cavalry company at Rice's ranch at Eagle Springs; one company of cavalry at Smith's ranch; three companies of cavalry and one of infantry at Fort Quitman; and two companies of infantry at El Paso. The line was important, for it connected the people of Texas with the rich gold, silver, and copper regions of New Mexico, Arizona, and California.[19]

By this time, the construction of Fort Stockton was well underway. During April and May a great deal of troop movement occurred.

[18] "Report of Major General W. S. Hancock," in House, *Report of the Secretary of War*, 40 Cong., 3 sess., 1869, House Exec. Doc. No. 1, pp. 210–211; Joseph Carroll McConnell, *The West Texas Frontier*, 2:212–235; "Statement of expeditions and scouts in the district of Texas and Fifth Military District (State of Texas) during the year ending September 30, 1868," in House, *Report of the Secretary of War*, 40 Cong., 3 sess., 1869, House Exec. Doc. No. 1, pp. 712–714.

[19] San Antonio *Herald*, February 20 and April 18, 1868.

On April 9, 1868, Company K, Ninth Cavalry, left Stockton for Fort Davis, but new troops soon arrived, including Company D, Ninth Cavalry, on April 17, Company G, Forty-first Infantry, on April 21, and Company A, Forty-first Infantry, on May 10. Company A had marched all the way from Brownsville. Camp Hudson was abandoned. Company D, Ninth Cavalry, left on April 10 for Fort Stockton, and Company G, Ninth Cavalry, left on April 12 for Fort Clark. Companies C and I, Ninth Cavalry, left Fort Davis on May 1 and arrived at Fort Quitman on May 8. The eighty-three men of Company I had passed through Fort Stockton, arriving on April 17, on their way to Forts Davis and Quitman, and on May 2 Troops A, B, D, and E, Ninth Cavalry, were at Fort Stockton. Captain George Gamble took command of the post in April and retained it for the remainder of the year.[20]

With the reestablishment of the forts, Ben Ficklin began a new line from Fort Stockton to Chihuahua, Mexico. By May of 1868, he was carrying passengers west at the low price of fifteen cents per mile, making the 650 miles from San Antonio to El Paso in six and one-half days, a rate of 100 miles per day.[21]

On June 4, 1868, a picket of fifteen men from Company G, Forty-first Infantry, under Lieutenant Lewis, was transferred from Castle Gap to China Ponds.[22] Apparently it was at this time that the stage line changed from the Horsehead route to the Horseshoe Bend and the present "S" Crossing on the Pecos, near the future location of a pontoon bridge.

Simultaneously, Peter Gallagher, the founder of Saint Gall (the original town site of the city of Fort Stockton), was investing in the area. Born in Westmeath County, Ireland, in 1812, Gallagher in 1829 went to New Orleans, where he became a stonemason. In 1837 he moved to San Antonio, where he practiced his trade until 1841, when he joined the Texan Santa Fe Expedition. With the other members, he was taken captive and sent to a prison in Mexico. After his release in 1842, he joined John Coffee Hays's Texas Rangers. After being in the

[20] U.S. Department of War, Post Returns, Fort Stockton, April and May, 1868; "Report of Major General W. S. Hancock," in House, *Report of the Secretary of War*, 40 Cong., 3 sess., 1869, House Exec. Doc. No. 1, pp. 707–709; U.S. Department of War, Post Surgeon's Report, Fort Stockton, April and May, 1868; U.S. Department of War, Post Returns, Fort Stockton, June–December, 1868.
[21] Haley, "Ben Ficklin," pp. 11–12.
[22] U.S. Department of War, Post Surgeon's Report, Fort Stockton, June, 1868.

mercantile business in San Antonio from 1846 to 1850, Gallagher returned to Ireland, married Eliza Conran, returned to Texas, and invested in real estate. From 1861 to 1864 he served as chief justice of Bexar
County.[23]

After the Civil War Peter Gallagher became for a short time a
leader in the movement to divide the state. Prior to the war most of
the proponents of division had been East Texans who wanted to shed
the responsibilities of frontier protection, but after the war the movement was led primarily by a small group of Unionists in San Antonio
and South Texas. The Convention of 1866 voted in favor of division but
took no further action, and the Eleventh Legislature, which met in August, 1866, refused to consider the governor's recommendation to sell a
portion of the public domain to the United States and voted against
division. After the victory of the radicals that fall in Congress, however, the divisionists refused to concede defeat. Edward Degener, a
prominent Unionist in San Antonio, wrote that the large German and
Unionist population would form a separate state at "a mere Congressional suggestion," and a few days later he and fifteen others addressed
to Congress a memorial asking for the division of Texas into two states.[24]

The most influential leaders in the movement were E. J. Davis of
Corpus Christi, who had attained the rank of brigadier general in the
Union Army, and James P. Newcomb, co-owner of the *San Antonio Express*, who had strongly opposed secession and now assumed the leading editorial voice in support of division. In the Reconstruction Convention, which met on June 1, 1868, division became the major goal of
the radical delegates, and by the end of the year the convention was in
a deadlock on the issue. In December, to promote the movement, a
group of citizens in San Antonio, including Gallagher, G. W. Brackenridge, and Samuel Maverick, held a mass meeting. Gallagher presided, and John James served as secretary. One of those attending
thought that the state should be called Bucola, which he said meant
"The Land of the Shepherd," but apparently Gallagher did not express
any preference for a name.[25]

[23] Webb and Carroll, *Handbook of Texas*, 1:661.

[24] Edward Degener to E. M. Pease, December 30, 1866, and January 21 and October 24, 1867, E. M. Pease Collection, Austin Public Library, Austin, Texas; Ernest Wallace, *The Howling of the Coyotes*, pp. 8–24.

[25] San Antonio *Herald*, February 25, 1868; Weston J. McConnell, *Social Cleavages*

In January, 1869, there were several other mass meetings in San Antonio on division, but Gallagher did not participate. Needing some productive land at a convenient location on which to produce supplies for the military posts in western Texas, Gallagher had speculated heavily in irrigable land near Fort Stockton. On December 5, 1867, in San Antonio, he and J. G. C. Lee contracted with the army to deliver 5,000 bushels of corn to Camp Hudson at $2.50 per bushel, 2,500 bushels to Fort Davis at $3.75 per bushel, and 15,000 bushels to Fort Stockton at $4.00 per bushel.[26] In addition to the army, mail stages, wagon trains, and travelers that far from the settlements would need and be willing to pay high prices for stock feed. Other men likewise were investing in potential farm areas in the Toyah Valley and San Felipe Creek (in the region of present Del Rio). William Russell established an extensive irrigated farm on the Rio Grande, near Candelaria, but a flood caused the river to change its course and to wash away his farm.[27]

Because of the great amount of water that flowed from Comanche Springs, Gallagher purchased a large amount of land on Comanche Creek. In addition, on February 2, 1868, he bought the property upon which Fort Stockton is now situated. To gain control of Comanche Springs and the property of Fort Stockton, Gallagher on May 6 also bought the José Montes Survey 150 and the John Flood Survey 151, and on the latter he built his mercantile establishment. His impressive store, a long, flat-roofed adobe, running lengthwise toward the north and south, was located just south of the present (1981) Elliott and Waldron Company's office. It had an appearance similar to that of the old Santa Fe capitol. A well, hand-dug, was at the northwest end of the building. Five years later, Gallagher and John James purchased 5,500 acres, some of it for cultivation with irrigation from Comanche Springs.

The enterprising Gallagher also managed to get the nearby land watered by San Pedro Spring. Because he was in Texas prior to March 2, 1836, Joseph Burleson, Jr., had received a "first class" headright cer-

---

in Texas: A Study of the Proposed Division of the State, p. 78; Wallace, Howling of the Coyotes, pp. 46–90.

    [26] "Contracts by the Quartermaster's Department," in U.S. Congress, Senate, Message of the President of the United States. Letter from the Secretary of War, 40 Cong., 2 sess., 1868, Senate Exec. Doc. No. 59, pp. 2–3.

    [27] Carlysle Graham Raht, The Romance of Davis Mountains, p. 194.

tificate for one square league (*sitio*) and one *labor* (4,605.5 acres). Burleson filed on only one *sitio*, and finally on September 18, 1860, he transferred the remaining 177 acres to Peter Gallagher, who in 1868 had the tract located and surveyed to include San Pedro Spring. Since the water from the small spring was easily harnessed for irrigation, he soon had a tenant, Pedro Ureta, raising corn for the market at Fort Stockton.[28]

John James, also from San Antonio and a friend of Gallagher, was another pioneer who obtained considerable property near Fort Stockton. James, born in England in 1819 while his parents from Nova Scotia were there on a visit, migrated in 1837 to San Antonio, where he soon became an assistant surveyor of Bexar County. He was in the Battle of the Salado when General Adrian Woll and the Mexican Army invaded Texas in 1842. In the spring of 1839, while surveying on the Frio River, five of his party were killed by Indians. In 1844, he surveyed the town sites of Castroville, D'Hanis, Boerne, Quihi, and Bandera. In Bandera, James established a sawmill, powered by horses, and furnished lumber for military posts. He also established the first lumberyard in San Antonio. His partnership mercantile business in San Antonio, under the name of James R. Sweet and Company, did a large volume of business prior to the Civil War. In 1855, James brought sixteen Polish families to Bandera, where he had a hotel. Before and during the Civil War, he owned the land upon which Fort Davis was built. Like Gallagher, he owned ranchlands in Bandera County, and the two jointly owned property in Fort Stockton. In Stockton James owned the James Hotel, stage stand, and corrals, which were located in the same block as and southwest of the present courthouse. To the north, in present Crane County, he acquired the salt lake.

Friends of James and Gallagher who were simultaneously developing property in the lower Pecos country included George Howard, N. T. Wilson, Paul Wagner, George H. Giddings, the Mavericks, the Herffs, and José Policarpo Rodríguez, the great scout and guide.[29]

---

[28] Pecos County, Deed Records, 18:284, 343; 20:20; Pecos County Land Patent Records, 2 (pts. 53 and 731), 17 (pts. 537 and 538), 35 (pt. 153); Webb and Carroll, *Handbook of Texas*, 1:20.

[29] Webb and Carroll, *Handbook of Texas*, 1:904; Clarence R. Wharton, *Texas under Many Flags*, 1:383; *Galveston News*, November 30, 1877; Vinton Lee James, *Frontier and Pioneer Recollections of Early Days in San Antonio and West Texas*, pp. 20–23, 30, 44, 48; *Fort Stockton Pioneer*, November 15, 1962.

In 1868 George M. Frazer and his family moved to Fort Stockton. Frazer, born in Brownsville, Tennessee, on January 5, 1828, came to San Augustine, Texas, with his parents in 1834. In Tennessee, the Frazers had been neighbors of David Crockett, and en route to the defense of the Alamo Crockett and his small party visited the Frazer family at San Augustine.

With the outbreak of the Mexican War, eighteen-year-old Frazer, in June of 1846, enlisted in Jo Bennett's company at Galveston, which immediately joined Albert Sidney Johnston's regiment. Later, he transferred to R. K. Goodlow's company in G. T. Wood's regiment. He returned home after the battle of Monterrey, but on March 11, 1847, he joined Benjamin F. Hill's company of John C. Hays's regiment. While scouting at a ranch known as Macunarti, he was shot through the thigh and rode for three days on horseback in order to obtain medical attention at Monterrey.

Following the Mexican War, Frazer in 1849 joined Colonel Joseph E. Johnston's large military force and survey crew as it traveled from San Antonio to Fort Bliss, where he remained until March of 1850. He then went to Socorro and later to Santa Fe, and during the following year he and about seventy other men prospected for gold at the confluence of the Gila River and San Francisco Creek. En route, the group visited with Apache chief Mangas Coloradas and his tribe at Tularosa Creek. Mangas informed his visitors that there was much gold in the country but none for the white men, but he did trade them some cattle. Along the San Francisco, the Frazer party panned for gold, finding "color" but no "pay."

For a time Frazer served at Santa Fe as a chief wagon master of the army. In March, 1857, he bought a stock of goods and started for Tucson, Arizona. En route, while helping an army patrol trail Indians, his wagon train was ambushed and all of his property, valued at $4,000, was lost to the Indians. He presented a claim against the government for this loss, but it was never paid because he was unable to identify the Indians who had been responsible. His only compensation was a certificate for gallant service.

On January 14, 1858, at Doña Ana, New Mexico, George Frazer married Miss May Edgar, the sister of John and James Edgar, whose adventures in the Pecos country have been previously narrated. The Edgar family had come from Fort Smith, Arkansas, when May was a child and, like Frazer, had moved across West Texas in 1849 with Colonel Johnston.

In 1860, while living in Mesilla, Frazer joined prospectors at Piños Altos and associated for a time with the well-known gold seeker Jacob Snively. Shortly after the outbreak of the Civil War, as previously related, a stage party, consisting of young Union sympathizers who were trying to reach California, was attacked in Cook's Canyon by Apache Indians led by Mangas Coloradas and Cochise. Frazer and a few others who were sent to investigate were the ones who found the bodies of Emmett Mills and his friends behind a stone fortification on top of a peak. Following his Civil War activities in the Territory of New Mexico, Frazer served in Louisiana under General Tom Green and Colonel George Madison.

After the war, Frazer moved to San Antonio, where he was employed by W. B. Knox to run a line of freight wagons between that city and Chihuahua, Mexico. Because it was centrally located on the long route, he moved his family to Fort Stockton, and for a time they lived in a tent on the banks of the creek. With the fort nearby, the family felt secure. At night, if the men were away, the top of a table was placed flat against the tent's opening to keep out varmints. One night the women and children heard a frightening scream; the next morning panther tracks were all around the tent.[30] Subsequently, there will be more about Frazer, the notable pioneer who became the first county judge of Pecos County, and the members of his family.

The Lower San Antonio–El Paso Road crossed the Pecos River, a treacherous stream of bad water, quicksand, and whirlpools, between Lancaster and Stockton, but the crossing was closed when the river was flooded. Consequently, in 1868 a bridge was constructed at a location near Lancaster, 4.65 miles down the river from Pecos Spring and about a mile above the mouth of Live Oak Creek.[31] On orders from General Hatch, Captain F. S. Dodge and thirty men of the Ninth Cav-

[30] James Cox, *Historical and Biographical Record of the Cattle Industry and the Cattlemen of Texas and Adjacent Territory*, 2:457; O. W. Williams, "An Old Timer's Reminiscences of Grant County," *West Texas Historical Association Year Book* 16 (1940): 135–140; Barney Riggs, Jr., L. F. Durrell, Myrtle Lewis, and other descendants of George M. Frazer, oral statements, to Clayton Williams, particularly relative to the tent dwelling.

[31] U.S. Department of War, Lieutenant Colonel Thomas Hunt, "Journal," Office of the Chief of Engineers, Q 154, p. 29, RG 77, NA.

alry from Fort Stockton, beginning on May 3, 1868, explored the area from Lancaster to Horsehead in search of a better route. Dodge returned to Stockton on May 15, after covering 350 miles, and recommended the relocation of the mail route by Flat Rock Ponds to the region of the Horseshoe Bend of the Pecos.[32] Since First Lieutenant Robert Neely, with Company A, Forty-first Infantry, left Fort Stockton on July 12 for temporary duty at Pecos Station near "S" Crossing on the Horseshoe Bend to guard the mail, the route apparently by then had been changed.

For a time thereafter, the military kept patrols in the area. Captain Lewis Johnson, Company D, Forty-first Infantry, arrived at Fort Stockton on July 17 from temporary duty at Horsehead Crossing. During the same month, Captain Dodge with twenty men scouted between the Pecos Station and Camp Charlotte at the headwaters of the Concho; Captain George Gamble, a lieutenant, and forty men of the Ninth Cavalry patrolled south to the vicinity of Independence Creek, and First Sergeant Henry James and twenty men of the Ninth Cavalry scouted in the direction of Fort Lancaster. The outpost at the Lancaster Crossing, eighty miles east of Stockton, had been established in March, and Camp Melvin, fifty-five miles east of the post, and Escondido (Tunas) Springs were set up in July, with plans to change the details every month.[33]

The military patrols, nevertheless, failed to keep the cattlemen and the mail coaches from being attacked by Indians. During the summer of 1868, John Dalton, Mose Terry, and Abe Denton drove a herd from the Palo Pinto country to Fort Sumner. On the return trip, they were attacked at the head of the Middle Concho; their horses, equipment, and money were taken; and they were left on foot.[34] D. M. Poer and A. G. Boyce were more fortunate. Poer drove 1,200 cattle from the Fort Concho area to the great Terrazas ranch in Chihuahua, and Boyce trailed a herd of 3,000 cattle by way of the Concho and Horsehead Crossing to California. Neither encountered any trouble with Indians.[35]

In August, 1868, while driving a mail stage between El Paso and

[32] U.S. Department of War, Post Returns, Fort Stockton, May, 1868.

[33] Ibid., July, 1868.

[34] McConnell, *West Texas Frontier*, 2:231.

[35] Raht, *Romance of Davis Mountains*, p. 157; Richard, "Ere the Coming of the Cattlemen," p. 193.

Fort Davis, Big Foot Wallace and his eight companions, upon sighting dust rising in the west, hurried to a better defensive position at a water hole (likely Van Horn's Well). After the first onslaught, the Indians withdrew a short distance, and Wallace and his men then killed a few of their own animals for use as a breastwork. The night passed without incident, but the Indians renewed the assault the next morning. In an effort to get within the barricade, the Indians concealed braves amid their thirsty horses and turned them loose to go to water. But the ruse failed and cost the Indians a number of mounts. The Indians then showered Wallace's party with arrows and bullets while circling the barricade at full speed and hanging on the sides of their horses. Fortunately for the stage group, a crashing thunderstorm struck, and the Indians left, but not before they had lost an estimated eleven of their comrades and wounded three of the whites. Soon after starting out again, Wallace encountered some cavalry scouts with a doctor, who attended the wounded. Wallace's next stop was Fort Davis.[36]

During the remainder of 1868, eight or ten herds of cattle were trailed by way of Horsehead Crossing and the Pecos to New Mexico without incident.[37] But not all were so fortunate. Robert Casey loaded his belongings, his wife, and his five children in a covered wagon and with the help of only one Mexican headed for New Mexico. Fortunately, he was acquainted with the trail and was soon joined by Ben Gooch with two cowboys and his cattle. Near the Pecos River, the party saw lights in the distance, sometimes to the north of the trail, sometimes to the south. Casey feared that they were made by Indians, but Gooch contended that they were made by other cow outfits.

One morning while Robert Casey was sleeping, after standing night guard, Mrs. Casey heard a low, rumbling noise and saw clouds of dust made by Indian horsemen racing toward the cattle. Abruptly awakened by his wife, Casey began shooting. Mrs. Casey put the children in the wagon, grabbed a muzzle-loading, double-barreled shotgun, rammed powder into one barrel and shot into the other. Evidently pulling the trigger to the barrel containing the shot, the frightened woman handed the weapon to the Mexican, who quickly discovered her mistake. Few men have risked life and limb for less than did one of

---

[36] Don H. Biggers, "From Cattle Range to Cotton Patch," *Frontier Times* 21 (1943): 71–73.

[37] T. U. Taylor, *Jesse Chisholm*, pp. 102–103.

the Gooch cowboys. His companions were retreating to the Casey wagon, but he had a new suit of clothes in Gooch's wagon and refused to abandon it to the Indians. He hid in the wagon with the suit and was not discovered by the Indians when they ransacked the back of the wagon.

When Mrs. Casey saw her pampered sheep being driven off by Indians, she grabbed a tin pan, ran out into the open, beat on the pan, and cried "Nannie! Nannie!" At this familiar sound, which signaled a generous supply of corn, the sheep broke away from the Indians and raced back for the feed. Had Mr. Casey not run to the rescue of his angry wife, she likely would have been taken captive. The other men had used most of their ammunition on game, but fortunately Casey and the Mexican had enough to keep the Indians away from the wagon. However, the raiders got away with 1,300 cattle and all the work oxen. The only known casualty was one Indian.

The travelers, left in hostile country in the winter with practically no ammunition and few provisions, gathered the few cattle the Indians had left and, with a new team of wild steers, continued up the Pecos. Progress, however, was difficult. The unbroken oxen sometimes refused to pull and at other times took off at a gallop and overturned the wagon and its occupants, but the Caseys nevertheless completed their trip and settled on the Rio Hondo, about twenty-five miles south of Fort Stanton, where they experienced many more adventures.[38]

[38] Raht, *Romance of Davis Mountains*, pp. 177–179.

CHAPTER 8

July, 1868, to June, 1869

DESPITE the military patrols, during the summer of 1868 the Trans-Pecos country continued to be unsafe for travelers and cattle drovers. On the night of July 10, the mail arrived at Fort Quitman with both the stage driver and the lone escort suffering from lance wounds. At the head of a canyon, fourteen miles east of the post, eight Apaches had leaped from concealment and had thrown their lances, wounding the two men, who, because of the fine team of horses, managed to escape.[1]

On August 19, Lieutenant Smith and a detachment of twenty-two men from Companies C and K, Ninth Cavalry, were dispatched from Fort Davis in pursuit of Indians who had stolen stock from the mail line at El Muerto. After riding 164 miles, they failed to contact the Indians and captured only one mule. Captain Burney's (probably First Lieutenant James G. Birney[2]) detachment of Ninth Cavalry, sent on a similar mission, had better success. It recovered all the stock that had been stolen from a government train but saw no Indians. After more stock had been stolen from the neighborhood of Fort Quitman, a detachment from Company H, Ninth Cavalry, left that post on August 24 and recovered nineteen head of stock as its reward for 250 miles of marching.[3] Farther east, on August 31, Captain George H. Gamble, Ninth Cavalry, of Fort Stockton, captured nine armed Mexicans, who after loitering for two weeks in the vicinity had stolen four horses from cattle herders at Horsehead Crossing, but three other Mexicans escaped in the

---

[1] San Antonio *Herald*, July 25, 1868.

[2] Francis B. Heitman, *Historical Register and Dictionary of the United States Army*, 1:220.

[3] U.S. Department of War, Post Returns, Fort Davis, August, 1868, Records of the Adjutant General's Office (AGO), Record Group (RG) 94, National Archives (NA), Washington, D.C.

direction of Mexico with the horses captured from some cattle drovers on their way to El Paso.[4]

Although the detachments were recovering stolen stock, no thieves were being punished. But this was about to change. The Indians attacked a wagon train of a Mr. Morales west of Fort Stockton at Leon Springs, drove off 100 of his mules, and set fire to his wagons. The drivers and owners escaped unharmed. When news of the incident reached the fort, the authorities held westbound emigrants at the post until there were enough to provide for their own protection. Among those detained was the family of Mrs. Reuben Allen, who recently had arrived from England and was bound for ranchlands near Ruidoso, New Mexico.

When First Lieutenant Patrick Cusack returned to Fort Davis from San Antonio, forty-five armed Mexicans that Morales had sent in pursuit of the Indians were there. They had found the encampment of the guilty Indians, but it was too large for them to attack. It numbered, they reported, about 200 warriors and their families, who had with them about 200 head of horses and mules. The Mexicans also reported that because of high water the Indians had been unable to cross the Rio Grande and were on their way to the Guadalupe Mountains. At that time, it turned out, the Indians were not far from Fort Davis. In response to their request for aid, Lieutenant Cusack, with a detachment of sixty black troopers from Companies C, F, and K, Ninth Cavalry, and fifteen days' rations, on September 8 left Fort Davis to search for the Indians. That evening the detachment camped at the old abandoned Músquiz quarters in Musquiz Canyon, where it was met by Mexican guides. The next morning the expedition headed east, but thereafter it traveled mostly by night, concealing its daytime camp in canyons and lighting no fires. On the morning of the fourth day, the troops rode up on the Indians, who retreated for about five miles to Horsehead Hill, which was too steep for the troopers' horses to climb.

During the resulting engagement on September 12 or 14, the soldiers killed twenty-five Indians, wounded twenty-five others, captured two Mexican boys, an Indian baby girl, 150 buffalo robes, 300 smaller skins, 198 horses and mules, some beef cattle, and other trophies. They then destroyed the wickiups.

[4] U.S. Department of War, Post Returns, Fort Stockton, August, 1868.

Some of the returning black troopers rode into Fort Davis with their faces painted and in full Indian regalia, and others bore long poles from which hung Apache scalps. The captive children were in good condition. The buffalo robes, skins, bows and arrows, and shields, from the ranchería of Chief Alsate of the Mescaleros and Chief Sabier of the Lipans, were sold at cheap prices, and the mules were returned to Morales and El Muerto.[5] For "conspicuous gallantry" in this engagement, Cusack was breveted a captain.[6]

To get a firsthand report from the frontier (and possibly for reasons of health), a San Antonio *Herald* correspondent, H. C. Logan, took the stage trip to El Paso during the latter part of 1868.[7] Logan wrote that the road was worst from Boerne to Comfort, that he had breakfast at the Nimitz Hotel in Fredericksburg, and that Loyal Valley in Mason County, twenty-five miles from Fredericksburg, which consisted of two houses, one a combination store, post office, and stage stand, was the most picturesque spot. Fort Concho, he thought, could accommodate six companies but was permanently garrisoned by only one of cavalry and two of infantry. A company of the Fourth Cavalry, headquartered there, was usually absent scouting and garrisoning minor posts. The quartermaster and commissary depots were completed, and the troops were quartered in large wall tents with stone fireplaces attached. Two miles above the post was the mail station, the home station of the El Paso line, and three miles farther, at the junction of the Middle Concho and the South Concho, was Bismarck, then about the size of Loyal Valley.

The next station, Camp Charlotte, a picket post with a garrison of one company of the Fourth Cavalry, was on the Middle Concho fifty-five miles from Fort Concho. At least 150,000 cattle, Logan estimated,

[5] Details of the incidents involving Cusack are from: U.S. Department of War, Post Returns, Forts Davis, Quitman, and Stockton, August and September, 1868; *Army and Navy Journal* 6 (October 10, 1868):114; San Antonio *Herald*, September 16, 22, and 29, 1868; "Statement of expeditions and scouts in the district of Texas and Fifth Military District (State of Texas) during the year ending September 30, 1868," in U.S. Congress, House, *Message of the President of the United States. Report of the Secretary of War*, November 20, 1868, 40 Cong., 3 sess., 1869, House Exec. Doc. No. 1, pp. 715–716, 774, 855–861; Mrs. Victor Smith, San Angelo, Texas, to Clayton Williams, March 17, 1971.

[6] Heitman, *Historical Register*, 1:347, and 2:432.

[7] Logan's articles appeared in the San Antonio *Herald*, October 20 and 26 and November 3, 10, 12, 17, 24, 26, and 27, 1868.

had passed there during 1868. Five herds, ranging from 1,000 to 3,000 head, had moved by the post during a twenty-four-hour period. Troops in the picket camps usually levied a tax of one beef from each passing herd to supplement their meager rations.

Thirty miles from the Pecos, the mail route left the Butterfield Road and went southeast to Pecos Station (near the present "S" Crossing on the Horseshoe Bend), halfway between Fort Lancaster and Horsehead Crossing. As previously mentioned, Captain F. S. Dodge during the previous May had found this place to be a better crossing than Horsehead, and in July he had spent ten days locating a route from there to the headwaters of the Concho. Soon afterward the mail stage was using the new route.[8] At Pecos Station, Logan wrote that his stage had traveled 120 miles from Fort Concho in forty hours. He left an excellent description of the crossing: "There is no sign of a river . . . no banks, trees, 'nor nothing,'—the result is, before you know it you are in it. It is a deep, turbid stream, very swift, very crooked, quite narrow—not more than thirty feet wide—and the muddiest stream I ever saw; the banks on both sides are about three feet high. A boat is used here to 'ferry' over the mail. Coaches being kept on both sides." Commenting further on this area, Logan wrote that the stage encountered some delay at the crossing, for it had to be taken across the river on a canoe. An order had already been received at Fort Stockton, however, to have the bridge near Fort Lancaster moved to Horseshoe Bend.

From the Pecos, Logan traveled about fifty miles westward by night across a virtually waterless and level prairie to Fort Stockton. Fort Stockton, he reported, was garrisoned with four companies of the Ninth Cavalry and one of the Forty-first Infantry, all black, quartered in temporary but comfortable, adobe structures. Permanent buildings were being erected, but it was difficult to obtain lumber. The commanding officer's quarters, the guardhouse, and the quartermaster and commissary depots were near completion. Plans called for five stables, each to hold 100 horses, but only one, "the finest in the state," had been completed. Logan was also impressed with the guardhouse. It was, he wrote, "the neatest thing of the kind" and the strongest he had ever seen, except perhaps the Nashville penitentiary.

[8] U.S. Department of War, Post Returns, Fort Stockton, May and July, 1868.

Five stacks of grama grass hay, each 230 feet long, 28 feet high, and 18 feet wide, had been stored for winter feed for the horses, but already (November 5) two stacks had been used. George Crosson, who had contracted to supply the post with 1,500 tons, had cut most of the hay by hand and hauled it over forty miles. The post had its own garden, some four miles down Comanche Creek, which produced a sufficient supply of vegetables and fruits. The reporter claimed that he saw several pumpkins over three feet in length and that the watermelons were small but fine.

Logan also reported that there was no timber and that "wood is not cut but dug, consisting entirely of roots." The contractor for the supply, "Don Pedro" Gallagher, had gotten between 200 and 300 cords of this wood and hauled it about forty miles to the fort. Gallagher, he further noted, was the postmaster and a post trader. (The job of post trader was rather remunerative. Notice was received at Fort Stockton on October 27, 1868, that Gallagher and Thomas Johnson had been appointed post traders there.[9]) George B. Lyles and Joseph Friedlander were unofficial post traders, and George M. Frazer was considering establishing a dairy to supply milk and butter to the post occupants.

Logan noted that Lieutenant Cusack, hero of the engagement over Alsate's Apaches, wore his "laurels with modest grace and dignity." Logan was greatly impressed with an Apache shield that he examined. The shields, he wrote, were made of "three thicknesses of rawhide, sewed together with rawhide strings, and covered with buckskin; are about the shape and size of the bottom of a barrel, and are impervious to pistol balls, point blank range, any distance above ten steps,—while a glancing shot at any distance, with even a musket, will fly off; these shields are hung over the neck, and readily held with the left hand. . . ."

About daylight on November 8, Logan left Fort Stockton in a "light, strongly built buggy with dashing teams." He passed the station at Barilla (Varela) Spring and within twenty miles of Fort Davis entered Limpia Canyon at Point of Rocks. "The scenery in viewing the mountains," he wrote, "is no longer just beautiful; it is sublimely magnificent." Winding around the canyon and crossing the creek about twenty times in half as many miles, he arrived in Fort Davis shortly after dark.

[9] Ibid., October, 1868.

As headquarters of the Ninth Cavalry, commanded by Lieutenant Colonel Wesley Merritt, Fort Davis was then garrisoned with six companies. During the Civil War, Merritt had been breveted major general for meritorious service. Another officer was Captain and Brevet Lieutenant Colonel William Thompson Frohock, whose company of black troops had withstood the attack of numerous Indians in December of 1867 at the ruins of Fort Lancaster.[10] Construction on the fort was proceeding slowly. Four or five stone officers' quarters had been erected. The commanding officer's quarters contained four large rooms, two in front that faced east with a hall between and two that extended back from the south end with a gallery on both sides. The stable was one grand corral about a hundred yards square. In spite of the fine water in Limpia Creek, dysentery was a serious problem among the troops; twenty men had died recently from it. The malady, it was later determined, was due to the lack of adequate vegetables in the diet.

Of the three mercantile establishments at Fort Davis, that of E. D. L. Wickes and Company was the best situated and monopolized the soldiers' business. "Don Patricio" Murphy had three large buildings at an excellent location. The buildings, each 130 feet long, formed three sides of a square, and on the fourth side there was a wall about 12 feet high. The enclosed plaza protected Murphy's goods and horses from marauders. C. H. Lesinsky and Company was ready for business but had not received a consignment of goods shipped from New York more than six months previously.

Freight charges on goods arriving at Fort Davis were almost prohibitive. The charge for a box of apples brought by stage from San Antonio had been thirty-one dollars, which the consignee had refused to pay, but Logan noted that a hay contractor at Fort Stockton had paid the charge of twenty-six dollars for a small package of scythe whetstones brought from San Antonio.

The scouting patrols were unable to prevent the Indians from attacking the stages and raiding the company teams. On October 22, 1868, at Van Horn's Well, eight Indians fired on a small detachment of Ninth Cavalry, which was escorting the mail company stock, and on the next day Indians, possibly the same party, fired several shots at the stage and its occupants between Eagle Springs and Van Horn's Well.[11]

[10] Heitman, *Historical Register*, 1:438, 706.
[11] U.S. Department of War, Post Returns, Fort Quitman, October, 1868.

On the evening of November 30, the stage that left the Concho Station for San Antonio failed to reach Kickapoo Station, the first stop. Several days later the occupants of the next stage discovered what remained of it about five miles east of Kickapoo Springs. Apparently the lone occupant, the driver, had been lanced and scalped before he was able to fire a shot. Although the stage was standing on its wheels, its curtains, leather, loose fixtures, and mail were missing. One month previously at Kickapoo Station, fifteen or twenty Indians had run off the herder, captured the station's ten mules, and then, while standing on the main road at a distance of 150 yards from the station, fired at every person they had seen. An attendant had escaped by hiding behind a hay stack.[12] No one at the station had been killed, but it had been impossible to save the stock.

The attempt to relocate the Lancaster bridge to the vicinity of Camp Melvin was unsuccessful. On December 8, Captain Gamble reported to the acting headquarters of the Fifth Military District that he had had the bridge moved, but the river within three or four miles of the mail crossing was too wide for it at any point, and, consequently, he had had it replaced at its previous location. It would require a bridge at least sixty-five feet long to span the river at the mail crossing, and it would cost $10,000. The nearest available lumber was the forest beyond Fort Davis, a distance of 170 miles. Furthermore, Gamble continued, the bridge near Lancaster was more beneficial because the ford there was often impassable, and without a bridge the stage would often be delayed ten days. He did not believe that it was "necessary to have a bridge at the mail crossing simply for the accommodation of a few pounds of mail, three times a week." Before the war the mail contractors had built flat boats for crossing streams and he thought that "Mr. Ficklin might provide one at this point that would only cost a few hundred dollars, as it is not a route that would be followed by any trains, either citizen or Government."[13]

Since most of the enlisted men of the Ninth Cavalry were former slaves and could neither read nor write, all the paperwork ordinarily done by the first sergeant and company clerk was handled by the commissioned officers. These chores added to their regular duties imposed

[12] San Antonio *Herald*, December 5, 1868.

[13] George H. Gamble, Fort Stockton, to Captain C. S. Roberts, December 8, 1868, in U.S. Department of War, Records of United States Army Commands, RG 98, NA.

a hardship on the officers. Disturbances among the enlisted personnel were frequent, and occasionally violence erupted. On July 4, Private George W. Johnson shot Private Isam Davis, who died within two weeks thereafter.

Furthermore, the military at Fort Stockton was the only law-enforcement agency west of the Pecos and had to deal with several civilian disturbances. When completed, the guardhouse served as a civilian jail, but before that lawbreakers were shackled and closely guarded. In March, two Mexican citizens at the post had an altercation; one, who had been shot in the leg, was placed in the post hospital, and the other was put in the guardhouse. In June, Matthew M. Ueter was killed, and the alleged murderer, Frank Carson, an employee of the quartermaster department, was placed in confinement. Conflicts between men with wagon trains were not unusual. As a result of one incident, one man with a bullet wound in the groin was placed in the hospital, but his opponent escaped. In another affray, in which several ineffective shots were fired, the two participants were both put in the guardhouse. After a fight between two other members of the same train, one participant, who had received a critical knife wound in the left lung, was placed in the hospital, and the other was confined. On July 28, three of those civilians were still in the guardhouse.[14]

The Pecos country was very hard on horses. As a result, the cavalry at Fort Stockton could seldom mount one-half of its troops. In a report in September, 1868, Captain Gamble, who had lost both his private horses, explained what, in his opinion, was the major cause for the mysterious deaths of the horses and what remedial action he had taken. In the past year, at least eighty horses at Fort Stockton had died. Of the twenty he had examined, the inner lining of the stomach was "entirely burned away, similar to poisoning with corrosive sublimate." The horses generally died, Gamble continued, in from one to two hours, "apparently in great pain being affected both in the stomach and head, the throat swelling, and running at the nostrils." Gamble believed that the ailment was caused by the Mexican corn furnished by contractors, which to prevent infestation by insects had been lime soaked and then dried. "For some months I [have] had all the corn

---

[14]Gamble to Lt. Charles E. Morse, A.A.A.G., Department of Texas, March 31, June 4 and 30, and July 28 and 31, 1868, Army Commands, RG 98, NA.

soaked at least five hours before feeding, and now lose but very few animals."[15]

On October 2, 1868, the headquarters of the Ninth Cavalry was transferred from Fort Davis to Fort Stockton and placed temporarily under the command of Major (Brevet Colonel) James F. Wade. Arriving at Stockton on December 15, Wade took command of the 261 men in Troops A, B, D, and E, Ninth Cavalry, and Company G, Forty-first Infantry. At Fort Davis, Merrit had three companies of the Ninth Cavalry and one company of the Forty-first Infantry, a total force of 249 men.[16]

Many Indian raids in Texas during 1868 resulted, at least in part, from governmental mismanagement. According to Richardson, "The conduct of the United States Indian service and military forces on the South Plains . . . was such as to puzzle the savage mind." Some chiefs maintained that the 1867 Medicine Lodge treaty did not restrict their activities south of Red River; others, inclined to honor the treaty, went to the reservation but found that supplies were inadequate and the agency was almost abandoned. Consequently, they returned to their customary raiding, even in the lower Pecos area in 1869.[17] The stage that left El Paso on January 5, driven by a Mr. Bass, did not arrive at Fort Davis. The next stage, which left El Paso on January 7, found, between Eagle Springs and Van Horn's Well, the mutilated body of Bass and, farther on, the empty stagecoach. The location became known as Bass Canyon. The body of the other occupant, Judge Hubbell of El Paso, was later found by members of a wagon train. No troops were sent in pursuit of the killers because those based at Forts Davis and Stockton were then reconnoitering the Pecos, Rio Grande, and Guadalupe mountains.[18]

On January 16, Major General E. R. S. Canby issued an order that placed western Texas under martial law. The order divided the

[15] Gamble to Roberts, September 4, 1868, ibid.

[16] "Report of the Adjutant General," in U.S. Congress, House, *Message of the President of the United States. Report of the Secretary of War*, November 20, 1869, 41 Cong., 2 sess., 1870, House Exec. Doc. No. 1, pp. 170–171; U.S. Department of War, Post Surgeon's Report, Fort Stockton, January 4, 1869, AGO, RG 94, NA.

[17] Rupert N. Richardson, *The Comanche Barrier to South Plain's Settlement*, p. 320; Clarence R. Wharton, *History of Texas*, p. 371.

[18] San Antonio *Herald*, January 16 and 17, and February 2, 1869.

area into six jurisdictions and granted post commanders authority superior to that of all local law enforcement officers within their respective jurisdictional boundaries. The commanders designated were at Forts Clark, Concho, Stockton, Davis, and Quitman and Camp Concordia (the temporary name of Fort Bliss). The order discontinued the use of Forts Mason and Inge and Camp Wood, placed Forts Concho, McKavett, Clark, and Duncan in the subdistrict of the Pecos, and placed Forts Stockton, Davis, and Quitman in the subdistrict of Presidio.[19]

By late January, 1869, the sawmill that had been moved from Fort Stockton to a canyon west of Fort Davis was producing lumber. Located where the El Paso road turned up the canyon in "the Fort Davis pinery" and a short distance west of the present Bloys Camp Meeting Ground, it must have been well guarded for, although it was isolated and no doubt supplied with horses and corn (which usually attracted Indians), Wade's report mentioned no Indian problems there. Other reports made the same day, however, showed that other civilians under Wade's jurisdiction were not so tranquil. On January 27, J. Tuft, a driver for the El Paso Mail Line, was arrested for the rape of Sergeant Jeffards' wife, while en route from Camp Melvin, and was placed in the Fort Stockton guardhouse. Only the day before, R. G. Hulbert, a post trader at Fort Davis who had been confined in the Stockton guardhouse, was returned to Davis for trial for an unidentified offense.[20]

After the death of the horses had been attributed to the Mexican corn, some of the posts would no longer use it, and an acute shortage of that grown in the United States developed. Thus, pursuit of Indian raiders became virtually impossible. At El Muerto, which had no corn after January 1, the guard often saw the smoke of Indian camp fires, but the horses were too weak for a pursuit. To remedy the situation, the quartermaster of the Fifth Military District advertised for bids to furnish Fort Stockton until May 31 with an adequate supply of good, clean shelled corn in sacks.[21]

Even when the horses were well fed and in good condition, In-

[19] Ibid., January 23, 1869.

[20] U.S. Department of War, Lt. Col. Thomas Hunt, "Journal," Office of the Chief of Engineers, Q 154, p. 14, RG 77, NA; James F. Wade, Fort Stockton, to Lt. Louis V. Caziarc, A.A.A.G., Fifth Military District, January 27, 1869 (three letters), Army Commands, RG 98, NA.

[21] San Antonio *Herald*, January 14 and February 2, 1869.

dian raiders usually escaped. At daylight on February 11, a large party of Apaches stampeded and drove off 150 head of stock from the ranch of a man named McIlvaine, near El Paso. Colonel Mason of "Concordia" with a detachment of forty men attempted without success to overtake the thieves.[22]

On February 21, 1869, a government wagon train under the charge of a Mr. Butler, while camped at Kickapoo Springs near Fort McKavett, was suddenly attacked by well-armed Indians. Surprised and without their guns, the three soldiers on guard and the Mexican drivers fled from the scene. While the Indians were unharnessing the teams, Davis Walker and several others arrived, shot to death three of the Indians, and rescued the stage, its occupants and contents, and the horses.[23]

Inspector Brigadier General Judson David Bingham the following month ordered Colonel Wade to adopt an economizing policy at Fort Stockton. He directed Lieutenant Jacob Lee Humfreville, the quartermaster, to complete the nearly finished officers' quarters but to stop the erection of any other permanent buildings. When the approved buildings were completed, the construction force was to be sent to San Antonio. At the time of this inspection, the post had a civilian payroll of $1,130 per month for building construction. Seventeen horses, 220 mules, seven oxen, four carts, and thirty-three army wagons were available for transporting materials. The post had no corn or grain on hand, the native hay had been hauled from a distance of twenty miles, and most of the cavalry horses were in poor condition. Mesquite roots for fuel and grain were purchased on the open market.

Construction on the post was well underway. The completed construction included one set of officers' quarters, a stone guardhouse, a commissary and quartermaster's offices, and a granary. The buildings in various stages of construction were two sets of officers' quarters, a quartermaster's storehouse, and workshops. The enlisted men and the adjutant were still housed in temporary structures, and the quartermaster's supplies, including clothing, subsistence stores, and corn

---

[22] Ibid., February 25, 1869. In February, 1869, when flood waters from the Rio Grande washed Fort Bliss away, the garrison was temporarily located at Concordia Ranch; hence, the name Camp Concordia until Fort Bliss was restored before the end of the year (Walter P. Webb and H. Bailey Carroll, eds., *The Handbook of Texas*, 1:620).

[23] San Antonio *Herald*, March 2, 1869.

(when there was any), were piled on the ground and covered with tarpaulins. Building material on hand included 160 doors, 134 door frames and casings, 14,900 lathes, and 385 window sashes; 120,000 shingles were en route. Whether this constituted an adequate or surplus supply for the completion of approved construction, the records do not state. The government edifices and other improvements at the time were valued at approximately $150,000. Near the post, traders owned and occupied four adobe buildings valued at about $1,000 each.

The land on which the post was located belonged to Peter Gallagher, and the government did not have it leased. Without the benefit of the post, the land would have been worth about ten cents an acre. Gallagher also owned all the land along Comanche Creek, and he offered to sell the whole to the United States for $4.00 per acre, lease it all for $2,000 annually, or negotiate a sale or a lease on less than the entire tract.[24]

During the spring of 1869, the Indians renewed their warfare all across the Texas frontier. Lipans and Kickapoos from south of the Rio Grande raided in the counties of Bexar, Frio, Uvalde, Zavala, Medina, and Atascosa, killing sixteen persons, stealing hundreds of horses, and damaging considerable property, then returned to the safety of Mexico with little or no loss.[25] The Comanches and Kiowas likewise wrought havoc all along the frontier, particularly in the northern and central segments. They were not always so fortunate, however, as to escape the vengeance of the whites. A detachment of troops from Fort Griffin surprised an encampment of about twenty-five Comanches in the region of Flat Top Mountain and the Double Mountain Fork of the Brazos north of present Snyder. In the resulting engagement fourteen Indians were killed, three or four possibly wounded, and fourteen horses were captured and given to the Tonkawa scouts.[26] That year thousands of Texas cattle were trailed to the northern and western markets, some without any trouble from Indians and some less fortunate. Damon Slater and a Mr. Moss drove 1,400 head of cattle to California by way of

[24]J. D. Bingham, Fort Stockton, to J. L. Humfreville, March 15, 1869, and Bingham to A.A.G., Austin, March 16, 1869, in "Fort Stockton," Consolidated File, Records of the Quartermaster General, RG 92, NA.

[25]William H. Leckie, *The Buffalo Soldiers*, p. 87.

[26]*Army and Navy Journal* 6 (June 5, 1869):658, and 6 (July 3, 1869):722.

the Llano, Concho, and Pecos rivers. D. H. Snyder trailed a herd from Georgetown by way of Horsehead Crossing to Bosque Redondo, and Henry Taylor, from the Sabinal Valley, drove a herd by way of Devils River, Howard's Well, Horsehead Crossing, and Fort Bliss to California, all without encountering any trouble from Indians.[27]

Frank Tankersley, however, was not so fortunate. With seventeen cowboys he left his Dove Creek ranch with a herd of 1,700 cattle for California but sold only 1,000 head in San Bernardino. Tankersley returned by boat and rail to Houston and thence by horseback to his home. Beneath the floor of his cabin, he deposited $25,000 in gold that he had brought from California. Two of the cowboys were killed by Indians on the return trip over the trail.[28]

Silas Gibson and his group from Blanco County were even less fortunate. Gibson and his brother had been among those who went to California after the discovery of gold. They had prospered and returned to Texas for their families and relatives. Accompanied by eighteen men, women, and children in four or five ox-drawn wagons, and with a herd of 1,500 steers and forty horses, Silas Gibson in May, 1869, started for California. The immigrant train went by the Upper San Antonio Road to Horsehead Crossing and from there up the Pecos along the Goodnight-Loving Trail. At the mouth of Black River, in New Mexico, it was attacked by a large party of Indians, probably Apaches.

While some of the men guarded the horses and cattle, the others helped the women arrange the wagons into a defensive fortress. The Indians were not able to overpower the wagon position, but they succeeded in stampeding the horses. Silas Gibson and a few companions pursued the raiders and recovered their horses. While the horses were being driven back to the encampment, Gibson and Thomas Shelly attempted to hold off the Indians. When Shelly's horse became exhausted, Gibson dismounted to fire at his pursuers and save his companion. Shelly escaped, but the Indians killed both Gibson and his splendid mount. What happened to the cattle is not recorded, but the next day Silas Gibson was buried beside the trail in a grave covered with rocks for protection against predatory animals. But before long that rude "monument to our pioneer forebearers' heroic efforts to

[27] J. Marvin Hunter, *The Trail Drivers of Texas*, pp. 846, 905–912, 1033.
[28] *New Encyclopedia of Texas*, p. 1114.

carve homes and security from the savage West" had forever been erased.[29]

Farther south, near Johnson's Run in the Trans-Pecos country, about 150 Indians at 3 P.M. on May 26 attacked the six-wagon train of José McVillereal. One Mexican teamster and two Indians were killed and the mules captured. Because the captured mules were driven toward Mexico, the Indians were thought to have been Kickapoos or Lipans. When several days later the news reached Fort Stockton, 160 miles from the site, Colonel Wade thought it useless to send troops in pursuit.[30]

Colonel Wade was obstinately determined to complete Fort Stockton. On June 4, 1869, he reminded the headquarters of the Fifth Military District in Austin that General Bingham had not authorized a post hospital. He had been using tents for hospital quarters, and he wanted authority to construct a permanent building before the construction crews were sent to San Antonio.[31]

[29] *El Paso Times*, June 29, 1962.

[30] James F. Wade, Fort Stockton, to C. E. Morse, May 31, 1869, Army Commands, RG 98, NA; *Austin Republican*, June 16, 1869.

[31] Wade to Morse, June 4, 1869, Army Commands, RG 98, NA.

CHAPTER 9

June, 1869, to September, 1870

O<small>N</small> June 11, 1869, a few days after he wrote for permission to construct a permanent hospital at Fort Stockton, Colonel James F. Wade requested authority to employ additional civilian workers. He wanted twenty teamsters for one month and ten carpenters, one plasterer, and one painter for four months. Only a short time before, he had been allowed to have one clerk, one forage master, a veterinary surgeon, a saddler, a wheelwright, four blacksmiths, a train master, a mason, and nine carpenters. Little by little, progress was being made on the unfinished buildings.[1] He needed to hurry, for the Indian problem was rapidly becoming more serious.

On June 7 troops from Fort Clark encountered about 100 Lipans and Mescaleros about fifty miles above the mouth of the Pecos. The military force, commanded by Colonel Ranald S. Mackenzie, Twenty-fourth Infantry, and Captain John M. Bacon, Ninth Cavalry, and consisting of detachments from Troops G, L, and M, Ninth Cavalry, a few civilian volunteers, and two guides, on the first charge killed two Indians. On the second charge, the Indians scattered to the adjoining escarpments and down the river. After destroying the ranchería, the troops pursued the Indians without success until their horses became jaded.[2]

Because the Comanches and Kiowas were increasing the intensity of their raiding in the counties of central Texas and the Apaches in far western Texas, military guards were assigned to most small stage stations.[3] The mail line stations guarded by details out of Fort Stockton

---

[1] James F. Wade, Fort Stockton, to Charles E. Morse, June 11, 1869, U.S. Department of War, Records of United States Army Commands, Record Group (RG) 98, National Archives (NA), Washington, D.C.

[2] *Army and Navy Journal* 7 (October 9, 1869):110.

[3] Joseph Carroll McConnell, *The West Texas Frontier*, 2:249–267.

were: the Pecos crossing at Lancaster, seven men; Camp Melvin, in the Horseshoe Bend area, eight men; Escondido (Tunas), five; and Varela, forty-eight miles west, six.[4] The number of soldiers was entirely inadequate, and, consequently, the Indians continued to raid the stations for livestock. An unidentified band surprised and drove off seventeen horses belonging to the two-wagon camp of the El Paso Mail Line and five horses of the soldier escort at the head of the Concho, near Camp Charlotte. During the exchange of gunfire, one Indian, killed or seriously wounded, was carried off by his comrades. Two miles from there, the raiders drove off the stock of two travelers. Lieutenant D. H. Cortelyou with a company of the Ninth Cavalry went in pursuit of the raiders, apparently without success.[5]

On July 27, Indians drove off six mules from the mail station at Camp Charlotte. Soon afterward, near Mustang Ponds, they met the eastbound stage, drawn by two mules. The driver and the black soldier escort jumped from the stage and hid in the bushes. The Indians took over the stage and continued with it to Centralia Station. There, unsuspecting Lieutenant Samuel E. Armstrong and the six soldiers of the Forty-first Infantry, the guard sent from Fort Stockton, failed to notice anything unusual until it was too late. Consequently, they lost ten animals and were left afoot. One horse overlooked by the Indians was used to send a messenger to Captain George Gamble at Fort Concho. The next morning, when Gamble with a small detachment of Ninth Cavalry rode out to the mail station and found that the Indians had headed west with the coach, he considered pursuit inadvisable and returned to Fort Concho. Simultaneously, J. M. Trainer and a party of citizens from Fort Concho who scouted the North Concho found no Indians but brought back two ponies.[6]

To better place these events, it may be helpful to give the location of some of the stations along the stage route between Fort Concho and Fort Stockton. From the head of the Middle Concho the road went by Mustang Ponds, Centralia Station, China Ponds, and Castle Gap to

[4] U.S. Department of War, Post Surgeon's Report, Fort Stockton, June 16, 1869, Records of the Adjutant General's Office (AGO), June 16, 1869, RG 94, NA.

[5] San Antonio *Herald*, July 2, 1869; U.S. Department of War, Post Returns, Fort Concho, July, 1869, AGO, RG 94, NA.

[6] *Texas State Gazette* (Austin), August 9, 1869.

Horsehead Crossing on the Pecos. Camp Charlotte was about fifty-five miles west of Fort Concho in present Irion County at the junction of Kiowa Creek and the Middle Concho and about two and a half miles west of the intersection of present State Highway 163 and the Middle Concho. Mustang Ponds, frequently mentioned in reports prior to the Civil War, is located on Captain W. R. Livermore's map of 1883 halfway between Camp Charlotte and Centralia. Centralia (also known as Central) Station was about twenty miles north and six and a half miles east of the southwest corner of present Reagan County.[7] China Ponds (or Wild China Ponds) is about fourteen miles east of Castle Gap, which is on the western line of Upton County between McCamey and Crane.

While at Centralia Station in 1869, Lieutenant Colonel Thomas Hunt noted that the water was hauled from the head of the Middle Concho, a distance of thirty-two miles. In 1868 or 1869, a southern branch of road was opened from Centralia Station to Camp Melvin at the Horseshoe Bend of the Pecos. This road passed by two locations both known as Flat Rock Ponds, one a half-mile southwest of the present town of Stiles and the second on the railroad right-of-way four or five miles east of Rankin. Salt Crossing of the Pecos was above Horsehead Crossing, at a point on the river that is four or five miles eastnortheast of Buena Vista in Pecos County. It was used to reach the abundant source of salt at Lake Juan Cordova in present Crane County.[8]

Indian troubles continued to plague travelers in the area. Late in 1869 Pat Dolan and Captain James G. Birney were nearing Seven Springs in Limpia Canyon, northeast of Fort Davis, when they recognized several "coyote yaps" as Indian signals. After a wild dash through a barrage of arrows, they reached the camp of a Mexican wagon train bound for Chihuahua. Although the Mexicans were surrounded by In-

[7]The ruins of Centralia Station are in the Centralia Survey, nine and one-half miles north of the Santa Rita Oil Well, Reagan County.

[8]Lieutenant Colonel Thomas Hunt, "Journal," Office of the Chief of Engineers, Q 154, p. 10, RG 77, NA; Dr. George W. Elliott File, Archives, Upton County Assessor's Office, Rankin, Texas; the U.S. Mexican Trust Company's map entitled "Pecos Palisades Tracts" and various other maps of the present counties of Pecos, Crane, Upton, Reagan, Irion, and Crockett. On January 21, 1870, the San Antonio *Herald* carried this advertisement: "A large lot of superior Pecos salt for sale (in sacks) at Fort Concho, Texas. For particulars apply to A. Bayless, Fort Concho, Texas." The Old Salt Trail from Ojinaga, Mexico, to the lake in Crane County had long been in use, but now a Texan hoped to commercialize it.

dians, Dolan and Birney succeeded in getting into their camp, and the two parties later managed to reach the safety of Fort Davis.[9]

Dolan, father of the late West Texas historian Mrs. O. L. Shipman, spent considerable time in the Trans-Pecos country. Born in Ireland in 1843 and brought to Texas seven years later, young Dolan had grieved to see his friends join the Southern forces, because, as his daughter later wrote, "he had practically grown up around Government headquarters in San Antonio and he overheard Colonel Robert E. Lee when he expressed to a fellow officer what a crushing blow it was to him to see the United States being divided. . . ." During the latter part of the war, Pat Dolan had joined the Union Army and participated in the final engagement at Palmito Ranch. In 1867, Dolan became a wagon master for the army at Fort Davis, where one of his duties was to oversee the hauling of timber from Sawmill Canyon.[10]

During the latter part of August, 1869, between Fort Davis and the Rio Grande, Indians captured most of a cattle herd belonging to a driver named Scott. Leaving a few men to guard the uncaptured remnant, Scott and some of his hands overtook the Indians within five miles. The cattlemen, with Winchester rifles, out-gunned the thieves and forced them to abandon the cattle.[11] During the following month, after Kiowas and Comanches had depredated in the Fort McKavett and San Saba regions, Captains Henry Carroll and Edward Miles Heyl, with ninety-five men of Troops B, E, F, and M, Ninth Cavalry, successfully campaigned in the region of the Brazos and killed a number of Indians.[12]

As a result of the increasing danger from Indians, stage companies requested additional escorts. In response, J. L. Humfreville, the quartermaster at Fort Stockton, on September 26 was ordered to send to Sergeant Joseph Miller, Company A, Forty-first Infantry, at Centralia

[9]Mrs. O. L. Shipman, *Taming the Big Bend*, pp. 109–110. First Lieutenant and Brevet Captain James G. Birney became a regular captain on December 1, 1869 (Francis B. Heitman, *Historical Register and Dictionary of the United States Army*, 1:220).

[10]Mrs. O. L. Shipman, *Letters Past and Present: To My Nephews and Nieces*, pp. 10, 13–18, 47, 51; Barry Scobee, *Fort Davis, Texas, 1583–1960*, pp. 156, 167; Allan A. Stovall, *Breaks of the Balcones*, p. 227; Will F. Evans, *Border Skylines*, pp. 248–249; *El Paso Herald-Post*, January 25 and February 13, 1930.

[11]San Antonio *Herald*, September 9, 1869.

[12]William H. Leckie, *The Buffalo Soldiers*, p. 88; *Army and Navy Journal* 7 (November 27, 1869):89. More than twenty years later both Carroll and Heyl received brevets for meritorious service in this campaign (Heitman, *Historical Register*, 1:286, 527).

additional men and a four-mule team and wagon, with sufficient forage to last through October 31. Consequently, on the next day, he sent there a noncommissioned officer and six privates of Companies A and G, Forty-first Infantry.[13] At the same time, the Varela Mail Station was transferred to the jurisdiction of the Fort Davis command, and Colonel Wade soon withdrew his guard from that station.[14]

On October 3, Humfreville was ordered to furnish "such materials as are on hand for girder plates and rafters for the company quarters now being erected, and such carpenter work as may be necessary. . . ."[15] Apparently Wade was very anxious to complete the post's building program.

General Edward Hatch, in command at Fort Davis, nevertheless ordered an expedition against the Comanches and the Kiowas. In October, Captain John Mosby Bacon with six companies of the Ninth Cavalry left Fort Concho. At the site of Fort Phantom Hill he was joined by a detachment of Fourth Cavalry and twenty Tonkawa scouts, and at Fort McKavett he was further reinforced by Brevet Captain Frederic William Smith with thirty-six men of Company F, and First Lieutenant Byron Dawson with twenty-seven men, Company M, both Ninth Cavalry. On October 5, the command started for the headwaters of the Colorado and the Salt Fork of the Brazos. On October 28, while in bivouac on the Freshwater Fork of the Brazos (White River), the command was attacked by about 500 Comanches and Kiowas armed with carbines, pistols, lances, and bows and arrows. In the engagement, which was renewed the next morning, the Indians had several warriors and horses killed, and the soldiers suffered several men wounded and two horses killed and twelve wounded before the Indians fled.[16]

While some of the men were risking their lives in the field, others at Fort Stockton, and perhaps elsewhere, were risking their health in another way. On November 9, the commanding officer there notified

[13] Francis Moore to J. L. Humfreville, Fort Stockton, September 26, 1869, Army Commands, RG 98, NA.

[14] Wade, Fort Stockton, to C. O. of Fort Davis, September 27, 1869, ibid.

[15] Moore to Humfreville, Fort Stockton, October 3, 1869, ibid.

[16] U.S. Department of War, Post Returns, Forts Concho and McKavett, October and November, 1869. More than twenty years later Bacon and Dawson received brevets for their meritorious service in the 1869 campaign. (Heitman, *Historical Register*, 1:179, 361). Smith probably would have received a similar honor, but he died at Fort McKavett from accidental gunshot wounds on December 22, 1869 (Fort McKavett, Post Returns, December, 1869).

the commanding officer at Fort Concho that he was sending five "undesirable colored females" to San Antonio via Concho and advised him to take steps to prevent these women from "afflicting your command."[17]

On November 24, a detachment of twenty men of Companies F and M, Ninth Cavalry, under Captain Heyl, attacked a small party of Apaches on the south fork of the Llano, forty miles west of old Fort Terrett. One Indian was killed, six horses and one mule were captured, and Heyl was seriously wounded.[18]

Indian raids led to an increase in the cost of freighting goods from San Antonio to the military posts in western Texas. To Fort Stockton the army contract with Adams and Wickes was at the rate of $1.52 per 100 pounds per 100 miles, or $5.48 for hauling a 100-pound sack of flour the 361 miles from San Antonio to Stockton.[19] Since it appeared that a farm irrigated by water from Comanche Springs could be a profitable investment, some industrious men from San Antonio started the first irrigation project near Fort Stockton. On land obtained late in 1869 and purchased with scrip and squatters rights early in 1870, Cesario Torres, Bernardo Torres, and Félis Garza constructed 2,885 yards of hand-dug ditches six feet wide and three feet deep, through Surveys 150, 160, and 215. In consideration for crossing their property with the ditch, John James and Peter Gallagher were granted the right to take eighteen cubic feet of water per second from it.[20] A log, rock, and brush diversion dam was built approximately three-fourths of a mile down Comanche Creek from the fort. The old ditch and the ruins of buildings involved, enclosed with a high adobe wall for protection against Indians, outlaws, and the elements, were still visible in 1981.

Johnson's Mail Station, west of Fort Concho, was attacked by Indians on December 25, and five horses of the guard were taken. Captain Ambrose Eugene Hooker and fifty men of Companies B and E, Ninth Cavalry, went in pursuit but failed to overtake the thieves.[21]

[17] Lewis Johnson, Fort Stockton, to C. O. of Fort Concho, November 9, 1869, Army Commands, RG 98, NA.

[18] U.S. Department of War, Post Returns, Fort McKavett, November, 1869.

[19] "Report of the Quartermaster General," in U.S. Congress, House, *Message of the President of the United States. Report of the Secretary of War*, November 20, 1869, 41 Cong., 2 sess., 1870, House Exec. Doc. No. 1, pt. 2, p. 214.

[20] Pecos County, Minutes of the Commissioners Court, 1:22.

[21] U.S. Department of War, Post Returns, Fort Concho, December, 1869; *Houston Telegraph*, January 7, 1870, quoting from the *San Antonio Star*, December 30, 1869.

On January 3, 1870, Captain John M. Bacon set out from Fort Clark to scout the Pecos from Lancaster Crossing to its mouth. He had in his command First Lieutenant and Brevet Captain Charles Parker, Lieutenant Francis Snelling Davidson, a Dr. Jackson, and detachments from Companies G and L, Ninth Cavalry—in all, about 100 men. On January 16, the soldiers spotted an Indian encampment five miles ahead, but the Indians, seeing the approach of the troops, hastily fled in the direction of Johnson's Run. The troops gave chase for fifteen miles, but when night came the Indians scattered like quail. Their encampment, which, according to a letter in the San Antonio *Herald*, consisted of about fifty lodges, "with the usual covering of dressed hides, &c., thousands of pounds of dried meats, together with a large quantity of the general paraphernalia pertaining to such places," was destroyed, and in their flight the Indians abandoned "about 100 animals, horses and mules, a large number of them with packs of provision, clothing, cooking utensils, hatchets, bows and arrows, &c." Having destroyed all the captured property that could not be sent to Fort Clark, Bacon continued his scout some distance farther before returning to Fort Clark on February 6.[22]

Meanwhile, 160 miles to the north, a Mr. Love and Walsh DeLong from Kickapoo Springs, while hunting hogs on the South Concho, about fifteen miles from Fort Concho, were fired upon by twelve or fourteen Indians who had hidden in tall grass. One bullet broke DeLong's arm and another hit Love in the ear.[23] Fortunately, DeLong could still use effectively his Winchester, but Love had a faulty rifle and managed to fire only one shot. The Indians fled, carrying with them one dead comrade. The following night the horses from the post at McKavett were stolen, supposedly by the same Indians.[24] The Walsh DeLong involved was probably G. W. DeLong, one of the earliest ranchers in present Tom Green County and a native Kentuckian. He had arrived in Texas either before or during the Civil War and had served during that conflict as a guide, minuteman, and Indian fighter. He had participated in January, 1865, in the battle with the Kickapoo Indians on Dove Creek.[25]

[22] San Antonio *Herald*, February 14, 1870.

[23] Parenthetically, the Indians were getting most of their guns from New Mexican traders (*comancheros*), but not nearly as many or as good as sometimes reported.

[24] *Houston Telegraph*, January 21, 1870.

[25] *New Encyclopedia of Texas*, pp. 3149, 3386, 3487.

By mid-January of 1870 Ficklin's weekly stage from San Antonio to El Paso had been captured by Indians only three times since its establishment. It had inaugurated a semiweekly schedule, and between Fort Concho and Fort Stockton it had installed coaches to replace its buckboard vehicles.[26]

From Fort Davis on January 20, 1870, Captain Francis Dodge with detachments from Companies A, C, D, H, I, and K, Ninth Cavalry, headed northwest, hot on the trail of the Mescaleros. Somewhere in the rugged country of the Guadalupe Mountains, during sleet and rain, the command surprised them at their ranchería. The Apaches fled and from the shelter of rocks on a nearby peak fired upon the dismounted troopers as they struggled up the treacherous incline. The troops reached the summit by nightfall, but by then the surviving Indians had escaped. Next morning, the troopers counted ten dead Indians, captured twenty-five ponies, destroyed the camp, and returned to Fort Davis.[27]

Vagabonds other than Indians were on the West Texas frontier. Early in February, a detachment of soldiers, en route from San Antonio to Fort Concho, spotted some horses being driven by a man who, seeing the soldiers, deserted his animals and ran. Suspecting him to be an Indian, the soldiers gave chase and killed the rider's horse. The captured man, a white, was wanted for killing a soldier. Some soldiers went for an ambulance in which to transport the prisoner. When they returned, the prisoner was gone, and all of the guards were dead except one who had managed to escape. The surviving trooper reported that fifteen men had surrounded them, killed the other guards, and rescued the prisoner.[28]

Meanwhile, the situation at Fort Stockton was quiet. The Comanches and Kiowas were busy plundering in North Texas, in Llano and Comanche counties, and at the deserted Camp Colorado. But Apaches skulking on the Pecos and on the Concho were ready to strike at every favorable opportunity. On or about March 2, J. F. D. Kruse and about ten men and their families, returning from New Mexico to Texas, had reached the Dagger Bend of the Pecos, on the common

[26] San Antonio *Herald*, January 13 and 17, 1870.
[27] Leckie, *Buffalo Soldiers*, p. 90; Robert M. Utley, *Fort Davis National Historical Site, Texas*, p. 34; *Texas State Journal* (Austin), February 13, 1870.
[28] San Antonio *Herald*, February 11, 1870.

border of present Ward and Loving counties, when they saw a mysterious smoke in the distance. Late the next day, another party returning from New Mexico came under Indian siege for a time.[29] The Fort Concho area, however, was at the time the favorite target of the Apaches. On one occasion the raiders, to avoid alerting the guard at the Fort Concho corral, first killed the bell mule with arrows and then drove off eighteen other mules and four horses. A short time later, fifteen mules and two horses were stolen from Bismarck Station on the Concho, almost on the doorsteps of the fort.[30]

Early in the spring, ninety-one troopers of Companies H and I, Ninth Cavalry, from Fort Quitman, commanded by Major Albert Morrow, headed toward the Guadalupe Mountains, expecting to establish a supply camp and at Pine Springs to be joined by more troopers from Forts Stockton and Davis. Along the way, Indian signal fires were seen, but the command reached Pine Springs without incident. There, Morrow was soon joined by Lieutenants Martin Briggs Hughes and Gustavus Valois and sixty troopers from Fort Stockton. (For some unknown reason, Valois, a Prussian, had changed his name from Gustavus Haenel.[31]) From Pine Springs, the contingent rode northwest through rugged canyons in the Guadalupes where some horses and pack mules had to be pulled from crevices into which they had fallen.

Eventually, an abandoned Mescalero ranchería of seventy-five lodges was found, with a large quantity of sotol bread, about 100 gallons of mescal, hides, robes, skins, and various utensils. The soldiers then circled back twenty-five miles west of their supply camp to bivouac at Cuervo Springs. After a short rest, the troops again rode north, passed between the Guadalupes and the Sacramentos to the Peñasco River in New Mexico, and returned to their supply camp along the eastern escarpment of the Guadalupes.

Since the Mescaleros had apparently abandoned their hideouts in the Guadalupe Mountains, Morrow headed south, skirted the foothills in the Sierra Diablo, and marched toward Apache and Rattlesnake springs. In that region, his command surprised a ranchería of thirty lodges and killed a few Indians. The survivors quickly hid among the nearby rocks, lechuguilla, and cacti. The camp and a large amount of

[29] McConnell, *West Texas Frontier*, 2:249–253.
[30] San Antonio *Herald*, January 17 and March 12, 1870.
[31] Heitman, *Historical Register*, 1:980.

supplies were destroyed, and twenty-two horses were captured. The troops had marched about 1,000 miles through mountainous and desert country in fifty-three days, indeed an amazing feat.[32]

Meanwhile, other Indians were striking near the posts. Three miles from Fort Concho, on May 1 the driver of a stagecoach, an escort, a passenger, and one road agent withstood an attack after killing six Indians. Four days later, the Fort Stockton–bound stage from Fort Davis was attacked in Dog Canyon in the foothills of the Davis Mountains.[33] At the time, Fort Concho had five cavalry and three infantry companies, Davis had three cavalry and two infantry companies, and Quitman and Stockton each had two companies of cavalry and one company of infantry.[34]

Early in 1870, Fort Stockton, a part of unorganized Presidio County, which was attached to El Paso County, experienced one of its first civil suits. The trouble was over the distribution of water from Leon Creek for irrigation purposes. In April a man named Pleasantier filed a suit with Justice of the Peace John Moczygemba against George B. Lyles, a post trader, for building a dam across the stream. Although he had not made bond and was not a qualified officer, Moczygemba found Lyles guilty, ordered him to remove the dam, and assessed a fine of ten dollars for each day the structure remained intact. When Lyles failed to abide by the order, a party, pretending to act under authority of the law, destroyed a part of the dam. Because the destruction would "stop all irrigation and cause the loss of all crops on Leon Creek," wrote Colonel Wade, "I sent a detachment of troops to that place with orders to take charge of the dam, have it rebuilt, and not to allow anyone to interfere with the same."[35]

Five days later, Sergeant Stance and ten troopers of Company F, Ninth Cavalry, from Fort McKavett, while on patrol to Kickapoo Springs, charged a band of Indians, who abandoned nine horses, and the next day, while returning to McKavett, the patrol surprised an-

[32] Leckie, *Buffalo Soldiers*, pp. 91–93.

[33] U.S. Department of War, Post Surgeon's Report, Fort Stockton, May 3 and 5, 1870, AGO, RG 94, NA.

[34] San Antonio *Herald*, May 4, 1870.

[35] Wade, Fort Stockton, to H. Clay Wood, May 6, 1870, Army Commands, RG 98, NA; U.S. Department of War, Post Surgeon's Report, Fort Stockton, May 6, 1870, AGO, RG 94, NA.

other party of Indians and added five more horses to its captured herd.[36]

About 400 miles to the west of Fort McKavett, Indians, apparently Apaches, struck a party of seven whites on its way either to or from El Paso. Charles Keerl, his wife, and four others were killed and their bodies mutilated. The trail of the perpetrators led to the Rio Grande, but beyond there Mexican troops under Colonel Terrazas were not able to follow it.[37]

About the same time, on May 25, at Varela Stage Station, between Fort Davis and Fort Stockton, a man named Polomio was seated by his horse and keeping an eye on the stage company's mules, which were grazing four or five hundred yards from the corral, when suddenly four mounted Indians appeared and in poor Spanish demanded the animals. Polomio refused and attempted to stop the Indians from driving away the mules. During the exchange of shots Polomio probably would have been killed had not black troopers on guard at the station rushed to his rescue.[38]

On June 1, in a mesquite flat four miles west of Fort Stockton, twenty-six Comanches approached a stage driven by A. J. Bobo, who was accompanied by two black soldiers and a single passenger, James D. Spears, an agent for the El Paso Mail Company. Bobo brought the gentle mules to a halt, Spears's rifle rang out three times, and three Comanches tumbled from their saddles. After this unexpected reception, the survivors withdrew, held a consultation, and then began their circling-and-firing maneuver. One large brave, bolder than the others, fell sprawling to the ground, his thigh broken by a ball from Spears's Winchester. He tried to hobble off, leading his horse, but Spears killed him with another shot. Bobo, while holding the whip and reins in his left hand and firing his carbine with his right, killed a dashing brave on a superb white horse. Moments later when a bullet wounded one of the stage mules, the frightened team dashed off at full speed and did not stop until it reached Fort Stockton. The Comanche raiders did not follow.

According to an account of the episode given several years later,

[36] Leckie, *Buffalo Soldiers*, pp. 93–94.
[37] McConnell, *West Texas Frontier*, 2:118.
[38] San Antonio *Herald*, June 7, 1870.

five Indians were killed and five were crippled. The warriors removed their dead and wounded as usual, but the bones of their horses were visible by the roadside for many years. The two soldiers were of no help. One "was so paralyzed with fright that his gun dropped from his hands, without a shot being fired by him, and the other, after shooting once at an angle of forty-five degrees upward, subsided in the interior of the stage. . . ." If the report is true, their behavior was an exception, for usually the black troopers displayed much gallantry. Spears, incidentally, became part owner of the Bismarck farm and was a partner of F. C. Taylor in the stage business and a general store at Ben Ficklin. After its organization, he became sheriff of Tom Green County.[39]

To supplement the inadequate and inefficient federal forces and to stop the Indians from raiding, the Texas legislature passed an act, approved June 13, 1870, providing for twenty companies of mounted Rangers of sixty-two men each and in August authorized the issuance of bonds in the amount of $750,000 to finance the organization. Although fourteen companies were organized, this defense effort was a failure because of the opposition of the federal government and the inability of the Texas officials to sell the bonds, so the loss of life and property continued—even increased.[40]

In the summer of 1870 the Torres Irrigation Company, owner and operator of farms in the vicinity of Fort Stockton, began using water from the Pecos River for irrigation. The pontoon bridge had been completed, and a settlement of Mexicans located there on June 2. The Mexicans, who were very poor, lived in "underground holes" (dugouts apparently), and used an ancient plow "consisting of a long beam, at one end of which a pointed stick is secured at an acute angle."[41] According to a survey by O. W. Williams in 1886, the pontoon was two miles up the river from the old "S" Crossing, where present State Highway 349 crosses the Pecos, between Iraan and Rankin. Williams, who in 1880 first crossed the Pecos on this bridge, later wrote, "At sun-

[39] *Galveston News*, May 20, 1877; Mary Bain Spence, "The Story of Benficklin, First County Seat of Tom Green County, Texas," *West Texas Historical Association Year Book* 22 (1946):36, 41.

[40] Ernest Wallace, *Texas in Turmoil, 1849–1876*, p. 249; H. P. N. Gammel, ed., *The Laws of Texas, 1822–1897*, 6:179–182; Ronald N. Gray, "Edmund J. Davis: Radical Republican and Reconstruction Governor of Texas" (Ph.D. diss., Texas Tech University, 1976), pp. 249–252.

[41] U.S. Department of War, Post Surgeon's Report, Fort Davis, June 2, 1870.

set we came to the Pecos River and crossed on a pontoon bridge swung by iron chains between banks, with movable platforms on either side as approaches to the pontoon to fit any stage of the water." [42]

By 1870 the civilian population along the Pecos and westward was sufficient for the organization of new counties. Along with El Paso and Worth counties, Presidio County (which included the present Pecos County) had been created by the legislature on January 3, 1850. Beginning at the confluence of the Pecos River and the Rio Grande, its boundary extended up the Rio Grande to its juncture with the Ford-Neighbors Trail (an undefined location), then northeast to the Pecos, and then down that stream to the Rio Grande. In the spring of 1850, Robert S. Neighbors, an Indian agent who with John S. Ford had explored a road from San Antonio to El Paso in 1849, was sent to organize Santa Fe, El Paso, Worth, and Presidio counties, but he managed only to organize El Paso County. Finally, in an election at Fort Davis on December 3, 1869, for officers of Presidio County, Peter Donnelly was elected sheriff, Peter Johnson, district clerk, and John Moczygemba, justice of the peace for Precinct No. 1. Donnelly, however, resigned on May 2, 1870, and on October 12 the district clerk was the only commissioned official, and the military was still the only effective law enforcement agency. The unorganized Big Bend area, however, was as large as Massachusetts, Connecticut, and one-half of New Hampshire combined, and smaller political units were inevitable. To bring this about, the legislature on July 10, 1870, again provided for the organization of Presidio County. The limits of the new county were to begin at the southeast corner of El Paso County, follow the Rio Grande to the mouth of the Pecos, then follow the Pecos to the northeast corner of El Paso County, and thence, the eastern boundary of El Paso County to the point of beginning.

Peter Gallagher, George B. Lyles, and Patrick Murphy were appointed as commissioners to hold the election. They were directed to meet at Fort Stockton on the first Monday in September, 1870, to divide the county into five precincts, and to order an election to be held at Fort Stockton for a justice of the peace for each precinct and for a sheriff and a clerk of the district court. Notices of the election were to

[42] Sketch 27, Pecos County, General Land Office, Austin, Texas; S. D. Myres, *Pioneer Surveyor—Frontier Lawyer: The Personal Narrative of O. W. Williams, 1877–1902*, p. 101.

be posted in three prominent places in each precinct (saloons probably were given priority) at least twenty days prior to the election. Voters were to write in a choice for a county seat, and a plurality would decide the location. The commissioners were to send the returns to the secretary of state within ten days after the election.[43]

But, alas, the commissioners failed to comply with their instructions. Perhaps they did not feel that a general election in little Fort Stockton was adequate for such a vast territory or were apprehensive that the expenses of the election and county business would have to be borne by them and a few other landowners and preferred to continue for a while longer with military law. Commissioner Lyles, no doubt, remembered that John Moczygemba, the self-styled justice of the peace, had destroyed his dam across Leon Creek and had imposed on him a heavy fine and that it had been Colonel Wade who had abrogated the sentence and had the dam rebuilt.

By then organized religion had reached Fort Stockton. The Catholics had erected a small, one-room adobe building on the creek between the fort and the farm cultivated by Torres, Torres, and Garza. Some ruins, visible many years later, were apparently the remains of that church, organized and financed by the Irish Catholics, including Peter Gallagher, George Frazer, and Francis Rooney.[44]

Other Catholic activities in West Texas were described by August Santleben, the noted freighter who operated between San Antonio and Chihuahua City. Early in 1870, Santleben rode the stage from San Antonio to Fort Stockton. A Sister St. Stephen, who was visiting the forts, was a passenger on the same stage from Fort Concho to Fort Stockton. Later, Santleben made some interesting comments about the trip and the sister:

The other passengers were Mr. Head [Heid] and Mr. Gallagher, residents of Fort Stockton; and our escort of two soldiers, [who] . . . rode outside with the driver. As we were well armed no uneasiness was felt on account of Indians.

Sister St. Stephens [*sic*] was an entertaining traveling companion, and she made herself agreeable throughout the trip. We sometimes presumed on her

[43] Gammel, *Laws of Texas*, 3:462, and 6:206; W. W. H. Davis, *El Gringo: Or, New Mexico and Her People*, pp. 110–111; Clayton Williams, *Never Again*, 3:47–48; 1869 Election Returns for Presidio County, Records of the Secretary of State, Archives, Texas State Library, Austin.

[44] Many years ago the author saw these ruins and was told by old-timers that they had been part of a church.

by making jolly remarks, but she did not resent the liberty and was always in a pleasant humor. Once I ventured to say that she could be of no service in case we were attacked by Indians. She laughed and replied that if such an event should happen her part would be attended to equally as well as ours; that we should do the fighting and she would do the praying.[45]

Santleben's route on the San Antonio–Chihuahua Trail was by Presidio and Forts Stockton, Lancaster, and Clark. Other freighters who operated along this route were the Edgar brothers (John, James, and William), John Davis, Ed Froboese, John Holly, Sha Hogan, John Burgess, William Brooks, Richard Daly, William Russell, and possibly the famous (or infamous) Roy Bean. Alozia Danda, possibly the most celebrated freighter over that route, was in demand because of his courage and ability as an Indian fighter.

Santleben's wagons were large, twenty-four feet in length, and of the prairie-schooner type. The back wheels were seventy inches high with tires six inches wide and one inch thick. The front wheels were twelve inches lower than the rear. The axles were of solid iron with spindles three inches in diameter. Bows attached to each bed were overhung with heavy tarpaulins on which the train owner's name and the wagon number were painted. The average load for such a wagon was 7,000 pounds. Each wagon had a powerful brake, controlled by the driver from his saddle on one of the wheel-mules. If the brakes went out (and occasionally they did), the heavily loaded wagon was uncontrollable on a steep hill, endangering the lives of both the driver and the mules.[46]

During 1870, the Indians launched a number of attacks on the freight trains. The Miguel brothers' train, en route to Fort Davis with supplies from San Antonio, was attacked eighteen miles east of Johnson's Run. The entire herd of mules was taken, and two Mexicans were killed and burned at the foot of a hill in a rude fortification. Soon afterward, August Santleben's wagon train was attacked near Beaver Lake. When the Indians roped the bell mare and led her off, the entire herd of mules followed her.[47] The white men trained their herd to follow an animal wearing a tinkling bell. Thus, depredating Indians needed only

---

[45] August Santleben, *A Texas Pioneer*, pp. 121–122.

[46] R. D. Holt, "Old Texas Wagon Trains," *Frontier Times* 25 [erroneously labeled 26] (1948):274–276.

[47] Ibid., p. 272.

to lead or drive off the melodic animal and the remainder would follow.

On at least one other occasion that same year, Indian raiders used a mare's bell to lure the animals of a wagon train into captivity. It happened at the Santa Niña water hole. In 1903, William M. Edgar, a former superintendent of transportation for the Adams and Wickes contracting firm, reminisced to a reporter about the trouble wagon trains had had with Indians. From 1867 to 1873, said Edgar, Adams and Wickes had a large number of trains running to army posts on the Texas frontier, which required at times as many as 1,500 mules and from 150 to 200 wagons. While one of his teamsters, a man named Gruington or Brewington, was stopped at the Santa Niña water hole, thirty-five miles north of the head of Devils River, Indians (Kickapoos, Mescaleros, or Lipans) in broad daylight drove off his mules, which had been side-lined. Gruington waited at the water hole until another train, in the charge of Hart Mussey, came by and pulled his wagons to Fort Stockton. According to Edgar, a Captain Wilcox, Ninth Cavalry (apparently John Andrew Wilcox, Fourth Cavalry) with a company of cavalrymen followed the trail of the raiders across the Rio Grande and attacked their camp but was forced to retreat by the Indians, whose number was estimated at about 135.[48]

When on September 27, 1903, San Antonio police sergeant John Fitzhenry read Edgar's account of the Santa Niña raid, he promptly wrote in far more detail for the *Express* his recollections of the affair. Fitzhenry stated that his westbound train of nine wagons, accompanied by an army paymaster with over $100,000 (apparently an exaggeration) and about twenty soldiers as guard, reached the Santa Niña water hole only a few hours after the Indians had left Gruington stranded.

In the early afternoon, from the top of the hill, Fitzhenry saw a camp of wagons and smoke at the water hole, but the mules were grazing "some miles" away in an arroyo. Concluding that there was no grass at the water hole and that the herd had been sent to the arroyo to graze, Fitzhenry turned his train in the direction of the grazing mules. In his words:

At the distance of a quarter of a mile I discovered . . . that they were Indi-

[48] *San Antonio Express*, September 27, 1903; Heitman, *Historical Register*, 1:1034.

ans and that we were almost in their hands. I immediately realized what had happened and . . . circled back to the waterhole.

When we got close enough, I recognized Gruington, or rather, Brewington, for I knew him by the latter name. . . .

"Brewington, why did you send your herd down the valley?" I called to him.

"That ain't my herd any more; the Indians came and got them this morning," he replied.

He then told me all about the affair. . . . The band of about 135 Indians was led by a big, powerful fellow who was signally brave. In the first heat of the attack he kept shouting in Spanish: "get the bell mare!" The bell mare was staked out, however, and the mules refused to be driven off. When the leader saw this he called out to kill the bell mare. Finally he made a dash through the fight on his horse, cut the bell strap and ran off in a hail of shots, tinkling the bell, and tolling the mules after him. But in ducking his head his queue caught in some sage brush and to the astonishment of Brewington, it was pulled off, revealing the fellow to be a red-headed, freckled-faced white man.

Fitzhenry thought that these Indians had a village of several hundred tipis on the Pecos but that they abandoned it soon after this.

To the *Express* reporter, Edgar recalled another 1870 event that occurred while he was working for Adams and Wickes. A fine train en route from San Antonio to Fort Concho camped for the night at Kickapoo Springs, thirty-five to forty miles from Fort Concho. Soon after sunset, a group of Indians, presumably Kiowas, swooped upon the train and drove off all the mules. A detachment of troops from Fort Concho discovered the trail left by the raiders, which led in the direction of the Kiowa reservations, but soon gave up the pursuit. Adams and Wickes had other losses, but only on these two occasions, as Edgar remembered, did trains lose all their mules.[49]

[49] *San Antonio Express*, September 28, 1903; M. L. Crimmins, "General Mackenzie and Fort Concho," *West Texas Historical Association Year Book* 10 (1934):22.

CHAPTER 10

September, 1870, to January, 1871

On September 5, 1870, Fort Stockton was garrisoned by Companies A and I, Ninth Cavalry, Company G, Twenty-fourth Infantry, and Company K, Twenty-fifth Infantry, under the command of Lieutenant Colonel James F. Wade. Wade's persistence in getting buildings constructed had been effective. The stone ammunition magazine was complete; the officers' quarters and storehouses had board floors and shingle roofs; the men's quarters, the workshop, and the granary had dirt floors and thatched (tule) roofs; and there were adjutant's and quartermaster's offices and quarters for employees. The quartermaster's adobe corral was back of the present "1876" Young store.

The activated neighboring posts were Fort Davis, 74 miles southwest; Fort Concho, 170 miles east-northeast; Fort Clark, 266 miles southeast; and Fort Quitman, 202 miles west-northwest. The nearest town was Presidio del Norte, 147 miles southwest. The closest Texas town of importance was Fredericksburg, 370 miles east. The nearest railroad was at Columbus, 575 miles east-southeast.[1] Although it had served as the temporary county seat since June of 1856, Uvalde, two miles south of Fort Inge, was only a small settlement.

The only tree in the vicinity of Fort Stockton was a cottonwood in the post garden. A good supply of watercress, used as an antidote for scurvy, had been transplanted in Comanche Creek. The creek, fed by six springs, headed about half a mile south of the post and ran nearly due north for about four miles, where it sank into the ground, forming a marsh. Eight miles west, three large springs, known as Leon Holes, averaging thirty feet in diameter and twenty feet in depth, provided water for the irrigation of a large tract of land farmed by Mexicans. The Escondido headspring, eighteen miles east of the post on the mail

---

[1] The mileage estimates are based on the routes in use at that time.

route to Fort Concho, was about ten feet square. Antelope Spring, later known as Agua Bonita, with pretty but bitter water that was a re-surfacing of Comanche Creek, was about twelve miles northeast of Fort Stockton on the Horsehead Crossing road.[2]

Peter Gallagher apparently had platted his 160-acre tract for the town site of Saint Gall. The area had been first surveyed in 1859 by Anson Mills of El Paso as a site for the original post. The platted sub-division shows "Initial Point Center of Plaza." Zero Stone, in the cen-ter of the plaza, marks the base point for all surveys in what became Pecos County.

According to the 1870 census, the population of the Fort Stockton region of Presidio County was 582, of whom 429 were civilians. This included Lylesville (at Leon Holes) and the Torreses' and Garzas' farms along Comanche Creek. Sometimes because the information-givers were illiterate, but more often because the census takers made guesses, many names were spelled incorrectly. For various reasons, several of those whose names were on the census roll are worthy of historical mention.

Peter J. Gallagher, born in Ireland and the nephew of Peter Gal-lagher, was a general merchant with two stores and a personal estate of $10,000. He had two store clerks, John Moczygemba from Prussia and Gerard Storms from Belgium. Although probably not a United States citizen, Moczygemba in 1869 had been elected, but never qualified as, the justice of the peace of Precinct No. 1. Gallagher had two other em-ployees, a Bavarian and a Frenchman, who was by trade a brick mason. He had two stores, one 1,000 yards from the parade ground, likely the present Koehler's store near the creek, and the other, 400 yards from the parade ground, a large establishment southwest of the present courthouse and diagonally across from the James Hotel. In the second block south of Gallagher's store, on the northeast corner of Block 22 of the Saint Gall Addition, is Holliday's trading post, the only building constructed in 1859 that remains intact.

Joseph Heid, from Baden, Germany, operated a saloon, and his wife, Wilhelmina, from Prussia, ran a boarding house for carpenters and mechanics, which still stands in the old part of Fort Stockton. In addition to their three children, the Heid household included a cook

[2]U.S. Department of War, Surgeon General, *A Report on Barracks and Hospitals with Descriptions of Military Posts*, Circular No. 4, December 5, 1870.

and a farmer from France. Many years later, daughter Emma Heid Werner wrote a short account about her arrival at Fort Stockton and her childhood. She stated that when Joseph Heid went to Fort Stockton to establish a home he took his young son, Frantz Joseph, with him, and that she and her baby sister came with their mother on the stage. As the stage neared the tiny village of Fort Stockton, "we saw a big man waving his white hat. We knew it was our Papa welcoming his family to their new home." Emma Heid Werner left some insights about her life in the frontier town.

Often times when the daily chores were finished and the children safely tucked in to their beds Mama and I would walk down to the lovely creek about a block from home to fish in the moonlight. It was a very good running stream and the fish we caught were delicious. The creek was very pretty as it meandered through the village. There was lots of green vegetation growing around.

Papa had the contract to furnish the local Fort with fresh meat. We kept the cattle at our small ranch at Leoncita [Leon] Springs. They would be brought to town and butchered there. Every year Papa would grow vegetables and fruit at the ranch. They were all of superior size and very good.

On one occasion, when Heid and his son Frantz were eating lunch, Indians sneaked up to their ranch house and stole the horses that they had been using that morning to work cattle. "Mama ran a boarding house," Emma continued, "for a few of the local residents and an occasional visitor. She served two bountiful meals a day. Upon my first visit back to the old home town over 40 years later the late Howell Johnson . . . said, 'Those sure were some meals.'"[3]

Other native Germans living in Fort Stockton included Constable Theo Vahldiek, from Prussia, and his wife, who was a dressmaker. Living with the couple were their three children and a young male cook from Mexico. Joseph Friedlander, a twenty-nine-year-old merchant, also from Prussia, employed two clerks and two cooks, all American-born, in his store at the site of the former Pecos County Library. The building, which fronted north, had a wing on the east running south and in the rear a courtyard surrounded by an adobe wall and outbuildings for servants or campers. Lewis Kordzik, a butcher from Prussia, had two laborers in his establishment. Thomas Johnson, from Pennsyl-

---

[3]Emma Heid Werner, "Memories of Emma Werner, Oldest Daughter of Wilhelmina Doz Grumbein and Joseph Heid, Born in San Antonio," manuscript in possession of Joseph Heid's granddaughter, Mrs. Berte Haigh, Midland, Texas.

vania, operated a general merchandise store about 1,000 yards from the parade ground.

Fort Stockton, even in 1870, had a sizeable Mexican population. Pedro Sosa, a brick mason from Mexico, in 1885 (perhaps also in 1870) lived in a large adobe house located on the block northwest of the present courthouse. In addition to his wife and four children, he had in his household two cooks, six laborers, five of whom were from Mexico, and another woman with some small children. José Moreno, a butcher from Mexico, and his wife from Texas, had in his household several laborers and their wives, all from Mexico, except two who were native Texans.

Located several miles east-northeast of the post, between State Highway 290 and the 7-D paved road and several hundred yards south of the old ditch, may still be seen (1981) the ruins of the settlement that was built defensively, with no outside doors or windows, in the form of a square around a large patio.[4] It was the property of Cesario Torres, a farmer from Mexico, who had a declared personal value of $4,000 and real estate value of $1,000. In addition to Torres' wife and five children, the settlement included eight families and fifteen or twenty other laborers, most of whom were from Mexico. Torres' home was near the post, about 1,500 yards up Comanche Creek on its east side from the parade ground. Establishments 19 through 29 were on a much smaller scale and likely were adobes for renters of farmlands.

George M. Frazer, from Tennessee, although involved in many activities, was registered as a farmer. His home was located on the bank of Comanche Creek, about 2,000 yards downstream from the parade ground. In addition to Frazer, his wife, and five children, two laborers were living in the home.

Thomas Jaques, a laborer and at age seventy the oldest resident in the Fort Stockton area, his wife, their four children, and several other families of laborers, all from Mexico, resided in one household.

The census taker made a separate listing for the people at Lylesville. George Lyles from Virginia, for whom the place was named, lived in Saint Gall but operated a farm at the Leon Holes. Two of his eight children were born in Mexico. In fact, most of Lylesville's adult

[4] This establishment was likely Survey 52, for which a patent was later issued under an "Act for Benefit of Actual Occupants of Public Land," approved on May 26, 1873 (H. P. N. Gammel, ed., *The Laws of Texas, 1822–1897*, 7:553–554).

population were natives of Mexico. These included Marcel Padilla, a farmer, and his wife, who had five children at home; Francisco Barron, a blacksmith and gunsmith from Chihuahua, Mexico, and his wife, who eventually left a large number of descendants in Fort Stockton; and Francisco Flores and his wife, who then had five children at home. There were two laborers, one with a wife and child, at the Flores residence. Most of the inhabitants in establishments 5 through 17 were from Mexico. Some of these residences housed two families or a number of laborers. Apparently, Lyles promoted this colony from Mexico, yet he had no title to the property nor did he ever obtain a deed to any land in Pecos County. His residence was in Fort Stockton, about 800 yards from the parade ground.

Establishment 37 on the census report included soldiers and civilians in the barracks and residences in or around the garrison. The commissioned officers were living either in the officers' quarters or in buildings rented from the elder Peter Gallagher. Lieutenant Colonel James F. Wade and his wife, both from Ohio, and their three-year-old son had a mulatto domestic servant. Other commissioned officers included First Lieutenant Francis Moore, from Scotland and unmarried, whose two domestic servants likely served both at his quarters and at the post; Captain Michael Cooney and his wife, both from Ireland, and their one-year-old son; First Lieutenant Patrick Cusack, from Ireland, his wife, and their sons; Captain Lewis Johnson, from Germany, and his wife; Captain Francis Dodge, from Massachusetts; First Lieutenant James Morgan, from Illinois; First Lieutenant William Brunton, from Iowa; Second Lieutenant Martin Hughes, from Pennsylvania; Captain William Welsh, from Ohio; First Lieutenant William McElroy, from Pennsylvania; and Second Lieutenant Edward Allsworth, from New York. Officers with families usually employed domestic servants. All the officers except young Hughes had graduated from the U.S. Military Academy and had won honors during the Civil War.[5] The civilian personnel at the post included Peter Donnelly, a brick mason, and his wife, both from Ireland, and their five children. Donnelly, as previously stated, was elected sheriff of the unorganized county but never qualified and soon resigned. The five laundresses, varying in age from

[5] U.S. Department of the Interior, Census Office, *Ninth Census of the United States, 1870. Population. Texas*; Francis B. Heitman, *Historical Register and Dictionary of the United States Army*, 1:160, 256, 325, 347, 376, 552, 576, 664, 722, 726, 991, 1018.

twenty-one to twenty-eight, were either black or mulatto, and two had small children. Reportedly, they lived in the back of a building near the shallow crossing of Comanche Creek.

The population was unusually cosmopolitan. Of the persons listed, more than half (298) were foreign-born. Most of the foreign-born came from Mexico (261), but nine other foreign nations were represented: Ireland, 15; Prussia, 8; France, 7; Scotland, 2; Baden, 1; Bavaria, 1; Belgium, 1; Denmark, 1; and Malta, 1. The majority of the enlisted men had been recruited in Louisiana after the Civil War.

It was a youthful population. The soldiers, of course, and most commissioned officers were young. Of the civilians, ninety-seven were between thirty and forty years of age; thirty-eight were between forty and fifty; twelve were slightly past fifty; and only three were over seventy; and there were many children.

Reportedly, the ranches and farms on Comanche and Leon creeks had a total population of about 500, mostly from Mexico. In 1870, the farms, according to reports by the post personnel, produced 12,000 bushels of corn that sold for $2.00 per bushel.[6] Wheat and oats had not been successfully cultivated, but melons and garden vegetables did well. The post garden, three or four miles northeast of the fort, was irrigated and cultivated by post personnel, and for three seasons it had furnished an abundance of vegetables, including okra, onions, melons, and cucumbers. Milk was $0.20 per quart; butter, $1.00 per pound; eggs, $0.75 to $1.00 per dozen; and chickens, from $1.00 to $1.50 each.

According to the surgeon general's report late in 1870, the three adobe barracks had stone foundations and thatched roofs, and each was eighty by twenty-four feet long. Each barrack was built to accommodate a full company, but seldom was any one building occupied by more than fifty soldiers. Each building was lighted and ventilated by eight large windows and two doors and warmed in winter by mesquite-root fuel burned in one large fireplace. There were no washrooms inside. The soldiers slept on straw-filled ticks and wooden bunks, two men to each. Two of the barracks had wings, each forty by twenty-four feet, for a kitchen and mess room. The occupants of the third were using a tent for a kitchen, in which a crude mud structure served as a

[6] James F. Wade, Fort Stockton, to A.A.G., February 17, 1871, in U.S. Department of War, Records of United States Army Commands, Record Group 98, National Archives, Washington, D.C.

cooking range. The mess rooms were unfurnished, and each man supplied his own seat, if any, knife, and fork. Meals were usually eaten out-of-doors.

Each of the five adobe, one-story officers' quarters had stone foundations, shingle roofs, front porches, and boarded floors, with walls plastered and whitewashed inside. Each room, eighteen by fifteen feet with a fourteen-foot ceiling, was heated by a fireplace. Water was supplied every morning by a water wagon, from which barrels were filled. Like the enlisted men's barracks, the officers' quarters had no bathing or toilet facilities.

The guardhouse, fifty-six by sixteen feet and of rock with a shingled roof, was located on the south side of the parade ground in view of the officers' quarters. There was one room for the guard and another, with arm and leg shackles, for the prisoners. The guard's room was ventilated by one door and two windows and heated by a fireplace. The prisoners' cell was not provided with any heat, and it was ventilated and lighted by only two openings in the wall, each eighteen by four inches. Such ventilation was adequate for only two persons, but more often a room held fifteen prisoners. It was confinement with punishment, for the prisoners were virtually deprived of light, ventilation, and warmth.

The report mentioned several other buildings. For a hospital, an old building, formerly an officers' quarters, was being used. A hospital building, however, would soon be completed. The post had a bakery, an adobe building twenty-two by eighteen feet with a shingled roof, but it had no laundry, chapel, library, or schoolhouse.

The stables were 100 yards to the rear and to the east of the men's quarters, not far from the creek. The original plans called for three large stables, but only one had been built. It was an excellent building, 250 by 30 feet, with stone foundations, adobe walls, and shingled roof. There were 100 apertures, each eighteen by ten inches, plus two large doors at the ends and one large door on each side.[7]

The isolation, the deprivations, and the routine chores of garrison, farm, and ranch life in 1870 might have been extremely boring for soldiers and settlers alike had it not been for the Indians. The constant threat of Indian depredation made it unnecessary to wish that some-

[7] Surgeon General, *Report on Barracks and Hospitals.*

thing exciting would happen. Especially imperiled were the people who traveled by stage—drivers, passengers, and scant soldier escorts—who had to traverse hundreds of miles of uninhabited and rugged country with the constant fear of attack. And when an attack occurred, as it often did, the travelers were nearly always at an extreme disadvantage. On the night of September 30, 1870, when twenty miles from Fort Concho en route to Fort Griffin, a stagecoach was attacked by about thirty Indians. The driver and one of the guards escaped by jumping off and hiding in the brush. An investigating patrol found the scalped corpse of the other guard and the coach riddled with bullets and arrows, indicating a severe fight, but the four mules were missing.[8]

During 1870 and 1871, many raids into Texas were made by Kickapoos from Mexico. In November of 1870, members of that tribe appeared in the vicinity of Uvalde, stole horses, plundered a cart train, carried off a Mexican boy, and killed David Adams, the brother of Captain W. C. Adams, and his Mexican employee. While searching for the depredators, nine men of Company E of the Rangers from Fort Inge on December 3 engaged seventy Indians with 300 horses on Pendencia Creek, not far from where Adams had been killed. In a desperate fight, one of the Rangers was killed, and supposedly eight Indians were killed or wounded.

Kickapoos crossed the Rio Grande again in December, killed D. G. Anderson at Carrizo, took all of the horses from the ranch of Santos Benavides at Charco Largo, from the W. W. Stewart spread at Fort Ewell, from the Lowe ranch on the Nueces, and from Joe Walker's ranch on the Frio River, and then escaped without any losses across the Rio Grande.[9] About the same time, some 150 miles to the northwest, Indians drove off twenty-two horses from the Tankersley ranch.[10]

North of Fort Stockton, at Dagger Bend on the Pecos, "fifty mounted Indians at daybreak on September 23 charged the camps of cattle drovers Rhodes, Sloan, and Chisum, who were returning home after delivering a herd, and got away with 56 horses and mules, all except two, in the camp of the Texans with no casualties on either side."[11]

[8] San Antonio *Herald*, October 6 and 13, 1870.

[9] Ibid., December 16, 1870.

[10] Ibid., December 7, 1870.

[11] *Daily New Mexican* (Santa Fe), November 3, 1870 (reprinted in the *Pioneer News-Observer* [Kerrville, Texas], December, 1972).

Not all activity in the area at the time was hostile or military, however. In 1870 Francis Rooney settled near Fort Stockton. Born in Castleblaney, Ireland, Rooney when fourteen ran away from home and, after remaining for some time in Scotland and England, embarked from Liverpool for New York. The vessel in which he sailed was three months crossing the Atlantic. In New York, his first job was unloading salt on the dock for twenty-five cents an hour. In Philadelphia, he enlisted in the U.S. Third Cavalry and was sent to Texas, where he served at Fort Quitman. When his enlistment expired, he settled in Sabinal, Uvalde County, and engaged in cattle raising and various other occupations. In the early 1860s, while in Uvalde, he met and married Jane McCarthy, a native of Ireland, who had come with her parents to the United States. During the Civil War, Francis Rooney served as a private in the Uvalde Company of the Texas Militia of the Confederate Army and was again stationed for a time at Fort Quitman.

Apparently Rooney made some arrangement with Peter Gallagher for a one-room adobe building near the San Pedro Spring, six miles north of Fort Stockton, which had been occupied by Pedro Ureta and his family, who irrigated a patch of corn from the waters of the spring and sold the corn to the military post. Supposedly the spring was named for Pedro Ureta, but how or when the site became "canonized" as San Pedro ("Saint Peter") is not known.

After familiarizing himself with his new surroundings, Rooney started a herd of cattle from the Sabinal country toward Fort Stockton. Within two days' drive of the Pecos River he got a message that his wife was sick, left the herd, and returned to Uvalde County. While he was gone, his foreman and three Mexican cowboys were killed, scalped, and thrown into the Pecos, and his cattle were taken by the Indians. A part of the herd later recovered by the troops was the beginning of his ranch operations. Rooney built a rock pen on the side of the hill west of San Pedro Spring to enclose the herd at night. This structure remained a landmark until recently, when the rocks were removed.

Francis Rooney and his family eventually became very prominent in West Texas, and subsequently there will be more about them. With boundless energy and ambition, Rooney, the poor immigrant boy, set forth to fulfill the American dream. He soon established and operated a large irrigation project, using the water from Comanche Creek. The forts provided a ready market for his products, and his labor and enterprise brought prosperity. In time he built on the farm a fine residence for his growing family, which by 1883 included five children.

Except for the lone cottonwood in the post garden, the first trees at or near Fort Stockton were grown on the Rooney farm. Rooney brought the slips for these trees, cottonwoods and willows, ox-drawn from Presidio del Norte, and planted them on the rim of his main ditches.[12] For at least eighty years, probably more, those willows and cottonwoods provided shade for an annual May Day picnic.

The property was sold by his heirs in the early 1900s, but until then the May Day affair was one of the social highlights of Pecos County.[13] Sack races, three-legged races, greased pig, greased pole, and other contests provided entertainment and fun, and lemonade in large wooden barrels was available. The main event, however, was the bountiful feast, prepared beforehand by the women and spread on tablecloths for the noon meal.

At least one menu (excluding meat and beverage) for a typical holiday affair at the Rooney farm (this one for July 4, 1900), has survived on three small pieces of paper with the following, almost forgotten letterhead:

> Neighbors and Johnson, Proprietors,
> "Pecos County Pickings"
> The Official Paper of Pecos County
> Devoted to the Best interest of Ft. Stockton and Pecos County
> Published every Thursday . . . subscription $2 per year
> Job Work a Speciality.

On these, Mrs. O. W. Williams on June 19, 1900, wrote:

We, the undersigned, whose names are hereto appended agree to furnish the following edibles for the fourth of July celebration to be held at the Rooney Grove on the 4th, July next.

Mrs. H. Butz—3 loaves bread, 3 cakes, 4 pies and salad;
Mrs. M. Adams—salads, 3 pies, cake;
Mrs. James Rooney—bread, pies, salad, cakes;
Mrs. W. C. Crosby—1 large cake, pies, 1 bottle pickles;
Mrs. Valentine—2 cakes, 6 loaves bread, pies;

---

[12] Frank Rooney, "Life of Francis Rooney," manuscript written for Rooney's sister, Mrs. Herman Butz, copy in possession of Clayton Williams.

[13] One of Francis Rooney's granddaughters, Mary Agnes Butz, nearly always managed to leave the grove with a good sunburn, and consequently she was nicknamed "May Day," and this evolved into "Maidie." Now Mrs. W. J. B. Dixon, she is still called that.

Mrs. Young—salad, pickles;
Mrs. Atcherberg—4 loaves bread, 1 cake, salad;
Mrs. Erwin—plenty;
Mrs. Moore—4 loaves bread, 2 cakes;
Mrs. Williams—4 loaves bread, 2 cakes;
Mrs. Howell Johnson—4 loaves bread, pickles;
Mrs. N. O. Royal—2 cakes, 4 pies, 4 loaves bread;
Mrs. L. Teel—2 cakes, 4 pies;
Mrs. S. B. Dees—2 cakes;
Mrs. John Adams—2 cakes, 2 loaves bread;
Mrs. Irene Scott—pickles.

For meat, the men barbecued as many beeves as needed. Although the Fourth of July picnic was no different, the May Day affair was always regarded as the outstanding social event of the year. As an outgrowth of the May Day celebration, the Pioneer Club was organized in Fort Stockton on November 10, 1933.

The major crops produced on the Rooney farm were corn, barley, and oats. These were sold at the fort or to the freight wagon trains. The trains, according to Rooney's son, Frank, consisted of twenty to forty wagons, each drawn by fourteen to eighteen mules. A single wagon carried as much as 14,000 pounds of freight. Frank recalled that farming in those days was usually carried on with oxen and Mexican plows. Small grains were harvested with a hand sickle. The threshing was done by piling the grain in a pen constructed for that purpose and driving horses round and round over it until the grain was out of the straw. Since shovels and pitchforks were scarce and expensive, substitutes were made from forked limbs of mesquite trees. Corn was either shelled by hand or placed in a woven net of rawhide supported by four forked sticks and the grain beaten off the cob with sticks.[14]

[14] Frank Rooney, "Life of Francis Rooney."

CHAPTER 11

January, 1871, to May, 1872

DURING January of 1871, Companies A and D, Ninth Cavalry, G, Twenty-fourth Infantry, and K, Twenty-fifth Infantry, were at Fort Stockton, still under the command of Lieutenant Colonel J. F. Wade. In September, Captain Lewis Johnson, Twenty-fourth Infantry, took temporary command until the arrival a month later of Lieutenant Colonel Wesley Merritt, Ninth Cavalry.[1] Born in New York and an 1855 graduate of the Military Academy, Merritt had had a brilliant military career during the Civil War and had received many honors for gallantry and meritorious service.[2]

As the soldiers went about their business, more civilians settled in or near the little community of Saint Gall, which Peter Gallagher had founded, adjacent to the post. As previously noted, Peter J. Gallagher, the nephew, was in charge of the elder Gallagher's two stores in the tiny settlement. Gallagher the uncle also owned two tracts of land that included the townsite on which the post was located and the springs and upper waters of Comanche Creek.

In San Antonio, the elder Gallagher had been an outstanding merchant, stockman, and builder. He had a store on Main Street and a three-story stone home, which was eventually razed and replaced by the Alamo Gardens. He built the old San Antonio post office and several buildings in the quadrangle of Fort Sam Houston. The Menger Hotel still stands as a monument to his ingenuity and craftsmanship. Twenty-five miles northwest of San Antonio, near Boerne, Gallagher's Circle G Ranch lay in the beautiful valley of the San Geronimo River.

[1] U.S. Department of War, Post Returns, Fort Stockton, 1871, Records of the Adjutant General's Office (AGO), Record Group (RG) 94, National Archives (NA), Washington, D.C.

[2] Francis B. Heitman, *Historical Register and Dictionary of the United States Army*, 1:706.

His story-and-a-half, four-room, stone ranch house was a small fortress. Its single outside door was of oak, and the windows were protected by iron bars and oak shutters. The house had both rifle slits and loopholes in the outside walls of the ground floor and the loft room. In February, 1871, Gallagher sold his stock of goods and, at age fifty-nine, moved his family to the Circle G Ranch. No Indian trouble was expected that close to the army's headquarters in Texas, but one misty morning, while the field hands were smoking bacon, the Indians, some dressed in soldiers' uniforms, opened the corral and drove out eighteen horses. In later years, Mrs. Griff Jones, Gallagher's niece, recalled the incident:

"Aren't those Indians?" I called to my uncle. One look and he hurried to snatch a rifle from the stack always kept behind the door. There were fifteen, riding in squads of five. Scarecrow figures, they appeared with pieces of rawhide in which holes had been cut for the feet, their only saddles. Those nearest the house . . . [wore] soldiers' uniforms, cast off or stolen.

Before my uncle could do anything, the party had gathered up the stock and was on its way. . . . We children grieved because our pet riding horses were gone.[3]

The depredators rode to Helotes Creek, chased six Mexicans into their dwellings, killed a woman who was washing laundry, and then south of Leon Springs stripped a Mexican man of his clothes and shot an arrow into his chest. Next, they appeared at the home of H. M. Schmidt and, while the parents watched, captured two boys, Clinton and Jefferson, who were herding sheep nearby. Schmidt leaped on a horse and galloped after the Indians, and a black workman alerted the neighborhood. The brothers, whose last name history has recorded as Smith, were eventually recovered.[4]

Shortly after the Gallagher family moved to the Circle G, leading West Texas pioneer Benjamin F. Ficklin died on March 10, 1871, at the home of his friend and partner, Sawyer, in Georgetown, Maryland. After having survived untold perils during the Mexican War and as a mail-stage rider and driver from Arkansas to far West Texas, Ficklin died ironically at the age of forty-four when a fish bone lodged in his

---

[3] Dade Rayfield, "Legend of the Circle G," *True West*, December, 1966, pp. 31–32.

[4] San Antonio *Herald*, February 1 and 28 and March 2 and 7, 1871; Dorman H. Winfrey and James M. Day, eds., *The Indian Papers of Texas and the Southwest, 1825–1916*, 4:426; Clinton R. Smith and Jeff D. Smith, *The Boy Captives*, ed. J. Marvin Hunter, p. 128.

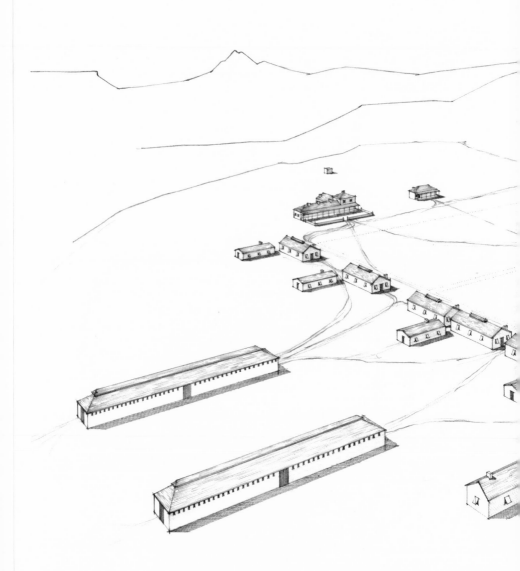

Military post of Fort Stockton. *Drawing by Larry McSpedden.*

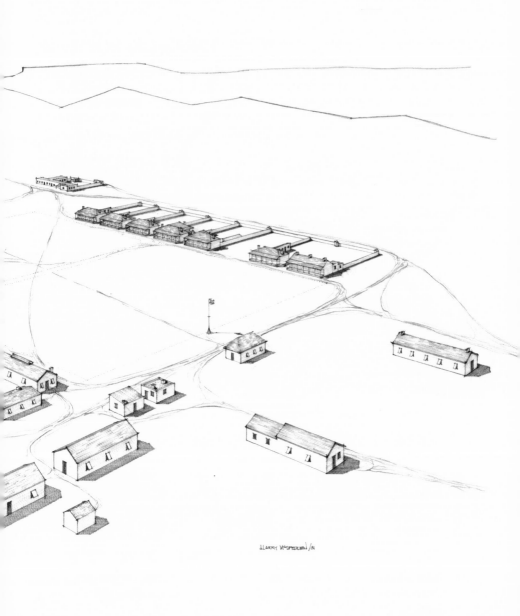

LARRY McSPADDEN/84

throat. The first county seat of Tom Green County was named Ben Ficklin (also spelled Benficklin) for him.[5]

Meanwhile, the Indian raiders struck all along the frontier with increasing fury. On April 13, 1871, about ninety miles east of Fort Stockton, two stagecoaches met at Central Station (Centralia). In the down-stage were a black woman, the stage agent, the guard, and the driver. In the up-stage were two unarmed passengers, an escort, and the driver. Upon sighting an Indian, one of the soldiers proposed to investigate. The agent urged him to stay near the station, but his advice was not heeded. The soldier and two escorts soon were in the midst of twenty-five to thirty charging Indians. One man retreated to the station; another took cover by a small tree and probably would have been cut off from his comrades had not the agent held the Indians at bay by rapid gunfire until the soldier could dash safely to the camp. The Indians continued the onslaught for nearly two hours, often coming within forty yards of the station. Each escort fired about fifty rounds, and the agent estimated five or six Indians were killed and several wounded and one member of the stage party was wounded.[6]

This incident is possibly the same as that reprinted from the *San Antonio Express* in the *Galveston News* on May 20, 1877, which involved James D. Spears, the indomitable El Paso Mail Company agent, whose fight with Indians took place in 1870 four miles west of Fort Stockton. The locations do not coincide, but some details are similar. According to this account, the eastbound and westbound stages had met and stopped for breakfast and the eight mules were grazing about seventy yards from camp, when the Indians suddenly appeared on a ridge and charged. The drivers and two guards got behind the coaches for protection, but Spears ran between the mules and the Indians and opened fire. Fortunately, not one of the Indians' shower of missiles struck him. Spears's fire from his own trusty Winchester was more effective, according to the account: "For as the Indians—who were lashed to their horses, as is often their custom when going into battle— wheeled and drew off, no less than seven of them dangled, head downwards, from their saddles, their horses being led away by their com-

[5] Walter P. Webb and H. B. Carroll, eds., *The Handbook of Texas*, 1:596; J. Evetts Haley, "Ben Ficklin, Pioneer Mail Man," *Shamrock*, Spring, 1959, p. 12.

[6] *Houston Telegraph*, April 27, 1871; San Antonio *Herald*, April 18, 1871; *Texas State Journal* (Austin), April 22, 1871.

rades. Besides those who were killed, several were wounded before they could get out of the range of Spears's rifle." The Indians retreated to the ridge, and there the chief, in full war dress, with a silver-plated queue hanging from his head to his heels, danced a war song of defiance. Waiting until the dancer momentarily paused, Spears fired, and, "before the echoes began to reverberate, the swift leaden messenger had done its fatal work, and the chief fell with his last war song on his lips. This ended the fight."

The fight and siege lasted about three hours. One bullet struck the muzzle of Spears's rifle, but he was unharmed. No one of Spears's party, the account continued, was hurt except one soldier who was slightly wounded in the foot, and no mules were lost. The Indians suffered an estimated ten or twelve killed or wounded. Both of these accounts and others describe Spears, who later became a Tom Green County sheriff, as a superhero. Although the stories may have been first told by Spears, they were probably embellished by the *Express* writer.[7]

Because of increased Indian activity in the regions of the Pecos and Devils rivers, Colonel Wade was ordered in April, 1871, to reestablish an outpost of three commissioned officers and sixty enlisted men at Fort Lancaster, and the commanding officer at Fort Clark was ordered to reestablish Camp Hudson with a similar force. Wade sent the designated number of troops to Fort Lancaster and made a number of improvements there. The post had corrals and an excellent water well, but its reestablishment sapped the strength of Fort Stockton. Lancaster required all available transportation about one-third of each month, thereby leaving insufficient hauling facilities for Stockton. For a time, ironically, Lancaster appeared to be the post and Stockton the outpost.[8]

During April, plans were made for counteracting Indian guerrilla activities. A detachment of the Twenty-fourth Infantry searched for a practical route between Forts Clark and McKavett, an area in which the Indians had vandalized and stolen stock. Three companies were

[7] *Galveston News*, May 20, 1877 (reprinted from *San Antonio Express*, n.d.).

[8] San Antonio *Herald*, April 30, 1871; James F. Wade, Fort Stockton, to A.A.G., July 11, 1871, U.S. Department of War, Records of United States Army Commands, RG 98, NA.

relocated: C, Ninth Cavalry, from Fort Davis to Fort McKavett; K, Fourth Cavalry, from Fort Brown to Fort Griffin; and L, Fourth Cavalry, from Ringgold Barracks to Fort Richardson.[9]

The organization of the counties west of the Pecos River was nearing completion. On May 2, 1871, the legislature amended the 1850 act that had created Presidio, El Paso, and Worth counties. The east-southeastern boundary of El Paso County was now to be from the intersection of the 32nd parallel of north latitude and the Pecos River down the western bank of that stream to the south bank of Delaware Creek, thence southwest to San Martin Springs, thence southwest to the Rio Grande where it crossed the 105th parallel of longitude.[10] On the following day the legislature created the county of Pecos. Its boundary line, beginning at the junction of San Francisco Creek with the Rio Grande, ran in a northwesterly direction to Varela Spring, thence northwest to San Martin Springs, thence northeast along the El Paso County line to the Pecos River, thence down the Pecos to the Rio Grande, and thence up the Rio Grande to the beginning point. Peter Gallagher, George Frazer, and Cesario Torres were appointed as a board of commissioners for the purpose of organizing and ordering an election of county officers.[11]

On May 12, the legislature repealed a previous act providing for the organization of Presidio County and passed a new act to organize that county. The boundaries established in the new act began at the junction of the Rio Grande and the 105th parallel, then went northeast along the line of El Paso County to San Martin Springs, thence southeast along the Pecos County line to Varela Spring, thence southeast to the junction of San Francisco Creek and the Rio Grande, and thence up that stream to the place of beginning. Patrick Murphy, Moses E. Kelly, and Daniel Murphy were appointed as a board to carry out the organization.[12]

In the spring of 1871 the Indians pillaged the Texas frontier with increased destruction, particularly the area from Montague and Young counties southward through Llano and Burnet.[13] Although Texans gen-

[9] San Antonio *Herald*, May 9 and 12, 1871.
[10] H. P. N. Gammel, ed., *The Laws of Texas, 1822–1897*, 6:972.
[11] Ibid., 6:975–976.
[12] Ibid., 6:988–989.
[13] Joseph Carroll McConnell, *The West Texas Frontier*, 2:268–288.

erally felt that the Rangers could resolve any conflict, they were unable to stem the hostile advance. Consequently, the legislature, on March 18, 1871, called on its congressional delegation to get the Kiowa-Comanche Reservation moved to a point at least 150 miles from the Texans' nearest settlements.[14] Nothing came of the proposal, but aid was obtained from another source.

To determine the true situation and what measures, if any, should be taken, General William Tecumseh Sherman made a personal tour of inspection of the entire frontier from San Antonio to Kansas. Accompanied by Inspector General William B. Marcy, two staff members, and fifteen cavalrymen, he headed north from San Antonio on May 2 by way of Forts Mason, McKavett, Concho, and Griffin, without visiting Fort Stockton or any of the posts in far western Texas. As the party on May 18 made its way across the Salt Creek prairie, between present Graham and Jacksboro, it miraculously escaped being annihilated by a band of about 150 Kiowa Indians. From their hiding place on a nearby hill, the Indians watched the soldiers pass because Do-ha-te (also known as Maman-ti or Sky Walker), the medicine man, after having made medicine on the evening before, had instructed his followers that two parties would pass the site the next day, that the first should not be attacked, but that an attack on the second would be successful. A few hotheads wanted to attack the first, which happened to be Sherman's party, but Do-ha-te warned that his medicine would not work with this group. Then came from the east Henry Warren's wagon train, twelve men and ten wagons loaded with contract corn for Fort Griffin. The Kiowas rushed from their hiding place, killed seven of the teamsters, one of whom was chained to a wagon wheel and burned, plundered the wagons, and captured forty-one mules. That night Thomas Brazeal, one of the five who escaped, although wounded, limped into Fort Richardson and told Sherman a pitiful story of what had happened. The general, not aware, of course, that his life had been spared as a result of the uncanny prophecy of a medicine man but obviously realizing that it could as well have been his mutilated body bloating in the hot sun on the Salt Creek prairie, quickly concluded that drastic military action was necessary. Fortunately, he had at Fort Richardson the brilliant and energetic Colonel Ranald S. Mackenzie and five com-

[14] Gammel, *Laws of Texas*, 6:1054–1055.

panies of the tough Fourth Cavalry, which had arrived in March from the southwestern posts to protect the North Texas frontier.[15]

To enable Mackenzie to take action against the Kiowas, Sherman immediately reshuffled the personnel of the frontier posts in Texas. Additional companies of the Fourth Cavalry from Brownsville, Laredo, McKavett, Concho, and Griffin were sent to Fort Richardson, and on June 17 General J. J. Reynolds, commander of the Department of Texas, ordered the Ninth Cavalry and the Twenty-fourth Infantry shifted to offset the removal of the units sent to Mackenzie. Company C, Ninth Cavalry, then en route to Fort McKavett, was sent instead to Fort Concho; Company B, Ninth Cavalry, was sent to Fort Griffin; Company G, Ninth Cavalry, was transferred from Fort Clark to Fort Griffin; Lieutenant Colonel William R. Shafter, the commander of the Twenty-fourth Infantry after Mackenzie was transferred in 1871 to the Fourth Cavalry, was sent with a detachment of his black troops from McKavett to Davis; Companies C and I, Twenty-fourth Infantry, were moved from Fort Clark to Fort McKavett; and Companies C and H, Twenty-fifth Infantry, were moved from Fort McKavett to Fort Clark.[16]

With the transfer of most units of the Fourth Cavalry to North Texas, the Kickapoos increased their raiding in South Texas. During May and June, Indians, presumably Kickapoos, stole more than 100 horses in the vicinity of Uvalde and San Miguel Creek, stole some horses from W. C. Adams (formerly of the Confederate Army), shot one of Adams' employees at his dwelling, and escaped down the Nueces.[17] About the same time, other Indians stampeded a New Mexico–bound cattle herd near Spring Creek in Coleman County. Two cowboys were killed, one was rescued by travelers who came upon the scene, and the others fled to safety.[18]

[15] Wilbur S. Nye, *Carbine and Lance: The Story of Old Fort Sill*, pp. 124–131; Ernest Wallace, *Ranald S. Mackenzie on the Texas Frontier*, pp. 29–30.

[16] Wallace, *Mackenzie on the Texas Frontier*, pp. 33, 39–41. The Texas frontier forts were Richardson, Griffin, McKavett, Clark, Duncan, McIntosh, Ringgold, Brown, Stockton, Quitman, and Davis; the outposts were Phantom Hill, Chadbourne, Terrett, Hudson, Camp Wood, and Lancaster; the picket stations were Mountain Pass, Head of the Middle Concho, Kickapoo Springs, Concho Mail Station, Bismarck, Splitgarbers, Brazos, Escondido Springs (near Fort Brown), Melvin, El Muerto, and Varela Springs (San Antonio *Herald*, June 17, 1871).

[17] San Antonio *Herald*, June 15, 1871.

[18] Warren Hunter, "Killing of Dan Arnold and Lapoleon Lemmons," *Frontier Times* 5, no. 3 (December, 1927):97–98.

The Indian raiders also continued their activity in the Trans-Pecos country. At Varela Spring, a Fort Davis picket station, about noon on June 17, 1871, sixty raiders ran off forty mules and three horses belonging to a detachment of Company A, Twenty-fourth Infantry, under Captain Frederick M. Crandal. On the following day, when Shafter at Fort Davis, who had no more than twenty-five men available for pursuit, learned that the raiding party had headed toward the Guadalupe Mountains, he requested the aid of Colonel Wade at Fort Stockton. Wade immediately sent Captain Michael Cooney, Ninth Cavalry, and First Lieutenant J. N. Morgan, Twenty-fourth Infantry, with a detachment of seventy-five enlisted men from Companies A and L, Ninth Cavalry, two guides, and rations for twenty-two days. The command rendezvoused at Varela Spring with Shafter, his lieutenant, a doctor, and twenty-four troopers from Fort Davis.

The combined force followed the trail northeast for twenty-six miles, passing Toyah Creek along the way, and made a dry night camp on June 22. The Indians, having crossed the Pecos River at Indian Crossing and gone thirty miles beyond to permanent water in the white sands of present Ward County, were still a few days ahead. During the next day, in an area unknown to the soldiers, Shafter followed a devious trail over shifting dunes, crisscrossed by the flood washes of recent rains, and made another dry camp. On June 26 Shafter followed the trail of shod mules eastward, out of the sand country, where he concluded that there was no water closer than Mustang Spring on the Staked Plains, and turned back in search of water. After a hot, dry seventy-five-mile ride that day, the command reached permanent water in the sand dunes.

There the party recuperated for two days and then, to minimize the effects of heat and thirst, it started at sundown toward the northwest. After eighteen continuous hours in the saddle, it encountered a fresh trail made by a large number of mules. Without rest, the exhausted and thirsty men followed the trail, which led toward the southwest to a large and recently deserted Indian camp. From there, Shafter followed the trail toward the northwest until daylight before allowing the men a short rest. A short distance farther, he discovered three braves in camp with a herd of horses. On seeing the soldiers, the Indians mounted and fled, their rides easily outdistancing the jaded army horses. The troopers, after rounding up the Indians' ponies, discovered another Indian camp a short distance away. When the soldiers approached, its occupants disappeared on foot into nearby sand dunes. After taking ten horses and five mules, burning the lodges and abandoned supplies, and confiscating seventy-five bars of lead and several flasks of powder, Shafter headed southwest toward the Pecos. Along the way the command captured an old squaw, who was riding a fine mule and herding a couple of old horses.

Discovering at this point a fresh trail, Shafter led his weary troopers in pursuit of its makers. At night, he stopped at a small stream of gypsum water, and the column straggled in at nine o'clock for a miserable, thirsty night camp. Scouts reported that the Pecos was within four miles, and before dawn the troops were off to quench their thirst. At the river, they found signs which indicated that on the previous day a party of about 200 Indians had headed up the stream. Shafter's men and horses, however, were totally exhausted, and after giving them a rest he headed for Fort Davis. The captured squaw informed the soldiers that fifteen Comanches, who had stolen the mules at Varela, were on their way to the Red River area, that three bands of Apaches had just ended their enmity with the Comanches at a meeting in the sand dunes, and that the Indians had acquired their lead and powder a few weeks before from comancheros at the head of the Colorado River.[19]

When they reached Fort Stockton on July 16, Captain Cooney and Lieutenant Morgan had marched 420 miles on their expedition. The destruction of camp equipage and their capture of only a few animals was a rather poor showing for their strenuous effort. Obviously, the Indians were still besting the soldiers. Consequently, the Texas legislature, on November 25, 1871, provided for twenty-four additional companies of minutemen for the protection of the frontier. Each company was to include an elected lieutenant, two sergeants, two corporals, and fifteen men, and the term of enlistment was to be twelve months.[20]

One major problem for the army was its inability to obtain adequate forage for its mounts. By 1871, however, this situation had improved at Fort Stockton. Colonel Wade reported that no oats and only a small quantity of barley were in the vicinity of the post, but during

[19] San Antonio *Herald*, April 9, 1871; Wade, Fort Stockton, to A.A.G., June 20, 1871, Army Commands, RG 98, NA; J. Evetts Haley, *Fort Concho and the Texas Frontier*, pp. 163–167; Regimental Returns, 24th Infantry, AGO, RG 94, NA.

[20] Gammel, *Laws of Texas*, 7:36.

the past two years the settlers had grown corn in "respectable quantities."[21] The mutual interdependence between soldiers and settlers was becoming well recognized. Without the military, settlers likely could not have survived; the settlers, in turn, furnished the soldiers with a considerable amount of their requirements.

Some of the first settlers in the Fort Stockton area were slow to obtain titles to the land on which they squatted (some others never did). Rooney accumulated his land by preempting.[22] A preemption act, passed by the congress of the Republic of Texas in 1838, provided that a holder of a valid certificate, who would settle upon and improve the land within three years, could obtain title to as much as 320 acres of the public domain. The cutoff date was later extended by the state legislature to January 1, 1854. Then, in 1854, the legislature passed a true homestead law that allowed a grant of 160 acres and required a residence of three years. Changes were made in 1866, 1870, and 1876, but the basic policy continued until the 1890s.[23]

One tract of 640 acres in Survey 258, originally a bounty certificate issued to the heirs of Manuel María in payment for military service, was transferred, apparently in 1871, to Francis Rooney, who through the aid of Peter Gallagher, it appears, obtained a loan from John T. Brackenridge, cashier of the San Antonio National Bank. With this money, Rooney in October, 1871, purchased three tracts of land totaling 1,600 acres, including the María certificate.[24]

Military law was still the only law west of the Pecos. Two men, Samuel Farkswell and William Henry, were arrested in Fort Stockton in July, 1871, and charged with theft of horses from a Mr. Peacock at Horsehead Crossing. Colonel Wade wrote his superiors for instructions regarding the civilian prisoners in his guardhouse.[25]

Meanwhile, despite the Indians, the mail stages continued to operate. On July 5, 1871, about four miles west of Eagle Springs, a driver lost his hat and had one mule wounded by Indians, and, later in the month, another stage was attacked some forty miles above Fort Con-

[21] Wade, Fort Stockton, to A.A.G., February 17, 1871, Army Commands, RG 98, NA.

[22] Frank Rooney, "Life of Francis Rooney," manuscript written for Frank's sister, Mrs. Herman Butz, copy in possession of Clayton Williams.

[23] Webb and Carroll, *Handbook of Texas*, 2:20–21.

[24] Pecos County, Deed Records, 1:59 (Release of Deed of Trust to Rooney), 20:25.

[25] Wade, Fort Stockton, to A.A.G., July 31, 1871, Army Commands, RG 98, NA.

cho, but this time not even a hat was lost. On July 13, 1871, the Sawyer and Ficklin El Paso Mail Line advertised its new schedule in the San Antonio *Herald*. Westbound four-horse coaches left San Antonio on Mondays, Thursdays, and Saturdays at 8 A.M. for Concho. From Concho they would depart on Wednesdays and Saturdays for Fort Stockton, Fort Davis, Fort Quitman, Toro, San Elizario, and El Paso. In addition, the schedule listed two-horse hacks from Fort Concho by way of Fort Griffin to Jacksboro and four-horse coaches from San Antonio by way of Castroville and Fort Clark to Eagle Pass.[26]

After the massacre on the Salt Creek prairie in May, General Sherman authorized Colonel Mackenzie to lead an expedition into western Texas with the objective of driving the Comanches to the reservation. In October Mackenzie, with eight companies of the Fourth Cavalry, two of the Eleventh Infantry, and twenty Tonkawa scouts, about 600 men in all, left old Camp Cooper, five miles north of Fort Griffin. After a skirmish with Quanah Parker's band of Comanches in Blanco Canyon, near present Crosbyton, he encountered a snowstorm while chasing the fleeing band across the unexplored Llano Estacado. He then sent the troops to the posts for the winter.[27] Not long after the troops had returned to their posts, on November 22, Indian raiders stole the mules and horses from a wagon train on Kickapoo Creek near Fort Concho. Soldiers followed the trail to the upper Colorado before deciding that pursuit was futile.[28]

During the early part of 1872 Lieutenant Colonel Wesley Merritt had at Fort Stockton Companies A and D, Ninth Cavalry, Company G, Twenty-fourth Infantry, and Company K, Twenty-fifth Infantry. On April 16 Merritt and Captain Cooney, with the headquarters detachment and Company A, Ninth Cavalry, departed for Fort Clark. Captain F. S. Dodge served as interim commander at Stockton until relieved on May 15 by Major Zenas R. Bliss, who arrived with Companies G and I, Twenty-fifth Infantry.[29]

Civilians in the Stockton area prospered, Peter Gallagher possibly most of all. The army had inadvertently constructed buildings on land

[26] San Antonio *Herald*, July 13 and August 8, 1871.

[27] Wallace, *Mackenzie on the Texas Frontier*, pp. 45–46.

[28] Haley, *Fort Concho*, pp. 178–193; Robert G. Carter, *The Old Sergeant's Story*, p. 70.

[29] U.S. Department of War, Post Returns, Fort Stockton, January–May, 1872.

to which he had a recorded deed. Thus, it was unable to prevent Gallagher from taking possession of the buildings and renting one to Thomas Johnson, a post trader. The building rented to Johnson was near the limits of "the reservation" and was likely the old Koehler Store on the banks of Comanche Creek.[30]

Although Pecos County had not yet been organized, a "county" election was held on January 13, 1872. Crafton F. Wilcox, Cesario Torres, Thomas Rife, Joseph Heid, and Francis Rooney were elected justices of the peace and qualified on February 29. On May 24, Edward Kornrumpf declined an appointment as sheriff, and on September 18 Heid, Rooney, and Thomas Johnson were commissioned as a board of appeal. They qualified on October 30, although technically there was as yet no Pecos County.[31]

Meanwhile, on January 15, 1872, the commander of Company D, Ninth Cavalry, at Fort Stockton, was requested to furnish a complete description of three men of that company who had been sentenced to prison and to accompany the prisoners to their place of confinement.[32] Their destination was probably Ship Island, Mississippi, where after the Civil War most soldiers convicted of crimes from all parts of the Southwest were sent. The prisoners, the majority of whom were black, were held in frame buildings under the constant guard of black soldiers.[33]

By 1872, it was becoming apparent to the Indian that he, like the buffalo, was an endangered species. In desperation the Kiowas and Comanches became even more ferocious. Their most infamous raid that year was the massacre at Howard's Well, in present Crockett County. Primarily in retaliation for the imprisonment of Satanta and Big Tree for their participation in the massacre of Warren's teamsters, the Howard's Well massacre began with a relatively quiet episode in the life of August Santleben. While returning from freight deliveries at Fort Davis, Santleben stopped at the Pecos salt lake to load his prairie

[30]Wade, Fort Stockton, to A.A.G., July 27, 1871, Army Commands, RG 98, NA.

[31]Pecos County, Texas, Records, January 13, February 29, May 24, September 18, and October 30, 1872, Records of Texas Secretary of State, Archives, Texas State Library, Austin.

[32]Lt. John S. Loud, Fort Stockton, to c.o. of Co. D, 9th Cavalry, January 15, 1872, Army Commands, RG 98, NA.

[33]Zenas R. Bliss, "Reminiscences," 5:50–59, Eguene C. Barker Texas History Center, University of Texas, Austin.

schooners from the free and unlimited supply of salt, which was in demand among ranchmen. The "lake," which covered about fifty acres, about eighteen inches deep and with a glittering surface of white salt about four inches thick, was situated among the sand hills in a desert two miles east of the Pecos River and six miles above Horsehead Crossing. The men cautiously placed the corral near the lower end of the lake, where there were no sand hills to obstruct the view. The mules were side-lined and turned loose to graze. On both the second and the third day, the men spotted about thirty Indians watching from a distance, apparently looking for an opportunity to drive off the coveted mules, but Santleben kept the mules heavily guarded at all times and did not allow them the opportunity. The Indians quietly bided their time.

After the wagons had been loaded and covered with heavy tarps, Santleben on April 18 resumed his journey. That evening, he crossed the Pecos at Salt Crossing and camped on the west side of the river without incident. During the next day, while proceeding toward Fort Lancaster, the teamsters saw Indians observing their movements. On the third day, Santleben stopped at Howard's Well. A short distance farther he met Anastacio Gonzales, of San Antonio, a wagon master with whom he was acquainted, informed him that Indians had been lurking around his train for two days, and advised him to maintain extreme caution.

At noon that same day, April 20, Gonzales stopped on level ground near Howard's Well and circled his wagons to form a corral. His ten large wagons, with high sideboards and large overhanging tailgates, each drawn by ten mules, were loaded with commissary supplies and kerosene (and lumber, according to one report). Two or three herders were sent with the mules, and the noon meal was prepared within the enclosure. While the men were eating, the herd of mules dashed by, pursued by Indians, who were shouting and shooting. Simultaneously, other Indians attacked the wagon train and slaughtered all of the men. The mule herders, all wounded, were lashed to wagon wheels, soaked with kerosene, and set afire. Marcela Sera, the pretty twenty-year-old wife of a teamster, her one-year-old baby, and her mother were taken captive. The Indians disposed of the baby by dashing its head against a wagon wheel. When soldiers were spotted in the distance, the Indians ordered the captive women to keep up with the fast-moving mule herd, but the older woman collapsed and was then lanced and scalped. An Indian at the same time pulled Marcela Sera onto his horse and deposited her with some squaws who had sought cover in a brushy ravine.

Four days previously, Colonel Merritt with his staff, the regimental band, and Companies A and H, Ninth Cavalry, had left Fort Stockton for Fort Clark to bolster that region's defenses against Indian incursions. By coincidence, Merritt arrived at Howard's Well while Gonzales' wagon train was still smoking. He found eight badly burned men lashed to wagon wheels, six of whom were dead. One of the survivors had two fingers burned off and a bullet wound through his foot; the other had a badly burned back and a bullet wound.

Captain Cooney with a detachment of Company A and Lieutenant Frederick R. Vincent with Company H started in pursuit of the Indians. While advancing up the steep incline, the troops encountered heavy fire. Nine of their horses were wounded. Cooney's horse fell but got up and started dragging the captain, whose foot was caught in a stirrup. Cooney was saved, however, by some of the troopers. The fury of the Indains' defense forced the troopers to fall back and dismount. Forming a skirmish line, they attempted another tortuous advance. This time Lieutenant Vincent was shot through both legs. Although bleeding profusely, Vincent continued for some time to direct his men. When a messenger arrived at Howard's Well with the news of Vincent's condition, Dr. Cleary, who was with Merritt, started to the rescue with an ambulance, but the lieutenant died before reaching the camp. Vincent, a native of Prince Edward Island, had progressed during the Civil War from private to captain. In the summer of 1867 he had joined the Ninth Cavalry as a second lieutenant and in 1869 had become a first lieutenant.[34]

During the engagement, the troops recovered Mrs. Sera, but, with the approach of darkness and short of ammunition, they retreated to their camp at Howard's Well, under the scrutiny of more than 100 Indians under the leadership of White Horse and Big Bow. Seeing that the soldiers had posted a strong night guard, the Indians left for the Llano Estacado. It was a decided victory for the Kiowas and Co-

[34] Heitman, *Historical Register*, 1:987.

manches, even though they failed to get away with most of the stock and had two of their leaders wounded. White Horse, who had killed Gottlieb Koozer and taken Mrs. Koozer and her children captive, was shot in the arm, and Tau-ankie, the son of Lone Wolf, was shot in the knee. Big Bow, the other leader, had participated in the Warren wagon train massacre but had escaped capture. Next morning the Indians departed, and the defeated soldiers buried their dead and, because they did not have adequate rations to reach their destinations, headed for Fort Clark.[35]

Although he was not personally a witness to the affair at Howard's Well, William Edgar, because he was an employee of Adams and Wickes, the firm that apparently owned the Gonzales wagon train, had considerable information about the incident. He may, of course, have forgotten many of the details, but in 1903 he recalled that Gonzales worked for Adams and Wickes. The train was technically owned by Gonzales, but Adams and Wickes held a mortgage on it. On its last trip, this time to Fort Stockton, at Howard's Well, about forty miles from the head of Devils River, Gonzales sent his herd of mules about one mile from camp to graze. Colonel Merritt, who soon afterward with two companies of the Ninth Cavalry arrived at the site, found "the wagons all on fire, the men killed and partly burned, and the mules all driven off, with various small bodies of Indians on the hilltops inviting him out to fight. But the Indians being about 135 in number, closed in about him, killed Vincent, and drove the company back to the support of the other company under General Merritt, when no further effort was made to recapture the mules."[36]

A few days after the Howard's Well episode, Major Bliss, while enroute from Fort Clark to Fort Stockton with several companies of the Twenty-fifth Infantry and the families of some of the officers, passed the site. In his account of the trip he supplied considerable information, seldom seen in official army records, relative to Fort Stockton.

[35] August Santleben, *A Texas Pioneer*, pp. 141–147; Bliss, "Reminiscences," 5:175–183; Haley, *Fort Concho*, p. 196; William H. Leckie, *The Buffalo Soldiers*, pp. 101–102; C. C. Rister, *The Southwestern Frontier, 1865–1881*, pp. 148–149; Rupert N. Richardson, *The Comanche Barrier to South Plains Settlement*, p. 348.

[36] *San Antonio Express*, September 27, 1903. A commemorative marker has been erected by the Crockett County Historical Society a short distance from Howard's Well.

On the journey of over 300 miles, he wrote, the train consisted of thirty-three wagons, some assigned to the field and staff of the regiment, some to the commissary, and some to the quartermaster, and two and one-half to each company. Since their families were not entitled to transportation, the officers "had gotten up some sort of a vehicle for the families to ride in. When we got straightened out on the road . . . there were about a dozen carriages of all kinds and description. . . . Because the wagons were not sufficient to haul all the officers' furniture, a great deal was left standing behind the road at our camp on the Pinta. . . . The fourth day out from Pinta we encamped at old Fort Hudson. The adobe buildings were nearly all down, but the picket buildings still had the walls standing."

Before the end of the fourteen-day march many men and officers had blistered feet and other afflictions. The women and children, although unaccustomed to reveille and breakfast before daylight, to riding in uncomfortable carriages, and to sleeping on beds placed on the ground—or, when it rained, between wet mattresses and blankets—were even less happy at the prospect of living in Fort Stockton. Bliss remembered that when "the ladies first got a sight of the Post, that some of them were to live in, for nobody knew how long . . . the sight caused many sad hearts. The post looked in the distance like a camp of Mexican carts. There was not a tree to be seen. . . . There was little if any grass, and the whole landscape had a grayish appearance."

In time, many of the soldiers and their families decided that their first impression of Fort Stockton had been wrong. The post was occupied by Company D, Ninth Cavalry, and Companies I, J, and K, Twenty-fifth Infantry, and said Bliss: "[The] Post Garden . . . was the best garden I have ever seen at a military post. We had more than the officers and men could possibly use, and sold quite large quantities of vegetables. The sweet corn and melons could not be surpassed. There were several hundred grape vines that supplied an abundance of grapes. Before we were ordered away we came to think that Fort Stockton was a very desirable station."[37]

Besides, Santleben was hauling thousands of pounds of copper, salt, potatoes, apples, and other supplies from the Terrazas ranch in

[37] Bliss, "Reminiscences," 5:187–190.

Chihuahua to Forts Davis and Stockton. On one trip from Chihuahua in 1872, he stated, he crossed the Pecos River at Horsehead Crossing, but he meant Horseshoe Bend, for he described the pontoon bridge that had been constructed by the military. The structure, he wrote, was not capable of supporting his heavily loaded prairie schooners, and he had to transport his freight, mostly copper and salt, in relays.[38]

[38] Santleben, Texas Pioneer, pp. 141–148.

CHAPTER 12

May, 1872, to July, 1874

FROM May, 1872, until July, 1874, Indian depredators kept army patrols busy. On May 20, 1872, a small detachment of Ninth Cavalry attacked a band of Kickapoos on Pendencia Creek in northwestern Dimmit County. A couple of days later, a detachment of the Fourth Cavalry was attacked by Comanches on Lost Creek in the eastern part of Coleman County, and on June 15 the guard at Johnson's Station, about twenty miles west of Fort Concho, while under attack, killed two Indians.[1]

Then, on July 6, 1872, a Dr. Bartlett and Matt Tucker, of Erath County, were en route up the Pecos River with 2,500 head of cattle. Above Horsehead Crossing, an estimated 300 Indians attacked the drovers just as they were preparing to water the cattle and make camp. Dr. Bartlett, who had previously lost a herd at Johnson's Station and was riding about 300 yards in advance, was overtaken by approximately thirty Indians, killed, and his body mutilated and burned. About a third of the raiders took possession of the herd while the remainder laid siege to the cowboys at the wagon. The Indians, decorated with paint, feathers, and buffalo horns and attired only in "yees" (perhaps breechclouts), kept at a safe distance from the wagon. Growing tired of the slow standoff, Tucker and his men decided to move their wagon and four horses to a better location. When they started, the Indians dashed closer, took a few broken-down animals, and then left behind the stolen herd.

[1]Francis B. Heitman, *Historical Register and Dictionary of the United States Army*, 2:437; "Record of Engagements with Hostile Indians in Texas, 1868 to 1882," *West Texas Historical Association Year Book* 9 (1933):103–104.

On the next day, Tucker, while returning downriver for help, encountered a herd of 2,000 cattle at Dagger Bend, about forty miles above Horsehead. The owners, Spiller and Miller, having seen Indians near their camp on the previous night and anticipating an attack, had driven there to wait until they were reenforced on the fifth by the arrival of a Mr. Hoffman of Brown County with seven men and 650 cattle. When Hoffman failed to appear, Spiller and a Mr. Roberts went to Horsehead Crossing to investigate. Discovering in the darkness that night a number of dead cattle scattered about a camp and knowing that Hoffman's party had only one rifle and one shotgun, they assumed that the herd had been captured and started to Fort Stockton for help but became lost and did not arrive there until four days after Tucker's herd had been captured.

As soon as they had reported, Major Z. R. Bliss ordered Captain F. S. Dodge to equip each man of his Company D with 100 rounds of ammunition and twenty-six days' rations, to proceed to Horsehead, and from there try to recapture the stolen herd. If no trail was found, Dodge was to escort the herd of Spiller and Miller for 100 miles up the Pecos. Dodge took one wagon and team and the six available pack mules. After recovering a part of Tucker's herd, Dodge and his black troops returned to the Dagger Bend and from there escorted the Spiller and Miller herd and the Taylor and Charley Vandeveer herd safely up the Pecos to the region of Seven Rivers.[2] Incidentally, while Dodge was protecting 7,000 cattle at Dagger Bend, the mail that left Fort Stockton on July 13 was captured by Indians near Johnson's Station, a site under frequent attack, and the letters and packages torn up. On his return, a short distance from Fort Stockton, Dodge discovered and followed an Indian trail to a ranchería of twenty lodges. The occupants escaped, but black troopers rode into Fort Stockton with Indian bonnets decorating their heads.[3]

Not long afterward, Jack Cureton, the renowned Indian fighter, and his train of ten wagons, while returning from California, found and buried the charred body of Dr. Bartlett. Farther along the road, Cure-

[2] U.S. Department of War, Post Surgeon's Report, Fort Stockton, July 11, 1872, Records of the Adjutant General's Office (AGO), Record Group (RG) 94, National Archives (NA), Washington, D.C.; Joseph Carroll McConnell, *The West Texas Frontier*, 2:296–297.

[3] William H. Leckie, *The Buffalo Soldiers*, p. 102.

ton met eight cowboys who had been with Tucker and Bartlett at the time of the attack.[4] In disregard of the Indian trouble in the vicinity, however, Company J, Twenty-fifth Infantry, on July 25, 1872, left Fort Stockton for Fort Gibson, Indian Territory.[5] During the summer the stage attendants continued to have their problems. On July 31, a stage driver and a corporal escort reported at Fort Stockton that at 2:00 P.M. three days previously, while the men were at dinner and the herd was grazing about 175 yards from the station, 180 to 200 Indians drove off 8 mules belonging to Central Station, 10 or 12 others ran off the herd, and another party of 30 or 40 approached the rear of the station to prevent any attempt to rescue the herd. Simultaneously, a larger group with between 200 and 300 horses and mules leisurely came over the hill from the north and watered the stock about one-half mile from the station, remaining in full view for three or four hours. In addition, Bliss wrote that:

The citizens at the station were poorly supplied with ammunition—there was no herder with the mules at the time they were taken. The Indians remained in the vicinity of the station until the night of the 29th ulto. . . . The Indians wore no clothes and all carried shields. Many of the horses they were driving were American horses—shod and had lariats dragging. . . . A Mexican stage attendant, who had been a captive of Apaches and Lipans, stated that the Indians were Kiowas or Comanches for they all had shields and drove their herd of horses with lariats tied to their horses' necks and with the lariats dragging behind. From all the shooting that was done by the soldier escorts only two horses were killed.[6]

The patrols were gradually becoming more successful in contacting Indians. While Colonel Ranald Mackenzie was preparing at Fort Richardson in the spring of 1872 for a campaign against the Comanches, a detachment of his cavalry from Fort Concho captured a *comanchero* who confessed that he was one of many New Mexicans employed to steal or to acquire from the Comanches Texas cattle. He stated that there was a good wagon road across the Staked Plains with plenty of water. Upon receipt of the report, General C. C. Augur, commander

    [4]J. Marvin Hunter, "Crossed the Desert in 1872," *Frontier Times* 6, no. 5 (February, 1929):180–181.
    [5]U.S. Department of War, Post Returns, Fort Stockton, July, 1872, AGO, RG 94, NA.
    [6]Zenas R. Bliss, Fort Stockton, to AAAG, August 1, 1872, Records of United States Army Commands, RG 98, NA.

of the Department of Texas, ordered Mackenzie, as a part of his campaign, to break up the cattle stealing. With six companies of his tough Fourth Cavalry, one company of the Eleventh Infantry, and twenty Tonkawa scouts, Mackenzie left Fort Richardson on June 19 and on July 1 established his supply camp on the Freshwater Fork of the Brazos (White River), eleven miles southeast of present Crosbyton. There, a few days later he was joined by Lieutenant Colonel William R. Shafter with three companies of the Twenty-fourth Infantry, Mackenzie's former troops, from Fort McKavett.

While Mackenzie's cavalrymen were scouting the eastern edge of the Staked Plains from near present Snyder to near present Clarendon, 200 of the Indians the troops sought on July 9 captured a herd of 1,500 cattle on the Pecos River twenty-three miles above Horsehead Crossing, and four days later another group stampeded a herd of 2,600 head only twelve miles from Fort Concho. Having accumulated his supplies, Mackenzie on July 28, with 200 troopers and 20 Tonkawa scouts, set out from his supply camp in pursuit of the cattle thieves. He trailed the thieves by way of Fort Sumner to Puerta de Luna, on the Pecos, where they had scattered. Foiled in his efforts to catch the thieves, Mackenzie recrossed the plains by way of the Palo Duro Creek to Palo Duro Canyon and then went south to his supply camp.[7] A few days later a small Fourth Cavalry detachment and two Tonkawa scouts skirmished in Jones County with about 50 Comanches, killing one, a Mexican, and capturing eleven horses that had been stolen.[8] After resting his men and horses, Mackenzie with approximately 300 troopers and scouts marched northward and on September 29 surprised a large village of Kwahadi and Kotsoteka Comanches on the North Fork of Red River, seven miles above its junction with McClellan Creek. In the ensuing battle, the troopers, with a loss of 2 killed and 2 wounded, killed 23 counted Comanches (the Comanches later set the number at 52) and destroyed 262 tipis and large stores of supplies. About 130, most of them women and children, were taken captive, and of these 124 were taken to Fort Concho and there held as prisoners. José Carrion, formerly a teamster with the train burned at

[7] Ernest Wallace, *Ranald S. Mackenzie on the Texas Frontier*, pp. 64–74. See also, Ernest Wallace, ed., *Ranald S. Mackenzie's Official Correspondence Relating to Texas, 1871–1873*, pp. 45–141.

[8] "Record of Engagements," p. 104.

Howard's Well, asserted that he recognized forty-three mules that had belonged to his train.[9]

While Mackenzie was campaigning against the Comanches, Captain Edward M. Heyl, with Company K, Fourth Cavalry, and Company I, Eleventh Infantry, was guarding a Texas and Pacific Railroad crew surveying a route toward the Pecos, and Captain Joseph Rendlebrock, with Company G, Fourth Cavalry, was busy escorting large herds of cattle (12,000 in one herd) from Fort Concho to Horsehead Crossing and for some distance up the Pecos. To help support these troop detachments, the commander at Fort Stockton sent supplies and forage to the mouth of Delaware Creek. On September 16, 1872, six wagons left, and on October 3, six more wagons, loaded with rations and forage, departed under the charge of Lieutenant James Pratt, Twenty-fifth Infantry. The wagons had to go 35 miles to Horsehead Crossing and then up the Pecos for 125 miles to the Delaware.[10]

With the garrison at Fort Stockton depleted of supplies, it was no time for any kind of emergency, especially a fire. The only waterworks consisted of a large wagon with a tank on it. Each morning water was hauled in it from the creek and distributed into barrels for drinking and cooking. The animals were watered at the creek. On the evening of November 18, the quarters of Lieutenant Michael Courtney, Twenty-fifth Infantry, were completely destroyed by fire, along with eight hundred dollars of his currency. Two adjacent quarters, one occupied by Captain Dodge and his family and the other by the paymaster, were only eighteen feet from the burning building. The soldiers saved these by placing wet blankets on the roofs. Without the quick thinking and rapid work of the soldiers, all five officers' buildings likely would have gone up in flames.[11]

On October 6, a fight occurred about half a mile south of Camp

[9] Wallace, *Mackenzie on the Texas Frontier*, pp. 74–87; Robert G. Carter, *The Old Sergeant's Story*, pp. 83–85; Rupert N. Richardson, *The Comanche Barrier to South Plains Settlement*, pp. 361–362. See also Wallace, *Mackenzie's Correspondence*, pp. 133–148.

[10] Jno. P. Hatch, Fort Concho, to AAG, Department of Texas (DT), August 2, 1872, and Joseph Rendlebrock to Post Adjutant, Fort Concho, June 23 and August 17, 1872, both in Army Commands, RG 98, NA; U.S. Department of War, Post Returns, Fort Stockton, September and October, 1872; Zenas R. Bliss, Fort Stockton, to AAG, September 16 and October 3, 1872, Army Commands, RG 98, NA.

[11] Bliss to AAG, November 19, 1872, Army Commands, RG 98, NA.

Charlotte when a band of Comanches descended on eight cowboys, who were driving a cattle herd, and their small military escort. When the Indians attacked, the remuda and the soldiers were two miles ahead of the herd. The horses, frightened by the gunfire, stampeded, and the Indians chased them into the hills. The raiders were pursued, however, and during their flight had one killed, two wounded, and three of their ponies killed. They also left behind a quantity of supplies, including some new blankets and haversacks filled with jerked buffalo meat. Apparently the blankets had been issued only a short time before at their agency.[12]

During the early part of 1873 Fort Stockton was occupied by Company D, Ninth Cavalry, and Companies F and K, Twenty-fifth Infantry, all under the command of Major Bliss until March, when Captain F. S. Dodge took command. Captain E. G. Bush, Tenth Infantry, relieved Dodge in September, but the change seems not to have become official until October. Dodge left the post with Troop D, Ninth Cavalry, on November 18, 1873, for Fort McKavett.[13]

In January, 1873, the Ninth Cavalry was scattered over a wide area, from the lower Rio Grande to far West Texas. General Edward Hatch and the headquarters were transferred from Fort Clark to Ringgold Barracks. Companies B, C, H, G, and L were stationed at strategic points to fend against Kickapoo and Lipan raiders from Mexico. The other units were left at Forts Concho, Stockton, Davis, and McKavett to chastise Comanches, Apaches, and Kiowas and to protect the mail and commerce route to El Paso.[14]

In February, Santleben and his family accompanied one of his westbound wagon trains. Soon after leaving Fort Clark, the train was joined by a Dr. Livingston and six men en route to California. At California Springs, Santleben encountered a detachment of troops, accompanied by some scouts, but ignored the suggestion of the commanding officer to hold up until the area ahead had been made safe. The next day at Beaver Lake the troopers again warned Santleben of danger ahead. At some unspecified site on the forty-five-mile stretch between Beaver Lake and Howard's Well, while Dr. Livingston and his

[12] C. C. Rister, *The Southwestern Frontier*, p. 297.
[13] U.S. Department of War, Post Returns, Fort Stockton, 1873–1875.
[14] Leckie, *Buffalo Soldiers*, p. 106; San Antonio *Herald*, January 7, 1873.

party were about a mile in advance, they and the train were attacked by an estimated forty Indians. Two men, Black and Jones, and one mule were killed, and the other mules were stampeded. Afterward, Livingston and his four surviving companions were content to stay close to the wagons. The cavalry, about three miles from the scene at the time, went in pursuit of the Indians but to no avail. Some miles farther, near present Sheffield, the Livingston party again saw Indians, but there was no engagement.[15]

The federal government had long encouraged the locating of railroad routes throughout the country, but in Texas it was the state government that provided the material aid. Both before and after annexation, several schemes were advanced, but the first significant incentive was in 1852 when the legislature provided for the donation of 8 sections (5,120 acres) of public land for each mile of rails constructed. But this was not enough, for only twenty miles, in the vicinity of Houston, were laid. Therefore, in 1854, the legislature raised the grant to 16 alternate sections for each mile of rails, the maximum not to exceed 800 sections. The recipient, in turn, was obligated to complete at least twenty-five miles, to bear the expense of the surveys, to have its line terminus on the Gulf Coast, its bays, or on Buffalo Bayou, and to dispose of these lands within twelve years.

In 1856, the legislature authorized the lending of school funds to the amount of $6,000 per mile of rails laid; and under this provision nearly $2 million was given out on loan to various companies. By 1861 Texas had approximately 468 miles of railroad, but at the end of the Civil War only four lines were intact, and those were in disrepair and the companies were facing bankruptcy. To make matters worse, construction was further hampered when, in 1869, the legislature forbade further land grants to railroads. Nevertheless, in 1872 the Houston and Texas Central Railway Company reached Dallas, which then had a population of no more than 3,000.

Early in 1873, the state constitution was amended to allow the legislature to aid railroad construction by grants of land not to exceed 20 sections per mile of tract. In March, Blocks 8 through 12 were surveyed for the Houston and Great Northern Railroad Company along

[15]August Santleben, *A Texas Pioneer*, pp. 149–151. Santleben wrote inaccurately. For example, he wrote that "General MacKenzie" was at Fort Clark in February, 1873, whereas Mackenzie did not in fact arrive there until April.

the west bank of the Pecos River in present Pecos County. In July, 210 sections were surveyed about twenty miles southwest of Fort Stockton in Block 3, with the Texas and Pacific as grantee. During the next eleven years, most of Pecos County was surveyed by the railroad companies.[16]

It was some years, however, before the rails and smoky engines appeared, and, meanwhile, engagements with the Indians continued with old-fashioned horse or foot power. On April 27, 1873, the mail station at Eagle Springs was successfully defended against an Indian attack by a small detachment of Company B, Twenty-fifth Infantry, from Fort Quitman.[17] Farther east, Jim Adams and five men from Brackett skirmished with Indians near Devils River. In this engagement four Indians and one cowpuncher were killed.[18]

Some Indians, including Tonkawas and Seminoles, served notably as scouts for the soldiers. Many of the "Seminole" scouts were "naturalized" blacks or half-blacks. "These Negroes," wrote Major Bliss, "were former slaves of the Seminole Indians, having been held as slaves by the Indians subsequent to their removal to Indian Territory. They had all of the habits of the Indians, were excellent hunters and trailers, and splendid fighters."[19]

In May, 1873, about twenty of those intrepid Muscogee Seminoles under John L. Bullis accompanied Colonel Mackenzie on a raid on a Kickapoo and Lipan village whose warriors had been depredating in Texas. The Kickapoos, who in 1865 had been unjustly attacked while migrating to Mexico by the Texans, once settled near Santa Rosa, Mexico, had struck back with savage fury. By 1870, aided by their Apache neighbors in Mexico, they reportedly had almost wiped out the livestock industry in the area between Del Rio and Laredo on the Rio Grande and Bandera and Bexar County on the north and had killed and wounded more than a hundred Texans. Two years later, a fact-

[16]Walter P. Webb and H. B. Carroll, eds., *The Handbook of Texas*, 1:852, 2:430; Eldon Stephen Branda, ed., *The Handbook of Texas: A Supplement*, 3:771–772; H. P. N. Gammel, ed., *The Laws of Texas, 1822–1897*, 3:1455–1459; Rupert N. Richardson, *Texas: The Lone Star State*, p. 350; Pecos County, Texas, Survey Records, A7:23–207, C2:47–238, C3:1–212, C4:1–64.

[17]Heitman, *Historical Register*, 2:438.

[18]D. C. McMeans, "The Battle of Devil's River," *Frontier Times* 7, no. 3 (December, 1929):109–111.

[19]Zenas R. Bliss, "Reminiscences," 5:105, Eugene C. Barker Texas History Center, University of Texas, Austin.

finding commission reported that the region had only one-tenth as many livestock as in 1865 and that alleged losses totaled more than $48 million.[20]

Since the young and daring Colonel Mackenzie and his tough Fourth Cavalry had convinced the Comanches and Kiowas that peace was preferable to raiding in Texas (primarily because of the imprisonment of the two Kiowa chiefs and the Comanche captives at San Angelo), President U. S. Grant, the war department, and Generals Sherman and Sheridan decided early in February, 1873, to put an end to the "unchecked and chronic spoilation of our population on the Mexican border."[21]

To carry out the task, which would obviously entail a dangerous and only questionably legal crossing of the international border, they moved Mackenzie, who had previously established his headquarters at Fort Concho, and most of his regiment to Fort Clark, because, Sherman explained, it was a more efficient scouting unit than the Ninth Cavalry. After getting oral orders to do whatever was necessary to clean up the situation, Mackenzie made thorough preparation for a raid on the Kickapoo and Apache villages near Remolino, Mexico, sixty miles south of the Rio Grande. Just as darkness settled around the command on the evening of May 17, Mackenzie at the head of a total of 515 enlisted men, officers, scouts, and citizens scrambled up the south bank of the Rio Grande onto foreign soil. All the long night, along mule and cattle trails that wound through dense chaparral, across rocky ravines, and over dusty, barren stretches, the command rode under a dim moonlight. At 6:00 A.M., on May 18, from the top of a slope, the men saw a Lipan and two Kickapoo villages no more than a mile away.

When the cavalry charge hit the villages, the surprised Indians—the warriors had left the day before—scattered panic-stricken. The destruction was complete. The lodges were all burned, at least nineteen Indians were killed, forty women and children and a Lipan chief were captured, and sixty-five horses, some wearing Texas brands, were taken. Mackenzie suffered one trooper killed, two others slightly wounded, and four horses killed. After a short rest the command headed for Texas, and, as the gray dawn of morning appeared on the nineteenth,

[20] Wallace, *Mackenzie on the Texas Frontier*, pp. 92–95.
[21] *Galveston Daily News*, December 15, 1872.

the exhausted blue-coated raiders forded the Rio Grande, just in time to avoid a Mexican cavalry unit that was in hot pursuit. The mission had been a daring display of bravery and a remarkable feat of endurance. Without sleep and with only hard bread for nourishment, the command had traveled more than 140 miles in thirty-eight hours, and the men of two companies had ridden 160 miles in forty-nine hours without removing the saddles from their horses.

As a result of the raid and the negotiations by United States commissioners, many of the Kickapoos returned to Indian Territory (Oklahoma). Mackenzie then had his troops patrol the Rio Grande, deployed other detachments to strategic points to prevent further depredations, and on several occasions sent his cavalrymen across the border when on a hot trail of the depredators. These tactics he continued until July, 1874, when he was sent with his Fourth Cavalry to participate in the Red River War. He had not permanently eliminated the depredations, but for the next two years the reports consistently stated that "affairs were quiet" in the region between Laredo, Del Rio, and San Antonio.[22]

Mackenzie's success, however, did not alleviate the Indian problem in the Trans-Pecos area. In fact, some of the Indians from Mexico apparently shifted their operations to that area, and the Mescaleros of New Mexico capitalized on the military emphasis in the Laredo–Del Rio area to step up their raids along and west of the lower Pecos.

In May, 1873, a small Mescalero party swept around the northeast rim of the Davis Mountains and made a pass at the small settlement of Toyah and another one at Varela Stage Station. Troop detachments from Fort Davis were unable to find the Indians' trail.[23] In defense of the Indians, especially in this instance the Mescaleros, it should be remembered that the Indians saw nothing illegal or immoral about taking and destroying the property of the white men; to them it was a war for survival.

In July, 1873, in the midst of the Indian raids, a "messy" situation developed at Fort Stockton between the authorities and the black soldiers. The post was garrisoned by Company D, Ninth Cavalry, and

[22] "Record of Engagements," pp. 104–105; J. Evetts Haley, *Fort Concho and the Texas Frontier*, pp. 209–210; Wallace, *Mackenzie on the Texas Frontier*, pp. 92, 95–111.
[23] U.S. Department of War, Post Surgeon's Report, Fort Davis, May, 1873.

Companies G and K, Twenty-fifth Infantry. In general, the soldiers' conduct had been good, and there had been no unusual number court-martialed.[24] Trouble began on July 14, when Captain Dodge received a complaint, "signed by a majority of the enlisted men [all black] of the command," against the post surgeon, J. A. Cleary, relative to his treatment of Private John Taylor, Company K, Twenty-fifth Infantry, who had died on July 10.[25] After giving some unsubstantiated details pertaining to the death of Taylor and commenting on remarks attributed to Cleary, the communication asserted that "we believed the deceased came to his death from intentional neglect on the part of the post surgeon, U.S.A., who from malicious feelings of a personal nature refused to give or allow him proper treatment from the 30th of April until the 7th of July, 1873."[26] The signatures were in "round robin" (in a circle around the document, thus making it impossible to determine the leaders or who signed first). When no action was taken against the doctor, a large number of the black soldiers became rebellious and were brought before a general court-martial at Fort Stockton on August 26, presided over by Major Bliss from Fort Davis.[27] Years later in an account of the affair, Bliss wrote that sixty-two, including some noncommissioned officers who had been put in the guardhouse, were arraigned on the same charge and all tried at the same time. Bliss held the court on the back porch of his old quarters, then vacant, and the prisoners sat in the backyard.

According to Bliss, the trouble started in April, when Taylor reported to Dr. Cleary that he was sick. Cleary gave him some medicine but did not regard him sufficiently ill to be excused from duty. His comrades, however, believed that he was ill and for some time did his chores without the captain's knowledge. The second time he reported sick, he was not excused, and, when he reported a third time, he was

[24] U.S. Department of War, Post Returns, Fort Stockton, July, 1873; Francis S. Dodge to A.A.G., July 3, 1873, Army Commands, RG 98, NA.

[25] Apparently this was Peter Joseph Augustine Cleary, a native of Malta who was living in New York at the time of his enlistment in the Union Army during the Civil War (Heitman, *Historical Register*, 1:309).

[26] Dodge to AAG, July 14, 1873, Army Commands, RG 98, NA. Since most of the troops were former slaves and illiterate, the letter may have been written by a white person.

[27] Bliss to A.A.G., July 18, 1873, Army Commands, RG 98, NA; Bliss, "Reminiscences," 5:205–209; San Antonio *Herald*, August 17, 1873.

placed in the guardhouse overnight for "malingering" and the next morning was sent to work. About 10:00 A.M. he became very ill and was taken to the hospital. Dr. Cleary sent for a Dr. Buffington, who by chance was passing through Stockton on his way to an assignment. Buffington likewise was unable to determine any cause for the illness, but in a few minutes Taylor was dead.

The explanation given for the death is a highly interesting revelation of the scientific ignorance of the medical profession and the superstitious nature of the illiterate blacks. Cleary and Buffington, Bliss continued:

made an autopsy, but found nothing to produce death. His spleen was slightly enlarged, but all his other organs were in a normal condition. There was no way to account for his death, except that he had been hoodooed, and it so preyed upon him, that he died from fright or from a sort of homesickness, and Dr. Cleary so reported.

These men were easily frightened by the idea of being hoodooed, and it made them sick, and perhaps this man died from that cause. The men thought the doctor had given him some dose to make him sick and had killed him. . . .[28]

The black troopers at the garrison became very excited, and had it not been for the capable handling of the situation by Captain Dodge might have mutinied. Prior to the letter of protest, fatigue groups talked loudly and boldly, when the wives of officers could overhear, about hanging Dr. Cleary, taking the lives of the officers, and taking command of the post. All those implicated in the affair were found guilty and received sentences ranging from five to fifteen years in the penitentiary.[29] The present revisionist historians likely would stress the injustice of the sentences, but it should be recalled that punishment then, even for minor violations, was severe.

Meanwhile, the Indians continued to depredate. A detachment of Company L, Fourth Cavalry, had an encounter with Indians on Lipan Creek, not far from Fort Concho, on July 14.[30] In this area, which was particularly hard-hit during July, Indians took fifty-five horses from Dick Robertson, forty-two from John Chisum, and every mule that G. W. DeLong owned. A short distance eastward, on Brady Creek,

[28] Bliss, "Reminiscences," 5:205–209.
[29] Ibid.
[30] Heitman, *Historical Register*, 2:439.

more than a hundred horses were stolen. But the Indians' take was nil in an attack on an emigrants' train at Lipan Spring, in southeastern Tom Green County.[31]

Several men, including two employees of James Trainer, while en route from New Mexico to Fort Concho, encountered about thirty Apaches from Fort Stanton, who carried forty-day permits to hunt on the plains. It was later suspected—but never proved—that it was these reservation Indians who on July 31 made a raid near the Pecos Mail Station at Camp Melvin. In that raid Juan Chabarilla, a herder, was killed, and two horses and twelve mules belonging to the stage company were driven off.[32]

About the same time, several drovers of cattle herds headed for the Pecos country were victims of Indian raiders. While delivering a herd of cattle to John Chisum in New Mexico, John Hittson, Sam Gholston, and Joe Franks were attacked on the Concho River, near the present town of Paint Rock. Their outfits, consisting of 75 to 100 men, were scattered up and down the river about half a mile apart. Near nightfall, Indians raided Gholston's crew, wounding one man and getting away with sixty horses. The engagement took place in plain view of the Franks outfit and was witnessed by J. B. Gillett. Two nights later, Franks's crew was attacked, but the horses were well guarded and none was lost.[33] William Keith from Menard County, was en route to New Mexico with 6,000 cattle when attacked by Indians near Horseshoe Bend on the Pecos. Keith was critically wounded, and his leg had to be amputated. He died a short time later, on August 3, 1873.[34] Only a short distance upstream, the Indians captured an entire herd driven by Mr. and Mrs. Joe Hay, George Gammel, Moody Doffman, and several others. During the exchange of shots, Mrs. Hay was wounded in

[31] *Galveston News*, July 19, 1873. Place names often cause problems. Even in official documents, the same place may have multiple names or the spelling may vary, such as Well or Wells and Spring or Springs. Nearly every "spring" (singular) mentioned thus far in this work appears on some document in plural form. Lipan, Eagle, Kickapoo, San Pedro are examples. The site near Guadalupe Peak today is always Pine Spring (singular), but it was not so in the past.

[32] Dodge to AAG, September 1, 1873, Army Commands, RG 98, NA.

[33] James B. Gillett, *Six Years with the Texas Rangers, 1875 to 1881*, p. 10. "Hitsons" was the name given by Gillett, but obviously he meant John Hittson, a well-known cattleman, who was associated with John Chisum.

[34] McConnell, *West Texas Frontier*, 2:309–310.

the leg, but she and all those in her party escaped by slipping into a ravine.[35]

Although Fort Stockton had been occupied by soldiers since 1867 and considerable money had been spent on the post's construction, the army had taken no steps to lease or purchase the land and buildings. In the summer of 1873, the owner, Peter Gallagher, insisted on some kind of settlement. Consequently, on September 17 Gallagher signed with Lieutenant Colonel S. B. Holabird, the quartermaster general, a one-year lease for an annual rental of $600 for 896 acres of Survey 204 and 80 acres in the north half of Survey 151. For an extra $200 the lease included the 25-acre garden, three or four miles northeast of Fort Stockton, and permitted the army to use water from Comanche Springs.[36]

Simultaneously, the new village of Ben Ficklin (or Benficklin), on the Concho and four miles from Fort Concho, had its beginning. The new settlement and the surrounding area were described in glowing terms by "H. C." in a letter published in the San Antonio *Herald*:

Some fine farm lands on the Concho River, which would be settled up if it were not for the Indians. . . . Mr. F. C. Taylor's Bismarck farm, a beautiful and desirable property, has a number of tenants. Mr. Taylor is building a town in a mile of the stage station, and calls it Ben Ficklin. It already has a neat store, a fine blacksmith and wood shop and buildings for families of mechanics. Henry Taylor, nephew to the old stager, is the postmaster.

The mail station is a beautiful little village itself, containing some twelve or fifteen buildings for animals and good stage shelter. . . . Notwithstanding the heavy and large rock walls enclosing the animals and buildings, a guard is on every night at nine o'clock for safety. . . . I suppose there are about 125 to 150 people at this place.[37]

For a time, it appeared that Taylor's new village would overshadow the civilian settlement adjacent to Fort Concho. The latter, which started as a trading post known as Over-the-River, saw its name changed to Santa Angela, Saint Angela, San Angela, and eventually to San Angelo because someone did not think that the combination of the masculine "San" and the feminine "Angela" was appropriate. For several

---

[35] Ibid., p. 310.

[36] "Lease of Fort Stockton, Tex.," July 1, 1873 (signed by Peter Gallagher on September 17, 1873), in U.S. Department of War, Records of the Quartermaster General (Consolidated File), RG 92, NA.

[37] San Antonio *Herald*, September 17, 1873.

years Ben Ficklin was the most important settlement in Tom Green
County and might have remained so had not a flood in 1882 washed it
away.[38]

The Indians, meanwhile, continued to raid. On September 16,
some ranchmen reported seeing red riders near Leon Holes, seven
miles west of Fort Stockton. Possibly this was the occasion when Indians shot an arrow through a greased-paper window of the Frazer half-
dugout building and wounded a Mexican woman.[39] Lieutenant John
Conline and fifteen men of the Ninth Cavalry from Fort Stockton found
the trail but were unable to catch the Indians. Soon afterward Captain
E. G. Bush, the post commander at Fort Stockton, wrote that G. M.
Frazer, a ranchman, while scouting for cattle had seen several trails of
Indians, some parties as large as twenty-five, leading toward the Pecos.

They are supposed to be Mescalero Apaches from the reservation at Fort
Stanton, N.M., which they are said to have left recently and from Presidio del
Norte, Mexico. The general direction of their trails is from Varela Spring to the
Pecos, about 35 miles north of this post, and they are either en route to kill
buffalo or to depredate in the settlements. They did no damage in this vicinity.
Mr. [M. F.] Corbett, post trader, will soon return from Presidio del Norte, and
from him I expect to ascertain if these Indians came from Mexico, or if these
are Indians on this side of the Rio Grande. . . .[40]

Although Bush did not always know the identity of the Indians or
where they came from, the patrols that fall became more effective. On
October 1, an attack on the Centralia Stage Station by fifteen Indians
was repulsed by Sergeant Benjamin Mew and a small detachment of
Company K, Twenty-fifth Infantry, from Fort Stockton. Reinforced by
the arrival of an estimated forty comrades, the Indians renewed the
attack, but again they were driven off. A few months earlier, Mew had
been brought before a court-martial on charges of trying to poison a
comrade. Because the evidence given by Martha Mew, the sergeant's
wife, and a Corporal Lee, was circumstantial and unconvincing, Mew
was acquitted but sent to chase Indians.[41] On the same day that Sergeant
Mew and his men repulsed Indians at Centralia, Troop C, Eighth Cav-

[38] Webb and Carroll, *Handbook of Texas*, 1:145, and 2:539.
[39] Descendants of G. M. Frazer, Fort Stockton, to Clayton Williams, oral statements made on various occasions.
[40] E. G. Bush to AAG, October 2, 1873, Army Commands, RG 98, NA.
[41] *Army and Navy Journal* 10 (June 7, 1873):681.

alry, killed three Indians and wounded one in the Guadalupe Mountains, and on December 31 a detachment of four men of Company B, Twenty-fifth Infantry, from Fort Quitman repulsed an attack on the stage stand at Eagle Springs, wounding one Indian during the brief skirmish.[42]

The worst defeat suffered by Indians during this period took place near the headwaters of the Nueces River, in Edwards County. There, a party of twenty-one Comanches and nine Kiowas hid their spare horses, hobbled and unguarded, and rode into Mexico, where they killed fourteen Mexicans, rounded up 150 horses and mules, and ravaged the country through which they passed. While returning along the Laredo–San Antonio road on December 6, they killed two Americans. Two Mexican prisoners, however, escaped and alerted Lieutenant Charles L. Hudson, who with forty-one men of the Fourth Cavalry was scouting in the area. The next day, Hudson located and confiscated the horses that had been left near Kickapoo Springs. He planned to wait in ambush but, learning of the Indians' movements, surprised them on December 9. After about ten minutes' hot fire, the Indians broke and ran, leaving behind eighty-one of their animals and nine dead comrades. Hudson had one trooper slightly wounded. On their way to the agency, the Indians suffered another loss of eleven warriors and sixty-five horses at the hands of Lieutenant Colonel George P. Buell near Double Mountain. Among the Indians killed were Chief Lone Wolf's favorite son and his nephew.[43] Ironically, although Lone Wolf did not know it, Lieutenant Hudson, who had shot his son, was also dead, having been shot accidentally in his quarters at Fort Clark by his roommate.[44]

When the weather warmed and the grass greened, Lone Wolf organized a party and went to Texas to locate and bring home the bodies of his son and nephew. Fearful that Lone Wolf might also seek revenge, Captain Eugene B. Beaumont with seventy men of Company A, Fourth Cavalry, went from Fort McKavett to the burial site, but the bodies

[42] Heitman, *Historical Register*, 2:439; *Galveston News*, October 21, 1873; "Record of Engagements," p. 105.

[43] Wallace, *Mackenzie on the Texas Frontier*, pp. 118–119; Haley, *Fort Concho*, pp. 184–193; Leckie, *Buffalo Soldiers*, pp. 79–80; U.S. Department of War, Post Surgeon's Report, Fort Clark, December 10, 1873; "Record of Engagements," p. 106, W. S. Nye, *Carbine and Lance*, p. 183.

[44] *Galveston Daily News*, January 4, 1874.

had been removed. When it appeared that the cavalrymen might overtake him, Lone Wolf left the remains of his son and nephew on a mountainside. Beaumont followed Lone Wolf's trail for 240 miles, finding water only twice, to Johnston's Station, twenty-eight miles above Fort Concho, where the fleeing Kiowa party had killed a Ninth Cavalry trooper and captured twenty-two horses. Fully aware that on his jaded horses he could never overtake his quarry, now on fresh mounts, Beaumont gave up the chase.[45]

By the end of 1873, the Fort Stockton buildings consisted of seven officers' quarters, adjutant and quartermaster's office, hospital, guardhouse, magazine, bakery, storehouse with a capacity for quartermaster and subsistence stores for 200 men for six months, a workshop, and a stable for 100 horses. The guardhouse and magazine were built of stone. Supplies and quartermaster and subsistence stores were sent in wagons from San Antonio. Other supplies came from Saint Louis, Missouri, via Denison, Texas. Salt, furnished by contract, was obtained from a salt lake thirty-five miles from the post. Subsistence to last from three to six months was kept on hand. At this time, the nearest telegraph line was at San Antonio.[46] The post was garrisoned by Company B, Tenth Infantry, Companies F and K, Twenty-fifth Infantry, and Company M, Ninth Cavalry. Detachments performed guard duty for the stage stations at Escondido, Centralia, and Melvin, escorted herds of cattle, and made scouting patrols.[47]

Discipline at frontier posts was usually severe. Early in 1874, Captain Bush, at Fort Stockton, recommended a remission of a portion of the punishment assessed one of his troopers. Blacksmith Henry Harrison, Company D, Ninth Cavalry, had been sentenced to be dishonorably discharged from the service and then confined at hard labor at Fort Stockton for eight months, wearing a twenty-four-pound ball attached to his left leg by a chain four feet long. Bush recommended that "in consideration of his good conduct, so much of the unexecuted portion of his sentence as related to the wearing of the ball and chain may be remitted."[48]

[45] Nye, *Carbine and Lance*, pp. 182–184, 188–189; Dorman H. Winfrey and James M. Day, eds., *The Indian Papers of Texas and the Southwest, 1825–1916*, 4:386–387; Wallace, *Mackenzie on the Texas Frontier*, pp. 119–120.

[46] Bush to AAG, December 4, 1873, Army Commands, RG 98, NA.

[47] Bush to AAG, December 31, 1873, Army Commands, RG 98, NA.

[48] Bush to AAG, January 20, 1874, Army Commands, RG 98, NA.

In March, 1874, Tom Green County was created out of Bexar County. Covering an area of 12,500 square miles, it extended westward to the Pecos River, and, even after twelve other counties have been carved from it, it still has an area of 1,503 square miles. Ben Ficklin became the first county seat, and after it washed away in 1882 the county government was moved to the present seat, San Angelo. The county was named in honor of Thomas Green, who came to Texas in December, 1835, and served as a private during the Battle of San Jacinto, where he helped man one of the Twin Sisters, the only artillery possessed by the Texans. Green was also the captain of the Travis Company Volunteers at the time of the Rafael Vásquez invasion in 1842, inspector general of the Somervell Expedition of 1842, a captain with John Coffee Hays's Rangers in the Mexican War, a colonel with Sibley's New Mexico Expedition during the Civil War, and a brigadier general later in that war. He participated in the recapture of Galveston and in the defeat of the Banks Red River Expedition, during which he was killed while trying to capture a federal ship on Red River on April 12, 1864.[49]

During the same month that Tom Green County came into existence, Indians struck again at Howard's Well. W. C. Johnson with a party of eight men and a number of pack mules left Fort Clark in March for Colorado. While encamped at Howard's Well, Johnson wrote in a letter to a friend: "We were attacked by a large party of Indians, who killed all our animals, wounded myself, and killed two of our party, one named Andy Parks, and the other named Henry Roben. . . . We had to eas [eat] mules until we reached Fort Davis. We are all now poor as a church mouse, and will have to walk from here to Santa Fe."[50]

In April, 1874, several men who were or had been post traders at Fort Stockton received army contracts. M. F. Corbett and Joseph Friedlander got the contract to supply hay, wood, and coal to most of the forts in the area. Friedlander also contracted to supply Forts Davis, Clark, Concho, and Duncan with flour, corn, meal, beans, soap, beef (part on hoof), vinegar, salt, candles, and bacon. Corbett, one of the lowest bidders, contracted to supply Fort Stockton beef (on hoof) at 4¢, mutton (on hoof) at 6¢, mutton (block) at 10¢, and salt at 4¢, each item per pound. G. M. Frazer agreed to furnish beef (block) at 6¢ per

---

[49] Webb and Carroll, *Handbook of Texas*, 1:727–728, and 2:787.

[50] W. C. Johnson, Fort Davis, letter, in *Denison Daily News*, April 14, 1874.

pound; Thomas Johnson, candles at 35¢; J. Landa, bacon at 18¢; H. Lesinsky, flour at 6½¢; and Friedlander, beans at 4½¢.[51] Surprisingly, candles were much more expensive, per pound, than any food item, and, considering the long and hazardous roads, prices were cheap at a frontier post.

Plenty of supplies were needed, because the Indians were still raiding in the area. On June 2, a group of Mexicans, headed by Cesario Torres of Fort Stockton, was attacked by about fifteen Indians near the mail station at Camp Melvin. The raiders shot Torres in the arm and drove off about thirty-five horses and mules. On the following day, Captain Bush sent a detachment of troops after the raiders, but apparently to no avail.[52]

A few days later, in the vicinity of old Fort Hudson, Herman (or Ramon) Hernandez, a resident of San Antonio in charge of an Adams and Wickes forage train bound for Fort Stockton, spotted ten Indians driving a herd of cattle toward the Rio Grande. Knowing that the drovers were not the rightful owners, the Adams and Wickes wagon master left six of his men to guard the corralled train and with seven others went after the cattle thieves. In a short time, he captured the herd of 160 cattle and thirteen days later delivered it to Fort Stockton, where G. M. Frazer took charge of the cattle until the owners were located.[53]

In June, 1874, the Southern Plains Indians opened a full-scale war on the whites, known as the Red River War. After the imprisonment of Chiefs Satanta and Big Tree for the Salt Prairie massacre in 1871 and the taking of Indian captives in September, 1872, in the Battle of the North Fork of the Red River, the Kiowas and Comanches remained peacefully camped on their reservation. They knew well that only by remaining at peace could they hope for the release of their people. Mistakenly convinced that the two tribes intended to remain peaceful, the Indian Bureau ordered the release of the prisoners. The Comanches were returned to Fort Sill in June, 1873, and the two Kiowa chiefs in October. Immediately, the warriors renewed their destructive raids

[51] San Antonio *Daily Herald*, April 23, 24, and 27, 1874.

[52] Bush to AAG, two letters, July 2, 1874, Army Commands, RG 98, NA.

[53] Bush to AAG, June 23, 1874, Army Commands, RG 98, NA; San Antonio *Herald*, June 29, 1874; *Denison Daily News*, June 21, 1874. Bush gave Herman as Hernandez's first name, but it is Ramon in the *Herald*'s account.

into Texas and Mexico, including the one that culminated in the battle with Lieutenant Hudson. The Indians in general, however, waited for warm weather to begin major warfare.

The situation at the agency in the spring of 1874 was unusually bad. Heavy rains interfered with freight service, and rations were in short supply or, at times, not available, and the Indians had to resort to killing their own horses and cattle for food, as well as cattle belonging to neighboring whites. Suddenly the more thoughtful Indians became aware that the buffalo were fast becoming extinct and that, as a result, their way of life (culture, traditions—everything) would vanish. In their despondency, a young and yet untried Comanche medicine man, named Isa-tai ("Coyote Droppings") renewed for a time their hopes. Isa-tai told his people that the Comanches could remain strong only if they killed all the whites, and he convinced them that he had enough power to provide the necessary cartridges and to lead them to victory.[54]

The target selected by the Indians was a buffalo hunters' camp known as Adobe Walls, in the Texas Panhandle. The camp, established in the spring of 1874, was actually a budding town, located about a mile from the ruins of the Adobe Walls where Kit Carson had battled the Comanches and Kiowas ten years earlier. At the time of the attack, on the early morning of June 27, twenty-eight men and one woman were present. The Comanches, some Cheyennes, and perhaps a very few Kiowas, all together numbering 200 to 250, were led by Quanah, the son of the famous captive Cynthia Ann Parker, and Isa-tai, the new Comanche prophet. Isa-tai claimed that his power would make the warriors impervious to the white men's bullets. When the battle ceased that afternoon, the raiders had killed only three whites, but they themselves had nine dead (whom the whites could count), possibly more, and a number wounded—a crushing spiritual defeat for the Comanches. The warriors lingered around Adobe Walls for several days but did not dare attack it again, and in time a detachment of troops rescued the buffalo hunters.[55]

---

[54] Richardson, *Comanche Barrier*, pp. 375–379; Wallace, *Mackenzie on the Texas Frontier*, pp. 115–120.

[55] Richardson, *Comanche Barrier*, pp. 379–381; Nye, *Carbine and Lance*, pp. 190–191; Webb and Carroll, *Handbook of Texas*, 1:9; G. Derek West, "The Battle of Adobe Walls," *Panhandle-Plains Historical Review* 36 (1963):1–36.

Although their initial attack on the whites had failed, the Southern Plains Indians were not dismayed; they opened a full-scale war over a wide area all along the frontier from Colorado to South Texas. This time, however, both the state and federal governments immediately took major steps to settle the Comanche and Kiowa problem. The Texas legislature, convinced that it could not rely on the army for protection, already had appropriated $300,000 to establish a Frontier Battalion, to consist of six companies with seventy-five Rangers each. By early July, all the companies were stationed at intervals between the main fork of the Brazos River and the Nueces River, and during their first six months of operations nearly every company had encounters with Indians.[56] Also in July the Indian Bureau turned the Comanches and Kiowas over to the war department, which in turn authorized a major campaign that would drive hostiles to and restrain them on their reservation.

[56] Webb and Carroll, *Handbook of Texas*, 1:651; Gillett, *Six Years with the Texas Rangers*, pp. 32–33.

CHAPTER 13

July, 1874, to January, 1876

$\mathbf{T}$HE battle of Adobe Walls in June, 1874, resulted in the termination of the Quaker Peace Policy on the southern plains. The interior department transferred control of the Comanches, Kiowas, Cheyennes, and Arapahoes to the war department, and on July 20, 1874, General William T. Sherman advised General P. H. Sheridan, commander of the Division of the Missouri, which included the Department of Texas, that the Secretary of War had ordered the punishment of guilty Indians "wherever found . . . the Reservation lines should be no barrier."[1] Sheridan immediately directed General John Pope, commander of the Department of Missouri and General C. C. Augur, commander of the Department of Texas, to have five columns of troops converge from as many directions on the headwaters of the Red and Brazos rivers in western Oklahoma and along the eastern edge of the Llano Estacado of Texas, where by September more than half of the Comanches and Kiowas were camped. Pope ordered Colonel Nelson A. Miles to move southward from Fort Dodge, Kansas, with twelve companies and Major William R. Price to move eastward from Fort Union, New Mexico, with four companies of cavalry until he joined Miles. Augur directed Lieutenant Colonel John W. Davidson to operate westward from Fort Sill with nine companies between the Red and Canadian rivers, Lieutenant Colonel George P. Buell with eight companies from Fort Griffin, near present Albany, to scout the area along the Red River headwaters, and Ranald S. Mackenzie with eight companies of his Fourth Cavalry and five of infantry to establish his base on the Freshwater Fork of the Brazos, near present Crosbyton, and scout his old familiar haunts along

---

[1]William T. Sherman to P. H. Sheridan, July 20, 1874, in Joe F. Taylor, ed., *The Indian Campaign on the Staked Plains, 1874–1875* (compilation of military records contained in Records of the Adjutant General's Office [AGO] 2815, Record Group [RG] 94, National Archives [NA], Washington, D.C.), pp. 11–12.

the eastern edge of the Llano Estacado, overlapping the other commands in the area of Palo Duro Canyon. Altogether forty-six companies, about 3,000 troops, were sent into the fields against the hostile
Indians.[2]

The campaign got underway in mid-August. The Indians, after retreating southwestward in front of Davidson and losing fights with
Miles and Price, took refuge in the Tule and Palo Duro canyons and
the nearby rough country. In a daring maneuver on September 28,
Mackenzie led his cavalry down a narrow zigzag path along the wall of
Palo Duro Canyon and destroyed five villages, an estimated 200 tipis,
of Kiowas, Comanches, and Cheyennes, where their principal medicine man had assured them they could never be found by the blue-
coats. The cavalrymen destroyed all their supplies, and captured 1,424
horses and mules, of which 1,048 were killed to make certain that the
Indians did not stampede and recover them. In mid-October, Buell
destroyed two encampments on the North Fork of Red River, a few
miles east of Palo Duro Canyon. From the Canadian River almost to
present Snyder the troops scouted every valley and watering place until Christmas, but the Red River War was over. Faced with an extremely harsh winter, without lodges, provisions, or robes, without
horses to renew their supply, and no longer able to find safety from the
blue-coated troopers, the Indians, band after band, straggled to their
reservation and surrendered. Quanah Parker, the last major holdout,
reached Fort Sill on June 2, 1875.[3]

By midsummer, only a few small parties were still at large, and
others occasionally stole away and stayed out for short periods, but,
according to R. N. Richardson: "These Indians never again participated in an outbreak. . . . The buffalo hunters were making the plains
dangerous for them . . . and if the braves followed their old trails to
Texas, the rangers were sure to pounce upon them."[4]

The Texas Rangers (the newly formed Frontier Battalion) were in
the field in 1874 before the army. On July 11, in a tough fight at the
mouth of the Concho River and near Rich Coffey's ranch, Major John

[2] Ernest Wallace, *Ranald S. Mackenzie on the Texas Frontier*, pp. 124–125.
[3] Ibid., pp. 125–170.
[4] Rupert N. Richardson, *The Comanche Barrier to South Plains Settlement*, pp.
381–395.

B. Jones and his men routed a band of Indians and captured 150 stolen horses.[5] In August, 1875, the Rangers encountered the Indians in the region of the present town of Big Lake. When within one hundred steps of the warriors, they were ordered to dismount, advance on foot, shoot low, and kill as many horses as possible. The first volley killed two horses, wounded one of the braves, and caused the Indians to flee in every direction. Ranger James B. Gillett, seeing a rider pull an old warrior with a Winchester up behind him, started in pursuit, firing with his Sharps carbine. As he drew closer, the brave dropped his Winchester and started using his bow and arrows. As their horse turned into a grove of mesquite trees, Gillett jumped from his mount, fired, and killed the horse. The older warrior hit the ground running. Gillett went in pursuit, but he also noticed that the other "Indian," who was struggling to get out from under his dead pony, was a white youth with long, red hair.

Gillett and Ed Sieker (who later became involved in outlaw troubles at Fort Stockton) killed the older warrior, but the white boy escaped. When the fighting was over, the Rangers had wounded two other Indians and captured fifty-eight horses and a Mexican boy about fifteen years old, who stated that the Indians were Lipans from Mexico.

Many years later, Gillett attended a pioneer reunion, where he met and visited with Herman Lehmann, who talked about his eight years with the Indians. During the exchange of tales of their experiences, Lehmann described in considerable detail a time when his horse had been shot from under him. He was the red-headed white "Indian" who had escaped from Gillett. Thus, after more than fifty years, the former Ranger and the former "white Indian" had again met. This time, they shook hands.

Herman Lehmann was almost eleven years old, had never been to school, and spoke only German when he and his younger brother, Willie, were captured by Apaches near Loyal Valley, Mason County, Texas. Willie managed to escape nine days later, but Herman grew into a roaming Indian. When he was about sixteen, his adopted Apache father was killed by a medicine man who then threatened Herman. To save his own life, Herman killed the medicine man, took his gun,

[5] San Antonio *Herald*, August 18, 1874.

gathered his bow and arrows, a blanket, and some provisions, and took off on the best horse in the herd. Thereafter, he spent many months alone on the plains of West Texas, living off game, tunas (the fruit of the prickly pear), sotol, and other vegetation.

After about a year of this solitude, he encountered and joined a party of Comanches. While with the Comanches, he went on raids and sometimes participated in battles against whites and their Tonkawa scouts. He was with the last remnant of Kwahadi Comanches who surrendered at Fort Sill. He was adopted by Quanah Parker and in 1878 returned to his family. He never completely readjusted and often embarrassed his family with his Indian ways. More than once, his brother Willie had to persuade him not to steal horses from the neighbors. Eventually, however, he worked as a trail driver, married twice, and fathered two sons and three daughters. Since he had been enrolled as a Comanche, he received an allotment of land in Oklahoma, and in late life he became a celebrity in the Texas hill country. He died in February, 1932, and was buried in Loyal Valley.[6]

Although the Comanches and Kiowas had been forcibly confined to a reservation, bands of other tribes made life and property insecure in southwestern Texas. From the west, the Mescalero Apaches continued to depredate and then rush back to their reservation, usually without the agent's having detected their absence. After Mackenzie was sent to North Texas in 1874, the Kickapoos and Lipan Apaches from Mexico resumed their lucrative practice of driving thousands of Texas livestock across the Rio Grande to a ready market. In July, 1874, within a mile of the customhouse at Presidio del Norte, Mescalero Indians stole twelve or fifteen animals and captured two children. Because the elder child was unable to travel on foot as fast as the mounted Indians desired, his captors killed him. Soon after, unidentified Indians raided a ranch run by a Mr. Smith, killed Smith, and burned his house. About the same time, Indians stole twelve of Milton Faver's finest oxen but failed to get his cows, because they were unable to uproot the pickets of the enclosure.[7]

[6] James B. Gillett, *Six Years with the Texas Rangers, 1875 to 1881*, pp. 38–44; Eldon Stephen Branda, ed., *The Handbook of Texas: A Supplement*, 3:517; Boyce House, *Cowtown Columnist*, pp. 65–66.

[7] *San Antonio Express*, July 20, 1874.

John Chisum's ranch on the Pecos River in New Mexico was a favorite target of the Mescaleros. Chisum claimed that in 1873 the Apaches stole thousands of his cattle and that in July of 1874 the same Indians got away with stock worth $47,675. In 1875, when the raiding was renewed, Chisum's men complained to the Mescaleros' agent, F. C. Godfroy. When the agent refused to be of assistance, the men, after killing some Mescaleros who resisted, drove the stolen Chisum stock away.[8]

On August 1, 1874, Santiago Talamantis camped his wagon train near Varela Spring, about twenty-five miles northeast of Fort Davis. He carried freight from San Antonio for points along the road to Chihuahua, including Fort Davis. Suddenly, a band of twenty-five or thirty Indians stampeded and got away with all his stock, including his only saddle horse. The freighters had to wait for a passerby for transportation into Fort Davis, from which the details of the incident were forwarded to the San Antonio *Herald*.[9]

In the fall of 1874, one hapless Frenchman found out that it was not yet safe to travel alone across West Texas. On November 30, F. C. Taylor, general superintendent of the El Paso mail route, sent the details to a friend in San Antonio, who, in turn, gave the story to the *Herald*. The unnamed Frenchman left Fort Concho on foot and unarmed with the hope of reaching Bosque Grande, New Mexico. He spent one night at Centralia Mail Station. On November 22, members of an eastbound wagon train, headed by a man named Everett, found the Frenchman's scalped body three miles west of Centralia. Everett told Taylor that he had seen several Indian trails that crossed the road in the area of Centralia and the head of the Concho and that an estimated one hundred Indians, reportedly heading south, had camped a few miles east of the head of the Concho.[10]

[8]"Indian Depredation Claims," in U.S. Congress, House, *Letter from the Secretary of the Interior*, March 22, 1882, 47 Cong., 1 sess., 1882, House Doc. No. 135, p. 3; *Democratic Statesman* (Austin), August 16, 1874; John A. Richard, "Ere the Coming of the Cattlemen," *Frontier Times* 6, no. 5 (February, 1929):193.

[9]"Bala Rasa," August 4, 1874, in San Antonio *Herald*, August 10, 1874. In Mexican Spanish *balarassa*, perhaps what the writer intended, is the word for rotgut liquor and also for a person who does not care about his own person or interest (Francisco J. Santamaria, *Diccionario de Mejicanismos*, p. 112).

[10]*Democratic Statesman*, December 8, 1874, an article reprinted from the San Antonio *Herald*, n.d.

Indians were also active near El Paso. During the same month that the Frenchman lost his life, they drove off the mules belonging to the wagon train of Gabriel Valdez while it was camped a short distance from El Paso, killed an ox near Fort Bliss, and stole two horses belonging to a Californian.[11] Then, on April 8, 1875, fourteen Indians charged the El Paso stage at Bass Canyon, between Eagle Springs and Van Horn's Well, and chased it to the Van Horn Station. At Eagle Springs, several days later, as the keeper and a sergeant were watering eight mules, Indians attacked the station and got away with half a dozen animals.[12]

Also in April, Lieutenant John Lapham Bullis would have lost his scalp had it not been for the loyalty of his Seminole scouts. The detachment from Fort Clark was trailing a raiding party and seventy-five stolen horses. It spotted the invaders in the process of crossing to the west side of the Pecos, at a shallow crossing known as Eagle's Nest, the future site of Judge Roy Bean's activities. With the exception of one woman, the Indians were dismounted. The soldiers slipped on foot quietly through the brush, close enough to fire on them. Although three Indians were killed and another wounded, the soldiers had to make a hasty retreat. Bullis' horse got away. Three of his men, upon seeing the predicament of their commander, dashed back under heavy fire to his aid. Sergeant John Ward managed to get Bullis mounted behind him, while the other two—Isaac Payne and Pompey Factor— fought off the Indians. Although his carbine sling and stock were hit by bullets, Ward carried Bullis to safety. Later the three who saved Bullis received high honors for their gallantry.[13]

On April 15, at the head of the Concho, a lone Indian caught prowling near the camp of a detachment of the Ninth Cavalry was killed, and two days later the driver of a westbound stage reported that he had seen some Indians about fifteen miles from Camp Melvin.[14] Then, early in May, twenty-five miles from Fort Concho, a detachment of the Tenth Cavalry chased seven Indians into a cedar brake. There it gave up the chase, but it did recover thirty-three stolen horses and

---

[11] San Antonio *Herald*, February 4, 1875.

[12] Ibid., April 22, 1875.

[13] Ibid., May 4, 1875; San Angelo *Standard Times*, September 27, 1964.

[14] M. M. Blunt, Fort Stockton, to A.A.G., May 1, 1875, Records of United States Army Commands, RG 98, NA.

mules. On May 24, an attempt to steal the horse herd at Fort Concho failed. While Captain T. A. Baldwin's herd of Tenth Cavalry horses was grazing near the post, guarded by a corporal and five privates, five thieves, one of whom was dressed like an Indian, attempted to stampede the horses. The corporal, however, spotted the thieves in time, charged them, captured one, and saved the herd.[15]

The Fort Davis area was also hit. One soldier was shot while working in the post garden, and sheep and goats in Patrick Murphy's corral were driven off. Because the Indians took his animals, Sam Miller, who had a farm at San Solomon Springs (Balmorhea) and a stage line from Fort Davis by way of Toyah Valley to the Seven Rivers country of New Mexico, had difficulty staying in business. Young Robert Lyles was involved twice within a short time in deadly Indian attacks. Near the present Seven Springs Ranch, he was wounded by Mescaleros, but Daniel Murphy rescued and took him to his Toyah farm. Not long afterward, he and some Mexicans rescued the survivors of a party in Limpia Canyon not far from Fort Davis, but not before three of their comrades had been killed.[16]

During June of that year, Martin Roival's wagon train, loaded with flour, while camped between Forts Davis and Quitman, was attacked by Indians. Roival escaped with his mules, but the Indians destroyed what flour they were unable to carry off. A short time later, the teamsters repulsed an attack on a wagon train belonging to Bonifacio Zuñiga, of San Elizario, between Van Horn's Well and Eagle Springs, but Alfonso Zuñiga, a herder with the train, was severely wounded.[17]

In the Presidio area, on July 31, four Indians raided Milton Faver's ranch. This time they ran off a thousand sheep, killed one man, and captured a couple, their two children, and an elderly woman. Pursuers found the bodies of the husband and the elderly woman within a few miles. Because the troops at Fort Davis were too distant to be of service, Viejo, the brother-in-law of the dead man, reported on August 8 that he had sent a party of thirteen men from Presidio del Norte to help Faver trail and punish the guilty Indians—but to no avail. Viejo also reported that he had received news from Chihuahua that Mexican

[15] San Antonio *Herald*, May 15 and June 7, 1875.

[16] Carlysle Graham Raht, *The Romance of Davis Mountains and Big Bend Country*, pp. 200–201, 203.

[17] San Antonio *Herald*, July 24, 1875.

soldiers under Colonel Terrazas, in a battle with a large group of Indians near Eagle Springs, Texas, had killed twenty-five and captured twenty-one but, in turn, had lost nine men. Although the details were unconfirmed, the Mexican people of Presidio del Norte, he added, "seldom get the wrong end of a story." [18]

Meanwhile, on April 30, Colonel Benjamin H. Grierson had assumed command of the military district around Fort Concho, and about the same time Lieutenant Colonel William R. Shafter had set up camp near that post and prepared for an expedition to penetrate the southern plains. Shafter moved out from Fort Concho on July 14 with nine troops of the Tenth Cavalry, two companies of the Twenty-fourth and one of the Twenty-fifth Infantry, Lieutenant John L. Bullis and his Seminole scouts, and Lieutenant C. R. Ward and his Tonkawa scouts. Taking sixty-five wagons, each with a six-mule team, 700 pack mules, and a beef herd, the command arrived at Blanco Canyon near present-day Crosbyton sixteen days later and established its supply camp. From that point, Shafter sent out scouting detachments that crisscrossed the South Plains and Edwards Plateau from present Plainview on the north, beyond the Pecos River on the west, and to the Rio Grande on the south. One trail was followed 150 miles west to the sand dunes and shinnery that border the east side of the Pecos, a region almost devoid of water. The troops then marched to the Pecos and down it to Horsehead Crossing. [19]

While resting his stock there for a few days, Shafter sent a courier to Fort Stockton with a request for rations. Captain S. T. Norvell replied, "I will furnish you with the articles requested in so far as we have them to spare," and assured him that his mail would be forwarded by transportation that left the next morning. [20]

On the return to his supply camp, Shafter went up the Pecos to the Great Falls, at the junction of present Reeves and Pecos counties, where he turned northeast and found what he called Dug Spring. From here, he followed an Indian trail, repulsed a surprise midnight

[18] Ibid., August 21, 1875.

[19] J. Evetts Haley, *Fort Concho and the Texas Frontier*, pp. 231–233; William H. Leckie, *The Buffalo Soldiers*, pp. 143–145; Paul H. Carlson, "William R. Shafter: Military Commander in the American West" (Ph.D. diss., Texas Tech University, 1973), pp. 142–179.

[20] S. T. Norvell, Fort Stockton, to Wm. R. Shafter, August 28, 1875, Army Commands, RG 98, NA.

attack by a small party of warriors, and then trailed them the next morning for twenty miles to an abandoned camp. He then led the troops to their supply camp, reaching there on September 25.[21]

Meanwhile, Captain Norvell, with Company M, Tenth Cavalry, and twenty-eight days' rations, made plans to leave Fort Stockton on September 2 to scout around Delaware Creek and the Guadalupe and Sacramento mountains for Indians on the run from Shafter. The scout, if made at all, was brief, for the captain was at Stockton on or before September 22.[22]

After recuperating at his supply camp, Shafter again sent out scouting detachments. On October 12, six companies of cavalry and two of infantry marched to the headwaters of Yellow House Canyon, northwest of the present city of Lubbock. From there, troops scouted the major watering places in the present counties of Lubbock, Lynn, Borden, and Howard. The detachment under Lieutenant Bullis went to Laguna Sabinas (Cedar Lake) in present Gaines County. That water was too saline to be potable, but good drinking water was located in dug wells north of the lake. Nearby, Bullis surprised an Indian encampment. Although he did not kill any Indians, he destroyed thousands of pounds of food, material, and equipment abandoned by the fleeing occupants.[23]

Later, when Shafter arrived at Cedar Lake, he ordered Lieutenant Andrew Geddes to pursue a large party of Indians. Geddes and his two companies of cavalry and Seminole scouts made one of the wildest chases ever recorded in West Texas history. The pursuit passed by the site of present Midland, by Centralia Station on October 24, and thence by Howard's Well and the intersection of the Fort Lancaster–Fort Clark road. There the lieutenant had his wagons move to Fort Clark for additional supplies, while he trailed the Indians, who were riding hard to reach the safety of Mexico. After crossing the Pecos below the mouth of Independence Creek, the route was rougher and rougher, but still Geddes trudged on. On November 2, near the Rio Grande, he and his

[21]Haley, *Fort Concho*, p. 233; Leckie, *Buffalo Soldiers*, pp. 143–147; Carlson, "William R. Shafter," pp. 162–163.

[22]Norvell, Fort Stockton, to A.A.G., September 1 and 22, 1875, Army Commands, RG 98, NA.

[23]Haley, *Fort Concho*, pp. 233–237; Leckie, *Buffalo Soldiers*, pp. 146–147; Francis B. Heitman, *Historical Register and Dictionary of the United States Army*, 1:450–451; Carlson, "William R. Shafter," pp. 142–179.

men overtook the Indians. They destroyed much of the Indians' loot, killed one brave, and captured four women and a boy.[24]

Previously, military endeavors had been greatly hampered by the slowness of communications. The white man's messages were not as rapid as the red man's smoke signals. In September, 1872, the army was ready to begin the installation of the new communication, telegraph, along the frontier from Fort Sill to Brownsville.[25]

Far western Texas, where the Apaches were still raiding, was a long way from the lines. The major problem in stringing the lines westward would be the acquisition of suitable poles. On April 28, 1875, the headquarters of the Department of Texas inquired about the possibility of procuring poles near Fort Stockton. Lieutenant Colonel M. M. Blunt, at Fort Stockton, advised that they could be obtained near Fort Davis, some 80 to 100 miles west, at a price of two to three dollars each. By June the north-south line was partially complete with a Fort Clark–San Antonio connection, and plans were being made for an extension to the western garrisons.[26] That fall Captain S. T. Norvell, at Fort Stockton, asked for bids for 500 pine poles. On November 10, 1875, when the line had been completed from Denison to Concho and from San Antonio to Fort Clark, Captain Daniel Hart, Twenty-fifth Infantry, was advised to take thirty men and construct the telegraph line from Fort Stockton toward Fort Concho.[27] In December, Major George W. Schofield, the Fort Stockton commander, reported that the telegraph line from Fort Concho had been completed to within 125 miles of Fort Stockton. "A company of infantry from this post is engaged in the construction on this end; ten miles of holes dug, and poles distributed: work at present is slow and inconvenienced for want of transportation."[28]

During 1875, the command at Fort Stockton was changed a num-

[24] Norvell, Fort Stockton, to AAG, November 1, 1875, Army Commands, RG 98, NA; Carlson, "William R. Shafter," pp. 168–171.

[25] *Democratic Statesman*, September 29, 1874.

[26] San Antonio *Herald*, June 30, 1875.

[27] Norvell, Fort Stockton, to A.A.G., November 1, 1875, Blunt and Norvell, Fort Stockton, to A.A.G., April 29, 1875, Norvell to Lt. A. W. Greely, October 14, 1875, and Lt. Owen J. Sweet, to Capt. Daniel Hart, Fort Stockton, November 10, 1875, all in Army Commands, RG 98, NA.

[28] George W. Schofield, Fort Stockton, to A.A.G., December 10, 1875, Army Commands, RG 98, NA.

ber of times. In January, Captain Edward Bush was in charge, and the garrison consisted of Companies M, Ninth Cavalry, B, Tenth Cavalry, and F and K, Twenty-fifth Infantry. Bush was replaced in April, when Lieutenant Colonel Matthew Marsh Blunt arrived with Company C, Twenty-fifth Infantry. Captain S. T. Norvell took command in September but was replaced in December by Major George W. Schofield. During the second half of 1875, the garrison consisted of one company of the Tenth Cavalry and three companies of the Twenty-fifth Infantry.[29]

Fort Stockton's soldiers had little reason to complain about the food. During 1874, the post garden produced an abundance of onions, carrots, beets, turnips, pumpkins, squash, yams, peas, radishes, cucumbers, beans, corn, lettuce, cabbage, watermelons, and canteloupes, some in surplus, which was sold to members of wagon trains. Watercress, previously planted in the springs, was also plentiful. During the fall and winter, the many ducks, snipe, cranes, and geese that appeared along the banks and marshes of Comanche Creek provided a variety of fresh meats.[30]

Early in 1875, twenty-two bodies of soldiers and government employees were removed from the old cemetery to a new post cemetery. Although some coffins had been in the ground for more than six years, all were in good condition.[31] For bathing facilities, the soldiers at Fort Stockton used the springs and creek, even in winter. In warm weather, Major Schofield required the soldiers to bathe twice a week, at least, "in the creek which in places is well adapted for the purpose." The officers, at their own expense, had constructed a small bathhouse "near the southeast corner of the post on the creek at the mouth of a large spring, the temperature of which averages 76 degrees from which fact it can be used nearly eight months in the year."[32]

During the summer of 1875, a water system at the post was completed—but for fire-fighting, not bathing. A 14,082-gallon underground cistern was constructed below the middle of the parade ground. By means of a hydraulic ram and 800 feet of pipe, water was conveyed from Government Spring (the later name of the site) to the cistern.

[29] U.S. Department of War, Post Returns, Fort Stockton, 1875, AGO, RG 94, NA.
[30] Post Surgeon's Report, Fort Stockton, December, 1874, AGO, RG 94, NA.
[31] Ibid., February, 1875.
[32] Schofield, Fort Stockton, to A.A.G., December 10, 1875, Army Commands, RG 98, NA.

The old ram, covered with rust, still rests (1981) at the original site, and the underground cistern remains in the backyard of Billie Rae Owen, but a horse trough, built of rock and placed near the cistern, has long since disappeared.

On May 30, 1875, a damaging hailstorm hit Fort Stockton. Lieutenant Colonel Blunt wrote that the hailstones averaged ten inches in diameter and that sixteen picked up by the post surgeon weighed over two pounds each. "The after effects of the storm," Blunt continued, "[have] been very serious to the shingle roofs—the store house will require a new roof over at least half the building. All the roofs of the officers' quarters . . . will require extensive repair." [33]

During 1875, Pecos County, which had been created four years earlier, was officially organized. The name derives, of course, from the Pecos River, the boundary of the county on the north and east, but the origin and meaning of the name remains a mystery. According to Adolph F. Bandelier, the word was first applied by Juan de Oñate, who in 1598 established the first settlement in New Mexico, to an Indian pueblo then known as Cicuye, but Bandelier added that the origin of the word was unknown. Several others have stated that the word is a corruption of a Mexican name for the stream, Río Puerco, meaning "dirty river." Elsie Parsons, another authority on New Mexico, claimed that the name is from the Jemez Indian name Bahkyush. It has even been contended that is a derivation of the Spanish word *pecoso* ("freckled"). [34] Puerco is the name of the river on most of the early Spanish maps of the area.

Pecos County was organized on March 9, 1875, at the little town of Saint Gall, adjacent to Fort Stockton. The 386 registered voters in the county on that date [35] elected E. W. Bates, district clerk; F. W. Young, county surveyor; Andrew Loomis, sheriff; Morris Jacobs, treasurer; Joseph Heid, inspector of hides and animals; and George M. Frazer, Cesario Torres, Francis Rooney, and Hipolito Carrasco, justices of the peace. All those elected soon qualified. Until the next year, the duties

[33] Blunt, Fort Stockton, to A.A.G., June 1, 1875, Army Commands, RG 98, NA.

[34] L. Tuffly Ellis, "Southwestern Collection," *Southwestern Historical Quarterly* 81 (October, 1977):219–220; Walter P. Webb and H. B. Carroll, eds., *The Handbook of Texas*, 2:314, 354–355.

[35] "M," Saint Gall, in San Antonio *Herald*, March 22, 1875. "M" also stated that Father Perry, the resident priest, was trying to organize a school at Saint Gall.

Hospital Guard House Trading Store & Court House

Old Fort Stockton's hospital (*left*) and guardhouse.

...oys leaving Ft Stockton - 1885

Company of Tenth Cavalry, stationed at Fort Stockton, passing in front of the officers' quarters.

Fort Stockton officers' quarters, west side of parade ground.

Enlisted men's barracks, east side of parade ground, Fort Stockton.

Camp of Company F, Sixteenth Infantry, at Santa Rosa Spring, 1885. *Photograph by Captain George Wedemeyer, courtesy of Mrs. Otto Anderson.*

Company F, Sixteenth Infantry, camped at Escondido Spring, 1885. *Photograph by Captain George Wedemeyer, courtesy of Mrs. Otto Anderson.*

Left: Captain Charles L. Pyron, Confederate Second Cavalry, who occupied Fort Stockton in June, 1861, and later operated a wagon train through the town. *From Gertrude Harris*, A Tale of Men Who Knew No Fear. *Right*: Captain William C. Adams, Confederate Second Cavalry, who occupied Fort Stockton in July, 1861. *Courtesy of Mrs. Brawley Adams.*

Fort Davis, 1890. *Courtesy of William Wilson.*

Freight wagon leaving Pecos for railroad delivery to Fort Stockton, around the turn of the century. *Courtesy of Barney Hubbs.*

Freight wagon arriving at Fort Stockton from railroad station, sometime between 1883 and 1912. *Courtesy of H. H. Butz.*

Post trader's building, Fort Stockton, 1870s. The store was operated by F. W. (Billy) Young, whose family is shown (*left to right*): Eloise, Lillian, Mrs. Young, Andrew, Aileen, and F. W. (others not identified).

Rooney and Butz General Merchandise Store, converted from storage room on south end of the Koehler Saloon. *Courtesy of H. H. Butz.*

Bob and Bill and six hundred steers against the
crowding pen,
When the T.P. freight came roaring by;
"Ride to 'em Cowboys then."

Cowboys heading off stampede. *Drawing by Waldo Williams.*

Mule Shoe (Presnall and Mussey) Ranch cowboys at the headquarters, four
miles northeast of Fort Stockton, 1885.

Judge O. W. Williams, ca. 1900.

of the commissioners court were handled by the four justices, with
Frazer presiding. Apparently a fifth justice was selected about six
months after the initial election, for on September 27, 1875, Martin
Hupmann's name appears on the court's records.

Frederick William (Billy) Young, the first elected Pecos County
surveyor, was born on November 16, 1844, in Magdeburg, Prussia, on
the Elbe west-southwest of Berlin. One of the four children in the
Jung family, F. W. anglicized his name in San Antonio before he moved
to West Texas. Possibly the entire Jung family migrated to this country
together and settled either in San Antonio or in Fredericksburg. According to family tradition, F. W. ran away from home (whether in
Germany or the United States is not known), because he did not get
along with his stepmother, and in May, 1860, he joined the Union
Army. He served in Company A, First Regiment of the U.S. Infantry,
and remained in the army until July 18, 1867. According to Captain
W. G. Wedemeyer, who knew him at Fort Stockton, Young was an
army musician and later a first sergeant. After his discharge, he became a quartermaster's clerk (a civilian job), and it was that position
that brought him from San Antonio to Fort Stockton around 1870 to
assist post trader Joseph Friedlander.

Young also spent some time in New Orleans. According to family
tradition, a little girl named Matilda Loeper was in a tree in her wealthy
family's yard on Canal Street when she first saw Young, who was staying at a nearby boarding house. She immediately announced, "When I
grow up, I'm going to marry that man." She kept her word. Matilda,
the daughter of Theodore and Sophie (Miller) Loeper, both from Prussia, was born in New Orleans on September 6 in 1853 or 1854. The
wedding took place on November 18, 1873, at the Loepers' home.[36] In
arid and untamed West Texas, the young bride had to adjust to a way of
life that was far different from the gentility to which she had been ac-
customed. On her first trip to Fort Stockton, the wagon train ahead of
her party was attacked by Indians, and several people were killed.

Billy Young eventually became the post trader at Fort Stockton.

---

[36] The 1880 census, probably taken before September 6, indicates that Matilda was
born in 1855, but if her death certificate is correct, she was born in 1853. The "Familien
Register" in the Young family Bible shows 1873 as the year she married, but one descendant stated that it was 1872.

His family occupied the post trader's building, located on the southwest corner of the parade ground, and there his first daughter, Eloise,
was born on November 21, 1874, reputed to have been the first Anglo
child born in the present city of Fort Stockton.[37] Young made his first
investment in Saint Gall in August, 1875, by purchasing a lot for twenty
dollars from M. F. Corbett, Peter Gallagher, and John James, all of
whom he had probably known in San Antonio. In 1879, he bought adjoining property, and eventually he acquired the Diamond Y Ranch.
The F. W. Young Building, where he ran his mercantile business, still
stands (1981) near where Comanche Creek once flowed, and in front of
the adobe structure also stands the trunk of a lone cottonwood tree.
The glass transom over the front door bears the inscription "1876,"
indicating the year that Young purchased the building. Previously, according to Theo Young Winfield, the south portion had been an officers' club, and the east and west wings had housed the laundresses.
Possibly it had been built by the army on land for which it had no lease.

Young was well liked and respected by both the military personnel and civilians with whom he associated. In addition to being owner
of one of the earliest mercantile stores in Fort Stockton and the first
elected county surveyor, he was also an early postmaster and was
elected to various other offices, including that of county judge.[38]

[37] Since there had been army wives at the post for several years, the statement
about being the first born in Fort Stockton is subject to question. In time, the Youngs
had six children, five of whose middle names were the last names of army officers who
were Billy's friends. Eloise Courtney Young was likely named for Michael Lewis Courtney, a native of Ireland, who entered the army from Illinois and was with the 25th Infantry. Aileen Maxon Young received her middle name from Mason Marion Maxon, who
served with the 10th Cavalry. Andrew Hart Young was certainly named for Daniel Hart,
who served in the 25th Infantry. Lillian McKay (Mackay?) Young probably received her
middle name from James Ormond Mackay, who served with the 3rd Cavalry. Theodora
George Young, whose first name came form Billy's father-in-law, Theodore Loeper and
possibly from Billy's sister Dora, probably got her middle name from Charles Peaslee
George, a second lieutenant in the 16th Infantry.

[38] The biographical sketch of F. W. Young is based on family statistics and tradition
from Mary Winfield McComb (wife of Dr. Asher McComb and daughter of Theo Young
Winfield), of San Antonio, some of which Mrs. McComb obtained from Edwin Young of
the same city, and on: 1880 census of Pecos County; data on the tombstone of F. W.
Young in Fort Stockton's East Hill Cemetery; Pecos County, Texas, death records, 1904;
death certificate for Mrs. M. L. Young, from the Texas State Health Department, Austin; Clarence R. Wharton, *Texas under Many Flags*, 5:165; two pages from the family
register in F. W. Young's Bible, copies courtesy of Mrs. McComb; Heitman, *Historical
Register*, 1:330, 451, 506, 670, and 698; U.S. Department of the Interior, *Eleventh Cen-*

All the others chosen for office at the first Pecos County election were prominent and industrious residents. Although mentioned earlier, some possibly deserve an additional comment. George M. Frazer at the time was ranching near Leon Holes, running a dairy, and doing contract work for the army. Francis Rooney, the energetic and frugal Irishman, operated a 1,500-acre farm, irrigated by water brought two miles by a ditch from Comanche Creek, and lived in an adobe residence, previously described. Since he was often busy with army contracts, he must have used many tenant workers on his farm.

Joseph Heid, the inspector of hides and animals, and his wife were operating a boarding house. Since nearly every store or establishment that sold meals or groceries also sold liquor, Heid was also a saloon keeper. One of Heid's houses still stands (1981), in the same block as and north of the F. W. Young Building. Heid later became sheriff and soon afterward purchased four lots in Saint Gall, which included the buildings used for the boarding house and the saloon.[39]

Cesario Torres, one of the elected justices of the peace, had been a prominent resident of San Antonio and with his brother had begun farming near Fort Stockton in 1869. Later he transferred most of his operations to the west side of the Pecos River, upstream from Pontoon Crossing. Hipolito Carrasco, another justice, whose descendants still live in Fort Stockton, operated a ranch at the San Pedro Spring. E. W. Bates, the district clerk, who previously had been a resident of New Mexico and Colorado, had arrived in 1873.

Pecos County now had its officers, but no jail. Previously, the army had supplied the only law enforcement, and thus a question arose as to the responsibility for the detention of civilian prisoners. In September, 1875, Captain Norvell, the commanding officer at Fort Stockton, who at the request of the sheriff had a civilian charged with murder confined in the post guardhouse, asked for instructions: "shall assistance be furnished and shall prisoners of the civil authorities be

---

sus of the United States, 1890. Special Schedule of Surviving Soldiers, Sailors and Marines, and Widows, etc. Texas, Pecos County, Supervisor's District No. 8, Enumeration District No. 16, p. 1; *Fort Stockton Pioneer*, November 13, 1977 (obituary of Mrs. Theo Young Winfield); data regarding Young's land purchases, Pecos County, Texas, Deed Records, 1:30, 423, 431, 451, and 529; and Capt. W. G. Wedemeyer's Diary, entry for January 22, 1884.

[39] Pecos County, Texas, Deed Records, 1:26.

confined in the guard house upon the application of the civil authorities."[40] The problem was not easily solved, because of considerable
difficulty in getting a jail constructed.

The commissioners court held its first session on April 12, 1875.
On one of the first issues considered—the foraging of stray livestock on
the farmers' crops (damages by stock from wagon trains were especially
heavy)—the court made it illegal for stock to run loose and unherded
from March until December 1 each year, thus leaving it unnecessary
for farmers to fence in their crop lands, and provided for an animal
pound in each precinct to aid in enforcing this ordinance. Then, at
its meeting on May 31, the court appointed E. W. Bates county tax
assessor-collector of the newly organized and penniless county. At the
June 4 meeting, Sheriff Loomis submitted his resignation, and the justices called for an election on June 24 to fill the vacancy. At the same
session, the court approved a salary of $150 a year for the county clerk,
established a poll tax of 50 cents, and set a tax of 33⅓ cents per $100
valuation of taxable property for the construction of a courthouse and
jail. Nothing was done, however, about the construction, and in 1877
the same rate was again established for that purpose. At the meeting
on July 26, 1875, Heid was declared sheriff, as a result of the election
on June 24. At the request of the county surveyor, the court made an
appropriation to pay the county surveyor of El Paso County for a tran-
script of the Pecos County surveys and another for $50 to refund to
Young for the express charge for county form books sent by stage from
Saint Louis, an amount equal to the cost of the books.

On September 27, the justices established an ad valorem tax of
five cents per $100 valuation for use on public roads and bridges; or-
dered a scholastic census to be taken of children between six and eighteen years of age, inclusive, and for the transmission of the results to
the superintendent of public instruction, accompanied by a communication relative to the appropriation for public schools in the county;
and requested the treasurer of El Paso County to forward all monies
then due Pecos County. The session of November 30 met in the John-
sons' house, then occupied by the district clerk, and officially designated
it as the courthouse of Pecos County. The building, which probably had
been used by Peter J. Gallagher, the nephew of the founder of Saint

---

[40] Norvell, Fort Stockton, to A.A.G., September 22, 1875, AGO, RG 98, NA.

Gall, was on Comanche Creek about three-quarters of a mile from the fort, and outside the present boundaries of the city of Fort Stockton. The first session of the district court, in Saint Gall, was scheduled for June 28, 1875, but delayed for two days until the arrival of Judge Charles H. Howard.

Four days after Pecos County's organizational election, the legislature authorized a convention to assemble on the first Monday in September in Austin for the purpose of framing a new constitution for the state. Saint Gall and Fort Stockton were in the Thirtieth Senatorial District, which included twenty-one other counties and the Bexar District.[41] It was also election year for state officials and time for party conventions. The Democrats, although few in number around Saint Gall and Fort Stockton, met on June 7, 1875. The meeting, after being called to order by George M. Frazer, chairman of the Democratic Executive Committee of Pecos County, named E. W. Bates secretary, adopted resolutions submitted by a committee of three, and selected Francis Rooney to represent the people of Pecos County at the district convention in Castroville on June 21. As alternates, it designated Judge Howard of El Paso and the delegate from Tom Green County.[42]

[41] San Antonio *Herald*, May 13 and June 16, 17, 20, 1875. Cameron, Nueces, Hidalgo, Webb, Zapata, Duval, Encinal, Starr, McMullen, Zavala, LaSalle, Dimmit, Maverick, Frio, Medina, Uvalde, Kinney, El Paso, Presidio, Pecos, Tom Green, and Crockett were the counties in the district.

[42] Ibid., June 16, 1875.

CHAPTER 14

1876

Dᴜʀɪɴɢ 1876 Fort Stockton was occupied by Companies M, Tenth Cavalry, and A, F, and C, Twenty-fifth Infantry. Major George Wheeler Schofield, Tenth Cavalry, commanded the post until July. Captain John William French, Twenty-fifth Infantry, who then commanded for about one month, was succeeded by Captain David Dougall Van Valzah, Twenty-fifth Infantry. Van Valzah remained in command during the remainder of the year. All three commanders had been breveted during the Civil War. Schofield, who also was breveted after the war, was a native of New York but entered the service from Missouri; French was from the District of Columbia; and Illinois-born Van Valzah entered the service from Pennsylvania.[1]

Because of numerous thefts of livestock in the vicinity of Fort Quitman during January, a detachment of the Twenty-fifth Infantry was sent on February 6 to reconnoiter the area. Under the command of Captain Charles Bentzoni, the detachment consisted of a lieutenant with twelve men, Company B, William Oakes, a hospital steward, and John Evans, a guide.[2] The command went down the Rio Grande to a point about thirty miles below Hot Springs and then to Eagle Mountains (or Eagle Peak) and Eagle Springs. Leaving the latter place on February 14, it found about twenty-five miles to the north, at Buckskin Springs, a fresh horse and mule trail. The trail led to the Carrizo Mountains, where on February 17 Bentzoni discovered an abandoned ranchería of twenty-five huts. From here the trail led northward

---

[1] U.S. Department of War, Post Returns, Fort Stockton, 1876, Records of the Adjutant General's Office (AGO), Record Group (RG) 94, National Archives (NA), Washington, D.C.; Francis B. Heitman, *Historical Register and Dictionary of the United States Army*, 1:437, 865, 984.

[2] Heitman, *Historical Register*, 1:213. Bentzoni, a native of Prussia, was another officer who had been breveted for Civil War service.

through the Carrizo Mountains. On the next day, two more abandoned camps were found, one of which contained a pit (twenty feet in diameter) of "mescal" (probably sotol) roasting.[3]

Close on the Indians' trail, on the eighteenth the troops camped at dark on a bitterly cold night and huddled around their fires. Two hours after midnight, Indians fired a dozen or more shots into the camp but did no more serious damage than killing the guide's horse. Getting an early start that morning, the soldiers soon found and destroyed a camp where three or four horses had been butchered, preparatory to making jerky. At 4:00 P.M. the command reached the top of a precipice, about 1,500 feet above the flats and salt lakes southwest of Guadalupe Peak, from which they spotted an estimated 500 horses and mules, possibly stolen, being driven down the slopes by about 100 Indian men, women, and children. Upon sighting the approaching soldiers, the Indians took cover in a protected canyon. Since the quarry greatly outnumbered his force and had reached a protected area, Bentzoni wisely chose to head home.[4]

Not long afterward, on March 5, Fort Davis suffered a severe windstorm, which commenced at 8 A.M. and increased in intensity until 11 A.M. Men were thrown to the ground; the walls of the corral were blown over; oak trees seven or eight inches in diameter were twisted off like straws; the ceilings of the officers' quarters were destroyed; windows of the barracks were blown in; one-third of the tin roof on the new hospital was blown away; and shingles were blown from other houses.[5]

In March, Lieutenant Colonel George Pearson Buell was sent from Fort Concho to reestablish Camp (or Fort) Hudson, on San Pedro Creek near Devils River, with two companies of cavalry. The post was to be used as a "summer camp, to protect the settlers, who are filling up that section of the state very rapidly." Then in April, German-born Lieutenant Louis Henry Orleman from the District of Columbia, who had joined the service in 1862, was ordered to Camp Hudson to take command of Company B, Tenth Cavalry. Orleman had received bre-

[3] Sotol is a southwestern plant resembling yucca, which the Apaches processed for food and drink. Numerous remains of "mescal pits," with charred rocks, are still visible in 1981 in West Texas.

[4] San Antonio *Herald*, February 24 and March 3, 1876.

[5] Ibid., March 18, 1876.

vets for his gallant service against Indians at Beaver Creek, Kansas, in October, 1868, and again in the battle at the Wichita Agency in August, 1874.[6]

Meanwhile, the military telegraph line had been completed and was in operation as far as Stockton. On May 18, 1876, the *Galveston News* published a telegram it had received from Denison on the previous day: "The frontier telegraph from Denison, via Jacksboro, Concho, San Antonio and Eagle Pass to Brownsville . . . was completed last night. . . . This gives connection with all frontier posts, there being a branch from Jacksboro to Fort Sill, and another from Concho to Stockton. All the wires are now in working order. They have been constructed in eighteen months by government troops." Construction of the line from Fort Stockton to Fort Davis was underway.

On January 31, the Pecos County precinct boundaries were established. At the time the county officials were George M. Frazer, county judge; James Johnson, sheriff; E. W. Bates, clerk; and Joseph Heid, Cesario Torres, Francis Rooney, and Hipolito Carrasco, commissioners. Johnson resigned on June 10, and the court replaced him on September 11 with Joseph Heid. Heid resigned as a commissioner on November 15, and M. F. Corbett was chosen to replace him on November 29. On March 1, 1876, the court received bids for the construction of a jail but let no contract, and it approved payment of $2.50 for printing to the Stockton *Telegraph*, the area's first newspaper.

Keeping the telegraph line in service was not an easy task. The San Antonio *Herald* of February 26, 1876, gave some reasons: "The buffalos use them to rub their backs on, and when there is a prairie fire, the poles assist materially in making the scene awe-inspiring. Occasionally the teamster or stockman cuts down a few poles with which to boil his frugal pot of coffee. . . ." Indians also found the poles useful as fuel. Consequently, the army later switched to iron poles. Some of the iron poles still (1981) support telephone lines east of Fort Stockton.

The Indians remained a serious problem in the area during the spring of 1876. Early in May, there were reports from Fort Clark of depredations in that vicinity. On Pinto Creek a Mexican herder was killed and another wounded. Colonel William R. Shafter's forces, in

[6] Ibid., March 25 and April 7 and 14, 1876; Heitman, *Historical Register*, 1:260, 760.

camp twenty-six miles above the mouth of the Pecos, were scouting in that area.[7] Farther west, about two weeks later, Second Lieutenant Charles Greenlief Ayres with a detachment of the Tenth Cavalry went in unsuccessful pursuit of some Indians who had killed one Mexican and wounded another near Fort Davis.[8]

During the full moon of July, Mexican Indians crossed the Rio Grande at Villa Acuña (now Ciudad Acuña), opposite the American town of San Felipe (present Del Rio). Fred J. Arno, a scout with Lieutenant John Bullis and his Seminoles at Camp Wood on the Nueces River, reported that such bands "invariably" went north from the Acuña crossing to the vicinity of the present Big Lake in Reagan County. From there, they traveled south and east by way of Kickapoo Springs to the headwaters of the Frio River or the Nueces and then returned to Mexico with their stolen stock. Bullis assumed that his band would return by the head of the Nueces, but instead it went by the Frio. While on a wide scout, Arno saw the Indians going down Frio Canyon, about twenty-five miles from Bullis' camp. He rode for camp as fast as his horse could travel over the rough country, arriving about midnight.

By daylight, Bullis and his scouts were riding down the Nueces Canyon, hoping to head off the Indians before they came out of the Frio Canyon, but the Indians, having the advantage of better terrain, reached open country seven or eight hours ahead of Bullis. Unburdened by any plunder other than horses and able to replace their jaded mounts, they easily recrossed the Rio Grande ahead of Bullis and his Seminoles. Bullis crossed into Mexico and followed the trail all night and into the morning. About ten o'clock he charged the surprised Indians at San Pedro, some fifty miles south of Eagle Pass. Arno reported that the Seminole-Negro scouts were almost uncontrollable in their ferocity, and that, consequently, an estimated 160 to 170 Kickapoos and Lipans were slain. Bullis had only 3 men killed.

After recovering about 150 horses, Bullis and his men headed north. Making a hasty return to avoid a fight with Mexican soldiers, Bullis and his command reached the border without incident and crossed in full view of the citizens of Piedras Negras, opposite Eagle

    [7] San Antonio *Herald*, May 11, 1876.
    [8] U.S. Department of War, Post Surgeon's Report, Fort Davis, May, 1876, AGO, RG 94, NA; William H. Leckie, *The Buffalo Soldiers*, pp. 145–150.

Pass.[9] Other units of the military were also active in the area. On August 4, Companies B, E, and K, Tenth Cavalry, from Fort Clark, under the command of Captain Thomas C. Lebo, crossed the Rio Grande, marched for eight days into the Santa Rosa Mountains, and destroyed ten Kickapoo lodges. Thereafter, from September until December, Grierson's troops searched the regions of the Pecos, Devils, and Concho rivers and the Guadalupe Mountains.[10]

Meanwhile, a congressional investigation had revealed that Secretary of War William W. Belknap was involved in the scandalous selling of post traders' contracts and other grafts. On March 21, Major G. W. Schofield of Fort Stockton complained to the headquarters at Washington about the exorbitant prices being charged by post traders M. F. Corbett and Joseph Friedlander. On May 21, Friedlander was replaced as post trader by F. W. Young but was allowed some time to sell all his goods except liquor. Young immediately notified the commanding officer at Stockton that his goods were to be shipped from San Antonio on May 14, but it was not until September 18 that he officially began acting as post trader.[11] As previously noted, Young bought a store in Saint Gall and installed the "1876" glass transom over the front door, or else added the date to the transom that already existed.

During the spring of 1876, a party that included seventeen-year-old William Louis Kingston was en route from Mason, Texas, to Fort Davis, with four wagons loaded with corn. About eighteen miles from Fort Davis, on the San Solomon (now Balmorhea) road, fifteen or twenty Mescaleros waylaid the train at a site known as Little Hell. The wagons were corralled, the teams were placed inside with a small guard, and then several members of the party climbed a nearby conical hill on the west and quickly put up a breastwork of rocks. The defenders held the Indians off with their buffalo guns for two days and nights before the siege was abandoned. No casualties were reported. On top

[9] *Fort Stockton Pioneer*, August 8, 1931; Grace Lowe Butler, "General Bullis: Friend of the Frontier," *Frontier Times* 12, no. 8 (May, 1935):360.

[10] Leckie, *Buffalo Soldiers*, p. 151.

[11] G. W. Schofield to AG, March 21, 1876, Owen J. Sweet to J. Friedlander, May 21, 1876, John W. French to A. J. Landa, July 11, 1876, Owen J. Sweet to A. J. Landa, July 27, 1876, D. D. Van Valzah to F. W. Young, August 11, 1876, Owen J. Sweet to M. F. Corbett, and Sweet to Joseph Friedlander, September 18, 1876, all in Fort Stockton, Texas, Records of United States Army Commands, RG 98, NA.

of that little conical hill, a mile and a half below Wild Rose Pass, the remains of the rock barricade are still visible (1981).[12]

During the first half of 1876, an estimated 311,390 cattle were driven out of Texas. Nearly two-thirds of these cattle went by Fort Worth and Red River Station, about 100,000 by Fort Griffin and Doan's Crossing, and about 12,000 up the Pecos.[13] That summer Charles Goodnight moved 1,800 head into Palo Duro Canyon. His closest neighbors were the Bugbees, some 80 miles away, and the nearest settlements were the small communities of Fort Griffin, more than 200 miles to the southeast, near present Albany, and Henrietta, even farther eastward, in Clay County.[14]

Some of the drovers were rustlers. When forty or fifty miles east of Fort Stockton, some drovers of one stolen herd went to that post, where they learned that the authorities were watching for them. When they returned to the herd, an innocent youth named Jim Downs, the cook, overheard the men talking and concluded that he was with a group of rustlers and should escape them. Knowing nothing about the country, he asked the boss if they were close to Fort Stockton. The boss replied: "Maybe we are and maybe we ain't. What's Fort Stockton got to do with this drive?"

Downs explained that he was almost barefoot and naked and that he very much needed to buy some clothes. Besides, he said, the chuck box was nearly out of baking powder, salt, and some other necessities, and he desired to go for what was needed. The boss, however, did not agree, and a worried Downs passed another sleepless night.

The next day, about a mile in advance of Downs's chuck wagon, a cattle inspector (probably H. F. Gasky, the Pecos County animal and hide inspector) and his men met the herd. While the officers were inspecting the cattle, one of the rustlers rushed to the wagon, got a few articles, and said to Downs: "Take care of yourself, young man. The jig's up and the other boys have escaped." Downs jumped on the chuck wagon and started the team at full speed in the opposite direction. He soon discovered that the officers were giving chase and were rapidly

[12] Charlie Stone, Fort Stockton, whose information came from Kingston, oral statement, to Clayton W. Williams.

[13] *San Antonio Express*, June 28, 1876.

[14] Joseph Carroll McConnell, *The West Texas Frontier*, 2:199–204.

gaining on him. When on a rough hill, about 500 yards in the lead, he circled around a small ridge until out of sight of his pursuers, grabbed a Winchester, jumped to the ground, and hid among the boulders and brush. Upon overtaking the wagon, the officers fired about fifty shots into the wagon sheet, just in case any rustlers were in the vehicle.

In his jump from the wagon, Downs had severely sprained an ankle. Though guilty of no crime, he was a fugitive from the law; his ankle was swollen; he was in Indian country with only three cartridges in his gun; he had no food. After going about two miles, he hid until dark. That night, he traveled about ten miles and at daylight almost walked into an Indian camp. On the tenth day, with his bleeding feet wrapped with pieces of his worn-out clothing, he discovered a Mexican riding toward him on a burro. Downs cocked his gun and called out, but the Mexican, who was on his way to a buffalo hunters' camp about thirty miles distant, was friendly and insisted that Downs take some of his provisions, including a blanket and his shoes (which did not fit), and directed the unfortunate youngster to a hunters' camp about sixteen miles away. On the following day, Downs hobbled into the camp and was properly cared for.[15]

Some six months after the Downs affair, two cowboy pals, Philip Rock and Lou Niel, both reportedly dangerous, shot each other to death in a Fort Stockton saloon. Niel, from Dallas, and Rock, from Columbus, Texas, had been with John Slaughter's large herd of cattle that had been driven up the Pecos to New Mexico. On their return, the two decided to break the monotony by riding into Fort Stockton. In the F. W. Young saloon, Rock, while under the influence of liquor, asked Niel and some black soldiers to have a drink with him. Niel replied that he did not drink with blacks and drew his gun. After a short argument, each shot the other in the chest. Niel fell to the floor. Standing over him, Rock said, "I'm shot in the guts and will die," and then emptied the remaining contents of his revolver into Niel's head. Rock died five hours later. The two bodies were buried in the same grave. Years later, a man appeared to take the remains of his brother home for reburial, but he was unable to make a positive identification, and the two bodies were reburied in the same grave.[16]

[15] Don H. Biggers, "Jim Downs' Tramp across the Plains," *Frontier Times* 5, no. 7 (April, 1928):312–315.

[16] *San Antonio Express*, October 18 and November 3, 1876. The story about the

In the fall of 1876, Phillip Halker Pruett bought forty head of shorthorn cattle in Santa Fe and drove them via the Pecos River (the Goodnight-Loving trail in reverse) to Ben Ficklin on the Concho. His outfit consisted of a wagon train, a few saddle ponies, four men, two women, and five children. When the outfit "camped near the falls on the south side of the Pecos River and 30 or 40 miles south of where Pecos City now is, a Mexican from the Torres farm [more likely from Rooney's farm between the Great Falls and the Grand Falls of the Pecos] rode up and offered Pruett a two-year-old heifer for a pound of coffee."[17] Pruett did not have a good cow pony, but after the Mexican agreed to stay with the herd until the heifer got used to being with the other cattle the deal was consummated. Thus Pruett obtained an animal that during the next twenty-three years "bore 19 heifers and one bull calf, and her increase led to over 200 head in a few years." Pruett estimated that the pound of coffee traded for the heifer "netted him a profit of at least $1,000."

Years later Pruett recalled another unusual incident at the Pecos on that trip. At Horsehead Crossing or Salt Crossing in mid-December he saw 250 wagons, loaded with dried buffalo meat, headed for Presidio, Mexico. Pruett stated:

These Mexican drivers were freighters from Mexico City and Chihuahua. They did not kill the buffalo themselves, but contracted with buffalo hunters to skin and stake out the hides to dry, in exchange for the meat.

They only used knives to skin the heads and split the hides on the leg[s]. Four mules were hitched to the buffalo's head, and four more mules to the hide they had skinned off the head, then they started the teams in opposite directions and pulled the hide off.[18]

On March 10, 1875, the legislature enacted a law, designed to encourage the development of natural resources, that destroyed the existing harmony among owners of irrigation systems north of Fort Stockton. Cesario Torres, Bernardo Torres, and Félis Garza had each preempted 160-acre tracts and in 1868–1869 together had built a 1,885-

---

man who came looking for his brother's remains was told by Roy Rooney, son of Frank Rooney, to Clayton Williams.

[17] "Traded Pound of Coffee for Heifer Back in 1876," *Frontier Times* 6, no. 2 (November, 1928):93.

[18] Ibid. The meeting was likely at Salt Crossing since the Mexicans probably got salt to preserve the meat at Salt Lake.

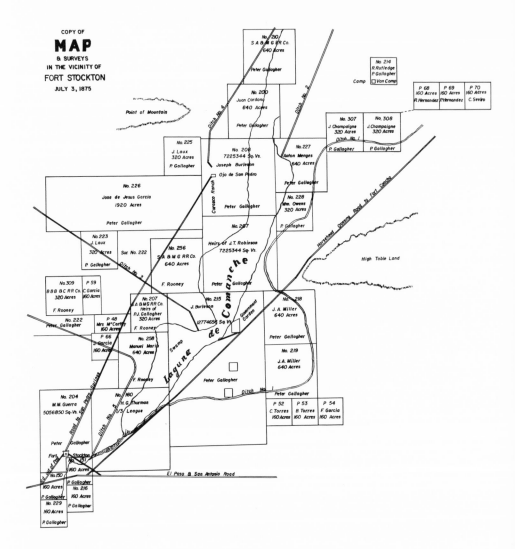

COPY OF
MAP
& SURVEYS
IN THE VICINITY OF
FORT STOCKTON
JULY 3, 1875

Point of Mountain

No. 210
S A B M G RR Co.
640 Acres

Peter Gallagher

No. 214
R. Rutledge
P. Gallagher
Camp   Van Camp

P 68   P 69   P 70
160 Acres 160 Acres 160 Acres
R. Hernandez P.Hernandez C. Seviro

No. 200
Juan Cordona
640 Acres

Peter Gallagher

No. 307   No. 308
J. Champaigne J. Champaigne
320 Acres   320 Acres
Ditch No. I
P. Gallagher   P. Gallagher

No. 225
J. Laux
320 Acres
P. Gallagher

No. 208
7225344 Sq. Vs.

Joseph Burleson

Ojo de San Pedro

Carvaco Ranch

No. 227
Anton Menges
640 Acres

Peter Gallagher

No. 226
Jose de Jesus Garcia
1920 Acres

Peter Gallagher

Peter Gallagher

No. 228
Wm. Owens
320 Acres

P Gallagher

No. 207
Heirs of J.T. Robinson
7225344 Sq. Vs.

Peter Gallagher

Horsehead Crossing Road to Fort Concho

High Table Land

No. 223
J. Laux
320 Acres
P. Gallagher

Sur. No. 222

No. 256
S A & M G RR Co.
640 Acres

F. Rooney

Ditch No. 3

No. 309   P 59
B B B & C RR Co. C. Garcia
320 Acres   160 Acres

F. Rooney

No. 207
S A & M G RR Co.
Heirs of
P.J. Gallagher
320 Acres

F. Rooney

No. 215
J. Burleson

12774655 Sq Vs.

Government
Garden

No. 218
J. A. Miller
640 Acres

Peter Gallagher

No. 222
Peter Gallagher

P 48
Mrs. M°Carthy
160 Acres

P 66
J. Garcia
160 Acres

No. 258
Manuel Maria
640 Acres

F. Rooney

Swamp

Laguna   de   Comanche

No. 219
J. A. Miller
640 Acres

Peter Gallagher

No. 204
M. M. Guerra
5056850 Sq. Vs.

No. 160
H. G. Thurman
1/3 League

Ditch No. I

Peter Gallagher

P 52   P 53   P 54
C. Torres   B. Torres   F. Garcia
160 Acres 160 Acres 160 Acres

Peter   Gallagher

Fort   Stockton
No. 151
160 Acres

El Paso & San Antonio Road

No. 150
160 Acres
P. Gallagher
No. 229
160 Acres

P Gallagher
No. 216
160 Acres

P Gallagher

P. Gallagher

yard ditch from Comanche Creek to their holdings. Then, in 1872 and 1873, they constructed an additional 880 yards. In 1872, Francis Rooney and Ann McCarthy (Rooney's wife's maiden name) constructed 4,784 yards of ditch, and two years later they added an additional 5,200 yards along laterals. Thus far, there was plenty of water for all.

The 1875 law authorized grants of land to builders of four types of canals, the classification based on width and depth. The amount of the grant was to be sixteen sections for each mile in the first class, twelve sections for each mile in the second class, eight sections for each mile in the third class, and four sections for each mile in the fourth class. To qualify, a minimum of three miles had to be completed. The act prompted existing owners to lengthen their existing canals and provided an incentive for a number of new diggers. By May 20, 1875, Cesario Torres, Bernardo Torres, Juan Torres, and Félis Garza had organized the Torres Irrigation and Manufacturing Company for the purpose of constructing a ditch on the west bank of the Pecos from about fourteen miles above the "stage bridge" (the area of Camp Melvin and the Pontoon Crossing) to Horseshoe Bend.

That same month, Samuel Miller, James Maloy, Theodore Wilson, and W. MacDonald, all residents of Presidio County, and George M. Frazer and Francis Rooney, both of Pecos County, organized the Toyah Creek Irrigation Company. They planned to take water from the Mescalero (San Solomon) Springs northeastward about twenty miles. Although this would not take water from the Pecos, the system could affect those who irrigated from the river, since San Solomon fed Toyah Creek and the creek drained into the Pecos.

Simultaneously, Peter Gallagher, M. F. Corbett, and John James, as owners of the Comanche Creek Irrigation Company, applied for a charter and the right to construct five ditches, about twenty-four miles in all, to take water from Comanche Creek. One ditch would take water from a point a short distance below one of Rooney's systems. Consequently, to protect his water right, Rooney, as president, applied for a charter, under the name of Comanche Irrigation and Manufacturing Company, for a ditch (which had already been constructed). During the first year of the company's existence, Ann M. McCarthy and Arthur Conroy were its directors.

Before the end of 1875, Torres and Garza complained that Gallagher, Corbett, James, and A. M. Rector were taking too much water and leaving them with too little. Then Rooney brought suit to prevent Gallagher, Corbett, and James from building the ditch that, he felt, would curtail his water. The suit dragged on for several years. Finally on October 12, 1878, the court allowed Gallagher, Corbett, and James to construct the outlet ditch below Rooney's. Consequently, Rooney's intake of water was somewhat curtailed.[19]

The irrigation conflict (a mini-feud in comparison with the devastating feuds in Pecos County during the 1890s) involved persons who had previously been good friends—and would be again when the trouble subsided. The conflict, however, was not without humor. Once Francis Rooney failed to appear for a hearing. As an excuse he gave later, Rooney explained that the Indians were then pretty bad and that he was afraid to come in because some redman "might stick his gun in me belly and blow me brains out." The judge, convinced that the Indians were a real danger or amused over the statement as to the location of the defendant's brain, let Rooney off without a fine.[20]

Later, Rooney, Arthur Conroy, and Jacob Jacobs chartered the Pecos Irrigation Company, with a proposed life of twenty years, for the construction and operation of a canal along the west side of the Pecos River from four miles above the Great Falls to about 300 yards above the Riffles. (Great Falls is the point on the Pecos that marks the common boundary of Reeves and Pecos counties.) A dam was constructed across the river, and six miles of ditch were dug alongside the west bank. Tracts of land irrigated from this ditch were farmed by Mexicans on a sharecrop basis, four-fifths to the farmer and one-fifth to Pecos River Irrigation Company.[21]

During 1876, some progress was made toward getting a railroad in the Fort Stockton area. As previously noted, Texas had consistently encouraged railroad construction by subsidies of public land or, for a

---

[19] John James died on November 27, 1876, and was buried in San Antonio (Walter P. Webb and H. B. Carroll, eds., *The Handbook of Texas*, 1:904).

[20] O. W. Williams, Fort Stockton, oral statement, to Clayton Williams.

[21] This sketch of irrigation has been compiled from Thomas Lloyd Miller, *The Public Lands of Texas, 1519–1970*, pp. 74, 83; H. P. N. Gammell, *The Laws of Texas, 1822–1897*, 8:449–451, 1089–1091; Pecos County, Texas, Minutes of the Commissioners Court, November term, 1875, and February 1, 1876; Pecos County, Minutes of the District Court, 1:116; Pecos County, Records of the Secretary of State, 1875 and 1876; Pecos County, Deed Records, 1:53–54; Reeves County, Deed Records, 2:150; and Will P. Rooney, son of Francis Rooney, oral statements, to Clayton Williams.

short time, of money (bonds), and the railroad surveys had gotten underway in present Pecos County in 1873. The state constitution of 1876 reestablished the granting of sixteen alternate sections of land for each mile of completed track. This eventually included large tracts in the present counties of Pecos, Tom Green, Crockett, Upton, Irion, Andrews, Ward, Loving, Winkler, Crane, Ector, Schleicher, Presidio, and El Paso. Already the Texas and Pacific Railroad had begun constructing its line from Texarkana to Dallas, and in anticipation of its extension across western Texas it had six Pecos County townships surveyed in July, 1876.[22] Tracks were not laid across the area for several more years, however, and, meanwhile, outlawry and Indian depredations continued to be a major problem.

[22] Webb and Carroll, *Handbook of Texas*, 2:752; Eldon Stephen Branda, ed., *The Handbook of Texas: A Supplement*, 3:772; Pecos County, Survey Records, D2:1–135, and D3:1–266.

CHAPTER 15

1877-1878

O N January 5, 1877, Fort Quitman was permanently abandoned, when Captain Charles Bentzoni and Company B, Twenty-fifth Infantry, left for Fort Clark. About the same time, Fort Stockton was occupied by Companies C, D, and F, Twenty-fifth Infantry, and Company M, Tenth Cavalry, with Captain David Dougall Van Valzah in command. Lieutenant Colonel Matthew Marsh Blunt took over the command in May, and on July 26 Company M, Tenth Cavalry, was transferred to Fort Clark. During October, a lieutenant and five infantry men were staking out the telegraph line to Varela Spring. The personnel at the post remained the same through the remainder of the year.[1]

Meanwhile, the Mescaleros, Kickapoos, and Lipans from both sides of the Rio Grande were raiding in Texas. As a countermeasure, on January 10, 1877, Lieutenant John L. Bullis, his Seminole scouts, and Captain A. S. B. Keyes with ninety men from Companies B and D, Tenth Cavalry, left Fort Clark to search for the Kickapoo and Lipan raiders in Mexico. After a difficult march, they found and destroyed a recently abandoned Indian camp in the Santa Rosa Mountains. On January 24, Captain Daniel Hart, Twenty-fifth Infantry, and Captain and Assistant Surgeon B. F. Pope, with a detachment of twelve enlisted men, returned to Fort Stockton after having been as far as the head of the Concho on a hunt for buffalo to get meat for the garrison. Two months later, in March, Lieutenant Pat Dolan's Company F, Frontier Battalion (Texas Rangers), while pursuing Indians along the rugged Devils River, recovered thirteen horses.[2] The Torres farm on the Pecos

---

[1] U.S. Department of War, Post Returns, Fort Quitman, January, 1877, and Fort Stockton, 1877, both in Records of the Adjutant General's Office (AGO), Record Group (RG) 94, National Archives (NA), Washington, D.C.

[2] William H. Leckie, *The Buffalo Soldiers*, p. 152; U.S. Department of War, Post Surgeon's Report, Fort Stockton, January, 1877, AGO, RG 94, NA; "Texas Frontier Trou-

was raided in April. On the twenty-second Indians drove off five horses, and a week later another party, presumably from the Mescalero reservation, stole nine horses and mules and all the work animals.[3]

After Company M moved from Fort Stockton to Fort Clark in July, there was no cavalry at Fort Stockton, and, consequently, the raids henceforth in the vicinity were usually successful.

Meanwhile, the stages carried more passengers, and the risks involved became less hazardous. A reporter gave an illuminating account of his trip from Fort Concho to Fort Stockton in June, 1877. From Concho the road was "over plains covered with a growth of mesquite trees and with luxurious grass." The Twin Mountains and Lone Tree Mountain "disappeared from view as the stage nears Johnson's Station . . . twenty-five miles from the post. This is the Dinner House, and here Ike Gilman, well known on the road as Double Thumbed Ike, disposes fresh eggs and hot coffee besides venison or buffalo steaks, fish and wild turkey, the game being the product of his own bow and spear." During the next afternoon, the reporter saw several small herds of buffalo, "a few hundred each." He also reported that from the head of the Concho it was twenty-five miles to Centralia Station, where he was told by the inn-keeper that "a large party of Indians had passed the station on the previous night. . . . Upon arriving at the Pecos Station [Camp Melvin at Pontoon Crossing] it was reported that all the horses and mules from the Torres farms on the Pecos had been stolen on the previous night."

The reporter was greatly impressed with possibilities of farming by irrigating from the Pecos River, especially when he learned that a couple of systems were already in operation. One, owned by Francis Rooney and others, at the Riffles, three miles above the Great Falls, utilized thirty Mexican families, and the other was the Torres' Irrigation Company, located fifteen miles above where the El Paso road then crossed the Pecos.

The former system was of recent origin. On January 19, 1877, Francis Rooney, Arthur Conroy, and Jacob Jacobs obtained a charter for the Pecos River Irrigation Company to construct an irrigation ditch in Pecos County, the water to be taken from the Pecos River on the

bles," in U.S. Congress, House, *Report and Accompanying Documents of the Committee on Foreign Affairs*, 45 Cong., 2 sess., 1878, House Report Doc. No. 701, p. 105.

[3] *San Antonio Express*, May 4, 1877.

west side. At the time the *Express* reporter wrote, two separate tracts, one containing 320 acres in the north half of Survey 22 and the other in the center of Survey 6, both in Block 8 of the Houston and Great Northern Railroad Company's survey, were being put into cultivation. The Torres Irrigation Company, on the other hand, the reporter wrote, by "primitive engineering backed by perseverance, has constructed a dam by dumping between three and four thousand wagon loads of rock into the stream, thus raising the water several feet and causing it to flow into a ditch nine feet wide." That system had, the reporter added, 500 acres planted in wheat, corn, barley, and other crops.[4]

The reporter also recorded that Escondido, "the Dinner Station," thirty-six miles west of the Pecos and eighteen miles from Fort Stockton, was at the head of an extensive valley. The water from Comanche Creek was being used to irrigate about 4,000 acres of wheat, barley, corn, rye, oats, vegetables, and grapes. Corn, previously obtained from Mexico at a cost of $2.50 per bushel, was now grown near Fort Stockton and cost about $1.00 per bushel. This amounted to a considerable saving to the military, which used about 20,000 bushels at Forts Davis and Stockton. The El Paso grape and the white grape imported from France by Peter Gallagher produced a good yield in 1876.

At the time of the observant reporter's visit, Fort Stockton was the western terminus of the telegraph, but plans were underway to extend the line to El Paso. The garrison had one company of cavalry and three of infantry, all black troops. The *Express* reporter avoided experiencing an attack by Indians—but not by much. On June 10, six company mules and the stage tender's horse at Varela Station, west of Fort Stockton, were taken.[5] On the same day, Mexican regulars reportedly attacked a party of *lerdistas* (followers of Sebastián Lerdo de Tejada, the political opponent of Porfirio Díaz) above the mouth of Devils River. Captain Joseph Kelley with Company E, Tenth Cavalry, from Fort Clark, who was on patrol in the region, captured fifty of the *lerdistas*, but the regulars had already dashed back across the Rio Grande.[6]

On June 21, a small party of Lipans and Kickapoos crossed the Rio Grande near San Felipe (present Del Rio), rode swiftly into Edwards

[4] Reeves County, Texas, Deed Records, 2:150; reporter's account, *San Antonio Express*, June 12, 1877.

[5] *San Antonio Express*, June 12, 1877.

[6] Leckie, *Buffalo Soldiers*, p. 153.

County, stole horses in Kerr and Kimble counties, and recrossed the Rio Grande without meeting any opposition. Sergeant E. A. Sieker and a detachment of Company D, Frontier Ranger Battalion, after following another Indian trail from June 26 to July 10 from Devils River to the Pecos, captured thirteen horses.[7]

The transfer of the cavalry from Fort Stockton provided an incentive for the Mescaleros to raid in that area. In August Francis Rooney and Cesario Torres lost stock. Twenty-five miles downstream from the Torres farm Thomas C. Nelson, the Pecos County surveyor, was ambushed by five Indians. One shot entered his left breast, one went through his hat, and one through his canteen. Nelson thought he either killed or wounded an Indian. He rode horseback to the Torres farm, where two weeks later he was still in serious condition.[8]

Meanwhile, on August 1, at El Muerto, thirty-eight miles west of Fort Davis, Luis Cardis' mail stock, consisting of eleven mules, was stolen, and one of his drivers, Hank Dill, was killed, apparently by Mescaleros. Colonel George L. Andrews, commander at Fort Davis, was severely criticized by some area citizens for his tardiness in sending troops in pursuit of the murderers. Even so, Andrews did direct Sergeant Joseph Clagget to take ten men of Company H, Tenth Cavalry, and proceed to the station at El Muerto and from there to follow the trail with the utmost vigor. Clagget, aided by a Pueblo Indian guide, followed the trail to the Carrizo Mountains, but five miles north of Van Horn's Well the tracks scattered, and the trail was lost. Clagget then headed for Rattlesnake Springs, the nearest water he knew about, where he hoped to pick up the trail again. Finding the springs dry, the sergeant and his men went north and then east to the Guadalupe Mountains, searching each water hole for signs of the Indians. At Horse Tanks, the mounts had gone without water for forty-eight hours, and Clagget abandoned the hunt.[9]

A few days later, Texas Rangers picked up James Beardall (Beardsall), who had been convicted for a murder near Fort Lancaster but had escaped from the San Antonio jail eighteen years before. The prisoner denied that he was Beardall, but the deputy sheriff at the time of the

[7] Ibid., p. 153; U.S. House, "Texas Frontier Troubles," 45 Cong., 2 sess., 1878, House Report Doc. No. 701, p. 106.

[8] *San Antonio Express*, August 14 and 30, 1877.

[9] Ibid., August 17, 22, and 30, 1877.

trial "readily recognized" him and had also recognized him three years before in Mexico. In 1858, Beardall, then a soldier at Fort Lancaster, and another soldier, named Draper, had been tried and convicted by a court in San Antonio of murdering and robbing Louis Vare. They had attempted to make it appear that the crime had been committed by Indians.[10]

Driving a stagecoach was a very hazardous job. The coaches went unescorted or had only one or two guards. One driver, Red Harte, was killed near El Muerto; "Spot" Bishop, another driver, and two passengers died from sunstroke near Fort Stockton. In mid-September, 1877, a mail coach from El Paso to Stockton was attacked by Indians in Bass Canyon, but the frightened team sped away so rapidly that no harm was done. About the same tme, six or eight persons were killed by mounted Warm Springs Apaches between El Paso and Fort Davis.[11] In the fall of 1878, United States troops entered Mexico several times in pursuit of Indian raiders. Bullis and his scouts crossed the Rio Grande near Fort Duncan on September 28 and again reached the headwaters of San Diego Creek, only to find the Lipan village deserted. Realizing that this band may have crossed into Texas, Bullis hastily returned to the north side of the river, but, finding no trails, on October 28 he again crossed into Mexico. This time he discovered and followed a horse trail that led to the foothills of the Santa Rosa Mountains. After an engagement in which he was outmanned and outgunned, Bullis returned to Fort Clark.

On his next crossing he had the support of a large contingent of troops under the command of Captain S. B. M. Young, Eighth Cavalry, and Lieutenant William H. Beck, Tenth Cavalry. Early in November, the column crossed the Rio Grande and moved into the rough regions of the Carmel Mountains opposite the Big Bend, where pack mules were roped together to prevent their toppling off the treacherously high and narrow trails. Even so, a number of mules fell. In the roughest portion of those mountains the command encountered Alsate's (Arzate's) Apaches. The siege was a stalemate until some of the troops executed an encircling movement. The Apaches thereupon abandoned twenty-three animals and their camp and escaped up a pre-

[10] Ibid., August 30, 1877; Clayton Williams, *Never Again*, 3:173–177.
[11] *San Antonio Express*, August 30 and September 17, 1877.

cipitous incline among the rocks and lechuguilla. The soldiers took the animals and destroyed the camp.[12] Mescaleros and Lipans were also raiding ranches and farms in the vicinity of Presidio Del Norte. Late in the summer of 1877, a small scouting party of Mexican troops found eighteen to twenty lodges near Eagle Springs. The Indians, assuming that it was an advance detachment of a larger force, abandoned their ranchería, and the Mexicans, not wanting to risk an encounter, returned to Mexico.

After a scouting party reported that it had discovered an Indian village on the north side of the Rio Grande, Mexicans from several villages and ranches on both sides of the Rio Grande planned for two expeditions against the Indians. From Presidio, one group would go downstream; the other, under the command of Narciso Anaya, from San Carlos (in northern Chihuahua, not far from the Texas village of Lajitas), was to scout upstream. Both groups were to move to the Mexico side but expected to find and to follow a trail that led into the United States.

In preparation for crossing the international border, Anaya persuaded Richard C. Daly, who lived on the Texas side of Presidio, to write to Colonel George L. Andrews, the commanding officer at Fort Davis, for permission. In his letter, dated September 23, Daly explained that Anaya's force would consist of 80 to 100 Mexicans, a "good many" of whom lived in Texas, and that he was under the impression that Anaya was acting under orders from the governor of Chihuahua. Preparations had been underway for some time, but the expedition had been delayed until a time convenient for the farmers. Since Anaya planned to start "on September 31 [*sic*]" and there was not enough time to obtain approval from the governor of Texas, he was sending the request to the nearest military authority. Perhaps to associate a prestigious name with the request, Daly added that "Mr. Favers" (no doubt Milton Faver) had given the Mexicans ten dollars' worth of powder and shot for the campaign.

After waiting a couple of days beyond his schedule without receiving a reply from Andrews, Anaya with seventy-eight men, including four Indian scouts, on October 2 headed up the Rio Grande. With or

[12]Leckie, *Buffalo Soldiers*, pp. 154–155; M. L. Crimmins, "The Mescalero Apaches," *Frontier Times* 8, no. 12 (September, 1931):552–553.

without permission, it was his intention to go by Eagle Springs and, if necessary, to the Guadalupe Mountains. There was no need, however, for Anaya to worry, for on October 4, the next day after receiving Daly's letter, Andrews gave his approval.

Shortly before Anaya started, an Indian woman resident of San Carlos, learning of his plans and knowing that her son was near Eagle Springs with the Indian raiders, slipped away to warn her son and his comrades. Thus Anaya failed to find his quarry there when he arrived a few days later. When his scouts found a fresh trail that crossed the Rio Grande, Anaya followed it. He crossed the El Paso road near Eagle Springs and followed it from the Eagle Mountains northward toward the Guadalupe Mountains and the Pecos River. Because the country was extremely dry, he traveled at night, so that the dust raised by the horses' hooves would not be seen. At a water hole in the Guadalupes, he discovered that the Indians were only a day or two ahead. After having been delayed one night by rain, he saw the Indians the next morning, October 16 or 17, only two or three miles ahead. Leaving the main body to reconnoiter a water hole, presumably the Indians' destination, the scouts got caught in a position where they could have been killed by the Indians. To save them, Anaya charged across the two miles that separated them from the Indians, and simultaneously the scouts attacked on the opposite side. During the battle, thirteen Indian women and three men escaped, but the Mexicans killed six braves and captured six women and sixty-nine horses and mules. One of the captives was the woman from San Carlos who had gone to warn her son. Anaya's only casualty was a man wounded in a hand-to-hand fight. Daly later reported to Colonel Andrews that the plunder captured by Anaya included "plenty of brown domestic, calico, brass kettles, powder, lead, perfumery, repeating arms and ammunition, sugar and coffee, government blankets, both white and grey." Daly believed that the Indians were from the reservation near Fort Stanton, New Mexico.

The captives told the Mexicans that a day or two before the battle, nine braves with five Henry rifles, three needle guns, and one Spenser had left the camp and headed in the direction of Fort Stockton. The dead braves were scalped for evidence in making claim in Chihuahua City for the $1,000 bonus being paid at the time for scalps of hostile Indians. The Mexicans, with the scalps, captive women and animals, and plunder returned to Presidio by way of El Muerto. All except one of the animals were identified as stock from various Mexican towns and ranches. The downstream expedition failed to find any Indians.[13]

Anaya's success did not check the raiders. During the same month Indians in broad daylight drove off two oxen from a wagon train near El Muerto and in Bass Canyon killed four or five men who were cutting hay for the stage company. On October 19, eleven Indians were seen stealing two horses on the Pecos, about forty miles north of Fort Stockton, and two nights later they stole two horses from the Torres ranch, near Camp Melvin. Then, the westbound stage that left Centralia Station at 3 A.M. on October 22 had not been heard from two days later. The missing stage was later found west of Flat Rock and about twelve miles east of Camp Melvin. The dead driver lay nearby. The horses, the canvas, the leather straps, and the mail, except for some registered packages, had been taken. Both Daly and Colonel Andrews believed that the raiders were those who had left the camp near the Guadalupe Mountains a day or two before Anaya attacked it.[14]

From September through December of 1877, serious trouble erupted over the ownership of the salt lakes west of Guadalupe Peak. The conflict, which had been brewing since the 1860s, occurred over an effort by some men to obtain private ownership of the lakes, while others felt strongly that the area was public domain. A feud developed between Luis Cardis, who controlled the Mexican vote in the El Paso area, and District Judge Charles H. Howard, who filed on the property in the name of his father-in-law, George B. Zimpleman, of Austin. In September, after Howard arrested two men who had threatened to go for salt, a riot ensued, and Howard was held by a mob at San Elizario for three days. He gained his freedom by promising under duress to relinquish his claim. This promise he did not keep.[15]

Involvement in the so-called Salt War reached as far east as Fort Stockton, where Andrew Loomis, the first elected sheriff of Pecos

[13] Richard C. Daly, Presidio, to Col. George Andrews, September 23 and October 7 and 27, 1877, Andrews, Fort Davis, to Daly, October 4, 1877, and Andrews, Fort Davis, to AAG, November 1, 1877, all in Letters Received, AGO (Main Series), RG 94, NA.

[14] *San Antonio Express*, October 4, 25, and 31, and November 2, 1877; Daly to Andrews, October 27, 1877, and Andrews to AAG, November 1, 1877, Letters Received, AGO (Main Series), RG 94, NA.

[15] Walter P. Webb and H. B. Carroll, eds., *The Handbook of Texas*, 2:536–537. See also "The San Elizario Affair," *San Antonio Express*, October 7, 9, 11, 13, 16, 25, and 31, 1877.

County, resigned as sheriff in order to join Judge Howard. The Mexicans on both sides of the border and the salt haulers, who were nearly all Mexicans, took the other side. June Peak told Judge O. W. Williams that he and another guard had to rest on the flat roof of an adjoining building to prevent trouble while Judge Howard was holding district court in Pecos County.[16] On October 10, 1877, Howard killed Cardis in an El Paso store. On December 1, while out on bail, Howard brought suit against "trespassers" who had left for the salt lakes with sixteen wagons. At San Elizario, where Howard had gone to press his case, he and several citizens sworn in as Rangers were besieged by an angry mob. To prevent more killings, on the fifth day, Howard gave himself up, but on December 17 he and two of the so-called Rangers were shot by a firing squad composed of Mexicans. The other Rangers were disarmed and allowed to leave.[17]

On November 9, the telegraph line between Forts Concho and Stockton was cut near where the stage driver had been killed the previous month, and two days later Indians were seen near Horsehead Crossing with pieces of telegraph wire and mail sacks. Apparently the same Indians stole four horses near Horsehead Crossing and at Francis Rooney's farm on November 14 killed two fine bulls and ran off four head of cattle. Ten of Rooney's men followed the thieves for about sixty miles but failed to overtake them. A Fort Stockton correspondent for the *San Antonio Express* facetiously remarked that Lieutenant Jones, with a detachment from Colonel Shafter's command, "passed down the Pecos on the 10th and came in here on the 11th. They reported having seen no Indians' trails, but it seems the Indians saw them." Understandably, Francis Rooney was even more critical. On November 14, 1877, he wrote to the *Express* that the Indians had made another raid through the Pecos country on August 10, taking at the time thirty-four horses and mules and killing two and driving off six head of his cattle. The thieves, he stated, were the same Indians who had stolen four horses from "Mr. Keasey," who had a cattle herd about fifteen miles downstream from him, and the same ones who had recently killed the stage driver. His pursuit party had found scattered along the trail pieces of

[16] June Peak to Judge O. W. Williams, Williams to Mary Ethel Dunn, and Dunn to Clayton Williams, oral statements.

[17] James B. Gillett, *Six Years with the Texas Rangers, 1875 to 1881*, pp. 195–197; Webb and Carroll, *Handbook of Texas*, 2:536–537.

the mailbags taken from the stage. Rooney then bitterly criticized the military for its failure to provide protection. "Our frontier is in a deplorable condition. We have no protection of property. . . . If every head of my cattle should be driven off tomorrow, I could not get ten men at the post to follow the trail. The commanding officer is left powerless, as he has no horses and but few men. So the Indians you see, have a free field for their operators. . . ."[18]

The "Mr. Keasey" possibly was either Whitaker or Otis M. Keesey, although neither of the brothers is remembered today as an owner of cattle. The Keeseys, who came from Virginia, both became leading merchants in Fort Davis. Otis became an early county judge of Presidio County, at Fort Davis, before the area was made a part of Jeff Davis County. Whitaker Keesey came to West Texas in 1867 as head baker (a civilian job) for Lieutenant Colonel Wesley Merritt, Ninth Cavalry. Even though his salary was small, by 1873 he had saved enough money to establish a mercantile store in Fort Davis. Eventually he became wealthy and built an elegant two-and-a-half-story "mansion" near Fort Davis as a gift for his wife, who unfortunately died before it was completed.[19]

Rooney's complaint brought no help from the army, and the Mescaleros continued to drive off his and other livestock in the area. On December 17, fourteen Indians, most of whom were on foot, took five saddle horses from Rooney's Pecos River ranch. Rooney appealed for aid to the post commander at Fort Stockton, who insisted that he did not have enough horses available for pursuit.[20]

An efficient mounted patrol from the post sent out even on that date might have prevented the next raid. Two days later, fourteen Apaches ran off all fourteen of some cattlemen's saddle horses at Horsehead Crossing. Three of the victims recaptured two of the horses, only

[18] *San Antonio Express*, November 22 and 23, 1877.

[19] Will F. Evans, *Border Skylines*, pp. 205–206; Carlysle Graham Raht, *The Romance of Davis Mountains and Big Bend Country*, pp. 159, 202; Barry Scobee, *Old Fort Davis*, pp. 3, 72; Barry Scobee, *Fort Davis, Texas, 1583–1960*, pp. 99, 131, 137, 153, 186–187. Mrs. Marie Gene McKnight of Austin, Mr. and Mrs. Keesey Miller of Fort Davis (and a ranch near Valentine), and Mrs. Keesey Kimball of Alpine also provided many details, especially regarding the "mansion." Keesey Kimball was named for Keesey Miller, and Keesey Miller was named for Whitaker Keesey, but neither Miller nor Kimball was kin to Mr. Keesey. Mr. Miller's father was a close friend of Whitaker Keesey and worked in his store.

[20] *San Antonio Express*, December 21, 1877.

to have them retaken by the Indians. Soon afterward, Gallagher's farm three miles north of Fort Stockton lost all of its horses and mules to the thieves. The trail went toward the Rio Grande. Since Sheriff Joseph Heid and a posse were searching on the Pecos, by the time another posse had been organized it was too late, for the thieves were far away on the Great Comanche War Trail that led into Mexico. Later that month, these or other Indians killed Gabriel Valdez, a road agent of the stage line, and a black man named Thompson, in a water wagon en route from Van Horn's Well to Eagle Springs, and took their six horses.[21]

Joseph Heid was one of the few men, during the early years of Pecos County, who was able to handle the office of sheriff. As noted earlier, when Andrew Loomis had resigned Heid had replaced him, and later when James Johnson resigned Heid again took over the badge. In the general election of November 5, 1878, Heid again was chosen as sheriff. At the same time the voters reelected George M. Frazer county judge, E. W. Bates clerk, and M. F. Corbett, Cesario Torres, and Francis Rooney commissioners. Emilio Lavedra was elected to replace Hipolito Carrasco as the fourth commissioner.

As the year 1878 opened, Indian raids continued as destructive as ever. In January, Indians (probably Apaches) killed a man and took stock from the Russell ranch, some forty miles north of Presidio. Thirty Mexicans pursuing the raiders were ambushed; only two escaped, and one of these was wounded. Because of this incident, Captain L. E. Edwards, with the geological surveying party of the Galveston, Harrisburg, and San Antonio Railroad Company, hired teams and took his crew to look for J. C. Tait and his survey party, who were in the Chinati Mountains. Edwards feared that the depredators, believed to be from the Fort Stanton reservation, might have attacked Tait and his party. However, Edwards found Tait and his men near Faver's ranch, all safe. They had seen no Indians. Tait, who had with him the son of Brigadier General E. O. C. Ord and the son of Colonel H. B. Andrews, vice-president of the railroad company, said that he needed about a week to complete his survey of the Chinati Mountains.[22]

Early in 1878, Cesario Torres' 600-acre farm near Pontoon Crossing employed fifty Mexican families, and his 1,400-acre farm near Fort Stockton, irrigated by water from Comanche Springs, required the la-

[21] Ibid., December 23, 1877, and January 15, 1878.
[22] Ibid., January 6 and 12, 1878.

bor of forty Mexican families. The Stockton spread was stocked with 350 head of cattle, 200 Mexican goats, 50 horses and mules, and 200 hogs, and its major crops were corn, barley, oats, beans, and other vegetables.[23]

By 1878, Mexican soldiers were often crossing to the Texas side of the Rio Grande in pursuit of thieves. There was little objection to this practice. A mutual understanding had developed that troops, both Mexican and United States, when in hot pursuit might cross the border without bothering to obtain authorization.

General E. O. C. Ord, commander of the Department of Texas, was given authority on June 1, 1877, to send troops across the river when pursuing, but the attempts were unsuccessful. Prominent Texans then began to pressure Washington to send Colonel R. S. Mackenzie and his Fourth Cavalry, which had finished its campaign against the Sioux and Northern Cheyennes and was then in Indian Territory, back to the Rio Grande. Late that year General William T. Sherman, having obtained permission to do this, ordered Mackenzie to move six companies of his Fourth Cavalry to Fort Clark and take command of the District of the Nueces. Leaving Fort Sill in mid-December, Mackenzie, upon arriving at Fort Clark, established eight subposts at strategic sites and in May began preparations to destroy the Lipan village near Santa Rosa, Mexico. He ordered his trustworthy lieutenant colonel, William R. Shafter, at Fort Duncan, to move the 150 miles to Santa Rosa and there establish a supply base as part of this expedition. Mackenzie organized into two columns a formidable force, consisting of three battalions of infantry, three batteries of artillery, eight companies of cavalry, a group of Seminole scouts, and forty wagons filled with a thirty-day supply of rations. On June 12, the scouting column crossed the Rio Grande fifteen miles above the mouth of Devils River and searched the regions of Burro Mountain and between the San Diego and San Rodrigo rivers without locating any Indians. The appearance of Mackenzie in Mexico with such a formidable force, however, apparently indirectly influenced President Porfirio Díaz, who was anxious to entice American capital into his country, to cooperate in breaking up the raiding across the border.[24]

Lieutenant Bullis, who crossed into Mexico in pursuit of Indians a

[23] *Fort Stockton Pioneer*, September 10 and 17, 1908.
[24] Ernest Wallace, *Ranald S. Mackenzie on the Texas Frontier*, pp. 174–176.

number of times, estimated that there were about 235 depredators from four tribes of Mexico operating in Texas. One of these parties during two raids into Texas in 1876 killed twenty-five men and one woman. The troublesome border area on the Rio Grande extended about 400 miles.[25]

Mackenzie's assignment to the Rio Grande, of course, called for some reshuffling of troops in the area. Some were sent to strengthen the posts farther west. At Fort Stockton, Companies C, D, and F, Twenty-fifth Infantry, were joined on January 18 by Company B, Tenth Cavalry. Lieutenant Colonel M. M. Blunt remained in command until April, when Captain D. D. Van Valzah relieved him. Company L, Tenth Cavalry, arrived in June. The force remained the same during the rest of the year, but Major Napoleon Bonaparte McLaughlin, a brevet brigadier general during the Civil War and one of Mackenzie's fine captains until he transferred to the Tenth Cavalry in May, 1876, took command in August. Van Valzah resumed command in October.[26]

On January 5, sixty miles northwest of Presidio, six men were killed by Mescalero Apaches from the Fort Stanton reservation. On the same day, Captain M. L. Courtney, Twenty-fifth Infantry, with Companies A and H of the Twenty-fifth and Company H, Tenth Cavalry, started from Fort Davis on a fruitless pursuit of Indians who had raided and killed four Mexicans and wounded three on Russell's ranch on the Rio Grande. On February 16, two other Mexicans, Victorio Rios and Sevoriano Elivano, were killed by Indians in Limpia Canyon near Fort Davis.[27]

After Mescaleros took twelve mules from a wagon train near Fort Davis, Andrew Geddes, Twenty-fifth Infantry, with ten men of Company K, Tenth Cavalry, rode out on April 15 from Fort Davis and followed a trail toward the Carrizo Mountains.[28] The same day, Lieutenant John Bigelow, with twenty-five men of Company B, Tenth Cavalry, of Fort Stockton, pursued Indians who had attacked the mail stage at Escondido Station, twenty-three miles east of Fort Stockton, killed a

[25] *New York Times*, January 9, 1878.

[26] Francis B. Heitman, *Historical Register and Dictionary of the United States Army*, 1:674.; U.S. Department of War, Post Returns, Fort Stockton, 1878.

[27] "Record of Engagements with Hostile Indians in Texas, 1868 to 1882," *West Texas Historical Association Year Book* 9 (1933):112–113.

[28] Heitman, *Historical Register*, 1:451. Geddes had been promoted to captain only a few days before.

Mexican passenger, and taken the mail and the mules. The driver had escaped into the brush and then walked four miles to the station. Bigelow found and buried the body of the victim and then followed the trail of the Indians southeast to the Rio Grande, where he gave up the pursuit because he "had no trailer or guide."[29]

On April 17, W. N. McCall was killed nine miles from Fort Quitman. Three days later, Lonjinio Gonzales, a mail rider, and two other men were killed near Point of Rocks, eighteen miles northeast of Fort Davis. These depredations were attributed to Mescaleros from Fort Stanton.[30]

During the summer of 1878, various outposts were established. Van Valzah left Fort Stockton on June 8 to establish a camp on San Francisco Creek, then in Pecos County. Company H, Tenth Infantry, Companies C, F, and H, Twentieth Infantry, and Company M, Fourth Cavalry, left Fort Clark on June 10 to unite with Companies A, B, and M, Eighth Cavalry, and Companies K and L, Fourth Cavalry, to garrison a temporary camp on Devils River, preparatory to trailing Indians into Mexico. But within two weeks the soldiers from Fort Clark were back at their post, as no hostile Indians had been located.[31]

As far as the settlers along the lower Pecos were concerned, the situation was bad. Indians raided almost unchallenged in the vicinity of Flat Rock, Camp Melvin, Castle Gap, Eagle Mountains, the Chinatis, San Francisco, El Muerto, the Guadalupes, Escondido, and elsewhere. The soldiers, often using Indian guides, rarely caught up with the raiders.[32]

Under such circumstances, General B. H. Grierson, with an escort of troops, made an extended scout from August 8 until October 8 from Fort Concho through the Pecos and Trans-Pecos region. He followed the Pecos upstream to Blue River, went through the Guadalupe

---

[29] D. D. Van Valzah, Fort Stockton, to AAG, April 16 and 21, 1878; D. D. Van Valzah, Fort Stockton, to General B. H. Grierson, April 25, 1878, Records of United States Army Commands, RG 98, NA.

[30] "Record of Engagements with Hostile Indians," pp. 113–114.

[31] U.S. Department of War, Post Returns, Fort Stockton, June, 1878, and Fort Clark, June, 1878.

[32] This dire situation can be seen in the following sources: U.S. Department of War, Letters Received (Fort Stockton correspondence), 1878, AGO, RG 94, NA; *Galveston News*, June 28, 1878; San Antonio *Herald*, June 29, 1878; "Record of Engagements with Hostile Indians," pp. 112–114; U.S. Department of War, Post Returns, Fort Stockton, 1878; and Heitman, *Historical Register*, 2:444.

Mountains, by Salt Lakes, Eagle Springs, El Muerto, Barrel Springs, and Fort Davis, continued his march to the Rio Grande, and returned by way of Fort Stockton. His report, upon returning to Concho, described a tragic situation. "The old round about stage road across the plains," he wrote, "from Camp Charlotte to Pecos Station, which traverses a comparatively desert country without water or vegetation of any value has been virtually abandoned." The stage company was contemplating moving its stations "to the new road and the telegraph line will also probably be changed and a repair station established at the spring [Maxon, later Grierson]."[33] This change from Camp Charlotte to Grierson Spring was soon made, but the stage did not always follow that route. During the fall of 1878, given the recent Indian activities, the road between Fort Davis and Fort Stockton was considered unsafe for small parties. But the families of Whitaker Keesey and George M. Frazer were not deterred by Indians. The Keeseys, who joined the Frazer wagon on an October trip from Fort Davis to Fort Stockton, reached Varela Spring about dark, having made a distance of twenty-eight miles since noon that day. Leon Springs, forty miles farther, was reached the second day, and the Frazer home on Comanche Creek, a mile from the fort, was seen about noon on the third day. The Frazer family then consisted of four girls and two boys. Annie Frazer Johnson, afterward Annie Riggs, also spent much time at her parents' home. The Frazers made an all-out effort to entertain the Keeseys during their fourteen-day stay. They drove around, went shopping, saw the sights, and held in their honor a dance that lasted for two nights.[34]

Lieutenant W. H. Beck, Tenth Cavalry, was accused of mercilessly marching his unmounted black troops in extremely hot weather through rough, stony country, covered with cactus, mesquite, and lechuguilla, near San Carlos Ford on the Rio Grande, without giving them adequate rest stops. When many of the exhausted men fell out, Beck declared that "the goddam lazy sons-of-bitches ain't worth hell room." (In the official report, *hell* was acceptable, but the rest had to be printed as "the G——d——lazy s——of b——. . . .") A day later,

[33] B H. Grierson, Fort Stockton, to AAG, December 25, 1878, in U.S. Department of War, Letters Received, AGO, RG 94, NA.

[34] Barry Scobee, "Social Life on Frontier Found to Be Strenuous," *Standard Times*, San Angelo, October 6, 1957. This article quotes a letter, dated October 7, 1878, from Annie Keesey to her sister in Wellsburgh, West Virginia.

only eight men were with Beck when he reached his camp at Peña Blanca (headspring of San Francisco Creek). At this point, Beck was accused of saying, "By G——, I'll fix them tomorrow so they won't fall out."

On October 15, while at the Peña Blanca camp, Beck reportedly said to one of his men: "You G——d—— black ignorant s—— of b——," and then after getting some back-talk he assigned the soldier to hard labor, which lasted until October 23, when Lieutenant John Bigelow assumed command at the post. Beck then got drunk and rode to Fort Stockton. Spurring his horse, he rode right into the store of M. F. Corbett, which adjoined the post. Eventually, Beck was returned to Peña Blanca—but allegedly for several days thereafter remained drunk.[35]

Also in 1878, the sixty-six-year-old Irishman Peter Gallagher, founder of Saint Gall, died in Bexar County on October 30. Besides leaving as a monument to his craftsmanship a number of prominent buildings in San Antonio, he demonstrated business ability in the successful development of farming property in West Texas.[36]

As previously noted, the Pecos County commissioners court on June 4, 1875, had established a tax of 33⅓ cents per $100 valuation of taxable property for constructing a jail and a courthouse, but nothing had been done immediately to get the projects underway. In February, 1877, the court asked for sealed bids for the jail construction to be submitted no later than April 2. On that date, the court awarded a contract to W. R. Mapes to construct a two-story stone building for $1,025. Then in May the commissioners again set a tax rate of 33⅓ cents to pay for both a jail and a courthouse. When it met on June 15, the court annulled its contract with Mapes, because of "nonfulfilment," and awarded a new contract to Thomas R. Robertson. This contract provided $975 for a one-story building, which was "to be finished and delivered to the county on or before September 15, 1877." Robertson, however, was unable to secure the construction materials as early as he had planned, and in August, before work on the project had begun, the court returned to the original plan for a two-story building and granted

[35] "Courts-Martial," in U.S. Congress, House, *Letter from the Secretary of War*, January 26, 1884, 48 Cong., 1 sess., 1884, House Exec. Doc. No. 104, pp. 109–113.

[36] Webb and Carroll, *Handbook of Texas*, 1:661.

Robertson "an additional contract," which allowed him an extra $500 for the change, to be paid with a county warrant "as soon as sufficient funds have been collected from the tax levied in 1877." The commissioners extended the completion date to November 1, with the provision that the first floor had to be finished by September 15. On September 13, Robertson proposed additional work, not included in his original bid, and requested another extension of time. The court agreed and approved an additional $250 for the proposed changes, for a total cost of $1,725, and specified that the building must be ready for occupancy by November 1.

The specifications required that a large portion of the lower floor be below ground level and accessible through a trapdoor. The late William Cope, who years later was a deputy under Sheriff D. S. Barker, recalled that Barker had said that the trapdoor was designed for hangings. The site of the original jail was southwest of and adjacent to the present jail.

In February, 1878, the court established a special tax of only ten cents for the maintenance of the courthouse and jail, and on March 25, declaring that the jail was ready for occupancy, authorized payment to Robertson. Apparently the building was not entirely satisfactory—at least not for long—for in January, 1880, it needed repairs, and county officials again requested that the army house civilian prisoners in the post's guardhouse.

CHAPTER 16

1879-1880

IN disregard of Indian raids and other hardships, pioneers tried to educate their children. Although an attempt by a Catholic priest to start a school in 1875 was unsuccessful, the first school at Fort Stockton was apparently established as early as 1879. The school, in an adobe building with a flat, mud roof, near the west bank of Comanche Creek and close to the site of the old concrete dam and water gates, was furnished with a few long, crude benches and had no desks. During the first year, the ten pupils held their tablets and slates on their knees while writing and had a tobacco-spitting teacher.

Thé second school, which was in the long room of a house later occupied by Pilar Durán and in 1981 the property of Mrs. Paschal Odom, had long, rough desks and benches. The teacher, a Miss Gorman, taught, among other things, geography, with the assistance of an ancient globe, to about twenty children of army officers and the more affluent Anglo and Mexican families.

A small adobe house west of the present courthouse and in the vicinity of the present Elliott and Waldron Abstract Company's office served as the third school. The fourth schoolhouse, a one-room adobe southwest of the courthouse, is generally regarded as the oldest school building in Fort Stockton. Jessie Williams, a sister of O. W. Williams, was the teacher. The fifth school structure (some crumbling adobes and a part of the stone foundation are still visible in 1981) was an abandoned soldiers' barracks. The sixth school, the one-room fourth to which a second room had been added, housed two teachers and about fifty pupils. When two teachers were needed, the county usually tried to hire a husband-and-wife team.[1]

---

[1] James Rooney, "History and Progress of the Fort Stockton Schools," *Fort Stockton Pioneer*, May 12, 1922.

Meanwhile, at Fort Stockton in January of 1879, Lieutenant Colonel Matthew Marsh Blunt was in command of Troops B and L, Tenth
Cavalry, and Companies C, D, and F, Twenty-fifth Infantry. From June 1
to September, during Blunt's absence, Captain D. D. Van Valzah served
as post commander. In February a detachment from the post was sent
to Grierson Spring for the purpose of "conducting materials for a telegraph line." From April 4 to June 25, Captain George Augustus Armes
and Troop L were in camp at and scouted the area around Santa Rosa
Spring, not far from Rooney's river farm. During August, Company C
was at Santa Rosa Spring, and later in the year it was relieved by Troop
B. That fall Company F was at Rainbow Cliff, better known by its
Spanish name, Peña Colorada ("painted rock"), located south of the
Glass Mountains on the headwaters of Peña Colorada Creek and a few
miles southeast of present Marathon.[2]

The Ninth Cavalry, which had formerly been in West Texas, in
1879 was scattered over a wide area of New Mexico and Arizona. It was
having trouble with Victorio and his Warm Springs Apaches (called
Warm Springs because of their earlier residence at Ojo Caliente in
southwestern New Mexico), who were often joined by their Mescalero
kinsmen. Its troopers had more than one encounter with this band
during 1879 in the Ojo Caliente area, in Las Cornudas Mountains, and
on Las Animas River.[3]

Reportedly, Victorio had been a "lieutenant" under Mangas Coloradas, a Mimbreño, and had become the leader when Mangas was
killed during the Civil War. Between 1871 and 1878, he was on and off
a reservation in the Ojo Caliente area and often visited the Mescalero reservation—perhaps for recruiting purposes. In 1879, he began
an all-out campaign of depredations in West Texas, Mexico, and New
Mexico.[4]

[2] U.S. Department of War, Post Returns, Fort Stockton, 1879, Records of the Adjutant General's Office (AGO), Record Group (RG) 94, National Archives (NA), Washington, D.C. On maps and in official reports, the name was usually corrupted to Pena Colorado, without the Spanish tilde and with a masculine adjective modifying a feminine
noun.
[3] Frederick Webb Hodge, ed., *Handbook of American Indians North of Mexico*,
2:916; Francis B. Heitman, *Historical Register and Dictionary of the United States
Army*, 1:444–445.
[4] Hodge, *Handbook of American Indians*, 1:282, 799, and 863, and 2:916; Walter P.
Webb and H. B. Carroll, eds., *The Handbook of Texas*, 2:841. Victorio Peak and Victorio
Canyon, both near present Van Horn, Texas, were named for this Apache chief. In spite

Victorio's kinsmen, the Mescaleros, also were depredating far and wide, particularly in the region of the lower Pecos and Devils rivers. As a deterrent, Lieutenant John L. Bullis on January 31 took thirty-nine of his Seminole scouts from their camp on Las Moras Creek, near Fort Clark, and set up a base at San Felipe (present Del Rio). About a month later, a scouting party from this camp discovered and followed an Indian trail up the Pecos River for thirty-four days and 300 miles to the Mescalero reservation. When it arrived there on March 8, 1879, the reservation agent, F. C. Godfroy, refused to surrender the marauders on the basis that only civilian authorities had the right to arrest reservation Indians.[5]

During the early summer southwestern Texas was continually victimized by raiders from both Mexico and New Mexico. On May 5, a band apparently from Mexico stole about twelve head of stock near Fort Davis. Lieutenant Robert D. Read and a detachment from the Tenth Cavalry immediately followed the trail southeast for eighty miles to the region of Peña Blanca Creek, in the Big Bend. There, they recovered six abandoned animals, but, because the trail scattered, pursuit was no longer possible. On May 18, John Clarkson was murdered, presumably by Indians, near Van Horn's Well. In a fight with Indians at the salt lakes in present Hudspeth County on July 27, Captain M. L. Courtney, Twenty-fifth Infantry, with a detachment of Troop H, Tenth Cavalry, captured ten and wounded three Indians, two mortally, but had two of his men wounded.[6]

On the morning of July 14 Apaches ran off with about fifteen ponies from the Dutchover ranch in Limpia Canyon and, reportedly,

---

of this fact, the peak had feminine name (Victoria) until 1959, when the United States Board on Geographic Names took official action and made the name masculine (Victorio) to reflect more correctly the origin of the mountain's name (Webb and Carroll, *Handbook of Texas*, 2:841; Eldon Stephen Branda, ed., *The Handbook of Texas: A Supplement*, 3:1067–1068.

[5] M. L. Crimmins, "The Mescalero Apaches," *Frontier Times* 8, no. 12 (September, 1931):553–554; Edward Hatch, Mescalero Agency, to Lt. John L. Bullis, March 10, 1879, and Bullis, Fort Clark, Texas, to AAAG, May 9, 1879, in U.S. Department of War, Letters Received, AGO (Main Series), RG 94, NA.

[6] General E. O. C. Ord, San Antonio, to AG, May 12, 1879, in U.S. Department of War, Letters Received, AGO, RG 94, NA; "Record of Engagements with Hostile Indians in Texas, 1868 to 1882," *West Texas Historical Association Year Book* 9 (1933):101–119; Ord to AG, Military Division of the Missouri, February 12, 1879, in U.S. Department of War, Letters Received, AGO, RG 94, NA.

killed a woman. Lieutenant Read with a detachment of cavalry and about a dozen citizens followed the trail toward the Fort Stanton reservation. In the highest part of the Apache Mountains, northeast of present Van Horn, Read recovered nine ponies but gave up the pursuit without contacting any Indians. A short time after the Dutchover ranch incident, Juan Gutiérrez was killed by Indians two miles from Fort Davis. During the next few weeks, large numbers of horses, cattle, and sheep were stolen from the William Russell ranch in southern Presidio County, and a Mexican was killed there.[7]

On July 26, in an effort to thwart the Indian activity in the lower Pecos area, the troops were again reshuffled. Troop D, Tenth Cavalry, was ordered to set up camp at the head of the North Concho; Troop E was sent to nearby Camp Charlotte; Troop F was moved to Grierson Spring; and Troop K was ordered to relieve Troop C in the Guadalupe Mountains. If a permanent water supply could be found in the Castle Gap region, Troop B was to establish a camp there. The detachments were not only to scout and to fight Indians, but also to locate all springs, pools, and other sources of water.[8]

Even with the new arrangement, the posts were too distantly separated for the troops to provide protection to all residents and travelers on the southwestern Texas frontier. Three stonemasons, who were walking from Ysleta to Fort Davis, were attacked by Indians within sight of Barrel Station. One outraced the Indians to the stage station, but the other two were killed. Fifty miles away, John Spencer and his son William, en route from Charco de Alsate (the present location of Alpine) to Fort Stockton, were attacked by Indians as they approached Leoncita Springs. Spencer's horse was shot, but he quickly sprang up behind his son, whose excellent mount then outran the Indian ponies to safety.[9]

The larger, well-protected groups were seldom bothered by Indi-

---

[7]Capt. Louis Henry Carpenter, Fort Davis, to AAG, July 14, 1879, and Col. B. H. Grierson, Fort Concho, to AAG, July 20, 1879, both in U.S. Department of War, Letters Received, AGO, RG 94, NA; "Outrages and Indian Raids in Presidio Co., from June 1, 1879, to June 1, 1880," Texas Adjutant General's Papers (AGP), RG 401, Archives, Texas State Library (TSL), Austin.

[8]Lt. Robert G. Smither, Fort Concho, to C.O., Co. D, 10th Cavalry, Fort Concho, July 26, 1879, in U.S. Department of War, Letters Received, AGO, RG 94, NA.

[9]Carlysle Graham Raht, *The Romance of Davis Mountains and Big Bend Country*, pp. 218–219.

ans. Colonel William R. Livermore's exploration crew traveled from Fort Clark to El Paso, seeking a route for a railroad and suitable sites for defense outposts. Accompanied by one company of the Eighth Cavalry, some Seminole scouts commanded by Lieutenants W. A. Shunk and J. W. Pullman, several wagons pulled by six-mule teams, and a large pack train, Livermore's group crossed the Pecos River at its mouth and climbed slowly northwest beyond Meyers Spring, generally following the route of the present Southern Pacific Railroad without encountering any trouble with Indians.[10] During the same period, however, a small, defenseless party of emigrants was massacred. When one day's ride from the Pecos River, a Texas and Pacific Railway Company survey crew, led by Murray Harris, and a detachment of troops encountered a westbound emigrant group. The soldiers and the surveyors advised the emigrants that Indians were especially troublesome in the area and that they should wait until they could all travel together to the Emigrants' Crossing of the Pecos (about fifteen miles below the present town of Pecos). The emigrants disregarded the warning. On the following day, the soldiers and surveyors found and buried the emigrants' scalped and mutilated bodies near the crossing.[11]

About fifty years later, the remains of the emigrants were discovered. Reeves County sheriff Ed Kiser, Deputy Louis Robertson, Barney Hubbs, and a couple of Mexicans with shovels investigated the site. Hubbs wrote that "we visited the mass grave at Emigrants' Crossing. Mr. [Earl] Ligon, owner of the site, had found some human bones. . . . The best I remember, we found 18 skeletons or 18 skulls and a bunch of bones. Realizing that no recent murders had been committed, they were reburied and we came back to town."[12]

From July 28 to November 30, 1879, Second Lieutenant John Bigelow, Jr., Troop B, Tenth Cavalry, maintained a camp at Santa Rosa Spring, about twenty-five miles north of Fort Stockton and about midway between Horsehead Crossing and Emigrants' Crossing. While

[10] Ibid., p. 220.
[11] A. B. Kelley, an engineer with the Humble Oil and Refining Company (Exxon), who obtained the information in an interview with W. H. Abrams, of the Land Department of the Texas and Pacific Railway Company, oral statement, to Clayton Williams, 1966. The location of the crossing is on a ranch currently owned by Earl Ligon, approximately forty-two miles northwest of Fort Stockton (Earl Ligon, oral statement, to Clayton Williams and others, October 29, 1977).
[12] Barney Hubbs, Pecos, Texas, to Clayton Williams, July 11, 1977.

scouting, the troops struck an Indian trail on August 6 and followed it up the Pecos to the camp of a Mr. Beckwith, a cattleman, where Indians had just stolen some of his horses. Spotting the Indians not far from there, the soldiers chased them over sand hills and dunes, without getting in firing range, to the reservation near Fort Stanton. The agent refused to allow the soldiers to arrest the thieves, but he agreed to let the owners, if they could make suitable identification, purchase their stolen horses for $2.00 a head. Under these terms, ten horses were retrieved; eleven others had been picked up on the trail.[13]

From August 23 to December 15, Lieutenant H. B. Quimby and Companies G and F, Twenty-fifth Infantry, from Fort Stockton, were busy in the area of Camp Peña Colorada. In addition to scouting over a large area, the troops built barracks, officers' quarters, a portion of the wall of a stable and forage house from stone quarried nearby, and a road from Burgess Water Hole (present Alpine) to Peña Blanca Creek.[14] The army needed several additional posts to stop Apache chief Victorio from raiding across the Trans-Pecos region.

Meanwhile, Victorio was giving army officers a lesson in strategy over a tremendously wide area, ranging from the Pecos River westward into Arizona and from Fort Stanton, New Mexico, southward deep into Mexico. Major Albert Payson Morrow and his troops on September 16 struck a two-day-old trail at the head of Sierra Blanca Canyon. Two days later, the troopers encountered Victorio and his 140 warriors in a well-fortified position at the head of Las Animas River. After an all-day battle the troops withdrew under cover of darkness with a loss of five men killed, including two Navajo army scouts and a civilian, one wounded, and thirty-two horses killed and six wounded.[15] After his victory, Victorio went to the Candelaria Mountains in Mexico, about fifty-five miles west of Ysleta, Texas. A party of fifteen Mexicans who stumbled upon and followed the trail were ambushed and killed. Another group of about thirty-five who went to rescue their kinsmen

[13] "Report of the General of the Army," in U.S. Congress, House, *Message of the President of the United States. Report of the Secretary of War*, November 19, 1880, 46 Cong., 3 sess., 1881, House Exec. Doc. No. 1, pt. 2, p. 145.

[14] Ibid., p. 146.

[15] J. S. Loud, Santa Fe, N. Mex., to AAG, Fort Leavenworth, Kansas, September 23, 1879, quoted in General John Pope, Fort Leavenworth, telegram, to AAG Williams D. Whipple, September 24, 1879, in U.S. Department of War, Letters Received, AGO, RG 94, NA; Heitman, *Historical Register*, 1:729, 1026.

were maneuvered into the same slaughter site, and twenty-six for certain, possibly twenty-nine, were killed. Another rescue party, consisting of forty men from El Paso, thirty-five from Guadalupe, eighteen from San Ignacio, thirteen from Saragosa, and Company C of the Frontier Rangers went to the scene, but by the time this group arrived the Indians had disappeared.[16] No doubt Victorio wanted to avoid an encounter with such a strong adversary.

Despite the increased activity of the troops, the Indians raided within sight of the forts. In October, 1879, they stole the horses of Charles Mahee, a soldier, three miles from Fort Davis, and in November, within a mile of that post, they attacked Beninio Flores and took his horses.[17]

In January, 1880, Fort Stockton was still the headquarters for Troops B and L, Tenth Cavalry, but during a part of the winter Companies C and F were on detached service at Camp Peña Colorada, where they were constructing buildings and improving roads. Lieutenant Colonel M. M. Blunt was in command of the post until June 27. Captain J. M. Kelley served as interim commander until the arrival of Major R. F. O'Beirne, Twenty-fourth Infantry, on July 9. O'Beirne was transferred to Fort Concho on November 23 and was succeeded by Major Charles A. Webb, Sixteenth Infantry. All mounted troops at Stockton during the year were in the Tenth Cavalry. Troops B and L were the regular units there, but they were at times on detached service or chasing Indians. Troop E was there for a short time during the summer, and late in the year Troops G and I were garrisoned at the post.

With the coming of spring, the several units were again sent into the field or to other camps. Of the Twenty-fifth Infantry companies, C left in April, D was transferred in May, and B, which left with Colonel Blunt in June, was replaced by Company I, Twenty-fourth Infantry, until December, when, in turn, it was replaced by Company K, Sixteenth Infantry.[18]

Meanwhile, from January 16 to April 27, Lieutenant Bullis with forty-six Seminole scouts accompanied an exploring and mining expe-

---

[16] George W. Baylor to John B. Jones, Austin, December 3, 1879, AGP, RG 401, TSL.

[17] "Outrages and Indian Raids," AGP.

[18] U.S. Department of War, Post Returns, Fort Stockton, 1880.

dition sent out by the Galveston, Harrisburg and San Antonio, the Texas and Pacific, and the International and Great Northern Railway companies. (The Great Northern never built any track in the lower Pecos country, but it owned considerable land in the region.) This fifteen-man party, organized in San Antonio, included E. S. Niccolls, assayer; E. F. Gray, engineer; Murray Harris and B. A. Freisenden, representatives for the Texas and Pacific; and Burr G. Duval (son of federal judge Thomas H. Duval and nephew of the noted historian John C. Duval), representative for the International and Great Northern. The party reached present Del Rio on January 6, Devils River on the next night, and Johnson's Run on January 11. Five days later, it passed the ruins of Fort Lancaster, where a man by the name of Tarde was operating a cattle ranch. Four miles farther, it crossed the Pecos River and then proceeded eighteen miles upstream to the Riffles, where it was joined by Lieutenant Bullis and his Seminole blacks. Although the Seminole scouts were considered ferocious, Duval, while at the Riffles, wrote in his diary: "Every night they [the Seminole scouts] have a sort of camp meeting, singing, prayer, and reading the Bible, which among these lonely hills sounds weird and peculiar."[19]

The party passed through Forts Stockton and Davis and by January 29 had established its camp near Presidio del Norte on Cibolo Creek, two miles from Milton Faver's ranch and four miles above an encampment of two troops of cavalry commanded by Captains L. H. Carpenter and C. D. Viele. From this base, almost daily exploring parties to the Chinati Mountains found some evidence of silver, bismuth, and lead.

The explorers returned by way of Fort Davis and Muzquiz Canyon and arrived at "Rainbow Cliff" (Peña Colorada) on March 23, where Captain Charles Franklin Robe, Twenty-fifth Infantry, from Fort Stockton, had his men busy constructing rock huts for quarters. The water there, Duval wrote, "is in large pools at the foot of a limestone ridge with a capstone of yellow limestone, hence the name 'Rainbow' or more properly 'Peña Colorado!'"[20]

At Meyers Spring, which poured out of the cliff some seven feet above the base of a high, over-arching cliff of limestone, Duval noted

[19] Sam Woolford, ed., "The Burr G. Duval Diary," *Southwestern Historical Quarterly* 65 (April, 1962):487–511.
[20] Ibid.

that the face of the cliff contained many Indian pictographs in red ochre, depicting men with a flintlock musket. Two days later, the party arrived at the Eagle's Nest crossing of the Rio Grande, and on March 31 Duval thought it worth noting that "the Pecos ford descent to river, [had been] well worked out by Uncle Sam's soldiers." From that point, the party continued to San Antonio. At no time did it encounter any problem with Indians, no doubt because of the protection provided. Although the expedition located traces of minerals, it was not until two years later that any effort was made to begin commercial development of silver in the Chinati Mountains.[21]

At the time the explorers were in the vicinity of the Pecos ford, on March 31, Colonel B. H. Grierson with a column of cavalry was at the Pecos Falls, where he learned that on the previous night some stock had been stolen from a nearby rancher (possibly Francis Rooney). Grierson dispatched Lieutenant Calvin Esterly and a detachment from Troops B and L, Tenth Cavalry, the latter from Fort Stockton, on a trail that led to the northwest. On the evening of the third day and in a dust storm, the troops overtook the Indians, killed one, and recovered eight head of stock.[22] On the next day, no longer able to find a clearly marked trail, Esterly gave up the pursuit. After a march of 220 miles, about 90 miles without water, the detachment rejoined Grierson's column near the mouth of Black River in the vicinity of present Loving, New Mexico.

A week later, on April 7, another contingent of troops commanded by Captain Henry Carroll discovered Victorio's band in the San Andreas Mountains. Carroll attacked, but in the ensuing fight received two wounds. Lieutenant Patrick Cusack took command, but the Apaches gained an advantageous position and had his men surrounded when Captain Curwen B. McLellan, Sixth Cavalry, arrived just in time and charged the Indians with his entire force. The battle raged until dark, when the Indians fled in three groups. A large number, according to the official report, returned to their Mescalero reservation.

On the previous day, Grierson had sent Captain T. C. Lebo, with Company K, Tenth Cavalry, from the Black River on a scout through the Guadalupe Mountains, and thence northward via Blue-water to

[21] Ibid.; Raht, *Romance of Davis Mountains*, p. 283.
[22] "Record of Engagements with Hostile Indians," pp. 115–116.

the central settlements on the Peñasco. At the same time Grierson had started with his main column via the Pecos and Seven Rivers for the Mescalero reservation. On the day after he started (the same day that Captain Carroll battled Victorio's band) Captain Lebo located an Indian trail. Following it through the Guadalupes, he suddenly on the ninth surprised a camp of Apaches at Shakehand Spring, about forty miles south of the Peñasco. In the ensuing engagement the chief was killed, four women and one child were captured, between twenty and thirty head of livestock were taken, and the camp, which was well supplied with provisions, apparently obtained from the Mescalero agency, was destroyed. Among the captives was a Mexican boy, Coyetano Garcia, who had been taken by those Indians in March near Presidio del Norte.

As long as the pillagers could easily find refuge in Mexico or on the Mescalero reservation, the army's work would be almost futile. Therefore the Indians at the agency had to be counted and disarmed. Grierson's entire command reached the Peñasco on April 10 and continued by way of Silver and Elk springs to the headwaters of the Peñasco. Two days later a courier from the agent, a Mr. Russell, informed Grierson that the Indians were camped on a mountain adjoining the agency at Tularosa. Some Indians, Russell said, were being escorted to the agency to avoid any misunderstanding between the hostiles and the peace advocates. Their camp was in timber on the opposite side of the stream and fully one-half mile from the agency building on the north side of the Tularosa.

According to Grierson, the agency for a long time had been "a sort of hospital for old, infirm Indians; and a commissary for Indian women and children; a safe refuge and convenient place for the younger and more active Indians to obtain supplies to enable them to continue their raiding and depredations in Texas and elsewhere." It had also become virtually a supply camp for Victorio's band, whose members were, "by a most remarkable manifestation of generosity on the part of the Indian Department, having their families fed and kindly cared for at the San Carlos Agency."[23]

On April 13, the time set for the disarming and dismounting of the

[23] B. H. Grierson to AAG, Dept. of Texas, May 21, 1880, in U.S. House, "Report of the General of the Army," *Report of the Secretary of War*, 46 Cong., 3 sess., 1881, House Exec. Doc. 1, pt. 2, p. 155.

Mescaleros, 320 persons were counted present. Hoping that others would arrive, the deadline was delayed until April 16. At 10:00 A.M. on that date, the army began disarming the Indians. When some Mescaleros attempted to escape among the trees and up the mountain, the soldiers killed 2 of the group and captured their stock. At 2:00 P.M., when the troops moved to surround the Indian camp, some Indians were detected riding, leading, and driving their ponies up the mountain, hoping to escape. Units of cavalry, however, quickly crossed the Tularosa in pursuit of the fleeing Indians, and the infantry attacked small groups that it overtook. Several Indians were killed, others were wounded, and a few horses were shot. All but 30 to 50 surviving Indians were driven back to the camp. Those who escaped immediately joined one of Victorio's nearby bands.[24]

Shortly before the disarming of the Mescaleros, O. W. Williams passed through Fort Stockton on his way to New Mexico—little realizing that four years later he would return to the small community and remain there for the rest of his life. On April 7, in Fort Worth he had boarded a fine Concord coach, drawn by six spirited horses. During the next two days and nights of hard traveling, he passed through Comanche and Brownwood and arrived at Fort Concho on April 9. On April 11 he and three other passengers left Concho in a small, open buckboard stage, drawn by two undersized mules. They reached the head of the Middle Concho by noon of the next day, passed the Centralia Flats soon afterward, and then moved by a water hole called Flat Rock, about four miles east of present Rankin and the site of a murder during the previous week, reportedly by Indians but the driver believed by a white man.

At sunset the party crossed the Pecos on the pontoon bridge, where Camp Melvin and the stage stand were located, on the east side of the river. Williams was more impressed with the mechanics of the bridge than anything else. The next stage stand, Escondido, was about thirty-seven miles distant. Here, the team was changed in the early hours of morning, and Williams met the stage attendant, a colorful character by the name of Ike T. Hock.[25] (These two were destined to

---

[24] The account of the Grierson episode is from ibid., pp. 154–158.

[25] A reproduction of the stage building now stands on Highway 290, very near the site of the original station. It was erected by Roland Warnock's highway crews on the basis of information supplied by Clayton Williams.

see a lot of each other in future years.) Hock told the passengers to wait a minute and he would have something for them to eat. While he was preparing the meal, Hock's pet skunk and her five babies strolled into the room. The passengers had to tolerate the critters' presence while they ate (or pretended to eat) a meal that cost each one dollar. After another eighteen miles, Williams later wrote, "At sunrise we passed through the beautiful water of Comanche Creek, just as we heard the morning trumpet notes from the Fort Stockton garrison." At 9:00 A.M., April 13, the mule team was being changed at Leon Water Holes. When the party arrived at Davis at 9:30 that evening, considerable uneasiness prevailed among the residents; a few days earlier Indian raiders in the vicinity had killed a number of people. The stage reached Barrel Springs at 3:00 A.M. on April 14 and was at El Muerto Station by 7:00 A.M. At Eagle Springs, between Van Horn Station and Fort Quitman, it encountered a number of Pueblo Indians, led by Chief Simón Olquín, who were scouting for Victorio's Apaches.

While Williams was riding through far western Texas, Grierson's Tenth Cavalry and General Edward Hatch's Ninth Cavalry by the sixteenth had disarmed 250 of the 400 Mescaleros and had appropriated their mounts. As previously noted, the escapees joined Victorio, who raided so frequently and furiously that, according to Apache historian Frank C. Lockwood, "the hearts of the settlers in New Mexico, Arizona and Chihuahua were filled with terror and they made little effort to resist the savages." [26]

This was the situation as O. W. Williams continued on the stage toward Santa Fe. Not far beyond Mesilla, he saw lying in their yokes the partially dried carcasses of twelve oxen and behind them the irons and charred fragments of a freight wagon, the aftermath of an Apache raid, and not far from that another very similar scene. The stage party, however, was watching for the site of a recent killing it had been told about in Mesilla. After nightfall and some twelve miles east of Fort Cummings, the stage reached the site where the attack had occurred. According to Williams, the victims included an army paymaster, probably carrying money for troops, his son, and the driver. Williams described the scene:

[26] William H. Leckie, *The Buffalo Soldiers*, pp. 216–223; Frank C. Lockwood, *Apache Indians*, pp. 230, 231.

We had come up a long, shallow canyon and out on an open stretch of country over which arose a forest of dead yucca flower stalks, when we saw ahead some white objects scattered not only on the road but also in the yucca bushes on the south side of the road. . . .

We got out and looked around. There were many tracks of horses and men in the road where the soldiers had taken up the pursuit on a trail leading to the southwest . . . we soon discovered . . . [that the] tops of the yucca flower stalks standing eight or ten feet above the ground, carried . . . markers plainly showing the direction of that trail as far as we could see. . . . [The] markers consisted of large white envelopes, out at one end and thrust down on the pointed tops of the stalks.

At Fort Cummings, Williams was informed that a troop of cavalry with Indian scouts that had followed the trail had been ambushed, had several wounded, and been defeated.[27]

After passing through Silver City, Williams had a wild and scary ride to Knight's Ranch, where some black soldiers of the Ninth and Tenth cavalries, commanded by Major George A. Purington, an elderly man, were shoeing horses, working at a camp fire, and going over the saddles and guns. Here, Williams afterward wrote: "I learned that the cavalry troop led by Indian scouts on the trail of hostile Indians had come that morning to Knight's Ranch and had relieved the inmates from a state of siege. Fortunately, the Indians had not been able to do any damage beyond wounding a horse in the corral, but they lurked around the house all the night before and had fired repeatedly into it and the adjoining corral. On the approach of the scouts and soldiers, the Indians had disappeared; but the soldiers . . . were not in shape to continue pursuit without resting their horses."[28]

Victorio's raiders soon swept across the Trans-Pecos country. About a month after Williams passed through the area, on May 12 or 13, a well-armed, westbound wagon train, consisting of about twenty wagons, was attacked by about twenty Apaches in Bass Canyon, east of Eagle Springs. The frightened drivers rushed away in disarray. Several wagons overturned and were plundered by the Indians. D. Murphy and his wife and child survived by jumping out of their wagon and hiding in the brush. News of this attack reached the stage station at Eagle

[27] S. D. Myres, *Pioneer Surveyor—Frontier Lawyer: The Personal Narrative of O. W. Williams, 1877–1902*, pp. 105, 106.
[28] Ibid., pp. 118, 119.

Springs when driver "Dutch Willie" with his team and wagon arrived at full speed. He had managed to escape, the driver said, but nearly all other members of the train had been killed.

Four men immediately started for the scene of the attack. Three were members of the stage station; the fourth was Robert Johnson, who was on his way from San Antonio to El Paso. On reaching the vicinity of the attack, the rescue party found the body of Hames (or James) Grant and the mortally wounded Mrs. Harry Graham. While Grant was being buried, Murphy, his wife, and child came out of the brush. Murphy had been slightly wounded twice. After hiding his wife and child, he had covered their retreat by bluffing the savages with a disabled rifle. Harry Graham, who had been shot through the hip, was found nearby.[29]

Apparently Harry Graham had a brother who also survived the attack. On June 8, Sergeant L. B. Caruthers of the Frontier Battalion (Texas Rangers), who had recently arrived at Fort Davis in search of outlaws, two of whom were named Graham but not connected in any way with the unfortunate members of the wagon train, reported that "the Graham boys of the Bass Canyon party are here, Harry the one who had his wife killed, is laying in the hospital shot through the hip, the post sergent [sic] thinks now, that he may recover. They are both destitute, the Indians carring [sic] off money and everything else. . . . The soldiers left here in pursuit of the Indians on the evening of the 5th day after the fight. How is that for an Indian pursuit? Of course they did nothing."[30]

About two weeks later a small party that passed through Bass Canyon saw evidence of the massacre. One of its members was George F. Grant (presumably no kin to James, or Hames, Grant) a former college roommate of O. W. Williams and a member of Williams' surveying expeditions on the Staked Plains.[31] Grant had intended to travel west

[29] Morve L. Weaver, "Overland Trip in 1880," *Frontier Times* 4, no. 4 (January, 1927):7–8; U.S. House, "Report of the General of the Army," *Report of the Secretary of War*, 46 Cong., 3 sess., 1881, House Exec. Doc. No. 1, pt. 2, p. 149; "Record of Engagements with Hostile Indians," p. 116. The dead man's name had been recorded as both Hames and James Grant, but the former appears to be correct.
[30] Sgt. L. B. Caruthers, Fort Davis, to Lt. C. L. Nevill, June 8, 1880, AGP, RG 401, TSL.
[31] On August 31, 1925, George F. Grant sent O. W. Williams an account of his 1880 trip, manuscript in possession of Clayton Williams.

with Williams in April but had been delayed. His party included a Judge Ewing, formerly of Missouri, seven other men, and a boy.[32] Judge Ewing, young Scott (who was afflicted with tuberculosis), and the driver rode in a covered spring wagon drawn by a team of horses; the others were mounted. Food, kept in a large dry-goods box, and camping equipment were carried in the wagon. The party had several rifles and a shotgun, and each probably had a pistol.

Fort Worth was then the western end of the Texas and Pacific Railway. From there westward, several Concord coaches, each drawn by four fine horses, passed the party, but beyond Fort Concho "it was a case of buckboards and broncos." At Fort Worth, the party was joined by Jim Mounts, from Missouri, who owned a wagon and two fine mules, and two other well-armed men from Denton. Mounts later discovered the Carlisle Mine in the Steeple Rock District of Arizona.

At Fort Concho, George Grant and his companions heard that west of the Davis Mountains they might expect Indian trouble, but they continued. They crossed the Pecos on the pontoon bridge, went through Fort Davis, and laid over at El Muerto Springs to let the animals rest. At night the animals were staked out but well guarded. On the next morning, a supply of water was placed in the calked dry-goods box, canteens were filled, and the journey was resumed. Shortly afterward, the Grant party met three men, including a Lieutenant Mills (apparently, Stephen Crosby Mills, Twelfth Infantry) who was in command of a group of Indian scouts, Troop D, Sixth Cavalry, some of the same that O. W. Williams had met at Eagle Springs a few days earlier. At Bass Canyon, Grant and his party barely escaped an attack, so narrowly that it was reported in Dallas, where he was known, that Grant had been killed. Fortunately, Grant and his party encountered no hostile Indians anywhere.

The Victorio War continued throughout most of 1880. In June, Lieutenant Mills and his detachment battled Apaches in the Chinati Mountains, southwest of Fort Davis and just north of where the railroad prospectors had searched for minerals. During the engagement, Simón Olquín, the leader of the scouts, was killed.[33]

---

[32] In addition, the party included a Mr. Cook, a painter; Henry Baldwin, from Meriden, Connecticut; a Mr. Quon from Louisiana; the boy's father; and three others, whose names Grant could not recall.

[33] Information pertaining to this period of the Victorio War is from Edward Hatch,

Upon completion of his tour of duty at the Mescalero reservation, Colonel Grierson returned to Fort Concho, but he did not remain there long. Soon afterward, Victorio and his warriors had fled into Mexico, but Colonel Adolfo L. Valle and 400 Mexican troops soon chased them back across the Rio Grande. When it was evident that Victorio was heading into Trans-Pecos Texas, Grierson, accompanied by his son and a small escort, left Fort Concho on July 10 and headed for that area. On July 23 he encountered Lieutenant Mills and his detachment of soldiers and Pueblo scouts at Eagle Springs. A few days later, Grierson's scouts spied some of Victorio's scouts in Quitman Canyon, and Captain John Curtis Gilmore, from Eagle Springs, reported to Grierson that he had been fired upon by Indians and that telegraph wires had been cut, insulators broken, and poles knocked down and dragged away.

Since it appeared that he was surrounded by Indians, Grierson "took position" at Tinaja de Los Palmas, about one-third the distance from Van Horn to Eagle Springs, and sent orders by stagecoach employees for reinforcements to come immediately to his aid. In response, Lieutenant Leighton Finley and fifteen men arrived early the next morning. Grierson immediately ordered Finley to take ten men and charge the hostiles. After about an hour of desultory fighting, Captain C. D. Viele and a small body of troops from Eagle Springs arrived. The Apaches kept the soldiers pinned down, however, until Captain Nicholas Nolan with a detachment of troops joined the fight. The Apaches, then greatly outnumbered, gathered up some of their wounded comrades and withdrew, leaving seven dead warriors on the field.

Grierson then ordered Troop K, Eighth Cavalry, from Fort Davis, to scout and occupy the Sierra Diablo northwest of Van Horn and

---

San Andreas Mountains, to AAG, April 8, 1880, and McLellan, Fort Bowie, to Lt. L. A. Craig, May 16, 1880, U.S. Department of War, Letters Received, AGO, RG 94, NA; Edward Hatch, Santa Fe, to AAG, August 5, 1880, in U.S. House, "Report of the General of the Army," *Report of the Secretary of War*, 46 Cong., 3 sess., 1881, House Exec. Doc. No. 1, pp. 93–98, 149, 154–163; Heitman, *Historical Register*, 1:286, 321, 340, 347, 450, 552, 676, 687, 714, 729, and 946, and 2:440. For details regarding the encounters Williams and Grant had with Pueblo scouts and Lieutenant Mills and the death of the scout Simón Olquín, see Myres, *Pioneer Surveyor—Frontier Lawyer*, pp. 103, 106; Grant, to O. W. Williams, account of his trip west, August 31, 1925; William D. Whipple, Chicago, to AG, June 15, 1880, U.S. Department of War, Letters Received, AGO, RG 94, NA.

Troop F, Tenth Cavalry, from Fort Stockton (but on detached service to Peña Colorada), to occupy the mountain passes and water holes between the Indians and their apparent destination—the Mescalero reservation. The wily Victorio, however, fooled everybody by crossing again into Mexico.

Grierson, convinced that Victorio would try to reach the Mescalero reservation by way of Bass Canyon, prepared to block his route, but in August Victorio passed through the Van Horn Mountains, avoided the prominent water holes and passes occupied by the troops, and then went through the rocky Sierra Diablo. Upon learning that Victorio had again slipped by his troops, Grierson marched sixty-five miles in twenty-four hours to Rattlesnake Springs, about thirty miles north of the present town of Van Horn, where he met Troop B, Tenth Cavalry, from Fort Stockton. There, the troops concealed themselves and hopefully awaited the arrival of Victorio and his band. By dawn of the next day, August 6, Indians were seen approaching, but Victorio was too crafty to rush into a trap. Instead, he forced the troops to fire from a distance, and little harm was done. The thirsty Indians thereupon attempted to reach a water hole in the canyon, but it too was defended by troops. The Apaches then scattered among the rugged slopes. A few hours later, they attacked a wagon train of emigrants near the canyon that led to Rattlesnake Springs, but they withdrew after having one of their group killed and several wounded.[34]

A few days after the battle at Rattlesnake Springs, fifteen Texas Rangers under G. W. Baylor arrived on the scene. Years later, one of those Rangers recalled that shortly after his detachment had passed the site on August 9 stage driver Ed Walde on the Quitman–Van Horn road encountered about 100 of Victorio's warriors. Walde, driving two spirited Spanish mules pulling a white, canvas-topped buckboard, had as a passenger retired General J. J. Byrne, who was employed by the Texas and Pacific Railway to locate lands granted to the company by the State of Texas. The Indians' first volley mortally wounded Byrne, and

[34]Grierson, Fort Concho, to AAG, May 21, 1880, Edward Hatch, Fort Craig, N. Mex., to AAG, June 8, 1880, and Lt. Gen. P. H. Sheridan, Chicago, to AG, August 2, 1880, all in U.S. Department of War, Records of United States Army Commands, RG 98, NA; Branda, *Handbook of Texas,* 3:1067; C. C. Rister, *The Southwestern Frontier, 1865–1881,* pp. 209–214; Leckie, *Buffalo Soldiers,* p. 223; and Grierson, Eagle Springs, Texas, to AAG, July 31, 1880, Army Commands, RG 98, NA.

Walde quickly turned his frantic mules and went at full speed toward Quitman, with the Apaches chasing and shooting at him for several miles. When the buckboard careened safely into the shelter of Quitman's adobe walls, it and its canvas top were literally shot to pieces. Even some of the wheel spokes had been shattered.[35] The people of Quitman gave Byrne the best burial they could and covered his grave with rocks to protect it from the wolves. With him, Byrne had a pathetic letter addressed to Mrs. Lilly L. Byrne, care of Major Fairfax, and endorsed with the following condition: "Ysleta, Aug. 4/80. This letter is only to be delivered to Mrs. Byrne in the event of my death, J. J. Byrne." The letter revealed that Byrne was fully aware of his perilous situation.

James J. Byrne, a native Irishman, had joined a New York infantry unit in 1862, as a first lieutenant, had become a colonel in a New York cavalry unit in 1864, and had received brevets as a brigadier and a major general before the end of the Civil War. Mustered out of the service in 1866, he became two years later a United States marshal for the eastern district of Texas, where he was mentioned as a conservative candidate for Congress. In the 1870s, when he began working for the Texas and Pacific, Byrne and his beautiful wife, the former Lilly Loving, daughter of a wealthy Mississippi planter, established their home in Fort Worth. As chief engineer of the railroad survey from Fort Worth to El Paso, Byrne had a crew of about thirty men. In charge of transportation and commissary was "a big-hearted, fearless, rough and ready Irishman" named Pat Dolan (not the same person as the Texas Ranger with the same name). Dolan and Byrne became close friends, and the two made a pact that if either were killed, the other would see that the corpse was returned to Fort Worth for burial.

In early August, 1880, Byrne was in Ysleta, near El Paso, preparing to rejoin his crew in the Guadalupe Mountains. The Victorio War was raging, and he had a premonition that he might be killed by Indians. Thus, on the night of August 2, he sat at a crude table in a shack in Ysleta and wrote what he felt would be his last words to his beloved Lilly. She must not conclude, he wrote, that the cramped and irregular lines and the incoherency of ideas in his letter of the previous evening were caused by his dissipation but by anxiety and tension, for "if ever

[35] James B. Gillett, *Six Years with the Texas Rangers, 1875 to 1881*, pp. 252, 253.

human emotions [were] too sad for words to tell, mine are at this moment. . . ."

Then he wrote his last goodbye: "I will leave here tonight to join my party. If accident should befall me, this will be my last goodbye, to *all* I love upon this earth. If God's mercy and protecting care, should avert the danger by which I am surrounded, then you will never see these lines and the remainder of my days on Earth will be offered in devotion and praise,—to prove my worthiness of your love and my thankfulness, for his grace in sparing me to share it. But if it is my fate to die without again meeting you on Earth, my spirit will be with you . . . and will remain and abide with you forever. . . ."

There followed a list of Byrne's landholdings, which were numerous, and suggestions as to how Mrs. Byrne should handle or liquidate them, and then a final farewell: "Goodbye—my darling,—wife,—my heart is breaking with the thought that I may see you no more. It may be that I have conjured up a horrid dream, but it is too sadly real for that. . . ."[36]

The letter was eventually sent to Mrs. Byrne in Fort Worth. By the time it arrived, Pat Dolan and the other members of the railroad survey party were there. To honor the pact he had made with his unfortunate friend, Dolan, with a coffin in a buckboard pulled by a couple of Spanish mules, traveled alone the 600 miles to Quitman. There he dug up the putrid remains of his friend, placed them in the coffin, and then made a frightening—but safe—return trip to Fort Worth.[37]

Had Byrne been able to delay his trip a couple of months, he would not have been a victim of the Victorio War. In fact, the final phase of that war was already underway. By then, Grierson was convinced that Victorio and his band (which included women and children, some on foot) were cornered. He had placed his forces, which included Indian scouts and Texas Rangers, on the north, east, and

[36] J. J. Byrne, Ysleta, Texas, to Mrs. J. J. (Lilly) Byrne, August 2, 1880, in J. J. Byrne Biographical File, Eugene C. Barker Texas History Center, University of Texas, Austin. The letter was typed when it was offered as the last will and testament of J. J. Byrne.

[37] In addition to Byrne's letter, the account of Byrne is from Heitman, *Historical Register*, 1:271; Webb and Carroll, *Handbook of Texas*, 1:260, 564; E. O. C. Ord, San Antonio, to AG, August 25, 1880, in U.S. Department of War, Letters Received, AGO, RG 94, NA; several articles in the J. J. Byrne Biographical File.

south of the holdouts. Hatch had a strong command blocking the trail toward the Mescalero reservation. Buell with a detachment of troops and Seminole scouts was positioned between the band and its western escape route. Finally, in the event the band should escape the Americans, a strong Mexican force was waiting for it at the Rio Grande. Nevertheless, Victorio outmaneuvered the troops and again crossed into Mexico. But the river was to be Victorio's Rubicon.

Before Victorio crossed the river for the last time, however, several minor engagements occurred between his followers and the soldiers. Somewhere in the Sierra Diablo (probably on or near Victorio Peak, about twenty miles north of present Van Horn), Captain T. C. Lebo and his detachment routed fifteen of Victorio's warriors and captured 150 animals, beef on pack horses, maguey food (probably sotol flour), and a quantity of berries. It was the last of Victorio's engagements on Texas soil.[38]

Victorio led his band into Mexico in August of 1880. There he managed to evade the Mexican troops for almost two months, but he was doomed. During the afternoon of October 14 Colonel Joaquín Terrazas surrounded his well-fortified band in the Tres Castillos (or Castillo) Mountains. The next morning, according to Terrazas, "we took his position leaving Victorio and 60 warriors and 18 women and children dead." In addition, sixty-eight women and children and two captives were taken prisoner, and 180 animals of different kinds were seized. "All the arms and plunder were also left in my possession," Terrazas continued; "I lost 3 men dead and 12 wounded." Terrazas also reported that thirty Indians who were absent when he made the attack were still at large.[39]

During the next few months, a few more encounters occurred between United States troops and either Victorio's men who had missed the battle with Terrazas or Mescaleros who, not knowing of Terrazas' victory, were trying to join Victorio. The worst occurred on October 29, when some of Captain T. A. Baldwin's men of the Tenth Cavalry were attacked by a group "thirty-five to fifty strong" near Ojo Caliente in West Texas. Baldwin lost one corporal and three privates. He trailed

[38] U.S. Department of War, Victorio Papers, Grierson to AAG, DT, August 14, 1880, Records of the United States Army Continental Commands, RG 393, NA.

[39] Joaquín Terrazas, Camp Agua Nueva, to G. P. Buell, October 18, 1880, in U.S. Department of War, Letters Received, AGO, RG 94, NA.

the marauders but was unable to prevent their escape across the Rio Grande. Finally, on January 29, 1881, on the western rim of Victorio Canyon, the last Indian battle ever fought on Texas soil took place. In this engagement the remnants of Victorio's band supposedly were annihilated.[40] At long last, the whites held unchallenged claim to the Fort Stockton and lower Pecos country.

[40] Ord, San Antonio, to AG, October 30, 1880, in U.S. Department of War, Letters Received, AGO, RG 94, NA; Branda, *Handbook of Texas*, 3:1067.

III.
Law, Outlaws, and Feuds

CHAPTER 17

1880-1881

D URING the Victorio War, the Fort Stockton region was also plagued by a band of outlaws, and, according to the 1880 census returns, considerable changes had occurred in and around Fort Stockton since 1870. Both topics deserve some consideration.

Indians were not alone in violating the Golden Rule. Armed white vagabonds robbed isolated ranchers and even commercial establishments in several towns. The residents of Presidio County were hit hardest, but those in Pecos County did not entirely escape. E. P. Webster's house was burglarized, and in February, 1880, S. R. Miller's horses and guns were stolen. In March, Moses Kelly's store in Presidio was robbed, and later George Garrett was assaulted and robbed by four men, two of whom were afterward arrested. In Pecos County, F. W. Young reported that two mules had been stolen from his ranch seven miles north of Fort Stockton.[1]

The notorious Jesse Evans gang was responsible for many of the robberies. Jesse Evans, a mysterious young man, reportedly was leading a rustler band in New Mexico in the late 1870s and taking part in the Lincoln County War, sometimes as a friend of Billy the Kid and sometimes as the Kid's enemy. After he and some cohorts escaped from jail in New Mexico, they moved their activities to the Presidio–Fort Stockton region, where an estimated twenty men were in the gang.[2]

On August 3, 1879, Evans had a run-in with Harry Ryan, the Pecos County sheriff. The details of the affair are not clear in the extant

[1]"Outrages and Indian Raids in Presidio Co., from June 1, 1879, to June 1, 1880," Texas Adjutant General's Papers (AGP), Record Group (RG) 401, Archives, Texas State Library (TSL), Austin.

[2]Barry Scobee, *Fort Davis, Texas, 1583–1960*, p. 130; Ed Bartholomew, *Biographical Album of Western Gunfighters*, entry for Jesse Evans (the entries are listed alphabetically, but the pages are not numbered).

records, but apparently, after remaining free for a time, Evans and John Banner, both charged with murder, were confined in the army guardhouse at Fort Stockton from December, 1879, until late April, 1880, while the county jail was undergoing repairs. During that time Evans' medical bills for treatment of a gunshot wound were paid by the county, as the prisoner claimed that he was a pauper. On April 21, the Pecos County grand jury indicted Evans on two counts of assault with intent to murder, Banner for murder, William Turner for murder, and Henry Burley for assault with intent to murder. Evans was tried immediately. District Judge Allen Blocker in his charge to the jury explained that a case of simple assault was punishable by a fine of not less than five dollars or more than twenty-five dollars. Assault, he continued, became aggravated when committed upon an officer during the lawful discharge of his duties, provided the defendant was aware that he was an officer of the law, or when committed with a deadly weapon without intent to murder.

On one count, the jury quickly found Evans guilty of simple assault and fined him five dollars, but on the other it returned a verdict of not guilty. Presumably Evans claimed that Sheriff Ryan did not properly identify himself at the time of the altercation. District Attorney T. A. Falvey charged that between the time the jury retired and when the verdict was rendered the jurors illegally had separated and held conversations with unauthorized persons, but he failed to get a new trial, and Evans was set free on or about April 28. William Turner and John Banner both were found guilty of murder and were given prison sentences.[3]

Two or three weeks afterward, the Evans gang went on another rampage. On May 19, three of the gang robbed a Fort Davis store owned by Charles Siebenborn and Joseph Sender of about a thousand dollars in cash and merchandise valued at one hundred dollars. According to Annie Keesey, who lived in Fort Davis at the time, the three robbers, well armed and mounted, rode up to the store one evening

---

[3] Pecos County, Texas, Minutes of the Commissioners Court, January to June, 1880; Pecos County, Minutes of the District Court, Cases 35 through 39. Blocker's charge to the jury, the jury's verdict, and Falvey's charge of malfeasance on the part of the jury were, in 1980, among old records stored, in no particular order, on the third floor of the Pecos County Courthouse. Many of the old county records had been lost or misplaced.

just before lamp lighting, dismounted, walked in, covered all those present with their pistols, had the owners open the safe, and appropriated "about 900 dollars," some guns, pistols, and ammunition. "They had the store people go out ahead of them and made them walk up the road while they rode off." Keesey then added an interesting comment: "One thing that gave them such a good opportunity was that the store is out in the prairie . . . and that time in the evening very few [are] likely to enter. It is so common for strangers to come in on horseback and well-armed that no one took any account of seeing them around. There are some pretty desperate characters on the frontier, [who] do not value their lives any more than you would a pin."[4]

The S&S building, a short distance east of the army post, was pretentious in size, one story, of thick adobe walls, and had a cellar. B. A. Johnson, who arrived in Fort Davis in 1910 and purchased the building in 1918 for $500, heard an amusing anecdote relating to the robbery. According to this story, a customer, unaware that a robbery was underway, entered the store and, seeing several persons on their knees at the bookkeeper's platform with their backs to him and heads bowed, called out: "Hey! What's going on here, a prayer meetin'?" "Right," said a man off to one side, pointing a revolver. "Jine 'em." The customer did so.[5] Two of the robbers were identified as brothers Bud and Charles Graham, alias Ace Carr and Charles Graves; the third was probably Evans.

On the following day, the home of August Diamond was burglarized. Before and after Evans was jailed in Fort Stockton, a large number of homes, ranches, and establishments were hit by robbers. The victims included Diedrick Dutchover, George Crosson, the Reverend Joseph Hoban, who had allowed the Crosson family, when it first arrived in Fort Davis, to live for a while in the old adobe church. Within less than two months in 1880, at least fourteen assaults and robberies were committed in and around Fort Davis. Since the local authorities were unable to stop the criminal activity, the county attorney of Presidio County on May 21 requested the governor to send Texas

[4] Annie Keesey, Fort Davis, to her sister, June 16, 1880, as quoted in Scobee, *Fort Davis, Texas*, p. 137. Annie and Isabelle arrived in Fort Davis in the late 1870s to live with their brother, Whitaker Keesey.

[5] Scobee, *Fort Davis, Texas*, pp. 136–138.

Rangers to Fort Davis. In his letter he explained that "many lawless men congregate around the cattle camps in New Mexico and from there they come in large parties to depredate upon the peaceable and law abiding citizens of . . . this county."[6]

Upon learning of the rampant crime in Presidio County, Judge George M. Frazer on May 24 wired Governor O. M. Roberts a report on the Siebenborn-Sender robbery and a request for ten Rangers to be sent to Fort Stockton. The judge even went with a posse of angry citizens in search of the outlaws, but some members of the posse thought that Frazer was more dangerous than the hunted. In this connection, Judge O. W. Williams later quoted John Rooney as saying that he was one of the search party among the tules on the creek, "when 'Billy' [F. W.] Young quit the hunt on the plea that Judge Frazer, who rode the path just ahead of him and carried a shotgun on his shoulder was more dangerous than the gang, because he carried the gun with his hand on the trigger-guard all the time, with the barrel lined on Billy's belly."[7]

On June 3, before the arrival of any Ranger, Judge Frazer reported to the adjutant general of the Frontier Battalion that on the previous day A. Carr (Bud Graham), one of the robbers of the Fort Davis store, had been arrested and that he was alleged to be one of the gang that previously had robbed the Pegleg stage station. The judge was rather optimistic. "The Robbers are afoot, their horses have been captured and it's likely that we will capture them if they do not get fresh horses before the rangers arrive." Graham was placed in jail at Fort Stockton.[8]

Within a short time, Sergeant Edward A. Sieker, Jr., arrived at Fort Stockton with ten Texas Rangers. Ranger Sergeant L. B. Caruthers was sent to Fort Davis. This was the same Sieker who in 1875 had skirmished with the band of Indians that included Herman Lehmann. Sieker, a native of Baltimore and for a time a resident of Virginia, had served as a messenger for the Confederates and, as a Texas

[6] Ibid., pp. 101, 131; "Outrages and Indian Raids"; John Dean, Fort Davis, to Gov. O. M. Roberts, May 21, 1880, AGP, RG 401, TSL.

[7] "Outrages and Indian Raids"; O. W. Williams, Fort Stockton, to George H. Lewis, Elyria, Ohio, March 1, 1933, copy in possession of Clayton Williams.

[8] George M. Frazer, Fort Stockton, to J. B. Jones, June 3, 1880, AGP, RG 401, TSL; "Outrages and Indian Raids."

Ranger, had survived many scrapes with Indians and outlaws. Twenty-nine-year-old Caruthers was serving as a Texas Ranger in Lampasas County at the time of the Horrell-Higgins feud.[9]

On June 8, two days after arriving at Fort Davis, Sergeant Caruthers reported to his commander, Lieutenant C. L. Nevill, that "everything is quiet now," but that the people were always on the alert for the outlaws from New Mexico and the Pecos who stole horses from the ranchers, the emigrants, and the freighters. A large number of outlaws, Caruthers had been told, congregated on the Pecos between Lancaster and Seven Rivers, especially between the New Mexico line and Horsehead. Caruthers also reported that the Fort Davis store had been robbed by two Williamson County men, Bud Graham (alias Ace Carr) and Charlie Graham (alias Charles Graves) and by Jesse Evans. A reward of $1,100 had been posted for them by the citizens of Davis and Stockton, and Bud Graham had been captured in a "badly managed" fight with the citizens, who let the other two escape. The two who escaped, Caruthers continued, were reported to be at Horsehead Crossing, and he assumed that Sieker already had gone for them. "The two Graham boys are indicted in Williamson Co. for murder. I have wired Capt. Strayhorn for capias. Stockton and this point seem to be roundevous [*sic*] for the gentry, who come in to get supplies, lay their plans and gamble, also lay over places for them on their way in and out of Mexico. . . ."[10]

Nearly a week later, in a second communication to the attorney general, instead of reporting that everything was quiet, Caruthers should have stated that he found there "the suppressed calm of absolute fear" of another attack by the Evans gang. The sergeant claimed that a plan to rob three stores had been foiled by the arrest of Bud Graham. Another Graham brother, Jessie (alias George Davis), was in town with a comrade called John Gunter, who had used the alias of John Gross in New Mexico, but whose real name, Caruthers believed,

[9] *New Encyclopedia of Texas*, p. 3680; Bartholomew, *Western Gunfighters*, entries for the Sieker brothers, Richard Russell, and L. B. Caruthers; biographical sketch of Edward A. Sieker by Mrs. Ruby Sieker, widow of Gay Sieker, Edward A. Sieker's grandson, Menard, Texas, February 16, 1977, to Clayton Williams; Clifford B. Casey, *Mirages, Mysteries and Reality: Brewster County, Texas*, pp. 50–51; Scobee, *Fort Davis, Texas*, p. 159.

[10] L. B. Caruthers, Fort Davis, to C. L. Nevill, June 8, 1880, AGP, RG 401, TSL.

was August Gross, of Fort Griffin. Gross (or Gunter), believed to have been born in Alabama and to have been a butcher at Fort Griffin, Texas, in 1878, was then a butcher in Fort Davis.[11]

Caruthers continued that Jesse Evans, who had several indictments against him in New Mexico, headed a band of twenty men and had agents in the towns of Fort Davis and Fort Stockton. The agent at Fort Davis was "Capt. Tyson," whose real name was John Selman. Caruthers had Selman, who was under indictment in Shackelford County and "was getting very scary," appointed deputy sheriff and jailer. The jailer had just resigned, fearing that if Carr (Graham) was brought there the band would attack the jail to rescue him.

> The sheriff [Caruthers continued] could not get a posse of six reliable men to guard the jail in this county, . . . his life has been threatened, and he is afraid to do his duty because he cannot get proper support. . . . Outlaws are lying out in the mountains in gangs of five to seven, watching this point and Stockton. I think their main objective is to release Carr. The Sheriff left Carr in Stockton . . . if he was brought here, they would not be able to hold him 48 hours without rangers . . . [for] it is impossible to get reliable men for service here. . . . S. Graham, formerly of Company A is the only man here that I would have. We need a squad of rangers here . . . this is the route the thieves are compelled to travel from haunts on the Pecos to the Rio Grande. . . .[12]

The Pecos County sheriff mentioned by Caruthers must have been Harry Ryan. Ryan had resigned on May 24 but apparently continued in office until succeeded by John Edgar early in 1881. The appointment of Selman as deputy and jailer has been generally regarded as an "incredible and monstrous joke." Selman was wanted by the "Shackelford County Mob" for rustling and butchering cattle there, but he escaped on a good horse. J. K. Dike related that, during his flight from Shackelford County to New Mexico, Selman stole 2,000 sheep and forced the two herders to drive them to El Paso, where he sold the sheep. "Within the next two years, Selman drove two or three sizeable herds of rustled stock from Lincoln County, New Mexico, to Arizona."[13]

[11] Bartholomew, *Western Gunfighters*, entry for Albert Gross.
[12] L. B. Caruthers, Fort Davis, to J. B. Jones, June 14, 1880, AGP, RG 401, TSL.
[13] Scobee, *Fort Davis, Texas*, p. 132; Walter P. Webb and H. B. Carroll, eds., *The Handbook of Texas*, 2:591; Bartholomew, *Western Gunfighters*, entry for John H. Selman;

On June 15, 1880, Sergeant Sieker informed the adjutant general that several bribes had been offered to get Bud Graham released from jail. Sieker arrived at Fort Davis with Graham, but Caruthers doubted that he could be held there without additional Rangers. The adobe combination courthouse and jail at Fort Davis had been completed only recently on land donated by Whitaker Keesey. For some reason, the building came to be known as the "batcave," even though none of the old-timers could recall ever seeing a bat there. After Sergeant Sieker arrived at Fort Davis, the other members of the Evans gang, deciding that they could not rescue their comrades, headed for Presidio. There, Evans bought a pair of boots, and then he and his three companions rode back to the Chinati Mountains. Tipped off regarding the whereabouts of the gang, Sieker and Caruthers with four privates (Sam Henry, Tom Carson, Dick Russell, and George Bingham) on the night of July 1 started in search of it.[14]

On July 3 the Rangers, while watering their horses in Cibolo Creek, eighteen miles from Presidio, spotted their quarry headed toward the mountains. After a running fight for a mile and a half, the outlaws took refuge in the mountains behind a ledge of rocks and from that position showered the Rangers with gunfire at a range of forty yards. Ranger Carson had his hat brim and stirrup leather hit and his horse wounded before Sieker shot his assailant "between the eyes." Finally, after about an hour of fighting, when the Rangers got the advantage and charged, the surviving outlaws surrendered—but not until they had killed Ranger Bingham with a shot through his heart and Sieker had killed Jesse Graham. That night, Sieker reported: "We were a sad sight . . . two bodies [Bingham and Graham] were covered with blankets, prisoners were tied with ropes, lying by a little brush fire, and in the evening, in that desolate place, a heavy rain began to

---

Scobee, *Fort Davis, Texas*, p. 132. Also useful were Mrs. L. E. Farmer, "Fort Davis on the Clear Fork of the Brazos," *West Texas Historical Association Year Book* 33 (1957): 117–119, 126; J. R. Webb, "Henry Herron, Pioneer and Peace Officer during Fort Griffin Days," *West Texas Historical Association Year Book* 20 (1944):32–33; J. K. Duke, "Bad Men and Peace Officers of the Southwest," *West Texas Historical Association Year Book* 8 (1932):55–56.

[14] Edward A. Sieker, Fort Stockton, to J. B. Jones, June 15, 1880, and L. B. Caruthers, Fort Davis, to J. B. Jones, June 22, 1880, both in AGP, RG 401, TSL; Scobee, *Fort Davis, Texas*, pp. 100–102, 133.

fall on us." Sieker sent a Mexican to Del Norte for a coroner, who arrived the following morning. The Rangers then buried their comrade on the side of the road and showed their respect by firing three volleys over his grave. Continued Sieker: "With saddened hearts, we wound through mountain passes, to Davis, arriving safely with our prisoners . . . people here are so happy with our success, they propose to give us 12 or $1,400 for capture, and they will have Bingham's remains buried here. . . . We confiscated four pistols and two Winchester carbines. The U.S. Govt. took the Springfield guns. Bingham died bravely, in the act of loading his gun. . . . Russell and Carson deserve great credit for their bravery."[15] The Rangers were unaware that they had captured Evans until he was identified at Fort Davis.

Despite the success of the Rangers, the citizens of the area feared that friends of the Evans gang would make an effort to free their pals. Evans wrote Billy the Kid asking for help, and the letter was smuggled out of the jail by John Selman. Selman, however, was arrested for return to Shackelford County, and the letter was never mailed.[16]

In October Evans was brought to trial in Fort Davis' new courthouse, was found guilty, and was sentenced to ten years for robbery and another ten years for the murder of Ranger Bingham. At Huntsville, where he became prisoner No. 9078, he was described as being about 5'7", of fair complexion with gray eyes and light hair, and about 150 pounds in weight, and as having scars on his left thigh and left arm, some supposedly received during a robbery in New Mexico.[17] What happened to Evans after he was sent to prison remains a mystery. Some sources claim that he served out his term; others, that he died in prison. Apparently he escaped, with a bit of bribery, for his name appeared on a "wanted" list published by the Texas prison system in 1886.[18]

What happened to the other outlaws captured with Evans is like-

[15] Bartholomew, *Western Gunfighters*, entries for Richard Robertson Russell and Tom Carson; Sieker, Camp Hancock (Menard County), to Jones, July 12, 1880, AGP, RG 401, TSL.

[16] Scobee, *Fort Davis, Texas*, p. 134.

[17] Bartholomew, *Western Gunfighters*, entry for Evans; Ed Bartholomew, *Jesse Evans, a Texas Hide-Burner*, p. 70; *San Antonio Express*, October 19, 1880.

[18] Scobee, *Fort Davis, Texas*, p. 135; Bartholomew, *Western Gunfighters*, entry for Evans.

wise not certain. The Grahams, released on bail, apparently skipped the country and were never tried. The reports on Gross and the other outlaws are too conflicting to disentangle.[19]

Soon after the capture of the Evans gang, Ranger Captain Charles L. Nevill arrived with reinforcements and camped in Musquiz Canyon. By then, however, as a result of Sieker's and Caruthers' activities, the remaining outlaws had dispersed or were in hiding.[20] On July 19, Nevill reported that he had just returned to Musquiz Canyon from a scout to the crossing of the Texas and Pacific Railroad on the Pecos River, where he had gone "to investigate the reports so numerous, that Wm. Antrum, alias 'Billie the Kid,' was depredating in that section with his crowd of 15 or 20 men." On the way, with seven Rangers he had gone by Fort Stockton to confer with the civil authorities relative to "getting papers for arrests," but he had found little verification of the rumors. At the Pecos crossing, he had received a warm welcome by the estimated 200 persons, because considerable "reckless shooting" had been done in the midst of their tent city. Nevill could obtain no evidence that the Kid had been there, and no one would sign a complaint.

About ten or eleven o'clock of the second night Nevill was there, James Venable started shooting into the Rangers' camp. On his fifth shot, the Rangers fired "at the blaze of his pistol," knocked the gun from his hand, and arrested him. Since the arrest was made on the east side of the Pecos, in Tom Green County, and there was no justice of the peace for that county closer than Concho, 200 miles distant, Nevill released Venable. He added that "Pecos City (as the place is called) is partly in Tom Green and partly in Pecos County so it will require two sets of [peace] officers or at least Justices of the Peace."[21]

Bud Graham had been moved to Presidio County's "batcave" (jail) none too soon; otherwise he probably would have escaped from the jail at Fort Stockton. In October three prisoners in the Pecos County jail, which supposedly had been repaired by Harry Ryan a short time earlier, made their escape by digging out one of the rocks in the jail's wall.

[19] Scobee, *Fort Davis, Texas*, p. 135; Bartholomew, *Western Gunfighters*, entries for Samuel Graham, Albert Gross, Albert Graham, Charles Graham, and Dolly Graham.
[20] Scobee, *Fort Davis, Texas*, p. 134.
[21] C. L. Nevill, Musquiz Canyon, to J. B. Jones, July 19, 1881, AGP, RG 401, TSL.

One of the escapees, a soldier named Robinson, had killed a fellow soldier and had been compelled by the military authorities "to dig the grave and bury his victim under a military guard." [22]

During all the excitement over outlaws, the 1880 census takers were gathering information in Pecos County. When the statistics had been compiled, the census for the county listed 1,689 persons (excluding soldiers), almost four times as many civilians as in 1870 (429). Of these, 948 were males, and 822 were under twenty years of age. There were 233 farmers, many evidently tenants, 8 stockmen, 279 laborers, 29 servants, 5 merchants, 3 blacksmiths, 2 Catholic priests, 3 tailors, 2 bookkeepers, and 2 cooks; only 1 person for each was listed as a carpenter, surveyor, schoolteacher, shoemaker, mason, wheelwright, saddler, store clerk, milliner, post guide, and saloon keeper. The last is misleading, for most merchants were then selling liquor and were virtually operating saloons. Some other entries are also questionable. It is difficult to believe that there were 3 tailors but only 2 cooks and 1 store clerk in the whole county, but census-taking in 1880 was slipshod, and some persons with more than one job apparently reported only one. All the civilians except ten blacks and nine mulattos were either Anglo or Latin American. [23]

The eight stockmen were George M. Frazer, Francis Rooney, Cesario Torres, Reuben Richards, F. W. Young, James Johnson, Lorenzo Lara, and Hart Mussey. There was, however, considerable discrepancy between the census and the tax rolls. The tax rolls show only four of the eight census-listed stockmen (Rooney, Torres, Young, and Mussey) as owners of any livestock in the county and that they owned altogether only 5,950 head of cattle; yet thirteen other individuals, partnerships, or companies, some of whom obviously were residents of Pecos County, were owners of 14,670 head of cattle. [24]

[22] *San Antonio Express*, October 7, 1880.

[23] U.S. Department of the Interior, Bureau of the Census, *Tenth Census of the United States, 1880. Population. Texas*, Pecos County.

[24] The 1880 tax rolls for Pecos County list the stockmen and number of cattle for each as follows: Paxton and Price, 1,400; Poyner and Powell, 500; Beckwith and Ward, 1,600; Creeling and Olinger, 1,000; Vanmick, 1,000; C. Slaughter, 1,000; Norbo and Gibson, 4,000; A. R. Robinson, 1,800; Hart Mussey, 4,000; Mrs. Heid, 150; F. Hernández, 200; F. W. Young, 250; Tom Nelson, a surveyor, 120; the Torres brothers, 400; H. C. Tarty, 1,800 (possibly the "Tarde" who was running a ranch in the Fort Lancaster area and who has been mentioned previously); and M. F. Corbett, 100. Corbett also had 400 sheep.

James Johnson, the stockman, had married George M. Frazer's daughter, Annie, on June 16, 1877, in a ceremony performed by Father Joe Ferra in the Catholic Church.[25] Johnson served as sheriff of Pecos County for a while in 1876, but on January 1, 1877, after the resignation of Arthur Conroy, the commissioners court appointed him county treasurer, to be paid on a commission basis.

Thirty-eight-year-old Mena Heid, the owner of 150 cattle (but not listed on the census as a stockman) and the mother of six children, was the widow of Joseph Heid, who had served as sheriff of Pecos County for several years. Heid had died suddenly of an unspecified cause on February 9, 1879.[26] Harry Ryan was appointed to succeed Heid as sheriff, but there seems to have been some delay, for the minutes of the commissioners court show that he was not bonded until April 10, 1879.

Incidentally, correspondent Styx, in his letter about Heid's death, also reported several other news items that add to the historical understanding of Fort Stockton. Saturo Gonzales had been shot, mortally, when he attempted to prevent a thief from taking one of his horses. A new bridge was to be built across the Pecos River at or near the old one, and the telegraph line was to be moved from the stage road to the new road by Grierson Spring, and iron poles would be used. Possibly of more local interest was the "social event of the season"—the marriage of E. W. Bates, district and county clerk and a former army officer, to Elvina Torres, the eldest daughter of Bernardo Torres, member of a famous Castilian family of Spain.

An analysis of the census by precincts provides worthwhile insights into the history of Pecos County. In Precinct 1, the site of Fort Stockton, there were 82 laborers, 97 housekeepers, apparently including wives of soldiers, 2 Catholic priests, 1 schoolteacher, 19 farmers, 1 surveyor, and a few others. Families that have descendants living in Fort Stockton a century later include Aniceto Pena, Pedro Sosa, John Valentine, and Macedonio and Francisca Lugo. Macedonio, who was born in El Mulato, Chihuahua, in 1850, had only one child, but Francisca by a former marriage had five children, all named Durán (incorrectly spelled Durand by the census taker), athough some, according to the Spanish custom, used their mother's maiden name, Cano. Fran-

---

[25] Pecos County, Texas, Marriage License Records, 1:58.

[26] "Styx," Fort Stockton, February 15, 1879, San Antonio *Herald*, February 23, 1879, reprinted from *News-Item* (Mason, Texas), n.d.

cisca was the daughter of Juan Cano, Sr., who had been killed in the 1850s, when Indians raided his small farm near San Carlos, Mexico, and made off with his herd of mares, and Desideria Ramos de Cano, who died in Fort Stocton at the age of 100. Francisca ("Pancha") spent considerable time at the farm of O. W. Williams, where she helped with the household chores.[27]

For Precinct 2, which included the Torres and Garza farms some three miles northwest of Fort Stockton and the Torres farms on the Pecos near Pontoon Crossing, the census listed 123 laborers, 62 farmers, 112 housekeepers, and 248 "at home" (children and some others), a carpenter, a blacksmith, and 2 stockmen. Of these people, those with descendants who have continued to live in or near Fort Stockton include Lorenzo Lara, Camito Sanches, Gabriel Luján, Félis Garza, Jesús Salazar, and Félis Olquín.

Precinct 3, which included the Francis Rooney farm three miles north of Fort Stockton, had 52 laborers, 63 housekeepers, 63 farmers, 7 servants, 1 stockman, and 129 "at home." In addition to the Rooneys, another family that contributed to the present population of Fort Stockton was that of Guellermia Gonzales and her six children.

Precinct 4, which included Great Falls and Grand Falls on the Pecos River and the Rooney and Reuben Richards farms, contained 89 farmers, 84 housekeepers, 22 laborers, 2 merchants, 21 servants, 1 clerk, 1 blacksmith, and 182 "at home." Among the farmers was Nestor Carrasco, whose descendants were still living in Pecos County a century later.

The big increase in the population was due largely to the development of irrigation projects. The continued growth in the population of Pecos County appeared questionable. The Indian danger in the area would soon be eliminated, and the Southern Pacific and Texas and Pacific railroads were both building across the Trans-Pecos country. When completed, they obviously would destroy the large and lucrative wagon-train business in Fort Stockton. To counter the impact on Pecos County, the commissioners court on April 28, 1880, approved an advertisement in the *Texas Sun*, a newspaper published in San Antonio by James P. Newcomb and A. W. Gifford, which set "forth the advan-

---

[27] Details from S. L. Gonzales and Joe Primera, Fort Stockton, descendants of this family, to Clayton Williams; Clayton Williams, *Never Again*, 3:67.

tages of the County to parties desiring locations for agriculture or stock raising [and] to induce emigration to Pecos County."[28]

Meanwhile, until the railroad was in operation, the mail and passenger stages continued to be of major importance to the Fort Stockton–area people. Between Fort Concho and El Paso, the stage in 1880 stopped (and apparently changed teams) at sixteen stations, including Stockton and nearby Camp Melvin on the Pecos, Escondido (about midway between the Pecos and Stockton), Leon Water Holes (seven miles west of Stockton), and Varela Spring (about midway between Stockton and Fort Davis and at the western corner of Pecos County).[29] Along this route, the mail very often arrived late, and occasionally it did not arrive at all. Because of rains, the westbound stages arrived very late at Fort Davis every trip from August 23 to August 31, except on August 25. During that wet spell, one stage was lost in Limpia Creek for seventy-two hours, and, when it was found, the mail "was a mass of pulp," and the driver had drowned in the creek.[30]

Although the army in the 1880s used the Grierson route from the Middle Concho to the Pecos, the route of the telegraph line, the stage occasionally went by way of Centralia, almost due north of Camp Melvin and about midway between the head of the Concho and the Pecos. Big Jim, apparently a famous landmark on the Grierson route, was a large rock a few miles south of the present town of Big Lake.[31]

One of the best remembered and most colorful stage attendants in the Fort Stockton area was German-born Herman H. Huelster, who had come to the United States in 1867 at the age of sixteen. Herman first went to Saint Louis but in the 1870s moved to the Concho country, where he worked for a while with cattle outfits. In 1878, he began

[28] Eldon Stephen Branda, ed., *The Handbook of Texas: A Supplement*, 3:649.

[29] The other stage stops along the route, from east to west, were Johnson, Head of the Concho, Centralia, Davis (where passengers had to change coaches), Barrel Springs, El Muerto, Van Horn, Eagle Springs, Quitman, Camp Rice (Fort Hancock), Hawkins, and Ysleta.

[30] "Star Route Investigations," in "Letter from the Postmaster General," February 21, 1884, in U.S. Congress, House, *Message of the President of the United States. Report of the Secretary of the Interior*, 48 Cong., 1 sess., 1884, House Exec. Doc. No. 100, p. 157; Webb and Carroll, *Handbook of Texas*, 1:626.

[31] Lt. T. W. Jones, Fort Stockton, to Sgt. Baker, August 25, 1881, Records of United States Army Commands, RG 98, National Archives (NA), Washington, D.C.; Captain W. G. Wedemeyer, Diary, entry for May 27, 1885, Marcus Whitman College Library, Walla Walla, Washington.

working on Daniel Murphy's farm in Toyah Valley, and two years later he took charge of the stage station at Leon Water Holes, adjacent to George M. Frazer's farm. While in Saint Louis, Herman had married Josephine Pene, also a native of Germany, who had also come to Saint Louis at the age of sixteen.

At Leon, the Huelsters had only an elderly Mexican to assist them with the chores; thus life for them there was a rather laborious and monotonous existence. The stand was a rudely constructed, two-room building. The only interest for the couple, other than their work, was the daily mail coach, an event they always looked forward to. They cared for sixteen mules, and, as the Indian trouble had abated somewhat, they were able to put the mules on grass. As a sentinel, they staked out an old gray cavalry horse with a bell jingling about its neck, and the mules stayed close.

During July and August of 1880, the Leon Water Holes had some very heavy rains, and the dirt roof of the Huelster stage station leaked so badly that the passengers and the Huelsters had to "move about inside and eat in a room almost knee-deep in water."

In 1881, the Huelsters moved from Leon Water Holes to Varela (Barilla) Spring Station, about thirty miles east of Fort Davis, where conditions were about the same. They lived in a similar two-room adobe building with a dirt roof. Apparently the Huelsters were moved from Leon to Varela because the stage attendants at the latter place had been killed by some of Victorio's Apaches. The stand at Varela was on land that later was a part of the McCutcheon brothers' JEF Ranch. The Huelsters' new home was reasonably secure, but the spring was at an unprotected site some distance away, too risky to use because of hostile Indians. Consequently, Herman Huelster erected another building a couple of miles away to serve as the stage station, and here he and his Mexican helper dug a well, nine feet deep, which supplied plenty of good water. To combat the high cost of living and to provide a full table for the stage passengers, as required, Mrs. Huelster tried to maintain a flourishing garden with a variety of vegetables for the table and to raise many chickens to furnish eggs and meat.[32]

---

[32] *New Encyclopedia of Texas*, p. 3624; Carlysle Graham Raht, *The Romance of Davis Mountains and Big Bend Country*, pp. 186, 220–222; Scobee, *Fort Davis, Texas*, pp. 24, 73, 157. Other details were obtained from Wade Reed (who got them from Bill Kingston); Sigfried William Huelster (called both Fred and Fritz), Fort Stockton; and

Although the Fort Stockton military garrison could not yet be abandoned, its usefulness was rapidly diminishing. On January 1, 1881, its personnel consisted of Company K, Sixteenth Infantry, and Troops B, G, I, and L, Tenth Cavalry, with Lieutenant Colonel J. F. Wade in command. Company I, Sixteenth Infantry, was transferred to Fort McKavett.[33]

After an inspection of the Stockton post in the middle of 1881, Major O. M. Poe reported its site was "unattractive" and that the westward extension of the Texas and Pacific Railroad made its importance "appreciably diminish, but . . . it will probably be some time yet before it can be abandoned." Because of the Indian situation, he felt that Fort Davis should have an outpost and that Fort Quitman should be reactivated or a new post established nearby.[34] As a result of Poe's report, General C. C. Augur recommended that Forts Concho, McKavett, and Stockton had been rendered unnecessary by the building of railroads and, therefore, should be abandoned.[35]

Possibly as a result of Poe's report, two companies of Sixteenth Infantry were transferred from the post, and on April 24 Troop B, Tenth Cavalry, went on detached service to guard the Texas and Pacific's construction line in the sand hills east of the Pecos River. Company A ar-

---

Loreine (Mrs. Louis) Collins, Balmorhea, Texas, the widow of Ludwig August Huelster, who supplied a rundown on Huelster's children from the family Bible. William Craig Huelster, Loreine Collins' son, Balmorhea, put the author in contact with his mother.

[33] U.S. Department of War, Post Returns, Fort Stockton, January and February, 1881, Records of the Adjutant General's Office (AGO), RG 94, NA. On March 31, 1880, the post's buildings were: one office, 18 × 51 feet; one commissary and quartermaster storeroom, 34 × 150 feet; one officer's quarters, 22 × 10 feet, with two wings, each 19 × 21; one officer's quarters, 27 × 50 feet, with a wing, 18 × 21; three officer's quarters, 22 × 50 feet; one officer's quarters, 22 × 50 feet, with a wing, 18 × 43; one officer's quarters, 22 × 64 feet, with a wing, 18 × 21; a guardhouse, 19 × 51 feet; hospital, 28 × 150 feet; kitchen, 22 × 22 feet; four enlisted men's barracks, each 28 × 84 feet; sergeant's quarters, 18 × 34 feet; grain house, 34 × 40 feet; carpenter and blacksmith shop, 20 × 76 feet; bakery, 20 × 27 feet; one corral, 50 × 250 feet, with a wing, 100 × 142 feet; two stables, each 34 × 250 feet; four mess rooms and kitchens, each 28 × 55 feet; magazine, 14 × 14 feet; a privately owned officer's quarters, 105 × 20 feet, with two wings, each 21 × 18 feet; and a cemetery, 172 × 180 feet (Lt. E. F. Glenn, Fort Stockton, report March 31, 1880, in U.S. Department of War, Records of the Quartermaster General (Consolidated File), RG 92, NA).

[34] "Report of the Chief of Engineers," in U.S. Congress, House, *Message of the President of the United States. Report of the Secretary of War*, November 10, 1881, 47 Cong., 1 sess., 1882, House Exec. Doc. No. 1, pt. 2, Appendix V V, pp. 2822–23.

[35] "Report of the General of the Army," in ibid., pp. 128–130.

rived at the post on May 6, Troop L departed for Fort Concho on May 30, and Troop B returned on August 5 from the sand hills. On September 7 Troop I went to Fort Davis for temporary duty, and from September 19 to November 19 that troop was repairing the telegraph lines between Forts Stockton and Davis. Troops G and L spent a part of the fall and winter at the head of the North Concho River. The end of 1881 found the post still under the command of Colonel Wade, who had four companies at the garrison, B and G, Tenth Cavalry, and A and I, Sixteenth Infantry.[36]

When construction of the Texas and Pacific Railway line reached the vicinity of the Pecos, troops from Fort Stockton took over the duty of guarding the crews. In the summer of 1881, they were guarding 350 men and sixty teams employed in laying the tracks. By July 29, the track-laying crew was only about thirty-five miles from the Pecos River, and the grading crew was some distance ahead of that, and other crews were constructing a railroad bridge over the Pecos River.[37]

When labor troubles erupted on the Texas and Pacific line, Captain T. J. Spencer, in command of Tenth Cavalry troops at White Sand Hills, was reminded, on May 13, that he and his men were there to protect the workers from Indians and were to take no part in any trouble between the contractor and workers. Simultaneously, to the south, troops from other army units and garrisons were guarding the construction crews for the Galveston, Harrisburg and San Antonio Railway Company's line, which was approaching the Pecos River from the east, and the Southern Pacific crews, who were working their way eastward toward the Pecos.[38]

A mail stage contract still provided triweekly service from Brackettville to Fort Davis, a distance of 271 miles, thus giving Fort Stockton two stage lines. An inspector, on May 31, 1881, complained bitterly about the operation of a twice-a-week side line from the Brackettville–Fort Davis line to the head of Devils River, where two speculators were attempting to found a colony.[39]

[36] U.S. Department of War, Post Returns, Fort Stockton, March-December, 1881.
[37] *Dallas Herald*, August 11, 1881.
[38] U.S. Department of War, Post Surgeon's Report, Fort Stockton, May, 1881, and Fort Clark, June, 1881, AGO, RG 94, NA; Webb and Carroll, *Handbook of Texas*, 1:665.
[39] "Star Route Investigations," in U.S. House, *Message of the President*, 48 Cong., 1 sess., 1884, House Exec. Doc. No. 100, pp. 34–36.

Although in 1881 the soldiers were mainly concerned with daily guard routine, Indian raids had not entirely ceased. On April 14, Lipans from Mexico killed a Mrs. McLaurens and looted her house on the Frio River, considerably east of Fort Stockton but close enough to cause concern there. Lieutenant John L. Bullis, with his detachment of Seminole Indian scouts from Fort Clark, followed the trail for six days to the raiders' ranchería, ten miles down the Rio Grande from the mouth of the Pecos, and, in an early morning surprise attack, killed four warriors and captured a woman and a child. Three of his scouts were wounded. The Indian woman informed the troops that her village was the home of about sixty Lipan families, whose warriors frequently crossed the Rio Grande to capture horses.[40]

Reportedly, "the last Indian affray" in the Trans-Pecos region took place in September, 1881.[41] This involved the livestock and family of P. H. Pruett, who, as previously stated, had traded a pound of coffee for a wild heifer. In 1880, Pruett and his family again moved, this time with 280 head of cattle to Limpia Canyon, a few miles from Fort Davis. There they rented a small, well-built adobe house (Agua Blanco) from Lonjino Silvas, a Mexican freighter, and acquired his small acreage of corn and other crops.

Mrs. Ora (Andrew G.) Prude, the daughter, later recalled that her mother tended the forty cows used in her dairy business and that officers and "their ladies came to our place on horseback and in hacks to drink buttermilk at a dime a glass. Mother kept the milk cool with wet clothes. In a little more than a year she took in $1500 on milk and butter sales, which was more than pin money in those years."[42]

Within a few weeks, Pruett had purchased some land in Musquiz Canyon and was building a home there in September when he was raided by Indians. His son Eddie, about eleven, who at the time was

---

[40]C. C. Rister, *The Southwestern Frontier, 1865–1881*, pp. 267–268; Frost Woodhull, "The Seminole Indian Scouts on the Border," *Frontier Times* 15, no. 3 (December, 1937):122–123; "Report of the General of the Army," in U.S. House, *Message of the President*, 47 Cong., 1 sess., 1882, House Exec. Doc. No. 1, pt. 2, p. 128.

[41]Heitman's "Chronological list of battles, actions, etc., ..." does not include any action on Texas soil from October 28, 1880, until December 21, 1891. The engagements that took place in Texas, on the lower Rio Grande, during the early 1890s were concerned with Mexican brigands and revolutionists, not Indians (Francis B. Heitman, *Historical Register and Dictionary of the United States Army*, 2:446–449).

[42]Scobee, *Fort Davis, Texas*, p. 141.

herding the dairy cattle near their Limpia Canyon place, saw two Indians shoot at the cows and raced home to give the alarm. His mother
sent Will (or Eddie) to apprise a "frontiersman by the name of McKinney, who, in turn, rode fast to notify Pruett in Musquiz Canyon. Pruett
then sent a workman some four miles to the Ranger camp near Mitre
Peak." [43] Meanwhile, during the night, an estimated eleven Indians
killed a sheepherder and some sheep forty-five miles to the east, near
the Leon Water Holes.

Around sunup, Captain C. L. Nevill and seven or eight of his
Rangers, along with Pruett and another man or two, started the pursuit from the site of the slain cow. The trail led by the carcass of one of
Pruett's steers the raiders had killed. After fifty miles of trailing, the
posse spotted the Indians near the site of the present town of Kent.
The warriors had become "dumfounded" because they suspected that
a "ridge of earth extending to right and left as far as they could see" was
a fortification behind which soldiers were concealed. Thus, they made
medicine for battle. The "fortification" turned out to be a newly erected
embankment made by the Texas and Pacific Railway construction crew,
but it caused the Indians to delay their flight long enough to be overtaken by their pursuers.

The warriors, upon spotting Nevill's advancing party, briefly froze
in their tracks but then fearlessly charged across the "fortification."
Upon their arrival at the embankment, Nevill and his men found two
abandoned burros laden with fresh sheep pelts. For nine more days,
Nevill and his men followed the trail to the Guadalupe Mountains, but
then, observing that the fleeing Apaches had been joined by another
large party, they voted to return to their camp. Apparently without
suffering a casualty, the Apache raiders in this "last affray" had killed a
sheepherder and some sheep and had escaped with some horses picked
up along the Pecos, in addition to a mare and two colts that belonged to
Pruett. [44]

Long before the Indian raids had ceased, some stockmen were
grazing their herds on the open range along the Pecos River far from
the protection of army garrisons. In mid-May of 1879, Captain George
A. Armes found a Mr. Beckwith ranching in the region of Pope's Cross-

[43] Ibid., p. 142.
[44] Ibid., pp. 141–143; Will F. Evans, *Border Skylines*, pp. 207–210.

ing, near New Mexico. This apparently was John Beckwith, the owner of a herd of cattle in the Peña Colorada area, whose wife and five children were living in Fort Stockton at the time of the 1880 census.[45] During the early 1880s, the Halff brothers, Mayer (or Meyer) and Solomon, moved a large number of cattle into the Peña Colorada region, and simultaneously half-brothers Alfred S. Gage and Edward L. Gage, who were associated with E. M. Powell, a land agent, moved cattle into the same region. During the next year Charles Mulhern, a soldier at Fort Davis, sent his son Robert to Fort Griffin for his cattle. He and Robert later owned and occupied the old Músquiz home.[46]

Texas Rangers L. B. Caruthers, James B. Gillett, Robert L. Nevill, and C. L. Nevill also became ranchers and landowners in the Trans-Pecos country. The Nevill ranch, about twenty miles south of Alpine, was first owned by C. L. but was later purchased by Robert. Much of this land had originally been taken up by George Crosson.[47]

George F. Crosson, Sr., and his associate (but apparently never his business partner), Lawrence Haley, each established a large sheep ranch in the Davis Mountain region, but both eventually switched to cattle. George Crosson had run away from his native Ireland at the age of nine and joined two older brothers at what one source called Fredericksburg (possibly Fredericton), New Brunswick, Canada. The three brothers had later moved to the United States, worked for a while in logging camps in Mississippi, and during the gold rush gone to California. During the Civil War, George was a wagon master in the Confederate service. In 1866, he married Elizabeth Healey and opened a mercantile business in San Antonio. This led to a partnership with Thomas D. Johnson in the operation of wagon trains between San Antonio and Chihuahua and Monterrey, Mexico. On at least one trip, Crosson was accompanied by Haley, who was raising sheep in the Uvalde area. In 1876, Crosson sold out his business interests, acquired some sheep, and joined his herd with Haley's. The combined herds were driven to the Davis Mountains. Later, after the arrival of the rail-

[45] George Augustus Armes, *Ups and Downs of an Army Officer*, p. 464; Raht, *Romance of Davis Mountains*, p. 225.

[46] Branda, *Handbook of Texas*, 3:369; Casey, *Brewster County*, pp. 103, 155, 365–366; Raht, *Romance of Davis Mountains*, p. 224; Scobee, *Fort Davis, Texas*, pp. 47, 102–103.

[47] Casey, *Brewster County*, pp. 155, 392.

roads, the two men acquired large ranches: Haley on upper Calamity Creek, in the vicinity of Cathedral Mountain (sometimes called Haley's Peak), south of Alpine, and Crosson some miles farther south.

Lawrence Haley, also a native of Ireland, had moved to Saint Louis in the 1840s with his family and likewise had made the gold rush. Later, he returned to Missouri but, failing to find his family, eventually moved to Texas.[48]

Farther north, the Hashknife, one of the most famous of the southwestern Texas ranches, in the late 1870s began grazing its cattle along the west side of the Pecos River, about twenty miles north of the present town of Pecos. The original owners, J. R. (Bob) Couts and John N. Simpson, had a herd of cattle in Taylor County, at the site of present-day Abilene, as early as the mid-1870s. Evidently in the late 1870s, Bob Couts sold his interest in the Hashknife to Simpson and William Edgar Hughes, and, in 1881, Couts became president of the Continental Land and Cattle Company of Saint Louis. The Continental then purchsed the Hashknife (Simpson became one of Continental's stockholders), and the Millet brothers' 20,000 head of cattle likely was the herd that Hughes and Simpson sent to graze west of the Pecos River. For some time, the owners did not bother to register the Hashknife brand in Pecos County.[49]

The Caseys, a brave but unfortunate family, began ranching north of Fort Davis during the Victorio War. As previously related, Robert Casey and his wife were attacked by Indians in 1868 while they were driving a small herd of cattle and a flock of sheep along the Pecos toward New Mexico. Casey's neighbors in New Mexico included the Horrell brothers (Mart, Tom, Merritt, Ben, and Sam), who had been involved in a serious feud in Texas. In New Mexico they again promptly

---

[48] *New Encyclopedia of Texas*, pp. 568, 1282, 3192; Casey, *Brewster County*, pp. 22, 154, 370–371; Scobee, *Fort Davis, Texas*, pp. 101–102, 131; Raht, *Romance of Davis Mountains*, p. 203.

[49] Webb and Carroll, *Handbook of Texas*, 1:1, 783, 861; Bill Leftwich, *Tracks along the Pecos*, p. 19. Also see the following articles from the *West Texas Historical Association Year Book*: Emmett M. Landers, "From Range Cattle to Blooded Stock Farming in the Abilene Country," 9 (1933):70; John Thomas Duncan, "The Settlement of Hall County," 18 (1942):72–76; J. R. Webb, "Chapters from the Frontier Life of Phin W. Reynolds," 21 (1945):126, 128; Naomi H. Kincaid, "The Founding of Abilene, The 'Future Great' of the Texas and Pacific Railway," 22 (1946):22–23; Robert W. Dunn, "The History of Loving County, Texas," 24 (1948):97; Naomi H. Kincaid, "Anniversary Celebrations of West Texas Towns," 32 (1956):137.

got involved in trouble, in the so-called Horrell War, a bloody affair during which at least seventeen men were killed, including Ben Horrell and a brother-in-law, Ben Turner. Robert Casey, a staunch ally of his fellow Texans, allowed the Horrells and their friends to fort up in his ranch house and gristmill when a sheriff's posse came after them. Consequently, Casey got into trouble and was soon murdered. His son, William D. Casey, moved the family and their livestock back to Menard County, but in 1880, during the Victorio campaigns, he moved his family, 100 head of cattle, and a few horses to a ranch in the northeast fringe of the Davis Mountains. One of the cowboys who worked later on Casey's ranch was William L. Kingston, who, in 1876 at age seventeen, was with a party that was attacked by Mescaleros near Fort Davis.[50] There will be more about Kingston.

Another young and soon-to-be-prominent cattleman who ventured into the lower Pecos River country before its safety was assured was William Perry Hoover. In 1881, at age twenty-seven, Hoover brought his small family and herd of 200 cattle to Crockett County. Hoover, born in Hamilton County in 1854, was the son of Buck Hoover, a rancher, who died when William was twelve years of age. Young William made his first trip "up the trail" before he reached his teens and later worked in Uvalde County. Eventually he inherited his share of his father's estate and became the owner of 200 cattle, which for several years he moved from place to place, first to Llano County, then to Kimble County, and eventually to the Pecos River. While he and a hired cowboy herded the stock toward the Pecos, a short distance above the mouth of Howard's Draw, Mrs. Hoover (Laura McNutt) and the two children (Arthur, two, and a baby girl) trailed along in a covered wagon. The Hoovers built a shack of cedar staves, sealed with mud, reportedly the first permanent house constructed in present Crockett County. On the free grass of the state's public domain, Hoover's herd increased. In time he leased and later bought land until eventually he owned 100 sections.[51]

[50] Phillip J. Rasch, "The Gun and the Rope," *West Texas Historical Association Year Book* 33 (1957):138–142; Webb and Carroll, *Handbook of Texas*, 1:836–837; Heitman, *Historical Register*, 1:815 (Randlett); Evans, *Border Skylines*, pp. 229–232; Raht, *Romance of Davis Mountains*, pp. 227–228; Scobee, *Fort Davis, Texas*, pp. 161–162.

[51] *New Encyclopedia of Texas*, p. 1130; Claude Denham, "Frontier Problems and Amusements in Crockett County," *West Texas Historical Association Year Book* 9 (1933): 35–37; *Ozona, Texas, Crockett County, 1891–1966*, p. 13.

Some stockmen, including Francis Rooney, were not so fortunate. Rooney obtained twenty-four certificates on October 19, 1881, as a bonus for the construction of six miles of ditch alongside the Pecos River. He located fourteen certificates in present Brewster County, near Leoncita Springs and Peña Colorada. The former site, he felt, would constitute the beginning of a ranch, and the latter would give him a foothold near the future fort.[52] He died, however, before deriving any benefits from the holdings.

Meanwhile, the general election on November 20, 1880, brought about some changes in Pecos County. John Edgar, Judge Frazer's brother-in-law, replaced Harry Ryan as sheriff. Jacob Jacobs replaced E. W. Bates as county clerk, and T. A. Falvey became district attorney. Allen Blocker remained the district judge, and James Johnson was retained as the county treasurer. (Johnson's wife, Annie Frazer Johnson, was running the Hotel Johnson, a popular boarding house.)[53] Cesario Torres, Francis Rooney, and M. F. Corbett were reelected as commissioners, but Corbett, for some unknown reason, chose not to qualify, and Joseph Friedlander was appointed to replace him. William Lempest replaced Emilio Lavedra as the other commissioner.

The most surprising change was the election of F. W. Young as county judge. Apparently Frazer had not sought reelection; his responsibilities had been great, and he had not been paid for his services during the previous year. The county finances were in bad shape, and it is likely that the Gallaghers' stores held many unpaid Pecos County warrants. The county funds had been heavily drawn upon for the expenses incurred in capturing and guarding outlaws. Furthermore, very few lands or other properties had been rendered for taxes, and consequently there had been very little income from taxation. The commissioners had also paid $500, which they could ill afford, to advertise the county's opportunities. Perhaps, since there was no bank in Fort Stockton, there was a financial motive in electing a county judge and a commissioner who happened to be storekeepers and whose businesses might be able temporarily to finance the county's business.

The new commissioners court consequently was primarily concerned with the county's financial dilemma. It took steps immediately

[52] David R. Reeves, Director of Records, General Land Office, Austin, to Clayton Williams, November 22, 1974.
[53] Armes, *Ups and Downs of an Army Officer*, p. 479.

to pay with warrants all the overdue accounts, instructed the sheriff to make a settlement with the county treasurer on or before March 1, 1881, for money collected by him, and ordered the treasurer to present a financial statement for the county in February and his books and accounts at a called meeting on March 15. Within another year the situation had improved, largely because of the addition of two railroads, which resulted in 1882 in Pecos County's having a rendered property value of $1,796,751, compared with $620,701 in 1881.[54]

In 1881, the name of the settlement known as Saint Gall became officially and permanently Fort Stockton. The name Saint Gall, which Peter Gallagher had given his first townsite subdivision, had never been universally accepted. Most people had tended to refer to the settlement as Fort Stockton. On August 13, 1881, in an election ordered by the commissioners court, the voters by a majority of sixty-four to twenty-nine favored Fort Stockton over Saint Gall. The same election also officially recognized Fort Stockton (the town) as the county seat.[55]

[54]A. W. Spaight, *The Resources, Soil and Climate of Texas*, p. 252.

[55]Pecos County, Commissioners Court Minutes, July 1 and August 13, 1881; Clayton Williams, "Fort Stockton's First 100 Years," *Fort Stockton Centennial, 1859–1959*.

CHAPTER 18

1882

I<small>N</small> 1882, Pecos County covered 11,279 square miles, bounded on the east by 300 miles of the Pecos River and on the south by 150 miles of the Rio Grande. After the remnants of Victorio's band had been subdued, stockmen had begun moving onto free range in the county, and by the following January county tax-assessment rolls listed 763 horses and mules, 34,806 cattle, 4,102 sheep, and 1,177 goats. The irrigated farmland was producing from twenty to thirty bushels of corn, eighteen to twenty bushels of oats, and thirty to forty bushels of barley to the acre. With two railroads being completed, the county's virgin territory was open for speculation and development.[1] The Texas and Pacific line had been completed through Pecos City and Toyah (then in Pecos County) to Sierra Blanca by late December, 1881, when O. W. Williams and his bride rode one of its first passenger trains from Dallas to El Paso. The couple changed to the Southern Pacific at Sierra Blanca and ended their trip to Silver City, New Mexico, on a stagecoach.[2]

When the Texas and Pacific completed its line through the northern part of Pecos County, George M. Frazer in May, 1882, obtained an annual contract to carry the mail both ways between the rail station at Toyah and Fort Davis, a distance of sixty miles, six times a week for $2,640. At the same time, Beriah Magoffin got a similar contract for a route between Toyah and Fort Stockton for $3,290.[3] Another mail-contract route was established between Del Rio and Fort Davis, via

---

[1] A. W. Spaight, *The Resources, Soil and Climate of Texas*, pp. 252, 254.

[2] S. D. Myres, *Pioneer Surveyor—Frontier Lawyer: The Personal Narrative of O. W. Williams, 1877–1902*, p. 17.

[3] "Offers and Contracts for Carrying the Mails," in "Letter from the Postmaster General," February 21, 1883, U.S. Congress, House, *Message of the President of the United States. Report of the Secretary of the Interior*, 47 Cong., 2 sess., 1883, House Exec. Doc. No. 93, pp. 213–214.

Fort Stockton, a distance of 241 miles, to provide triweekly service, but in December this route was deemed unnecessary and abandoned.[4]

Meanwhile, a transcontinental railroad was nearing completion. By September, 1882, the Southern Pacific had built its rails eastward through El Paso to within five miles of Eagle's Nest (Langtry), and the Galveston, Harrisburg, and San Antonio cars were running to Seminole Cave, four miles east of the Pecos River. At the end of the latter line, Chinatown was an encampment of some 3,000 Chinese laborers, who reportedly were treated much like slaves.

In this area of cactus- and rock-covered mountains and valleys, Bernardo Torres, a Fort Stockton resident, started the town of Eagle's Nest, later made famous by Judge Roy Bean. Torres, as previously mentioned, had been one of the first to establish a farm irrigation system from the Comanche Springs, and afterward he had been an associate in the construction of the Torres dam on the Pecos, about twelve miles upstream from Camp Melvin, and the irrigation ditches to carry diverted Pecos water to nearby farms. For these developments, he had received from the state thirty-seven sections of land, a portion of which he located at the juntion of the Pecos and the Rio Grande and on the route of the Galveston, Harrisburg, and San Antonio line. There he built one wooden shack and two adobe buildings on a ledge 300 feet above the Rio Grande. Until the railroad arrived, Torres' town was called Eagle's Nest, after a town on the opposite side of the river, which got its name because of the many aeries under a nearby crag high above the stream. To obtain water, Torres constructed a road from his settlement to the river.

In 1882, the rails from the east were laid across Devils River at its mouth and to the Pecos. For the crossing at the mouths of both rivers, the crews had to tunnel through mountains. These great tunnels, cut out almost entirely by Chinese coolies, nearly a century later are covered by the waters of the Amistad Reservoir, a joint creation in the 1960s of the United States and Mexico.[5]

[4]"Curtailment in the Service," in "Letter from the Postmaster General," January 25, 1884, U.S. Congress, House, *Message of the President of the United States. Report of the Secretary of the Interior*, 48 Cong., 1 sess., 1884, House Exec. Doc. No. 84, p. 486.

[5]Jack R. Skiles, "Eagles Marked the Site That Became Langtry," *Standard Times* (San Angelo, Texas), January 26, 1964; Eldon Stephen Branda, ed., *The Handbook of Texas*, 3:27.

Willow Spring, about six miles northwest of Eagle's Nest, and Meyers Spring, twenty-five miles northwest of Willow Spring, both then in Pecos County and in extremely rough country, had long been the escape route to Mexico for raiding Lipans, Mescaleros, and Kickapoos. For this reason, Eighth Cavalry units from Fort Clark and their Seminole scouts in 1882 were at times on patrol duty in the regions of Meyers Spring and the lower Pecos to protect the railroad workers and and other citizens from Indian intruders.[6]

Since troops were needed in the Rio Grande border posts and other posts along the westward-moving frontier, the army decided in 1882 to abandon Fort Stockton. In January it was occupied by Troops B, G, and L, Tenth Cavalry, and Companies A and I, First Infantry, under the command of Lieutenant Colonel J. F. Wade. Employees included a foragemaster, a guide, a wheelwright, a blacksmith, and two teamsters. Now that the Indians in New Mexico had been subdued, the soldiers were occupied largely in garrison and escort duty. On April 20, Companies A and I, First Infantry, departed Fort Stockton for New Mexico; and Troop B, Tenth Cavalry, was detached to Fort Davis. In May, Company B, Sixteenth Infantry, was moved on detached service from Fort Concho to Stockton, and, during June, the situation was so quiet that Colonel Wade turned command temporarily over to Major Curwen Boyd McLellan and was on leave. In July, further preparations for abandonment got underway. Company B, Sixteenth Infantry, was transferred to Fort Concho; Troop B, Tenth Cavalry, was sent to Fort Davis; and Companies A and I, First Infantry, were transferred—at least on paper—to Arizona. As a precautionary measure (or because they were not needed elsewhere), Troops G and L, Tenth Cavalry, were retained for a while longer, but the headquarters of the Tenth Cavalry was moved from Fort Concho to Fort Davis.[7]

No chronicle of southwestern Texas would be complete without

[6] U.S. Department of War, Post Surgeon's Reports, Fort Clark, 1882, Records of the Adjutant General's Office (AGO), Record Group (RG) 94, National Archives (NA), Washington, D.C.

[7] U.S. Department of War, Post Returns, Fort Stockton, 1882, AGO, RG 94, NA; "Report of the General of the Army," in U.S. Congress, House, *Message of the President of the United States. Report of the Secretary of War*, November 14, 1882, 47 Cong., 2 sess., 1883, House Exec. Doc. No. 1, pt. 2, p. 104; William H. Leckie, *The Buffalo Soldiers*, p. 238.

some mention of Judge Roy Bean.[8] Bean was known as the "Law West of the Pecos," and the law he enforced was strictly Roy Bean's law. Roy Bean, born in Mason County, Kentucky, about 1825, and his brother, Samuel G. Bean, in 1848 organized a trading expedition to Chihuahua, where evidently for a short time they operated a small saloon. There, it seems, Sam married the daughter of the notorious scalp hunter James Kirker, who had a contract with the governor of Chihuahua to exterminate the Apaches. Kirker and his hunters, finding it easier and less dangerous, began bringing in scalps taken from Mexican peasants. According to one story, Roy killed a customer for denouncing Kirker for this practice and then to escape an angry mob fled the country.

At any rate, some sort of trouble did cause the Beans to leave Chihuahua in haste. Sam then operated a saloon and hotel business in Mesilla and at Piños Altos, New Mexico, near Las Cruces and Silver City, respectively, and Roy went to California where another brother, Joshua, was an influential citizen. In February, 1852, Roy was arrested in San Diego for fighting a duel, but he escaped from jail a couple of months later and went to nearby San Gabriel, where he joined Josh Bean in operating a saloon. After Josh was murdered, Roy became the sole proprietor and prospered for several years, but in the late 1850s he showed up with no money at Sam Bean's home in Mesilla. He claimed that a rival for the affection of a Mexican girl had strung him by the neck to a tree, but the girl had cut him loose.

Until the outbreak of the Civil War, Roy helped Sam with his businesses, which, in addition to the saloon and hotel, included retail merchandise. Apparently, the two made a profit in just about everything, including their fine billiard table. Roy may have served in some capacity with the Confederates during the campaigns in New Mexico, but if so it must have been insignificantly, for he was not to become

[8]The account of Roy Bean is from the following sources: Walter P. Webb and H. B. Carroll, *The Handbook of Texas*, 1:129–130, and 2:26, 564; C. L. Sonnichsen, *Roy Bean, Law West of the Pecos*, pp. 75–96, 113–114; Skiles, "Eagles Marked the Site"; Noel B. Gerson, *Because I Loved Him: The Life and Loves of Lillie Langtry*, pp. 10, 214; Myres, *Pioneer Surveyor—Frontier Lawyer*, p. 171; Dorothy Watson, *The Pinos Altos Story*, p. 5; O. W. Williams, Fort Stockton, to J. W. Ballard, December 8, 1930, copy in possession of Clayton Williams; Richard King, "Lillie Langtry in Texas," *West Texas Historical Association Year Book* 37 (1961):82–98; Ralph A. Smith, "Poor Mexico, So Far from God and So Close to the Tejanos," *West Texas Historical Association Year Book* 44 (1968):102.

involved in anything that was not profitable. His activities during the next few years are even more difficult to disentangle. Some reports claim that after the Battle of Glorietta he went to San Antonio, where he variously worked as a freighter, butcher, wood contractor, dairy operator, and saloon keeper and schemed to avoid the payment of his rent. Others claim that he appropriated money from Sam Bean's saloon and slipped into Mexico but returned when financially able to establish a freighting business. Unquestionably, Roy did operate as a freighter for some time before settling in the area of Eagle's Nest. On one occasion his wagons sustained considerable damage in the Pecos River at Horsehead Crossing. His Mexican hand Pancho, after examining the contents of the wagon, announced: "Señor Bean, the can goods, heem soaked; the bacon shees wet." When queried about the whiskey, Pancho replied, "Hees fine." "Hell," snorted Bean, "there ain't nothing to worry about then."

In October, 1866, Roy Bean married Virginia Chavez, and in time the couple had four children. Financial and domestic difficulties eventually influenced Bean to leave San Antonio and, probably at the suggestion of his friend, W. N. Monroe, the contractor who was building the Galveston, Harrisburg and San Antonio railroad westward, to set himself up in business near the railroad construction camps.

As previously noted, hundreds of Chinese and other laborers were employed in the construction of this railroad line, and many others, including professional gamblers, thieves and pickpockets, and whiskey salesmen were also there. This was the kind of environment to which Roy Bean seems always to have gravitated. During the summer of 1882, the camps along the twenty miles of railroad construction in the lower Pecos area contained about 8,000 people. Eagle's Nest (later Langtry) was fifteen miles west of the Pecos. Ten miles east-southeast of Eagle's Nest was Vinegarroon (named for a harmless scorpion, popularly believed to be venomous, that emits a vinegary odor when disturbed), and between it and Eagle's Nest was Soto City (named for the sotol plant, which resembles a yucca, but most people who do not speak Spanish pronounce it *soto*, a corruption of the Spanish name). All three settlements were then in Pecos County.

By the spring of 1882, Bean had set up his tent saloon in the railroad construction area. On June 6, probably while Roy was still selling booze at Vinegarroon, Major Converse, the railroad contractor at the mouth of the Pecos, wrote to the Texas adjutant general that the hard characters who populated the camps were getting out of hand and that eight or ten Rangers were needed to maintain order. A short time later, the Rangers, under the command of Captain T. L. Oglesby and Lieutenant L. P. Sieker, arrived and quickly closed nine saloons and one store. Oglesby reported that the area had only one deputy sheriff and no justice of the peace and recommended that Roy Bean be appointed to fill the latter job. The appointment was made on August 2, but Bean and the Rangers did not bother to wait for it. On July 25, Bean rolled into Eagle's Nest, set up his whiskey business, and proceeded to administer justice. He did not qualify until December 6, over four months after the Pecos County commissioners court made the appointment. Thus, there was no legal authority for his "justice" during the interval. Bean began his activities at Eagle's Nest by erecting a sign that read: "On the Banks of the Rio Grande, Eagle's Nest Springs, Pecos County Headquarters Depot Saloon, Monroe Camp No. 6." On the same day, the Rangers brought Joe Bell before Judge Bean's court, charged him with aggravated assault, and obtained the first conviction under Bean's "Law West of the Pecos."

Although Judge Bean's decisions were often unreasonable and without any legal basis and he pocketed more fines than he sent to Fort Stockton, the Rangers liked very much having the cases settled on the spot to avoid the expense and the twelve days required to transfer prisoners and witnesses the approximately 600 miles to and from Fort Stockton.

Bean later moved back to Vinegarroon. There, the Vinegarroon Dance Hall, a large tent over a rock floor, served as Ranger headquarters, courtroom, gambling hall, and saloon, and frequently it was the scene of violence. Occasionally corpses were dragged out of the place to the tune of rowdy music and amid the noise of shattering beer bottles. Reportedly, two women were shot there, one of whom was killed instantly.

Before the end of the year, the contractors were shipping their equipment and men to other areas, and Vinegarroon was becoming a ghost town. Consequently, Bean decided to move to a new settlement, called Strawbridge (soon afterward renamed Sanderson). But Charlie Wilson, who operated a saloon there and did not like competition, determined to get rid of the intruder. A Mexican, hired by Wilson, slipped into Bean's saloon and laced the whiskey barrel with a strong dose of kerosene. Since, thereafter, his customers were few and far between, Bean soon packed up and moved back to the Pecos area. Ordinarily Roy Bean knew how to handle competitors, though. Once, when a competitor erected a shack near his own tent, the judge induced him to make a hasty departure by ventilating the proprietor's shack with bullet holes. With that done, Bean invited the spectators to guzzle up the man's booze and to bring whatever was left to his own establishment.[9]

At the end of 1882, Bean was back at Eagle's Nest, and his judicial decisions and eccentric behavior were well on the way to becoming legendary. He obtained a copy of the 1879 *Revised Statutes of Texas*, but he made use of it only when it suited his purpose; otherwise, he twisted the wording to fit his own interpretation of the law. The lawyer who attempted to defend a client in Bean's court nearly always had his objections overruled, and if he persisted in objecting he was threatened with the hangman's noose. Defendants who had the audacity to complain about a fine usually obtained stiffer punishment. On one occasion, three gamblers cheated a stage driver, and the driver sold the company vehicle and mules to the gamblers to get money for a comeback. Unfortunately, he was again the loser, and the town of Vinegarroon lost both stage and mail service. When the stage owner arrived and discovered what had happened, he had the gamblers brought before Bean's court on a charge of interfering with a public conveyance. Bean ruled that the gamblers had to return the stage, the team, and the money. When they sarcastically demurred, Bean fined each thirty dollars for gambling. They left the court without paying the fines, but Bean had a Ranger return them. When they again complained bitterly about the fines, Bean informed them that he had indeed made a mistake and raised the fine of each to fifty dollars. Back-talk from defendants could be very profitable for the judge.

Bean's friends fared no better in court than his enemies. It was a violation for a person to carry a pistol or other concealed weapon unless he was traveling; as long as he was not standing still, no law was broken. In the case of a friend charged with carrying a concealed

[9]O. W. Williams, account in possession of Clayton Williams; Sonnichsen, *Roy Bean*, pp. 82–83, 92–96.

weapon, Bean ruled that at the moment of arrest he was standing still and therefore was guilty as charged. One of Bean's most bizarre decisions, which may or may not be true, dealt with a man who was killed when he fell from a bridge. Upon discovering that the victim had a pistol and forty dollars on his person, the judge fined the corpse forty dollars for carrying a concealed weapon—the corpse was not traveling when the pistol was found on it.

Another well-known legend deals with the death of a Chinese man.[10] According to one version, the man, who was working as a cook for the railroad construction crews, took special pride in the pies he baked. When these culinary delights were removed from the oven, he placed them in an adjoining tent to cool. Soon some began disappearing. Arming himself with a meat ax, the indignant cook hid in the cooling tent and waited. When a large Irish track worker sneaked in and snatched a pie, the cook raised his ax and charged the thief, who fled to his own tent, grabbed his ancestor's broadsword, and literally cut off the Chinese man's head as he entered the Irishman's tent. When the Irishman appeared in court, Judge Bean consulted the statutes applicable to decapitation. His decision was: "I see where it is homicide to kill a man. But I don't see where it is against the law to kill a Chinaman." Case dismissed!

Some who witnessed the eccentric decisions considered them practical and wise. The Irishman's friends were prepared to start a riot had he not been released. In the case of the pistol-toting corpse, the forty-dollar fine was more than was needed for the burial—Bean, of course, kept the difference. To assuage tempers, Bean during the court recesses often acted as bartender to the jury, the prisoners, and the bystanders.

In 1930, the late O. W. Williams, in a letter to a friend, recalled still another of Bean's interesting decisions. An engineer on a passenger train had been killed in a rear-end collision at Eldridge (between the present towns of Sanderson and Dryden). Eldridge was not in Bean's precinct, but it was in Pecos County, and Bean held the inquest. Bean had with him a bright young man, who wrote a good hand and had some knowledge of technical legal terms. From the return, Williams continued, "written in a beautiful long hand and signed by

[10] Alice Evans Downie, *Terrell County, Texas: Its Past—Its People*, p. 77.

Bean as 'Crowner'," it appears that a freight train going west had side-tracked at Eldridge to allow the westbound passenger train to pass. The freight train had stopped at Dryden and accidentally had left there the rear brakeman, whose duty it was to close the switch at Eldridge. Therefore the switch was not closed. The engineer of the passenger train should have blown his whistle on approaching the siding but did not, and the rear-end collision killed the engineer of the passenger train. The finding of coroner Bean was to the point: "The rear brakeman, left in Dryden, was guilty of the death of the engineer, because he was not on hand to close the Eldridge switch, and the engineer, himself was an accessory after the fact to his own death, because he had failed to blow the whistle at Eldridge."

In response to criticism that he was illegally marrying and then divorcing some couples, Judge Bean claimed that he had a right to rectify his errors when a marriage he performed did not "take." When a visiting judge informed Bean that he was exceeding his authority and might be arrested and jailed in Fort Stockton, Bean supplied money for gambling to his visitor, who, after running up a debt of $500, departed without again mentioning the illegal divorces.

As previously noted, on January 12, 1883, the Galveston, Harrisburg and San Antonio Railway line finally connected with the Southern Pacific west of the Pecos, a short distance east of Tunnel No. 2, some 227 miles west of San Antonio. "There, Colonel T. W. Pearce drove a silver spike in the last tie and the 'Sunset Route' became a reality."[11] When the trains began to operate on a regular schedule, to attract passengers to his liquor establishment Bean set up in front of his saloon a row of cages in which he kept bear, wildcats, panthers, coyotes, and other native animals. When a passenger train stopped at the station, the judge handed one large bear a bottle of beer, and the bruin sat on his haunches, tipped the bottle to his mouth, and guzzled. Bored passengers, tired of viewing rock gulches, sand hills, and lechuguilla, piled out of the train to watch the bear guzzle the suds and, of course, to quench their own thirst in the saloon. Bean would delay giving the passengers their change until the whistle announced that it was time to board. A few passengers invariably failed to wait for their change. Bean also used his beer-drinking bear to help enforce his decision. As one

[11] Mrs. O. L. Shipman, *Letters Past and Present: To My Nephews and Nieces*, p. 75.

example, he had a Mexican who had failed to support his wife and children chained to a post so that he could barely stay beyond the reach of the animal until he agreed to support his family.

Bean's use of his pet bear, however, according to O. W. Williams, came to an untimely end. A disgruntled drummer, who had been shortchanged by Bean more than once, decided to get revenge. When Roy went to Del Rio on a drinking spree and left his son Sam in charge of the business, the drummer sent a telegram to Roy, signed with Sam's name, that stated: "The bear is dead. What shall I do with it?" The inebriated judge passed the telegram around among the men in the Del Rio saloon, who suggested that he keep a sentimental souvenir of his furry benefactor. Consequently, the judge wired his son to skin the bear, and the son, of course, killed the bear before it was skinned.[12]

The drummer was not the only man to turn the tables on Bean. Another was Francis Rooney, at the time a resident of the Marfa and Alpine area, grandfather of the Francis Rooney who in 1981 lives near Marathon, nephew of the pioneer Francis Rooney of Fort Stockton, and a practical joker. Very chagrined over having had to leave $19.50 in Bean's possession in order to catch a train, on his return from San Antonio Rooney got off the train at Langtry with an empty gunnysack and told Roy that he wanted some cold beer for the boys on the train during the remainder of the trip. While the beer was being counted and sacked, Rooney held in view a $20.00 bill. "The purchaser," a chronicler wrote, "hefted the bag; he thought perhaps he might take a few more. Deliberately, he put in a half-dozen additional bottles. No, he decided that would be too heavy. He took out a couple." Rooney continued to delay the sale until the "all aboard" call. "As the train puffed down the track, Francis Rooney sprinted after it, 50 cent beer bottles bumping his long legs, his $20 bill clutched in his fist. And to the astonished ears of Roy Bean floated back the parting words, 'Sorry, no change'."[13]

Bean reached the peak of his notoriety when he staged the Fitzsimmons-Maher heavyweight championship fight. The bout had been forbidden in Texas, New Mexico, and Arizona, but Bean outwitted the

[12] O. W. Williams, Fort Stockton, oral statement, to son Clayton Williams.
[13] Dorothy Forker, "On Nueces River, Immigrant Vied with Judge Bean," *San Antonio Light*, January 4, 1941.

Rangers, who had been sent to prevent the fight, by building a ring on the south side of the Rio Grande. Fitzsimmons won in less than two minutes.

Perhaps the most famous of the Bean myths concern his infatuation with the famous British actress (who, critics quipped, "couldn't play dead if you shot her") Lillie Langtry. In her prime, long before she toured Texas, Lillie's pictures were widely posted, and both men and women were agog at her beauty. Contrary to myths, Bean never met the famous "Jersey Lillie," but he became infatuated with pictures of her and named his saloon the Jersey Lilly. In letters and telegrams to the actress, he claimed, falsely, that he had named "my town" for her. (Actually, the town was named for a civil engineer in charge of a construction crew on the railroad line.)[14]

Apparently Lillie Langtry believed Bean's statement and was delighted. After ignoring Bean's letters and telegrams for some time, she eventually replied, before her tour of Texas in 1888, that she would be unable to visit Langtry, but she would send twenty-five dollars for the erection of a drinking fountain in the town's public park. To this, Bean is reported to have replied: "We ain't got no public park, and in the second place, if it's anything these hombres drink, it ain't water."[15]

Miss Langtry started on her 1888 tour of Texas with much trepidation. Fearing that cowboys would be shooting their guns off all the time and that bandits would rob her elegant train, she left her jewelry in New Orleans. However, she was pleasantly surprised—or so she later claimed—that city after city, including Austin, San Antonio, Waco, Fort Worth, Dallas, and Galveston, was a place of culture; perhaps she felt this way because she concluded that everybody loved her.

Actually, after seeing the plump thirty-five-year-old lady on stage in such dull productions as *A Wife's Peril*, which required very little more of her than to be on stage and look lovely in chinchilla, not everyone did love her. Yet, to see her, Texans in large numbers went through rain and sleet and paid high prices. Texas critics generally agreed with a writer for the *Austin Statesman* that she was neither an actress nor a beauty, that she was overweight, clumsy, and "by no means graceful,"

[14] King, "Lillie Langtry in Texas," p. 92; Webb and Carroll, *Handbook of Texas*, 2:26.

[15] George Hendricks, *The Badman of the West* (San Antonio: Naylor Company, 1959), p. 95, quoted in King, "Lillie Langtry in Texas," p. 92.

that her rich and beautiful costumes "partly redeem[ed] her performance from total failure," and that her large audience was due to "little more than curiosity."[16]

In 1903, the citizens of Langtry learned that the "Jersey Lillie" would be passing through Langtry on her next tour. According to Miss Langtry, "the bigwigs of the township . . . besought me to take advantage of passing through Langtry to bestow half an hour on a reception."[17] Arrangements were made with the Southern Pacific for the stopover. A couple of hundred men, women, and children were on hand to welcome Lillie—by then about fifty years of age and probably more plump than in 1888—when the train she was on arrived about 5:00 P.M. on January 4, 1904. Laura Torres, the thirteen-year-old daughter of the founder of the settlement, made a nice speech, and Sam Bean was in the reception line. Roy Bean, Jr., then twenty-one, apparently got frightened and hid out to avoid a part in the reception. Lillie shook hands with everybody, shuffled cards in the saloon, promised to donate fifty dollars for repair of the school, which was about to topple, and accepted a number of gifts, including Bean's pistol and items of flora and fauna. One gift, a bear, stubbornly resisted being put on the train. All in all, it was a lovely occasion, enjoyed by the crowd, most of whom believed that the town had been named for the famous lady. Unfortunately, Judge Roy Bean, who would have gloried in the occasion most of all, was not present. Upon her arrival, Lillie Langtry reportedly asked to meet "that funny old man who had been writing to me all these years," but she came too late.[18] That "funny old man" had died about ten months before of lung and heart complications, aggravated by a trip to San Antonio, and had been buried in the Del Rio cemetery. A legend has it that the Mexican caretaker at the cemetery, who saw Bean's grave the morning following Miss Langtry's brief stop at Langtry, reported that it looked as if it had been disturbed. The caretaker's statement became the basis for an often repeated tale that "the Law West of the Pecos had turned over in his grave when the Jersey Lillie came to his town."[19]

[16] Quoted in King, "Lillie Langtry in Texas," p. 86.

[17] King. "Lillie Langtry in Texas," p. 92.

[18] Stuart N. Lake, "Vinegarroon and the Jersey Lily," *Saturday Evening Post*, February 7, 1931, quoted in King. "Lillie Langtry in Texas," p. 97.

[19] King, "Lillie Langtry in Texas," pp. 97–98.

Judge Roy Bean has been the subject of many books and articles and several motion pictures. Many people have believed that he was a scoundrel; others have praised him as a symbol of law and order. Either way, Bean left an indelible mark on the history of southwestern Texas.

Roy Bean and the people with whom he dealt, however, were not typical of the majority of their contemporaries in the region of the lower Pecos. Most of the people there were hardworking, responsible citizens, whose principal means of livelihood in 1882 was ranching or stockraising. One of those was cattleman Monroe B. Pulliam, who with his brother-in-law, W. L. Holmsley, operated adjacent to and on the west side of the Pecos River in the vicinity of Pontoon Crossing. Pulliam, a native of McKinney, moved to Uvalde County with his parents when he was still an infant. There, as a teenager, he took part in a number of Indian battles, worked on several ranches, including his father's, and accumulated a small herd of cattle. In 1876, he moved his stock to the Fort Concho area, eventually acquiring thousands of acres there and along the Pecos. For twelve years he also had cattle on leased land in the Indian Territory. Holmsley, a native of Uvalde County, at age thirteen went up the trail with a herd of cattle partially owned by his father. For several years, he managed his father's ranch in Fisher County. He joined Pulliam on the Pecos in 1882, but he had some cattle of his own. After ten years, he acquired his own ranch on Live Oak Creek but later sold it and bought another ranch near Rankin. Holmsley's brand was the letter A on both the left side and the left hip; Pulliam's was the letter S, from which a Pecos River crossing got its name. Pulliam retired in 1916, Holmsley in 1927.[20]

Another pair of prominent cattlemen who grazed their stock on a large amount of free range in Pecos County in 1882 were James Dunn (J. D.) Houston and his brother Robert A. (Bob) Houston, Jr. Born in DeWitt County in 1850 and 1849, respectively, the Houston brothers, after their rancher father died during the Civil War, began hiring out to go up the trail. By the time he was seventeen, Dunn had become a trail boss, responsible for getting several thousand cattle to the Abilene, Kansas, market. Money earned from these trips enabled the

[20] *New Encyclopedia of Texas*, p. 1262; Mrs. Octavia Downie Smith, "Charles Downie," typed manuscript, 6 pp., 1936, copy in possession of Clayton Williams.

brothers to build their own herds. In 1871, Dunn placed his cattle in the region of Santa Rosa Spring and grazed them alongside the Pecos River. During the next few years, he went into partnership with George W. Littlefield, acquired vast herds of cattle, and purchased thousands of acres in Pecos County and elsewhere in Texas.

Dunn and Bob drove or sent many herds to northern markets, and quite a few cowboys and later ranch owners got their first trail-driving experience with Houston outfits. One of these was Robert L. Anderson, who started going north with herds in 1880, when he was about sixteen. Beginning about the same time, Anderson spent three years at line camps on a ranch Dunn Houston owned between the North Pease and Red rivers.[21]

Three others who worked for Dunn Houston during this period, Shipton Parke, James Livingston, and Morgan Livingston, became stockmen and prominent citizens of Pecos County, and their involvement in some major events that occurred there in the 1880s and 1890s is subsequently narrated. Shipton Parke, the son of Hezekiah and Elizabeth (Cruze) Parke, was born in Richmond, Kentucky, on March 10, 1848. When the boy was five years old, the family moved to Gonzales, Texas. In 1878, Shipton moved to Houston's ranch on the Pecos River and afterward made a number of cattle-trail trips. In the early 1880s, he went to work on Houston's Pecos County ranch.[22]

James Archibald and John Morgan Livingston were the sons of Hugh G. (for McGoogan) Livingston and Mary Elizabeth (Finney) Livingston. After migrating to Gonzales in 1854 and teaching school there a couple of years, Hugh G. Livingston in 1856 married and then farmed on the land owned by his wife and her three children by her former marriage. James and Morgan Livingston, born in Gonzales in 1857 and 1863, respectively, while still in their teens and following their father's death, had to go to work. Both became cowboys on the Houston ranch on the Pease. Like Shipton Parke, they drove herds "up the trail" to the northern markets and moved in the early 1880s to the Houston ranch in Pecos County.[23]

---

[21] J. Marvin Hunter, ed., *The Trail Drivers of Texas*, pp. 924–925.

[22] Clarence R. Wharton, *Texas under Many Flags*, 5:169–170.

[23] Hugh Rooney Livingston (grandson of Hugh G. Livingston), comp., "A Genealogical Study of the Livingston and Related Families," manuscript, copy provided Clayton Williams by the compiler; *New Encyclopedia of Texas*, p. 3267.

No history of Fort Stockton and Pecos County would be complete without an account of the early sheepmen. One of the first to make a profitable business out of raising sheep was Charles Downie, who eventually became one of the most successful ranchers in West Texas. Born on November 9, 1851, in Detroit, Michigan, three years after his parents had arrived in the United States from Scotland, young Charles and his father invested in the grocery business in Detroit. In 1872, the father died from injuries received in an accident, and the twenty-year-old youth was left to support the family. For a time, Charles served as a bellboy on night shifts at a hotel, and later he worked in the railroad yard, but, whenever possible, he read to augment his education. In the mid-1870s, Downie was advised by a physician to seek a healthier climate and an outdoor life. Like many others who sought to rehabilitate their health in the mid-nineteenth century, he moved to Texas and worked for a while as a drygoods clerk in Austin. In time, he managed to save enough money to buy about 900 sheep. While still living in the Austin area, Downie married Miss Josephine Roessler, and eventually the couple became the parents of three children.

During the early 1880s, Downie free-grazed his sheep to Kimble County, where he managed to lease a pasture. When the lease expired, he moved his flock through the regions of Rock Springs and Sonora and then into Pecos County, where he arrived in 1882. At Eagle's Nest, Downie pawned his shotgun to purchase some groceries and then camped with his flock a short distance to the northwest, probably at Willow Spring. The crop of wool from his spring shearing provided sufficient funds to retrieve his shotgun and to purchase enough groceries to move his sheep farther west onto the free range. After grazing the herd for some time in the vicinity of Maxon Spring and Longfellow (in the southern tip of present Pecos County), he established what came to be known as the Old Rock Pens, some twelve to fifteen miles north of Sanderson, built by Mexican sheepherders to safeguard their flock at night. The "gates" of the pens consisted only of brush stacked against the openings to keep the sheep in and the varmints out. Downie lived nearby in a tent. At times he kept a fire burning all night as a protection against panthers, coyotes, and bobcats.

For a while, Downie had to haul water for himself and his sheep from the railroad station at Haymond. Once, while riding beside the railroad tracks, he encountered three tired and hungry Italians who had walked all the way from San Antonio, about 300 miles. He took them to his camp, fed them, and through his partner, Robert Paxton, who was able to communicate with the Italians in French, put them digging a water well by hand at the Rock Pens camp. At a depth of approximately 300 feet, the Italians struck water. Downie then established his headquarters near the well. Later, after making a road from there over the Big Hill, Downie obtained his supplies from Sanderson and had his mail placed in a box in one corner of Charlie Wilson's Old Cottage Bar, where the post office was located.[24]

Charlie Wilson, the saloon keeper who had discouraged Roy Bean from doing business there, had earlier founded the town, originally called Strawbridge. In 1881, a roundhouse constructed there was named Sanderson, after Thomas P. Sanderson, a construction engineer, and when the railroad arrived in May, 1882, the settlement too became known as Sanderson.[25]

In time, two other ranchers, Robert Paxton, a well-educated fellow Scot, originally from Edinburgh, and Sam A. Purinton, from Maine, became associated with Charles Downie. In 1878, Paxton, then twenty-five, left his home in County Fife, Scotland, and made his way to Florida. After contracting malaria, he moved to the dry, open-air country of Pecos County, where in 1882 he and Downie bought thirty-eight sections of ranchland from J. S. Myrick and A. S. Johnson, trustees. Soon afterward, Downie and Paxton bought twenty-five additional sections, but in January, 1884, they started segregating their interests, and Downie bought twenty-five sections from Paxton.[26] Purinton acquired Pecos County land from time to time from 1887 to 1910.[27] Care must be taken to avoid confusing S. A. Purinton with George Augustus Purington. Purington, a career military officer who for a time was stationed at Fort Stockton, acquired more than fifty sections by a tax title through the commissioners court, a large amount of land in Pecos County during the 1880s. Purington, who apparently never did any

[24] *New Encyclopedia of Texas*, p. 1262; Octavia D. Smith, typescript.

[25] Webb and Carroll, *Handbook of Texas*, 2:564.

[26] Smith, "Charles Downie"; Jesse A. Paxton (son of Robert Paxton), County Fife, Scotland, to Mrs. Herbert A. Smith, Lafayette, California, October 29, 1951, copy in possession of Clayton Williams; various transactions recorded in Pecos County, Texas, Deed Records, vols. A-2 and A-3, and in Pecos County, Deeds of Trust, vol. 1.

[27] Pecos County Deed Records and Deeds of Trust between 1887 and 1910 have considerable space devoted to Purinton's land transactions.

ranching, sold the entire holding in 1885 and 1886, much of it to J. D. Houston.[28]

Downie, Paxton, and Purinton were good judges of grazing land, and their ranches covered some of the best stock country in Pecos County. Brush corrals were placed so that the flocks could be grazed by day over widespread regions and penned at night, surrounded by kerosene lanterns to help keep away the predators. During his expansion, Downie's old shotgun was again used to obtain needed funds, this time for a well dug by the Charles brothers. This well made it possible for his stock to graze the surrounding grass that had been bypassed for lack of water. In time, Downie also acquired a large goat herd and became one of the biggest West Texas producers of wool, mohair, and mutton.[29] Downie and S. A. Purinton were also active in the civil affairs of Pecos County. Purinton was appointed as a commissioner in January, 1887, and he was elected to that office in November, 1890; Downie was elected to the same office in 1894.

In 1882, William Davis (Billy) Kincaid and Joseph M. Kincaid, sons of David G. and Talatha Adline (Davis) Kincaid, started sheep ranching in Pecos County. Billy and Joseph eventually formed a partnership with Davis St. Clair Combs, and in time they acquired about 200,000 acres in West Texas. Combs, a Missourian born in 1839, came with his family to Texas in 1854 and settled near San Marcos. He fought as a Confederate in a number of battles, including the last, at Palmito Ranch. From 1866 to 1879, he took cattle and horses up the trail to the railhead markets and even to the Dakotas. In 1880, he and the Kincaids were ranching near San Angelo, but soon afterward they moved farther west and began acquiring land.[30]

In the general election on November 7, 1882, in Pecos County, T. A. Falvey, then district attorney, was elected to succeed Allen Blocker as district judge, and C. F. Neill won the office formerly held by Falvey. G. M. Frazer was elected to replace F. W. Young as county

[28] Francis B. Heitman, *Historical Register and Dictionary of the United States Army*, 1:809; Pecos County, Minutes of the Commissioners Court, 2:157; Pecos County, Deed Records, vol. 3 (various passages pertaining to Purington's sales of 1885 and 1886).

[29] Smith, "Charles Downie"; *New Encyclopedia of Texas*, p. 1262.

[30] *New Encyclopedia of Texas*, pp. 502, 1555, 2011–2012; Branda; *Handbook of Texas*, 3:188.

judge. For commissioners, the voters in Precinct 1 elected Corbett to replace Joseph Friedlander; in Precinct 2, they retained Cesario Torres; in Precinct 3, they returned Francis Rooney; and in Precinct 4, they elected James Murphy to replace William Lempest. John Edgar and Jacob Jacobs were reelected as sheriff and clerk, respectively.[31]

[31] Pecos County, Commissioners Court Minutes, November, 1882, 1:184–188; Pecos County, Election Returns, 1882, Records of the Secretary of State, Archives, Texas State Library, Austin.

CHAPTER 19

1883-1885

BY 1883, the Fort Stockton garrison was no longer on the frontier, and the garrison was serving only to furnish supplies to Peña Colorada, an outpost for soldiers assigned for escort and occasional scout duty. Throughout the year, Lieutenant Colonel J. F. Wade, who was in command—except during August—had there Troops G and L, Tenth Cavalry.[1] Wade's biggest problem that year was Captain G. A. Armes. In fact, Armes was also a problem to the army and to Congress.

George Augustus Armes, a native of Virginia, who during the Civil War rose from a private to a captain and a brevet major, had an outstanding record and received special recognition for his gallantry in the battle at Hatchers Run, Virginia, on December 9, 1864. Mustered out of service in September, 1865, he reenlisted as a second lieutenant in the Second Cavalry in April, 1866. Three months later, he became a captain in the Tenth Cavalry, then stationed in Missouri. His frequent controversies with his fellow officers finally resulted in his discharge in June, 1870. Although the discharge was honorable, Armes was resentful.

After the discharge, Armes lived in Washington, D.C., where his wife's family apparently had considerable influence. Although he became very successful in the real estate business, he persistently petitioned Congress to reinstate him, and he spent much time attacking Secretary of War W. W. Belknap. Later, he claimed credit for exposing Belknap's graft and for his removal from office. In May, 1878, Armes, by an act of Congress, was reinstated as a captain. In August he, his wife, and their small children arrived in Fort Stockton, where he assumed command of Troop L, Tenth Cavalry. It was not long before

[1] U.S. Department of War, Post Returns, Fort Stockton, 1883, Records of the Adjutant General's Office (AGO), Record Group (RG) 94, National Archives (NA), Washington, D.C.

Armes was again in conflict with his fellow officers. Most of the time during his almost five years at Fort Stockton, he was under house arrest on charges of breaking regulations or was involved in courts-martial. Troop L did field duty during the Victorio campaigns of 1880 and 1881, but apparently its captain was with it very little. Armes did some scouting up the Pecos and probably around Castle Gap but never where there was any action, apparently because his superior officers did not trust him.[2]

On April 14, 1883, upon receipt of news that Indians from Mexico were raiding along the lower Pecos, Wade ordered Armes to march with his command to Mussey's ranch at Pear's (Tunas, Escondido) Spring and from there to follow W. H. Echol's 1860 camel-train trail to Independence Creek, a distance of fifteen miles. If a fresh Indian trail was found, Armes was to endeavor to overtake and punish the Indians; otherwise, he was to notify stockmen in the vicinity of Independence Creek and Shut Valley of the threat, ascertain the direction taken by the Indians and the movements of other troops (two companies of cavalry were sent from Fort Clark toward the Pecos during the night of April 13–14), and act as seemed best under the circumstances. In case the trail from Pear's Spring was not practical for wagons, he was to leave his wagon at Mussey's and to take pack mules. If he should find that no Indians had been in the vicinity of Independence Creek and he could get no news regarding them, he was to ask by telegram from Thurston Station for further orders.[3]

Armes stated that he took forty-two mounted men and four mules, packed with fifteen days' rations, and the first afternoon marched the twenty miles to Escondido. By nightfall on the fifteenth, after having traveled fifty-five miles, he arrived at Pecos Spring, close to present Sheffield, where he dined with Hart Mussey, the cattleman, who furnished a cowboy to act as a guide. From Mussey's, Armes continued down the Pecos, joined along the way by a rancher named Ramsey, to the Weaver ranch. There a note on the table stated that Weaver had gone to Meyers Spring. While the troops were confiscating a quantity of dried beef, Weaver returned, added a sack of flour to the beef, and

[2] Francis B. Heitman, *Historical Register and Dictionary of the United States Army*, 1:169; George Augustus Armes, *Ups and Downs of an Army Officer*, pp. 518–521.

[3] U.S. Department of War, Post Returns, Fort Stockton, April 14, 1883; Armes, *Ups and Downs of an Army Officer*, p. 520.

informed Armes that he had heard that other "soldiers had been sent to their rescue."

On April 18, at Thurston Station, Armes reported by telegram directly to the adjutant general of the Department of Texas that he had scouted to "Musils Ranche," had seen a few pony tracks, had found an Indian horse on Ramsey's range (but one of his horses had been stolen), and from the top of a mountain had seen in Richland Valley (but had not followed) two mounted men, presumably Indians. He had marched nearly 200 miles and would leave the next day for Eagle's Nest with two Seminole guides and from there would scout up the Rio Grande to Shafter's Crossing and try to intercept the Indians.[4] None of the latter plans were in his orders.

On that same day the commanding general at San Antonio instructed Armes to return to Stockton by the "most direct and advantageous route." On his return, while at Meyers Spring on the eighteenth, Armes wrote: "We have marched about fifteen miles today. I marched out across the Rio Grande and overnite into Mexico, where the Indians have taken refuge, as I had driven them very far into that country, and returned to camp."[5]

Armes contended that he had forced the Indians to seek refuge in Mexico, but his superior maintained that he had accomplished nothing and that during the scout he had violated his orders. Consequently, Armes was brought before a retiring board in August of 1883 and forced to resign from the army.[6]

While Colonel Wade was attending the meeting of the Armes retiring board in San Antonio, Major Horace Jewett, Sixteenth Infantry, served as commander at Fort Stockton. Company F, Sixteenth Infantry, had arrived from Fort Concho on July 6. During the remainder of 1883, the post was occupied by Troops G and L, Tenth Cavalry, and Company F, Sixteenth Infantry. On December 15, 1883, Captain William George Wedemeyer, after a leave of absence, rejoined his Company F.[7]

[4] Armes, *Ups and Downs of an Army Officer*, p. 520.
[5] Ibid., pp. 520, 521.
[6] Ibid., p. 521.
[7] U.S. Department of War, Post Returns, Fort Stockton, July–December, 1883; Capt. W. G. Wedemeyer, Diary, February 29 and May 25–28, 1884, Marcus Whitman College Library, Walla Walla, Washington.

During 1884 Jewett was in command whenever Wade was absent. That spring, when trouble appeared to be brewing among the Ute and Navajo Indians in Utah and Arizona, the military commander of the department at San Antonio asked the post commanders how quickly they could condition and prepare their troops for the field. To find out, Wade on May 25 took the soldiers at Stockton on a conditioning trip. He went by Young's ranch on the salty waters of the Diamond Y Draw, Monument Springs, Santa Rosa Spring, and the abandoned ranch and irrigation ditches of Francis Rooney to the Grand Falls of the Pecos and then returned to Fort Stockton. The mounted troopers, of course, did better than the weary foot soldiers. Captain Wedemeyer noted in his journal that the Pecos River, in the vicinity of Rooney's holdings, was about 200 feet wide and quite deep and that the water at the Grand Falls passed over a ledge of rock to fall about 10 feet.[8]

Finally, after a long delay, Colonel Wade with Troop L, Tenth Cavalry, on March 27, 1885, departed for Arizona, leaving Major Jewett in command of Troop G, Tenth Cavalry, and Company F, Sixteenth Infantry.[9] There was to be only a short time left for the other troops at Fort Stockton. The end of Indian troubles and the arrival of the rails had brought about many changes. The great wagon-train and stage-coach traffic no longer existed, and the military market for locally grown food, corn, and hay had dwindled to insignificance. The soldiers had been replaced by stockmen as the major inhabitants of the area.

In June, 1883, the firm of Jesse H. Presnall and Hart Mussey bought some 22,000 acres in the valley of Comanche Creek, including the great Comanche Springs and the site of the post of Fort Stockton. Much of this land was irrigated. Previously, only Hart Mussey had been involved in the venture. After the purchase, a portion of their herd of 15,000 head of cattle was moved from the region of Escondido and Pecos springs to the salt grass flats north of and around their new headquarters, three miles northeast of Fort Stockton.[10]

Another stockman, Alfred Gage, whose arrival has been mentioned previously, began with a small herd of 100 cattle, which grazed

[8] Wedemeyer, Diary, May 25–28, 1884.

[9] U.S. Department of War, Post Returns, Fort Stockton, March, 1885.

[10] O. W. Williams, Fort Stockton, to Jesse C. Williams, Hankow, China, September 6, 1934, in possession of Clayton Williams; land purchases of Mussey and/or Presnall, Pecos County, Texas, Deed Records, A-2:311–507.

around his half-cave, half-cabin home, located about five miles south of Marathon and near the Peña Colorada post. Gage later bought 5,000 head of longhorn cattle from Milton Faver to start his Presidio Live-stock Company. He and his half-brother, Edward L. Gage, became very active in the real estate business in the Big Bend, making some sixty land transactions in Pecos County alone. During the late 1870s, Edward Gage was in partnership with E. M. Powell in a land-locating business with headquarters in Dallas. When surveying lands in the late 1870s, O. W. Williams at one time was in the employ of Powell and Gage.[11]

In 1883, the four McCutcheon brothers, Beau, Willis, William, and James, began ranching in the Davis Mountains. During the same period, L. M. and John Kokernot, James Cotter, W. B. Hancock, and J. D. Jackson drove their stock to the region of Murphysville (Alpine). Simultaneously, Mayer and Solomon Halff were ranging their stock from the mouth of Live Oak Creek, in present Crockett County, north-ward for a distance of eighty miles under a twenty-year cash lease from the State of Texas. They also established their 1,280-acre Circle Dot Ranch in Presidio County, but in 1883 they leased a small part of that land to the army for a military post.[12]

In 1883, A. D. McGehee, in association with J. M. Nance, H. Hillman, W. T. Jackson, and W. C. Johnson, started a cattle venture in Pecos County, but McGehee later "consolidated with the Toyah Land & Cattle Company, headed by M. Lookse of Galveston." His associates soon sold their 3,200 cattle to Ike T. Pryor and delivered them to him at Brady City.[13]

The late Fred J. Arno, who worked for the Halff brothers, had some interesting recollections of his employers. During the winter of 1883–1884, he and Mayer Halff obtained thirty-three good saddle horses and shipped them by train from San Antonio to Marathon. At Marathon Arno and Halff were met by some cowboys with a buckboard

[11]Clifford B. Casey, *Mirages, Mysteries and Reality: Brewster County, Texas*, pp. 22, 365; S. D. Myres, *Pioneer Surveyor—Frontier Lawyer: The Personal Narrative of O. W. Williams, 1877–1902*, p. 51.

[12]Barry Scobee, *Fort Davis, Texas, 1583–1960*, p. 157; *Standard Times* (San Angelo), August 29, 1954; Eldon Stephen Branda, ed., *The Handbook of Texas: A Supplement*, 3:369.

[13]J. Marvin Hunter, ed., *The Trail Drivers of Texas*, p. 489.

and team and escorted to their ranch house, adjacent to Camp Peña Colorada, where they spent the night. The Halff brothers owned a small store and cantina about a mile from their house and sold supplies to neighboring sheepherders, cowboys, and occasionally detachments of soldiers. That night, Arno recalled, "all hell broke loose" in the cantina, "with much shooting and yelling," but there was lots of room and no one was hurt. It made old man Halff a little nervous, but the ruckus quieted down about eleven o'clock.[14]

At daybreak the following morning, four or five cowboys had a difficult time harnessing two small, black Spanish mules, not much larger than burros, to a buckboard loaded with guns, bedding, and chuck box and driven by Arno and Halff. When released, the spirited mules raced through the gate, as though shot from a cannon, and covered the four miles to Marathon in a very short time. The two men continued along the dusty road at a fast clip, following the trail that had been made by Halff's herd of horses. By lunchtime, they had reached Gap Tank, a distance of forty-five miles and only twenty-five miles from Fort Stockton. From there, the mules were easily handled until they topped the hogback escarpment nine miles from Fort Stockton and sensed the end of the journey. The team rushed into town, scattering children and dogs in all directions. Pulling up in front of Young's store, Halff unharnessed the mules, set up camp in Young's corral, and sent his horse herd on ahead to his ranch on the Pecos River. He also instructed his men to have a wagon and team meet him at Pecos Spring. The spring in front of Koehler's store, as Arno later recalled, was then full of water. Two hundred yards north of Koehler's was the big spring then known as Comanche Chief, and the roar produced as the water gushed out could be heard for a considerable distance. Small boys delighted (and have since) in jumping into the Comanche Chief and experiencing the thrill of being shot out by the tremendous force of the water.

After laying over one day at Stockton, Halff and Arno found it necessary to enlist the aid of five or six Mexicans to get the rambunctious team of mules into harness. During the effort, the mules dashed off through the Garza and Torres farming district (newly acquired by Presnall and Mussey) with a pack of baying dogs at their heels. When they were finally brought under control and the journey was resumed, the

[14] Fred J. Arno, oral statement, to Clayton Williams.

little mules again covered seventy miles before dark, reaching Pecos Spring. Leaving Arno and the Spanish mules in camp to await his return, Halff took a wagon and team from there to Lancaster Crossing.

After spending some time inspecting his land and livestock in the Live Oak Creek area, Halff rejoined Arno and the little mules at Pecos Spring. From there, Arno and Halff, instead of using the regular roads, headed more directly across the rough countryside. Steep hills, deep canyons, and scarce water made for a difficult trip to Haymond Station. Although often delayed by having to tie the buckboard's back wheels to the body of the vehicle to act as a brake as they skidded down steep descents, they made it in two days.[15]

In frontier days, a cowboy had to be exceedingly good at roping. He took pride in his abilities and competed to be as good or better than any other. One June day in 1883 at a general store in Pecos (then still in Pecos County), some cowboys started arguing about who was the best roper, broncobuster, and other related cowboy activities. The argument ended in the "world's first rodeo." On the following July 4, cowboys from several ranches gathered near Pecos to settle the issues in a friendly way. That rodeo was nothing in comparison with the colorful pomp of those of the present, but it was a beginning. A number of hands from Dunn Houston's NA Ranch participated, including Morgan and Jim Livingston, and probably Shipton Parke. The steers roped were wild longhorns, three and four years old and weighing about 1,200 pounds each. For winning first in the steer-roping contest, Morgan Livingston received twenty-five dollars; Trav Windham, boss of the neighboring Lazy Y Ranch, was second and received fifteen dollars. Although this was the official beginning of the American rodeo (the only big-time sport in the United States to spring directly from an industry), it was not until 1929 that the cowboy tournament finally emerged as a nationally organized event.[16]

In 1884, Daniel G. Franks moved his cattle by train from Atascosa County, south of San Antonio, to Thurston, a railroad station east of Dryden. Franks, who was associated in the cattle business with John F. Camp, expected to range on Indian Creek, south of Dryden, but, find-

[15] Ibid.

[16] "Knight and Midnight," *Sports Illustrated*, August, 1955, p. 62; Hugh Rooney Livingston, comp., "A Genealogical Study of the Livingston and Related Families," copy in possession of Clayton Williams.

ing all the vegetation had been burned off that area, trailed his cattle to Shafter's Crossing on the Rio Grande. Franks and Camp later sold their interest in the herd to the Pecos Land and Cattle Company, but Franks continued as manager of the ranch until 1893. Franks and Camps also were sometimes associated in business with another colorful stockman, John M. Doak, who in 1889 became Franks' son-in-law.

The Pecos Land and Cattle Company, with which Franks was associated for many years, became the owner of 106 alternate sections of land, lying from Dryden to two miles north of King Springs, and it leased other lands from John L. Bullis, the army officer in charge of the Seminole scouts, who owned Richland, Geddis, Independence, Cedar, and Meyers springs. In 1884, it bought out the King Springs Cattle Company. In regard to Bullis and his land acquisitions, Captain Wedemeyer noted that: "Bullis owns a large quantity of land all over that portion of Texas through which he formerly marched, while in command of the Seminole Indian Scouts. Wherever Bullis saw fine land he located it with script [*sic*] which was in the market at 12-½ to 15 cents per acre."[17]

Bullis and fellow army officer William Rufus Shafter owned the silver mines at Shafter, in Presidio County, now a ghost town, but in time they had a disagreement over ownership. Shafter claimed that Bullis had no right to the property because he had already located as much land as the law allowed. Bullis, on the other hand, claimed that the land had been purchased with money his wife, Alice, had inherited from her father, Ambrosio Rodríquez (a prominent descendant of a family of Canary Islanders who had migrated to San Antonio in 1731) and that it was his wife's separate property. In the midst of this litigation, Alice Bullis died without issue. By rights, some members of the Rodríquez family believed, the land should pass to them, since Bullis claimed that purchase had been made with money Alice had inherited. María de Jesús Olivarri Rodríquez, Ambrosio's widow, however, aware that her son-in-law had spent much time, money, and effort to develop the land, permitted him to take over the property.[18]

[17] Wedemeyer, Diary, December 16, 1884.
[18] *New Encyclopedia of Texas*, pp. 1180, 2047; R. J. Lauderdale and John M. Doak, *Life on the Range and on the Trail*, pp. 45–47; Wedemeyer, Diary, December 16, 1884; J. M. Rodríquez, *Rodriquez Memoirs of Early Texas*, pp. 44–45, 49–51; Bullis' land transactions are recorded throughout volumes 1, 2, and 3 of the Pecos County Deed Records.

During the 1880s, the T5 outfit, with 12,000 cattle, ranged the area around Independence Creek and the Pecos River. Along the Pecos north of Fort Stockton, the Mule Shoe outfit, owned by Presnall and Mussey and managed by Taylor Stephenson, grazed 17,000 cattle. The NA outfit, ranging from Santa Rosa Spring, was owned by Dunn Houston and managed by Bill Mathis. Nub Pulliam grazed his S-brand cattle around the Pulliam water hole, about ten miles northwest of the present Iraan and a few miles from the Pecos. Bill Holmsley, Pulliam's brother-in-law, was the manager. The TX outfit, with 30,000 cattle in the vicinity of Horsehead Crossing, was managed by Sid Kyle.[19] George M. Frazer had his herd at Leon Water Holes, and F. W. Young used the Diamond Y Draw, north of Fort Stockton. Dunn Houston also made use of the Diamond Y Draw. To obtain water from the draw and to better secure rights to free-grazing between there and his NA Ranch, Dunn bought land in the vicinity of the Diamond Y Draw. He also bought $10,250 worth of cattle form Reuben Richards.[20]

In 1884, Jim P. Wilson came from Beeville with a herd of cattle to the region of Alpine, then known as Murphysville. At that time the antelope were still in big herds and unfamiliar with trains. One day Wilson observed a terrible encounter between a freight train and a large herd, which had been grazing at the base of the Glass Mountains. The frightened antelope, moving at full speed, met the train head-on, and the fast train "plowed its way through the solid mass of living animals." The result was almost unbelievable. "Antelopes were hurled and tossed in all directions for hundreds of feet; some were thrown high into the air by the impact, falling atop the train, through the cab-windows of the engine and into the caboose. Members of the train crew were besmeared with blood." There were piles of dead and dying antelopes. Jim Wilson and others killed some of the badly crippled.[21]

That same year, George Evans started his ranch about eight miles west of Fort Davis, near the head of Limpia Canyon. His 3,000 yearlings were driven from the San Antonio area by Uvalde, Devils River, Beaver Lake, and the Pecos River.[22]

[19] Lauderdale and Doak, *Life on the Range*, pp. 66, 70.
[20] Pecos County, Deed Records, 3:149–150, 152, 399, 596.
[21] Will F. Evans, *Border Skylines*, pp. 250–251.
[22] Hunter, *Trail Drivers of Texas*, p. 804.

Sheep had entered the West Texas picture, too. As previously narrated, sheepmen Downie, Purinton, and Paxton had placed their flocks between Sanderson and Haymond, north of the Southern Pacific. Their herders grazed the animals in the daytime and penned them at night in brush corrals, surrounded by lanterns to keep predators away. They also kept trappers busy catching wildcats, coyotes, panthers, and other enemies. The corrals could be used again and again as the sheep were rotated from range to range. Sheep sometimes could go for days, even months, without visiting a watering place, as cattle would need to do, for they were able to obtain moisture from vegetation and from small puddles and in the winter from snow. Consequently, while the cowmen held their cattle close to large quantities of water, the sheepmen sought the grass farther beyond.

Relative to civil matters in Pecos County, Judge Roy Bean, despite his reputation for quick and heavy penalties, actually paid into the county treasury only a very small sum. The minutes of the commissioners court, on November 16, 1883, show the fines for that year collected through convictions in his court had been $89.00. Of that amount, Bean was allowed $35.00 for expenses, and Sheriff John Edgar collected $36.65. Thus, Bean still owed the county $17.35. In March, 1884, the court appointed James S. Callahan justice of the peace in Precinct 6, which included Sanderson. Two months later, on May 13, it refunded Sheriff Edgar $107.60 for his expenses in connection with the closing of McCafferty's place at Vinegarroon (closed for selling liquor without a license); even so, Edgar was out $482.00 in legal fees involving the closing.

In 1883 Pecos County was considerably reduced in size. On April 14 the legislature created and provided for the organization of Reeves County out of that portion of Pecos County within a line extending from the Great Falls on the Pecos River west to Varela Spring, thence northwest to San Martin Springs, thence northeast to the mouth of Delaware Creek on the Pecos River, and thence down the river to the Great Falls. The new county, which included the town of Pecos, was named for George R. Reeves, who had moved his family from Tennessee to Arkansas in 1835, and then, about 1845, to Grayson County, Texas. Reeves had served Grayson County as tax collector, as sheriff, and afterward, from 1855 to 1861, in the legislature. During the Civil

War, he had been a colonel in the Confederate Army. He had died on September 5, 1882, while serving as Speaker of the House.[23]

The new county was to bear the expense of its boundary survey and to pay a pro rata share of the existing debt of Pecos County. To organize Reeves County, the commissioners court of Pecos County, within sixty days after the new county's creation, was to divide the proposed county into election precincts and designate polling places. Pecos County Judge George M. Frazer was instructed to order an election for the selection of county officers and the county seat and to appoint the election officials. The election returns were to be delivered to Judge Frazer for certification. Frazer also had to approve the bonds and to administer the oath of office to those elected.[24]

Meanwhile, the citizens of Pecos County decided that they needed a new jail (although the one they had was only about five years old) and a courthouse. To that end, the commissioners court on February 15, 1883, awarded a contract to J. W. Archer of Dallas for the construction of a two-story rock jail for $10,000 and a two-story rock courthouse for $34,000, payment to be made in Pecos County courthouse and jail bonds. The buildings were to be completed by June 1, 1884, and Archer put up a bond in the amount of $50,000.

Archer began construction on the courthouse and jail as scheduled. The court issued twenty-eight bonds, each of $1,000 denomination, to the contractor, and on May 13, 1884, extended the completion time from July 1 to August 25. In June it issued eight more bonds to Archer, bringing the total to thirty-six. On July 26, members of the court examined the construction of the courthouse and jail and concluded that the masonry did not meet specified standards and, consequently, on August 12, the court turned down an order from Archer to William Cameron and Company for eight bonds, subject to the proper performance of the contractor. On September 2, the court, noting that the buildings had not been completed as agreed, ordered the clerk to notify Archer and his bondsmen that, unless the buildings were finished by October 1, suit would be instituted.

The court decided not to initiate a suit in October, however, possi-

[23] H. P. N. Gammel, ed., *The Laws of Texas, 1822–1897*, 9:411–412; Walter P. Webb and H. B. Carroll, eds., *The Handbook of Texas*, 2:455.

[24] Gammel, *Laws of Texas*, 9:411.

bly to await the outcome of the election or perhaps in hope that legal steps would not be necessary. All four commissioners were reelected. Consequently, on November 14, the court instructed its newly appointed county attorney, Robert D. Gage, to institute action against Archer and his bondsmen for Archer's failure to complete the jail and courthouse on schedule. Then, at its session on December 10, the court agreed to a settlement; it issued a county warrant for $5,000 to Cameron and cancelled Archer's $50,000 security bond.

On March 5, 1884, a petition bearing a number of signatures was presented to the Pecos County commissioners court for the organization of Reeves County. Although steps to organize were, under law, supposed to have been taken within sixty days after creation of the new unit, the Pecos County court postponed action on the basis that the petition contained questionable signatures, and on May 13 the commissioners rejected the application on the grounds that it was not in proper form. On August 11, three petitions, one against and two for organization, from citizens of the proposed new county were placed before the court. On the following day, the court again postponed until September 1 a decision in order to obtain from the attorney general an opinion on the matter. On that day, Commissioners Hart Mussey and W. F. Youngblood voted for and Commissioners Cesario Torres and Francis Rooney voted against organization; Judge Frazer cast the deciding vote in favor of the proposal. By September 4, the voting precincts had been defined and the election date set for November 4, to coincide with the general election.

Much of the land in Pecos County was still the property of the state and, therefore, unrendered for taxes. A large portion of the county's income was derived from taxes paid by the Texas and Pacific and the Southern Pacific railroads. The organization of Reeves County would eliminate all tax payments to Pecos County from the Texas and Pacific. Quite naturally, some of the commissioners did not want to lose this revenue, especially those members who, a few years previously, had received no salary because of insufficient revenue.

The Archer contract, a land squabble, and the organization of Reeves County were the major concerns of the voters when they went to the polls on November 4, 1884. F. W. Young won over the incumbent, G. M. Frazer, for county judge by a vote of 288 to 8. (Perhaps

Frazer had not announced for reelection, and the eight votes were write-ins.) Frazer was for the creation of Reeves County, and it is probable that he had already decided to become a citizen of the new county. E. W. Bates defeated L. W. Durrell (Frazer's son-in-law) for county surveyor by a vote of 292 to 9 (Bates subsequently appointed Durrell his deputy). Of the slightly more than 300 votes cast in the election, John Edgar (Frazer's brother-in-law) received 295 for sheriff, Jacob Jacobs was reelected county and district clerk with 299, James Johnson (another of Frazer's sons-in-law) won the treasurer's office with 298, and Herman Koehler became tax assessor with 300. In Precinct 6, which did not have many voters, Roy Bean was reelected justice of the peace with 56 votes over J. S. Callahan's 38.[25]

Herman Koehler, born March 17, 1849, in Germany, when six years old crossed the Atlantic on a sailboat with his parents and two sisters in fifty-six days. Landing at Galveston, the family traveled by wagon to New Braunfels, where Herman attended school. Afterward, young Koehler spent a number of years in San Antonio, where he worked as a bookbinder and became acquainted with Joseph Friedlander. As a result of his relationship with Friedlander, Koehler moved to Fort Stockton to work in Friedlander's store. Later, F. W. Young replaced Friedlander as the Fort Stockton post sutler, and in 1882 Koehler made a trade with M. F. Corbett, who represented the heirs of John James, to take over their store.[26]

Not long after the 1884 general election, Oscar Waldo Williams arrived in Pecos County, which was to be his home until his death in 1946. In the 1880s, according to C. L. Sonnichsen, "the mouse in his [Williams'] lungs, to quote Ralph Waldo Emerson (who had one of his own), commenced gnawing again [and it became] necessary for him to get to a drier climate." Williams' opportunity to move there came as a result of the election. The surveyors were elected and, said Sonnichsen, "not much was expected of them, but the deputies were appointed and had to know something about the business." Deputy Surveyor Durrell had offended some of the big cattlemen by surveying blocks in their favorite pastures and opening them up to settlement.

[25] Pecos County, Texas, Minutes of County Commissioners Court, 1:194, 199, 201, 209, 225–228, 231, 241, 247, 267, 280, 282, 286, 303, 305, 308, 313.

[26] Mrs. Bill ("Maidie") Dixon, manuscript, Fort Stockton.

Durrell had to go. Somehow Williams heard of the opening, applied, and was hired.[27]

All in all, it was a time of conflict in Pecos County. Stockmen were irritated over surveys; Archer had not finished the jail and courthouse on schedule, and it appeared that the issue would have to be resolved in court; the organization of Reeves County had not progressed beyond the stage of labor pains; many Pecos County citizens were angry over the prospects of losing a lot of tax money to a prospective neighbor; and the Pecos County commissioners were not in agreement on the issues. This was the situation when F. W. Young took office as county judge on November 12, 1884. On the following day, some of the citizens of the proposed Reeves County appeared before the Pecos County court and made objections regarding the Reeves County election returns. The election, they contended, had not been ordered legally; the election officers had not been properly appointed by the Pecos County judge; the election had not been conducted by legal officers; and some unqualified persons had voted in the election. Some of the complaints were justified. In at least one case, possibly more, the number of votes far exceeded the number of residents. Captain Wedemeyer noted in his diary that: "The election in Reeves County, formerly a part of this county, besides electing county officers, was to decide the location of the county seat. It has been decided in favor of Pecos City. That [place] polled 200 votes out of a population of 40 residents."[28]

On December 11, the Pecos County court accepted the Reeves County election returns. The town of Pecos received 263 votes over Toyah's 184 votes for the county seat. Some of the citizens of Toyah, unhappy with the results, rode into Pecos and proceeded to shoot up the place.[29]

On February 9, 1885, the commissioners appointed Howell Johnson as the county attorney of Pecos County. Johnson, born on July 13, 1863, in northeast Texas, had studied law in offices in Texarkana and had been admitted to the bar in Bowie County prior to his twenty-first

[27] Myres, *Pioneer Surveyor—Frontier Lawyer*, pp. 14, 17, 18 (quote from Sonnichsen on p. 17).

[28] Wedemeyer, Diary, November 5, 1884.

[29] Bill Leftwich, *Tracks along the Pecos*, p. 26.

birthday. After practicing in Colorado City a few months, he moved to Fort Davis and lived there for about a year before accepting the position of county attorney at Fort Stockton. An affable and very popular gentleman, Howell Johnson served as either county attorney or county judge for most of his remaining years.[30]

By 1885, the Indians were no longer a problem to the citizens of Pecos County; they had generally accepted life on reservations and were adapting to the "white man's road." Thus, there was no longer any need for soldiers at Fort Stockton or its outposts. More than once the government for one reason or another had postponed its plans to abandon them. In December, 1883, Captain Wedemeyer wrote: "The post [Fort Stockton] is in bad condition. Last June nearly all of the Government stores were shipped away preparatory to abandoning the post, but as the citizens promised to furnish money for the rent for the land the post was kept up."[31] By mid-1886, however, the soldiers, like the Indians before them, were gone, leaving the destiny of the lower Pecos country to the bold and hardy pioneers and a flood of arriving settlers.

[30]"Death Closes Long Public Career, Judge Johnson," *Fort Stockton Pioneer*, May 27, 1938; *New Encyclopedia of Texas*, p. 3488.

[31]Wedemeyer, Diary, December 15, 1883.

CHAPTER 20

1885-1888

O<small>N</small> the night of June 29, 1885, tragedy struck the George M. Frazer and Pedro Sosa families. Two members of those families were killed in a fight that evening and two others in the aftermath. The former Pecos County judge and his wife were in San Antonio; their eighteen-year-old son, James Lee, who attended Saint Mary's College in San Antonio, was home for the summer to work on the family ranch at the Leon Water Holes. At the time, the Frazers' home was an adobe building in the Saint Gall addition, and the Sosas lived a short distance northwest of the new courthouse. It was Saint Peter's Feast Day, and the occasion was being celebrated with a dance in the Sosa home. About dark, James Frazer, his brother Bud, and a cousin, W. B. (Bill) Clark, started for the ranch to gather some cattle to slaughter for beef the next day. Upon reaching the Sosa home, they stopped to watch the gaiety and were invited in.

Accounts of what then transpired vary considerably. The *San Antonio Express* reported that only Bud, then a deputy sheriff, accepted the invitation, that there was a misunderstanding about Bud's joining the crowd, that the forty-five-year-old Pedro Sosa struck Bud with a bottle, that Bud tried to ward off the blows with his pistol, and that James and Bill, both unarmed, rushed to the aid of Bud. Four or five Mexicans then joined the fracas. Pedro Sosa's twenty-three-year-old son, Crispín, cut James's throat, and Bud then shot Crispín, but neither died until after leaving the house.[1]

The *Dallas Herald*, in a more detailed account, reported that the Frazers and Clark joined in the celebration and that all went well until about eleven, when Bud, during an argument over the procedure of a dance, struck twenty-one-year-old Pablo Sosa, the son of Pedro Sosa,

[1] *San Antonio Express*, July 8, 1885.

in the face with his fist and soon afterward, when Pablo renewed the row, struck him on the head with his pistol. At this point Crispín Sosa, Pedro Bosilio, and Pedro Sosa rushed Bud. James tried to aid his brother, but Pablo, Crispín, and Pedro Bosilio attacked him with knives, while Pedro Sosa engaged Bud. Bud, however, managed to empty his pistol of its three shots, one bullet severing Crispín's jugular vein.[2]

James made his way about fifty yards to the home of his brother-in-law and sister (James and Annie Johnson), knocked on the windowpane, and then fell dead. The next morning Crispín was found dead in a nearby house. Pedro Sosa and Bosilio were jailed. Apparently Pedro was freed; Bosilio, reportedly, while trying to escape, was shot and killed by custodian William Clark. Pablo Sosa escaped and, according to Sam Scott, hid for some time in a cave near Scott's goat camp, west of the Seven Mile Mesa. Eventually Pablo went to Presidio. Ernest Riggs, grandson of Judge Frazer, once stated that "the Frazers were very bitter over the death of James. When they learned of Pablo Sosa's whereabouts, they sent someone down there, who killed Sosa, hacked his body to pieces, fed the remains to the hogs, and brought back evidence of his death in the form of a small pocket-change purse made from the scrotum of the victim."[3]

During the time of the Frazer-Sosa tragedy, Deputy Surveyor O. W. Williams was busy trying to correct the overlapping surveys made by previous surveyors. Surveyor E. W. Bates, who was not a professional surveyor, had discharged Durrell because of trouble that arose over his surveys and because some of the "claims conflict with Bates' interest."[4] In the fall of 1885, Williams, Durrell's successor, made surveys from Escondido Spring eastward to the Pontoon Crossing, where he found numerous conflicts in the earlier surveys.[5] In 1885 or 1886, Maximo Alvarez, a cowboy in the employ of Jesse Presnall's Mule Shoe outfit, as he recalled many years later, met "George Williams, a land surveyor," in the Pecos Spring area in company with

[2] *Dallas Herald*, July 9, 1885.
[3] Ibid.; *San Antonio Express*, July 8, 1885; Sam Scott, Fort Stockton, oral statement, to Clayton Williams; Ernest Riggs, oral statement, to Clayton Williams.
[4] Capt. W. G. Wedemeyer, Diary, April 6, 1885, Marcus Whitman College Library, Walla Walla, Washington.
[5] Pecos County, Texas, Sketch 27, General Land Office, Austin.

"Crespin Sosa [if Crispín Sosa, then the meeting occurred before June 29, 1885, the date he was killed by Bud Frazer], Pentalion Rivera and Dolaras Viscarro."[6]

Maximo Alvarez, a native of South Texas, started early as a cowboy with a Mr. McAllen, a neighbor of "Captain King" (presumably Richard King, of the King Ranch), and afterward worked for a year on a ranch near San Antonio. In 1882, he helped Jesse Presnall move a herd of horses from the San Antonio area to Pecos Spring, near the site of present Sheffield. He returned to San Antonio in November, got married in Mexico in February, 1883, and soon afterward returned to Pecos Spring, this time with a herd of cattle for Presnall's Mule Shoe ranch. It was on this occasion that he met the Williams survey party. He continued to work for the Mule Shoe until November 25, 1887, when his runaway horse fell on him, breaking his collarbone and an arm and injuring his back, and then, he said: "My horse got up with my foot caught in the stirrup. In this condition and unconscious I was dragged by the horse until a rescue party found me" about eight hours later. At that time, Alvarez recalled, mail was received at Fort Stockton from Toyah six times a week, and supplies were shipped from Murphysville (Alpine), but no public conveyance went to that place. He also mentioned that Juan Torres was the owner of a sizeable holding of cattle, land, sheep, and hogs and that the army blacksmith shop employed Petronilo Martínez and Faustino Luján.[7]

During the fall of 1885, Susan A. Williams arrived at Fort Stockton, where her brother, O. W. Williams, lived, to teach school. Many years later, she recalled her arrival in a newspaper article. She was drawn to Fort Stockton, she wrote, by "the munificent salary of seventy-five dollars a month" and by the desire to visit her brother and his family. O. W. Williams met his wife and their two children, who were just joining him, and Susan at Toyah with an army ambulance he had borrowed from the officials at the fort. Upon driving into town, Susan continued, her brother "showed them their new home—the Pecos County jail! No other housing was available at that time. The residents

---

[6] Maximo Alvarez, an article dictated in Spanish for Waldo Williams, who gave it to his brother, Clayton Williams, trans. by Joe Primera, Fort Stockton. Alvarez inadvertently said "George" rather than "Judge." After November, 1886, when he was elected county judge, O. W. Williams, the father of the author, was called Judge Williams.

[7] Ibid.

lived on the lower floor and were expected to provide meals for the prisoners who should occupy the upper story." Susan, disappointed with such a dreary, drab country, went to her room, fell on the bed, and wept. Her brother offered no consolation upon finding her in tears. "Well, Sue," he remarked, "you had better have a good cry while you are about it. I have just heard that there is a case of smallpox next door. . . ."[8]

Susan's life in Fort Stockton was in fact rather dull, partially because of the prevailing restrictive social customs that governed the behavior of young women. Although the stores of Koehler and Young were nearby, for instance, after three years in Fort Stockton Susan could not remember ever having been inside a store in that town.

Susan's description of her school is very informative. Her schoolroom was equipped with long rows of crudely made benches, with something like eight desks to each row. "If a child seated on the inside needed to stand to recite, all the other pupils on one side must slide out first to allow an exit for that one. . . ." Some of the pupils Susan taught were Olga, Mary, and Charlie Heid; Vida Johnson and her brother; Tom Edgar and Mary Valentine; Nora and George Purington; Frank Rooney and his sisters, Mary and Katie; Andrew, Eloise, and Aileen Young; Severa and Carlos Pena; and Raphael Scott. Five-year-old Raphael, who "came to school just to look and listen," was regarded as a near genius. Being informed by some of the older children that Raphael could name and point out on the map of the United States all the state capitals, Susan placed him upon a chair and handed him the pointer. To her "amazement it was found that he could do what had been claimed for him. On the next program for visitors, Raphael was a star performer, and Sue's reputation as an expert teacher was established."[9]

During the mid-1880s, more stockmen moved into Trans-Pecos Texas, and a number of large ranches were established. In 1886, J. D. Jackson without mishap drove his 800 cattle the 400 miles from Williamson County to free range in Green Valley of Brewster County. The 73-mile dry stretch east of Horsehead Crossing was successfully nego-

    [8]"Pecos County's Early Teacher, Now 92, Recalls Experiences at Old Fort and in Schoolroom," *Fort Stockton Pioneer*, December 16, 1954.
    [9]Ibid.

tiated by driving the herd at night. Some stockmen who attempted the stretch during the heat of the day suffered. Jackson later recalled that one owner who attempted the drive by day lost 1,000 of his herd of 2,500. Crazed by thirst, the cattle began milling (moving in a circle), and, unable to get them to advance after another two days, the thirsty drovers to save their own lives abandoned the herd and rode to the Pecos River.[10]

Jackson, who had served as a Texas Ranger, was associated in the ranching business with Sam D. Harmon. During his many years in the Alpine area he was very active in civic, political, and church affairs, and he played a major role in getting Sul Ross State Normal College (now Sul Ross State University) established at Alpine. The Jackson-Harmon Cattle Company lasted until 1935, and at various times it controlled over 200 sections of land, ran over 10,000 head of cattle, and had a remuda of from 500 to 600 head of horses. "It was largely through Mr. Jackson's influence that Congress appropriated five thousand dollars to establish a laboratory for experimental purposes in finding a chemical agent for the destruction of a poisonous weed growing in Texas, New Mexico and Arizona."[11] In 1885, John Doak, Dan Franks, and Jasper Lauderdale gathered a herd of cattle, sold it, and delivered it to the owners in Pecos County, and the next year Lauderdale and Jesse Presnall gathered a herd at Fort Stockton and drove it to New Mexico.[12]

Most owners of herds, even those who owned land, made use of the unfenced, free range. Cold winds, sleet, and snow caused the cattle on the open ranges to drift southward for hundreds of miles, making it necessary each spring for the owners to conduct gigantic roundups to locate and separate their cattle and to drive them back to their respective ranges. These roundups were joint efforts on the part of the owners. The largest began on the Rio Grande and slowly moved up the

[10] *Rio Grande* 1 (March, 1912):18.

[11] Jackson's son-in-law, James E. Casner, a prominent civic leader and auto dealer in Alpine, has spent much money and many years on similar research and experimentation but for a different purpose—to find worthwhile *uses* for the so-called obnoxious plants that have plagued the stockmen of West Texas.

[12] *New Encyclopedia of Texas*, p. 518; Clifford B. Casey, *Mirages, Mysteries and Reality: Brewster County, Texas*, pp. 374, 378–379; Walter P. Webb and H. B. Carroll, *The Handbook of Texas*, 1:901; R. J. Lauderdale and John M. Doak, *Life on the Range and on the Trail*, pp. 55–57, 169, 172.

Pecos River to the New Mexico–Texas border with a "that's one of mine—that's one of yours" operation. This procedure continued until fencing put an end to the open range.

The Pecos roundup was a big operation. On hand, there were men from the NA, the T5, the TX, the Mule Shoe, and many other outfits. By mutual consent, Taylor Stephenson of the Mule Shoe generally straw-bossed the whole operation. The work started at dawn, or earlier, and by ten o'clock the recovered stock were herded in mass to the campsite. The various owners then "cut-out" from the herd their respective stock, and the calves were branded. Because of the close attachment between mother and offspring, the ownership of the calf was usually obvious, since its mother wore a brand.

It was during the big Pecos roundups that the word *sleeper* was incorporated in cattlemen's terminology. An unethical cowboy, while in an isolated area sometimes used a running iron (a small branding iron) to put his own brand on a calf old enough to survive on its own and left it tied down until the cattle on the roundup site had been inspected, separated, and sent their respective ways. The cowboy then untied the calf. At the next roundup, the guilty cowboy could claim the falsely branded calf (now a yearling) as his own. It was not uncommon for an old-timer, often grudgingly, to mutter: "Well, now, I knew that old son-of-a-bitch when he didn't have two cows to his name. And I can tell you for a fact, he got his start in the cattle business with a running iron and sleepers."[13]

Other ranchmen who moved into the Trans-Pecos country in 1885–1886 included William Louis Kingston and Lucas Charles Brite. Bill Kingston, the son of Tennis Kingston, a native of Ireland, and Martha Sheltonburger Kingston, from Illinois, was born in Mason County in 1859. Tennis Kingston had come to the United States at a young age, had enlisted in the army, had been stationed during the 1850s at Fort Davis, had later ranched in the vicinity, and in 1859, when Bill was only six weeks old, had been killed by Indians. Mrs. Kingston soon remarried. Following the Civil War, Bill and his family fled with other Confederates to Mexico, where they remained for two years. Soon after the family returned to Texas, Indians killed Bill's stepfather. Sev-

[13] Doug Adams, Fort Stockton, to Clayton Williams, oral statements regarding the term *sleeper*.

enteen-year-old Bill Kingston came close to suffering a similar fate when he was attacked, while with a party en route from Mason to Fort Davis with four wagons of corn, by Mescaleros at a place known as Little Hell, about eighteen miles from Fort Davis.

In 1885, Bill and his wife, Annie (whom he had married at Fort Davis in December of 1884), combined their cattle with those of friends in Mason County and headed west for Arizona. After working for a time as a cowboy for W. D. Casey, he established his own ranch at the mouth of Madera Canyon. Eventually, he became one of the biggest cattle raisers in the area and served for twenty years as a county commissioner of Jeff Davis County.[14]

Lucas (Luke) Charles Brite, who also arrived in West Texas in 1885, was born in 1860 in Caldwell County. Left fatherless at an early age, Luke started working, while still a boy, for cattlemen in La Salle, Frio, and Coleman counties and along the Concho River. One of his associates later wrote: "Luke and I lived together in the bush a long time. We had no tent or protection of any kind. We would put our grub in a sack and tie it to a rope and draw it up in a tree when we would leave camp."[15]

In 1885, back in Frio County, Brite and some friends combined their herds for a total of 730 cattle and headed west. When they reached the area of Capote Peak, in northwestern Presidio County, Brite separated his stock from the combined herd and located in that region. Eventually, he developed a ranch of some 125,000 acres, but he is remembered primarily for his association with cattle organizations, on both the state and national levels, and for his generous contributions to Texas Christian University.[16]

In 1885, J. W. Prude and his two sons, John and Andrew, and several other stockmen drove about 3,000 cattle from McCulloch County to an old lake site in the Davis Mountains just north of the present McDonald Observatory. Within a short time, "running-iron artists" had grotesquely altered the brand on many of the Prudes' cattle and had butchered a large number of their calves under the pretense that

[14] *New Encyclopedia of Texas*, p. 1305; Will F. Evans, *Border Skylines*, p. 227; Barry Scobee, *Fort Davis, Texas, 1583–1960*, pp. 36, 161–162.

[15] Noel L. Keith, *The Brites of Capote*, p. 2.

[16] Webb and Carroll, *Handbook of Texas*, 1:218; Keith, *The Brites*, pp. 14–15.

they were mavericks. With the help of the Rangers, the cattlemen retrieved several hundred cattle, but they had other problems. In 1886,
an estimated seventy percent of the cattle they originally brought
westward died because of a drought. Undismayed, however, some of
the group persevered and succeeded in becoming leading stockmen in
Trans-Pecos Texas.[17]

In the mid-1880s, Fred Millard and some associates who crossed
the Pecos near the Pontoon Crossing, probably at "S" Crossing, met a
"Mr. Prude, Lit Walder, and Ed Crockett with a herd of 2,700 cattle
headed for the Davis Mountains." Apparently this was the herd that
J. W. Prude and his associates moved from McCulloch County, since
Millard mentioned that half of the cattle had been lost. Millard, however, attributed the losses to heel flies and the fact that the cattle stampeded and fell over cliffs.[18]

In September, 1886, Prude (presumably J. W.) became involved
in an altercation in Fort Stockton with a man named Holland. The two
men had combined their herds, but here they intended to separate,
with Prude going to the Davis Mountains and Holland to the Seven
Rivers region of New Mexico. While their cattle rested nearby, the two
owners went into Fort Stockton. Later that day, when Howell Johnson,
the young county attorney, walked into Koehler's saloon and observed
some strangers involved in a monte game with large stacks of bills and
silver on the table, he decided to join the game. He placed a silver
dollar on the table as a bet, but dealer Zack Light (who was with another cattle herd resting near the town) stated that it was a private
game and refused to accept the bet. Johnson, without a protest, headed
for the courthouse.

About dusk, Johnson returned to Koehler's, where he met and
stopped to visit with Sheriff John Edgar and County Clerk George H.
Lewis. Meanwhile, the poker game had moved from Koehler's to the
store and saloon of Billy Young (the county judge), about 200 yards distant. Soon the men at Koehler's heard gunfire at the Young establishment. Edgar and Johnson went there immediately. When Johnson
reached the front door, Light pointed his pistol at Johnson and declared, "That is the sheriff." But Bill Clark, who had been involved in

---

[17] Evans, *Border Skylines*, pp. 202–204.
[18] F. S. Millard, *A Cowpuncher of the Pecos*, p. 15.

the tragic Frazer-Sosa affair, grabbed Light's pistol and yelled: "That ain't the sheriff; there he is behind the post." Light then persuaded Sheriff Edgar to enter the saloon and have a drink with him. While the two were sipping their drinks, Johnson, very displeased over Light's behavior, went to the post office section of the store, got a shotgun, returned, and confronted Light. Sheriff Edgar intervened, and, after some persuasion by Prude and Holland, Light left for his cattle camp. On the next day, Judge Young accepted Light's guilty plea (delivered by his trail boss, since Light was unable to make a personal appearance) and fined him ten dollars.[19]

Later that year, Light was fatally shot in a saloon at Seven Rivers, and the killer went free on a verdict of self-defense. Zack Light, a "good fellow" when sober but "bad" when drunk, had been "on a spree" for about a week when he entered the saloon operated by Les Dow, "a very quick gunman," and, said Dow, "demanded a hundred dollars from me. I told him I could let him have twenty-five but not a hundred. He then drew his revolver, but I threw my hand under it and the discharge went above my head. I shot at the same time and killed Zack."[20]

Funerals in the Fort Stockton area in the 1880s, unlike those today, were not well organized and were often a quite heedless affair. George Lewis, a former Pecos County clerk, many years afterward wrote a longtime mutual friend about the death of one of their contemporaries. The deceased had taken a dose of asafetida and then a big dose of laudanum. Lewis, who was on the deathwatch from midnight to daylight, stated that the body was laid out in the room next to the post office. The scene is described well in Lewis' own words:

I sat in the post office for a time with a hell of a stench coming in from somewhere. I opened the door but it still kept coming. Finally I took the lamp and went in, uncovered the deceased, and found that his stomach was boiling over and the assafetida [sic] just boiling out of him. So I covered him up again, went into the store, got a bottle of toilet water, knocked the neck off and poured it over him. That helped some, but when my partner wanted me to shave him, I quit.

[19] Howell Johnson, "An Almost Fatal Encounter," *Frontier Times* 6, no. 8 (May, 1929):351.
[20] Ibid.; Leonard Passmore, "Memoirs of Lafe McDonald," *Frontier Times* 6, no. 4 (January, 1929):172.

Remember, we got a Mexican to make a coffin for him. He tried to make a fancy lid and the thing did not fit down at all corners. When three went down, one was up. At the funeral, after we loaded the body into a spring wagon, one man noticed that a corner of the coffin was up and got in with a screw driver to close it down, but was not getting anywhere, when another man, pretty well soused, noticed what was trying to be done. He said "Tha's all right. Tha's all right. He can't get out of there." So with that, we took the body down where they had prepared a grave and buried him 6 feet deep. I don't suppose he got out of there either.[21]

As previously related, the army had not entirely abandoned the Fort Stockton garrison. With the country filled with cattlemen and the communities growing, however, some additional troops were ordered to move to Fort Concho in May, 1885. On that march, with his Company F, Sixteenth Infantry, Captain Wedemeyer made some noteworthy comments in his diary. Having left Escondido at 5:30 A.M., at 11:00 A.M. he reached some adobe walls, likely built by Cesario Torres but abandoned when the railroads arrived. There, his company marched down the river to the ford two miles below the old pontoon bridge, obviously unusable at the time. Here, Wedemeyer wrote, he ordered the mounted men to ride "at the head of the teams to keep them from going down stream with the strong current."[22]

Meanwhile, O. W. Williams in September, 1885, filed his survey of Block O. W., the last big vacancy in Pecos County. Block O. W. covered a rectangle about 4½ miles east-west by 26 miles north-south. To verify the location of the west line of this vacancy, Williams surveyed to the southeast corner of New Mexico Territory. By digging in the sand dunes, his party located the corner marker, a burnt barrel stave. He then established the validity of this marker by surveying both west and north until his lines coincided with other established markers.[23] While running this survey, Williams was charged by a black Spanish cow. He saved his transit from damage by throwing it into a mesquite bush, but the cow got him down and had nearly torn off all of his clothes before he was rescued by John Valentine, his mounted flagman. Block O. W. included the Leon Water Holes and the ranch operated by George M.

---

[21] George Lewis, Elyria, Ohio, to Howell Johnson, December 12, 1929, copy in possession of Clayton Williams.

[22] Wedemeyer, Diary, May 24, 1885.

[23] Pecos County, Sketch 19, General Land Office, Austin.

Frazer. The old stage stand was very close to the northeast corner of Survey 242.

From January until late June, 1886, the garrison at Fort Stockton consisted of Troop G, Third Cavalry, and Companies J and K, Sixteenth Infantry, with Major George A. Purington in command. Purington, a native of Ohio, rose during the Civil War from sergeant to lieutenant colonel with an Ohio cavalry unit before being mustered out in November, 1864. In 1866 he became a captain in the Ninth Cavalry and in 1883 a major in the Third Cavalry. By the time of his death in 1896 (he remained in the army until 1895), he had acquired much land in West Texas. He was the last commander of Fort Stockton. On June 26, 1886, Troop G departed for Eagle Pass. The following day, Companies J and K, along with the post band, headed for Fort Davis.[24] Thus, after nineteen years, taps finally sounded for the Fort Stockton post. Since 1867, the presence of the army had helped to provide a living for a large number of farmers, stockmen, freighters, mechanics, laborers, and merchants in its vicinity.

Gaynell Williams Miller, of El Paso, Texas, who was a daughter-in-law of O. W. Williams, wrote that Judge Williams, while in his late eighties, still remembered well the occasion when the last of the post personnel left: "The cavalry [were] mounted and the infantry riding in wagons and hacks along the western portion of the trail, heading into the sunset with a shroud of dust boiling up into the sky as each vehicle followed another over the unpaved, winding alkali road, their destination Fort Hancock [Camp Rice], leaving behind gaping windows, empty walls, a battered bugle, and a lonely life. Children followed the column to the edge of town, among them his own son, thrilling to the spectacle and determining to one day, be a brave soldier himself."[25]

In the general election on November 2, 1886, the following were elected to office in Pecos County: T. A. Falvey, district judge; J. M. Dean, district attorney; O. W. Williams, county judge; John Edgar, sheriff; George H. Lewis, county and district clerk; Howell Johnson,

[24] U.S. Department of War, Post Returns, Fort Stockton, January–June, 1886, Records of the Adjutant General's Office (AGO), Record Group (RG) 94, National Archives (NA), Washington, D.C.; Francis B. Heitman, *Historical Register and Dictionary of the United States Army*, 1:809.

[25] Gaynell Miller, El Paso, Texas, November 4, 1974, to Clayton Williams.

county attorney; R. W. Mussey, county treasurer; Herman Koehler, county assessor; and Francis Rooney, Charles Downie, and Hart Mussey, commissioners of Precincts 1, 2, and 3, respectively. For some unexplained reason, W. P. Matthews became the commissioner of Precinct 4 on November 8 by appointment, and on January 17, 1887, S. A. Purinton was appointed commissioner of Precinct 2 to replace Charles Downie.[26]

Religion was a major facet of the lives of the people in the Fort Stockton community. Land for a Catholic church was donated by Peter Gallagher in 1871, but it was not until 1876 that Father Joseph Hoban, of Fort Davis, took possession of the property for the church, made his first baptism on the site, and began keeping records. The cornerstone for a church was laid in the summer of 1877. When found by Father Manual Cuadrodo while repairs were being made on the old building in 1930, the inscription was still clearly legible.

August 1, 1877, R. B. Hayes, president of the United States; M. M. Blunt, commandant of the fort; R. B. Hubbard, governor of Texas; Father [Anthony Dominic] Pellicer, Bishop of San Antonio; G. M. Frazer, Judge of Pecos County; M. F. Corbett, Justice of Peace; Rev. Joseph Ferra, Church of St. Joseph.

Father José Ferra left before a roof was added to the large structure and the construction was completed by a Mr. Corbett in 1878. After Father Ferra's departure, the nearest priest was Father Hoban, at Fort Davis, but he rarely visited Fort Stockton. From 1881 to 1885, the church was served by several priests, who came only occasionally.[27]

Soon after the fort was abandoned in 1886, Mrs. Oscar W. Williams initiated Protestant Sunday school services in the county courthouse, which was being used already as a community center for dances and the annual Christmas tree. Mrs. Williams was superintendent and her sister-in-law, Sue A. Williams, was secretary. At the first service the twenty-three persons in attendance donated fifty cents, were divided into two classes, and for their lesson studied the Ten Commandments, Exodus 20:1–17. Later, a third class was formed for the children of Catholics, with a teacher of that faith, who used the Catholic version of the Bible.

With the departure of the military, many of the people at Fort

---

[26] Pecos County, Minutes of the Commissioners Court, November 8, 1886.

[27] Alvin Wilde, *St. Joseph Catholic Church of Fort Stockton*, pp. 15–16.

Stockton were left with no means for a livelihood. Some had depended on the army for trade or employment, the farmers lost the major market for their products, and the livestock industry was not large enough to provide jobs for the whole population. Consequently, some of the people left. However, stockmen were moving in, and some of those who had lost jobs soon found other employment. When the Mule Shoe outfit (Presnall and Mussey) bought land close to Fort Stockton and moved their cattle to the salt grass country, other stockmen also moved into the region. F. S. Millard, Ike T. Hock, Bryan Swain, and Bill Hobbs took a grazing lease with headquarters at Escondido Spring. Hock was familiar with the Escondido (Tunas) region, for he had tended the stage station there in 1880. Many years later, Millard wrote about some of his ranch experiences there. When he and his partners first arrived, they rode the line to keep back the neighboring Mule Shoe cattle. The Mule Shoe people refused to cooperate, however, so Millard's group stopped patrolling after the first winter and began branding "all the mule shoe mavericks we could. . . ." It was customary then "when you found somebodys else [*sic*] calf following your cow to stripe its legs with a hot iron and brand one of theirs. I never bothered anybody's calves but the mules shoes and TX." They were "the biggest out fitts [*sic*]," he continued. The Mule Shoe claimed 18,000 head, and the TX, 10,000 on the west side of the Pecos and 20,000 on the east side.[28]

Once when the TX failed to pay its taxes, Sheriff Edgar attached enough to sell for the amount due. Seven men, including Millard, who wanted to buy the cattle at the tax sale framed up not to bid against each other. As a result, they "got 1027 head, if I reckilict [*sic*] they cost 17 cents a head." Accompanied by Deputy Sheriff Stearly Pulliam, the buyers went to where Sid Kyle was gathering TX cattle below Horsehead Crossing. Upon being informed of the situation, Kyle reportedly said he thought it was "all wright [*sic*] if the TX outfit did not have sense enuf to pay their taxes to take them so we . . . gathered enuf to make our number." The new owners took the cattle to Escondido and branded them. The TX got back the cattle, however, because Sheriff Edgar had not gathered and held them for twenty days prior to the sale, as legally required.[29]

[28] Millard, *Cowpuncher of the Pecos*, p. 31.

[29] Ibid., pp. 38–39.

Despite his apparent softness when confronted by the inexper-
ienced and ill-advised deputy sheriff, Sidney J. Kyle was a good stockman and business manager. The town of Kyle was named for his father,
Ferguson Kyle, who came to Texas in 1865, settled in Hays County, and
afterward became a prominent state legislator. Kyle Field, the athletic
stadium at Texas A&M University, is named for a brother, E. J., who
was a renowned horticulturalist, a dean at Texas A&M College from
1911 to 1944, and at various times from 1904 to 1944 chairman of the
Texas A&M Athletic Council. Sid, however, punched cattle in Midland, Pecos, Reeves, and Loving counties. After managing the TX
outfit at Horsehead Crossing and the large T&L Ranch in Midland
County, he bought and stocked a 150-section spread in northern Loving County. Later, after his death, this ranch became dotted with oil
and gas wells.[30]

Millard also wrote at length about Herman Koehler and his establishment in Fort Stockton. Koehler, he stated, "was one of the best
men I ever saw." The store was in one end of his building, the saloon
and billiard tables in the other end. Koehler marked the price clearly
on each item for sale, and he never sold for less. His standard reply to a
complaint about the price was "By god don't take it." In the saloon two
slates were used to record the names of customers and the amount
each owed. At closing time, Koehler transferred the accounts to his
books. He spread quilts and blankets on the floor for the men, sometimes as many as twenty to thirty, who wanted to spend the night or
were too inebriated to leave. Mrs. Heid, who ran the boarding house
for Koehler, had but one small bedroom for rent, and no one but "a sick
man or a district judge" was allowed to sleep there. Koehler had an
employee named Alberto, who tended the customers' horses. Reportedly, there was no charge for the feed and care as long as a roomer
stayed. Possibly a majority of the cowboys who returned to Fort Stockton in the spring were broke. According to Millard, "They would draw
on Koehler for 40 or 50 dollars and I never knew of him turning one of
them down."

In 1887 or 1888, Millard remembered, there was a large migration

[30] Webb and Carroll, *Handbook of Texas*, 1:977; Clarence R. Wharton, *Texas under Many Flags*, 4:299; *Memorial and Genealogical Record of Southwest Texas*, p. 276; *San Antonio Express*, May 20, 1906; Lauderdale and Doak, *Life on the Range*, pp. 72, 175; Henry C. Dethloff, *A Centennial History of Texas A&M University, 1876–1976*, 2:506.

Left: Pecos County Courthouse, built in 1883. *Right*: Pecos County Jail, built in 1883.

The Old Picnic Ground on the Francis Rooney farm on Comanche Creek.

Left: Francis and Jane Rooney, who settled on Comanche Creek in 1870. *Right*: George M. Frazer, who moved to Fort Stockton in 1868 and in 1876 was elected first Pecos County judge. *Courtesy of Gene Riggs.*

Barney Riggs (*left*) and Annie Frazer Johnson Riggs (*right*), who after their marriage in 1891 lived both in Reeves County and at Fort Stockton.

The H. Koehler General Merchandise Store, 1885, with Comanche Springs in foreground. The building is now the first floor of the Pecos County Community House, Fort Stockton.

Fort Stockton in 1884, with Friedlander building (*front*) and Joseph Heid's saloon (*right*). *Photograph by Captain George Wedemeyer, courtesy of Mrs. Otto Anderson.*

Fort Stockton scene, 1899, with Koehler Hotel (now the Annie Riggs Museum) under construction (*front, center*). Other buildings identifiable are (*from left*) Grey Mule Saloon, post hospital (just under the horizon), Heid Saloon and boarding house (then operated by Mrs. Taylor Stephenson), Rooney and Butz and F. W. Young stores (behind hotel), James Rooney residence, and newly built H. H. Butz house.

Fort Stockton scene, 1900, with the F. W. Young store (*right, foreground*) and footbridge leading to the courthouse.

Grey Mule Saloon, opened in early 1894 by Sheriff A. J. Royal and Ed Montieth.

Orient Saloon, Pecos, where Barney Riggs shot two of "Deacon" Jim Miller's men. *Courtesy of Barney Hubbs.*

Group of Fort Stockton citizens. *Left to right, standing*: John Edgar, Andrew Jackson Royal, Jesús Jaramilla, and W. P. Matthews; *seated*: Hart Mussey, Charley Wilson (Sanderson), George Hawthorne, Reuben Mussey, and Herman Koehler.

Group of Pecos citizens, ca. 1883. *Left to right, standing*: Bud Frazer, Tom White, George M. Frazer, Allen Heard, John Rooney, and Tom Babb; *seated*: Lee Heard, Herman Koehler, and unidentified. *Courtesy of Gene Riggs*.

Left: Early Fort Stockton settlers; *left to right*, *standing*: Tom Riggs, Stamp Robbins; *seated*: Maye ———, Barney Riggs, and John Chalk. *Courtesy of Barney Hubbs. Right*: Edward Armon Sieker, Jr., one of the Texas Rangers who served in the Fort Stockton area during the late 1870s and 1880s. *Courtesy of Mrs. E. G. Sieker and Robert J. Sieker.*

Company D, Texas Rangers, Frontier Battalion, 1894. *Left to right, standing*: Deputy U.S. Marshal F. M. McMahon, William Schmidt, James V. Latham, Joe Sitter, Edward Palmer, T. T. Cook; *seated*: unidentified prisoner, George Tucker, J. W. Saunders, Sergeant Carl Kirchner, and Captain John R. Hughes. *Courtesy of Rose Collection in the Western History Collection, University of Oklahoma, Norman.*

Judge O. W. Williams in his mid-eighties, about 1940. *Courtesy of Mrs. George T. Abell.*

to New Mexico, and many of these people were broke when they reached Fort Stockton. Often when they asked for only a little, Millard wrote, "Koehler would say, 'well its a good ways to where you are going, you had better take more', and they would say they didn't have any money and Koehler would say 'that's all wright [*sic*], when you gets there and makes some money you can send it back to me'." Two years later Koehler told Millard, "all dem men sent me the money but vun and I think some bad luck overtook him."[31]

Since there was no bank in Fort Stockton, Koehler always kept on hand from three thousand to ten thousand dollars and cashed checks and loaned money without security. According to Howell Johnson, a fellow townsman, Koehler "was known to be the most humane and charitable person West of the Pecos."[32]

In 1887 Presnall and Mussey's huge Mule Shoe cattle company went out of business. The preceding year had been unusually tough on all West Texas cattlemen. The terrible blizzard early that year had taken an exceedingly heavy toll of cattle, and many surviving cattle had drifted southward for hundreds of miles, creating problems and additional expenses for the owners. In the lower Pecos country, rustlers seemed to be unusually active. Furthermore, that year Presnall lost about 611 steers that were being driven from Presidio County to market in Missouri by way of the Pecos and Canadian rivers. Losses occurred during night stampedes at Toyah, at the Hashknife Ranch, and at the treacherous Pecos River crossing, where many steers bogged and drowned. Then, on another drive, 1,000 cattle froze to death en route from Pecos County to Montana. As a result of these losses, Presnall's credit hit bottom.[33]

Presnall and Mussey's Mule Shoe herds were taken over by the Western Union Beef and Land Company.[34] With R. J. Lauderdale employed to tally the cattle, the roundup commenced at the Mule Shoe pens at Agua Bonita (previously shown on army maps as Antelope Spring), fifteen miles northeast of Fort Stockton, with Taylor Stephenson, of the Mule Shoe, acting as straw boss and superintendent.

[31] Millard, *Cowpuncher of the Pecos*, pp. 33–35.
[32] Howell Johnson, Fort Stockton, reminiscences, *Fort Stockton Pioneer*, April 5, 1956.
[33] J. Marvin Hunter, ed., *The Trail Drivers of Texas*, p. 388; O. W. Williams, oral statements, to Clayton Williams.
[34] Pecos County, Deed Records, 2:102.

To protect their respective interests, Dunn Houston's NA Ranch sent Bill Mathis, Morgan and Jim Livingston, Shipton Parke, and Bob Anderson; the TX outfit, from the Horsehead region, was represented by the Kyle brothers, Bill, Sid, and Albert, Ed Stuckler (often spelled Steuckler or Stueckler), and Martin Nester; and Henry Mansfield represented F. W. Young's Diamond Y Ranch. At various stages in the roundup, the operation was joined by some of the hands from the "S" ranch on the Pecos River, John Doak and a couple of other men from the Pecos Land and Cattle Company, and several cowboys from the Halff ranch on the east side of the Pecos River near Pontoon Crossing.

At each roundup station, from 1,000 to 1,500 cattle were run through a chute, branded, had their tails bobbed, and tallied, for a final tally estimated between 14,000 and 15,000 head. The Western Union Company paid twelve dollars a head for the cattle; it also bought and rebranded 180 saddle horses, 125 stock horses, and 50 unbroken horses. Presnall and Mussey sold their ranchlands and town property to the Fort Stockton Live Stock and Land Company, but in 1890 this property also was acquired by the Western Union Beef and Land Company.[35]

The minutes of May 9, 1887, of the Pecos County commissioners court reflect its first large sales of land for delinquent taxes. As noted earlier, G. A. Purington at this sale bought more than fifty sections (32,000 acres) of land at a cost of approximately $263—slightly more than eight cents an acre. George Hawthorne, the clerk at Koehler's store, purchased twenty-three sections at the same rate. Judge Williams noted in the minutes that the money from these sales was used to pay salaries and expenses to himself, Sheriff Edgar, Howell Johnson (the county attorney), John Valentine (the janitor at the courthouse), George H. Lewis (the district and county clerk), and the commissioners.

A statewide campaign by prohibitionists in the mid-1880s no doubt had some effect on the Pecos County general election in November, 1888. As a result of the campaign, the Texas legislature in 1887 approved the submission of a proposed amendment to the state constitution. Pecos County voters did not care to have their drinking habits legislated. In August, 1887, in Precinct 1, the vote was seventy-one

[35] Lauderdale and Doak, *Life on the Range*, pp. 174–176; Pecos County, Deed Records, A-4:101–102, 447, 449, and 26:30.

against and one for; in Precinct 3, it was three for and three against; and in Precinct 4, it was seventy-four against and four for. In Precinct 2 no votes were recorded. Of the 190 counties voting, only 29 gave a majority for prohibition.[36]

It must have been obvious to everyone in Pecos County who had cast the one and only vote in Precinct 1 for the amendment, for County Judge O. W. Williams was well known as a rabid foe of Demon Rum. Even had he known that the vote would cost him his job, he would not have voted otherwise, for he was not one to violate his principles. Nevertheless, in November, 1888, he was a candidate for reelection. The voters had not forgotten his stand on prohibition; R. W. Mussey defeated Williams by a vote of 123 to 44. In the other races, Winchester Kelso became the district judge; Walter Gillis was elected district attorney; John Edgar and George Lewis survived as sheriff and clerk; and Francis Rooney, H. W. Miller, Hart Mussey, and W. P. Matthews were elected commissioners. The election of Hart Mussey as a commissioner, Fred B. Mussey as surveyor, and Pope Presnall as county treasurer (over F. W. Young) clearly indicated that many voters were sympathetic toward and wanted to help the unfortunate former owners of the Mule Shoe Ranch.[37]

At the end of 1888, the people of Pecos County were relatively peaceful and congenial. Millard wrote that, when he left Fort Stockton in the late 1880s, "all got along like a bunch of brothers."[38] But it was the calm before the storm, for several violent and bloody feuds, which culminated in the killing of the Pecos County sheriff—in broad daylight, in the courthouse—soon were to begin.

[36] Webb and Carroll, *Handbook of Texas*, 2:414–415.
[37] Pecos County, Commissioners Court Minutes, November 12, 1888.
[38] Millard, *Cowpuncher of the Pecos*, p. 39.

CHAPTER 21

1889-1892

Fᴏʀᴛ Stockton experienced hard times during 1889. Nothing had regenerated the trade and employment lost when the army left. In addition, both the Texas and Pacific and the Southern Pacific railroads had bypassed the town by more than fifty miles from the nearest tracks. The Southern Pacific, the county's only railroad in 1889, had its roundhouse at Sanderson, the only town of consequence along its Trans-Pecos route. Dryden and Haymond contained only a few houses. Furthermore, there was no longer the wagon-train and stagecoach commerce. Pecos County, largely as a result of these factors, had lost the majority of its population. In 1880 it had more than 360 "house-keepers" (wives, widows, single women), and possibly about the same number of families, but eight years later the county had only 85 heads of family and an assessed county property value of $3,095,938.[1]

In 1889, Francis Rooney, at age sixty-two, was old from the hard-ships of his vigorous frontier life. After the fort had been closed, the railroads had been completed through the Trans-Pecos region, and the Overland Trail had been abandoned, Rooney disposed of his farm on the Pecos. He still owned the large farm three miles north of Fort Stockton, but with no nearby market for its products it was now a lia-bility. During the early part of the year, Rooney went to Peña Colorada to try to sell mesquite-root wood to the army outpost there. He took along his six-year-old son, Will, who got to see the noted frontiersman Big Foot Wallace, whose feet were not as large as he had expected.[2]

Rooney had three other sons, John, Frank, and James, ages twenty-

[1] Pecos County, Texas, Minutes of the Commissioners Court, August 26–27, 1889; U.S. Department of the Interior, Census Office, *Tenth Census of the United States, 1880. Population. Texas.*

[2] W. P. (Will) Rooney, youngest son of Francis Rooney, oral statements, to Clayton Williams.

five, eighteen, and sixteen, respectively, and four daughters, Ella, Kate, Mary, and Agnes, twenty-two, fifteen, thirteen, and eleven. Six or seven years previously, he had sent to Ireland for John, Rose, Kate, Francis, and Elizabeth, the children of his deceased older brother. When the children arrived at San Antonio, John and Frank, who were attending Saint Mary's College there, met their cousins at the Saint Leonard Hotel but found the Irish brogue difficult to understand.[3]

In addition to supporting a large extended family, the kind and noble pioneer had many other financial expenses. On one occasion, when Rooney and two other men were sureties on a politician's bond, one of the bondsmen died, the other left the country, and consequently Rooney had to pay the entire amount of the defaulted bond. Thus in 1888, because of the financial pinch, Rooney had to sell much of his ranchland in Brewster County, in the vicinity of Leoncita Springs.[4] The next year, while on a trip to the Williams farm on the Pecos, he became violently ill and subsequently died on October 27, 1889. To this pioneer, who had been instrumental in the organization of Pecos County, had served continuously since then as one of its commissioners, and had developed two large irrigation projects in the county, the commissioners court, during its November 11–14 session, paid a well-deserved tribute. Among other things, the resolution stated that: "We as members of the Commissioners' Court of Pecos County, State of Texas, mourn his loss as an active, honored and influential member. . . . And be it further Resolved, That the Court House of this County remain draped in mourning for a period of thirty days."

The Rooney estate tax renditions for 1890 showed 120 horses and mules, forty head of cattle, 5,587½ acres of land, and four wagons. The land was valued at $10,461; possibly between 1,500 and 2,000 acres were under irrigation. Rooney's oldest son, John, was running the ranch at Leoncita (what was left of it), and following his father's death Frank returned from San Antonio to run the large farm three miles north of Fort Stockton.

Many Pecos County citizens were occupied with raising cattle or sheep or both. The 1890 tax rolls of the county show that the fourteen

[3] Roy Rooney, son of Frank Rooney, oral statement, to Clayton Williams.
[4] H. H. Butz and W. P. Rooney, oral statements, to Clayton Williams; Brewster County, Texas, Deed Records, 1:164, 167, 173.

cattlemen reported 6,195 head, the herds ranging from 100 to 1,200 in numbers. Three owners had Spanish names, and two ranches were partnerships.[5] The four principal sheepmen reported that they owned a total of 18,400 sheep.[6] Many others owned smaller numbers.

Although John H. Anderson provided the name for an important draw (Six-Shooter Draw) in Pecos County, he apparently neither owned or leased any land nor rendered or paid any county or state taxes. He used a pistol design for his brand, placed on the right thigh of his cattle and on the left thigh of his horses.[7] Travis Roberts of Marathon, Texas, recently stated that it was generally understood among the old cowboys of this region that Six-Shooter Draw was named for a stockman who used such a brand in that locality. According to a different version, probably fiction, Ike T. Hock was told that he could not carry a pistol into Fort Stockton. Later Hock rode into town dragging a six-shooter attached to the end of a rope, the other end attached to his saddle horn. When asked the reason for his dumb stunt, he supposedly replied: "Well, if you can't carry a six-shooter, maybe you can drag one," and, pointing to what is now known as Six-Shooter Draw, added: "All the way from that draw, just to make it legal."

Cattleman R. B. Neighbors became involved in the Pecos County feud of the mid-1890s by being elected sheriff before Sheriff A. J. Royal was willing to give up the office. Neighbors' father, Robert Simpson Neighbors, a native of Virginia, who became an orphan when only four months old and thereafter lived with relatives until he came to Texas at the age of twenty in 1836, served in the Texas Army and in John C. Hays's company of volunteers in San Antonio during one of the invasions by Mexican troops. Neighbors and about forty other persons, including Big Foot Wallace, were taken prisoner by General Adrian Woll in 1842 and were imprisoned in Mexico. After his release in March, 1844, Neighbors returned to Texas, became the agent for the Lipan and Tonkawa Indians, in 1849 with John S. (Rip) Ford scouted out the

---

[5] Henry Packingham, 1,000, on Independence Creek; F. W. Young, 1,200; Robert Anderson, 600; Robert Anderson, J. M. Livingston, J. A. Livingston, and Shipton Parke, 600; H. H. Rhodino, 500; T J. Henderson, 400; Fred Mussey, 350; R. S. Neighbors and R. B. Neighbors, 300; Ike T. Hock, 300; A. L. Wallace, 295; Juan Torres, 200; W. P. Matthews, 200; Rosario Ureta, 150; and Camilo Terrasas, 100.

[6] Charles Downie, 6,400; S. A. Purinton, 5,500; M. A. Ellis, 3,000; and John Savage, 3,500.

[7] Pecos County, Brand Book, No. 1, November 12, 1889.

northern route for a San Antonio–El Paso road, organized El Paso County in 1850, afterwards had charge of all of the Indians in Texas, and finally served as the superintendent of the Brazos and Comanche reservations in Texas. After getting the reservation Indians removed to Indian Territory in 1859, he returned to Fort Belknap, where he was murdered by a stranger before he had an opportunity to see his infant son, Ross Simpson Neighbors.[8]

Brothers Ross Simpson and Robert Barnard Neighbors first registered their brand in Presidio County and then on May 8, 1885, in Pecos County. Apparently they neither owned nor leased any land, a common arrangement. At that time, much over-grazing was done by stockmen who merely drifted where grass was convenient. The first lease recorded in Pecos County by the Neighbors brothers was on February 21, 1889, from W. R. Ellis, who ranched between Haymond and Fort Stockton. This lease, which was to run until February, 1893, contained 2,560 acres, a windmill, a water trough, and some fences. R. B. Neighbors also acquired some land in a delinquent tax sale on March 6, 1891.[9]

Another colorful—and controversial—figure in Pecos County in the 1890s was Barney Kemp Riggs, the son of Thomas Riggs, Jr., a native of Alabama, and Hannah Felton Riggs, a native of Tennessee. Before moving to Texas, the Riggs family lived in Arkansas, where son Brannick (often spelled Branick) was born in the early 1850s and Barney on December 18, 1856. Richard, the third child, was born in 1858, after the family moved to Texas. During the next sixteen years, several other children were born, in either Bell County or Coryell County: Thomas (probably Thomas III), who in time married Mary Jane Johnson, daughter of Annie Frazer Johnson; Martha (Mattie), who married Bud Frazer, Annie Johnson's brother; Mary Emma, who married John Sterling Teague Baker; and James Monroe, who married Dollie May Mitchell.[10] Thomas Riggs, Jr., the father of this clan, had at least two brothers who came to Texas. John Riggs was killed by Indians in Coryell County in 1859. Brannick Riggs, for whom Thomas named his

[8] Kenneth F. Neighbours, *Robert Simpson Neighbors and the Texas Frontier, 1836–1859*, pp. 7–10, 15–17, 19, 23–24, 68, 70, 108, 283, 287.

[9] Pecos County, Deed Records, 4:436.

[10] Since Barney Riggs married Annie Frazer Johnson, and Barney's sister married Annie's brother, and Barney's brother married Annie's daughter, the Riggses and the Frazers were rather closely related by marriage.

firstborn son, moved from Texas to Colorado and afterward, in 1879, settled near the Chiricahua Mountains in Arizona. While still living in Bell County, Barney Riggs may have accidentally killed a man. The Austin *Democratic Statesman* of September 5, 1875, which perhaps carried the first notice of the shooting, stated: "Hugh Armstrong was shot, perhaps fatally, last Monday, near Salado [Bell County], by his friend Barney Riggs. The pistol was empty and Barney was only 'fooling with it'. Empty guns and pistols kill almost as many people as non-explosive coal oil lamps." It is not certain, however, that this Barney Riggs was the same man who later was involved in the Pecos County feuds, for more than one "B. Riggs" lived in Bell County. If it was Pecos County's Barney, he was about nineteen years old at the time.

In 1880, or possibly earlier, the Thomas Riggs family moved to Kimble County, near Junction. In March, 1880, Riggs became the postmaster at Viejo (later named Cleo), a tiny community twelve miles northwest of Junction. During the next few years, the Riggs family acquired property both in Junction and along Viejo Creek (also known as Bear Creek), a tributary of the north fork of the Llano River.

Not long after Thomas Riggs moved his family to Kimble County, son Barney joined his uncle Brannick Riggs in the livestock business in Arizona. Although he apparently prospered for several years, eventually he was confined in the Yuma Prison. In the meantime, Barney's brother Brannick was having problems with the law in Kimble County, Texas. In October of 1885, Brannick was charged with two felony counts, one for murder and the other for assault with intent to kill. The details are skimpy, but the cases dragged on for over a year. Then in March, 1887, a jury found Brannick Riggs not guilty of the murder charge. Apparently, the assault charge was dropped.

Thomas Riggs died in Kimble County in March, 1885. Not long afterward, Hannah Riggs and her children started selling some of their land, apparently with the intention of moving farther west. The land sales were completed, with Richard Riggs acting with power of attorney and Barney and wife Vennie signing documents before a notary public in Cochise County, Arizona. Hannah signed with an X, an indication that she was illiterate rather than infirm, since she lived for almost another fifty years. After disposing of the larger part of the Kimble County land, Hannah Riggs and her children moved to Pecos County, where they were to have an important role in the life and affairs of the community. There the family eventually was joined by Barney, who had gotten into trouble in Arizona. Although officials refuse to release official information about Barney, he shot to death a man at Willcox, was convicted for murder, and was sentenced to life imprisonment in the state penitentiary at Yuma. At the time he was married to Vennie and had one child, William Earl Riggs.

Barney soon became a prison trusty. His duties included going into Yuma to purchase food for the prisoners. One day, in 1889, while Barney was in the office of the prison secretary, several other convicts attempted a breakout. At the time, Frank M. King and another guard were outside the walls. On hearing the bell, a signal for all guards to assemble, they rushed to the prison, carrying their six-shooters but without their Winchesters. Near the main entrance a big, husky life-termer had caught Warden Gates around the neck, held a knife against his back, and told Frank Hartley, another guard, that he would stab the warden if he attempted to prevent his escape. Nevertheless, Hartley fired, killing the convict as the knife penetrated deeply but not mortally into Gates. When King and his companion reached the scene, another convict was holding Fred Fredley, the prison yardmaster, as a shield and maneuvering toward the river. When he exposed his side, they both fired and killed the convict. When the firing was over, three other convicts lay dead inside the main entrance of the prison. Tradition has it that Barney Riggs killed them. Riggs, who had obtained a pistol in the secretary's office in the commissary, rushed out and shot in the back of the head a convict who was standing by the commissary building with a gun aimed at Hartley. Thus Riggs, no doubt, saved Hartley's life and also likely saved the life of the warden. Later, as a reward for his loyalty and quick action, Barney Riggs was given a pardon and released from prison.[11] It has often been said that Barney

[11] This study of the Riggs family has been compiled from the following sources: U.S. Department of the Interior, Bureau of the Census, "Eighth Census of the United States, 1860. Population. Texas," Bell County; U.S. Department of the Interior, Bureau of the Census, *Tenth Census of the United States, 1880. Population. Texas*, Kimble County; Lee Riggs, son of Barney's brother Tom Riggs, oral statement, to Clayton Williams; Mary Larson (granddaughter of Barney's uncle, Brannick Riggs), Lowell, Arizona, to Clayton Williams, December 16, 1959; Frederica Wyatt, "Cleo's Lifeblood—Its Post Office— Will Close," *Standard Times* (San Angelo), October 22, 1974; Dick Roberts, "Heirship of Mrs. H. M. (Hannah) Riggs," undated manuscript, Midland, Texas, copy in possession of Clayton Williams; Glenn Shirley, *Shotgun for Hire: The Story of "Deacon" Jim Miller, Killer of Pat Garrett*, pp. 22–25; Frank M. King, *Wrangling the Past, Being the Reminis-*

Riggs "killed one man to get into prison and killed another [or more] to get out." His release obviously pleased many of his friends, who believed that the original killing had been justifiable.[12] Today, the old Yuma Prison is a museum, and one of its exhibits is a plaque commemorating Barney Riggs for his action during this episode.

On obtaining his pardon, Barney in 1890 joined his mother and her family in Pecos County. It is not known whether he made any effort to find Vennie, who had gone, or later went, to live in California. When he arrived in Pecos County, his brother Tom was operating a horse ranch and owned 160 head of horses. Soon circumstances, unrecorded but probably including existing family intermarriages, brought together the firebrand Barney Riggs and the strong-willed Catholic widow, Annie Frazer Johnson. Barney and Annie were married by County Judge R. W. Mussey on September 23, 1891, but the legality of the marriage was questionable.[13] The Pecos County probate records for 1902 show that after Barney's death Vennie F. Riggs filed a petition in Los Angeles County, California, claiming to be the "lawful and only surviving widow of B. K. Riggs."

From the time he arrived in West Texas until he was killed, Barney Riggs remained in and around Pecos County. It was a tumultuous decade for the Riggs and Frazer families, and more than one person died from Barney's "lead poisoning." Although Riggs was a gunfighter, it should be noted that at times he was acting in self-defense or on the side of the law and was never the waylay killer. "One story often reported," wrote Ed Bartholomew, "is that Riggs once killed a man in a gunbattle, and it was whispered that the man was shot in the back. . . ." Riggs, the story continues, to prove that such was not the case, dug up the body and brought it back to the saloon.[14]

---

cences of Frank M. King, pp. 192–194; Kimble County Historical Survey Committee, *Recorded Landmarks of Kimble County* (regarding the two courthouse fires), p. 179. For charges against Brannick Riggs in cases 347 and 348, see Kimble County, Texas District Court Minutes, 1:90–91, 94, 123, 167, 183, 201; for the Riggses' land transactions, see Kimble County, Deed Records, A:19–20, 383–385, 1:23, 329–330, 2:148–150, 172, and 4:474–475.

  [12] Ed Bartholomew, *Biographical Album of Western Gunfighters*, entry for Barney Riggs.

  [13] Pecos County, Marriage License Records, 2:42.

  [14] Bartholomew, *Western Gunfighters*, entry for Barney Riggs.

Another who had a major role in the Pecos County conflicts of the 1890s was Judge Oscar Waldo Williams.[15] Descended from a long line of frontiersmen, dating from the early 1600s, Oscar Williams was born in Mount Vernon, Kentucky, on March 17, 1853, the son of Jesse Caleb Williams, a prosperous merchant. Four years later, the elder Williams moved his family to Carthage, Illinois, where he established a merchandise store and engaged in other business ventures, including a pork-packing plant in Keokuk, Iowa. Many years later, Judge Williams recorded some fond memories of his early years in Carthage—among them the time, when he was about five years old, that he had gone with his father to the courthouse square to listen to a speech by political candidate Abraham Lincoln, "a long, angular figure, dressed in a long-tailed black coat, and topped by a tall, stiff hat which was known in those days as a stovepipe hat. . . ."[16]

The Williams family, Southern and Democratic, was on the wrong side of the Mason-Dixon line when the Civil War began, and, during the conflict, it had little contact with its Confederate kinfolk. When the war was over, Oscar spent a year at Liberty, Missouri, attending William Jewell College (a preparatory school). Following that, he attended Christian University (presently, Culver-Stockton College) in Canton, Missouri, where he studied Latin, Greek, astronomy, higher mathematics, chemistry, and a "Scientific Course." Outside classes, he played baseball, the flute, and practical jokes. In the fall of 1870, he entered Bethany College, in West Virginia, a "Campbellite" institution, where he excelled in baseball, did well in Latin, Greek, astronomy, mathematics, and some other courses, but failed in chemistry. (His excuse was that his chemistry teachers at Christian University had been as bored as he with the subject.) In lieu of a laboratory science, he studied civil engineering—a fortunate decision, since he later made use of the knowledge learned in the course to make a decent living in West Texas.

After Bethany, Oscar returned to Illinois, where his father was serving as a state senator. During the summer of 1871, he worked as a civil engineer on a railroad construction project, which soon turned

---

[15] The author's father.

[16] S. D. Myres, *Pioneer Surveyor—Frontier Lawyer: The Personal Narrative of O. W. Williams, 1877–1902*, p. 6.

out to be "a misguided venture that 'broke up in disaster. . . .'." Later, in Carthage, he served as a deputy county clerk of Hancock County.

In 1872, Oscar enrolled in Harvard to study law, and in June, 1876, he received a law degree from that institution. After working at several jobs and discovering that he had lung trouble, he left for Texas.

Early in 1877, Williams arrived in Dallas, a small community of about 2,500 souls. Unfortunately, a rather large number of those souls were qualified attorneys, but fortunately for him there was a need for surveyors on the wild plains of northwest Texas. Therefore he took a job as a surveyor and made surveys in the counties of Lubbock, Swisher, and Hale. At the time, there was hardly anything out there but the buffalo and the buffalo hunters, many of whom became even less "civilized" than the marauding Indians. Later, Williams prospected in New Mexico. Somewhere, during this time, he met and fell in love with Sallie Wheat, the daughter of a prominent Dallas citizen. He was attracted for one thing, no doubt, by her musical ability and fine soprano voice. Like Oscar, she had a Kentucky background and belonged to the Christian Church.

Oscar and Sallie were married in Dallas on December 15, 1881. A short time later the newlyweds were living in New Mexico. Soon they moved to East Texas, where Oscar made a living by examining titles and estimating timber for a Michigan lumber company, but for health reasons he needed to be in a dry climate. When he learned that Pecos County needed a deputy county surveyor, he applied for and got the job.[17]

As noted earlier, Williams and his party surveyed the last large vacancy in Pecos County, which he identified as Block O. W. In 1886, he surveyed the region along Comanche Creek, a few miles north of Stockton, and also a large area in present Culberson County for the University of Texas, consisting of Blocks A to N and amounting to about 500,000 acres. During the same year, he also ran for the state a traverse in Pecos County from Escondido Spring to Pontoon Crossing to determine the overlapping of previous surveys. During the spring of 1887, while serving as county judge, he surveyed another large part of Pecos County. In December, 1888, shortly after he was defeated for

[17] Ibid., pp. 5–18; O. W. Williams, Fort Stockton, to his son Jesse C. Williams, Hankow, China, June 3, 1925, copy in possession of Clayton Williams.

reelection as judge, he completed surveys in other parts of the county, and in 1892 he surveyed a large block along the Pecos River.[18]

Judge Williams soon loved the Fort Stockton country and rarely strayed far from it. Not long after his arrival there, he began a life study of the semidesert, its geography, history, culture, and folklore, and he put his observations on paper.

In 1889, Judge Williams became one of the owners of the Pecos River Irrigation Company, which had been incorporated twelve years previously by Arthur Conroy, Jacob Jacobs, and Francis Rooney. The brush dam on the Pecos River was originally constructed in Pecos County, but the area later became a part of Reeves County. As previously noted, the owners dug six miles of ditch along the west side of the river to a farm being worked by Mexican tenants. In September, 1883, Rooney and his partners sold the company to J. D. Houston, owner of the NA brand and stock, for $1,920, and on February 22, 1889, J. D. and W. B. Houston sold the project to A. P. Wooldridge, of Austin. Wooldridge immediately sold to T. J. Ray thirteen shares of the capital stock and about 375 acres of the company's land. A few days later, Judge Williams bought into the project. As payment for land and interest, he made to Wooldridge two promissory notes, each for $1,250, payable on March 1, 1890, secured by a deed of trust that included various surveys in Block O. W. and a small amount of land in Block Z, all in Pecos County, and all the material property he had. With an amended charter, the new organization planned to dig about eight additional miles of ditch adjacent to and on the west side of the Pecos. Ditches were also to be constructed from Santa Rosa Spring to the farms operated by Tom Ray and the Levi Scott family.

In March, 1889, the Texas legislature passed an act for the appropriation of the waters of the state rivers. A ditch right-of-way of 100 feet was to protect prior appropriators of river water, and within a specified time thereafter irrigation companies were to file a report in the counties of their operations. In compliance with the act, on September 30, 1889, O. W. Williams, as president of the Pecos River Irrigation Company, in an affidavit filed in Reeves County, declared that the company

[18] Pecos County, Sketches 19, 19½, 21, 25, and 27, General Land Office, Austin, Texas; O. W. Williams, Fort Stockton, to Dr. T. D. Wooten (President of the University of Texas), Austin, December 1, 1886, File 1594, General Land Office, Austin.

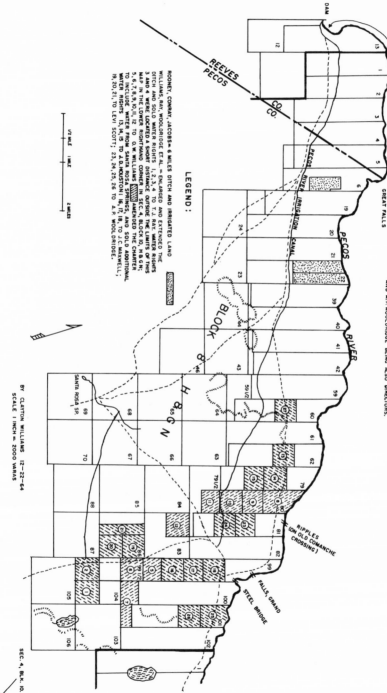

PECOS RIVER IRRIGATION CO — 1877 TO 1901

SECOND IRRIGATION PROJECT IN TEXAS TO USE THE PECOS RIVER WATER: I—25—1877 TO 9—18—83—FRANCIS ROONEY, ARTHUR CONROY AND JACOB JACOBS, DIRECTORS; THEN SOLD TO J.O. HOUSTON, WHO SOLD TO A.P. WOOLDRIDGE ON 2—22—1889; REORGANIZED AT THAT TIME, WITH O.W. WILLIAMS, PRESIDENT, T.J. RAY SECRETARY AND A.P. WOOLDRIDGE BEING ALSO DIRECTORS.

LEGEND:

ROONEY, CONRAY, JACOBS—6 MILES DITCH AND IRRIGATED LAND

WILLIAMS, RAY, WOOLRIDGE ET AL. = ENLARGED AND EXTENDED THE DITCH AND SOLD WATER RIGHTS 1, 2, 3, 4 TO T.J. RAY. WATER RIGHTS 3 AND 4 WERE LOCATED A SHORT DISTANCE OUTSIDE THE LIMITS OF THIS MAP IN THE LOWER RIGHTHAND CORNER IN SEC. 4, BLOCK 10, H & G N; 5, 6, 7, 8, 9, 10, 11, 12 TO O.W. WILLIAMS AMENDED THE CHARTER TO INCLUDE WATER FROM SANTA ROSA SPRINGS, AND SOLD ADDITIONAL WATER RIGHTS 13, 14, 15 TO J.O. HOUSTON; 16, 17, 18, TO J.C. MAXWELL; 19, 20, 21, TO LEVI SCOTT; 23, 24, 25, 26 TO A.P. WOOLDRIDGE.

BY CLAYTON WILLIAMS 12—22—64
SCALE 1 INCH = 2000 VARAS

was a corporation with its office in Fort Stockton, that the company's headgate was located in the Houston and Great Northern Surveys 11 and 12 of Block 7 in Reeves County, that the construction of the first ditch had commenced before January 1, 1878, that the proposed extension would enlarge the canal to a width of forty feet at the bottom, with a four-foot depth at or near the headgate, and that the carrying capacity of the canal would be 500 cubic feet per second. Then, on February 8, 1890, Williams made an affidavit in Pecos County, which declared the company's intention of supplying its canal with water from the Pecos River, Santa Rosa Spring, a number of artesian wells, and other sources, as authorized by the corporation's amended charter.[19]

In the latter part of 1889 or the early part of 1890, the Williamses moved to the site of the canal to supervise construction. The family first occupied two tents, and later had a brush arbor nearby, where its members could go to escape the summer heat of the tents. It was a new experience for Mrs. Williams and her two small children, Oscar Waldo, Jr., and Mary Ermine. Varmints and rattlesnakes, a shortage of necessities, an occasional "gully-wash" that covered the ground in and around their tents with two inches of water, and the total lack of luxury combined to make life difficult.[20]

Williams, now deeply in debt, was looking for every opportunity to get ahead. During the summer of 1890, he recorded that he had purchased 637 bushels of Kafir corn, kept a time sheet for twelve men, and reminded himself to see about some abstracts in Lubbock County and a cotton gin in Colorado City. In December he noted a passing interest in possible irrigation projects from Monument Springs and other sources and wrote himself a note to "see about Postal Route."[21]

Mrs. O. W. Williams purchased from the State of Texas all of Survey 80 in the Houston and Great Northern's Block 8, located near the end of the extension of the irrigation ditch. After the completion of the ditch, Judge Williams built on this land and alongside the canal a five-room, flat-top adobe home. Since the hand-dug well produced water fit only for nonpotable purposes, such as the laundry, every few days a

[19] Pecos County, Deed Records, A-2:351–352, A-4:618–620, and 4:419–421; Pecos County, Deeds of Trust, 1:147; Reeves County, Texas, Deed Records, 2:15; Pecos County, Irrigation Records, 1:301; Reeves County, Irrigation Records, 1:5; H. P. N. Gammel, ed., *The Laws of Texas, 1822–1897*, 9:1128.

[20] Ermine Williams Garnett, undated manuscript in possession of Clayton Williams.

[21] O. W. Williams, Fort Stockton, notes, in possession of Clayton Williams.

wagon with three empty barrels went to Santa Rosa Spring, about three miles away, for water for drinking and cooking. Handicapped by lack of a bank in Pecos County, Williams had his own coins made, with which he paid his laborers, who in turn used them to purchase groceries and other necessities at the store-room of the ranch home.[22]

Adjacent to Williams' land lay the NA Ranch, which extended from Santa Rosa Spring to the Young Ranch on the Diamond Y and westward to Coyanosa Draw. Ike T. Hock, in 1880 a stage attendant at Tunas, had become the wagon boss of the NA. Years later, Judge Williams told some interesting tales about Hock. Being a heavy drinker, Hock was often in Koehler's Saloon. One day he arrived there with a leg badly swollen from a rattlesnake bite. When asked what he had done for it, he said: "Nothin'. The liquor in me took keer of it." As an afterthought, he added, "The same liquor killed the snake."

A young cowboy named Pilar Durán also worked at the NA headquarters at Santa Rosa Spring. The 1880 census shows him to have been the eleven-year-old son of Francisca "Durand" Lugo. Francisca (or Pancha, as she was usually called) helped Mrs. Williams at the farm with household duties and also delivered Mrs. Williams' third child, Susan Kathryn. Pancha's father, as mentioned previously, had been killed in the 1850s near San Carlos, on the Mexican side of the Rio Grande, by Indians who, at the same time, had run off all his livestock. Pilar, a very energetic and affable lad, made a favorable impression on everybody in the region when he made an almost impossible horseback ride during an emergency. Pilar, who was at Santa Rosa Spring when Morgan Livingston, another NA employee, was shot through the left lung, helped the victim to his bed and then galloped over a large part of both Pecos and Reeves counties to get medical help. Judge Williams many years later in a letter to a friend gave a detailed account of the affair. As a young *vaquero* for the NA Ranch, Pilar did his best to learn to speak English and "did things for his white employers that the white man thought beneath his dignity." A youth named Ximenes slipped up to a window and through the glass shot Morgan Livingston in the back, the bullet passing through the victim's lungs. Ximenes ran into the *monte* ("brush"), but before he was out of range, Livingston had gotten out of the house and had fired two shots at him, wounding

[22] George Bentley, Monahans (formerly of Grandfalls, Texas), oral statements, to Clayton Williams.

him in the hand. He then told Pilar, the only other person present, to saddle up a horse and go after Judge Williams as fast as he could ride.

Williams was then building the upper portion of the present Imperial Canal and had his camp a little over three miles from the NA house. "It was just after noon," Williams wrote, "and I was in my buggy driving back to the working force, when I met Pilar rushing up on his sorrel horse. Hurriedly he told me the news and then galloped back." When Williams reached the ranch house, he found Pilar saddling another horse to go to Fort Stockton for a doctor. "At that time we had a county doctor under salary, . . . who was a feeble old man of some seventy years or more, but considered a good doctor." Livingston, who was lying in a bed, complained that blood in his throat might choke him, and Williams "got onto the bed and began to turn him over from side to side, and to press down on the lungs, hoping to start the blood running out of the wounds."

It was a guess on my part [Williams continued], and you know how much I felt relieved when the blood began to come through the wounds. Just then Mr. Maxwell came in. Before I had left the camp I had sent word to him to come to my help as he was an old Confederate Soldier, and must have had some experience with wounds of this kind. But the moment he came into the room and saw the blood over Morgan, the bed, and me, he became sick and was forced to leave us. . . . I had to work in the same way until finally Morgan said that the surging of blood in the throat had ceased.

About 6:00 P.M., Pilar returned from a 56-mile trip with word that the doctor had said he was physically unable to come. Williams then sent Pilar on a fresh horse to Pecos City, 40 miles away, for a doctor. A couple of hours later, Jim Livingston and Bill Matthews arrived, having heard in some way that Morgan had been shot. Pilar got to Pecos at 3:00 A.M., and, after trouble finding the proper house and getting a Dr. Homer Powers' promise to start right away, he tied and unsaddled his horse and lay down on his saddle blanket in the public street for a well-earned rest. He had ridden a total of 104 miles in fourteen hours, using four grass-fed horses, and was "*mucho cansado*" ("very tired"). Miraculously, Morgan lived, "pay enough for his [Durán's] loyal soul," and there will be more later about these two and about Dr. Powers.[23]

Pioneer farming along the Pecos was a risky business. Williams

[23] O. W. Williams, Fort Stockton, to George H. Lewis, January 13, 1930, copy in possession of Clayton Williams.

had considerable trouble with mustang herds. Wild horses would slip among his domestic animals and lure them away. He lost three work mules in this manner. Only one was recaptured, after being chased back and forth for three days from Horsehead Crossing to Santa Rosa Spring, and it then died from excessive running. The other two remained with the mustangs. Soon Williams raised cattle and hogs. The hogs went wild, but many were recaptured, driven to Pyote, and shipped to the Fort Worth market in two freight cars. Some of the cattle died from what was then called alkali, an ailment later attributed to their having eaten goldenrod. What was possibly Pecos County's first cotton crop was raised on the Williams farm. The seed cotton was hauled by wagons that broke a new trail across the dunes to Monahans. One of Williams' cotton crops was totally washed away when the Pecos River flooded. In places, the river was over a mile wide during a flood. Williams had an orchard and garden at the tail end of the irrigation ditch, but each year he lost much of its produce, particularly watermelons and cantaloupes, to hungry crows, coyotes, and other varmints.

Since he had no ranching or farming experience, Williams' hindsight became better than his foresight. The influx of farmers irrigating with water from the Pecos River above him meant less water for Pecos County farms and, except during flood times, the water Williams got was heavily saturated with salt. Unfortunately, he had no reservoir to catch flood water for later use. Consequently, to earn extra income, he spent considerable time in Fort Stockton doing clerical work at the courthouse or in the field on surveying jobs. While doing this, he rented one of the officers' houses of the abandoned fort for living quarters and on weekends walked the twenty-eight miles to his home. In his absence, Mrs. Williams had to see that crops were planted, range stock attended, cows milked, butter made, washing done, meals cooked, and the children reared. Although raised in Dallas without any knowledge about farms and ranches, she apparently did a fair job.

To make pioneer farming even more hazardous, herds of freegrazing sheep occasionally traversed the farms. In the spring, herders grazed them to New Mexico and returned them to the lower Pecos in the fall. These sheep consumed grass that was needed by Williams' stock, and they frequently pushed under the barbed wire fences to trample and eat the crops. Once, when a herd of sheep was headed toward her fields, Mrs. Williams had a team hitched to a hack and with a shotgun across her lap drove out to meet the herder. "I'll not shoot you," the staunch lady declared, "but I'll start shooting the first sheep that go under that fence." The herder wisely saw that his sheep avoided the cultivated land.[24]

Neighbors were important in the desolate Pecos area. A few miles southeast of the Williams farm, Tom Ray, a bachelor, and his two spinster sisters occupied a three-room, frame house, covered on the inside with newspapers to insulate it against cold weather. Ray's tract of land in the Pecos River Irrigation Company got good ditch water from Santa Rosa Spring. The irrigation company was sometimes referred to as "Austin's Colony in Pecos County," since many of the landowners, including the Rays, had come from the city of Austin. The Rays had a well-tended farm, surrounded by cottonwood trees. After a twice-a-week mail service went into operation by horseback from Fort Stockton to Monahans, the Santa Lucia post office was placed on Tom Ray's farm. Reportedly, it was pleasant to deliver the mail there at any time, day or night.

In 1890, or soon thereafter, a steel truss bridge was built across the Pecos on the road from Fort Stockton to Grandfalls. This bridge expedited the scheduled mail service between the two towns and the railroad town of Monahans. Subsequently, not far above the bridge, on the east side of the river, a cooperative cotton gin was established by Williams and the Grandfalls farmers. The location was chosen to obtain power for the gin from the ten-foot falls, but later a raging flood washed away the gin, other structures and machinery, the dirt approaches to the bridge, and the falls themselves. Williams was then working 600 acres of farmland and eight or ten sections of grazing land, all located in the salt-grass and brush country in the Pecos River area, but not all that land was actually owned by the family.

While the Williams family was engaged in farming, the yet-unsolved murder of Andrew Jackson Royal in the Pecos County courthouse occurred. Before moving to Fort Stockton, Andrew Jackson Royal and his wife, the former Naomi Obedience Christmas (Christmas Canyon, near Junction, was named for her family) lived in Junction, the county seat of Kimble County. Andy and his father, E. J., acquired considerable property, beginning in 1885, in and around

---

[24] Ermine Williams Garnett, oral statement, to Clayton Williams.

Junction. In 1892, he and a partner won a contract to build a new jail, and for several years thereafter he continued to acquire property in Junction.[25]

The first extant deed record in Kimble County for A. J. Royal, dated November 10, 1884, was for town property. During the next few years, he bought more land, both in and near town. One piece of town property, the Star Saloon, was owned jointly by Andy, his wife, and D. T. (Tom) Carson, a former Texas Ranger, who had served with Ed Sieker in the Trans-Pecos country during the Jesse Evans affair.[26]

By the late 1880s, A. J. Royal had been involved in a number of serious offenses. A former Kimble County official (who asked not to be identified) is of the opinion that more than one man was buried in Junction's oldest cemetery as a result of some conflict with A. J. Royal. In 1888, A. J. Royal and his wife began selling their property.[27] Likely, Andy had decided to move from Junction—perhaps, because of his run-ins with the law.

Most of Andy's troubles in Junction had occurred in or around the saloon that he and Tom Carson operated. In 1885, A. J. Royal, E. J. Royal, D. A. Townsend, Bill Clements, George Graves, and Jack Wood got into trouble with the law for playing cards. The two Royals (an indication that E. J. Royal was also a partner) and Bill Clements, a former Texas Ranger who operated a nearby saloon, were charged with permitting gambling on their premises. One of the alleged gamblers, George Graves, a freighter, got into an argument with W. W. Baker, a bartender who worked in Clements' saloon. When he arrived and heard the circumstances from the bartender, Clements went to the Star Saloon, where he found Graves, got into a fight with him, and shot him in the heart. A jury later quickly acquitted Clements of the murder charge.

The litigation that arose as the result of the death of another man,

[25] Frederica Burt Wyatt, a Kimble County historian, oral statements, to Gaines Kincaid, Austin; Kimble County Committee, *Recorded Landmarks*, pp. 24, 48, 138, 141, 179.

[26] Kimble County, Deed Records, A:141–143, 490–491, 1:211, 331, 346, 488–489, 2:359–360, 368, 587, 590, and 4:65–66, 167–168, 401. For details regarding the saloon, see O. C. Fisher, *It Occurred in Kimble: The Story of a Texas County*, p. 199.

[27] Kimble County, Deed Records, 2:369–370, 585–586, 588, 4:66–67, 198–201, 227, 513–514, 574, 5:496, 528, 6:345, 8:130.

Jim Stout, was probably the major reason that A. J. Royal left Kimble County. Stout, a likeable gambler, arrived in Junction, went to work as a bartender, and gained the respect of the town toughs, who learned quickly that the friendly stranger was very handy with his fists. Those with whom he had trouble over gambling included Andy Royal and Tom Carson. One winter night at closing time, Royal, Carson, and Stout left the Star Saloon together. Suddenly, Carson (for reasons not made clear) pulled a pistol and shot Stout. In his defense, he claimed that Stout had a gun under the sleeve of his overcoat and was reaching for it when he fired. To some bystanders, who moved him to a more comfortable place, the mortally wounded gambler said: "I went to that saloon tonight on their invitation to have a little game. I thought Tom Carson was the best friend I had. . . . Boys, don't ever put too much confidence in a man—not even a friend." Both Carson and Royal were indicted for murder. Although justice then was often swift, these cases were unnecessarily prolonged. Eventually, the district attorney dropped the charges against Royal for lack of evidence, and a jury found Carson not guilty. Meanwhile, Royal was also charged with "neglect of official duty," but the extant records do not specify his official duty. By the time he moved to Fort Stockton, this charge and others against him had been resolved.[28]

After moving to Fort Stockton in 1889, Andy Royal soon began acquiring property. On April 11, he obtained from George M. Frazer a deed to over 1,800 acres of Pecos County land at Leon Springs, a trade that involved 30 head of cattle branded AUS and 235 head branded BURT. The land included a large farm, irrigated from Leon Springs, some seven miles west of Fort Stockton. On April 1, 1890, Royal purchased 60 head of the TX-branded cattle (registered under the name of the American Land and Cattle Company) in one of Sheriff Edgar's tax sales (legal, this time) for a total price of $11.84. The TX owners were still being negligent about paying their taxes. Then, on July 17, 1893, Royal bought the establishment of the former post trader, Friedlander, which consisted of a very large building (on the site of the former li-

---

[28] Kimble County, District Court Minutes, 1:41–42, 48, 51, 55–58, 62–66, 173, 223, 226, 249, 255–256, 289–290, 318, 331. For details regarding the deaths of Graves and Stout, see Fisher, *It Occurred in Kimble*, pp. 233–234; for the death of Carson, see Bartholomew, *Western Gunfighters*, entry for Tom Carson.

brary) and several smaller houses, all within the limits of lots 1, 3, and 6, in the Saint Gall addition.[29]

Royal immediately began expanding his irrigation projects. On March 1, 1892, he applied for permission to construct the Casa Blanca Ditch, seven feet wide and three feet deep, "to conduct water from the Salt Creek, Sulphur Creek and Sutter Springs," some ten to fifteen miles north of Fort Stockton. At the same time, he made similar applications to build ditches from San Pedro Spring, seven miles north of Fort Stockton, and, in July, for still another to be called Naomi in honor of his wife.[30]

Meanwhile, as a result of an election, resignations, and appointments, the political situation in Pecos County had changed considerably. The minutes of the commissioners court indicate that in May, 1889, George H. Lewis resigned as district and county clerk, and George P. Hawthorne was appointed to replace him. Hawthorne, after serving little more than a year, resigned on June 30, 1890, and was replaced by Jacob Jacobs. On October 27, 1889, Commissioner Francis Rooney died and was replaced on November 14 by F. W. Young, another noble Pecos County pioneer, who resigned the office on August 25, 1890. The court then appointed A. J. Royal to fill the vacancy.

In the general election of November 10, 1890, incumbents Winchester Kelso and Walter Gillis (district judge and district attorney) were unopposed. For county judge, R. W. Mussey defeated O. W. Williams, whose prohibition views were still unpopular, by a vote of 193 to 54, and Frank Rooney defeated J. Jacobs for district and county clerk. F. W. Young and Howell Johnson were elected county treasurer and county attorney, respectively, and for assessor of taxes, A. J. Royal defeated C. M. Wilson by a vote of 169 to 79. The newly elected commissioners were W. H. Mansfield, S. A. Purinton, Hart Mussey, and W. P. Matthews. Matthews, who was also running for the office of sheriff and tax collector, was defeated in that race by the incumbent, John Edgar, 126 to 120. Edgar, however, failed to make bond within the required time, and on December 2, 1890, the commissioners declared the office vacant, ordered Edgar's bondsmen to pay the indebtedness, and appointed Matthews to fill the vacancy. When Matthews' bond

[29] Pecos County, Deed Records, 4:33, 433–435, and 5:603.
[30] Pecos County, Irrigation Records, 1:3, 86.

was approved two weeks later, the court appointed Shipton Parke to replace him as commissioner. Parke's sureties were Royal, Mansfield, Morgan Livingston, and Purinton. For various reasons, Mansfield resigned from the commissioners court on May 11, 1891, and was replaced by Rosario Ureta; Parke resigned on November 9, 1891, and was replaced by C. C. Harwell; Mussey resigned on September 30, 1892 (less than two months before the election), and was replaced by Thomas P. Baylor.

The first of many charges against Royal (disturbing the peace) appeared on the county court docket on August 18, 1890, but was postponed. Royal was tried and discharged on November 17, 1890. During its March, 1891, term the Pecos County grand jury, with O. W. Williams as foreman, indicted A. J. Royal for assault on S. P. Peterson and for carrying a pistol on January 17, 1891.[31] Then, on May 25, 1891, Royal was tried on the two charges, but a jury found him not guilty on both. Back in county court on April, 1892, Royal cited eleven men (all with Spanish names and probably all tenants on his farm) in a civil suit for the collection of rent. On May 16, 1892, he again appeared before the county court, this time to answer to three charges: carrying a pistol, assault and battery, and disturbing the peace. This case was continued until November 23, 1892, after the forthcoming election. By then there was a new judge, O. W. Williams, and all three charges were dismissed.

Meanwhile, according to Judge Williams' statement, on May 20, 1892, Royal shot to death Apollinar (or Apolinar) Mendoza.[32] According

[31]The author has certified copies of the grand jury indictments of A. J. Royal for beating up S. P. Peterson on January 17, 1891, and striking, wounding, and bruising him with a pistol (pistol-whipping), and an indictment against A. J. Royal for carrying a pistol on or about the seventeenth day of January, 1891, both signed by O. W. Williams, foreman of the grand jury.

[32]There are three versions, two by Judge O. W. Williams, of the account of events surrounding Mendoza's death. The oldest, written by Judge Williams, was done in pencil on ruled legal sheets. This account was discovered by the author among the files of his father (Judge Williams) after the death of his mother in 1936. Judge Williams said that he had prepared this account as accurately as he knew it for the grand jury. The second, edited version was typed by Judge Williams in the late 1930s. After the judge's death in 1946, the author read this typed account to W. P. Rooney and H. H. Butz, both of whom had lived in Fort Stockton at the time, and they agreed that, to the best of their recollection, the details were correct. Upon learning later that the Pecos County records differed in some details from his father's statement, the author employed Dr. H. H. Tracy, Fort Stockton, to search those records. Tracy spent several days during November and

to Williams' informants, Mendoza, while standing in front of the door to Koehler's Saloon, was shot in the back with a buckshot-loaded, double-barrelled shotgun by A. J. Royal. Mendoza died instantly.

Although he was not indicted for this by the grand jury, the deed contributed to Royal's reputation as a dangerous person. Williams wrote that, since he lived thirty miles from Fort Stockton and had little business in town, he knew very little about Royal before the murder of Apollinar Mendoza, except that he had a reputation for being quarrelsome and that people were afraid to talk about him.[33] At the inquest before Justice of the Peace F. Sanders on May 21, Royal faced the witnesses with a double-barrelled shotgun across his lap and a pistol in his scabbard. Long afterward, Williams wrote that "he [Royal] had threatened witnesses, Pilar Duran and John Southworth with death if they testified . . . against him. Pilar himself afterward told me that he testified with his eyes on Royal and his answers to questions were determined by a nod or a shake of the head of Royal. In consequence of threats, Southworth left the County a few days later and never returned, but is now [late 1930s] in Pecos."[34]

Williams also learned afterwards that "John Valentine having made some comments on the impropriety of Royals appearing before J. P. armed—he was threatened by Royal with death if he did not keep his mouth shut. So," Williams concluded, "he established an almost wholesale intimidation of people."[35]

Testimony at the preliminary examination was apparently hearsay, circumstantial, and conflicting. Statements by "witnesses" W. P. Matthews, John Southworth, Otto Robitz, W. T. Osgood, and Pilar Durán indicate that none of them saw the actual shooting of Mendoza. For instance, Robitz stated: "I did not see anyone shoot the first shot. The shots were in the direction of Mr. Koehlers. When I heard the second shot Mr. Royal was standing at the corner of Mr. Koehlers coral [sic]. . . . Mr. Royal had a gun in his hand and a pistol."[36]

December, 1980, examining the extant records in the attic of the courthouse and in the top story of the Pecos County jail. The account presented here synthesizes the three versions but draws most heavily on the 1930s typescript.

[33] Williams claimed little knowledge of Royal even though the previous May he had been foreman of the grand jury that had indicted Royal for pistol-whipping Peterson.

[34] Williams, 1930s typescript account of Royal-Mendoza incident.

[35] Williams, manuscript account of Royal-Mendoza incident.

[36] Pecos County records of Royal-Mendoza incident, gathered by H. H. Tracy.

Mr. Osgood's statement indicated that he was in the Koehler store and "did not go out for some time afterward. . . . Mr. Royal did not have a gun—he had a pistol—he had the pistol in his hand." Matthews' sworn statement read in part: "I was inside of Mr. Koehlers store and heard a shot and in a minute or two more shots. I came out of the door and saw the deceased Apolinar Mendoza lying on his face on the ground. When I came out I saw Mr. Royal—When I saw him he had a pistol—I did not see any shot gun. . . . I did not see him shoot. I went to deceased & I saw he was dead & I laid him back. There was a hole in the back of the vest. I did not strip him or see any other holes."[37]

Royal's own sworn account of the affair presented at the inquest stated that a Mexican (Mendoza) had asked him to go to Koehler's to pay him and others for some work they had done. Royal said that he agreed and that at Koehler's Mendoza and two other Mexicans wanted to be paid. When he handed one of them his money, Royal continued, Mendoza "reached his hand to his side like he was pulling his shirt up—and about that time I let him have it. . . . I know that I saw the bulk of his pistol."[38]

He had known the deceased about three years, Royal continued, and had heard of threats Mendoza had made against his life. He had been informed, on the evening of May 17, 1892, that Apollinar and two other Mexicans planned to kill him (Royal), and on the next night Natividad Ramírez had warned him that Mendoza and another Mexican intended to kill him. Royal claimed that the next morning, when he was 700 or 800 yards from his house Apollinar and another Mexican "raised up from behind a large cat claw bush . . . [and] opened fire on me and I laid down on the side of my horse and got away from there as fast as I could . . . then [when] I rode back towards them they . . . broke and run. . . ."[39]

Royal then stated that he went to his house and got his gun, and that he and Will (Bill) Osgood, whom he met in the field (and who was later a deputy when Royal was sheriff), trailed the Mexicans to within sight of the Rooneys' ranch but then returned to his farm and went to work. That evening, after having gone to the head of the ditch, Royal

[37] Ibid.
[38] Ibid.
[39] Ibid.

stopped, he swore, at the house of a Mr. Harris, where the same three Mexicans appeared, and one asked him where he intended to stay that night. Royal stated that he then went into town but, when he returned the next morning, other Mexicans told him those same three Mexicans and one other, Refugio Gamboa, had heard him leave and had attempted to cut him off "and they did not expect to see me back there alive."[40]

Royal's statement leaves some unanswered questions. A short time earlier, he had brought suit against eleven Mexicans for failure to pay rent. Why, then, did he not go to Sheriff Matthews or some other county official and file charges when the three Mexicans threatened to kill him? In any event, at the conclusion of the inquest, Royal was placed under bond, reportedly in the amount of $1,000, pending action by the grand jury.

In September, with Williams again serving as foreman, the grand jury investigated the matter. Royal's defense, Williams wrote, was the same as at the preliminary examination, namely "that 3 days prior to the killing—Apollinar and 2 other Mexicans had waylaid him on the road near his ranch in broad daylight and had attempted to assassinate him, and that, on the day of the killing, they had sent for him to come to Youngs [Koehler's] Store ostensibly to pay them some money he owed them but really to assassinate him, and that he killed Apollinar— when he—Apollinar—was about to shoot—Royal."[41] The earlier attempt at assassination by Mendoza and his associates was "corroborated by one Bill Osgood," who apparently worked for Royal.[42]

Since there was no evidence to refute Royal's claim of self-defense, Williams continued, there was no indictment. Indeed, only two members of the grand jury voted for indictment, and Williams believed both then and afterward that those two knew something that was not in the evidence but "feared to bring these things out."[43] It was not until long afterward that Williams learned of the threats against Durán and Southworth and that Mr. and Mrs. Refugio Gambera (or Gamboa), "whose testimony would have shown that the claimed . . . assassination [attempt] had never taken place," had been driven out "under

[40] Ibid.
[41] Williams, 1930s typescript.
[42] Williams, manuscript.
[43] Williams, 1930s typescript.

threats of death." All of these facts, Williams concluded, did eventually come out, though slowly, "and probably contributed to his [Royal's] end."[44]

About the same time as the murder of Apollinar Mendoza, Royal harassed and abused Mr. and Mrs. F. W. Young, the former county judge, who operated a store in Fort Stockton. According to Williams' statement, Young had reason to believe that Royal had branded and appropriated a colt of his. Young, a nonviolent, kind, and considerate person, dropped the matter when Royal denied the allegation, but Royal uttered threats against him and then went to his store, "yelling and shooting his pistol as he went." He asked for some cartridges and, when he turned around with them, Young faced "a cocked 6 shooter. For an hour or more Royal subjected him and Mrs. Young . . . to outrageous abuse."[45]

With his manuscript about Royal, Williams had a number of notes. In one note, apparently added as a reminder to bring up the matter of Royal's stealing horses and cattle, possibly before a grand jury, Williams wrote that late in 1892 he had begun to hear a good deal about Royal's stealing horses and killing cattle. Some "Mexicans living or having lived at his place—the Leon—have asserted to me that Mr. Royal killed cattle there regularly and claimed to them that it was toll for the water used by the cattle from the Leon." Williams added that he had some personal knowledge that Royal's man Osgood had killed cattle. Howell Johnson "tells me that he knows personally of Royal stealing 2 calves, 5 mares and 1 mule and had knowledge of acts indicating the stealing of other animals by him."

In the summer of 1892, according to Williams' notes, a number of owners of horses in the west end of this county and in the adjoining counties of Reeves, Jeff Davis, and Brewster banded together and rounded up the stock near Royal's ranch. "They found a great many of their horse stock with brands burnt into Royals brand, and carried their stock away, leaving word for Royal of their actions and inviting him to claim any horses they had taken away." After consulting County Attorney Howell Johnson, Royal dropped his claim to the stock. This little-known episode, Williams added, was "almost wholesale in its character."

[44] Ibid.
[45] Ibid.

Although Barney Riggs was Royal's chief aide, Riggs's in-laws, the Frazers, were not directly involved. George M. Frazer, Pecos County's first county judge, had long since moved to Toyah, where he had become the county judge of Reeves County. Mrs. Frazer, a devout Catholic, died in October, 1893, and was buried at El Paso.[46] George A. ("Bud") Frazer also moved to Reeves County, where he married Barney Riggs's sister, Mattie, on December 29, 1887, and continued to be an officer on the side of the law.[47] Some writers incorrectly have asserted that during the early 1880s he served as a Texas Ranger.[48] Beginning in 1890, Bud Frazer served for a number of years as the sheriff of Reeves County, and his activities up to the time he was slain, in 1896, were pretty much limited to that region.[49] His brother-in-law, Barney Riggs, on the other hand, was in trouble in both Pecos and Reeves counties.

[46] James Cox, *Historical and Biographical Record of the Cattlemen of Texas and Adjacent Territory*, 2:457–458.

[47] Reeves County, Marriage Records, 1:14. Cox states that the marriage was on December 31 (Cox, *Cattlemen of Texas*, 2:456).

[48] One account claims that he joined the Rangers in 1880 at age sixteen; another, that he joined at the end of the Victorio campaign, for several years was based at Ysleta, and then was transferred to Nolan County to fight the fence cutters before returning home to serve as a deputy sheriff (Cox, *Cattlemen of Texas*, 2:456; Bartholomew, *Western Gunfighters*, entry for George A. Frazer). The author has not been able to find in the Ranger files (Adjutant General's Papers) in the Archives, Texas State Library, any evidence that Bud Frazer was ever a Texas Ranger.

[49] Cox, *Cattlemen of Texas*, 2:456.

CHAPTER 22

1892-1894

THE 1892 election campaign in Pecos County was hotly and violently contested. O. W. Williams and R. W. Mussey were running for county judge; R. B. Neighbors and A. J. Royal, for sheriff; Frank Rooney and W. P. Matthews, for district and county clerk; Taylor Stephenson and George Hawthorne, for assessor; F. W. Young and H. Koehler, for treasurer; and Morgan Livingston, John Doak, and R. N. Baker for hide and animal inspector.[1]

Early in November, Corporal Carl Kirchner and two other Rangers arrived in Fort Stockton to keep the peace during the election. On November 7, the day before the election, Royal filed several complaints. He charged Frank and James Rooney, sons of the late Francis Rooney, with intimidating voters. On the following day, the Rangers arrested the Rooneys and delivered them to C. B. Teague, a deputy sheriff. Royal also filed complaints against Juan Gonzales for selling liquor without paying an occupation tax and Isidro Befie for unlawfully selling liquor. These cases were thereafter transferred to Williams' county court. Befie did not appear as summoned on December 4, and his bail bond, made by R. W. Mussey and Frank Rooney, was ordered forfeited. However, on February 6, 1893, this judgment was set aside in favor of the sureties.[2]

On November 8, while the election was being held at the Santa Lucia schoolhouse on the Ray farm near the Pecos River in Precinct 4, a belligerent Maximo Alvarez (the Presnall and Mussey cowboy who had been badly injured when his horse dragged him for several hours)

---

[1] Pecos County, Texas, Election Returns, 1892, 1:4–5.

[2] Monthly Returns for Co. D, Texas Rangers, November, 1893, Texas Adjutant General's Papers (AGP), Record Group (RG) 401, Archives, Texas State Library (TSL), Austin; Pecos County, Justice Records, November 7, 8, and 22, 1892, and February 6, 1893.

decided to see that his patron, A. J. Royal, received justice at the polls. O. W. Williams and his son Waldo, who was not yet a teenager, were present when the incident occurred. Many years later, Waldo recalled the event:

To bolster his courage, he (Maximo) drank too much. About 4:00 P.M. he decided to take charge of the voting polls. Father blocked Maximo when he tried to climb in through a window. This act incensed Maximo. He followed father as he turned away, and finally called him an unforgivable name. Father laid him out. Maximo recovered, went to his bed-roll, got out a Winchester, and started in toward the polls. I slipped out to my saddle pony, got my Winchester out of my saddle boot. I was relieved when Hiram Stephenson made Maximo surrender the gun.

Ten days later, Walter Ray, justice of the peace for Precinct 4, officially charged Alvarez with unlawfully carrying a gun at a voting place on election day.[3]

Despite his reputation as a troublemaker, Royal proved to be politically strong in the election. R. B. Neighbors won the Fort Stockton precinct, where most trouble occurred, by a vote of 84 to 58, but Royal carried the Sanderson precinct with 49 over Neighbors' 18, and in the county as a whole he won 193 votes to Neighbors' 137.[4] Other winners were Walter Gillis, district judge; C. C. Thomas, district attorney; O. W. Williams, county judge; W. P. Matthews, county and district clerk; H. Koehler, treasurer; John Odom, county attorney; John Doak, hide and animal inspector; and E. M. Teel, C. M. Wilson, T. P. Baylor, and C. C. Harwell, commissioners. Harwell, however, resigned on February 28, 1893, and was replaced by T. J. Ray, who qualified on May 8. O. W. Williams and A. J. Royal were sworn in by the commissioners court as county judge and sheriff, respectively, on November 17, 1892. After Odom failed to qualify, the court on December 1 appointed Howell Johnson as county attorney.[5]

   [3] Waldo Williams, manuscript, in possession of Clayton Williams; Pecos County, Justice Records, November 18, 1892.
   [4] Pecos County, Election Returns, 1892, 1:4–5.
   [5] Pecos County, Minutes of the Commissioners Court, November 17, 1892. According to the minutes of the Commissioners Court, S. A. Purinton and Herman Koehler were sureties for Williams. Sureties for Royal, who made a $5,000 bond, were C. W. Harwell, O. W. Williams, Eli M. Teel, Mary E. Sanders, and Herman Koehler. Teel, a native of Illinois, lived in Anderson and Runnels counties before moving to Pecos County. Royal's daughter, Lenora Exia (Lennie) Royal later married Teel's son, Robert Newton (Newt) Teel (U.S. Department of the Interior, Census Office, *Tenth Census of*

When Williams took office, some of the first cases involved the new sheriff. As previously noted, Royal had been charged on May 16 with carrying a pistol, assault and battery, and disturbing the peace, but Judge Mussey twice had postponed the cases, and they were still pending. On November 23, Judge Williams ruled for dismissal of all three cases because no one came forward to offer "good cause supporting affidavit." Not one of those who had preferred the charges appeared, possibly because the defendant had been elected sheriff.

Also during the November term of the county court, R. N. Baker (Royal's sometime friend) was charged with carrying a pistol and with assault. These cases were thrice continued, each time because Sheriff Royal's office failed to serve the papers. In August, 1894, before the cases had been tried, Royal and Baker would have a confrontation, and then the sheriff would be quick to file additional charges against Baker.

Meanwhile, in September, 1893, Sheriff Royal created a serious uproar by a brutal attack on one citizen and by his involvement in the mysterious disappearance of another. Judge Williams' lengthy statement about Royal also covered these incidents. On September 4, 1893, Royal, an armed officer, made "a brutal assault and unprovoked" on Elsa (Elza) White, "an unarmed, unresisting private citizen," striking him "with the butt of his pistol 3 times on the head." The blows, according to the doctor, "came near fracturing his skull." The assault created some enmities against Royal that "may have culminated in his death." Indicted by a grand jury for the assault, Royal became very angry, "particularly at R. L. Anderson, R. N. Baker, James Livingston, Shipton Parke and Frank Rooney, . . . and Francis Rooney, a witness for State." From that time on, Williams continued, Royal "commenced a series of threats and persecutions" against these men.[6]

When the case came up in county court in November and again in the following February, there was no trial because no jury was present. Judge Williams then had a jury drawn for the May term, but, when the

---

the United States. 1880. Population. Texas, Anderson County; Mrs. Maurice Owen Teel [Lennie and Newt's daughter-in-law], Junction, Texas, oral statement, to Gaines Kincaid, copy in Clayton Williams Papers).

[6] Williams, 1930s typescript of account of incidents concerning A. J. Royal. Both the typed and the earlier manuscript versions of Judge Williams' account covered the events discussed below. Again, the typescript is the version more heavily relied on herein. Frank and Francis Rooney were the son and nephew, respectively, of the late Francis Rooney.

time arrived, Royal did not appear and he had filed no bond. The judge thereupon appointed W. H. (Henry) Mansfield as a special bailiff to take his bond for appearance at the August, 1894, term, but Mansfield never did. Thus, when the Rangers arrived in August, Judge Williams sent word to Royal that unless he gave bond, as required by law, he would "put a new writ in the Rangers hands and have him re-arrested." Royal then made bond, with F. W. Young and Ed (or Ned) Monteith as sureties. Sometime earlier (according to the manuscript account, in June or July), Howell Johnson told Williams that Royal had said that if Johnson "argued strongly against him [Royal] he would assault him in Court and that if I [Williams] ruled against him he would shoot me in the Court Room, and wanted to know what we . . . could do. . . . I told him we would have to prepare to defend ourselves, as I did not know of anything else we could do."[7]

Another serious incident in which Royal was implicated was the disappearance of José Juárez.[8] In his narrative about Royal, Judge Williams also included an account of this case. In September, 1893, Juárez was arrested for stealing a watermelon from one of Royal's tenants.[9] When he got out of Royal's buggy at the jail just at dark, Juárez made a break for liberty. Royal, shooting as he followed, caught him in a marsh at the back of the jail, and a struggle ensued. Having fired his last shot, Royal "yelled for help," and Juárez was put in jail. In November, Juárez received a three-day sentence in jail. When his term expired, Williams continued: "Royal and Bill Osgood took the mexican in a buggy towards 12 mile mountain. Nobody ever saw the mexican after this—so far as I can learn. Royal claimed that he gave him a thrashing with a horse whip and told him never to show up again in Pecos County, and added in my hearing once, significantly, 'He never will'."[10]

[7] Williams, 1930s typescript.

[8] Below the heading about the Juárez incident in the manuscript account, an added line was squeezed in, which said, "Johnson in regard to 1-mule—5 mares & 2 calves." This was probably another of Williams' reminders of details he wanted to add later. Howell Johnson's claim that Royal had stolen a mule, two calves, and five mares was included in the typed version.

[9] Although Williams did not mention it in his statement, José Juárez had previously been charged with assault with intent to rape. This case, number 44 in county court, came up on August 21, 1893, before Judge Williams, who noted that Juárez was placed in the custody of the sheriff to make bond for appearance at the grand jury session on the third Monday in September.

[10] Williams, 1930s typescript.

There are reports that other Mexicans were victims of Royal's displeasure. The late Aubry Price of Fort Stockton once stated that Antonio Sánchez, a Mexican cowboy who worked for his father, showed him a grave beside the old road from Fort Stockton to Escondido in which was buried, Sánchez said, a Mexican whom Royal had killed. Royal, he said, had chased the man out of town, shot him, led the Mexican's horse back to Fort Stockton and ordered several other Mexicans to bury the body. And Douglas Adams, a native of Fort Stockton who worked alongside Pilar Durán in the Rooney Mercantile Company, has stated that "Pilar Duran told me that anytime any of Royal's Mexicans, who worked for him, began to press Royal for money he owed them, he [Royal] would kill them."[11]

In another case, Royal, it appears, displayed considerable favoritism toward one of his tenants. On June 19, 1893, Royal filed a complaint against Antonio Portio for "aggravated assault" on a woman. Royal, however, never served the writ, "always claiming that the man was out of the County." The case was continued on the docket, however, and after Johnson saw Portio, Royal promised "to arrest the man, but he never did so, and he was not placed under arrest until we had a new Sheriff in Nov. 1894."[12] Indeed, it seems that Howell Johnson saw Portio repeatedly and learned that he was a tenant on Royal's farm. "He [Johnson] said Royal had told him that his case was arranged."[13]

The troubles between Judge Williams and Sheriff Royal became increasingly tense, beginning probably when Williams tried to collect money Royal owed him, until the two eventually came to blows. It is not known exactly when the fight between them occurred, but years later two onlookers, Pilar Durán and H. L. Hatchette, who represented Royal as counsel during the feud, recalled a few details. Durán said that Williams was doing pretty well with his fists, cutting Royal's face, until Royal closed in and got Williams down. Hatchette said that when Royal got Williams down and started gouging at an eye with his thumb, Williams told him to stop or he would kill him. Royal did stop but later told Hatchette that he should have killed Williams while he had him down.[14]

[11] Aubry Price and Douglas Adams, oral statements, to Clayton Williams.
[12] Ibid.
[13] Williams, manuscript.
[14] Pilar Durán and H. L. Hatchette, oral statements, to Clayton Williams.

After Royal became sheriff, it was not uncommon for him to file charges against his enemies for the illegal possession of a weapon. Early in 1894, he charged Hiram Stephenson with unlawfully displaying a pistol in a public place and disturbing the peace. Stephenson pleaded guilty and was fined.[15] It was Stephenson who had prevented Royal's supporter Maximo Alvarez from taking over one of the polling places during the election of 1892.

According to the Williams' statement, Sheriff Royal on his own initiative also freed a jail inmate before he had completed his term of confinement. Egenio (Eugenio) Aguilar, arrested in May, 1894, for aggravated assault on a woman, was sentenced in county court to two months in the county jail, but, wrote Williams, "Royal turned him out after 34 days imprisonment without any authority." Williams said that he brought this to the attention of the grand jury, considering his own testimony sufficient for an indictment, but "that Grand Jury was not there apparently with any idea of doing anything against Royal. This . . . 'bad' mexican . . . had killed his man and had a certain influence at election, and it was generally believed that Royal had turned him loose in order to get his aid in the coming election."[16]

Sheriff Royal's escapades thus far, however, paled into insignificance in comparison with a feud between him and a prominent Fort Stockton pioneer family that split the community asunder and culminated in the Rooney-Royal shooting and, perhaps, the killing of Royal.

Enough had happened already to provide the fireworks; Royal, of course, did not hesitate to ignite them. In a frontier society, in which individualism was a pervasive character trait, no man, regardless of how powerful, domineering, or feared, likely could go indefinitely without his challengers. This particular feud had its origin in February, 1894, when Royal, in partnership with Ed Monteith, opened the Grey Mule Saloon, in competition with Herman Koehler. According to Williams' account, Royal, wanting his competitor out of business, not only threatened him but beat him with a walking cane within the hearing of at least four citizens.[17] The intimidated Koehler would do nothing, but Francis Rooney, Livingston, and Parke, all from the AB or 7 ranch, and

---

[15] Pecos County, Justice Records, February 25 and April 2, 1894.

[16] Williams, 1930s typescript.

[17] "Mansfield & Taylor Stephenson on the street heard the blows & I think Pilar saw it also" (Williams, manuscript).

some of Koehler's friends thereupon boycotted Royal's saloon. When Royal learned of their decision, he said he would make them drink at his bar and "would kick them out of the saloon and then fill them full of holes as they went out."[18]

Among those present in Koehler's store at the time of the shooting were Ed Stuckler (or Stueckler) and Pilar Durán, who about that time were involved in an incident involving Stuckler's newborn baby. Stuckler, after a long and stormy courtship, had married temperamental Candelaria Garza, who greatly resented her husband's weakness for strong drink and gambling. One night, when Ed was gambling in the Grey Mule Saloon, with quite a jackpot on the table, in came Candelaria with her baby and with a frantic gesture threw him on the pot and told Ed, with curse words in Spanish, "to take his old baby." Then out she went. The group assigned Pilar to take care of the child while they hunted his mother—who perhaps had gone to drown herself. Pilar took the baby to his home, but his wife, suspicious of his faithfulness to her and of his story, locked him out of the house. Pilar got the Sosas to take the child and returned home, but his wife kept him locked out until she later learned the truth. Incidentally, the baby grew into a good boy and became a railroad employee; the mother ended up living in San Antonio and "no one would suspect that she [once] had been the toast of the garrison at Fort Stockton."[19]

Ironically, the situation became more tense after Koehler's death on July 26, 1894. Koehler, as county treasurer, had in his trust over $5,000 of the county funds at the time. On the day Koehler died, John Odom was named treasurer to serve out the unexpired term. Judge Williams appointed Francis Rooney of Alpine, the nephew and namesake of the Pecos County pioneer, who in his opinion was the best qualified, as temporary administrator of the estate. The appointment did not please Royal, who was indebted to the Koehler estate in the amount of about $700, was preparing a counter-claim, and wanted as the permanent administrator someone who would be more responsive to his wishes.[20]

[18] Williams, 1930s typescript. According to Williams' manuscript version, the threats were made in the hearing of Stuckler and Johnson.
[19] O. W. Williams, Fort Stockton, to George H. Lewis, January 13, 1930, copy in possession of Clayton Williams.
[20] The counterclaim is said to have been based on Royal's having won the Koehler

On August 6, Sheriff Royal jumped on R. N. Baker, who was so drunk that he was "hardly able to stand," after Baker had let drop some words about the grand jury indictment of Royal for the assault on Elsa White. Royal "beat him up." At the same time he began "cursing and threatening" R. L. Anderson, James Livingston, and Shipton Parke, who were also on the same grand jury, and told Baker (perhaps also Valentine and Young, who were there) "to go to those 's o s of B———s' [*sic*] at Koehlers store and tell them that he was coming down . . . to 'wipe them out'." Young and his wife were too intimidated to relate the affair before a grand jury, and Royal "denied sending such a message," but Pilar Durán and Baker both told Judge Williams that they delivered the message. Regardless, the Rooneys apparently were "on the look out all day for trouble."[21]

Shortly after the confrontation with Baker, Royal appeared at the courthouse, where Justice of the Peace Hatchette was about to try a suit, *Young* vs. *Torres*, but, because Royal's "appearance and talk were so wild and vindictive," Hatchette, he afterward testified, "in fear of life," postponed the hearing until later in the day.[22]

Early that afternoon, Williams' statement continued, Royal went to Koehler's saloon; at the door he spoke briefly with a Macario (possibly Macario Gonzales), who "commenced to hurry away from the store," presumably because "he saw Royal draw a pistol." Rooney, who was in another room, Williams wrote, said that he heard Royal stop at the bar and a pistol being cocked and then saw Royal go into the store. Rooney claimed that, upon seeing no one in the store, Royal "exclaimed 'where are the S———s of B———s anyway'." As he "turned to go back, . . . he saw Jimmie [Rooney] with a shot-gun and started to throw his pistol down on him, when Jimmie fired and the row commenced."[23]

store in a poker game (H. H. Tracy, Fort Stockton, November 30, 1980, personal communication to Clayton Williams).

[21] Williams, 1930s typescript.

[22] Juan Torres, who married into the Sosa family in 1881, and F. W. Young had countersuits against each other for payment of a debt. Although only a small amount of money was involved, the legal hassle continued for several years (Pecos County, Marriage License Records, 1:127; Pecos County, Justice Records [Civil Cases Closed], Nos. 44, 49, 56, and 1149). Apparently Young also filed a criminal charge against Torres, but the packet that should contain the relevant papers is now empty (Pecos County, Justice Records [Criminal Cases Closed], No. 2, F. W. Young vs. Juan Torres).

[23] Williams, 1930s typescript.

Years later rumor had it that Royal beat a hasty retreat toward his home, as a few ineffective shots were fired at him from behind the walls of Koehler's adjacent feed yard. Whether that is myth or reality is really of no importance, but after getting together a few men, according to the Williams statement, Royal tried to purchase a barrel of coal oil from Young "to burn the [Koehler] store down in order, as he said, to shoot the men down as they came out." Without placing himself in danger, he had his men surround the store, and finally, after Francis Rooney had escaped, James Rooney and W. P. Matthews surrendered and were taken to the courthouse for a preliminary hearing before Justice of the Peace Hatchette on a charge that they "did make an assault with the intent . . . to murder . . . Royal by shooting him with a gun. . . ." During the hearing, according to Williams' statement, Royal, while armed, "abused" and threatened "to get them." [24] The two prisoners, convinced that they would not find justice at the examination before Justice of the Peace H. L. Hatchette, made bond to appear before the grand jury at its September term—the Rooneys making bond on that day with Shipton Parke and J. H. Lemons as sureties, and Matthews on the following day with Morgan Livingston and Taylor Stephenson as sureties. [25]

On August 6, when the shooting at Koehler's occurred, Judge Williams was with his family at his home on the Pecos River. After a fast messenger arrived with the news, Williams traveled over the sand dunes to Monahans, twenty-five miles distant, where on the next day he sent a telegram to the state adjutant general, asking that he send

[24] Indeed, according to the earlier, manuscript version of Williams' account, Royal threatened "to get them & get them in the face."

[25] Pecos County, Justice Records, August 6 and 7, 1894. H. L. Hatchette, a former school teacher in Fort Stockton, was appointed justice of the peace on November 15, 1893, made bond on February 12, 1894, with W. H. Mansfield and Taylor Stephenson as sureties, and in March, 1894, petitioned for permission to practice law. An examining committee, composed of C. C. Thomas (Pecos County district attorney), County Judge Wigfalls Van Sickle of Brewster County, Howell Johnson, an H. E. Crowley, appointed by District Judge Walter Gillis, recommended that he be granted a license to practice law. The Pecos County commissioners also recommended the granting of a license, adding that Hatchette was "a man of good standing and character as to morals, and of intellectual attainments worthy of merit," and on the same date as the application Judge Gillis granted the license. These Hatchette documents, dated March 19 and 20, 1894, once were in Packet No. 45, but that packet has since been lost or misplaced (Pecos County, District Court Minutes, September, 1894, 1:495–496).

"rangers at once to Fort Stockton. Serious trouble yesterday. Sheriff involved in the trouble."[26]

After wiring for the Rangers, Williams traveled in his buggy to the Rooney farm, about three miles north of Fort Stockton. The headquarters and other buildings were surrounded by an adobe wall that had many openings through which guns could be fired. The judge later told the author that when he arrived the Rooneys were expecting violence by Royal and that the defensive walls were fully manned by armed Mexicans. From there, Williams went to Fort Stockton and appointed a number of men as peace officers to control the situation until the arrival of the Rangers.

Judge Williams was not the only person to ask for Rangers. Two days after the judge sent his request, Sheriff Royal sent a telegram from the railroad stop at Haymond to Governor James S. Hogg for "four rangers at once. I want them to help enforce the law as I am powerless as sheriff."[27]

Meanwhile, the Williams statement continued, the Rooneys had sent for Judge Williams, and Matthews had sent for Anderson and the cowboys from the 7 Ranch ("the 'AB' boys") to aid them "in getting the protection of the law. . . ." Francis and Jimmie had to remain in town to care for the Koehler store, since Francis was temporary administrator. The judge noted that "one evening Morgan, Ship, Johnny R., Matthews, Francis, Jimmie, Frank and I went to boarding house together. . . ," but, although he had made a note to himself in his manuscript to relate some incident that happened there, he did not report it.[28]

The boarding house was that of Mrs. Ann Elizabeth Stephenson, formerly operated by Mrs. Heid. Mrs. Stephenson, born near Oakville, Texas, in 1853, the daughter of Elijah Votaw, a veteran of the Battle of San Jacinto, and Cynthia Jane Butler Votaw, was first married to Muir Macdonald, a native of Edinburgh, Scotand. The Macdonalds had two daughters, both born in Oakville. Nueces ("Essie"), born in 1876 and named for the river that flowed nearby the home, later became Mrs. James Rooney, and Jennie, born in 1877, became Mrs. Morgan Livingston. Mrs. Macdonald also raised her niece, Willie Maud Hobbs,

[26] O. W. Williams, Monahans, to Adjutant General, August 7, 1894, AGP, RG 401, TSL.
[27] A. J. Royal, Haymond, to Gov. J. S. Hogg, August 9, 1894, AGP, RG 401, TSL.
[28] Williams, 1930s typescript.

who first married a Mr. Dillard and later married James Livingston. Muir Macdonald died in 1878.[29]

As soon as he received Judge Williams' telegram, Adjutant General W. H. Mabry wired the first sergeant of Company D, at Ysleta, to go immediately by train with some of his men to Fort Stockton. Sergeant Carl Kirchner with four Rangers arrived at Haymond some time before daylight on August 9 and at 6:00 A.M. left there on the stage for Fort Stockton.[30] Since Sheriff Royal sent his telegram to the governor at 9:40 A.M., he and the stage carrying the Rangers likely passed between Haymond and Stockton.

On the following day, Kirchner reported to Mabry, on stationery having as a letterhead "Office of H. Koehler, Dealer in General Merchandise," that he had found the people at Fort Stockton were still considerably excited. Sheriff Royal and the Rooney brothers had been on opposite sides in the last election and had had trouble ever since, "Royal being a very overbearing & dangerous man when under the influence of liquor." It seems, Kirchner continued, that someone told the Rooneys that Royal was "coming down to clean them out & a short while after Royal stepped in pistol in hand & Rooney fired a load of shot at him but missed." Royal returned the fire but also missed and then tried to get a posse to arrest the Rooneys but could get only four or five men. "Rooneys are law abiding men & would have given up but say they were afraid of being murdered." They had surrendered, he added, when provided protection, and had posted bond to await the action of the next grand jury. Kirchner had not seen the absent sheriff, but he concluded from the information he had obtained, "Almost the entire County seems to be against the Sheriff & I think he will realize that he has no strength & behave for the present at least."[31]

During the next few months, several Texas Rangers, all from Company D at Ysleta, had roles in connection with the Pecos County

[29] Hugh Rooney Livingston, comp., "A Genealogical Study of the Livingston and Related Families," undated manuscript, in possession of Clayton Williams; Pecos County, Probate Minutes, 2:324; Mrs. Christine Stephenson, Santa Ana, Calif., to Gaines Kincaid, March 3, 1977. By his first marriage, G. Taylor Stephenson had three children, all raised by relatives in California. Christine Stephenson, the daughter-in-law of Hiram Stephenson, who was no kin to Taylor Stephenson, obtained some details regarding Taylor's early life from his granddaughter, Mrs. West, who lives in California.

[30] Carl Kirchner, Haymond, to Gen. W. H. Mabry, August 9, 1894, AGP, RG 401, TSL.

[31] Kirchner, Fort Stockton, to Mabry, August 10, 1894, AGP, RG 401, TSL.

feuds. From 1885 until 1893, Company D had been under the command of Frank Jones, an extremely able but superstitious man, who was mortally wounded on June 30, 1893, in a skirmish with bandits. Jones was replaced by Sergeant John R. Hughes, and Corporal Carl Kirchner was made the first sergeant. Carl Kirchner, one of the three Rangers who had come to Fort Stockton to help maintain peace at the time of the 1892 election, was born in Bee County, Texas, on November 19, 1867, the son of Christian H. and Martha Burditt Kirchner. Sometime after Carl's birth, the family moved to Fredericksburg, where Christian established a vineyard. Later Kirchner moved his family to Edwards County, where he served as a county commissioner. On May 18, 1889, at age twenty-one, Carl Kirchner enlisted in Captain Frank Jones's Company D, Frontier Battalion, of the Texas Rangers. A brave, quiet man, six feet two inches tall, with a splendid physique and striking appearance, he participated in a number of gunfights during his Ranger career and reputedly killed several men in the line of duty.[32]

Private Joseph R. Sitters, who went with Kirchner to Fort Stockton, was born in Medina County, Texas, around 1863. After working several years as a cowboy, on August 1, 1893, one month after Captain Jones was killed, Sitters enlisted in Company D at Comstock, Val Verde County.[33] Ranger J. W. Fulgham had enlisted in Company D on December 14, 1892. In August, 1893, while he and Reeves County Deputy Sheriff George Leakey were searching for stolen horses, Fulgham killed Charles Carrol, who resisted the officers' attempt to disarm him.[34] Private William Schmidt had enlisted on September 1, 1893, and Ed Palmer enlisted during the summer of 1894.[35]

On the twelfth of August, 1894, Judge Williams wrote a confidential letter to General Mabry, describing in more detail the situa-

---

[32] Robert W. Stephens, *Texas Ranger Sketches*, pp. 63, 65, 68–69, 77–80, 108; Allan A. Stovall, *Breaks of the Balcones*, pp. 117, 225; Robert E. McNellis, "Bass Outlaw: Lawless Lawman," *Guns*, December, 1976, pp. 46, 69.

[33] Service record of Joseph R. Sitters and various muster rolls and payrolls for Co. D, AGP, RG 401, TSL; Jack Shipman, "The Killing of Ranger Hulin [Eugene Hulen] and Inspector Sitters," *Voice of the Mexican Border*, 1936, p. 66; *El Paso Herald*, May 25, May 27, and June 8, 1915.

[34] Co. D, Muster Rolls for 1892, and Co. D, Monthly Returns for August, 1893, AGP, RG 401, TSL.

[35] Co. D, Muster Rolls and payrolls for the 1890s, AGP, RG 401, TSL.

tion and pleading for Texas Rangers to be stationed at Fort Stockton until after the November election. Much of the letter was a recapitulation of the situation and need not be repeated. Five Rangers from Ysleta had arrived on the ninth; there had been no trouble since the shooting on the sixth. On the seventh Williams had appointed some determined men as peace officers, and there had been no further trouble, but the matter was not ended, for the "sore was too deep to be healed at once." The trouble, he explained, was the result of a series of "outrages, abuses, and threats on the part of our Sheriff" against some of "our best citizens." As a candidate for reelection, the sheriff "is opposed by the great bulk of white population, . . . is favored by some white . . . of hard reputation, and depends upon the Mexican votes which he can cajole or bulldoze into voting for him . . . [and] he tries by every means fair or foul to avoid legal penalty . . . by threatening witnesses & courts & nullifying the processes of court." [36]

Royal was under indictments, Williams continued, to answer a charge in county court, and a number of matters against him were to be considered by the grand jury when it convened in September. Rangers were "absolutely necessary" for three months to preserve the peace, and he felt quite certain that the commissioners would appropriate forty dollars per month for three months to cover their expenses. "If we do not [have Ranger protection] blood is almost certain to flow. . . ." [37]

Two days after Judge Williams' appeal for Rangers, on August 14, Sergeant Kirchner, on Sheriff Royal's stationery, made a lengthy report on the situation to his superior, Captain John R. Hughes, at Ysleta. Since his report to Mabry, he had visited with and had heard Royal's version of the trouble. Baker, who had got on a drunk, he believed, had caused all the trouble by telling the Rooneys that "Royal was coming down to clean them out, which I don't think Royal ever said. . . ." When Royal, a few minutes later, came into the store, "Jim Rooney fired a load of shot at Royal but only grazed him. I think County Clerk Matthews also shot at him with a pistol & Royal fired 1 or 2 shots as he retreated. . . . No one was hurt." Royal's assailants had made bond

[36] O. W. Williams, Fort Stockton, to Mabry, August 12, 1894, AGP, RG 401, TSL.
[37] Ibid.

pending a grand jury hearing, he wrote, and he was convinced that
Royal "will be quiet now until court meets in Sept." Since his (Kirchner's) expenses were very high, he recommended that the Rangers be
removed until court met in September.[38]

Ranger Privates Bryant and Brown arrived back in Ysleta on August 15; Kirchner and the other two Rangers reached there on August
19 and reported to Hughes that the trouble at Fort Stockton had been
settled temporarily and that there would be no need for any Rangers
there until district court met on September 17. Hughes, in transmit-
ting the report to General Mabry, recommended that a detachment of
Rangers be stationed in Fort Stockton during the session of the district
court.[39]

According to Williams' statement, Royal did not live up to Kirchner's prediction. Even before they left, some of the Rangers and at
least two citizens, Williams wrote, heard Royal "threaten to take up his
gun and neither to eat nor sleep until he had killed 8 men if the Grand
Jury did not indict the Rooneys."[40] Pat Dowy (perhaps Downy), who
had worked in Royal's saloon earlier in the year, warned the Rooneys
that Royal "had threatened them in his hearing." Royal was also working to prevent Francis Rooney from becoming the regular administrator of the Koehler estate. He was planning to put in a claim for $500 of
cash he had loaned Koehler and also for $600 to $800 worth of other
items. Since Koehler's books showed no such indebtedness, Royal
knew, Williams asserted, that Francis Rooney would not allow it, and
he (Royal) wanted as administrator F. W. Young, who, he thought,
would be more amenable. "He had already intimidated Pilar Duran (as
he himself told me) into agreeing to testify that he saw Royal loan
Koehler $500."[41]

Then, on August 20, the day after Hughes reported that no Rangers
were needed in Fort Stockton until the district court convened, Judge
Williams again appealed to Mabry for Ranger protection for three

[38] Kirchner, Fort Stockton, to Capt. John R. Hughes, August 14, 1894, AGP, RG
401, TSL.
   [39] Co. D, Monthly Returns for August, 1894, and John R. Hughes, Ysleta, to W. H.
Mabry, August 19, 1894, both in AGP, RG 401, TSL.
   [40] Morgan Livingston, Ship Parke, W. P. Matthews, Judge Williams, and the four
Rooneys.
   [41] Williams, 1930s typescript.

months. "We are on the verge of serious trouble at County Court, and tomorrow may witness a killing. Everybody goes armed, . . . [even] citizens, ordinarily peaceful and law abiding. The feud is liable to become open war at any time. . . ." As a sort of postscript, he added that County Clerk Matthews was afraid to go to his office in the courthouse for fear of assassination and that some Fort Stockton citizens had refused lucrative employment and were preparing to move.[42]

In response to General Mabry's request for additional information, Hughes on August 23 replied that the Rangers had been moved from Fort Stockton because matters were settled there until the district court convened and because of the expense of boarding the men at the hotel. If Mabry wanted to have Rangers in Fort Stockton during the session of the district court, he wanted to send them by horseback because it would be less expensive. He was of the opinion that the court would not last more than three or four days.[43]

Mabry ordered Hughes to send a detachment of Rangers to Fort Stockton immediately. Consequently, Sergeant Kirchner with four men (Sitters, Palmer, Fulgham, and Schmidt) left Ysleta by horseback on August 26, and a few days later Hughes asked Mabry for permission to use state vouchers to purchase rations and horsefeed for the unit, possibly until after the election.[44] Actually, the Rangers would do much of their "camping out" in vacant rooms of the courthouse.

Upon his arrival, Kirchner found that Royal, contrary to his promise, had not allowed matters to remain quiet. For one thing he was harassing his erstwhile and sometimes drunken friend, R. N. Baker. For a couple of years, Royal had never found it convenient to arrest Baker on two criminal charges, but friendship turned to enmity after the grand jury of which Baker was a member indicted Royal in the Elsa White case. Whether Baker made up his story that led to the shooting at Koehler's store, as Royal asserted and Ranger Kirchner believed, or whether he was serving as Royal's messenger remains an unanswered riddle. At any rate, on August 21, Royal filed charges against Baker for

[42]O. W. Williams, Fort Stockton, to W. H. Mabry, August 20, 1894, AGP, RG 401, TSL.

[43]Hughes, Ysleta, to Mabry, August 23, 1894, AGP, RG 401, TSL.

[44]Co. D, Monthly Returns for August, 1894, and Hughes, Ysleta, to Mabry, September 8, 1894, AGP, RG 401, TSL.

carrying a pistol and disturbing the peace near Koehler's store, and four days later he filed a second charge that Baker "did . . . enter into a positive agreement to murder . . . A. J. Royal, and did unlawfully conspire . . . to murder . . . Royal." On September 9, Justice of the Peace Hatchette fined Baker $6 plus court costs on the weapon charge but found him not guilty of the conspiracy charge. Two days later Royal refiled the conspiracy charge. This time Baker waived a hearing and made bond in the amount of $3,000 to appear before the grand jury on September 19, at which time there was a "no bill."[45]

A majority of that grand jury, Judge Williams wrote in his lengthy statement about Royal, had reason to favor Royal. Three were Royal's candidates for office: R. W. Mussey for county judge, E. M. Teel for county treasurer, and M. A. Ernst for commissioner of Precinct 3. John Crosby was the son of his candidate for clerk, R. B. Barnes was a former tenant, and Charles T. Carter was an intimate friend of the Musseys. Others included John H. Anderson, whom Royal could ruin with a judicial execution, W. H. Strickland, who was negotiating for and later purchased Royal's interest in a saloon, and Taylor Stephenson, who was "in favor of indicting the Rooneys to prevent further bloodshed." Two Williams regarded as "impartial and independent," J. H. Lemons and E. M. Powell, and W. L. Cranfill was a newcomer, whose views were not known. Several stayed at Royal's home during the session of the court. Furthermore, the district attorney, Williams thought, was prejudiced in favor of Royal.[46]

The grand jury indicted Matthews for acting as a land agent without paying an occupation tax, and it indicted Judge Williams for practicing law, although Williams claimed he had never practiced law in Pecos County. It indicted, on the testimony of Royal and Royal's hired hand,

[45] Pecos County, Justice Records, August 21, August 25, September 3, and September 5, 1894.

[46] Williams, 1930s typescript. Grand jury minutes show variants on some of the names: J. B. (not R. B.) Barnes, J. (rather than W. H.) Strickland, and W. R. Cranfield (for W. L. Cranfill, the more likely name since it appears on various records of the period). The reference to Thomas, the district attorney, is not in the original version of Williams' account. However, in that version Thomas is mentioned in this section in a sentence, apparently an afterthought, which was squeezed in between two other lines, but the word following his name is illegible: "They refused—Thomas —— to let Jimmie Rooney testify to threats by Royal."

Bernardo Ruiz, a servant of Matthews, "for fornication,"[47] without indicting his female partner, who also "was supposed to be very intimate" with one of Royal's hired men, refused to indict Royal for the
Aguilar affair or for the "appropriation of lumber from School House in
Stockton, although testimony was clear on both and witnesses," and
indicted the Rooneys. "It was now believed [Williams continued] that
Royal . . . could murder and shield himself from the consequences under the forms of law. . . . Apparently there was only one of 3 things for
any threatened man to do—vis—to leave the country, to kill Royal or
be killed. . . . We bent our energies instead to prevent his re-elec-
tion. . . ."[48] Although Judge Williams did not mention it in his
narrative, the grand jury on September 22 did indict Sheriff Royal for
"assault and battery" on R. N. Baker on August 6 and on Henry Mansfield on September 17.[49]

A few days after court adjourned, Royal charged Frank and James
Rooney with having stolen a horse in 1892. This charge was brought
before Justice of the Peace Hatchette, who also served as Royal's counsel. It seemed rather strange that Royal should have waited until after
the lapse of two years and the adjournment of a grand jury, and the
Rooneys averred that "if any stealing was done at that time, Royal was
the guilty party."[50]

During the last ten days of September, the Rangers at Fort Stockton were busy making arrests. On the twentieth, they arrested J. M.
Watts and County Attorney Johnson on a charge of being "drunk and
disorderly" and turned them over to a justice of the peace, probably
Hatchette. On the twenty-second, they arrested James and Francis
Rooney on a charge of "assault to murder" and turned them over to
District Judge Gillis. On the twenty-fourth, Kirchner arrested Bernardo Ruiz on the fornication indictment and placed him in jail and, on
the next day, William Lemons (presumably, William H. Lemons, the
sixteen-year-old son of John H. Lemons[51]) for assault and battery. On

[47] Pecos County, District Court Minutes for September 17 and 22, 1894.

[48] Willaims, 1930s typescript.

[49] Files No. 158 and No. 159, indictments by the Grand Jurors of the County of
Pecos, September 22, 1894, certified copies in possession of Clayton Williams.

[50] Pecos County, Justice Records, September 26, 1894; Williams, 1930s typescript.
The packet containing these charges had "No Bill" written on the outside.

[51] Alice Evans Downie, ed., *Terrell County, Texas: Its Past—Its People*, p. 495.

the twenty-sixth, they picked up Matthews and Williams for failing to pay an occupation tax and also Sheriff Royal on an assault and battery charge. They turned Royal over to a justice of the peace—no doubt, his own attorney, H. L. Hatchette.[52]

In his typescript account of the affair, Judge Williams stated that the bonds for him, Johnson, and Williams were fixed at $200, with Young, John M. Odom, Taylor Stephenson, "Menier" or "Meniers" (probably J. E. Minear), and Thomas W. "Peake" (probably Parke) as sureties.[53] The bonds, Williams claimed, were probably worth $23,000 ($25,000, according to the earlier manuscript), but Royal alleged "it insufficient," and ordered the Rangers to take them to jail. Williams was released on a writ of habeas corpus.[54] Royal had Young make bond for him in Del Rio in an amount valued at $10,000.[55]

Williams also stated that, when it was necessary "for any of us under threats to go to the Court House, we went in pairs if possible, in order to give mutual protection." Matthews had about ceased going, sending Frank Rooney when he had to have something done. Royal was building an adobe wall around his saloon property that looked as though it was "to shoot from," and he then had with him Barney K. Riggs, "understood to be a 'bad' man," as his chief aide.[56]

Barney K. Riggs and Mrs. Annie Stella Frazer Johnson, the divorced former wife of James Johnson, were married by Judge Mussey on September 23, 1891. Thereafter, they probably spent much of their time in Reeves County, where Mrs. Riggs's father, George M. Frazer, was the county judge and her brother, Bud, who had married Barney's sister, was the sheriff. There, more than once, Riggs was arrested for carrying a pistol, once by his brother-in-law. Because of Judge Frazer's relationship, the case was transferred to the district court (the good judge must have been exasperated at times over the actions of his unruly son-in-law), but the charge was quashed. Later, in September,

---

[52] Co. D, Monthly Returns for September, 1894, AGP, RG 401, TSL.

[53] Minear was a farmer in Gonzales County who spent some time in Pecos County, where he married the niece of Shipton Parke and either then or later went into the cattle business with his wife's uncle. He did not actually settle in Pecos County until 1900 (*New Encyclopedia of Texas*, p. 3267).

[54] Williams said in his manuscript version that he uderstood Royal to have been "very angry over this."

[55] Williams, 1930s typescript.

[56] Ibid.

1893, Ranger Fulgham on temporary duty in Pecos arrested Riggs on a charge of murder or assault with intent to murder (the records are not clear). In March, 1894, Barney stood trial in the Reeves County district court for "assault with intent to murder . . . with malice aforethought," possibly the same alleged offense. Supposedly, Agustín Polanco had gone to the Riggs home to get his burro, when Riggs fired a pistol at him. This prompted Polanco to use profane language, and in turn Riggs struck the Mexican with his pistol. The prosecutor asked for a dismissal on the basis of insufficient evidence, and the jury took only fifteen minutes to find Riggs not guilty.[57]

In 1894, only three of Annie Riggs's six children by her first marriage were still minors. Two of these, Mary Jane, sixteen, and Thomas G., fourteen, were living with their mother, but the youngest, James C., twelve, was with his father, James Johnson. On October 17, 1894, the Riggs and Frazer families became even more interrelated when the teenage Mary Jane Johnson and her stepfather's brother, Tom Riggs, were joined in matrimony.[58]

[57] Pecos County, Marriage License Records, 2:42; Reeves County, District Court Minutes, 1:341, 399, 413, 418, 438; Co. D, Monthly Returns for September, 1893, AGP, RG 401, TSL.

[58] Pecos County, Probate Minutes, 1:170–171; Pecos County, Marriage License Records, 2:62.

CHAPTER 23

1894

THE five Rangers in Pecos County, however, had more important work than to "haul in" all those against whom Sheriff Royal filed a charge. They had instructions to be on the alert for horse thieves, which entailed some scouting, and during October, 1894, they were involved in an incident that got Pecos County officials and feuds entangled with international affairs—the arrest and escape of Victor L. Ochoa.[1]

Although a native of New Mexico and a citizen of the United States, Victor Ochoa had a passionate hatred for the regime of President Porfirio Díaz. In October, 1893, Ochoa and an underground group in the regions of Tomochic and Santo Tomás, Chihuahua, Mexico, mounted an intense press campaign against the Díaz government. After defeating their opponents in some other districts, the rebels on November 8, 1893, captured the customhouse at Palomas, near Columbus, New Mexico. There they issued a manifesto in which they proclaimed a slogan of "Down with Profirio Díaz—Long live the Constitution of 1857." Soon afterwards, United State officials in El Paso charged Ochoa with violating the neutrality laws. Ochoa, they claimed, had accepted a commission to serve Santa Ana Pérez, a Mexican rebel leader, and had hired men and provided means for them to go beyond the limits of the United States to make war against the Republic of Mexico.

On January 20, 1894, six columns of Mexican troops defeated the rebels, killing all except Ochoa and three others. Ochoa escaped by donning the uniform of a soldier he had killed and made his way into the United States. In Brewster County, he was joined by a Mexican

---

[1]Co. D, Monthly Returns for October, 1894, Texas Adjutant General's Papers (AGP), Record Group (RG) 401, Archives, Texas State Library (TSL), Austin.

fugitive who had escaped from jail in San Angelo and killed a tramp for his clothes and money. While riding with Ochoa one dark and rainy night, the jail escapee killed Jeff Webb, a cowboy from Alpine, although the details of this murder were a mystery until later revealed by Ochoa. Webb was a nephew of Fine Gilliland, who had killed H. H. Power in an argument over the ownership of a steer, on which some of the cowboys immediately afterward burned the brand MURDER. One evening, after a drinking session in an Alpine saloon, he headed on horseback for a cow camp north of Alpine. As he left town, he picked up (or stole) a friendly little bear, attached to a small chain, placed it in front of him on the saddle, and rode into the dark and stormy night.

Meanwhile, Ochoa and his companion (perhaps companions) were making their way toward town. Unaware that anyone was near until his horse bumped another, Webb ordered the strangers to halt. The convict thereupon fired, and Webb fell from his horse mortally wounded. Next morning, passersby discovered Webb's horse grazing nearby and the little bear sitting on the dead cowboy's face. Afterward, several men were charged with the murder, but none was found guilty. The murderer crossed the Rio Grande and disappeared into Mexico.[2]

Hearing that Ochoa was in El Paso, Captain John R. Hughes sent E. D. Aten, second corporal, Company D, and two other Rangers to assist Deputy United States Marshal George Scarborough in making the arrest. The Rangers returned to Ysleta, however, without the elusive rebel, who always had the backing of local Mexicans wherever he went, including Fort Stockton.[3]

From late in September until October 9, Ranger Sitters was away from Fort Stockton on an unsuccessful scout for horse thieves. During a part of the time, at least, Sheriff Royal was with him. Two days later Ranger Fulgham arrested one of the suspected horse thieves, Pancho Alvarado, and placed him in the Pecos County jail.[4] On the same day, Sheriff Royal and the Rangers arrested another suspected horse thief, who turned out to be the badly wanted Ochoa.

[2] Ricardo García Granados, *Historia de México*, 2:262; Francisco R. Almada, *La Revolución en el Estado de Chihuahua*, 1:103–104; Ira J. Bush, *Gringo Doctor*, pp. 62–71; Mrs. O. L. Shipman, *Taming the Big Bend*, pp. 123, 125–126, 128; *El Paso Times*, October 18, 1894; Carlysle Graham Raht, *The Romance of Davis Mountains and Big Bend Country*, pp. 306–308.
[3] Co. D, Monthly Returns for August, 1894, AGP, RG 401, TSL.
[4] Co. D, Monthly Returns for October, 1894, AGP, RG 401, TSL.

That drama had its beginning at the long, flat-roofed, adobe establishment of Pedro Sosa, northwest of the courthouse. Sosa, a rock mason who had moved to Stockton from Mexico during the construction of the fort, had built his home in 1877, not only for his own family but also for the convenience of travelers. It was here, during a *baile* ("dance") in 1885 that James Frazer and Crispín Sosa had been killed. Now, in October, 1894, a half-witted boy who lived with the Sosas walked into the Ranger camp near the courthouse and talked about a mysterious stranger who had arrived in the night and was planning to leave at daybreak. Private Fulgham, commander of the detachment in the absence of Sergeant Kirchner, concluded that it was probably another horse thief.[5] Fulgham and two other Rangers, joined by Sheriff Royal, went to the Sosa place and requested an interview with the guest. The stranger politely stated that he was W. C. Blode and that he was a cattleman looking for rangeland. The lawmen, dubious of his story, arrested Mr. Blode, gathered up his guns from a table, and took him to jail. There, from the papers he carried, they learned that they had on their hands Victor L. Ochoa. Ochoa then confessed his identity. Both Royal and Fulgham informed Captain Hughes of their prize. Consequently, on October 13, United States Marshal R. C. (Dick) Ware, who, as a Texas Ranger, had killed Sam Bass in 1878, sent his deputy, George Scarborough, to Fort Stockton to make a federal arrest if he confirmed that the prisoner was Ochoa. Unfortunately, Ranger Fulgham, who had the mistaken idea that the Pecos County sheriff was also a deputy U.S. marshal, turned Ochoa over to him. With the election less than a month away, Royal was not inclined to do anything to displease the local Mexicans.[6]

George Scarborough, the deputy marshal who had tried to arrest Ochoa in El Paso, was born in Louisiana in 1859, came to Texas as a boy, grew up in McLennan County, and worked as a cowboy in McCulloch County and other areas. Beginning in 1885, he served for a time as the sheriff of Jones County before becoming a deputy U.S. marshal.[7]

On Tuesday, October 16, Williams wrote in his account of Royal's doings, Royal had Ochoa make a speech in the courthouse advocating

[5] John R. Hughes, Ysleta, to W. H. Mabry, October 27, 1894, AGP, RG 401, TSL.

[6] Co. D, Monthly Returns for October, 1894, and Hughes, Ysleta, to Mabry, October 13, 1894, AGP, RG 401, TSL; *El Paso Times*, October 14 and 26, 1894.

[7] Ed Bartholomew, *Biographical Album of Western Gunfighters*, entry for George Scarborough.

his reelection, and at the same time he promised the fifteen or twenty Mexicans on hand to get Ochoa out of jail in return for their support and votes for reelection.[8] Several Mexicans later stated that such an agreement was made. On Sunday, October 21, Scarborough arrived at Fort Stockton to take custody of the prisoner. Royal, after some hesitancy, finally agreed to release Ochoa on Monday morning, but on Sunday night "Royal proceeded to shoot up the town unmolested altho 3 Rangers were stationed at the Court House," and Ochoa escaped. At least two persons later stated that they had seen among Royal's papers "a check for $2,600 drawn by Ochoa on his brother-in-law in favor of Royal."[9]

The account in the El Paso *Times* stated that when Scarborough reached Fort Stockton, the Mexican-Americans were having their "bailee" or dances and that the candidates in the forthcoming election were furnishing plenty of "red-eye." The *Times* continued, "It turns out that the prisoner was not held there so much on account of a big reward from Mexico, nor on account of stealing a horse, as he was to help . . . with the Mexican vote at the election."[10]

Ochoa later claimed that in his speech to the Mexicans in Spanish (which Royal did not understand very well) he "devoted himself almost exclusively to the subject of the recent revolution. It mattered little to him who wore the star in Pecos County." The candidates, however, reportedly "were highly pleased" with what they supposed to be their endorsement.[11]

Ochoa also related the details of his escape, which he thought very amusing. After the jailer got drunk on that Sunday night, about twenty of Ochoa's friends "took the keys from the sub and after liberating me put the fellow in my cell and locked him up. . . . My friends furnished me with a good horse and I made up my mind to strike for Carthage, New Mexico."[12]

[8] Again Judge Williams' long account of Royal is the best source for a narrative of the events that followed, and, again, the account given here follows the later typed and edited version. Significant differences in the manuscript version are shown in the footnotes.

[9] Williams, 1930s typescript. As will be seen shortly, the brother-in-law, John P. Meadows, was one of the men accused of assisting in Ochoa's escape.

[10] *El Paso Times*, October 24, 1894.

[11] Ibid., October 25, 1894.

[12] Ibid., October 26, 1894.

Many years later, Pilar Durán stated that he was among those who provided Ochoa with a horse on which to escape. That horse, however, mired in the creek at Toyah. Ochoa then confiscated another mount, but he did not get far. Meanwhile, two pairs of lawmen from Fort Stockton were searching for him. Marshal Scarborough and Ranger Sitters scouted in Brewster County for two days unsuccessfully before returning to Fort Stockton, having covered 80 miles. Rangers Fulgham and Schmidt, with better success, followed the trail, captured the fugitive as he rode into Toyah, and took him to jail in El Paso. In seven days they covered 560 miles, a seemingly impossible feat.[13]

Sheriff Royal was arrested for allowing Ochoa to escape, but, in the meantime, he continued to harass and threaten several citizens of the Fort Stockton community, including Judge Williams. On October 30, because Taylor Stephenson, the presiding election officer at Fort Stockton, refused to serve, the commissioners court, to avoid bloodshed and to conciliate as much as possible, selected as his replacement John Crosby, son of "Royal's candidate" for clerk. Royal, Williams stated, "came into the meeting and bitterly and vehemently opposed the selection of Crosby or anyone." A Ranger who was present left soon afterward.[14]

Williams stated that while he and Frank Rooney, the deputy clerk, were alone in the office, waiting for the clerk to finish the minutes for Williams to sign, Royal came into the room, "with gun in hand, thumb on hammer and finger on trigger." With an "insulting" gaze fixed on Williams, he stood there "5 or 10 minutes, then went out without having uttered a word." The next morning, Williams continued, Hatchette told the judge that Royal "had told him that he was going to kill me on first chance, and that he had gone into the clerk's office . . . for that purpose, but had not had a good chance . . . [and] that he was going to kill several others. . . . We heard of threats against us many times."[15]

The deputy marshal returned to Fort Stockton about November 1, Judge Williams recalled, and "arrested Royal for aiding U.S. Prisoner to escape." On the next day, Williams said that he was told by R. L. Anderson that Hatchette had stated that "he was afraid to be seen talk-

[13] Pilar Durán, oral statement, to Clayton Williams; Co. D, Monthly Returns for October, 1894, AGP, RG 401, TSL.

[14] Williams, 1930s typescript account of incidents concerning A. J. Royal.

[15] Ibid.

ing to me . . . that he had a long talk with Royal [who] . . . said he was going to kill me the first opportunity, and that he ought to have killed me a year before, that if he had done so, he would not have had all this trouble."[16]

On the twenty-seventh of October, Captain Hughes wrote General Mabry that Sergeant Kirchner would leave for Fort Stockton on the next day, and that he expected Fulgham and Schmidt to be detained in El Paso to testify against Ochoa and Royal. The captain miscalculated: Royal was not taken to El Paso, and Privates Fulgham and Schmidt returned to Stockton with their sergeant, where during the first days of November they were busy making arrests. On the first, the Rangers arrested Barney Riggs for assisting a prisoner to escape; on the second, Sheriff Royal, on the same charge; on the third, Camilio Terrazas and John P. Meadows on the same charge, Morgan Livingston for receiving stolen horses, and Judge Williams for receiving smuggled mules; and on the fourth, Shipton Parke for receiving a stolen horse. All these cases were referred to Marshal Scarborough for disposition.[17]

Judge Williams, in his narrative, provided some additional information pertaining to the arrests. On November 2, Royal had Severiano Gonzales swear out "a warrant against me for stealing 3 burros from him in 1892. That this was perjury . . . [for] I have had intimations that Royal paid the Mexican $15.00 for this. . . . I thought I could find witnesses enough in town to clear me of this, so I got the case continued until the next day at 10 A.M."[18] The next morning, while on his way to court, however, Williams was again arrested, this time by the deputy marshal. Royal had sworn out a warrant charging Williams, Morgan Livingston, Ship Parke, and Jim Livingston "with knowingly dealing in smuggled stock in 1890." Morgan was in town and gave himself up; Jim, who was in the country at the time, escaped; and Parke was at Haymond, "where he was arrested on our way to Del Rio."[19]

In the midst of all these affairs, Herman H. Butz, a teenage nephew of Herman Koehler, arrived in Fort Stockton. For many years, Butz was to play a vital role in the public affairs of Pecos County. Herman H.

[16] Ibid.
[17] Hughes, Ysleta, to Mabry, October 27, 1894, and Co. D, Monthly Returns, November, 1894, both in AGP, RG 401, TSL.
[18] Williams, 1930s typescript. In the manuscript account Judge Williams adds that he had given bond to appear the next morning.
[19] Williams, 1930s typescript.

Butz, born in New Braunfels on July 12, 1877, was the son of Theodore and Augusta (Koehler) Butz, natives of Germany. Theodore Butz came to Texas when young and later served in the Confederate Army. After his death in the early 1880s, Mrs. Butz moved to San Marcos and became the wife of Carl (or Charles) Meiners. Herman attended the public schools of San Marcos and was living there at the time of his uncle's death in 1894. After Herman Koehler died, Carl Meiners and his stepson went to Fort Stockton to take over the store and estate affairs. Augusta Meiners and her sister, Mrs. Meta Thomas, of Coahuila, Mexico, who also spent time in Stockton, were Herman Koehler's sisters and his only heirs. Although the seventeen-year-old Herman Butz was unaware of the seriousness of the Pecos County feuds, he was a keen observer. In letters to his sister, Emma Butz, he described the activities in Fort Stockton and some of the people. He was clerking in the store and had been introduced "to nearly half of Fort Stockton here. There are two Rangers here yet and many cowboys. . . . Pilar [Durán], the Mexican working here, is a very good man and so is Mr. Mussey the bookkeeper. . . . We have a good dinner at Mrs. Stevenson's [Stephenson's]."[20]

Mrs. G. T. Stephenson, the former Mrs. Macdonald, operated the boarding house formerly run by Mrs. Heid. This structure, the present Achterburg building and Boy Scout headquarters, was located just west of Koehler's store and just north of Young's store. At the time young Butz was eating at Mrs. Stephenson's, the boarders were understandably jumpy. Even while eating, the men kept their guns on their laps or otherwise handy and at times posted at the corner of Young's store a sentinel, who was to signal by waving a white handkerchief if Royal approached. On one occasion, the boarders were thrown into a small panic when the sentinel pulled a handkerchief to blow his nose.[21]

After a shooting affair, Carl Meiners decided that Fort Stockton was too rough for him and returned to San Marcos, but Herman liked the place and decided to stay. To Emma, he wrote that "they have balls here very often. I got acquainted with the Misses Rooneys, Stevensons and about ten others already. There are many more girls than boys here." The "Stevensons" were Essie and Jennie Macdonald, Taylor

[20] Herman Butz, Fort Stockton, to Emma Butz, October 29, 1894, copy in possession of Clayton Williams.

[21] Ibid.; the late Judge H. H. (Herman) Butz, oral statement, to Clayton Williams.

Stephenson's stepdaughters, but young Herman eventually became more interested in the Rooney girls. Four years later he married one.[22]

Butz was amused over some of the situations he experienced or heard about in Fort Stockton. On one occasion, Sheriff Royal preferred charges against Matthews, who was crippled and walked with a cane, for shooting at Koehler's store. While hobbling from the footbridge on the trail from Young's store to the courthouse, Matthews was fired upon by an unknown assailant, and the bullet lopped off one of his fingers. The gossip afterward was not so much about the shooting as about how incredibly fast the crippled Matthews could run. Then there was Mansfield, who was courting Miss Lemons; the wags about town referred to him as the "would-be Lemon squeezer."[23]

Even while in jail, Royal reportedly continued to make threats. Judge Williams, in his narrative, wrote that Royal told W. R. Ellis that "he [Royal] had plenty of money to buy witnesses with and would send us to hell, referring particularly to those of us he had sworn out warrants against." He also made "threats against out lives," Williams continued, to some of the Rangers, and "Johnson had left the County on account of them. No one I think doubted for a moment Royal's intention to kill any of [or] all of us that he had a good safe chance at."[24]

The lawmen, apparently because of the improbability of obtaining fair hearings in Fort Stockton, took their prisoners to Del Rio for an appearance before a justice of the peace. Judge Williams failed to relate any details of the hearings, but the entire group seems to have been released. After the hearing and before leaving, the Rangers advised Williams, Parke, and Livingston to arm themselves "on account of the threats Royal was making and they expected trouble on the train." There was no trouble on the train, however; Williams got off the train at Sanderson. There the next morning, election day, Royal and Riggs were "both marching around armed with guns and pistols [and]

[22]Herman Butz to Emma Butz, October 29, 1894; H. H. Butz and Mrs. W. J. B. ("Maidie") Dixon, oral statements, to Clayton Williams.
[23]Clarence R. Wharton, *Texas under Many Flags*, 5:164–165; Pecos County, Probate Minutes, 2:193; Herman Butz to Emma Butz, October 29, 1894; Mrs. W. J. B. Dixon and H. H. Butz, oral statements, to Clayton Williams.
[24]Williams, 1930s typescript. Additional details appear in Williams' manuscript account. Royal's particular targets are there identified as "the AB boys, me, Mathews, the Rooneys & Johnson, who had now left the county in fear of his life." Threats are said to have been made specifically "to Palmer of the Rangers."

we expected trouble."[25] About midmorning Royal left for Dryden, about twenty miles to the east, but Riggs "remained around the polls all day, armed but quiet." That night Royal and Riggs went to Haymond, the nearest railroad stop to Stockton. Williams laid over one day at Sanderson and then was several days on the road to Fort Stockton, stopping along the way at the ranch of S. A. Purinton to pick up the election boxes. Upon arrival at Fort Stockton, he learned that Royal had assaulted George Miller and Riggs had attacked Parke. According to the accounts, Royal "had been raging like a maniac," but he had left before Williams arrived, presumably for Laredo "to bring back hired desperadoes." While in Del Rio, Williams stated, "he had tried to hire Jim Reagan and it was supposed he was negotiating with others."[26]

In the voting precincts at Purinton's ranch, Sanderson, and Santa Lucia (near Judge Williams' farm) there was much opposition to A. J. Royal. The incumbent sheriff, however, fared better in Fort Stockton, where most of the trouble had taken place; there, Royal beat R. B. Neighbors 97 to 76. But the total vote in the county gave Neighbors 203 and Royal 121. For county judge, O. W. Williams received 195 votes to R. W. Mussey's 129; for county attorney, Howell Johnson defeated H. L. Hatchette 199 to 123; and for clerk, Frank Rooney won over Charles A. Crosby by a vote of 207 to 117. The Pecos County voters reelected Walter Gillis as district judge and C. C. Thomas as district attorney. Taylor Stephenson and Charles Downie became the commissioners of Precincts 1 and 2, respectively. The voters of Precincts 3 and 4 retained their incumbent commissioners, T. P. Baylor and T. J. Ray.[27] Clearly, Sheriff Royal and the candidates he backed had suffered a major defeat.

In the days immediately following the election, Royal did not accept its results quietly. Charges and counter-charges were filed. Two

[25] Williams, 1930s typescript. In his manuscript account, Williams adds, "As we understood Royal had sworn out warrents before Hatchette etc."

[26] Williams, 1930s typescript. According to Williams' earlier, manuscript account, "We knew he had offered Jim Reagan a good salary—And these threats plainly showed that he would have us killed by hired men, if not by himself." The Reagan brothers, John, Jim, Frank, and Lee, were cattlemen who operated between the Rio Grande and Sanderson and especially around Reagan Canyon, in the Big Bend, which was named for them. For a while, Jim Reagan owned and operated Charlie Wilson's old saloon in Sanderson (Alice Evans Downie, ed., *Terrell County, Texas: Its Past—Its People*, pp. 64, 587).

[27] Pecos County, Commissioners Court Minutes, November 12, 1894.

days after the election, Riggs charged Jim Livingston and Shipton Parke with assault upon himself. On the ninth, George C. Miller preferred charges of assault and battery against Sheriff Royal. The warrant was placed in the hands of Sergeant Kirchner. For some unexplained reason Royal did not file a similar charge against Miller but, instead, had Riggs plead guilty for him in the justice court and pay the five-dollar fine.[28]

In a final effort to remain in power, Royal tried to get the Rangers at Fort Stockton replaced. As previously stated, both Judge Williams and Sheriff Royal had sent a request for Rangers, and at first Kirchner had been inclined to believe that R. N. Baker was the main troublemaker. The Rangers had even cooperated with Sheriff Royal in searching for horse thieves and in making arrests. After Victor Ochoa escaped from jail, however, the Rangers no longer trusted Royal and began to work with the Rooney-Williams faction. After the election, Royal decided to get rid of that batch of Rangers. His opponents, however, took steps to circumvent the scheme. On November 11, Judge Williams wrote Captain Hughes at Ysleta of Royal's plan to obtain a new detachment of Rangers and of opposition to the change. Sergeant Kirchner and his men, he wrote, had conducted themselves "with great prudence & moderation, and have gained the respect and confidence of the law abiding people here." They had learned the "inside history of our troubles" and how to prevent trouble, and "we would view with alarm any proposed change, as some good men might be sacrificed before the new men would catch on the situation."[29]

On the same day, the sentiments expressed in Judge Williams' letter were incorporated in a petition to Adjutant General Mabry, signed by Williams, W. P. Matthews, John M. Odom, Jim and Morgan Livingston, Howell Johnson, R. B. Neighbors, Shipton Parke, and George C. Miller. Williams stated that "many more names could be added to the Petition, but time presses, and the letter must go tonight."[30]

Two days later, Captain Hughes wrote Mabry that he approved the way Kirchner had handled affairs at Fort Stockton. "I have met a

---

[28] Pecos County, Justice Docket, November 8 and 9, 1894.

[29] O. W. Williams, Fort Stockton, to Hughes, November 11, 1894, AGP, RG 401, TSL.

[30] Williams et al., Fort Stockton, to W. H. Mabry, November 11, 1894, and Williams, Fort Stockton, to Mabry, November 11, 1894, both in AGP, RG 401, TSL.

great many of the best citizens of Pecos county lately," Hughes told
Mabry, "and they are very much pleased with Sergt. Kirchner & the
men with him."[31]

In response to a written request by some citizens of Pecos County
(probably those who signed the petition), District Judge Walter Gillis
in Del Rio on November 16 wrote General Mabry that Rangers were
still needed at Stockton and that it would be far better to leave Kirchner
and his men there than to send in a new group of strangers. Gillis
added that "he strongly believed that Rangers are much more necessary to protect some of the good citizens of the County from violence at
the hands of Royal and his lawless Deputies, than to assist him in pre-
serving the peace and enforcing the law. . . . You may think it strange
that a sheriff would be charged with creating the necessity of Rangers
by his own lawless acts but unfortunately we sometimes have the worst
men in the County to fill that office in this end of the State. . . ."[32]

Judge Williams had cause, he wrote, to believe that Sheriff Royal
was "waylaying the Koehler store at night," perhaps for an opportunity
to shoot the judge. Williams frequently played dominoes, chess, or
checkers at Koehler's saloon at night. On one such occasion, someone
warned him to go home by a different trail. Taking heed of the warning, he chose another route and arrived home without incident. The
next morning, he heard that someone had stepped out of the darkness and held a gun on another man who was walking along the trail
Williams usually used. After a moment the gunman, reportedly Sheriff
Royal, lowered his gun and said, "I'm sorry, I've got the wrong man."[33]

In the 1890s newly elected officers assumed their new duties as
soon as the votes had been counted and they could qualify and be
sworn. For this purpose the Pecos County commissioners court convened on Monday, November 12. Those present were Judge Williams,
T. P. Baylor, T. J. Ray, and lame ducks E. M. Teel, C. M. Wilson, and
W. P. Matthews. R. B. Neighbors qualified and took the oath of office
as sheriff with Jim and Morgan Livingston, Shipton Parke, and I. T.
Hock as sureties on his bond in the amount of $5,000. H. L. Hatch-
ette's resignation as justice of the peace of Precinct 1 was accepted.
With that done, Williams later wrote, "we were somewhat easier,"

---

[31] Hughes, Ysleta, to Mabry, November 14, 1894, AGP, RG 401, TSL.
[32] Walter Gillis, Del Rio, to W. H. Mabry, November 16, 1894, AGP, RG 401, TSL.
[33] O. W. Williams, oral statement, to Clayton Williams.

since Royal had been expected to return and make trouble. "He had offered to bet $700 that Neighbors would never qualify as Sheriff." That evening, Williams continued, Royal returned to town, "drinking and threatening," but he made no appearance in court during its remaining three days.[34]

Quiet apparently prevailed in Fort Stockton for the remainder of the week. Then, on Monday, November 19, 1894, the county court again convened. On its docket, Royal was under indictment in three cases and was to be the complaining witness in five others.[35] Just after it adjourned in midafternoon two days later Royal was dead—shot by a never-identified assailant as he sat at a desk in the sheriff's office in the presence of at least two persons and with a number of others in the hall and in various nearby rooms.

According to Williams' lengthy narrative, Royal was under indictment for his assaults on White, Mansfield, and Baker, and trial was set for four cases in which he was the complaining witness. Royal, however, did not appear, and, after an attachment for the witness had been issued, court was adjourned until ten the next morning. Royal failed to appear. The sheriff explained that the writ had been served on Royal at the Leon and that Royal had said he would be there. Hatchette, his attorney, stated that he did not know his whereabouts. Court was held open until noon, and, after Hatchette made several trips to the saloon and toward Royal's home to no avail, an attachment for Royal's appearance, "returnable instantly," was issued. Court was then adjourned until ten the following morning. (Twenty-nine years later, James Happle, who married one of Royal's daughters in 1901, told the author that Royal did not go to the courthouse during the two days because he feared that he would be killed.) That afternoon, according to the Williams narrative, Royal, while drinking, sent one of his former deputies for Hock, to whom he told his troubles, said he was going to move to the Leon, and stated that he "was going to pick us all off." Hock reported the "threat" to the "7 boys," who, in turn, passed the word on to Williams and others.[36]

[34] Williams, 1930s typescript; Pecos County, Commissioners Court Minutes, November 12, 1894.

[35] Williams, 1930s typescript.

[36] Ibid. The manuscript version adds that Royal was planning to pick off his victims "one at a time." In that account, Williams opines that "this looks very probable, as he has

On the morning of November 21, Deputy Sheriff MacFarland and Ranger Palmer found Royal at his Leon farm and returned with him in time for the afternoon session of the court. The court postponed action on the three cases against him, and after testifying in each case in which he was a witness he returned to the sheriff's office. "He was [Williams wrote] plainly armed in Court—the pistol showing its form under the vest."[37]

Thirty-five years later Morgan Livingston remarked that: "One of the Rangers asked Judge Williams, 'Shall we disarm the prisoner?' After scratching his head, Williams replied, 'I guess not, for if we did, he probably would be the only unarmed man in my court'." And, in the early 1920s, O. W. Williams reminisced that during a recess as he, a couple of Rangers, Royal, several witnesses, and some spectators were returning up the stairs to the courtroom, they heard a gunshot above them. The men who were armed (probably most of them) pulled their guns and were advancing carefully when Hatchette suddenly rushed out of the courtroom, pistol in hand, and exclaimed, "An accident! An accident!" As soon as things calmed down, the hearings were resumed.[38]

Hatchette, a former schoolteacher who had had his license to practice law only a short time, made a vigorous defense for Royal during that afternoon but reportedly made everybody more nervous than they already were by picking up his pistol from the table and pointing here and there. Finally, Jim Livingston, deciding that he had had enough, jumped up, shouted a few cuss words, and told Hatchette to "point that damn thing in some other direction!" Thereafter, Hatchette kept his hands off the pistol.[39]

When the court adjourned about 4:00 P.M., Judge Williams, according to his narrative, went into the clerk's office to determine a point of law. While thus involved, he continued, he heard a voice call out "Royal" and "about 5 or 6 seconds" later,[40] "I heard the muffled sound of

a gang with him that he could apparently influence to do anything, & no man knew who would be sent to assassinate him nor where to look for them."

[37] Williams, 1930s typescript.

[38] Morgan Livingston, oral statement, heard by Clayton Williams, ca. 1929; O. W. Williams, oral statement while reminiscing with friends, heard by Clayton Williams, early 1920s.

[39] O. W. Williams, oral statement while reminiscing with friends, heard by Clayton Williams, early 1920s.

[40] The manuscript account says ten seconds.

a gun shot" in the direction of the east door of the courthouse and then a noise towards the sheriff's office. Concluding that Royal had shot someone, Judge Williams ran into the hall, where a number of people were congregating.[41] Williams was looking for Royal, he wrote, for "I knew he would shoot me on any chance like this." A haze of smoke could be seen at the door of the sheriff's office, from which came Charles A. Crosby, Royal's unsuccessful candidate for county clerk in the recent election, calling "Where is the Sheriff? Royal is dead." By then, Williams said, there were ten or twelve people in the hall. About that time Rangers Kirchner and Schmidt came on the run through the east door, followed by the sheriff. Williams then went to the door of the sheriff's office. According to his accounts (both the original and later typed versions), Royal was sitting in a chair at a desk, with his pistol on and his gun close by, his back to the door, his head resting on the desk, blood coming from his mouth and also streaming down his left arm, which was hanging by the chair, onto the floor. The right arm rested on the desk and on a pen holder, with the tip of the pen broken. The lower part of Royal's left shoulder showed "5 or 6 round bullet holes close together," apparently made, Williams believed, by buckshot, that "ranged toward the neck."[42]

Among those Judge Williams remembered seeing at the time, in addition to those named above, were Johnson, Ranger Palmer, Ship Parke, James and Morgan Livingston, Frank and James Rooney, Odom, and possibly Matthews, but he was unable to recall whether they were all there when he first rushed into the hall after the shooting. "Some were saying 'I wonder who did it'—'How did it happen.' But no one seemed excited and there was nothing in the appearance of anyone of them to lead me to suspect that he was the party who did the killing." Williams wrote that he saw no one come from the sheriff's office ahead of Crosby, and he could not recall seeing at that moment anyone with a shotgun or a rifle. A few minutes afterward he saw some people, including perhaps Matthews and Parke, get their guns in the clerk's office, where he too (and perhaps Frank Rooney) had a shotgun in the vault, which he had carried there when county court convened, as he

[41] Noticeably missing in the typed version are these lines from the original: "As I jumped up & ran out in the hall, I thought I heard among other noises steps going toward & into the Commissioners Court Room & I saw the door partially open" (Williams, manuscript account).

[42] Williams, 1930s typescript.

expected "to be assaulted and killed by Royal. I got my shotgun . . . later that evening. It was still loaded with 2 loaded shells. One barrel looked as though it had recently been fired, but I did not think . . . that it had been fired that day."[43]

At the time the shot was fired two men were in the office with Royal. Crosby told Williams, and apparently the Rangers and others, that he was sitting at the same desk where Royal was writing but did not recognize the voice of the gunman and that "all he saw was the barrel of a gun looking like a Winchester shotgun thrust through the door and a glimpse of someone in dark clothes at the door." Hatchette told Williams and the Rangers that he was in the corner of the room near the vault at the time and saw only "a small section of the end of the gun" and that he did not recognize the voice. Ranger Kirchner's account and Williams' were almost identical.[44]

In his report of the shooting to Adjutant General Mabry, Kirchner explained that "the feeling between the two parties was so bitter I knew it [presumably, a shooting] would come before much longer." At the time Royal was shot, Kirchner and Schmidt had gone to a nearby saloon "to see if everything was quiet there," and Ranger Palmer was in the courthouse office where the Rangers slept. Royal had become "very unpopular" as sheriff of Pecos County, Kirchner continued, and "all the good people agree that there would have been much trouble & bloodshed before now if it had not been for the presence of the rangers here." Two days later, Captain Hughes reported to his superior many of the above-mentioned details, adding that Royal "never spoke a word after he was shot" and that Kirchner and his men were doing all they could to ascertain and catch the killer.[45]

Judge Williams wrote afterward in his narrative about Royal that someone in the courthouse who "was under threat from him [Royal]" had killed him."[46] A number of men, including Williams, had been

[43] Ibid.

[44] Ibid.; Carl Kirchner, Fort Stockton, to W. H. Mabry, November 22, 1894, AGP, RG 401, TSL.

[45] Kirchner to Mabry, November 22, 1894, and Hughes, Ysleta, to Mabry, November 24, 1894, both in AGP, RG 401, TSL.

[46] Williams, 1930s typescript. In his manuscript version, Williams added: "& I would have considered that I or any of them would have been justified in killing him on sight in self-defense—We were perfectly satisfied—or I was at any rate—that the only

threatened by Royal "with death," and Williams knew, he stated, that Royal had waylaid paths traveled by those persons after night. In his narrative Williams then added several other serious grievances against Royal. "I had some personal knowledge of 1 cold blooded murder committed by him and had heard of another"; he had intimidated some witnesses into perjury, had perjured himself in court, twice, at least; he had "worked a Grand Jury into a course of injustice and oppression"; and it was believed that the district attorney "was strongly prejudiced in his favor . . . [for] he had been so far no obstacle to Royal working anything he desired through the Grand Jury." This situation, Williams felt, "forced every man under threat from Royal to realize no protection to his life. . . ."[47] Although he suspected that someone in the courthouse had done the shooting, yet Williams was unable, he wrote, to detect anything that led him to suspect anyone more than any other.[48]

In his typed 1930s version of his narrative of the affair Judge Williams added an additional comment as to how Royal may have planned to kill him. After the shooting, Ed Monteith, Royal's deputy, returned a pistol, which Royal had taken from R. N. Baker when Baker was arrested in September, to Ship Parke, its owner. On it had been scratched O. W. W., "probably by Royal," Williams concluded, "with intention of dropping it after shooting me in order to work up a case of self-defense."[49]

Charles A. Crosby, who was sitting at the desk beside Royal at the time of the shot and who apparently had been Royal's deputy, was the son of Stephen Crosby, the land commissioner of Texas from 1851 to

---

reason we had not been killed already was because Royal was simply waiting his time to kill us, without any show on our part of hurting him."

[47] Williams, 1930s typescript. The manuscript version summarized the situation: "In short it was plain to us that he thought & had reason to think that he could go harmless in the courts for a murder of any of us, & that he intended to kill us when he could do so without personal injury to himself. I knew this to be the feeling of those of us whom he had threatened. And I knew too that none of us hoped or believed in any safety of life except in his [Royal's] death."

[48] Williams, 1930s typescript.

[49] Williams, 1930s typescript. A warrant had been issued on August 21, 1894, by Justice of the Peace Hatchette for Baker's arrest for "unlawful display of pistol" on August 6 and for firing it near Koehler's store (Warrant No. 10, Fort Stockton, Pecos County, August 21, 1894, Red File #62, certified copy in possession of Clayton Williams).

1858, for whom Crosby County, Texas, is named. C. A. and his wife, Ophelia (Cleveland) Crosby, had four sons, three of whom moved to the Trans-Pecos country. Will C., the oldest, for some time operated the former government hospital, just east of the guardhouse, as a hotel. Richard H., whose son Bob became a world-famous rodeo performer, and John Everett, were stockmen. Before becoming a rancher, John worked for several outfits, including the NA. When in Fort Stockton, he and his family lived for a time in the old army guardhouse, a rock structure on the south side of the parade ground.[50] John's daughter Margaret, however, was born at her Uncle Will's hotel (the former government hospital) in 1896. Her family moved from Pecos County a year or two after Royal was shot.[51]

Since Charles A. Crosby was sitting at the desk beside Royal, questions regarding his failure to provide some information about the killer are logical, especially since the gunman called out "Royal" clearly and distinctly and his head, at least, would have been in a line of vision with the victim. Crosby in 1894, however, was an old man, partially deaf and almost blind, and Margaret Crosby recalled hearing that her grandfather had had trouble with his eyesight long before he moved to Fort Stockton.

Since the sheriff was also tax collector, the transmission of some of that business to the new sheriff had not been finished, and Royal died intestate. Judge Williams appointed Charles Crosby as temporary administrator of the A. J. Royal estate.[52]

The families of the men involved in the feuds had lived in dreadful fear much of the time, especially during the almost three months prior to Royal's death. Following Royal's defeat in the November election, Mrs. O. W. Williams took her three children and went to the Rooney farm, three miles north of Fort Stockton, where they stayed during

[50]The building, which is still well preserved in 1981, has served as a residence for a number of families. Among the best remembered were "Old Man" John Valentine who served as a courthouse janitor and a part-time deputy under Royal, a man named Carsy, the director of the first band at Fort Stockton, and his family, and the Rollins family, who lived there while constructing their home on the site of the former government hospital.

[51]Eldon Stephen Branda, ed., *The Handbook of Texas: A Supplement*, 3:210; Margaret Crosby, Austin, Texas, oral statements, to Gaines Kincaid, 1977.

[52]Pecos County, Probate Minutes, 1:196, 230. Incidentally, two days after Royal's death Robert N. Baker married John Valentine's daughter Mary, and the ceremony was performed by Judge Williams (Pecos County, Marriage License Records, 2:62).

the remainder of that period. Waldo Williams and Will Rooney, both around ten years old, had ridden on horseback to town and happened to be near the Royals' home when the tragic message was delivered to his family. For the rest of his life, Waldo had a vivid memory of the distress and weeping of Mrs. Royal and her children.

Who killed A. J. Royal? Eighty-five years later, the question cannot be answered, but rumors and speculations have been numerous and persistent. The majority of those who have expressed opinions say that a drawing took place to determine who would pull the trigger. In most stories, straws were drawn; in others, it was small pieces of paper, pebbles, or something else. Some say that five or six men were involved, but the most persistent tale had only three, from among the two Livingstons, two Rooneys, and Parke. The most frequently told version had Frank Rooney drawing the "killing straw" but then declaring that he could not do it. Thereupon, another of the trio (according to rumor, Jim Livingston, who was known to be an excellent marksman) said, "Well, I can—give me the straw!" Others, however, insist that it was Shipton Parke. Many years ago, the author told his father, Judge Williams, that he had heard a rumor that Ship Parke had done the shooting and asked if he knew the identity of the killer. He replied that he suspected Parke but added, "I absolutely do not know who the killer was."

Another bit of weak evidence is traceable to someone who attended Parke's funeral in January, 1916. This informant (who wants to remain anonymous) stated that more than one person heard Morgan Livingston, with a gesture toward Parke's casket, declare, "There goes the man who killed A. J. Royal." Recently Morgan's son, Hugh R. Livingston, wrote that his father never had anything to say as to the identity of the killer of Sheriff Royal: "After his death I asked my mother if he had ever told her anything about it. She said no." [53]

Another rumor, told in Alpine, had two of the three potential assassins not know which of the others drew the job. According to this story, three pieces of paper, of equal size, were used, with the assignment indicated on one, and after drawing each man destroyed his piece of paper without showing it to the others.

According to another bit of folklore, nine prominent men of Fort

---

[53] Hugh Rooney Livingston, El Paso, to Gaines Kincaid, Austin, May 30, 1977.

Stockton banded together for the purpose of eliminating Royal. On the afternoon of the shooting, the nine, wrote C. L. Sonnichsen, "are said to have been stationed from top to bottom of the courthouse to be sure their victim did not escape." Then, after the shot was fired, "the nine men, if there were nine men, and if the nine men were in the courthouse, came running from all directions asking what had happened."[54]

Other tales have persisted that a Texas Ranger was hired to do the shooting. Certainly there was some basis for speculation, since considerable antagonism had developed between the Rangers and Sheriff Royal, primarily over the Ochoa affair. In one account the late Pete Ten Eyck, while sheriff of Pecos County, said that, not long after he arrived in the county as a very young man, an oldtimer told him that the shot had been fired by a Ranger named Outlaw, who had been paid $500 (the sum always mentioned in connection with a Ranger's killing Royal) to do the job. The only Ranger by that name on record, however, is Bass Outlaw, who had been killed in El Paso by John Selman over seven months before the death of A. J. Royal.[55]

There were at least two other rumors during the 1930s that a Ranger was Royal's assassin. Will Rooney, while serving as the sheriff of Pecos County, told the author that he had heard "on good authority" that a group of Fort Stockton men had paid a Texas Ranger to kill Royal, but he would not elaborate. More recently, Roy Rooney, son of Will's brother Frank, who lives near McCamey, told the author a story, both intriguing and frustrating, that he had heard from Judge H. H. Butz. During a visit to Fort Stockton about 1960, Butz had told him that he had received a letter from a man named Smith (which could have been Schmidt), who stated that he wanted to reveal some information that had bothered him for many years. Others had been accused of killing Royal, he wrote, but the accusations were false, for he had done the shooting, for which he had been paid $500, while he was a Texas Ranger. In a telephone conversation in the summer of 1978, Karl Butz, Herman's son, said he knew of no such letter, but later, in another telephone conversation, Roy Rooney stated that Judge Butz, who was then

[54] S. D. Myres, *Pioneer Surveyor—Frontier Lawyer: The Personal Narrative of O. W. Williams, 1877–1902*, pp. 23–24.

[55] The late Pete Ten Eyck, as told to Gaines Kincaid during a conversation in the Pecos County sheriff's office, January, 1977; Robert E. McNellis, "Bass Outlaw: Lawless Lawman," *Guns*, December, 1976, pp. 69–70.

well into his eighties, had complete control of his mental powers at the time (although soon afterward the judge began to deteriorate in mind and body), that the judge had indicated that he had received the letter not long before, possibly a few years, and he was not certain of the name of the letter writer. But Smith (Schmidt) was still the name he had in mind, although, he added, "it could just as easily have been Jones." Roy was certain that the amount of money involved was $500, and he was not certain but thought the postmark on the letter was Pleasanton, Texas, which is south of San Antonio.

Rangers Sitters and Fulgham left Fort Stockton about November 18, three days before Royal was killed, and arrived at Ysleta on November 27. At the time Royal was shot, according to Kirchner's report, Palmer was in the courthouse office where the Rangers slept, and Kirchner and Schmidt had gone to Royal and Monteith's Grey Mule Saloon, almost adjacent to the courthouse, or to Koehler's, a bit farther away, and arrived together back at the courthouse soon after Royal was shot.[56] If Private William Schmidt killed A. J. Royal (under a contract), then it must follow that Kirchner knew of the plot and supplied Schmidt with an alibi, but in view of his fine reputation this possibility does not seem plausible. Furthermore, why would the aged Schmidt, if he wrote the aforementioned letter, choose the aged Judge Herman Butz as his confessor?

Also, what happened to the gun? C. L. Sonnichsen, in an introduction to S. D. Myres's book on O. W. Williams, wrote that "the assassin put the gun down by the door and vanished" and that Judge Williams "remembered later that the washroom door was slightly ajar as he passed it."[57]

So, "Who killed A. J. Royal?" Since several men had one or more motives to do so, it appears doubtful that the answer will ever be known with any certainty.

When Andy was buried in the old cemetery in Fort Stockton, Naomi Obedience Royal did not have enough money to place a monument at his grave. As soon as possible, however, she erected a marble tombstone with this inscription:

[56] Co. D, Monthly Returns for November, 1894, and Kirchner, Fort Stockton, to Mabry, November 22, 1894, both in AGP, RG 401, TSL.

[57] Myres, *Pioneer Surveyor—Frontier Lawyer*, p. 24.

In Memory of
A. J. Royal
Born
Nov. 25, 1855
Assassinated
Nov. 21, 1894
Sleep husband dear and
take thy rest
God called thee home.
He thought best.
It was hard indeed
to part with thee
But Christ's strong arms
support me.
Gone but not forgotten.

The devotion displayed by Naomi, along with statements and writings by some family members, portray A. J. Royal as a loving and devoted husband and father, who did not burden his family with his troubles, and indicate that they believed that Andy could do no wrong. This is normal. For some descendants, the passage of time has not appreciably obscured that memory. One descendant recently wrote: "The Royals were never people who indulged in feuds."[58] Not all members of the family, however, agreed. A great-great-grandson of Royal remembers, "My grandfather, Jones Black, told me that Royal was a 'mean son-of-a-bitch but that there were also other mean sons-of-bitches here then'."[59]

[58] Downie, *Terrell County*, p. 611.
[59] James Black, great-great-grandson of A. J. Royal and a Fort Stockton business owner, oral statement, to Clayton Williams (with permission to quote), 1980.

IV.
Tragedy and Success

CHAPTER 24

The Fate of the Fort Stockton Pioneers

CHARLES A. Crosby was temporary administrator of Royal's estate until late in the year, when Royal's parents, Ethel Joseph and Mary Frances (Ousley) Royal, moved from Junction to Stockton, and E. J. became the administrator. E. J., born in Virginia in 1834, and Mary Frances, born in North Carolina in 1836, were married in 1853. Andrew J., born in Lee County, Alabama, on November 25, 1855, was their only son, but they also had five daughters.[1]

The estate of A. J. Royal, as appraised by F. W. Young and E. M. Teel, consisted of 1,120 acres of farm and ranch land, valued at $3.00 an acre; 100 stock horses, worth $7.00 each; twenty-five head of cattle, worth $10.00 each; one wagon, worth $30.00; and three town lots.[2] The family residence, the old Friedlander place, Naomi Royal continued to run as a rooming and boarding house to support her family and to pay her husband's debts. Royal had long owed Judge Williams some money for clerical work (about which the two had had a physical encounter), but Williams never billed the estate for the amount. When asked why, he replied, "If I couldn't collect it from him, I'd surely not try to collect it from the widow." On October 26, 1898, Andrew Roy, the Royals' son, not quite six years old, died of diphtheria and was laid to rest beside his father.[3]

Sometime during 1900, Dr. Homer Powers, a widower with several sons and daughters, who had been everybody's friend, including A. J. Royal's, moved into Naomi Royal's rooming house. Powers was, by the way, the doctor summoned by O. W. Williams in 1889 from Pecos to care for Morgan Livingston's gunshot wound. He and Mrs.

[1] Alice Evans Downie, ed., *Terrell County, Texas: Its Past—Its People*, pp. 416, 611; Pecos County, Texas, Probate Minutes, 1:226.
[2] Pecos County, Probate No. 16.
[3] Downie, *Terrell County*, p. 611.

Royal were married in Fort Stockton on June 12, 1901, by a Baptist minister. The couple had one child, Naomi, who is now Mrs. Rudy Grossenbacher, of Waco.[4]

Following A. J. Royal's death, there was no further antagonism between his family and that of Judge Williams. For a while, Naomi sent daughters Carrie and Aileen to take music lessons from Mrs. Williams in her home. Sometime after Naomi married Dr. Powers, the family moved to the Leon and for a few years operated the Royal farm. They then moved to Cloudcroft, New Mexico, and sometime later to Rankin, Texas, where Dr. and Mrs. Powers lived out their lives.

A final note on the era pertains to the desk at which Royal was sitting at the time he was shot. According to the late Sheriff Pete Ten Eyck, the desk, ordered from Saint Louis, Missouri, and the first piece of furniture purchased by the officials of the newly created Pecos County, had been obtained for the use of the county clerk, but on becoming sheriff Royal had appropriated it for his own office. A few years ago, when the sheriff's department was moved to a new building south of the courthouse, the desk was placed in a hallway there. (The pigeon-hole structure on its top must have been added after Royal was killed.) Occasionally, a visitor would stop to examine the blood stains in the top right drawer, but those finally faded away. In the summer of 1978, the desk was loaned to the Annie Riggs Memorial Museum, across the street from the courthouse, where it still (1981) remains on display in the front hall.

The Pecos County general elections in 1896, 1898, and 1900 were far more peaceful than those previously in the 1890s. Judge Williams, Sheriff R. B. Neighbors, and Clerk Frank Rooney were reelected to their respective offices in 1896 and 1898. In November, 1896, Taylor Stephenson and Charles Downie were succeeded by James Rooney and George C. Miller, and, in February, 1898, when T. P. Baylor moved out of the county, Morgan Livingston was appointed to fill the vacated place. In November that year the newly elected commissioners were James Rooney, C. M. Wilson, Taylor Stephenson (who had moved to Precinct 3), and T. J. Ray. Rooney resigned in May, 1900, and Will Crosby was appointed to take his place. A month later, Stephenson

[4]Ibid., pp. 416–417, 419, 611; Pecos County, Marriage License Records, 2:106.

resigned and was replaced by Jim Livingston. After the election in November, 1900, James Rooney was the only one of those familiar names who reappeared as a commissioner.

The detachment of Rangers stayed in and around Fort Stockton for three months after Royal was killed.[5] The feuds ended with Royal's death, although some of the participants harbored grudges and grievances for many years.

In the Fort Stockton area, a few of the old landmarks still exist, although some have been greatly altered. East of town, the Tunas (Escondido) stage station, made of stone, is a replica built in recent years. Within the city limits, the surviving structures include the "Oldest House in Fort Stockton," Young's store, Koehler's store, which has been remodeled beyond recognition into a two-story community hall, the Grey Mule Saloon (after Royal's death operated by Monteith and Strickland), the old cemetery, the guardhouse, which is well preserved, a few of the officers' quarters, which are now being used as private residences, and several residences of old Saint Gall. The army's hospital, which started falling apart while Will Crosby was using it as a hotel, was torn down during the winter of 1903–1904.

The Pecos County jail and courthouse, although old and interesting, are not the buildings constructed in the 1880s. A contract was signed on August 12, 1912, with Jack Richardson, architect, and the Falls City Construction Company of Louisville, Kentucky, for the construction of new buildings. They were to be rebuilt from scratch with an "all new foundation," but the courthouse was to retain some of the old foundations and the old stones. Thus, the sites are the same, but the buildings, completed in 1913, are different.[6]

Across the street from the courthouse, on the eastern side, the Annie Riggs Memorial Museum attracts more visitors than any other building in Fort Stockton. The building was originally built for a hotel. Upon seeing a need for a hotel, Jim and Morgan Livingston with one-fourth interest, James Rooney and Herman Butz with one-fourth interest, and Ike T. Hock and R. B. Neighbors, each with a quarter interest,

[5] Co. D, Monthly Returns for March, 1895, Texas Adjutant General's Papers (AGP), Record Group (RG) 401, Archives, Texas State Library (TSL), Austin.
[6] Pecos County, Minutes of the Commissioners Court, 3:547–554, 580–581, and 4:16, 21.

organized the Fort Stockton Hotel Company. The company purchased the site from Mrs. Augusta Meiners, Butz's mother, and in 1898 started construction on a building. Completed the following year at a cost of $5,000, the new hotel (now the Annie Riggs Museum) was named, fittingly, Koehler Hotel in memory of the late Herman Koehler.[7] Perhaps Mrs. Meiners stipulated its name. In 1904, S. C. Vaughan was the proprietor, and Mrs. Annie Riggs was "agent." Apparently, Annie leased and started managing the hotel soon after she divorced Barney Riggs in 1901. In 1904, she purchased the property, changed the name to the Riggs Hotel, and operated it for the remainder of her life.[8]

Although the Fort Stockton area was generally more peaceful after the mid-1890s, Annie Riggs and several of her kin continued to suffer strife and heartache. Her father, George M. Frazer, the first county judge in Pecos County, had moved to Toyah in 1885 and thereafter spent most of his remaining years in Reeves County. There, he served as county judge from December 3, 1888, to November 14, 1894. His wife, May Edgar Frazer, died in El Paso on October 27, 1893, and was buried there. The judge died on August 27, 1908, at age eighty in Alpine, at the home of his daughter, Caroline (Mrs. L. W.) Durrell, wife of the local postmaster, and his body was taken to Pecos for burial.[9] Frazer died intestate, and his daughter, Annie Stella Riggs, asked the court to appoint her as administratrix. She stated that Frazer's estate consisted only of horses and cattle worth $500, but later she reset the value at $1,500.[10]

George A. (Bud) Frazer, Annie Riggs's brother, had a bloody and tragic life. Soon after Reeves County was created, Bud moved there and in 1890 was elected sheriff. During the following year James Brown Miller appeared and became Bud's nemesis. Sheriff Frazer apparently was not aware that Jim Miller was a killer long before he moved to Pecos City. At age twenty-two, while living in Coryell County, Miller

---

[7] Pecos County, Deed Records, 7:279; D. S. Beeman, curator of the Annie Riggs Memorial Museum, to Clayton Williams, oral statements, leaflets, pamphlets, etc.

[8] Pecos County, Deed Records, 12:110.

[9] James Cox, *Historical and Biographical Record of the Cattlemen of Texas and Adjacent Territory*, 2:457–458; Reeves County, Texas, Commissioners Court Minutes, December 3, 1888, and November 15, 1894; *San Antonio Express*, August 30, 1908.

[10] Reeves County, Commissioners Court Minutes, 2:13, 34–35.

was tried and sentenced to life in prison for the murder of his brother-in-law, John Coop. The case was appealed, Miller won a reversal, and no retrial was ever held. Later, Jim went to work as a cowboy for Emanuel (Mannen) Clements and became friendly with Mannen, Jr. (Mannie), who was involved in the "Murder Steer" episode. In 1884, the elder Clements was killed in Runnels County by a city marshal, Joe Townsend. Jim Miller retaliated by shooting Townsend from ambush with a shotgun. Townsend recovered, but Jim's deed endeared him to the Clements family. Later, in fact, he became a member of the family.

Because he went to church regularly and talked and acted like a preacher, Jim came to be called "Deacon" Miller. According to Bud Baker, Bud Frazer's grandson, it was the churchgoing people of Pecos who talked Sheriff Frazer into hiring Miller as a deputy. The sheriff began having doubts about Jim Miller after he killed a Mexican prisoner he was taking to Fort Stockton. Deputy Miller claimed that the Mexican had tried to escape, but Sheriff Frazer did not believe him. According to Bud Baker, Miller was told by Frazer to clear out, but he refused. That was the beginning of a feud.

After various charges, counter-charges, and close encounters, Sheriff Frazer concluded that Jim Miller, Mannie Clements, and Martin Q. Hardin were conspiring against him. (Clements and Hardin were both related to John Wesley Hardin.) Having been warned by some local citizens that his life was in danger, Frazer sent for Ranger Captain John R. Hughes, who arrested the trio of alleged conspirators in May, 1893. Clements and Hardin were soon out on bail, and, in June, Sheriff Frazer and Clements were involved in a fight, after which Clements charged the sheriff with assault. Bud Frazer was charged also with the theft of two mules, but this case was later dismissed. On April 12, 1894, the feud came to a head when Bud and Jim had a gun battle, in which Miller was seriously wounded. Soon afterwards, Bud sought safety in New Mexico.

In December, Frazer returned to Pecos. A few days later, he and Miller had another gun battle. Again Miller was wounded, and again Frazer left town. Having wounded Miller, but not fatally, in two separate gunfights, Frazer decided, according to Barney Riggs, Jr., that the Deacon had a charmed life, but he later learned that his adversary wore a bulletproof vest under his scissortail coat. Bud was indicted in

March of 1895, and the case was transferred to El Paso County, where at Miller's request John Wesley Hardin, who had acquired a knowledge of law while in prison, helped in the prosecution. Since the jury could not reach a verdict, the case was moved to Colorado City, where Bud was acquitted.

In September, 1896, Bud went to Toyah, a small Reeves County settlement in which lived his father, his wife, Mattie (who was the sister of Barney Riggs), and his little daughter, Eula Lee Frazer. A few days later someone told Jim Miller that Bud was back in Toyah and often visited a saloon there to play cards and pass the time of day. On September 14, while Bud was enjoying a card game in the saloon, the Deacon entered with a double-barreled shotgun, fired both shells, and nearly blew away the back of Bud Frazer's head. At Miller's trial, some witnesses, including George A. Scarborough, testified that Frazer had threatened the life of the defendant and had assaulted him on more than one occasion. Miller won a change of venue to Eastland County, and eventually he was acquitted "because of the conflicting nature of the testimony."[11]

After he had killed Bud Frazer, Miller and his friends decided that they ruled the roost in Reeves County, and, having been told once by Bud to clear out, Miller gave the entire Frazer family, including Barney Riggs, such an order. By then the good Judge Frazer was too old to strap on a gun and clean out a town—and besides it was not his style. But it was Barney Riggs's style. Taking a lesson, perhaps, from the charmed life of Deacon Miller, Riggs procured some protective covering. "When Dad and his family came to the outskirts of Pecos," Barney, Jr., related, "Dad got out of the buggy in which were Mama [Annie Frazer Riggs], two-year-old Ernest, and me, went into the brush and put on the bulletproof vest. After that, with his pistol in hand, he walked into Pecos ahead of the team, while Mama with a shotgun across her lap held the lines." Such precautions seemed necessary, for

[11] A considerable amount of the information relative to Bud Frazer's trouble with Miller was in oral statements made by Bud F. Baker to Clayton Williams. Baker gave to Williams a signed statement that his information was told to him by his mother, Eula Lee (Frazer) Baker, the daughter of Bud Frazer. Other helpful sources include Bill C. James, *Mysterious Killer, James Brown Miller, 1861–1909*; Cox, *Cattlemen of Texas*, 2:456; Bill Leftwich, *Tracks along the Pecos*, pp. 48, 50–56, 59.

Riggs had heard that Miller had delegated to Bill Earhart and John Denison, both of whom had been involved in the plot to kill Bud Frazer, the job of doing away with him. On the previous day, when supposedly warned that Miller's men sometimes wore metal vests, Barney laughed and declared: "That's all right, I'll just shoot them in the head." And so he did. When Riggs walked into the Orient Saloon, both Denison and Earhart were standing at the bar. Barney shot Denison in the ear and Earhart in the back of the head as he ran out.

On October 31, 1896, Barney Riggs was arrested by Ranger Sergeant Ed Aten and charged with murder, but he was eventually acquitted. His action, however, and the antagonism of the Reeves County citizenry, including Bud Frazer's "guntotin' sisters," caused Deacon Jim Miller to seek a healthier clime. He and his wife moved to Fort Worth, where Mrs. Miller ran a rooming house while rearing her children. During the next few years, Miller was involved in a number of killings, but he always managed to go free. The hypocritical Deacon was a gunman-for-hire, historians have generally agreed, who killed, for large sums, a number of men with whom he had no personal quarrel. Captain John R. Hughes believed that it was Miller who killed Pat Garrett, the killer of Billy the Kid.

Early in 1909, two men in Ada, Oklahoma, Joe Allen and Jesse West, supposedly hired Miller to kill Angus A. (Gus) Bobbitt, with whom they were feuding. Bobbitt was killed from ambush on February 27. Later, Allen, West, Miller, and Berry B. Burrell were arrested. On April 19, 1909, angry citizens of Ada took the four men from jail and lynched them.[12]

The marriage of Barney Riggs and Annie Frazer Johnson ended in a "feud"—in this case, between husband and wife. The couple were married on September 23, 1891, and within seven months the honeymoon was over. Still, the marriage lasted another decade. In her first

[12] Glenn Shirley, *Shotgun for Hire: The Story of "Deacon" Jim Miller, Killer of Pat Garrett*, pp. 6–13, 21–25, 30, 38–49, 101–116; James, *Mysterious Killer*, unpaginated; Leftwich, *Tracks along the Pecos*, pp. 59–61; Jack Martin, *Border Boss: Captain John R. Hughes, Texas Ranger*, p. 150; Co. D, Monthly Returns for October, 1896, AGP, RG 401, TSL; Barney Riggs, Jr., Ernest Riggs, and Bud Frazer Baker, oral statements, to Clayton Williams. Baker's information about the Riggs-Miller affair was told to him by his mother, Eula Lee (Frazer) Baker, the daughter of Bud Frazer, and by his great-aunt, Ella Frazer, the sister of Bud Frazer.

petition to obtain a divorce, in June, 1900, Annie declared that around April 1, 1892, Barney Riggs began "disregarding his marriage vows and his duties to plaintiff and their children [and] began a series of excesses, cruel treatment, and outrages toward plaintiff of such a nature as to render their living together longer insupportable," and as a result, she had "quit the conjugal duties of wife" on or about June 7, 1900. Although living with Barney was "insupportable" after only seven months of marriage, Annie had continued to bear his children for several years and even carried a gun into town to use, if necessary, in his defense. The specific charges she listed were many and rather serious. Since on or about June 7, 1900, she stated, her husband on "many occasions" and "continuously" had come home intoxicated, denounced his wife and children with "vile epithets and assaulted and otherwise maltreated and abused" them—so much that her married life "became a burden and a curse." This he also did even when "not intoxicated" and "without provocation." On or about July 20, 1898, the defendant had struck the plaintiff in her "face with a cartridge belt," and afterward he had whipped their seven-year-old son "unreasonable" and had "struck" her when she tried to get him to stop. Afterwards, on "many occasions" her husband, while intoxicated, had applied to her and to their children "the vilest and most obscene epithets," too "disgusting . . . to repeat," and, at all times, he had such a "violent temper" that their children "feared him with all the terror fear can produce." Furthermore, according to Annie's charges, her husband was "not a fit or proper person to have the care, custody, and education" of their children as he was "without parental affection." She added that he was "easily angered and of a violent and ungovernable temper, and [was] dangerous to his own family when angry" and that he was "addicted to habits of dissipation and improper associations."

Annie Riggs also stated that she and her children were "wholly without means of support or maintenance," except her interest in the property she and her husband owned together. This property included ranchland, owned and leased, over 200 head of cattle, over 500 head of horses, some of which she owned individually, and nearly 5,000 sheep, some of which were hers alone. She also stipulated what Barney was to pay for the care and education of their children.

For some undisclosed reason, Annie dropped the divorce proceedings a few days before the case was scheduled to be heard. The reconciliation—for whatever reason—was short. On February 14, 1901, Annie separated from Barney and immediately refiled for divorce. Her attorney, A. L. Camp, after listing the same charges set forth in the previous divorce petition, added some others. On or about February 13, 1901, Annie charged, the defendant came home "intoxicated and began to abuse" her and the children and "threatened to take the youngest child and leave the place."[13] When she protested, he "became wild with rage," "threatened" her with "bodily harm," and began to "kick and destroy the furniture by setting fire" to it. Furthermore, when she protested this action, he "thrust" her upon a sofa, held her there, and "attempted to pour coal oil from a can upon her and to set fire to her clothing, and would have succeed [ed] . . . had it not been for the assistance of other persons."[14] Then the defendant, the charges continued, declared he would "kill" her and their children and "ran to get a gun," whereupon Annie fled with the children into the darkness, "and wandered on the prairie all that night in great terror." Because of having to remain out all night without warmth or sufficient clothing, she and the children "became sick and suffered great agony, both mental and physical." After Annie and the children had fled into the night, Barney Riggs, Annie also charged, had "destroyed a great portion of their household goods, shot holes into the house, and into her hat, and otherwise destroyed" her things.

In this petition, Annie again pointed out that she had no means by which she could support herself and their children, that her husband had told the shopkeepers in town not to give her any credit, and that to keep her children alive she was having to turn to friends and relatives. This time Annie estimated the family worth at about $25,000, considerably more than in the previous June. The community property consisted of about 800 horses, 300 head of cattle, household goods, buggies and hacks, a piano, a grass lease of seventy sections of land, of which twenty sections were only two miles from Fort Stockton and the

[13] The children at that time were Barney, age nine, Ernest, age five, Eva, age four, and George, age two.

[14] Many years later, Ernest Riggs stated: "And, I as a little kid (five years old) picked up a rock and made Daddy stop trying to put Mamma on that coal oil can and set it on fire."

other fifty fourteen miles distant, where they had "a good five room house, wells, tanks and wind mills, . . . and one house and lot or lots situated in the town of Pecos."[15] At the time of her marriage to Barney, Annie claimed, she had owned 700 head of sheep and 20 horses; all these, her husband had sold and had invested the proceeds in other stock. She was unable to list the property that Barney Riggs owned at the time of their marriage.

In his reply, Barney Riggs denied many of the allegations, particularly those that Annie was destitute and that he was an unfit father. The community property was much less than she stated, his personal property was much more, and Annie's personal property was less. Furthermore, he wanted custody of the children, and he wanted all community property for their "maintenance and education." Should the plaintiff win custody of the children, Riggs wanted to make periodic payments toward their support and education through a third party designated by the court.

The divorce was granted on March 27, 1901. Barney Riggs did well. He was awarded the leased land, the place in Pecos City, most of the livestock, and all of the household goods at the ranch house near Fort Stockton, except the piano, which had belonged to Annie before the marriage. Annie also got 125 head of cattle and forty horses, and a cash settlement by which Barney was to make periodic payments toward the support of the children until 1904, totaling $2,000. The trustee was to be J. R. (Buck) Chadborn, who was married to Annie's daughter (by her prior husband), Nita Johnson Chadborn.

The trustee arrangement did not work. In March, 1902, Chadborn told the court, "I want out and you get somebody else." On the following day, Annie, through her attorney Walter Gillis, a former district judge, filed a petition that declared she had received no part of the payments, Chadborn had refused to act as the trustee, she and her children were consequently destitute, and she knew of no one, other than herself, who could serve as the trustee.

In his rebuttal, two days later, Barney Riggs declared that the court had no jurisdiction over the matter because there had been no final judgment in the divorce case, that within ten days after the di-

---

[15] Doug Adams states that the "good five-room house" occupied by the Riggs family was located west of town, approximately at the present site of the Firestone Test Center.

vorce he had tried unsuccessfully to give Chadborn $500, the amount of the initial payment, that he had never been able to get Chadborn to accept any payment, and that he objected to Annie's being named the trustee because she was not capable of taking care of either the money or the children.[16] Less than two weeks later, the conflict ended abruptly when Buck Chadborn killed Barney Riggs.

There had been considerable ill feeling between the two, because Buck had sided with his mother-in-law. After Buck resigned as the trustee, the ill feelings between the two grew even worse. At the time of the shooting, on April 7, 1902, Buck and Nita Chadborn lived in what is now known as the Oldest House in Fort Stockton, located southwest of the courthouse and behind the old schoolhouse. According to another of Annie Riggs's daughters, Myrtle Johnson Lewis, Buck Chadborn parked his buggy and team in front of his home to pick up his mother-in-law and some of the children. Barney, looking out from Mart Adams' nearby saloon, did not like the idea and started for the Chadborn home. Bob Neighbors, the sheriff, hoping to prevent trouble, talked Riggs into leaving his pistol in the saloon. Myrtle Lewis, who was standing near the buggy, years later stated that when he came near Riggs "started remonstrating and shaking his finger at Buck. He then reached back to get a handkerchief or something. Evidently afraid Barney was reaching to pull his six-shooter, Buck grabbed his gun from the seat of the buggy and shot Barney." At the sound of the shot, the team ran away, and Buck hurried to retrieve it. "Barney staggered down into the arroyo," between the Chadborn home and the schoolhouse, she continued, "and then barely got up and out. . . . He lay down there, mortally wounded."

A number of the young pupils at the nearby schoolhouse heard the shooting and witnessed at least a part of the scene. Theodora (Theo) Young, about twelve years of age, was seated in a privy when she heard the shot. She ran outside and saw the wounded man staggering toward the arroyo.[17] Little Barney, Jr., rushed to the arroyo and

[16] Minutes of the 83rd District Court in Pecos County, March, 1902, 2:63–69, 125–132; Josephine Buchanan, 1953, account of the killing of Barney Riggs, to Bill Riggs, copy in possession of Clayton Williams.

[17] Myrtle Lewis, oral statement, to Clayton Williams; Mary Winfield McComb, oral statement, to Gaines Kincaid, as told to her by her mother, the late Theodora Young Winfield.

found his father bleeding profusely but still conscious. Knowing that he was dying, Barney, Sr., made his son promise to revenge his killing. (More than one of Barney's sons eventually considered this idea but never followed through.) Annie Riggs had her former husband carried to the Koehler Hotel, where he died on the following day.

In 1953, Josephine Buchanan, who was then the district clerk in Fort Stockton, at the request of Bill Riggs, a grandson of Barney Riggs, Sr., wrote the details of the shooting as she had heard them from her mother, Mrs. J. L. Moore, and her brother, Elmer Moore. Barney, she wrote, had been trying to get Annie to come back to him. He hated Chadborn, and on the day prior to the murder he had "whipped Buck Chadborn with his walking cane at the livery stable," located just north of the courthouse. Barney, Josephine Buchanan continued, "had rheumatism badly and used a cane. . . ." Riggs "perhaps never thought that Buck would use a gun." At the time, Chadborn was loading Mrs. Riggs's belongings into a hack hitched to a span of mules to take her to the ranch. The Buchanan version claims that the shooting occurred in front of the house owned by Matilde Peña (which was afterward lived in by the Peñas), "back of the schoolhouse" and southwest of the courthouse. It was during recess, and Mrs. Buchanan's brother Elmer and sister Mary heard the shot and "saw Barney Riggs fall." The startled mules broke and ran around the schoolhouse. "Buck circled and came back to where Barney was lying. Barney [had] walked over . . . to the house where Mrs. Riggs was living . . . and walked up to the hack and pulled back his walking cane to hit Buck. . . . Buck was in the hack alone and he had his loaded gun beside him and shot Barney near the heart." Riggs, Mrs. Moore recalled, with his finger stuck in the wound, "bleeding and cursing Buck," staggered more than one hundred feet to the edge of the arroyo back of the schoolhouse. Riggs was taken to the hotel, later purchased by Mrs. Riggs, where he died, "cursing Buck to the last."[18]

Annie Riggs took over the supervision of her former husband's funeral. Since there was no priest available, she got Will A. Hadden, the deputy county clerk, to read a few verses from a Protestant hymnal as the last rites at the graveside.[19] In September, the grand jury indicted

---

[18] Buchanan to Bill Riggs, 1953.
[19] Will A. Hadden, oral statement, to Clayton Williams.

Buck Chadborn for second-degree murder. The case was transferred to Alpine, where Buck was tried and acquitted.[20]

Barney Riggs died intestate. His estate consisted of 600 horses and mules, eight jacks, forty head of cattle, one wagon, one buggy, harness gear, a mowing machine and rake, household effects, 1,000 shares of the Pecos Valley Standard Oil Company, one saddle, a Winchester shotgun, a Winchester carbine, and a considerable amount of land (either owned or leased).[21]

Annie Stella Frazer Johnson Riggs is remembered for her strength, her endurance, her devotion to the Catholic faith, and her great love for and loyalty to her children and grandchildren, of whom she raised several. She purchased the Koehler Hotel, renamed it the Riggs Hotel, and continued to run it as long as she was physically able. By frugal management and hard work she saved and invested in ranchland, which eventually produced oil and gas for the benefit of her heirs. The stalwart pioneer died on May 17, 1931.[22]

Another pioneer whose last years were tragic and pathetic was Robert N. Baker. Baker, who had been involved in A. J. Royal's trouble at Koehler's store in 1892, on June 8, 1898, killed Rosario Ureta in front of Koehler's store. According to the victim's son, Cosme, his father was killed by a crazy man in a dispute over a laundry bill. For some reason, Baker was not indicted until March of 1899. Shipton Parke, G. T. Stephenson, and Morgan Livingston went on his bond but were released in December. In Eagle Pass, on May 28, 1900, a jury was selected, and Baker was found not guilty—all in one day. Once a small boy, Clayton Williams, while looking over the family adobe-wall backyard fence, saw a man fall from his wagon seat and the wheels of his wagon run over him. He was told afterward that the man was Baker, that he was drunk at the time, and that his head was badly injured in the accident.

Acting on a complaint filed by Mary Valentine Baker on April 23, 1903, against her husband, a Pecos County jury concluded that R. N. Baker, age thirty-nine, was of unsound mind, that insanity ran in his family, that the present attack had lasted for nine days, and that he should be confined to a lunatic asylum. Thus, on July 18, Baker was

[20] Buchanan to Bill Riggs, 1953.
[21] Pecos County, Probate Minutes, 2:131–132.
[22] Pecos County, Death Records, 1:71.

sent to the State Hospital at Terrell, near Dallas. He was discharged in 1905, readmitted in 1906 after a new complaint by his wife, then, in 1908, he was discharged, readmitted, and discharged, all within the year.[23]

This narrative cannot be ended without at least a brief account of what happened to a number of other pioneers of the Fort Stockton area who have been mentioned prominently. W. P. Matthews, who served as a commissioner and during the Royal era as the county clerk, moved to Sanderson and bought Charlie Wilson's old saloon from the Reagan brothers.[24] W. H. Mansfield, the "would-be Lemon squeezer," helped to organize Terrell County, and a street in Sanderson is named for him. After working for various cow outfits in Pecos County, he established his own spread in 1895 and the next year married Mary Jane Lemons. Mansfield retired from ranching in 1927 and moved with his wife to Uvalde, where he died in 1934. Mary Jane died at the old Mansfield ranch in 1944 and was buried beside her husband in the Sanderson cemetery. Mary's father, John H. Lemons, died in Brewster County in 1898.[25] George C. Miller, who was allegedly assaulted by A. J. Royal during the tumultuous period in 1894, built one of the largest ranches in Brewster County. He retired in 1916 and settled in Marathon.[26] Howell Johnson, the young county attorney who left the Fort Stockton area for a while because of Sheriff Royal's threats, eventually became one of the most popular and respected men in West Texas. In 1898, he married Violet Eudaly, with whom he had four sons. After serving as county attorney for twelve years, he entered private practice. Then, in 1912, he was elected county judge, an office to which he was reelected several times. During his lifetime, he acquired a considerable amount of land and an irrigated farm near Fort Stockton.[27] F. W. Young, the noble pioneer who settled in the Pecos County area long before most of those involved in the feuds, died on November 12, 1904. Sheriff R. B. Neighbors, who was married to Young's daugther Aileen, died eleven days later.[28]

[23] Pecos County, Probate Minutes, 2:165–166; O. D. Flemster, Fort Worth, to John Garza, Fort Stockton, August 28, 1972, copy in possession of Clayton Williams.

[24] Downie, *Terrell County*, pp. 37, 145, 433, 514.

[25] Ibid., pp. 495, 506–507.

[26] *New Encyclopedia of Texas*, p. 1269.

[27] Ibid., p. 3488.

[28] Pecos County, Probate Minutes, 2:297, 317.

Shipton Parke married Emma Shelton, from Illinois, on February 26, 1896.[29] After working for some years in the cow business with R. L. Anderson and the Livingston brothers, Parke and the Livingstons established their own ranch. This partnership was dissolved in the late 1890s, but Parke continued to operate and develop his ranch business. At the time of his death, on January 3, 1916, he was president of the First State Bank in Fort Stockton, vice-president and a member of the Board of Directors of the Rooney Mercantile Company, and in various capacities associated with other enterprises. Parke died from a malignancy of the right eyelid, and his mourning friends had an impressive funeral ceremony for him. According to one of his biographers, Parke had "an unsullied reputation for business integrity and for fidelity. . . ," was a devout member and generous supporter of the Presbyterian Church, was a devotee of the outdoor sports, particularly baseball, and above all else loved his home and family. Shipton and Emma Parke were the parents of four children.[30]

The lives of the Livingston brothers, Herman Butz, Taylor Stephenson, the Macdonald girls, and the Rooneys cannot easily be separated because of intermarriage. Mrs. Annie E. Votaw Macdonald Stephenson, who ran a boarding house at the old Heid place (in recent time, the Achterburg building and the Boy Scout headquarters), died on February 27, 1895, and left Taylor Stephenson with two stepdaughters, Essie Macdonald, 19, and Jennie Macdonald, 17.[31] Within two months after their mother's death, both girls were married. Essie became the wife of James Rooney on April 22, 1895, and on the following day, Jennie married Morgan Livingston. Both ceremonies were performed by the Reverend William B. Bloys, who, a few years earlier, had founded the annual Bloys Camp Meeting.[32] Before her marriage, Essie taught school at the Rooney farm, just north of Fort Stockton. Young Will, one of the students, apparently was unaware that his teacher was being courted by his brother, James. During one Christmas season, mischievous Will, to relieve the classroom boredom, tossed a whole string of firecrackers into the fireplace. Pandemonium reigned

[29] Pecos County, Marriage License Records, 2:74. Judge O. W. Williams performed the ceremony.
[30] Clarence R. Wharton, *Texas under Many Flags*, 5:169–170.
[31] Document #15, Pecos County, Probate Minutes, 1:226, 227.
[32] Pecos County, Marriage License Records, 2:65.

for a few moments. As one explosion succeeded another, live coals and ashes showered the room, and teacher and pupils dived for cover. Later, when James asked who had done the dirty deed, young Will admitted his guilt, but his emulation of George Washington did not save him from the "darndest dressing-down" a kid brother ever received. Years later, Will told his son Bernard, "I should have known that James had more serious intentions concerning Essie than that small firecracker incident."[33] On May 13, 1905, a decade after the Macdonald sisters were married, Taylor Stephenson filed his will in Pecos County, and six weeks later, on June 29, he died in Santa Ana, California.[34]

James and Essie Rooney were the parents of six children. In his relatively short life, James became one of the most prominent businessmen in Pecos County. A large part of his business was in partnership with his brother-in-law, Herman H. Butz. Butz had married James's sister, Agnes Rooney, in 1898, and they became the parents of three sons and one daughter. Starting out together by buying Koehler's store, the two brothers-in-law remained partners for more than thirty years. The firm of Rooney and Butz was later incorporated into the Rooney Mercantile Company, a new building was constructed on Main Street, and other partners, including Shipton Parke, joined the business. The company erected the Rooney Office Building across the street from its mercantile building.

Rooney and Butz contributed the land at the corner of the present Water and First streets and a portion of the building for the first Protestant church in Fort Stockton. They also donated land to the Kansas City, Mexico and Orient Railway Company to aid the construction of its line into Fort Stockton, but this contribution backfired; the company subdivided the donated land into town lots and laid the rails into that area instead of into the older part of town. In time, the partners were also hurt by their practice of extending credit to stockmen, who too often failed to pay their debts. The partners were instrumental in establishing a banking system in Fort Stockton. As previously mentioned, the area's first "bank" had been the Koehler store, but that gentle German, Herman Koehler, the uncle of Herman Butz, "banked" only for the convenience of his customers. James Rooney was president

[33] Bernard Rooney, son of the late Will Rooney, oral statement while attending a reunion in Fort Stockton, April, 1977.

[34] Pecos County, Probate Minutes, 2:321, 324.

of the First State Bank for a number of years. Butz served as its cashier until 1914 and thereafter as a member of the board of directors until it was sold in 1924. Both men were instrumental in bringing the first telephone to Pecos County.

Butz became even more successful in real estate and insurance. For many years, he was the very able Pecos County treasurer, he was several times president of the Fort Stockton school board, and he was instrumental in bringing the first cotton gin to the county. He is best known, however, as a county judge of Pecos County.[35]

When only nineteen years old, Frank Rooney became the district clerk of Pecos County and discharged well the duties of that office, even though he was simultaneously operating a farm. He was still in his early twenties at the time of his feud with Royal. In May, 1895, in Hope, New Mexico, he married Mary Sanders, with whom in time he had three children. After operating the family farm for a decade, he turned it over to his brother Will and moved to his own irrigated farm seven miles northwest of Fort Stockton. In 1906, however, he moved back into town in order for his children to be close to school. In 1902, Frank Rooney was elected county judge, but for some unknown reason he resigned after serving only five months. Thereafter, he again served as the county and district clerk until he retired in December, 1920, altogether about twenty-six years. As far as his fellow citizens were concerned, he could have served indefinitely, but his health had failed. Afterwards, in pursuit of health, he moved to San Diego, California, and then to Inspiration, Arizona, where he died on April 24, 1926. His funeral, in Stockton, was one of the largest and most impressive ever held in the region.[36]

Previous references to Jim and Morgan Livingston have been numerous, but these have not adequately told the story of these two remarkable pioneers. As previously narrated, both had been cowboys with one of the large ranch outfits, and afterward they had their own ranch. On December 23, 1896, James Archibald Livingston was married in Fort Stockton to Willie Maud Hobbs Dillard (a cousin of Essie

[35] *New Encyclopedia of Texas*, pp. 3433, 3647; Hugh Rooney Livingston, comp., "A Genealogical Study of the Livingston and Related Families," copy in possession of Clayton Williams; Pecos County, Deed Records, A-4:417, 7:297, and 10:141; Wharton, *Texas under Many Flags*, 5:164.

[36] Wharton, *Texas under Many Flags*, 5:173–174. Frank Rooney was survived by his wife, Mary Sanders Rooney, two sons, Vernon and Roy, and a daughter, Frankie.

and Jennie Macdonald) by Brother Bloys.[37] Early that year Livingston
had killed a sheepman at Hawthorne's store. On January 28, Pilar Durán had gone to the home of Justice of the Peace Charles A. Crosby and
reported that a sheepman named Joseph Brutinel (Butinel in some records) had been killed at Hawthorne's store as a result of a serious argument over a waterhole or spring. Many years afterward, the late H. H.
Butz said that he had been in the entrance to Hawthorne's store and
had seen the sheepman running away from Livingston. Butz shouted
and waved his arms in an effort to keep Brutinel from entering the
store. But he did enter and died shortly afterward. After hearing the
testimony of W. P. Matthews, Taylor Stephenson, Frank Rooney, and
Herman Butz, the jury concluded that Brutinel was killed by "two or
more pistol shot wounds inflicted by J. A. Livingston" and that "Joseph
Brutinel fired the first shot with a pistol at the said J. A. Livingston."[38]
People who knew Jim Livingston allowed that Brutinel virtually committed suicide when he fired the first shot and missed, since Jim could
throw a dime into the air and hit it with a pistol bullet.

During the 1890s, Jim and Morgan Livingston terminated their
employment with J. D. Houston, and they, with Shipton Parke, went
into the cow business on their own. Their main range was in the Tunas
(Escondido) Creek area. Not long afterward, the three divided their
interests, and the Livingston brothers established a new ranch farther
north and about thirty miles east of Fort Stockton. Reportedly, this was
the first ranch in Pecos County to be fenced with barbed wire. In November, 1901, Morgan moved to Wagoner, Indian Territory, where Jim
joined him the next year, leaving Hiram Stephenson in charge of their
Pecos County ranch. In Indian Territory, the brothers engaged in the
cattle business on a big scale, but unfortunately both suffered tragic
accidents, Jim's mortal. In 1909, Jim Livingston drowned near Wagoner, in northeast Oklahoma, while attempting to swim across the
Grand River with his eight-year-old son, Earl, on his back. When Jim
disappeared, Essie Rooney, who happened to be visiting there and was
the only adult present who could swim, brought Earl to safety.

Morgan had a leg crushed by the wheels of a railroad stock car. He

[37] Pecos County, Marriage License Records, 2:76.
[38] H. H. Butz, oral statements, to Clayton Williams; Pecos County, Justice Records, 1:4.

had climbed to the top of the car, lowered himself through a porthole, "tailed" up a fallen animal, climbed out of the car, and descended by the handrail to the ground, when his right foot was caught on the rail by a moving wheel of the car. His right ankle and foot were mutilated, and his right leg had to be amputated about four inches above the ankle. He eventually returned to Fort Stockton, where he ranched on a smaller scale. During his latter years, he lived with his children in El Paso until 1940 and then in Houston until his death on July 27, 1941.[39]

Among the other prominent pioneer citizens of Pecos County who have had a share of this narrative previously were three sheepmen— Charles Downie, Robert Paxton, and S. A. Purinton. Downie and his wife became the parents of two sons and two daughters. Early in the twentieth century, he turned the management of his ranch over to his son Edward and, with his wife and younger children, moved to Berkeley, California, where he bought a fine home. Charles, however, continued to spend much time in Texas; then, in October, 1927, when his health began to fail, he moved to San Antonio, where he died during the following May. At the time of his death, his ranch consisted of some 150,000 acres. During the height of his ranching career, he had run about 20,000 sheep, a few thousand goats, and approximately 2,500 Aberdeen Angus cattle, which he had introduced to his lands during the 1890s.[40]

Much less is known about Robert Paxton, who for a while had been Downie's partner. In the early 1900s, he and Purinton both sold out, and their ranches became the nucleus of the gigantic West-Pyle Cattle Company. Paxton and his wife eventually returned to his native Scotland.[41]

S. A. Purinton died on September 21, 1914. He left a wife, Jackobina Noffett Purinton; a son, Edgar R.; and a daughter, Glenn E. His estate, in real and personal property, was assessed at about half a million dollars.[42]

[39] Livingston, "Genealogical Study"; Hugh Rooney Livingston, El Paso, to Gaines Kincaid, May 30 and July 9, 1977.

[40] *New Encyclopedia of Texas*, p. 1265; Downie, *Terrell County*, pp. 51, 336–339, 702.

[41] Downie, *Terrell County*, p. 575.

[42] Pecos County, Probate Minutes, 3:133, 138–139.

The best-known of all the Pecos County pioneers (except, perhaps, Judge Roy Bean), however, was Oscar Waldo Williams—surveyor, farmer, small-scale rancher, legal clerk, county judge, attorney,
and historian. Williams, the only participant in the Royal-Rooney feud
to write anything on the subject, continued to serve as county judge
until he was defeated for reelection in 1900. During the feud years,
and for some time thereafter, his small ranch and large, irrigated farm
near the Pecos River came close to bringing him to financial ruin, because farmers upstream in Loving, Reeves, and Ward counties were
not leaving enough water for his needs. Consequently, Williams returned to the occupation that earlier had gotten him through many
hard times—surveying. His surveys, sometimes alone and sometimes
in the company of state and federal geologists, centered in the Big
Bend area. Among his other accomplishments there, he helped complete the surveys that put an end to the disputes involving claims to
the rich quicksilver (mercury) area around Terlinqua. In addition to providing some income when the farm and ranch did not, the survey work
provided Williams with a vast knowledge of land values and with the
geography, folklore, and history that he afterward recorded.

Because of financial adversity, in 1903 he sent his family to his father's home in Carthage, Illinois, for about a year. During this adversity Williams started practicing law, and simultaneously Pecos County
began to show renewed signs of prosperity. Williams soon had as cli-
ents some of the leading ranchers and livestock firms of the area, many
homesteaders, and more absentee landowners than any other attorney
in Fort Stockton. In 1905, he began to buy scattered tracts of cheap
land, hoping to benefit from the investments. Not long before his
death, oil production on his land became a reality.

In the early 1940s, Judge Williams fell and suffered a concussion,
an injury from which he apparently never fully recovered. At age
ninety, his eyes were still piercing, his complexion aglow with health,
and his walk upright, but his mind had begun to show the strains of
age. Physical deterioration followed soon, and in the Fort Stockton
hospital he developed pneumonia, lapsed into a coma, and died quietly
on October 29, 1946, at age ninety-three years and seven months.[43]

Pecos County pioneer O. W. Williams lived frugally and contrib-

[43] S. D. Myres, *Pioneer Surveyor—Frontier Lawyer: The Personal Narrative of
O. W. Williams, 1877–1902*, p. 317. O. W. Williams was preceded in death by his wife,

uted liberally to churches, public improvements, and deserving students. He organized the Athletic Club of the Fort Stockton school and wrote a brochure, "To the Boys and Girls of the Fort Stockton School," that J. Frank Dobie rated as a classic.[44] While employed by the University of Texas and working with several scientists in the Big Bend area, Williams called their attention to a small habitation of the rabbit mouse, far removed from its place of origin,[45] and he identified two new varieties of ants, one of which bears his name.[46] He was an active participant in the West Texas Historical Association for many years, a life member of the Texas State Historical Association, and a thirty-second-degree Mason.

Many citizens of Fort Stockton still remember Judge Williams as an uncompromising, straight-laced, genial old gentleman with piercing, blue eyes under white, bushy brows, with a white mustache, and a face burned red from years of exposure to the West Texas sun and wind. In reminiscing, Williams once aptly penned his feeling during his last years: "When you have come to white hairs you will understand the longing with which old men look back on friends and scenes of the golden youth."[47] The quantity and quality of Williams' collections of information is probably his greatest contribution to posterity—outranking even those he made as a surveyor and as a jurist. He recorded his experiences, what he saw, and what he heard from the days of his youth, and this practice became for him in late life an absolute compulsion. His collections and writings have become essential for historians who deal with far western Texas. He realized more than most people that he lived in an age of rapid transition and that his experiences were unique, and he had the skill and talent to express that situation superbly.

We had left a people of quakers [he wrote], wearing the garments of peace and harmony; we had come among a people of war, frozen by some magic with sword in hand and armor buckled for the fray. Lance or sword or dagger peeped out from almost every bush, and where we saw a shrub without weap-

---

Sallie Wheat Williams, who died suddenly of a heart attack on August 25, 1936. The couple had five children, three sons and two daughters.

[44] J. Frank Dobie, oral statement, to Clayton Williams.

[45] Ray Williams, game warden of the Big Bend, oral statement, to Clayton Williams.

[46] O. W. Williams, oral statements, to Clayton Williams.

[47] O. W. Williams, Fort Stockton, to Jessie C. Williams, Hankow, China, March 10, 1930.

ons in sight we scrutinized it with a strong suspicion, that somewhere in its drab and russeted bosom there lurked some secret deadly missile. . . .[48]

And the experiences associated with all this he fervidly and anxiously endeavored to preserve for later generations.

[48] O. W. Williams, *The Honca Accursed* (brochure).

Bibliography

ORAL INFORMANTS

VERY few persons were formally interviewed; rather, the author, who has lived in Fort Stockton for more than eighty years, heard most informants relate the information for which they are cited at sundry (and some several) times without recording or now being able to recall the date. Approximate dates are shown where possible. All informants, unless otherwise shown, are, or were for many years, residents of Fort Stockton. Gaines Kincaid (Austin, Texas) served as a researcher for the author.

Adams, Douglas.
Arno, Fred J.
Baker, Bud.
Baker, Mrs. J. T. (1959).
Beeman, D. S.
Bentley, George, Monahans, Texas.
Black, James.
Butz, H. H.
Collins, Loreine (Mrs. Louis), Balmorhea, Texas (to Gaines Kincaid, 1977).
Cordero, Joe.
Crosby, Margaret, Austin (to Gaines Kincaid, 1977).
Dixon, Mrs. W. J. B. ("Maidie").
Dobie, J. Frank, Austin.
Dunn, Mary Ethel.
Durán, Pilar.
Durrell, L. F., San Antonio.
Frazer, George M., descendants of.
Garnett, Ermine Williams, Oklahoma City.
Gonzales, S. L.
Hadden, Will A.
Hatchette, H. L., Meridian, Mississippi.

Huelster, Sigfried.
Kelley, A. B. (Humble Oil and Refining engineer, who obtained the information from W. H. Abrams, Land Department, Texas and Pacific Railway Company).
Kimball, Mrs. Keesey, Alpine, Texas (to Gaines Kincaid, 1977).
Lewis, Myrtle.
Ligon, Earl (to Clayton Williams and others, October 29, 1977).
McComb, Mary Winfield, San Antonio (to Gaines Kincaid).
McKnight, Mrs. Marie Gene, Austin (to Gaines Kincaid).
Miller, Mr. and Mrs. Keesey, Fort Davis, Texas.
Primera, Joe.
Reed, Wade.
Riggs, Barney, Jr.
Riggs, Ernest.
Riggs, Lee.
Rooney, Bernard, Carlsbad, New Mexico (April, 1977).
Rooney, Roy, McCamey, Texas.
Rooney, W. P.
Scott, Sam.
Stone, Charlie (who obtained the information from William Louis Kingston).
Teel, Mrs. Maurice Owen, Junction, Texas (to Gaines Kincaid, 1977).
Ten Eyck, Pete (to Gaines Kincaid, January, 1977).
Whetstone, A. M. (ca. 1940).
Williams, O. W. (the author's father, who related his experiences at various times over a period of many years).
Williams, Ray.
Wyatt, Frederica Burt, Junction, Texas (to Gaines Kincaid, 1977).

LETTERS

Unless otherwise shown, each of the following letters was to and is in possession of Clayton Williams.

Butz, Herman H., Fort Stockton, Texas, to Emma Butz, October 29, 1894 (In possession of Maidie Dixon, Fort Stockton, Texas).
Byrne, J. J., Ysleta, Texas, to Mrs. J. J. (Lilly) Byrne, Fort Worth, Texas, August 2, 1880 (In J. J. Byrne biographical papers, Eugene C. Barker Texas History Center, University of Texas, Austin).
Coffer, Mrs. Paul, Lovington, New Mexico, April 3, 1967.
Conner, Truman H., Fort Worth, Texas, to O. W. Williams, Fort Stockton, Texas, n.d.
Durrell, L. F., San Antonio, Texas, February 26 and April 30, 1967.

Flemster, O. D., Fort Worth, Texas, to John Garza, Fort Stockton, August 28, 1972 (Original in possession of John Garza, copy held by Clayton Williams).

Gage, John C., Kansas City, Mo., February 26, 1964.

Hubbs, Barney, Pecos, Texas, July 11, 1977.

Larson, Mary, Lowell, Arizona, December 16, 1959.

Lewis, George, Elyria, Ohio, to Howell Johnson, Fort Stockton, Texas, December 12, 1929.

Livingston, Hugh Rooney, El Paso, Texas, to Gaines Kincaid, May 30 and July 9, 1977.

Mason, Fay Tankersley, Colorado Springs, Colorado, April 14, 1965.

Miller, Gaynell, El Paso, Texas, November 4, 1974.

Paxton, Jesse A., County Fife, Scotland, to Mrs. Herbert A. Smith, Lafayette, California, October 29, 1951.

Reeves, David R., General Land Office, Austin, Texas, November 22, 1974.

Sieker, Ruby (Mrs. Gay), Menard, Texas (a biographical sketch of Edward A. Sieker, February 16, 1977).

Smith, Mrs. Victor, San Angelo, Texas, March 17, 1971.

Stephenson, Christine, Santa Ana, California, to Gaines Kincaid, March 3, 1977.

White, Wm. P., Fort Davis, Texas, to Dr. W. E. East, Hallettsville, Texas, August 24, 1861 (In Archives, University of Texas, Austin).

Williams, O. W., Fort Stockton, Texas, to George H. Lewis, Elyria, Ohio, January 13, 1930, and March 1, 1933.

———, to Jesse C. Williams, Hankow, China, June 3, 1925, March 10, 1930, and September 6, 1934.

———, to J. W. Ballard, December 8, 1930.

———, to Dr. T. D. Wooten, President of the University of Texas, Austin, December 1, 1886 (In File 1594, General Land Office, Austin, Texas).

UNPUBLISHED MATERIALS

A great deal of primary material is contained in two voluminous collections held by the author in Fort Stockton, Texas. The Clayton Williams Papers include interviews, letters, short unpublished manuscripts, and notes relating to Fort Stockton and the surrounding area. The O. W. (Oscar Waldo) Williams Papers, gathered by the author's father, contain addresses, autobiographical sketches, business records and notes, documents, essays about local birds and animals, historical articles, journals and accounts of travel, memoirs and reminiscences, narrative accounts (handwritten and typewritten copies) of Sheriff A. J. Royal and the Texas Rangers in Pecos County, and more than twenty pamphlets (some unpublished) on a variety of subjects. Selected items from these two collections are included in the list below.

Adams, William C. Papers. In possession of Mrs. Brawley Adams, Balmorhea, Texas.

Alvarez, Maximo. Account of O. W. Williams–Maximo Alvarez incident, November 8, 1892. Transcribed by Waldo Williams, Fort Stockton, Texas, n.d. In Clayton Williams Papers.

Bliss, Zenas R. "Reminiscences." 5 vols. Eugene C. Barker Texas History Center, University of Texas, Austin.

Brewster County, Texas. Deed Records. Vol. 1. Brewster County Courthouse, Alpine, Texas.

Buchanan, Josephine. Account of killing of Barney Riggs, to Bill Riggs. Fort Stockton, Texas, 1953. Copy in Clayton Williams Papers.

Carlson, Paul H. "William R. Shafter: Military Commander in the American West." Ph.D. dissertation, Texas Tech University, 1973.

Dixon, Mrs. Bill ("Maidie"). An account of some early settlers in Fort Stockton, Texas. Fort Stockton, n.d. Copy in Clayton Williams Papers.

Elliott, Dr. George W. File. Archives, Tax Assessor's Office, Upton County Courthouse, Rankin, Texas.

Garnett, Ermine Williams. An account of personal experiences on the O. W. Williams Pecos County farm, n.d. Copy in Clayton Williams Papers.

Grant, George F. An account of a trip made by George F. Grant across the Trans-Pecos country in 1880. Fort Worth, Texas, August 31, 1925. O. W. Williams Papers, in possession of Clayton Williams.

Gray, Ronald N. "Edmund J. Davis: Radical Republican and Reconstruction Governor of Texas." Ph.D. dissertation, Texas Tech University, 1976.

Kimble County, Texas. Deed Records. Vols. A, 1, 2, 4, 5, 6, 8. Kimble County Courthouse, Junction, Texas.

———. District Court Minutes. Cases 347 and 348, Vol. 1. Kimble County Courthouse, Junction, Texas.

Kinder, L. S. "A Chapter in the Life of Col. Charles Goodnight." Plainview, Texas, typewritten, n.d. O. W. Williams Papers, in possession of Clayton Williams.

Livingston, Hugh Rooney, comp. "A Genealogical Study of the Livingston and Related Families." Undated manuscript. Clayton Williams Papers.

"Outrages and Indian Raids in Presidio Co. from June 1, 1879, to June 1, 1880." Adjutant General's Papers, Texas, Record Group 401, Archives, Texas State Library, Austin.

Pease, E. M. Collection. Austin Public Library, Austin.

Pease, Governor Elisha Marshall. Papers. Archives, Texas State Library, Austin.

Pecos County, Texas. Records. Pecos County Courthouse, Fort Stockton:
Brand Book, No. 1 and Vol. 1.
Death Records, Vol. 1.

Deed Records, Vols. A-2, A-3, A-4, 1-5, 7, 10, 18, and 20.

Deeds of Trust, Vol. 1.

Election Returns, 1892 (Vol. 1).

Grand Jury Records, Files No. 158 and 159, September 17 and 22, 1894.

Irrigation Records, Vol. 1.

Justice Records, 1892, 1893, 1894.

Land Patent Records, Vols. 2 (pts. 53 and 731), 17 (pts. 537 and 538), and 35 (pt. 153).

Marriage License Records, Vols. 1 and 2.

Minutes of the Commissioners Court, 1875, 1876, 1880, 1881, 1882, 1884, 1885, 1886, 1888, 1889, 1892, 1894, 1912, and 1913.

Minutes of the District Court, 1880 (Vol. 1, cases 35–39), March, 1894, September, 1894 (Vol. 1), and March, 1902.

Probate Minutes, Vols. 1–3.

Sketches, 19, 19½, 21, 25, 27.

Survey Records, A7, C2, C3, C4, D2, and D3.

Tax Rolls, 1880.

Warrant, No. 10, August 21, 1894, Red File #62.

———. Election Returns, 1882. Records of the Secretary of State, Archives, Texas State Library, Austin.

———. Records, 1872, 1875, 1876. Records of the Secretary of State, Archives, Texas State Library, Austin.

———. Sketches 19 and 27, Pecos County. General Land Office, Austin.

"Pecos Palisades Tracts" (map). Kansas City, Mo. [?]: U.S. Mexican Trust Company, ca. 1911. Copy in O. W. Williams Papers.

Presidio County, Texas. Election Returns, 1869. Records of the Secretary of State, Archives, Texas State Library, Austin.

Reeves County, Texas. Marriage Records. Vol. 1. Reeves County Courthouse, Pecos, Texas.

———. Deed Records. Vol. 2. Reeves County Courthouse, Pecos, Texas.

———. Irrigation Records. Vol. 1. Reeves County Courthouse, Pecos, Texas.

———. Minutes of the Commissioners Court. November, 1884, December, 1888, and Vol. 2, 1908. Reeves County Courthouse, Pecos, Texas.

———. Minutes of the District Court. March, 1894, Vol. 1 Reeves County Courthouse, Pecos, Texas.

Roberts, Dick. "Heirship of Mrs. H. M. (Hannah) Riggs." Midland, Texas, n.d. Copy in Clayton Williams Papers.

Rooney, Frank. "Life of Francis Rooney." Copy in Clayton Williams Papers.

Sieker, Ruby (Mrs. Gay). Biographical sketch of Edward A. Sieker. Menard, Texas, February 16, 1977. In Clayton Williams Papers.

Smith, Octavia Downie. "Charles Downie." 6 pp., typewritten, n.d. Copy in Clayton Williams Papers.

Texas. Militia. Muster Rolls, 1861. Archives, Texas State Library, Austin.

Texas Adjutant General's Papers. This file includes papers relating to the battle with the Kickapoo Indians at Dove Creek, January and February, 1865, and for Texas Rangers correspondence, muster rolls, monthly returns, orders, payrolls, reports, and service records, May–July, 1880, and 1890–1896. Record Group 401, Archives, Texas State Library, Austin.

Thompson, Jerry Don. "Henry Hopkins Sibley: Military Inventor on the Texas Frontier." Paper presented at meeting of West Texas Historical Association, Abilene, Texas, April 7, 1973.

Throckmorton, Governor James Webb. Papers. Archives, Texas State Library, Austin.

Upton County, Texas. George W. Elliott File. Archives, Assessor's Office, Upton County Courthouse, Rankin, Texas.

U.S. Court of Claims. Indian Depredation Case Records. Claim No. 2626 (J. D. Hoy). Records of the United States Court of Claims, Record Group 123, National Archives, Washington, D.C.

U.S. Department of the Interior. Bureau of the Census. "Eighth Census of the United States, 1860. Population. Texas." National Archives, Washington, D.C. Microcopy U58C, T355.

———. "Eleventh Census of the United States, 1890. Special Schedule Enumerating Union Veterans and Widows of Union Veterans of the Civil War." National Archives, Washington, D.C.

U.S. Department of War. Department of Texas. Letters Received. Records of the Adjutant General's Office (Main Series, 1871–1880), Record Group 94, National Archives, Washington, D. C. Microcopy 666.

———. Letters Received. Records of the Adjutant General's Office, Record Group 94, National Archives, Washington, D.C.

———. Lieutenant Colonel Thomas Hunt, "Journal," 1868. Office of the Chief of Engineers, Q 154, Record Group 77, National Archives, Washington, D.C.

———. Military Division of the Missouri. Letters Received (1879–1880). Records of the Adjutant General's Office, Record Group 94, National Archives, Washington, D.C.

———. Post Medical [Surgeon's] Reports. Records of the Adjutant General's Office, Record Group 94, National Archives, Washington, D.C. Microcopy 489:
Fort Clark, Texas, December, 1873, June, 1881, and 1882;
Fort Davis, Texas, May, 1872, and May, 1876;
Fort Quitman, Texas, August, 1868–December, 1869;
Fort Stockton, Texas, April, 1859–June, 1886 (no returns April, 1861–June, 1867), Books, 362–363.

———. Records of the Quartermaster General (Consolidated File), Record Group 92, National Archives, Washington, D.C.

———. Records of United States Army Commands, Record Group 98, National Archives, Washington, D.C.

——— Regimental Returns, Twenty-fourth Infantry. Records of the Adjutant

General's Office, Record Group 94, National Archives, Washington, D.C. Microcopy 665, Roll 245.

————. Returns from the United States Military Posts, 1800–1916. Records of the Adjutant General's Office, Record Group 94, National Archives, Washington, D.C. Microcopy 617:

Fort Chadbourne, Texas, August, 1867;

Fort Clark, Texas, June, 1878–December, 1881;

Fort Concho, Texas, October–December, 1869;

Fort Davis, Texas, August and September, 1868;

Fort Inge, Texas, September, 1867;

Fort McKavett, Texas, October and November, 1869;

Fort Quitman, Texas, January, 1867;

Fort Stockton, Texas, April, 1859–June, 1886 (no returns April, 1861–June, 1867), Rolls 1229, 1230.

————. Victorio Papers, August 14, 1880. Records of the United States Army Continental Commands, Record Group 393, National Archives, Washington, D.C.

Walker, Mr. and Mrs. John. Biographical Sketch of James Walker. Midland, Texas, n.d. Copy in Clayton Williams Papers.

Wedemeyer, W. G. (Captain). Diary (entries from December, 1883, to June, 1885). 4 vols. Marcus Whitman College Library, Walla Walla, Washington.

Werner, Emma Heid. "Memoirs of Emma Werner, Oldest Daughter of Wilhelmina Doz Grumbein and Joseph Heid, Born in San Antonio." Undated manuscript in possession of Mrs. Berte Haigh, Midland, Texas.

Young, F. W., and family. "Familien Register." Family Bible. In possession of Mrs. Asher McComb, San Antonio, Texas; partial copy in Clayton Williams Papers.

Young, Mrs. M. L. Death Certificate. Texas State Health Department, Austin.

NEWSPAPERS AND PERIODICALS

Army and Navy Journal, October 10, 1868–June 7, 1873.

Austin Republican, April and July, 1867; June 16, 1869.

Dallas Herald, March and April, 1867; September 4, 1869; August 15, 1874; August 11, 1881; July 9, 1885.

Democratic Statesman (Austin), August 16, September 29, and December 8, 1874.

Denison Daily News, April 14 and June 21, 1874.

El Paso Herald, May–June, 1915; March 17, 1923.

El Paso Herald-Post, January 25 and February 13, 1869.

El Paso Times, October, 1894; June 29, 1962.

Fort Stockton Pioneer, September, 1908; May 12, 1922; May 27, 1928; August 8, 1931; May 27, 1938; December 16, 1954; April 5, 1956; November 15, 1962; November 13, 1977.

Fort Worth Record, July 24, 1904.

Galveston Daily News, March 29, 1867.

Galveston News, July 19 and October 21, 1873; January 4, 1874; May 20 and November 30, 1877; June 28, 1878.

Herald (San Antonio), March, 1866–February, 1879. Frequently entitled *Daily Herald.*

Houston Telegraph, March 14, 1865; January 7 and 21, 1870; April 27, 1871.

New York Times, January 9, 1878.

Pioneer News-Observer (Kerrville), December, 1972.

Rio Grande, March, 1912.

San Antonio Express, January, 1868–October, 1880; July 8, 1885; September 27 and 28, 1903; February 14, 1904; May 20, 1906; August 30, 1908. Frequently entitled *Daily Express.*

San Antonio Light, January 4, 1941.

Southern Intelligencer (Austin), April 26, 1865.

Sports Illustrated, August, 1955.

Standard Times (San Angelo), November 30, 1930; August 29, 1954; October 6, 1957; January 26 and September 27, 1964; January 10, 1965; January 25, 1970; October 22, 1974.

State Gazette (Austin), June 12, 1852; March 9, 1861; August 9, 1869. Frequently entitled *Texas State Gazette.*

Texas State Journal (Austin), February 13, 1870; April 22, 1871.

BOOKS AND ARTICLES

Almada, Francisco R. *La Revolución en el Estado de Chihuahua.* Chihuahua, Mexico: Talleres Gráficos de la Nación, 1964.

American Heritage Civil War Chronology. New York: American Heritage Publishing Co., 1960.

Armes, George Augustus. *Ups and Downs of an Army Officer.* Washington, D.C., 1900.

Banta, William, and J. W. Caldwell. *Twenty-seven Years on the Texas Frontier.* Revised by L. G. Park. Council Hill, Okla., 1933.

Bartholomew, Ed. *Biographical Album of Western Gunfighters.* Houston: Frontier Press of Texas, 1958.

———. *Jesse Evans, a Texas Hide-Burner.* Houston: Frontier Press of Texas, 1955.

Baylor, George Wythe. *John Robert Baylor: Confederate Governor of Arizona.* Edited by Odie B. Faulk. Tucson: Arizona Pioneers' Historical Society, 1966.

Biggers, Don H. "From Cattle Range to Cotton Patch." *Frontier Times* 21, no. 2 (November, 1943): 61–76.

———. "Jim Downs' Tramp across the Plains." *Frontier Times* 5, no. 7 (April, 1928): 312–315.

Branda, Eldon Stephen, ed. *The Handbook of Texas: A Supplement.* Vol. 3. Austin: Texas State Historical Association, 1976.

Broaddus, J. Morgan. *The Legal Heritage of El Paso.* El Paso: Texas Western College Press, 1963.

Bush, Ira J. *Gringo Doctor.* Caldwell, Idaho: Caxton Printers, 1939.

Butler, Grace Lowe. "General Bullis: Friend of the Frontier." *Frontier Times* 12, no. 8 (May, 1935): 358–362.

Carter, Robert G. *The Old Sergeant's Story.* New York: F. H. Hitchcock, 1926.

Casey, Clifford B. *Mirages, Mysteries and Reality: Brewster County, Texas; The Big Bend of the Rio Grande.* Hereford, Tex.: Pioneer Book Publishers, 1972.

Conkling, Roscoe P., and Margaret B. Conkling. *The Butterfield Overland Mail, 1857–1869.* 3 vols. Glendale, Calif.: Arthur H. Clark Company, 1947.

Cook, James H. *Fifty Years on the Old Frontier.* Norman, Okla.: University of Oklahoma Press, 1957.

Couch, Josephine. "At the Ruins of Old Fort Lancaster." *Pioneer Magazine of Texas* 4 (November, 1923): 20.

Cox, James. *Historical and Biographical Record of the Cattle Industry and the Cattlemen of Texas and Adjacent Territory.* 2 vols. St. Louis, Mo.: Woodward and Tiernan Printing Co., 1895. Reprint. New York: Antiquarian Press, 1959.

Crimmins, M. L. "Fort Lancaster, Crockett County, Texas." *Frontier Times* 10, no. 5 (February, 1933): 196–198.

———. "General Mackenzie and Fort Concho." *West Texas Historical Association Year Book* 10 (1934): 16–31.

———. "The Mescalero Apaches." *Frontier Times* 8, no. 12 (September, 1931): 551–561.

Davis, W. W. H. *El Gringo: Or New Mexico and Her People.* New York: Harper & Brothers, 1857.

De Long, Sidney R. *The History of Arizona.* San Francisco: Whitaker and Ray Co., 1905.

Denham, Claude. "Frontier Problems and Amusements in Crockett County." *West Texas Historical Association Year Book* 9 (1933): 35–47.

Dethloff, Henry C. *A Centennial History of Texas A&M University, 1876–1976.* 2 vols. College Station: Texas A&M University Press, 1975.

Downie, Alice Evans, ed. *Terrell County, Texas: Its Past—Its People.* Sanderson, Tex.: Terrell County Historical Commission, 1978.

Duke, J. K. "Bad Men and Peace Officers of the Southwest." *West Texas Historical Association Year Book* 8 (1932): 51–61.

Duncan, John Thomas. "The Settlement of Hall County." *West Texas Historical Association Year Book* 18 (1942): 72–76.

Dunn, Robert W. "The History of Loving County, Texas." *West Texas Historical Association Year Book* 24 (1948): 93–119.

Edgar, William M. "One Wagon-train Boss of Texas, An Adventure with Indians on the Frontier." *Outing* 39, no. 4 (January, 1902): 381–383.

Elkins, John M. *Indian Fighting on the Texas Frontier*. Amarillo, Tex., 1929.

———. *Life on the Texas Frontier*. Beaumont, Tex., 1908.

Ellis, L. Tuffly. "Southwestern Collection." *Southwestern Historical Quarterly* 81 (October, 1977): 215–234.

Evans, Will F. *Border Skylines*. Dallas: Cecil Baugh, 1940.

Farmer, Mrs. L. E. "Fort Davis on the Clear Fork of the Brazos." *West Texas Historical Association Year Book* 33 (1957): 117–126.

Fisher, O. C. *It Occurred in Kimble: The Story of a Texas County*. Houston: Anson Jones Press, 1937.

Freehling, William W. *Prelude to Civil War: The Nullification Controversy in South Carolina*. New York: Harper and Row, 1966.

Gammel, H. P. N., ed. *The Laws of Texas, 1822–1897*. 10 vols. Austin: Gammel Book Company, 1898.

García Granados, Ricardo. *Historia de México*. 4 vols. in 2. Mexico: A Botas a hijo, 1912[?]–1928.

Gerson, Noel B. *Because I Loved Him: The Life and Loves of Lillie Langtry*. New York: William Morrow & Co., 1971.

Gillett, James B. *Six Years with the Texas Rangers, 1875 to 1881*. New Haven: Yale University Press, 1925.

Gregory, Doris. "Seven Rivers." *New Mexico Magazine*, May, 1961, pp. 25–29.

Haley, J. Evetts. "Ben Ficklin, Pioneer Mail Man." *Shamrock*, Spring, 1959, pp. 8–12.

———. *Charles Goodnight: Cowman and Plainsman*. Boston: Houghton Mifflin Company, 1936.

———. *Fort Concho and the Texas Frontier*. San Angelo, Tex.: San Angelo Standard Times, 1952.

Hall, Martin Hardwick. "The Formation of Sibley's Brigade and the March to New Mexico." *Southwestern Historical Quarterly* 61 (January, 1958): 383–405.

Hanscom, Otho Anne, ed. *Parade of the Pioneers*. Dallas: Tardy Publishing Co., 1935.

Harris, Gertrude. *A Tale of Men Who Knew No Fear*. San Antonio: Alamo Printing Co., 1935.

Heartsill, W. W. *Fourteen Hundred and 91 Days in the Confederate Army*. Edited by Bell I. Wiley. Jackson, Tenn.: McCowat-Mercer Press, 1953.

Heitman, Francis B. *Historical Register and Dictionary of the United States Army*. 2 vols. Washington, D.C.: Government Printing Office, 1875.

Hodge, Frederick Webb, ed. *Handbook of American Indians North of Mexico*. 2 vols. Washington, D.C.: Government Printing Office, 1907–1910.

Hoffman, Allen W. "Findings along a Segment of the California Trail of 1849." *West Texas Historical Association Year Book* 33 (1957): 113.

Holden, W. C. "Frontier Defense in Texas during the Civil War." *West Texas Historical Association Year Book* 4 (1928): 16–31.

Holt, R. D. "Old Texas Wagon Trains." *Frontier Times* 25 [erroneously labeled 26], no. 12 (September, 1948): 269–278.

House, Boyce. *Cowtown Columnist*. San Antonio: Naylor Company, 1946.

Hunter, J. Marvin. "The Battle of Dove Creek." *West Texas Historical Association Year Book* 10 (1934): 74–87.

————. *A Brief History of Bandera County*. Bandera, Tex.: Frontier Times Museum, 1949.

————. "Crossed the Desert in 1872." *Frontier Times* 6, no. 5 (February, 1929): 180–181.

————. *100 Years in Bandera, 1853–1953*. Bandera, Tex.: Privately printed, 1953.

————. *Pioneer History of Bandera County*. Bandera, Tex.: Hunters Printing House, 1970.

————, ed. *The Trail Drivers of Texas*. 2nd ed., rev. Nashville, Tenn.: Cokesbury Press, 1925.

Hunter, Warren. "Killing of Dan Arnold and Lapoleon Lemmons." *Frontier Times* 5, no. 3 (December, 1927): 97–98.

James, Bill C. *Mysterious Killer, James Brown Miller, 1861–1909*. Carrollton, Tex., 1976.

James, Marquis. *The Raven: A Biography of Sam Houston*. Indianapolis: Bobbs-Merrill Company, 1929.

James, Vinton Lee. *Frontier and Pioneer Recollections of Early Days in San Antonio and West Texas*. San Antonio: Privately printed, 1938.

Johnson, Howell. "An Almost Fatal Encounter." *Frontier Times* 6, no. 8 (May, 1929): 351.

Keith, Noel L. *The Brites of Capote*. Fort Worth: Texas Christian University Press, 1950.

Kimble County Historical Survey Committee. *Recorded Landmarks of Kimble County*. Junction, Tex., 1971.

Kincaid, Naomi H. "Anniversary Celebrations of West Texas Towns." *West Texas Historical Association Year Book* 32 (1956): 135–148.

————. "The Founding of Abilene, The 'Future Great' of the Texas and Pacific Railway." *West Texas Historical Association Year Book* 22 (1946): 15–26.

King, Frank M. *Wrangling the Past, Being the Reminiscences of Frank M. King*. Rev. ed. Pasadena, Calif.: Trail's End Publishing Co., 1946.

King, Richard. "Lillie Langtry in Texas." *West Texas Historical Association Year Book* 37 (1961): 82–98.

Landers, Emmett M. "From Range Cattle to Blooded Stock Farming in the Abilene Country." *West Texas Historical Association Year Book* 9 (1933): 69–81.

Lauderdale, R. J., and John M. Doak. *Life on the Range and on the Trail*. San Antonio: Naylor Company, 1936.

Leckie, William H. *The Buffalo Soldiers: A Narrative of the Negro Cavalry in the West*. Norman: University of Oklahoma Press, 1967.

Leftwich, Bill. *Tracks along the Pecos*. Pecos, Tex.: Pecos Press, 1957.

Lockwood, Frank C. *Apache Indians*. New York: Macmillan Company, 1938.

Lomax, John A. *Cowboy Songs and Other Frontier Ballads*. New York: Sturgis & Walton Company, 1910.

Longfield, Katie. "Pioneer Woman Tells of a Perilous Trip." *Frontier Times* 14, no. 2 (November, 1936): 56–57.

McConnell, H. H. *Five Years a Cavalryman: Or Sketches of Regular Life on the Texas Frontier, Twenty Odd Years Ago*. Jacksboro, Tex.: J. N. Rogers & Co., 1889.

McConnell, Joseph Carroll. *The West Texas Frontier*. 2 vols. Palo Pinto, Tex.: Texas Legal Bank and Book Co., 1939.

McConnell, Weston J. *Social Cleavages in Texas: A Study of the Proposed Division of the State*. New York: Columbia University, 1925.

McCoy, Raymond. "Victory at Fort Fillmore." *New Mexico Magazine*, August, 1961, pp. 20–23.

McMeans, D. C. "The Battle of Devil's River," *Frontier Times* 7, no. 3 (December, 1929): 109–111.

McNellis, Robert E. "Bass Outlaw: Lawless Lawman." *Guns*, December, 1976, pp. 46, 69–70.

Martin, Jack. *Border Boss: Captain John R. Hughes, Texas Ranger*. San Antonio: Naylor Company, 1942.

"Memoirs of Mrs. Ruth Clarinda Joff." *Frontier Times* 12, no. 3 (December, 1934): 99–104.

Memorial and Genealogical Record of Southwest Texas. Chicago: Goodspeed Brothers, 1894 and 1895. Reprint. Easley, S.C.: Southern Historical Press, 1978.

Millard, F. S. *A Cowpuncher of the Pecos*. Bandera, Tex.: *Frontier Times*, n.d.

Miller, Thomas Lloyd. *The Public Lands of Texas, 1519–1970*. Norman: University of Oklahoma, 1972.

Mills, Anson. *My Story, 1834–1924*. Edited by C. H. Claudy. 2d. ed. Washington, D.C.: Privately printed, 1918.

Mills, W. W. *Forty Years at El Paso, 1858–1898: Recollections of War, Politics, Adventure, Events, Narratives, Sketches, Etc.* Privately printed, 1901.

Moore, Ike, arranger. *The Life and Diary of Reading W. Black: A History of Early Uvalde*. Uvalde, Tex.: Privately printed, 1934.

Myres, S. D. *Pioneer Surveyor—Frontier Lawyer: The Personal Narrative of O. W. Williams, 1877–1902*. El Paso: Texas Western College Press, 1966.

Neighbours, Kenneth F. *Robert Simpson Neighbors and the Texas Frontier, 1836–1859*. Waco: Texian Press, 1975.

New Encyclopedia of Texas. Composed and edited by E. A. Davis and Edwin H. Grobe. Dallas: Texas Development Bureau, [1927].

Noel, Theophilus. *Autobiography and Reminiscences*. Chicago: Theo Noel Company, 1904.

Nye, Wilber S. *Carbine and Lance: The Story of Old Fort Sill*. Norman: University of Oklahoma Press, 1938.

Ozona, Texas, Crockett County, 1891–1966. Ozona, Tex.: Crockett County Historical Committee, 1966.

Passmore, Leonard. "Memoirs of Lafe McDonald." *Frontier Times* 6, no. 4 (January, 1929): 149–152, 171–172.

Raht, Carlysle Graham. *The Romance of Davis Mountains and Big Bend Country.* El Paso: Rahtbooks Company, 1919.

Rasch, Phillip J. "The Gun and the Rope." *West Texas Historical Association Year Book* 33 (1957): 138–142.

Rayfield, Dade. "Legend of the Circle G." *True West*, December, 1966, p. 30.

Richard, John A. "Ere the Coming of the Cattlemen." *Frontier Times* 6, no. 5 (February, 1929): 192–194.

Richardson, Rupert N. *The Comanche Barrier to South Plains Settlement.* Glendale, Calif.: Arthur H. Clark Co., 1933.

———. *Texas: The Lone Star State.* New York: Prentice-Hall, 1943.

Rister, C. C. *The Southwestern Frontier, 1865–1881.* Cleveland: Arthur H. Clark Company, 1928.

Rodríquez, J. M. *Rodriquez Memoirs of Early Texas.* 2d. ed. San Antonio: Standard Printing Company, 1961.

Santamaria, Francisco J. *Diccionario de Mejicanismos.* Mexico City: Editorial Porrúa, 1959.

Santleben, August. *A Texas Pioneer.* New York: Neale Publishing Co., 1910.

Scobee, Barry. *Fort Davis, Texas, 1583–1960.* Fort Davis, Tex.: Privately printed, 1963.

———. *Old Fort Davis.* San Antonio: Naylor Company, 1947.

Shipman, Mrs. O. L. *Letters Past and Present: To My Nephews and Nieces.* N.p., n.d.

———. *Taming the Big Bend: A History of the Extreme Western Portion of Texas from Fort Clark to El Paso.* Marfa, Tex.: Privately printed, 1926.

Shipman, Jack. "The Killing of Ranger Hulin [Eugene Hulen] and Inspector Sitters." *Voice of the Mexican Border* (1936; Marfa, Texas), p. 66.

Shirley, Glenn. *Shotgun for Hire: The Story of "Deacon" Jim Miller, Killer of Pat Garrett.* Norman: University of Oklahoma Press, 1970.

Smith, Clinton R., and Jeff D. Smith. *The Boy Captives.* Edited by J. Marvin Hunter. Bandera, Tex.: Frontier Times, 1927.

Smith, Ralph A. "Poor Mexico, So Far from God and So Close to the Tejanos." *West Texas Historical Association Year Book* 44 (1968): 78–105.

Smithwick, Noah. *The Evolution of a State: Or, Recollections of Old Texas Days.* Austin: Gammel Book Company, 1900. Facsimile reprint. Austin: Steck Co., 1935.

Sonnichsen, C. L. *Roy Bean, Law West of the Pecos.* New York: Macmillan Company, 1943.

Sowell, A. J. *Early Settlers and Indian Fighters of Southwest Texas.* Austin: Ben C. Jones & Co., 1900.

———. *Early Settlers and Indian Fighters of Southwest Texas.* New York: Argosy, 1900. Reprint in 2 vols. New York: Antiquarian Press, 1964.

Spaight, A. W. *The Resources, Soil and Climate of Texas. Report of the Commissioner of Statistics, etc.* Galveston: A. H. Belo and Company, 1882.

Spence, Mary Bain. "The Story of Benficklin, First County Seat of Tom Green County, Texas." *West Texas Historical Association Year Book* 22 (1946): 27–46.

Stephens, Robert W. *Texas Ranger Sketches.* Dallas: Privately printed, 1972.

Stovall, Allan A. *Breaks of the Balcones.* Barksdale, Tex.: Privately printed, 1967.

Strong, Henry N. *My Frontier Days and Indian Fights on the Plains of Texas.* N.p., n.d.

Taylor, Joe F., ed. *The Indian Campaign on the Staked Plains, 1874–1875: Military Correspondence from War Department Adjutant General's Office, File 2815.* Canyon, Tex.: Panhandle-Plains Historical Society, 1962.

Taylor, T. U. *Jesse Chisholm.* Bandera, Tex.: Frontier Times, 1939.

Texas: A Guide to the Lone Star State (American Guide Series). Sponsored by the Texas Highway Commission. New York: Hastings House, 1940.

Thomas, William Stephen. *Fort Davis and the Texas Frontier: Paintings by Captain Arthur T. Lee, 8th U.S. Infantry.* College Station: Texas A&M University Press, 1976.

Townsend, E. E. "Deed of a Frontier Hero." *Frontier Times* 5, no. 9 (June, 1928): 368.

———. "The Mays Massacre." West Texas Historical and Scientific Society Publications *Bulletin* 48, no. 5 (1933): 29–43.

"Traded Pound of Coffee for Heifer Back in 1876." *Frontier Times* 6, no. 2 (November, 1928): 93.

United States. *War of the Rebellion: Official Records of the Union and Confederate Armies.* 130 vols. Washington, D.C.: Government Printing Office, 1891–1901.

U.S. Congress, House. *Letter from the Secretary of the Interior.* 47 Cong., 1 sess., 1882, House Document No. 135.

———. *Message of the President of the United States. Report of the Secretary of the Interior.* 47 Cong., 2 sess., 1883, House Exec. Doc. No. 93.

———. *Message of the President of the United States. Report of the Secretary of the Interior.* 48 Cong., 1 sess., 1884, House Exec. Doc. No. 84.

———. *Message of the President of the United States. Report of the Secretary of the Interior.* 48 Cong., 1 sess., 1884, House Exec. Doc. No. 100.

———. *Message of the President of the United States. Report of the Secretary of War.* 39 Cong., 2 sess., 1867, House Exec. Doc. No. 1.

———. *Message of the President of the United States. Report of the Secretary of War.* 40 Cong., 2 sess., 1868, House Exec. Doc. No. 1.

———. *Message of the President of the United States. Report of the Secretary of War.* 40 Cong., 3 sess., 1869, House Exec. Doc. No. 1.

———. *Message of the President of the United States. Report of the Secretary of War.* 41 Cong., 2 sess., 1870, House Exec. Doc. No. 1.

———. *Message of the President of the United States. Report of the Secretary of War.* 46 Cong., 3 sess., 1881, House Exec. Doc. No. 1.

———. *Message of the President of the United States. Report of the Secretary of War.* 47 Cong., 1 sess., 1882, House Exec. Doc. No. 1.

———. *Message of the President of the United States. Report of the Secretary of War.* 47 Cong., 2 sess., 1883, House Exec. Doc. No. 1.

———. *Message of the President of the United States. Report of the Secretary of War.* 48 Cong., 1 sess., 1884, House Exec. Doc. No. 104.

———. *Report and Accompanying Documents of the Committee on Foreign Affairs.* 45 Cong., 2 sess., 1878, House Report Doc. No. 701.

U.S. Congress, Senate. *Message of the President of the United States. Letter from the Secretary of War.* 40 Cong., 2 sess., 1868, Senate Exec. Doc. No. 59.

U.S. Department of the Interior. Bureau of the Census. *Seventh Census of the United States, 1850. Population. Texas.* Washington, D.C.: Government Printing Office, 1850.

———. Census Office. *Eleventh Census of the United States, 1890. Special Schedule of Surviving Soldiers, Sailors and Marines and Widows, Etc. Texas.* Washington, D.C.: Government Printing Office, 1890.

———. Census Office. *Ninth Census of the United States, 1870. Population. Texas.* Washington, D.C.: Government Printing Office, 1870.

———. Census Office. *Tenth Census of the United States, 1880. Population. Texas.* Washington, D.C.: Government Printing Office, 1880.

U.S. Department of War. Surgeon General. *A Report on Barracks and Hospitals, with Descriptions of Military Posts, December 5, 1870.* Circular No. 4. Washington, D.C.: Government Printing Office, 1870.

Utley, Robert M. *Fort Davis National Historical Site, Texas.* Washington, D.C.: National Park Service, 1965.

Walker, Olive Todd. "Major Whitfield Chalk, Hero of the Republic of Texas." *Southwestern Historical Quarterly* 60 (January, 1957): 358–368.

Wallace, Ernest. *The Howling of the Coyotes: Reconstruction Efforts to Divide Texas.* College Station: Texas A&M University Press, 1979.

———. *Ranald S. Mackenzie on the Texas Frontier.* Lubbock: West Texas Museum Association, 1964.

———. *Texas in Turmoil, 1849–1876.* Austin: Steck-Vaughn, Co., 1965.

———, ed. *Ranald S. Mackenzie's Official Correspondence Relating to Texas, 1871–1873.* Lubbock: West Texas Museum Association, 1967.

———, and E. A. Hoebel. *The Comanches: Lords of the Plains.* Norman: University of Oklahoma Press, 1952.

Watson, Dorothy. *The Pinos Altos Story.* Silver City, N.M.: Silver City Enterprise, 1960.

Weaver, Morve L. "Overland Trip in 1880." *Frontier Times* 4, no. 4 (January, 1927): 7–8.

Webb, J. R. "Chapters from the Frontier Life of Phin W. Reynolds." *West Texas Historical Association Year Book* 21 (1945): 110–143.

———. "Henry Herron, Pioneer and Peace Officer during Fort Griffin Days." *West Texas Historical Association Year Book* 20 (1944): 21–50.

Webb, Walter P., and H. B. Carroll, eds. *The Handbook of Texas.* 2 vols. Austin: Texas State Historical Association, 1952.

Webster's New International Dictionary of the English Language. Springfield, Mass.: G.&C. Merriam Company, 1924.

West, G. Derek. "The Battle of Adobe Walls." *Panhandle-Plains Historical Review* 36 (1963): 1–36.

Wharton, Clarence R. *History of Texas.* Rev. ed. Dallas: Turner Company, 1935.

———. *Texas under Many Flags.* 5 vols. Chicago: American Historical Society, 1930.

Wilde, Alvin. *St. Joseph Catholic Church of Fort Stockton.* Fort Stockton, Tex.: Privately printed, [ca. 1972].

Williams, Clayton W. "Fort Stockton's First 100 Years." *Fort Stockton Centennial, 1859–1959.* Fort Stockton, Tex.: Centennial Committee, 1959.

———. *Never Again.* 3 vols. San Antonio: Naylor Company, 1969.

Williams, O. W. *The Honca Accursed* (brochure). Fort Stockton, Tex.: Privately printed, n.d.

———. "An Old Timer's Reminiscences of Grant County [N.Mex.]." *West Texas Historical Association Year Book* 16 (1940): 135–140.

Williams, R. H. *With the Border Ruffians: Memories of the Far West, 1852–1868.* Edited by E. W. Williams. London: John Murray, 1907.

Wilson, Steve. "Indians and Treasure Don't Mix." *Frontier Times* 48, no. 1 (January, 1974): 8–13, 40–41.

Winfrey, Dorman H., and James M. Day, eds. *The Indian Papers of Texas and the Southwest, 1825–1916.* 5 vols. Austin: Texas State Library, 1959–1966.

Winkler, Ernest W., ed. *Journal of the Secession Convention of Texas, 1861.* Austin: Texas Library and Historical Commission, 1912.

Woodhull, Frost. "The Seminole Indian Scouts on the Border." *Frontier Times* 15, no. 3 (December, 1937): 118–127.

Woolford, Sam, ed. "The Burr G. Duval Diary." *Southwestern Historical Quarterly* 65 (April, 1962): 487–511.

Wooten, Dudley G., ed. *A Comprehensive History of Texas, 1685–1897.* 2 vols. Dallas: William G. Scarff, 1898.

Wyatt, Frederica. "Cleo's Lifeblood—Its Post Office—Will Close." *Standard Times* (San Angelo, Texas), October 22, 1974.

Yoseloff, Thomas. *Battles and Leaders of the Civil War.* New York: Thomas Yoseloff, Publisher, 1956.

Index